THE GREENLAND TRILOGY

by Christoffer Petersen

Published by Aarluuk Press

This book is a work of fiction. The names, characters, places and incidents are products of the writer's imagination or have been used fictitiously and are not to be construed as real. Any resemblance to persons, living or dead, actual events or organisations is entirely coincidental.

ISBN: 978-87-93680-14-2

www.christoffer-petersen.com

Sun has failed me,
Light has bolted,
Polar Night's Darkness,
On Earth folded.

Far off, where I lie low,
ICE-GLARES envelop me,
Memories hound me,
— them I must tend,

strictly I am judged
but I will Endure;
oh, they who have pressed
to have convicted
to See: who I fabricated
amid all my musing.

Author's translation from
ISBLINK
by
LUDVIG MYLIUS-ERICHSEN (1872-1907)

Solen har svigtet mig,
Lyset er stængt,
Polarnattens Mørke
paa Jorden sænkt.

Fjernt, hvor jeg dølger mig,
ISBLINK ombølger mig,
Minder forfølger mig,
— dem maa jeg dyrk,

de dømmer mig strængt
men giver mig Styrke;
o, de har trængt
til at faa sigtet sig …
Se: jeg har digtet dig
alt, jeg har tænkt.

THE ICE STAR

Book 1 in *The Greenland Trilogy*

AUTHOR'S NOTE

The Sirius Sledge Patrol (Slædepatruljen Sirius) is an elite special forces unit within the Danish military with the primary mission of maintaining Danish sovereignty in Northeast Greenland. Since 1814, Greenland has been recognised as a part of Denmark, with Home Rule established in 1979, and Self Rule since 2009. When Climate Change finally captured the interest of the world's politicians in 2007, the question of who owned Hans Island - a tiny piece of barren land in the Nares Strait between Ellesmere Island (Canada) and Greenland (Denmark) - had already been dramatised with Canada and Denmark both laying claim to the island. Today, the political battle for ownership of Hans Island has been superseded by a far greater goal: ownership of the North Pole itself. In 2017, Canada and Denmark are both allies and players in the great stakes game of Arctic Sovereignty.

The Ice Star is written in British English and makes use of several Danish and Greenlandic words.

The Cabin

NORTHEAST GREENLAND

Chapter 1

ITTOQQORTOORMIIT, EAST GREENLAND

The wheels of the AugustaWestland AW139 slammed onto the gravel helipad of the remote arctic settlement with a bloated squeal of rubber and ice. The rotor chop of the phoenix-red twin-engined helicopter thundered through the fog. As the side door of the aircraft slid open, two men clad in arctic camouflage jumped down onto the gravel. A crewman inside the aircraft fiddled with the gun holstered on his belt as he dragged a woman from the helicopter's functional interior and out of the door. The camouflaged men hauled the woman out of the aircraft and dumped her limp body into the back of a pickup truck, nodding at the crewman and waving at the pilot as he twisted the collective and pulled the aircraft up and into the fog. The walls of the wooden houses dotted about the settlement shook until the aircraft was clear of the long, broad, frozen fjord.

The woman stirred in the bed of the pickup. Thick strands of her matted chestnut hair falling across her wind-bronzed and blood-speckled face in the aircraft's wake. There was more blood clotted between the fibres of her wool sweater, crusted in patches on her windpants, and grooved in the frost fractures of her hands. The shorter of the two men, a Nepalese man similar in height and skin tone to the Greenlanders, jumped into the back of the pickup and pressed his knee into the woman's spine. His breath misted in the cool air as she coughed beneath him. The second man, tall and blond with a build that challenged the seams of his Arctic smock, yanked the passenger door open and slid his muscled frame onto the torn leather seat. He stared out of the cracked window as the Greenlandic driver turned the pickup in a tight circle around the helipad and accelerated along the gravel road.

The driver, wearing the dark overalls of Mittarfeqarfiit, the Greenlandic Airport Authority, jerked through the gears, braking to a stop outside a frost-beaten wooden house at the top of the hill above the fjord. The flaked timbers and paint of the house, once red, was now salmon-coloured, skinned and gutted by Arctic hurricanes. The blond man and his Nepali partner exited the pickup, splashing through the meltwater streaming along the side of the road as they carried the woman up the wooden steps and into the vacant house. The Nepali closed the door as the driver crunched the pickup into gear and drove down the hill, as the last *whop* of the helicopter disappeared. He watched the pickup drop out of sight and turned to nod at his partner.

In the dusty silence of the house, they bound the woman's hands with a length of puppy chain and dragged her across the bruised wooden floor to the wall opposite the door. They gripped her arms and pulled her into a sitting position, wrapped the end of the thin chain around a thick nail in the wall, ripped the boots from her feet and tossed them into the centre of the room.

"Wake her up," said the tall man. He handed his partner a syringe of milky fluid.

The Nepali unscrewed the cap and pressed the needle into the woman's neck. He injected the fluid into her body, tossed the empty syringe into the corner of the room, rocked back onto his heels, and waited.

The woman noticed the chain first as the thin rusted links bit into her pale bloody wrists. She opened one eye and blinked until the room stopped spinning. In the dim interior of the house the woman tugged at the chain and closed her eyes. Images of dogs in harness, blood-spattered snow, the smell of burning wood and cordite fumes chattered through her mind. The memories jolted to a stop with a chain rattle as she tried to wrap her arms around her knees.

The first backhand slap across her face split her lip. Her head rebounded off the wall. She licked the blood from her lips, opened her eyes and stared at the short Nepalese man leaning over her. He hit her again. She snorted blood out of her nose and wiped it from her face with her sleeve. The Nepali took a step back; the floorboards creaked beneath his stubby polar boots.

Soft polar light persevered through the salt-grimed windows, edged with tired wood, flecked with fly shit. The woman winced as she stretched her legs, one eye on the Nepali man with the brutal backhand, the other on a glass of water on the floor. She jerked her head backwards as the blond man stepped into view and his large military boot connected with the glass, kicking it against the wooden wall where it smashed, showering her in jagged shards and splinters.

"Konstabel Fenna Brongaard, my name is Burwardsley. We met on the ice."

The man crouched in front of Fenna. He picked a shard of glass from her knee, studied it in the light. "You probably don't recognise me," he said. "I was wearing a ski mask. However, you might remember my friend, Bahadur." Fenna shrank into the wall as the short Nepali stepped forward, the wicked curve of his kukri knife in its black scabbard prominent upon his white camouflage fatigues. "Ah, yes," Burwardsley said with a grin. He flicked the glass onto the floor. "You *do* remember Sergeant Bahadur. I call him *Bad*, for obvious reasons," he laughed. "Sergeant?"

"Yes, Saheb?" Bahadur said and smoothed the wrinkles of his combat smock.

"Piss off outside and check on the neighbours."

"Yes, Saheb," Bahadur nodded and left the room. He pulled the door closed with a quiet snick of the lock.

"You are here so we can have a little chat," Burwardsley said. The floorboards creaked as he stood. "There are some things that need clearing up."

Fenna stared up at Burwardsley, the ceiling of the room less than half a metre above his head. His thick northern accent irritated her. *He's definitely English*, she thought. *And that name, something upper class, way back in the family tree.* She pushed her observation to the back of her mind, focused instead on the physical, more immediate details, and threats.

Burwardsley tucked his hands into the broad webbing belt around his waist, a Browning *Hi Power* 9mm fighting pistol hung in a canvas holster at his right hip. "Bahadur," Burwardsley said and nodded toward the far window, "found your partner." Fenna shivered. "Gregersen, wasn't it?"

Fenna focused on a patch of dried blood on her trousers, covering her right knee, she tried not to think of Mikael.

"Oversergent, I think his rank was. It doesn't really matter; he died by a bullet from *your* Glock." Burwardsley walked over to the wall and leaned against it. "Did you hear what I said, Konstabel? He was killed with *your* personal weapon. You killed him with a bullet to the head."

"No," Fenna thrust her chin forward. *That's not right.* "I didn't kill him."

"Back of the head," Burwardsley rubbed his palm through his blond hair just above his neck. "Execution style. Then you pulled his body into the cabin and set fire to it."

"No," Fenna said with a shake of her head. "I didn't kill Mikael."

That doubt again, lurking in the splintered memories of the past twenty-four hours.

"You didn't?" Burwardsley pushed his body away from the wall with his shoulder. Dust puffed from beneath his boots as he clumped around the room. "Somebody did. It took four hours for me and Bad to get to the cabin. That damned storm, the one that grounded your unit, I've never seen anything like it." He stopped in front of Fenna. "Convenient, eh?"

"Mikael was alive when you and your gun-thug stepped out of that helicopter."

"Really?" Burwardsley shook his head. "I don't know about the Danes, but in my navy we don't kill our mates, no matter how big the pay off."

"I didn't kill him."

"You just keep telling yourself that, love."

"I'm not your *love*," Fenna spat.

Burwardsley pulled his hands free of his belt and crushed Fenna's stocking feet beneath his boot. He gripped the chain and pulled her arms straight above her head. Fenna choked for air as Burwardsley punched her in the stomach with his free hand.

"You, *my love*, will be anything I want you to be." Burwardsley released the chain and Fenna slumped to the floor. He strode out of the room, ducked into the tiny kitchen and returned with a wooden chair. Burwardsley herded Fenna into the corner, slamming the legs of the chair onto the floor, pinning her shins beneath the cross bar. He sat astride the chair, his long legs bent higher than the seat, the back facing Fenna. "It's time for a more intimate chat, Konstabel."

Fenna's knees pressed tight against her chest, her elbows caught in the gap between the slats of the chair back. She stared around her forearms, wiped sticky strands of hair away from her cheeks and stuck out her chin. *I will not be afraid.* Her eyes flickered across Burwardsley's face. "I did not kill Mikael."

Burwardsley leaned forward, his breath tickled the ragged cuffs of Fenna's greasy, wool sweater. "The evidence suggests otherwise. Do you have another version of events? A witness perhaps?" Fenna pulled her head back behind her arms, strands of her hair caught in the chain pressing into her wrists. "Tell me, Konstabel." Burwardsley gripped Fenna's metal leash between thick fingers. "Where is the Greenlander?"

"What Greenlander?"

Burwardsley yanked the chain. "Don't get smart, *love*. Where is the fucking girl?"

"I don't know," Fenna shook at the end of the chain.

"She was there. At the cabin. I saw her," Burwardsley pointed to the door as Bahadur walked in. "*He* saw her. Where the fuck is she?" Burwardsley pulled at the chain, the nail ripped out of the wall. Fenna smacked her forehead on the back of the chair. "Come on, Konstabel. Where is she?" Burwardsley stood. He threw the chair against the wall and pulled Fenna onto her chest. "Grab her feet, Bad."

"But, *Saheb*," Bahadur took a step forward.

"Just fucking do it." Burwardsley dragged Fenna across the floor to the opposite wall. He wrapped the chain around the radiator and reached for the kukri at the Nepali's waist. He ripped it free of the scabbard and gripped Fenna's sweater. He pressed rough, frost-chapped knuckles into the small of her back. "Where's the fucking girl, Fenna?"

"*Saheb*," Bahadur gripped Burwardsley's arm.

"Shut up and hold her legs, Sergeant."

"Yes, Saheb," Bahadur said and lowered his eyes.

"No." *Not like this*, she thought. Fenna screamed as the Nepali Sergeant gripped her legs, one on each side of his waist. He stretched her, pulling her legs tight against his body. The chain rattled around the radiator. Burwardsley nicked a strip of Fenna's skin from her back with the tip of the kukri as he pared the sweater in two. It hung from her shoulders like a matted fleece.

"It's your thermal top next, love. How about that?"

"No," Fenna cried as tears stung her chapped lips.

"Then your bra."

"Please, God, no," she mouthed. She twisted her head to stare at Burwardsley, glaring at him through her tears.

"Then tell me, Konstabel, where is the girl?"

"I don't know where she is." Stretched taut, Fenna squirmed within Bahadur's grip.

"I warned you, love," Burwardsley said with a renewed grip on Fenna's leash. "Now I'm just getting started." Fenna screamed as Burwardsley pressed the tip of the kukri into the tear in her thermal layer.

She wasn't trained for this. *But he is*, Fenna realised as Burwardsley gripped the chain and Bahadur stretched her legs.

Chapter 2

Fenna screamed one more time. She bit back another and forced herself to stare straight ahead. She looked out of the window and caught the eye of a young Greenlandic girl standing astride the iron pipes insulating the water supply between the houses. The girl held a toy dog whip in her hand. Sledge dog puppies tugged at the frayed plastic rope curled on the dirt-speckled snow at her feet. The girl's deep, brown eyes widened as her mouth opened. Fenna shook her head. The girl turned, disappearing into the fog rolling in from the sea, trailing a wake of fat puppies in front of a dark blue police Toyota that slewed to a stop in the gravel outside the house.

"*Saheb.* Police," Bahadur said and dropped Fenna's legs to the floor. She crumpled onto her knees and elbows.

"Fuck," Burwardsley said and slapped the handle of the curved blade into the Nepali's palm. "Unchain her." He strode to the door, slamming it shut behind him.

Bahadur sheathed the kukri and unwound the chain from the pipes. Fenna collapsed against the radiator. "Put on clothes," he roughed Fenna's sweater around her shoulders. She flinched at his clipped English – sharp like the kukri. "If can't put on, hold in place. Now stand up." Bahadur stood behind Fenna. He pulled her to her feet. The sweater fell from her shoulders. He kicked it into the corner of the room, turning Fenna to face the door as the men entered the house. The Toyota's engine growled outside.

"Here she is," Burwardsley said and gestured at Fenna as he opened the door, standing to one side to allow three men to enter the room – two Danes, both wearing naval uniform, and a Greenlander. The Greenlander, a policeman, slipped in past Burwardsley. He leaned against the wall and cast a glance at Fenna, taking in the room. "We held her here until you could take her into custody." Burwardsley addressed the Danish officer, the senior of the two Navy men entering after the policeman.

Fenna watched the Danes strut into the room. *Not Sirius*, she thought, *but my own people at least.*

The officer, his uniform partly hidden beneath a bulky Canada Goose parka, turned his head toward Burwardsley, wiped his glasses and pointed at Fenna. "You said something about evidence?"

Burwardsley walked into the kitchen, unwrapping an oil cloth as he returned. He presented the officer with a *Glock 20* pistol, the magazine lying next to the pistol grip.

"Petersen will take care of that," said the officer. He watched as Burwardsley wrapped the pistol in the cloth and handed it to the Danish Sergent standing at the door. Petersen carried the pistol out of the house, the echo of his footsteps rumbling through the floor as he left.

"Konstabel Brongaard," the officer said and stepped forward. "My name is Premierløjtnant Vestergaard. I'm the investigating officer for your case and you are now in my custody," Vestergaard said and waved the policeman forward. "Cuff her, Maratse."

Fenna watched the Greenlander as he walked towards her. About the same height as Fenna, he wore the classic Greenlandic look of casual indifference together with a matching swagger. Fenna studied him as he approached. She glanced at Vestergaard and then flicked her eyes back to the policeman. *He is Greenlandic. He understands this place.* She allowed herself a breath as Bahadur let go of her arm. *He might understand me.*

Maratse unclipped a pair of handcuffs from the leather pouch on his belt as he approached Fenna. He circled the metal around her wrists, pausing to examine the red marks on her skin, the blood on her face. Fenna sagged under his scrutiny as her body shivered from the memory of the Nepali's backhand and Burwardsley's interrogation technique. He nodded at Vestergaard and locked the handcuffs, tightening them with a click.

"Premierløjtnant," Fenna said.

Vestergaard wagged his finger. "Don't speak, Konstabel," he said and nodded at Maratse. "Take her out to the car."

Fenna stood firm as the policeman guided her towards the door. "What about my boots?" she said and pointed to the middle of the room with her foot.

"Get her boots, Maratse," Vestergaard said with a sigh.

Fenna stumbled forward. Struggling with the handcuffs, she whispered to Maratse. "Can you help me?" The policeman nodded and crouched on one knee. He squeezed Fenna's left foot into her worn boot. He fumbled with the right one. Fenna tried a smile, but the Greenlander ignored her.

"Don't leave town, Lieutenant," Vestergaard said and shook hands with Burwardsley.

"I can't," he said. "Our ride flew out just ahead of the fog."

"Yes, the helicopter. Is your pilot going back for the body?"

"Yes. Until your lot get back in the air, we'll continue to help."

"Good," said Vestergaard. "And I'll need a copy of your report."

"I'll have Bad bring it over later."

Vestergaard gave a quick nod and followed Fenna as Maratse steered her out of the house. At the steps, Burwardsley waved to Fenna as the policeman helped her into the back seat of the Toyota. Dirty fumes from the exhaust mixed with the fog, staining the melting snow. The fog chilled the air, the peaks of unclimbed bergs of ice locked in the frozen surface of the sea poked through the gaps in the huge fjord below the village.

"See you soon, *love*," Burwardsley called as Maratse closed the car door.

Fenna slumped onto the cushioned car seat. Her hands in her lap, she sank into the soft fabric and sighed. She closed her eyes and rested her head on the dog guard separating the back seat from the rear compartment. She tried to block Burwardsley from her thoughts.

"Konstabel Brongaard?" said the Sergent in the front passenger seat. "My name is Petersen. I'm with the naval legal bureau. I will be helping the Premierløjtnant with the investigation."

Fenna squinted at the Sergent through dirty lashes, her eyes drifting to her *Glock* bundled in leather on the dash. "When do we go to Daneborg?" she said.

Petersen shook his head and tapped the window. "The fog is too thick. We were lucky to get in yesterday on the Air Greenland flight. There are no naval ships in the area," he said with a shrug. "We are at the mercy of the Scoresbysund police."

The low growl of the engine rocked the Toyota with a gentle vibration. Fenna stared past Petersen to look through the windscreen at Burwardsley joking with his Nepali Sergeant. He turned to look at her and she stiffened at Burwardsley's predatory looks. Fenna looked away as the rear passenger door opposite her was opened.

"Stop talking to the prisoner, Sergent Petersen," Vestergaard said as he ducked inside the car and sat next to Fenna. His shoulder pressed into hers as he struggled with the bulk of his parka, cursing as he closed the door. Maratse climbed in behind the steering wheel, slamming the driver door shut three times before it caught. Vestergaard leaned forward to tap the policeman on the shoulder.

"Take us back to the station."

The Toyota spat gravel from beneath its wheels as Maratse backed the car onto the dirt street and set off down the hill.

"Listen closely, Konstabel." Fenna stared out of the window as Vestergaard talked. "You are to be detained here in Scoresbysund," he said and raised his voice above the click of gravel missiles raking the underside of the Toyota. "What is the Greenlandic name?"

"Ittoqqortoormiit," Maratse said as he braked to avoid a string of puppies crossing the road. The larger of the puppies, Fenna observed, its tail beginning to sag, would soon be put on a chain.

"This is a Danish military investigation," Vestergaard continued. "Whereas the Greenlandic police are structurally Danish, Maratse will not be questioning you."

Fenna stared out of the window as they passed a hunter pushing an outboard motor on a weathered wooden sledge behind a dog team. The runners grating up the dirt road reminded Fenna of training her team on the beaches near Daneborg - jagged mountains on the land, behemoths of ice dogging the shore. There was more flex in the hunter's sledge, she noted, watching the roll of the hunter's gait and the wobble of the uprights in his hands. She leaned forward to look at the bindings. The sledges preferred by the Sirius patrol were broader and longer, more like the sledges of the west coast than the raised runners designed to cope with the deep snow of Greenland's east coast.

"Konstabel, are you listening?"

Fenna turned in her seat as they passed the hunter. He stopped to adjust his trousers, sewn from the skin of the ice bear. He winked at Fenna.

"Konstabel?" Vestergaard said and tapped the policeman on the shoulder. Maratse glanced at the Dane's fingers. "Stop the car." The Toyota slowed to a stop outside the bright red wooden walls of the *Pilersuisoq* supermarket and Vestergaard turned to look at Fenna. "I don't wish for this to be a difficult investigation, Konstabel Brongaard." He waved at the children playing on top of the RAL shipping containers outside the supermarket. "This is the first time since the Second World War that a Sirius Patrolman has been shot and killed on patrol. What's more, this is the first time that a fellow patrolman has been accused of doing the shooting, *and* the very first time that a Sirius patrol has included a woman." Vestergaard turned away from the window and looked at Fenna. "All these facts make for a very interesting and unique case." He paused to clear his throat. "Am I making myself clear, Konstabel?"

Fenna turned to look at Vestergaard. "My partner was killed, Premierløjtnant," she said and stabbed her fingers in the direction they had driven. "You should be talking to that British bastard and his Sergeant. They are the ones who..." Fenna fell back into the chair.

"Who *what*?" Vestergaard said. He waited for Fenna to look at him. He took a long breath before resuming. "Unfortunately for you, the British have a solid alibi with plenty of witnesses."

"Witnesses?"

Vestergaard leaned forward between the driver and passenger seats. "Excuse us, gentlemen." He waited until Petersen and Maratse were out of the car and the policeman had succeeded in closing his door. "Your mission was classified, Konstabel. You were tasked to retrieve a sensitive piece of hardware."

"It was a satellite," Fenna said. She looked out of the window as Petersen bummed a cigarette from Maratse. "Canadian. But then you must know that already."

"Yes," he said with a sigh. "Yes I do." He paused. "Konstabel Brongaard, you must understand. We are cut off from the world. The fog has seen to that. If you want a shot at clearing your name, you have to tell me everything before the weather lifts, before the helicopters and ships start to arrive." He paused once more. "Before any journalists get hold of the story."

Fenna flinched at the mention of the press. "And Burwardsley? What about him?"

"You are in my custody now," Vestergaard said. He pointed at Maratse. The Greenlander stood, hands in his pockets. His cigarette, tucked in the gap of a missing tooth, smouldered between his lips. "And his."

Fenna watched the Greenlander. She noted the way he nodded to the people passing on the street, the way he kicked stones at the packs of sledge dog puppies, and the way he ignored the Dane.

"The weather report says we have two days before the fog lifts. Maratse says three."

Fenna watched Maratse, holding his gaze as he turned and caught her eye. "Premierløjtnant?"

"Yes?"

"Can I trust you?"

Vestergaard fluffed at the tails of his jacket. "This is Denmark," he said. "Not America, Konstabel. We are very far from Hollywood, and happen to be on the same side."

"Actually," said Fenna as she bit at a flake of skin on her chapped lips. "It's Greenland," she said and the corners of her mouth twitched with the faint suggestion of a smile.

Chapter 3

Maratse unlocked the door to the tiny police station. Vestergaard followed him inside, leaving Petersen and Fenna on the steps, sheltered from the breeze but exposed to the inquisitive nature of the children scrabbling toward them over the rusted pipes between the houses. Wearing little more than thin sweatshirts and an assortment of scruffy trousers, the children were impervious to the chill fog draped around the buildings.

"They're curious," Petersen said as a squirm of four children and a toddler approached them.

"They're children," Fenna said and waved at them. She looked at Petersen. *Why did they leave me outside*, she wondered.

"What about you? Any family plans?" Petersen glanced at Fenna. Behind the bruises, the matted fringe, the spots of dried blood and grime, Fenna's hair framed a pretty face with steel blue eyes like ice.

"I'm with the Sirius Patrol," she said and smiled at the children who were teasing them with cheeky faces. "That will have to do for now."

She looked up as ravens scratched along the bitumen roof of the house opposite the police station. The birds dropped down to the rocky foundations and assailed the rows of halibut heads, impaled on nails through the lower jaw and hanging from wooden racks on the balcony to dry. Fenna watched as two sledge dog puppies and three ravens tussled for possession of a fish head that had ripped from its nail and fallen to the ground. Too heavy to carry away, the ravens croaked and cowed the puppies away from their prize.

Maratse joined them on the steps. "*Iserniaa*," he said and nodded at the door, turned and went back inside.

Petersen shrugged at Fenna before gesturing at the door. "After you." They followed the policeman. The children swarmed after them, beating the door with small, grubby fists and poorly shod feet, before scrambling over the pipes to play in the street.

"I've put you in here," Vestergaard said and guided Fenna into a small room with a cot and a washbasin the size of a football.

"It's a cell," Fenna said as she stopped at the heavy door. She spun the flap on the peephole. "Do you want my belt and laces?"

"That's cute, Konstabel." Vestergaard motioned to Maratse to remove Fenna's cuffs. She rubbed her wrists where the cuffs had irritated the rusty lacerations from Burwardsley's chain.

"We'll start in here," he said and led the way out of the cell and into the kitchenette next to Maratse's office. Fenna glanced at the picture of the Danish Queen Margrethe hanging on the wall above the policeman's desk. Vestergaard wrinkled his nose as he picked up the ashtray from the table squeezed between the wall and the refrigerator in the corner of the kitchen. He handed it Petersen. "Do something with this." Maratse lit a cigarette, took the ashtray from Petersen's hands and retreated into his office. He smoked quietly in the corner beneath the queen.

"Cosy," Fenna said as she squeezed past Vestergaard into the kitchen.

"Sit at the table, Konstabel. Petersen will stand over there," Vestergaard pointed at the kitchen counters.

"What is he going to do?"

"He will record our conversation. When the *Knud Rasmussen* arrives, he will get to work on your service pistol aboard the ship." Vestergaard paused, one eye on Fenna's face. "He'll do a ballistics check, to make sure it was your bullet. Once we retrieve the body."

Fenna looked around the small kitchen, avoiding Vestergaard's scrutiny. She suppressed the image of Mikael's body inside the burning cabin, and the smell of roasting flesh. She focused instead on the proximity of one of the Danish Navy's two offshore patrol vessels patrolling fishing grounds and enforcing sovereignty in the Arctic. *The Knud Rasmussen is close. More of my people.* She looked up. "Okay," she said.

Vestergaard steered Fenna into the chair by the wall, returning with a second chair from Maratse's office. He pushed the chair up close to the table to give Petersen room to make coffee. Vestergaard removed his jacket. He draped it over the back of the chair and sat down.

"Is Maratse the only policeman?" Fenna asked.

"No, there is a Dane, a summer replacement, but he is stuck in one of the other settlements. The fog is notorious on the east coast."

"It doesn't get much better further north," Fenna said and placed her hands on the table. "How far north have you been?"

"This is my first visit to Greenland."

"Oh," Fenna said.

"Greenland was never on my career map, Konstabel."

Vestergaard turned at the sound of fresh coffee percolating through the filter. "How long have you been with the navy?"

Fenna tapped the table with an idle rhythm. She stopped to study her hands. The fingernails were worn and chipped, the skin scratched and scabbed through the rigours of sledging, the pores were stained dark with the blood of her partner. "Can this wait? I could really use a shower."

"We'll see about that." Vestergaard took two mugs of coffee from Petersen and placed one in front of Fenna. "You were telling me about your service?"

Fenna lifted the coffee to her mouth and winced as the hot liquid singed her dried lips. She put her mug on the table. "I was twenty-two when I tried out for Sirius. It was in the spring of 2014. I shipped out to Greenland in the summer and completed my first patrol as a *fup*, a first-year-man, last November."

"So this patrol, with Oversergent Gregersen, was your second patrol?"

"My third. We had a training run in November, a short spring patrol early this year. And then another spring patrol - the mission - following that. Mikael," Fenna swallowed. "Mikael was the second year man."

"He is quite the Sirius legend, getting separated from his team during *his* first spring patrol."

"Yes."

"I read an article about his experience, how he survived. You were lucky to have him as a mentor."

Fenna bit her lip. "He was a good man. He..."

"Yes?"

"He saved my life."

"Really?" Vestergaard said. The chair creaked as he leaned back and sipped his coffee. "Tell me."

"You wanted to hear about my service record?"

Vestergaard looked out of the window at the fog. "I need to understand your relationship to Gregersen, Konstabel. If it's relevant then we have the time."

"All right," Fenna said. She took a breath. Mikael's death was still so close. "It was my first spring patrol, and I had just fallen through the ice."

NORTHEAST GREENLAND NATIONAL PARK

Mikael kicked off his skis, his breath smoking in the glare of his headlamp. The light caught the icicles tugging at his full red beard. The black wind jacket merged with and was lost in the black polar night. He pulled the wrist-thick brake rope from his shoulders and slipped along the length of the patrol sledge to where Fenna struggled to keep her head above the black water. A sledge dog gripped in each hand by the wet ruff of its neck, Fenna felt as though her lungs were being hammered on an anvil. She kicked at the water, kicked to stay alive.

"Keep kicking," Mikael shouted. He pushed past the sledge dogs closest to the hole, slipped onto his stomach and crawled forward, the loop of rope gripped in his right hand, the light from his lamp reflecting on the surface of the ice. "Let go of the dogs."

"No," Fenna said through trembling teeth.

"Let go of the dogs, Fenna."

The two dogs behind the leaders clawed at the fractured ice. They whined as they slipped. Mikael gripped the gangline in his left hand. Tossing one end of the braided rope to Fenna, he held onto the other with his right hand.

"Fenna. Let go of the dogs. Grab the loop," Mikael shouted as Fenna floundered in the freezing water. The dogs in her grasp started to sink. "Forget the fucking dogs and grab the line."

Fenna let go of the dogs. She struggled to circle her fingers around the thick braid.

"Put your arm through it," said Mikael. "Get the loop in the crook of your arm. That's it. Now hold on." Mikael pulled Fenna towards the edge of the hole. He squinted in the beam from Fenna's headlamp as her body ploughed a wedge in the ice until it thickened. "That's it. I've got you." Mikael held the rope tight. He released the gangline with his left hand and grabbed Fenna's jacket in his fist. He pulled her out of the water and onto the ice. "Kick you bastard. Kick."

Fenna kicked, generating feeble splashes of frigid seawater with barely a ripple on the surface.

"I've got you. Fucking hell, I've got you." Mikael slid onto his backside and dragged Fenna onto his legs. "Got you." He slipped onto his feet. What little heat she had left steamed out of Fenna's body in the lamplight. Mikael dragged Fenna alongside the sledge towards the rear. "Take hold of the uprights. Pull yourself up. Stamp your feet."

He left Fenna at the rear of the sledge and worked his way along the gangline. He pulled the dogs away from the hole. The line bit into the edge of the ice and stopped as the two lead dogs, sodden and near-drowned, anchored the team at the water's edge. Mikael drew his pistol. With one hand on the line, holding the team in place, he shot the first and the second lead dog in the head. Mikael holstered his pistol and cut the line with his knife. He hurried along the length of the sledge to where Fenna shivered at the uprights.

"Come on Fenna. Strip for fuck's sake." Mikael pulled a grab bag from beneath the cord binding the equipment to the sledge. He opened the canvas bag, pulled out dry thermal underwear, socks, and a wool sweater. He looked at Fenna. "Come on. Keep moving."

"Trying," said Fenna as her body shivered, her fingers rigid and useless.

Mikael hung the clothes on the back of the sledge. "Arms up." He tugged Fenna's sodden sweater over her head. Fenna's eyes locked on Mikael's as he tossed the sweater onto the ice. He grinned.

"What?" Fenna said with a slur of blue lips.

"The boys placed bets as to when I would see you naked." The beads of ice in his beard sparkled as Mikael's mouth twitched into a smile. He tugged Fenna's thermal top over her head, and pulled her trousers, long johns and panties to her ankles. "These aren't regulation underwear," he said and lifted her feet to remove her sodden panties.

"Bastard," Fenna said. She smiled though stiffened cheeks.

Mikael towelled his partner with brisk and rough movements, before helping her into dry clothes. "Get your socks on." The Oversergent tugged a chocolate bar from the cargo pocket of his trousers and pushed a piece into Fenna's mouth. As Fenna crawled onto the sledge, he pulled a sleeping bag out of a stuff sack. "Wrap this around you."

"Okay."

Mikael poured Fenna a cup of coffee from the patrol flask. "It's cold. I'll make more." Fenna shivered the coffee to her lips, splashing brown spots upon her knuckles.

"Where's Hidalgo?"

"Dead," Mikael said as he fiddled with the MSR stove. "I shot him. Pyro too. You didn't hear the shots?"

Fenna shook her head. "They were gone?"

"Yep." The stove spat, Mikael adjusted the fuel regulator. "Drink up. I'll have a fresh brew for you in a minute."

"Who's our lead dog? Betty?"

"Worry about that when your teeth have stopped chattering."

Fenna twisted on top of the sledge. "Mikael?"

"Yes?" he said and looked up.

"Thanks."

"Don't mention it." Mikael smiled. "Bad ice. We'll get going once you've warmed up." Mikael reached for Fenna's empty cup as steam drifted out of the pan on the stove. He dropped a teabag into the mug and poured hot water over it, handing Fenna the mug as he turned his head to save her from the glare of his headlamp.

"Thanks," Fenna said as she reached out from inside the folds of the sleeping bag and cupped the mug between her hands.

Mikael turned off the stove and made a coffee with the remaining water. He looked up as Fenna pulled the dry thermal top over her head, covering her breasts. The white light of the headlamp flickered across her stiff nipples.

He looked at Fenna and his eyes softened. "You had me worried for a minute."

"Me too," she said and tugged the sleeping bag around her shoulders.

Mikael packed away the stove. "You ready to move on?"

"Yes," Fenna said.

"Good. Get dressed. I'll stow the rest of the gear."

At the rear of the sledge, Mikael collected his skis before checking the dogs. Fenna watched as he walked the length of the gangline, stopping to make a fuss of each dog as he passed them. She looked beyond Mikael and stared at the hole in the ice. Fenna shivered as the moonlight danced upon the tiny floes bobbing in the black water.

Chapter 4

ITTOQQORTOORMIIT, EAST GREENLAND

Fenna's mug burred the tabletop as she turned it between her fingers. The thought of Mikael being reduced to a memory angered her. She stopped turning the mug and looked up, the memory of the chill of the Greenland Sea goose-bumping her skin. The men were silent and Petersen looked away as Fenna caught his eye. Vestergaard coughed and gestured to Petersen for more coffee.

"So," Vestergaard said as Petersen refilled his mug. "The Oversergent saved your life?"

"Yes," Fenna said. She shook her head as Petersen leaned over with the coffee jug. "I'm fine."

"You're fine?" Vestergaard looked up.

"I mean I don't want more coffee."

"Right." Vestergaard shuffled through the pages of his notebook and pulled a pen from his shirt pocket. He scribbled a note in the margin. "Oversergent Gregersen had an outstanding service record," he said as he wrote. "I had not heard, however, of him plucking you from an icy death." He looked up. "Your record, Konstabel, is a tad less notable."

"This is my first year of patrol."

"Yes. First," Vestergaard said and scribbled another note. "You are the first woman to ever pass selection for Sirius?"

"Several have tried, but the physical selection is where they drop out."

"You didn't."

"I was a biathlete at Esbjerg Gymnasium. I competed in the under 21s for Denmark."

"That explains your physical abilities, shooting and skiing," he said and circled something on the page of his notepad. "What drew you to Sirius?"

Fenna paused. "What about that shower?"

"Later," Vestergaard said with a wave of his hand. "The water tank needs refilling, so I hear. In the meantime, you can continue, Konstabel."

"All right," Fenna said and straightened her shoulders. "It was the challenge. Competing in a biathlon is one thing, but I always wanted something more. Maybe it's my father's fault?"

"Ah, yes," Vestergaard nodded. "He was military too, wasn't he?"

"Yes. Special Forces, Jægerkorps. He was killed in Afghanistan in 2006." *Dad*, she thought. *How come everything always comes back to you?*

"You were..."

"Fourteen," Fenna picked at the blood and grime beneath her fingernails. "All the men in my life seem to die young." Fenna looked up but Vestergaard ignored her.

"You were fond of your father?"

"Most of the time."

"He raised you?"

"In his own way." Fenna shivered as she recalled the early morning exercises and discipline he enforced to push her to excel in sports. *And I was only fourteen. What was the bastard thinking?*

"He was a bit of a character, so I've heard."

"Try living with him."

Vestergaard snickered as he made a note in his pad. "What about your mother?" he said and stopped writing with a click of the pen.

Fenna turned her attention to her nails and picked at the blood beneath them. *My mother*, she thought. Fenna could almost smell the alcohol on her mother's breath as she remembered her goodnight kisses. *With a mother like her, there's no wonder I choose to live in a world surrounded by men.* She was silent until Vestergaard got the message.

"Mikael then. What about him? You had feelings for him?"

"Yes." Fenna looked up and caught the quizzical look on Vestergaard's face. "No, not like that. There was no time for that."

"You have a boyfriend back in Denmark, I presume," Vestergaard said with a smile.

"I did have. Ravn and I split up a few months after I was posted to Greenland." Fenna paused as Vestergaard sipped at his coffee. "It seems some men aren't cut out to be sailors' wives." She laughed as Vestergaard spluttered coffee over his jacket. It felt good to laugh.

"But Mikael," Vestergaard said as he dabbed at his jacket with a handkerchief. "There really was nothing between you?"

"I've answered that," Fenna said with a sigh. "Mikael was my patrol partner. My mentor. He taught me everything I needed to know."

"And then you killed him?"

"What? No," Fenna slammed her palms on the tabletop. The

table rocked as she pushed herself up, the coffee spilling onto the floor.

Vestergaard leaned back in his chair, his palms open in front of his chest. "You didn't kill him, Konstabel?"

"What is this? An ambush? You ambushed me, with all this..." she waved her hands at the table. "This coffee and small talk bullshit."

"Calm down, Konstabel," Vestergaard said. He nodded to Petersen to stand down.

"You asked me to tell you about the time Mikael saved my life. Then you accuse me of taking his. What kind of officer are you *Premierløjtnant*?" Fenna spat Vestergaard's title through clenched teeth.

Vestergaard raised his eyebrows and waited. Maratse, a cigarette between his lips, appeared in the doorway.

"Sit down, Konstabel," Vestergaard said and gestured at the chair. "Finish your coffee." He lifted her mug from where it lay on the table. "Petersen, can you get the Konstabel some more coffee?"

"I don't want more coffee."

"Okay," Vestergaard said and lowered the mug. He turned around to look at the policeman. "Is there enough water in the tank for one shower?"

"*Iiji*," said Maratse with a nod.

Vestergaard scuffed his chair away from the table. "I think we can take a short break while I get set up here. Petersen will show you to the shower. Can we trust you not to jump out of the window?"

"Where the fuck would I go?" Fenna said. The skin of her left cheek flickered, just below her eye.

"Funny," he said and slipped his notebook into the pocket of his jacket. "One more thing before you go. The English Lieutenant, Burwardsley." Vestergaard paused as Fenna's body stiffened. "He mentioned something about a witness. A young woman? A Greenlander? Perhaps Maratse can locate her while you shower?"

Fenna turned from Vestergaard and looked at the police officer. Maratse pulled another cigarette from a crumpled packet of *Prince*.

"I'm sure I don't have to remind you, Konstabel, that a witness in your favour could make all the difference."

Fenna watched as Maratse lit his cigarette. "Her name is Dina."

"*Iiji*," Maratse said and puffed a cloud of smoke from between his lips. He rolled the cigarette into the gap between his teeth. With a nod towards Fenna he turned and left the room. The door to the police station swung shut behind him as Maratse clumped down the steps to the Toyota.

"Good," Vestergaard said as he scribbled a note onto a fresh page in his notebook. He tore it out and gave it to Petersen as the Sergent pushed past him.

"There is soap in the shower," Petersen said as he led Fenna out of the kitchen. He stopped to pick up a pile of clothes from the cupboard in Maratse's office. He pressed them into Fenna's arms. "There are towels upstairs. Used ones."

"I'll be fine. I just need a shower." Fenna looked around Petersen's shoulder as Vestergaard tore another page from his notebook. He folded the note into his jacket pocket, followed them to the doorway, and leaned against a filing cabinet at the entrance to the kitchen. "Do you require medical attention, Konstabel?"

"No," Fenna glanced at her wrists.

"Nothing," Vestergaard said and paused, "internal?"

"They didn't rape me, Premierløjtnant. If that is what you mean."

Vestergaard nodded. "That's just as well. The doctor is stranded in Kulusuk."

"The fog," Petersen said and shook his head.

"Twenty minutes, Konstabel. Petersen will wait outside the door."

"It's this way." Petersen led Fenna up the stairs to the first floor. "It really is just a shower. If you need the toilet, it's one of those bucket jobs downstairs." Petersen ducked his head and leaned against the window as Fenna squeezed past. "It's right in there. I'll wait here."

"It's not necessary, Sergent. I'm really not going to run away."

"I'll wait here," Petersen said and leaned against the wall.

Fenna entered the bathroom and shut the door behind her. Attached to the wall with clips and screws, the water pipes served as shelves with a blunt razor tucked behind one pipe, a dirty sponge behind another. Fenna turned on the water, peeled off her clothes and stepped beneath the shower head. She tugged the shower curtain around a rusty rail and distanced herself from the outside world. She twitched as the hot water sluiced the cuts and grazes on her skin and rinsed the blood and grime from her hair. Fenna worked up a lather of soap between her hands and smoothed it into her body, the Arctic ichor of blood, grit and grime streamed down her skin and pooled at her feet. She ran a soapy hand over her body, tracing the bruises around her ribs and stomach with a finger. Her thighs were untouched but her shins bore yellow shields of old haematomas from the prod and stab of sledge runners and the trials of sledging around boulders, across the ice. She lingered over the dog bite healing on her forearm and smiled.

"Lucifer," she said and traced the bite with her fingers. She pushed her face under the shower head and let the water rinse the slow well of tears from her eyes. "Where the hell are you, Lucifer?"

"Fenna?" Petersen knocked on the door. "Vestergaard says it's time."

"Two minutes," Fenna said and turned off the water. "I'll be down in two minutes."

She stepped out of the shower and wiped the mirror above the clothes hook and looked at herself with tired eyes. Her gaze lingered over her bruised cheek until the steam disguised her face as the mirror was obscured. She towelled her body with brisk movements, then stepped into Maratse's police trousers, securing them as tightly as possible at the waist with the draw cord she removed from his hooded sweatshirt. She pulled on the sweatshirt and socks and stepped into her boots, tying most of her hair into a ponytail, letting the wayward strands cling to her face. Petersen stood up as she opened the door to the bathroom.

"Better?" he said as his eyes lingered over Fenna's hair clinging to her cheeks.

"Much," Fenna said and nodded at the stairs. "Shall I go first?"

"Yes, I'll follow you."

Fenna descended the narrow staircase. She waited at the bottom as Petersen clumped down the stairs behind her.

"Handball?" Fenna said and pointed at the Sergent's left leg.

"Yes, I ripped a ligament in my knee."

"Same thing happened to my mother. That's why I chose skiing and shooting."

"Smart move," Petersen said and pointed over Fenna's shoulder. "He's ready."

Vestergaard stood to one side as Fenna entered the kitchen. As she sat down Petersen set up a microphone in the middle of the table.

"This is the formal part of our conversation. It will be recorded in full. You are encouraged to tell me everything. It might feel informal, given our surroundings, but anything you say may of course be used for the purposes of your prosecution and defence. I'm not your lawyer. I do, however, represent the navy in this case. Do you understand what I have said so far?"

"Yes," Fenna said. She poked at the tripod beneath the microphone.

"Then you will also understand that it's in your best interests to tell the truth," Vestergaard said and waited as Petersen placed a Thermos of coffee on the table. "As regards the sensitive nature of your mission, Petersen has full clearance and you can speak freely."

"How do I know that?"

"What?"

"That he has clearance?"

Vestergaard turned to Petersen. "We'll need the letter from the Admiral's office. It's in my briefcase."

"Actually," Petersen said and folded his hands behind his back, "I think it's in your overnight bag, in Maratse's car."

"It's okay," Fenna said and shrugged. "You said it was formal. I just wanted to be sure."

"We can show you the letter later. As for now, if we are to get this done before the fog lifts, we must begin."

"I'm ready."

"Coffee?"

"Yes," Fenna held the mug as Vestergaard unscrewed the Thermos and poured. Petersen reached around Vestergaard and switched on the microphone. He returned to the sink, rested against the kitchen units and waited.

"Start from the beginning of your patrol, when you were first tasked with the mission." The Thermos lid squealed as Vestergaard screwed it closed and placed it on the table.

"Well," Fenna said as she warmed her hands around the mug. "There was a storm coming, but we had a window to get as far north as possible. Hauksson was the pilot's name."

Chapter 5

NORTHEAST GREENLAND NATIONAL PARK

The tundra tires of the Twin Otter bounced along the gravel landing strip at Daneborg. As the pilot pulled back on the control stick Lucifer sank his canine teeth into Fenna's arm. She smacked the dog between the eyes once, twice before it let go. In the confines of the cabin, squeezed between the long, broad, wooden sledge, patrol gear and twelve sledge dogs, Fenna watched the blood stream between her fingers. After a brief halt between the fibres of her cargo trousers the blood dripped on the packing cases, traced the scratched surface of the aluminium deck and ran beneath crates and sledging boxes towards the rear compartment of the aircraft. Fenna clamped her hand on the wound, leaning back as the aircraft peeled from the earth into the polar sky. The wind whistled through the airframe. Lucifer squirmed and received another clout on the head.

At the front of the cargo area, closest to the open cockpit, Oversergent Mikael Gregersen tugged at the pilot's trouser leg, twisting an invisible dial back and forth with his hand in the air between them. The pilot nodded, reached forward to the console and turned the heat up to full. Mikael unclipped the first aid kit and a bottle of saline from the bulkhead. He squirmed his feet for the deck between the dogs and worked his way towards Fenna, bracing himself halfway. His knuckles bruised the plastic veneer of the ceiling as the aircraft bounced in a patch of turbulence. The two Sirius Sledge Patrollers grinned. Mikael pointed at Fenna's arm. She lifted a bloody palm from the puncture wound with a shrug. Several sledge dogs yawned as Mikael pushed off from the ceiling and stumbled over to kneel beside her.

"We forgot to turn up the heat," he shouted.

"What?"

"Heat, to make them drowsy," Mikael repeated, his mouth but a finger's width from Fenna's ear. "How bad?"

"It's okay," Fenna said and drew the ragged sleeve of her sweater and thermal top above the wound. Mikael passed her the saline with a squirting motion and Fenna diluted the blood seeping out of her punctured skin.

"More," he shouted.

With one squeeze Fenna emptied the bottle, cleaning the bite and loosening the clumps of blood within the wool fibres. Mikael dried the wound with a square of lint from the first aid kit. The two patrollers butted heads during another bout of turbulence. Mikael fell onto Lucifer and the dog squirmed beneath the Oversergent's body before flopping back onto all fours on the deck. Mikael pushed himself off the dog. He pulled a packet from the kit, tore off the top and dumped the white powder contents onto the open wound. He pressed his mouth to Fenna's ear as he dressed the wound.

"Antibiotics," he shouted. "Keep an eye on it. I'll give you a shot when we land."

"What?"

Mikael pressed two fingers and a thumb together in front of Fenna's face.

"Okay," she said and flashed the thumbs-up sign.

Mikael slapped Fenna on the shoulder and picked his way through the dogs to his seat by the cockpit. He clipped the first aid kit in place and nodded to the pilot before picking up the spare headset.

"Everything's okay," he said. Mikael leaned into the cockpit and pulled a pen from the pilot's chest pocket below his name tag. He tugged a laminated section of the aerial chart for northeast Greenland from under a bungee screwed into the dashboard. With the pilot's pen he traced their route with the nib.

"About an hour," said the pilot. "See that?" Hauksson pointed at the anvil of clouds in the vast, moonlit distance.

"We'll be all right," Mikael said and stowed the map.

"*You* might be. Make sure you have your shit together when we land."

"Not a problem," Mikael said and slipped the pen into Hauksson's pocket. He pulled off the headset and lurched onto the sledging box by the door. Mikael steadied himself with a hand on the sledge and grinned through his beard at Fenna. He tickled the ears of Betty, the lead dog at his feet, closed his eyes and listened to the drone of the engines.

Hauksson slid the Twin Otter to a halt. The engines idling, he teased the aircraft within a tight arc pointing the nose of the aircraft north. Fenna and Mikael extricated themselves from the dogs, the sledging boxes, and the webbing straps securing everything inside the cargo area. They pulled ragg wool mittens over thin thermal gloves and popped open the door, coughing with the first intake of dry polar air. The thermometer on the inside of the door began its steady contraction to minus thirty-nine degrees Celsius. Fenna jumped after Mikael through the fog of their breath onto the ice. The dogs' eyes flashed green and blue in the torchlight from their headlamps as they reached into the cargo area, grabbed an ice axe each, and a length of travelling chain and cord.

Mikael dug the first loophole in the ice closest to the aircraft. He removed his mittens and fished the cord through the arch in the ice, tying a bowline knot through the last link of chain, securing it. Fenna pulled the chain into one long length, digging loopholes at intervals, threading a cord through the closest link at each before stretching the chain taut at the final loophole. Her breath frosted on the chain and beaded the cord. The freezing metal burned through the thin fingers of her thermal gloves as she tied the last knot and slipped her hands into her mittens. Mikael worked behind Fenna, untangling the short lengths of chain branching out of the main line. As Hauksson killed the propellers, the hush of fur inside the Twin Otter leaked out of the aircraft with silent anticipation.

As Fenna trotted back toward the aircraft Mikael stopped her.

"All set?"

"Yep."

"How's your arm?"

Fenna rolled up her sleeve, her arm pale in the lamplight, shrouded in the fog of the patroller's breath. Mikael gripped Fenna's wrist and smoothed his thumb across the bandage.

"Sore?"

"It's okay. It wasn't too deep, more a panic-bite than anything else."

"All right," he said as he tugged Fenna's sleeve over the bandage. "We'll have a look at it in camp tonight and I'll give you a quick jab in the arse."

"You'll try," said Fenna.

"You'll love it," Mikael said and grinned behind a mask of mist. He nodded at the aircraft. "Let's get to work. Hauksson gets twitchy the longer we stay on the ice."

As Fenna clambered into the cargo hold the dogs erupted in flashes of bared teeth, whimpers and growls. Too closely related to the wolf to bark, the dogs half-barked and whined with abandon.

"Shut your noise," Hauksson shouted from the cockpit. Fenna grinned back at him, ignoring the finger the pilot flashed in return.

Fenna found Betty and wrestled her out of the canine mass. She tripped on the dog's tail and stumbled the lead dog out of the aircraft. Mikael caught Betty by the collar as Fenna tossed her out of the cargo door. Betty bounced on the balls of her hind feet as Mikael crunched the air from the surface snow in massive strides along the full length of the chain. He reached the end of the anchor line, fumbled for the karabiner clip and secured the team's lead dog at the collar. Betty stood rigid on the ice as Mikael returned for the next dog. One by one, Fenna bundled the dogs out of the aircraft and Mikael danced them into position. With a rap on the nose here and there, the Oversergent avoided the territorial arcs of piss marking the boundaries of each dog. Lacking trees, the dogs pissed on each another.

Fenna slid onto the floor of the Twin Otter, her legs, weighed down by the boots on her feet, dangled out of the doorway. Strands of fur floated in the light of her headlamp, twisting in the frigid breeze as Mikael joined her.

"How's Hauksson?" he said.

"Crotchety."

"Have you told him about the whisky?"

"I thought I'd leave that to you."

"I heard that," said Hauksson from the cockpit.

Mikael cuffed Fenna to one side as he leaned in through the doorway. "Are you going to earn it?"

"I'm not shifting boxes for one lousy bottle of *Jack*," said Hauksson. "How many have you got?"

"Two bottles," said Mikael. "They're yours as soon as you get off your arse and help us."

The wrench of worn springs masked another round of cursing as Hauksson carped out of the pilot's seat and staggered into the cargo bay.

"You're a sucker for a drink," said Mikael.

"There's fuck all else to do up here," said Hauksson. "Which box?"

"The last one."

"Bastards." Hauksson straightened up and pushed past Fenna.

He picked up a rectangular wooden box and hefted it onto his knee. "Come on then, dog-fuckers." Hauksson shoved the box at Fenna, forcing her out of the door as he dumped the first sledging box of patrol equipment out of the aircraft and onto the ice. Fenna arranged it on the ice a few metres from the aircraft. Mikael checked each box and item on a list tucked behind a flap of canvas in the sleeve of the patrol document wallet. It took all three of them to get the sledge out of the aircraft. They slid it out of the door and onto the ice alongside the equipment. Mikael fastened the canvas sledging bag between the uprights of the sledge with a webbing loop over the left and right wooden handles. The frosted links of chain rattled as the dogs shifted within the limits of their tethers.

As Hauksson and Fenna swept the aircraft interior for forgotten items, Mikael performed a thorough check of the sledge, scrutinising each of the bindings with his fingertips and eyes. He smiled when his fingers smoothed into the well of a cosmetic dent on the third cross-thwart.

"Found it," he said as Fenna hopped out of the aircraft.

"My dent?" she said and laughed at the memory of Mikael's exasperation at her carpentry skills. "Hey, I never said building a sledge was my forte."

Mikael cuffed Fenna on the shoulder. "She's going to have more than a dented cross-thwart when we've finished with her." He turned to wave at Hauksson.

"We've got two minutes before he starts prepping the Otter," said Fenna.

"Did you give him the whisky?"

"Just the one. See for yourself."

Back in the cockpit, Hauksson waved the bottle of *Jack Daniels* in the window.

Mikael pulled a pipe from his jacket pocket and tamped a twist of tobacco into the bowl. He thrust the pipe into his mouth. Fenna lifted the sledge boxes onto the sledge and Mikael shuffled them into position. He slid the first box between the wooden uprights at the rear of the sledge. Sanded and smoothed in the shape of a woman's breast and firm belly, the nipple on each upright made for a quick tease when cupping the tit on downward slopes and through gullies. In the harsh light of the Twin Otter the shadow of the sledge swelled on the ice. Fenna turned away from the aircraft to read the call-sign

Fever Dog stencilled the length of each sledge runner. The mission, she realised, was just about to begin.

Chapter 6

The cough of a propeller hurried the two patrollers as they fixed the sleeping mats and tent on top of the load, securing the canvas tarpaulin with trucker's hitches, passing the cord through heavy eyelets and around the thwarts sticking clear of the sledge runners. Mikael slid the padded rifle holster between the cord and the load, Fenna organised the skis. The second propeller coughed – a hoarse bark that caught their attention. Hauksson waved from the cockpit window and the patrollers continued their work. Mikael hung thick rope, woven into coils, over each of the uprights. The coils, the only piece of equipment designed to slow the sledge's progress, would be slipped over the runners when going downhill. Fenna and Mikael would wear them across their chests once they started the patrol. Like the sledge and almost everything else the patrol carried, they were easily repaired.

As the engines of the Twin Otter spun into an idle rhythm, Mikael and Fenna dug out the second bottle of *Jack Daniel's* tucked into the heavy canvas sledge bag hanging at the back of the sledge. Hauksson blotted the interior light of the aircraft as he filled the doorway.

"Hmm," he said. "Sledge bag, eh?"

Mikael shrugged. "You're getting old."

Hauksson nodded. "Too old for that," he said with a nod toward the sledge. "You want to get back on board?"

Fenna shook her head and grinned.

"She's eager, Gregersen. You want to watch her."

"She'll be all right. How about you?"

"Weather's holding for the moment. It's you who should be worried. I don't know why you couldn't wait a day." Hauksson turned in the doorway. "You've got my frequency?"

Mikael nodded.

"Fine then," Hauksson said and took the bottle. He yanked the door closed, clapping his last visible breath in half. Hauksson grinned through the window and flipped his middle finger. Mikael and Fenna returned the gesture.

They stepped back to the sledge as Hauksson revved the Twin Otter's engines in a tight circle, the arc from the wing lights blinding the patrol. The aircraft lurched to a stop as Hauksson applied the brakes, holding them firm as the engines whined, releasing them at fever pitch to roar down the short stretch of smooth ice before leaping into the black air. Fenna and Mikael watched as the Twin Otter traced a low and lazy circle in the sky returning to buzz the patrol with a waggle of wings. They waved and watched the aircraft disappear in the night sky. All was still. The polar air sank around them, they switched off their headlamps and the dark enveloped them.

ITTOQQORTOORMIIT, EAST GREENLAND

Vestergaard looked up as Petersen walked into the kitchen waving his mobile.

"All telecommunications are still down, sir. But I'll keep trying."

"The fog?" Vestergaard said and reached into his jacket pocket for his mobile.

"No, sir. The *TELE Greenland* guy at the store says it's a fault and they're working on it."

"How long?"

"They're working on it, sir. I have no idea."

"Very well," Vestergaard said and checked his mobile once more before slipping it back into his pocket. "Konstabel, did you have any experience of working with dogs before Sirius?"

Fenna smoothed the fabric of the sweatshirt over the dog bite. "No. Not so much."

"So, tell me the nature of your mission. What was it you were tasked to do?" Fenna glanced at Petersen. "It's all right, Konstabel. I assure you Petersen *is* cleared for this."

Fenna looked at Petersen. She watched as Vestergaard clicked the button on his ballpoint pen back and forth. "You'll show me the letter when Maratse returns?"

"As soon as he gets back," Vestergaard said and smiled. "Okay?"

Fenna took a deep breath. "At our second briefing, when the location of the satellite was confirmed, we were told to retrieve certain parts of the satellite, if we couldn't get it all."

"Just parts of it?" He looked up from his notes. "The satellite is called *Sapphire*. Correct?"

"Yes."

"I understand the Canadians launched it back on the 25th of February, 2013." Vestergaard closed his notepad and took a breath.

"*Sapphire* is a surveillance satellite."

"I know," said Fenna.

Vestergaard frowned and continued. "It's part of the Canadians' programme to improve their ability to patrol their Arctic territory, something that I understand is becoming increasingly important as the ice retreats and shipping lanes are freed."

"Kjersing told us that *Sapphire* is the first spy satellite the Canadians have ever launched," Fenna looked up. "Since we've been flirting with the Canadians over Hans Island, and not forgetting the *Xue Long* incident..."

"*Xue Long*?"

"A Chinese icebreaker that arrived in Tuktoyaktuk, in the far north of Canada, without them noticing," Fenna said and paused. "The Canadians have been having sovereignty issues in the Arctic for quite some time now."

Fenna remembered the briefing, with details about the Canadians and their snow machines getting stuck in bad ice in the far north. It had been a good joke at the time. Something for Sirius to feel proud about, proving once again, that as long as the sea continued to freeze, dogs were the only way to patrol the Arctic. That might change, Fenna realised, if the ice continues to retreat to the pole. *Who will have the last laugh*, she wondered.

"The Chinese," Vestergaard said and looked up from his notepad. "I assume you were also briefed on the Chinese cargo plane that flew over the area around the same time the satellite was reported lost?"

"Yes," Fenna said. "Kommandør Kjersing was quite concerned."

"It strikes me as strange they would only task you to bring back a piece of it."

"I think they were worried about the storm and the Chinese," Fenna said. "And our ability to get in and out with the entire satellite."

"*They*?"

"Kommandør Kjersing's seniors, sir."

Fenna paused as she thought about the briefing at Daneborg, when they were first tasked with the mission. Mikael, she remembered, had been as close to insubordination as a second year man could get. He'd made it crystal clear that picking up a piece of space junk was the last thing he wanted to do, especially when it shortened the patrol. *He lived for the wild*, she thought and sniffed to ward off a round of tears. *Shit, Mikael, what the hell did we get ourselves into? And,* she added as an afterthought, *did Kjersing know?*

"Tell me again why did they not just send a helicopter?"

"Okay," Fenna said and flexed her shoulders. She shifted her position on the chair. "All aircraft were about to be grounded due to a storm rolling in from the east. Hurricane strength. What the East Greenlanders call a *piteraq*."

"But you can operate in that kind of weather?"

"The dogs can cope with temperatures in the minus fifties."

"And the men?"

"That's the challenge," Fenna said. "Yes, we can do it. We *do* do it."

"And your mission?"

Fenna paused for a sip of coffee. She let her eyes drift across the tabletop, letting her mind wander as the coffee stains grew into lichen clustered outcrops of rock, pits in the surface of the table became ravines, scratches transformed into contour lines on the map, and the edge of the table became the ice foot rising and falling with the tide as the table rose and fell with Fenna's breaths.

"Konstabel?" Vestergaard said and tapped his pen on the table. "The mission?"

Fenna shook her head before answering. "We planned to sledge from our insertion point – where Hauksson dropped us off. Locate the satellite and retrieve the components before they were lost in the storm or buried in the snow." She looked up. "Total mission time: three to five days to reach the area. At which point we anticipated being contacted by helicopter."

Petersen shuffled for a better seat on the kitchen counter as Fenna waited for Vestergaard's next question. She took another sip of coffee and recalled the *shush* of sledge runners in the snow compared to the grating noise they produced when the dogs pulled them smartly across pure sea ice. Not the inland ice sheet that people thought they patrolled, but the sea ice along the coast of Northeast Greenland. Wild and untamed – polar bear territory.

"Was there any indication of a credible threat?"

"What?" Fenna said and looked up.

"Were you informed of any hostile groups interested in the satellite?"

"No," Fenna shook her head. "Perhaps that was our biggest mistake."

Fenna closed her eyes tight as the picture of Burwardsley, striding across the snow with the Browning pistol in his hand, invaded her mind. As the image focused, the details flooded back. As he'd approached the hut, he had pulled down the hood of his white camouflage jacket. He wore a green beret on his head and a low-cut mask that hid most of his face bar the blond hair flicking out from under the beret. Fenna recognised it now from a photo she had seen in one of her father's books. It was a British Royal Marines uniform. The shorter man with a machine gun, the one he called *Bad*, also wore a beret, green or black, it didn't matter. Fenna focused her memory on the eighteen inch sword at the man's waist, a kukri, a Gurkha blade. *A credible threat?* She opened her eyes and breathed out with a long breath as she focused on Vestergaard. *A Royal Marine and a Gurkha. I'd say that was a pretty fucking credible threat.*

"You seem a little preoccupied," Vestergaard said.

"It's just the questions. It brings everything back," she said. "They drugged me, you know?"

"Who? Burwardsley?"

"Who else. I think I'm still working the effects out of my body. The coffee helps," Fenna said and nodded at Petersen.

"There's plenty more," he said.

"Please continue, Konstabel," Vestergaard said with a click of his pen.

Chapter 7

NORTHEAST GREENLAND NATIONAL PARK

The constant shush of the sledge running across the crusty surface of the snow, hardened by the evaporating effect of the wind, thrilled Fenna. The dogs had found their rhythm, the patrol had established a routine and, with their fourth camp looming, they were making good progress despite the cold, despite the long hours of darkness. The rhythm of life in the far north, Fenna mused, came down to discipline, experience, and common sense.

They skied with short methodical strides, Mikael and Fenna each on opposite sides of the sledge, one hand on the uprights, the nipples already forgotten. Fenna breathed through the ice-laden fleece looped around her neck. She glanced at the yeti skiing beside her and grinned.

"One more laugh out of you and I swear," said Mikael.

Fenna smirked and picked at the ice beading on her eyebrows. She studied the line of dogs before them and picked out the rump of each, noting the position of its tail and gait. Lucifer at the front, just behind Betty.

"Lucifer is a little lazy today," she said. "I'll check his pads tonight."

"I checked them this morning, clipped a little more of the fur between his toes. He had a few marble-sized balls of ice at the end of yesterday. We might try him with socks tomorrow." Mikael's breath misted before him adding another layer of ice to his weighty beard.

The sledge slowed, causing Fenna and Mikael to look up and around. Each of the dogs in the team ran with a light-hearted lift of their feet. Tails wagging the dogs stopped pulling and the sledge ground to a languid stop. Betty sniffed and glanced back at Mikael.

"Go on girl," said Mikael. "Go on."

Fenna scanned the horizon as Mikael slipped his hold of the uprights and skied to the front of the line. His hands unhindered by sledge poles he slid to a stop and took hold of Betty by the ruff of fur around her neck. Mikael glanced back at Fenna.

Fenna lifted a hand and rested her finger on her nose. "There," she pointed, arm straight. "Eleven o'clock. A wolf?"

Mikael stood and looked in the direction Fenna indicated. The sledge shuddered as the dogs tugged. "Hold them, Fenna."

Fenna slipped the anchor coil from around her chest and looped it over the left-hand runner. On her return, halfway along the length of the sledge, the sledge shrugged and slipped past her. Fenna caught the left hand upright and slipped her skis in line behind the sledge. To the right, Mikael hopped towards the sledge as it turned away from him. The anchor coil ploughed the light coating of snow into a shallow furrow, lifting the upright and creating more drag on the surface. Not enough, Fenna realised as the sledge picked up speed when the dogs caught the wolf's scent, their erratic course dragging the sledge further from Mikael.

With both hands on the uprights, Fenna braked her broad-bladed skis in a V-shape, the dead man's rope trailing from the sledge between her legs. The rope tightened as Mikael took hold. It slid along the ice layered within his woollen-gloved palm. He pressed his cold hand into a fist and wrapped the rope twice around it.

Fenna felt the rope press against the inside of her right boot, travelling up the inside of her leg. She lifted one ski from the ice to free her leg. The rear of the ski caught in the rope, the binding opened and Fenna's ski cart-wheeled onto the ice.

"What are you doing?" said Mikael.

"Nothing. Fuck."

Fenna turned her left ski to follow the sledge and pushed the toe of her right boot onto the thwart between the uprights. The sledge increased speed as the dogs pursued the wolf down a slight hill. The wolf loped towards the ice foot and Fenna knew the sledge had to be stopped before it reached the smooth black ice. *If they get on the ice, we'll never stop them.*

"Roll the sledge, Fenna," Mikael shouted. "Roll it."

As the sledge crested the hill, Fenna pulled on the right upright facing downhill. The sledge tipped onto its side and she threw herself clear. Like an anchor the sledge slowed the team, frustrating the dogs to a halt. Mikael skied up to Fenna and offered her a hand.

"Fucking dogs," she said.

"It's not every day they meet a wolf."

"Where is it?"

"Somewhere beyond that mound – close to the ice foot. Thirty metres, maybe." Mikael clapped the snow from Fenna's back. "We'll see it again."

"I thought it would be frightened off."

"No chance. We're the most interesting thing out here. Come on; let's get the sledge turned around. We'll be ready next time."

Mikael loosened the sledge boxes while Fenna anchored the sledge. The dogs took turns to yawn and curl into a ball, watching Fenna and Mikael through the thick brush of their tails. The wolf lay down and watched from afar. When the sledge was ready, the boxes lashed, the gangline checked, Mikael skied to the end of the line and held Betty by the collar.

"We'll try again, shall we?" he said and brushed beads of ice from the lead dog's eyes.

"Wait a minute," Fenna said. "I need my ski."

Mikael shook his head. Betty nudged into his legs and he tugged gently at the dog's ears while they waited.

"Got it."

Mikael roused the dogs with a shout and pulled Betty in an arc, back up the hill. As the dogs turned the sledge, Fenna glanced back at the wolf. It lay with its head down on its front legs stretched flat on the ice. As Fenna kicked off and guided the sledge back on course, the wolf stretched and loped after the team.

The stars picked at the black canopy, the moon purged the ice of shadow. Fenna fed the dogs in a mist of breath. She pulled her hat firmly onto her head and looked at the tent, smiling as the glow of the tent light painted Mikael's movements on the dirty canvas walls. Fenna could hear the stove; she could almost smell the evening meal. It was the same routine every night. Tasks were completed in the same order, regardless of the weather. Anchoring the dogs and pitching the tent together before taking it in turns to work outside or inside. Tonight it was her turn to be outside and feed the dogs, while Mikael organised the tent and the evening meal. She smiled as she approached Lucifer. After just four days, despite the wolf, the team was beginning to gel.

Lucifer whined as she clumped towards him. The other dogs became restless. They had eaten particularly quickly, she had noticed. Faster than usual. Fenna whirled at a glimpse of white as the wolf circled the dogs and the camp. Betty, the bitch, whimpered, jogging in circles at the very limit of her chain. It was not long before the team began to howl. Sporadic and broken at first as the dogs found their voices in the frigid polar air, it became stronger and plaintive as the team found their rhythm. Fenna, her moon shadow cast on the ice before her, threw back her head and howled with the dogs. They stopped; Fenna howled alone for a few moments before the team took up the howl once more. In another unforeseen lull, she heard the answering howl of the wolf. In the far distance, the wolf sat upright between the lines carved by the sledge runners.

"How's dinner?" Fenna said as Mikael poked his head out of the tent baffle.

"Close. Was that the wolf?"

"Yep. Over there." Fenna pointed at their tracks in the snow.

"Got it." With one last look, Mikael crawled back inside. Fenna gave Lucifer a last hug, secured the dog food on the sledge and made her way to the tent.

"Bloody hell," she said as she closed the baffle behind her. "What died?"

"Your socks. My thermals," said Mikael. "You decide."

"Dinner ready yet? I'm starving."

"Salt needed, and then we're good."

Fenna pulled off her boots and hung them upside down from the tent loft. She crawled onto her sledge bag and looked around the tent. "I like what you've done with the place."

Mikael grinned and stirred the pot one more time. Steam evaporated in damp clouds, the vapours clung to the ceiling to form beads of ice.

"I thought I saw some blood on the trail today," said Fenna.

Mikael picked at his beard. "I can't believe Betty is coming into season. When the hell was she last in heat?"

Fenna shook her head. "I'll check the diary." She reached over to the wooden sledging chest that doubled as both bedside table and office space. While she flipped through the pages, Mikael melted snow for their coffee.

"Here we go," she paused for a moment. "Yep, she was last in heat in December. Just before Christmas." She looked up. "So, we have a problem."

"No more than usual," Mikael shrugged. "We should have thought about it but…"

"What?"

"The wolf," said Mikael.

"She must be just starting. You want to bring her in the tent tonight?"

"Not tonight. Give it one night and see what happens." A wicked grin parted Mikael's red beard. "Of course, it's only a myth, but Greenlanders used to tie their bitches out on the ice when they wanted new blood."

"Wolf blood," said Fenna.

"Not sure what the boys back at Daneborg would have to say about that."

"Would they know?"

"Ever seen a hybrid?"

Fenna shook her head.

"Me neither. But it would be interesting to see what we got out of it."

"We're leaving her outside tonight then?"

"I think so," Mikael said and handed Fenna her food. He paused at the first howl of the wolf.

ITTOQQORTOORMIIT, EAST GREENLAND

Vestergaard closed his notebook and tapped his pen on the tabletop. He wiped his hand over his face. "This is all very interesting, Konstabel," he said and inspected his fingers. "But what does it have to do with the mission?"

"The dogs *are* the mission," Fenna said. "Without them we won't get anywhere, we won't survive." She paused and said, "You don't understand, do you?"

"I need facts, not an encyclopaedic knowledge of the ins and outs of sledge dog breeding."

"That's funny, because that is exactly what Sirius needs. But, hey," she said and shrugged. "You're asking the questions. You wanted to know about the patrol."

"Have you forgotten, Konstabel, that you're being investigated for murder?"

Fenna slumped into the chair and fidgeted. "No," she said. "How could I forget?"

"Then why don't we get back to the mission, and away from this stuff about wolves and puppies."

"Sure, but if I leave something out, you'll only wonder at it later."

"Cut to the chase, Konstabel. Before the fog lifts and you are out of time."

Fenna leaned forward and slapped her hand on the table. "When the fog lifts, I expect someone from Sirius to arrive." She lifted her head and stared at Vestergaard, searching his face for the root of his impatience. "Is that it? You want the details in a hurry before the fog lifts?"

"I want the facts as they are fresh, so that I can compare them with the British version of events."

"Burwardsley," Fenna said. She struggled to stop her bottom lip from curling. "Who is he anyway?"

"We'll get to that," Vestergaard said and picked up his notebook. He turned to a fresh page and nodded for Fenna to continue. "The wolf then. If we must."

Chapter 8

NORTHEAST GREENLAND NATIONAL PARK

Stars of ice fractured from the canvas loft and whispered onto the sleeping bags, showering Fenna and Mikael with intricate crystals. Fenna turned several times in the night. During the coldest hour she woke to see Mikael sitting up straight on his camp bed. He placed a grubby finger upon his lips and nodded toward the wall of the tent. Fenna sat up, shedding the top portion of her sleeping bag and sending a light avalanche of ice onto the tent floor. They listened to the sound of dogs coupling outside the tent.

"He's stuck," Mikael said. "Hear that?"

Fenna nodded. "Betty's whimpering."

"Now the fun stuff begins. He has to keep the others at bay while they are joined. We should get a photo."

Fenna nodded and fumbled inside her sleeping bag for the camera battery. She unzipped it from a pocket within the down hood of the bag. Mikael listened to the dogs as the team began to challenge the wolf. The anchor chains rattled as the wolf turned to face the excited males. The dogs' complaints increased as Fenna thrust her feet into her boots, glanced at Mikael and untied the tunnel entrance.

Under the glow of the moon, the white arctic wolf shone greater than its shadow. The wheel dogs anchored next in line to Betty tugged at their chains in frustration and lupine energy. The wolf snapped, incisors bared, nostrils flared and gums pulled so far back its red maw burned in the moonlight. As Betty and the wolf danced to the limit of her chain, Fenna crept closer and exposed the pair. In the sudden glare of the flash, the wolf pulled at the bitch, their hindquarters lapping and overlapping in his frenzy. The team howled and the wolf, maddened with flight instincts, finally ripped its penis from the team's lead dog and cut a path across the ice, its black shadow three feet to the left of a blur of white.

Fenna slipped the camera in-between the thermal upper layers of her clothes. As she approached Betty she reached down and stroked a thumb over her nose and between her eyes. Betty nuzzled into Fenna's legs. She knelt down in the snow and Betty buried her head in the crook of her arm. As Fenna stroked the dog's fur, cold and dry, encrusted with snow and the wild scents of feral sex, she glimpsed the wolf in the distance, sitting on its haunches, silent, waiting. Fenna slipped free of Betty and retreated to the tent. The smell of coffee drifted through the tunnel entrance as she wormed her way inside.

"Everything alright?" said Mikael as he handed Fenna a mug of coffee, steaming in the lamplight.

"They were locked tight," said Fenna. "You didn't look?"

"I stuck my head out of the tent for a bit. Came back in to make another coffee. He was a big fella. His paws must have been the size of my hands," Mikael said and held them up in the light. "A little scrawny though."

"He was," Fenna said and took a sip from the mug. "Are we getting up?"

"I thought so. Seeing as we're all awake." Mikael collected the ingredients for breakfast. "Besides, I didn't like the look of the clouds in the east, yesterday. I want to crack on. Let's get this satellite and get home."

"Sure." Fenna placed her mug on top of a sledging box. "Pass me the diary. I'll make a note of the day. It's going to be pretty interesting to see what we've got seven weeks from now."

Mikael stabbed a spoon in the air between them. "I've yet to meet a single fire-breathing hairy bastard that didn't go week at the knees at the sight of a puppy. You, my friend, are going to be just one more gooey mess of glee when Betty whelps. There, I said it."

"And you won't?"

"We're not talking about me, rookie."

"Fine," she said and blew on the surface of the coffee. With her first sip she caught sight of Mikael's prized Webley revolver, hanging in its holster by the side of his sledging bag. "Shouldn't that be outside?"

"What?" Mikael turned in the direction Fenna was pointing. "Oh, the Webley." Mikael pulled it onto his lap, set his coffee mug down on the box and drew the revolver. "Yeah," he said. "It might freeze a little, but it's not as critical as the rifle." The Enfield lay underneath the right side of the tent, close at hand, but far removed from the condensation within the tent that might freeze the working parts and block the barrel. While the rifle was necessary to protect the patrol from chance encounters with bears, the patrol's service pistols were used as a last resort to put down a dog that could not complete the patrol.

"I thought the Glock 20 was our only sidearm?" Fenna commented. Her pistol was secure within a metal sledging chest still fastened to the sledge as ballast in the event of an unexpected arctic storm.

"It is," Mikael said and presented the Webley to Fenna, "This is more of an heirloom. A little bit of unnecessary weight passed down from one patrolman to the next." He smiled as Fenna tested the weight of the pistol. "It's yours when we're done with this patrol."

"Mine?"

"Yours to pass on to your first-year patrolman, next year, if you think he deserves it."

"If *he* deserves it, eh?" said Fenna. "*He* might be a *she*, you know?"

"You're the first woman ever to make it through selection. I won't hold my breath."

"We'll see. Got any ammunition?"

"Plenty," said Mikael. "Well, enough anyway. Never had to use it. And I don't remember it ever being used for more than target practice. It's a museum piece you know? Some collectors out there would pay a lot of money for a Webley."

"eBay?" said Fenna.

"eBay? Sod that," Mikael scoffed. "Anyone selling this would want to put it into the classifieds of an international gun magazine or sell it at auction." Mikael snatched the revolver out of Fenna's hands. "It's not yours yet, mate. And you're not bloody selling it."

Fenna held out her hands in apology as Mikael tucked the revolver back in its holster and hung it out of reach. As silence settled once more within the tent they grinned at each other over their mugs.

"eBay?" Mikael said and shook his head.

ITTOQQORTOORMIIT, EAST GREENLAND

Petersen tugged at the doors of the sticky cupboards in the tiny kitchen, searching for more coffee as Vestergaard read through the last page of his notes. Fenna glanced from the microphone to Vestergaard and back again. She pursed her lips and tapped a finger on the table.

"I'll be with you in just one moment, Konstabel," Vestergaard said without looking up.

"I was just wondering," Fenna said as she pointed at the

microphone. "Why are you making such thorough notes when you are recording the whole thing?"

Petersen paused mid-search and turned to glance at the microphone. Vestergaard raised his eyes and peered at Fenna.

"Actually," Fenna said. "I'm not even sure it's switched on."

"Petersen," Vestergaard said.

Fenna watched as Petersen leaned around Vestergaard to fiddle with the microphone. She turned to look at Vestergaard as he closed his notebook. Petersen nodded and removed the battery cover. He showed it to Fenna.

"Needs a new battery," he said with a shrug. "Must have forgot to replace it after the last time we used it."

"When was that?" Fenna asked.

Petersen closed the battery compartment. He looked up. "When was what?"

"The last time you used the microphone?"

"Last month," Vestergaard said. He leaned back in his chair and crossed his legs. "I was recording notes for my memoir. I must have left it on." He shrugged. "I'm not the most proficient with technology as any of my daughters will tell you."

Fenna folded her hands on the table and waited. Petersen removed the microphone and placed it on the counter. There was the sound of raven claws on the roof of the police station as Fenna waited for Vestergaard to continue.

"It's still official," he said with a wave of his notebook.

"But with no guarantees for me," Fenna said.

"Very well." Vestergaard nodded at Petersen. "How is your shorthand, Sergent?"

"Rusty, I'm afraid, sir."

"Well, do your best, for the benefit of the Konstabel." Vestergaard said and folded his hands upon the notebook in his lap. "Is that acceptable?"

Fenna bit at the inside of her lip and waited. She glanced at the wall, pressing her thumbnail into her fingertips as she thought.

"Can we continue, Konstabel?" Vestergaard said. He clicked the top of his pen.

"Yes," Fenna said with a nod. "Let's get on with it."

NORTHEAST GREENLAND NATIONAL PARK

Call-sign *Fever Dog* ran ahead of the storm for three days before it drove them onto the ice. Fenna cursed stubby digits as the wind chilled the blood from her fingers. The fascination of skin freezing on metal was short lived as they concentrated on routine in the flurry of snow, the ferocity of ice splinters and the fury of an arctic storm. As the dogs curled deeper and deeper into the snow at night the temperatures dropped below fifty. Mikael risked more fuel and they added more fat to their diet. The dogs devoured frozen chunks of seal blubber, waiting out the storm, insulated with every layer of snow that buried them. Inside the tent, Fenna prodded her finger at the tumours of snow bulging at the canvas walls. The wind shrieked as it wrestled with the tunnel baffle and whipped loose guy lines into blind flails of icy cord. The patrol was grounded, buried and alone.

Fenna woke to a rumbling spatter of bowels. The stale air moved around the inside of the tent as the walls buffeted in the arctic gale. She shifted onto her back and retrieved her headlamp from inside her sleeping bag.

"Don't turn on the light," said Mikael.

"Are you all right?"

"It's messy but I'll live. Just so long as it's just the shits, we can't afford to get sick out here."

"Something we ate?"

"Yeah, that curry you ordered, I think we can get our money back."

Fenna chuckled.

"Laugh it up, mate. It'll be your turn later."

Fenna listened as Mikael tied a knot in the plastic bag. "Are you going to throw it outside?"

"No. I thought I would use it as a pillow. Stupid fuck," said Mikael.

"Well, see you in the morning."

"Yeah," said Mikael.

Fenna listened as Mikael finished pulling up his thermals and crawled into his sleeping bag as gusts of wind buffeted a fetid combination of coriander and herbs around the tent.

ITTOQQORTOORMIIT, EAST GREENLAND

"Very descriptive, Konstabel. Thank you."

"You're welcome," Fenna said and grinned at the memory.

"So that was the storm? The *piteraq*, I think you called it," Vestergaard said as he checked his notes.

"That night and the following day were the worst. The storm just made everything that bit more difficult."

"So, how heavy is a typical patrol sledge?" Vestergaard asked as he checked his mobile. He frowned and returned it to his jacket pocket. Fenna watched him.

"About 350 to 400 kilos." Fenna pushed the base of her mug with her fingertips. "Maratse has been gone a long time."

"Yes," Vestergaard said and turned in his chair. "Petersen?"

"I'll see if I can find him," Petersen said with a quick drum of fingers on the kitchen counter. "If I can't, I'll be back within the hour."

"Bring something for dinner," said Vestergaard.

"I'll see what I can find. Although I don't imagine there'll be much before the first supply ship breaks through the ice." Petersen left the kitchen, pausing at the entrance to Maratse's office to lift his jacket from the hook.

"Lucifer pulled well the next day."

"Lucifer?"

"We put Betty in a canvas bag on the sledge. Less of a distraction."

"And Lucifer was the new lead dog?"

"Yes. That was the day the storm really hit us. Mikael and I took it in turns to lead the way, the dogs following, Lucifer always on our heels."

"It sounds tough," Vestergaard poured more coffee.

"It was."

Chapter 9

NORTHEAST GREENLAND NATIONAL PARK

Fenna lifted her foot, a sudden gust of wind pushed her off balance. She fell onto her side and broke her fall with a splayed hand. Lucifer licked her cheek. Fenna pushed herself up, wiped her goggles and brushed swathes of snow from her arms and thighs. The wind whipped snow darts at her body. She pushed on, breaking the trail, one mulish metre after the other. Fenna led the team as Mikael struggled to guide the sledge from the rear.

At the top of a steep gully she braced her hand, palm up, against the wind. She took hold of Lucifer's collar and halted the team's progress. Mikael clumped through the snow. He slipped one hand along the sledge, all the way to the gangline, and then followed that all the way to Fenna's side.

"What do you think?" Fenna shouted and pointed at the slope.

"Steep." Mikael looked back at the team, the wind snapping at his collar. "The sledge will take them out on the way down. We'll have to tip it." He cracked a smile through his beard of ice. "I'm having fun now. How about you?"

"What?" Fenna leaned in towards Mikael.

"Having fun?" he shouted in her ear.

"If I had bollocks they'd be sweating."

Mikael grinned, his teeth flashing between the icicles hanging from his beard. "Then let's keep going before you cool down. I'll go back and anchor the sledge, hold the team until you work your way back to me. We'll tip the sledge on its side and let the dogs pull it over the lip. We can hang onto the dead man's rope."

"Say again. That last bit?"

Mikael stumbled into Fenna, fighting the wind. "Rope."

"Okay," Fenna shouted. "I'll get ready." Lucifer jumped up, tugging at his harness. Fenna clicked a foot out of her skis and stamped down on the gangline. "He's pretty keyed up."

"They all are."

"Let's do it then."

Fenna watched Mikael work his way back along the sledge. She waited as he lifted Betty from the holdall securing her to the sledge. He slipped her free to let her run beside the team. Fenna clicked her heel back into her skis and skied the length of the team. She tugged at the gangline, pulling the dogs back, holding them in check. When she reached Mikael, she made ready to help tip the sledge on its side. The sledge sloped down to the right, its left runner knifed into a snow bank. The gear shifted ever so slightly within the ropes securing it to the thwarts.

"Get on the downward side," Mikael shouted. "Pull it over. I'll lift it as it comes up."

Fenna moved behind and around the sledge. She gripped one of the ropes securing the equipment to the sledge in a criss-cross pattern, and leaned back.

"Come on, Fenna." Mikael squatted on the opposite side of the sledge, fingers under the runner.

The wind snapped at her jacket. Fenna swore. She tugged harder. *I'm about twenty kilos too light for this*, she cursed. She threw her weight away from the sledge and felt it move. "It's coming."

Mikael grunted as the sledge started to tip. "Clear," he yelled. The left hand runner started to slip out of the patrolman's hands. "Fenna? You clear?"

"Let it go," Fenna scrabbled out of the way. She worked her way back to the rear of the sledge, and picked up the trailing line. The sledge slumped onto its side in the snow. Fenna looked along the gangline at the dogs.

Mikael joined her at the rear of the sledge and pulled the rifle out of its holster. He slung the rifle over his chest, positioning it so it hung comfortably from his shoulder to the opposite hip. The spare sling after the buckle cracked like a whip in the wind. "Don't want to damage it," he said.

"Are we ready?"

"Yes," Mikael said and adjusted his goggles. "Let's get started."

"Come on now, boys," Fenna shouted to the dogs. "Let's go." Lucifer tugged at the line, his harness taut, the traces vibrating along the length of the team as each dog pulled. "Let's go." Fenna and Mikael gripped the upright angled horizontally before them, pushing as the dogs pulled. The sledge inched forward.

"Come on, boys," Mikael said. His breath frosted another layer of ice in his beard.

The dogs dragged the sledge through the snow. It inched towards the lip of the slope. Fenna lifted her head, watching as first Lucifer then Piska and the team bully, Ninja, dropped over the lip and out of sight. The wind blasted a fresh salvo of ice into her face.

"Here we go," Mikael said and took a bight of the dead man's rope. "You ready?"

"We'll try and turn it? Maximum drag?" Fenna shouted.

"We don't want it to roll. Keep it straight. Kick off your skis. Slide them under the rifle bag."

As the last of the dogs crested the lip, Fenna and Mikael slipped their skis under the ropes on the sledge. One hand on the upright, the other on the rope, they prepared to guide the sledge down the slope.

"Keep an eye on the dogs. I'll look out for boulders." Mikael leaned into the wind. "When the slope starts to level off, we'll stop the team and pull her back onto her runners."

"Got it," Fenna said and moved out to the left of the sledge, the front of her jacket pressed flat in the wind. She watched the wheel dogs, Cisko and Nansen, closest to the tips of the runners. Mikael leaned out to the right. The runners of the sledge crested the slope as the dogs pulled. The sledge slid free until, see-sawing in the wind, it crashed down onto the slope, picking up speed as the dogs jogged down the thick layer of frost-packed snow on the surface. "She's going." One hand on the upright, Fenna staggered around the side.

"I got it," Mikael shouted and lengthened his strides, crunching air from the snow with his heels as he broke the surface. "Boulder to the right."

"What?" Fenna kicked snow into the wind as she descended the slope. "Mikael?"

"We missed it," Mikael shouted over the sledge. "We're clear until the..."

"What?"

"Let go of the rope," Mikael yelled. He yanked the rope out of Fenna's hand and bounded the length of the sledge. Mikael ducked in front of it and pulled the rope taut around the runners. He waited the second it took for Fenna to join him. "Pull," he said and thrust the rope into Fenna's hands. With snow pillowing under their heels, they hauled on the rope as the sledge pendulumed around the human anchor. The sledge quivered onto both runners as gravity clawed at it. "Keep hold of the rope," Mikael said and leaped after the sledge. He reached for the runners, stumbling as his feet broke the surface crust of snow, pinning him to the spot. "Fenna?"

She tossed the rope at Mikael and took off after the sledge as it slid into position, streamlining behind the string of dogs running before it. As Fenna caught the sledge the tip of the left-hand runner slid up and over Cisko, crushing the wheel dog. Fenna dug her heels into the snow, and hung low from the uprights. With the seat of her trousers dragging like an anchor, she stalled the sledge. Mikael pulled the trailing line over one shoulder and under the opposite arm, belaying the sledge to a stop as Fenna sat down in the deep snow.

"Whoa," Mikael called to the dogs. "Whoa, now." The sledge stopped. The right-hand runner less than a dog's width from Nansen. "Fenna? You okay?"

"I'm fine," she said, both hands gripping the uprights. *Barely okay*, she thought and worked hard to control her breathing, coughing icy air into her lungs.

"Have a look at Cisko," Mikael said as he fed the rope around his body. He worked his way down to the sledge, snow flurrying from his shoulders in the wind. He watched Fenna move along the left-hand side of the sledge. She stopped halfway. "How is he?"

"Not good," Fenna said as she crouched next to the wheel dog. Cisko lay panting beneath the runner. "At least one of his back legs is broken." She pulled the frozen fleece neckie below her chin and stood up. "A few ribs."

"Shit," Mikael said as he reached the sledge and gripped the uprights.

"Shall I do it?" Fenna shouted into the wind.

"I can if you want," Mikael said and tossed the trailing line behind him.

"No. I can do it." Fenna crouched down in the snow beside Cisko and stroked the dog's fur, smoothing his ears flat along the side of his head. "It's okay, fella." Fenna popped the flap of her holster, pulled out the Glock. "It's okay." She stepped back, holding the pistol in a firm two-handed grip. The team shuddered in their traces as she put a bullet through the wheel dog's skull. The crack of the shot pierced the wind, rebounding between the indifferent granite walls of the gully. She took a breath. *It needed to be done.* Fenna holstered the Glock and unclipped Cisko's lines from his harness and collar. She stood up. "We'll have to let the sledge run forward before I can pull him out."

"All right. Come back here and help me." The sledge slid

forward as they pushed from the rear. The dogs tugged until they called them to a stop. Fenna stooped to remove Cisko's harness.

"Fenna, you okay?" Mikael said. He held Cisko's body as she tugged the harness over the wheel dog's head. Free of the dog's body it snapped in the wind.

"I'm okay," she said with a weak nod of the head. "He was a good dog." She patted the dog's side and stood up. Fenna looped the harness and Cisko's collar over the upright. "What shall we do with him?"

"Leave him for the foxes and ravens," Mikael said and fiddled with his goggles. He cast a glance over the team at the way ahead. "See where it flattens out?" he said and pointed. "It's only a few kilometres to the ice. We'll make camp just off the ice foot. We can skirt around the next headland on the sea ice and make better time."

"Okay." Fenna reached down and smoothed her fingers over Cisko's eyes.

"Let's go then." Mikael slipped the rifle from his shoulder and returned it to the holster as Fenna clicked her heels into her skis. He put his own skis on and nodded to Fenna that he was ready.

"Come on, boys," Fenna shouted into the wind. The dogs pulled the sledge down the slope, snow from the runners spinning into Arctic dervishes in the wind all the way to the sea ice.

Chapter 10

ITTOQQORTOORMIIT, EAST GREENLAND

The tiny kitchen was cramped and stuffy with stale smoke and old coffee. Fenna longed for the fresh air and open skies of the sledge patrol. She stared at the tabletop until Vestergaard spoke.

"That was the third dog killed during your first year with Sirius," Vestergaard said. He paused to write a note. "There was nothing you could do?"

"Cisko was in pain," Fenna said and drummed her fingers on the surface of the table. "We have an intensive veterinarian course during training. We can pull teeth and stitch bites and that kind of thing. But you can't fix a broken leg on patrol, and a dog can't pull with broken ribs."

"So you killed Cisko."

"I put him down. There's a difference," Fenna said and took a breath. "You need to understand these are 'working dogs'. The Greenlanders understand it better than anyone. We love our dogs. We talk to them, and confide in them on patrol when our partners are driving us nuts. But they're still working dogs."

"I don't know," Vestergaard said and shrugged. "I'm pretty sure my wife would disagree."

"I'm sure she would." Fenna stood up. "I need to pee."

"Okay." Vestergaard pushed back his chair and leaned back as Fenna squeezed past.

She locked herself in the toilet next to the cell, lifted the lid and stared at two days' worth of human ablutions. Fenna sat on the toilet, a plastic bag lining the bucket beneath the seat, rested her elbows on her knees and held her head in her hands.

"Damn, Mikael. I'm sorry," she said and wiped a tear from her cheek. She sat in silence on the toilet and thought about the camp they had made that night near the ice foot, how the tidal creaks and groans in the ice vibrated through the tent as the wind *whumped* at the tent sides and wrenched at the guy lines.

NORTHEAST GREENLAND NATIONAL PARK

"Fenna? Are you done?" Mikael shouted, slapping his hand on the outside wall of the canvas tunnel tent. "I'm finished with the dogs. Ready to come in."

"Yeah, I'm done."

Mikael crawled through the baffle at the entrance to the tent, rolled onto his backside and removed his boots. "I like what you've done with the place," he said as the ice from his beard began to melt in the heat of the tent. Fenna gave him the finger and stirred the evening meal over the gas burner.

"How are the kids?" she said and leaned to one side as Mikael crawled onto his camp bed.

"They're fine. I gave them your regards," he said and checked his watch. "Is the radio ready?"

"All set. It's tuned to the normal patrol frequency. We don't have to use any of the code words before we get to the cabin." *It's a real shame*, she thought, a smile on her lips. "It'll be nice to get the news from base, hear what's going on with the other teams." Fenna passed Mikael a bowl of beef stew.

"This is good," he said as he wiped his thawing beard and spooned stew into his mouth.

"I know." Fenna leaned back against her camp bed. She checked her watch and turned on the radio, a robust relic from a decommissioned submarine, increasing the volume to compete with the wind.

"Calling all Sirius teams, this is Daneborg," the radio hissed. "We start with a storm warning. Easterly winds increasing from thirty to forty-five metres per second in the course of the night, reaching forty-seven metres per second in the early hours of the morning. Temperatures increasing to minus sixteen. Heavy snow forecast along the coast south of Mestersvig."

"That's us," Mikael said. He held his spoon poised over his bowl.

"It's going to be a hell of a day tomorrow."

Mikael shrugged and took another spoonful of stew as the radio operator in Daneborg read aloud letters and emails from home. He tilted his bowl and spooned the remaining stew into his mouth. "This is really good."

"You've said that already."

"I have," Mikael said and nodded. He tapped the back of the spoon on his chin. "And, considering your cheeky response to your senior..."

"Cheeky response?"

"To a senior officer, yes," Mikael continued. "I think it only fair that it's you who crawls out into the abyss and gives the dogs a cube of blubber."

"Because you forgot?"

"Because I forgot."

"I was the inside man today."

"You were, that is correct. Now you are making amends for hinting that your senior officer has a touch of senility."

"A touch?" Fenna tossed her empty bowl into Mikael's lap. "Seeing as we just switched roles, you're on dishes, coffee and dessert."

"I think I can manage that." Mikael paused at the smile creeping across Fenna's chapped lips. "What?"

"I don't know," she said and shrugged. "It's just..."

"Spit it out, Fenna."

"All right," she said and took a quick breath. "I didn't expect our relationship to work like this."

"Like what?"

"Like two guys on patrol. I thought the weak woman thing would get in the way." Fenna studied Mikael's face as he returned her look. She felt a slight tremor of embarrassment as he opened his mouth to speak.

"You've seen the movie?"

"God," Fenna said and rolled her eyes. "*G.I. Jane*? They called me that during training. Are you saying I'm Demi Moore?"

"Hardly," Mikael said with a cheeky grin. "She is far better looking." He flinched as Fenna looked around the tent for something to throw at him. "And I'm better looking than Viggo," he said and caught the spoon Fenna threw at his head. "I'm just saying that there's a reason you're here. I don't give a shit what they called you in training. We took two new men last year – and one of them was a woman. If you couldn't do the job, you wouldn't be here. But I'm not going to dwell on the woman-in-a-man's-world, crap. Honestly, I haven't got time for that. Sure, we had the meeting..."

"There was a meeting?"

"Don't be naive – of course there was a meeting. You're the first woman to join the patrol. I volunteered to have you on my team, mostly because I was curious. How would the dogs respond to a female patroller? How would I?"

"And?"

"Hah," Mikael said and threw the spoon at Fenna. "Not so fast, rookie. You'll get my evaluation when we're done, and not before. Now, get outside and see to the kids."

Fenna turned to study the walls of the tent, composing her smile as they bowed and flattened with each gust of wind curling in across the frozen surface of the Greenland Sea. She pulled on her outer layers and crawled past Mikael.

"Thanks," she said and squeezed his shoulder on her way out.

"You're welcome," he said and watched as she crawled out through the tent baffle and into the storm.

Fenna staggered among the dogs, treading on those she couldn't see as they lay, all but buried, beneath a thick layer of wind-blown snow. Fléchettes of snow bored into the pores of her jacket, stinging her face in gusts of tiny needles as she bent over each dog, slipping a large cube of seal fat between eager jaws. She made her way back to the tent, kicking the worst of the snow from her boots, clapping great clumps from her mittens, before burrowing into the baffle and pulling the stiff fleece neckie away from her face to breathe. She tied the baffle closed behind her and crawled into the living space of the tent.

"Hot drink," Mikael said and pushed a mug of tea into Fenna's mittened hands.

"It's tea," she said as she sniffed the contents of the mug.

"And?"

"We have plenty of coffee."

"And too much tea," Mikael tossed the teaspoon into an empty bowl. "I'm doing my best to get rid of it."

Fenna leaned forward. She sniffed Mikael's mug. "You have coffee."

"Yes," he said and leaned back on his camp bed. "I didn't pack the tea."

Fenna sat on her heels, placed her mug on the floor and removed her mittens, pearls of ice frozen within the wool fibres rattled as she tossed them onto the floor.

"We made good time today, despite the weather. We are relatively close to the crash site," Mikael said and sipped his coffee. "If we push on through the storm to the cabin, we can dump the gear and be at the site by midday tomorrow. Weather depending."

"Should we push on in this?" Fenna baulked at the thought.

"That's why they sent us. Because we can."

"But should we?"

Another gust of wind buffeted the tent, with a shower of ice grating over the cotton like a swathe of sandpaper.

Mikael swung his legs over the side of the bed. "I think it's implied."

ITTOQQORTOORMIIT, EAST GREENLAND

When did we start calling them kids? Fenna brushed her hair from her eyes as the hollow clump of boots on the stairs roused Fenna from her thoughts. She washed her hands and left the bathroom. Petersen and Vestergaard stood close to one another in Maratse's office, talking quietly. They stopped as Fenna closed the door to the toilet.

"Ah, Fenna," Vestergaard said with a nod to Petersen. He left the younger man in the office. "Something has come up." He gripped her elbow and guided her to the kitchen.

"What?"

"It seems that Maratse has been busy, and his search has been productive." He gestured to the chair. "Sit down, Konstabel."

"Has he found Dina?"

"Not exactly."

"So what is the problem?"

"Petersen found Maratse talking with an older hunter down by the ice. From what he can make out, it would appear that Dina is missing. We presume she is dead."

"Dead?" Fenna said and sank into her chair.

"The details are sketchy," Vestergaard said and put on his most sympathetic look. "This information does put us in a bit of a bind."

"What kind of bind?"

"Well," he said and sat down, "If Dina was the only witness who would be willing or able to corroborate your side of the story..."

"My side of the..."

"You understand? Until we know anything for certain," he paused. "Perhaps you would continue from where you left off?"

Fenna stared at the floor beneath her chair. Her hair fell over her cheeks, hiding her eyes. *She can't be dead, or I may as well be.*

"The fog is clearing, Fenna," Vestergaard prompted.

Chapter 11

NORTHEAST GREENLAND NATIONAL PARK

The descent to Loch Fyne cabin was uneventful, despite the wind peeling layers of exposed skin from their faces. Mikael helped Fenna to anchor the dogs to the travelling chain before grabbing the shovel and digging the snow from the cabin door. A testament to the determination of the pre-war Danish hunters, the cabin had lasted well, and was a favourite of many of the Sirius patrolmen. The name was carved into a broken ski, the tip tapering above the red wooden door. A muskox skull kept watch from its mount beneath the apex of the roof. The teams repaired the cabins during the summers, caching supplies in preparation for the spring and autumn patrols. Once the door was dug out, Mikael stepped onto the bench to remove the shutters from the window to the right of the door and made a quick inspection for signs of polar bears. Fenna joined him.

"Are we going inside?" she said, her words whipped from her mouth by the wind.

"We'll move the gear inside. Then I'll feed the dogs while you cook dinner." Mikael punched Fenna on the arm. "You get to sleep in a real bed tonight." Fenna grinned, took a breath and turned back into the wind.

The dogs were already half-buried in the snow by the time they had moved all but the essential survival equipment inside the cabin. Fenna closed the door behind Mikael as he returned to feed the dogs. She pulled off her outer layers and left her boots by the door, hanging her clothes on the nails behind it. She turned to explore the interior of the cabin, following the strings and pegs hung from the simple rafters to the map of Greenland pinned to the back wall of the cabin. The dark and aged wood panels framed a long thick mattress dressed with coarse sacking. She ran her hand along the cold metal surface of the Morsø wood-burning stove and smiled at the box of matches by the side of the kindling. Three matches stood proud of the box. Easy to grip and strike, she realised. Even with numb fingers. The stove was ready to be lit, just as the teams had left it the previous summer.

Fenna lit the stove and took a moment to explore the tiny bookshelf as the fire crackled into life, light from the flames licking at the nudes pinned to the walls. The bookshelf wedged a selection of literature between the bruised wooden sides. The titles ranged from airport thrillers to polar texts, some of which belonged in a museum, but it was the cabin diary that caught Fenna's attention. She cracked the spine and let her finger drift over the first few lines, and then slipped it back onto the shelf to read after dinner.

She returned to the stove and closed the glass door before hunting through the supplies piled in the centre of the cabin. She found what she was looking for and lit the propane gas cooking stove the teams had fixed the previous summer. An hour passed before Mikael was finished feeding the dogs and checking their feet for ice. Fenna beamed as he opened the door and sniffed.

"Bread?" he said.

"We have a stove."

Mikael organised his clothes and flopped into one of two armchairs. He picked at the battered leather padding on the arms, crossed his feet and nodded.

"Best place in the park," he said and closed his eyes.

ITTOQQORTOORMIIT, EAST GREENLAND

Fenna clasped her hands together and rested her elbows on the table. She hid her mouth behind her hands and stared at Vestergaard over her fingers. He looked up as he finished making a note. Petersen had long since given up on his shorthand, and Fenna was beginning to wonder if it was even necessary.

"Loch Fyne," Vestergaard said as he closed his notebook. "Is this *the* cabin?"

Fenna dipped her head and blinked slowly, affirmatively.

"*Best place in the park*," Vestergaard read from his notes. "It's a shame there's nothing left. Of course," he said as Fenna let her hair fall in front of her eyes, "We won't actually know the extent of the damage before the helicopter returns with Oversergent Gregersen's body, will we?"

Fenna took a few measured breaths. If there was pity in Vestergaard's eyes, she couldn't see it, and then her vision was clouded with tears.

NORTHEAST GREENLAND NATIONAL PARK

An hour had passed since they tethered Betty outside the cabin and sledged in the direction of the satellite. Fenna could still hear the bitch's howl of protest. It echoed in her ears as she studied the compass clasped in the palm of her mitten.

"Use the GPS, Fenna. Forget the bloody compass," Mikael shouted. With both hands on the uprights of the lightly-laden sledge, he leaned into the wind. "Did you hear what I said?"

Fenna staggered back from the front of the team and placed one knee on the sledge, sheltering the GPS between her back and the sledge bag.

"How far are we?" Mikael said as he joined her. He licked at the ice hanging like candy canes from the hairs above his lip.

"We should be within a few kilometres. I'm using the waypoints to box the coordinates," Fenna said and tugged her neckie down under her chin. "I plotted them last night, but the temperature is playing hell with the batteries. That's why I'm using this," she said and held up the compass secured around her wrist on a thick spectra lanyard.

"Okay, but we need to keep moving."

"I know, but..." She blinked at the stark white landscape. The team had been sheltered from the wind when ascending the gully. On top of the plateau, nearing the crash site, there was no escaping the needle-sharp wind and the freezing temperatures.

"The wind is ripping through us here," Mikael said. "So long as we have reasonable visibility we have to keep moving."

"I know. We should keep going." Fenna pulled her neckie over her nose and cheeks and walked back to the front of the team. She leaned into the wind. With her skis bound to the sledge, Fenna led the team on foot. Mikael pushed the sledge from the rear. After ten minutes of slow progress, a lull in the wind allowed the team to secure their position with the GPS and begin boxing the location of the crash site.

"There," Mikael said and slowed the sledge to a stop. Fenna turned, looked in the direction he was pointing and took a bearing on a black object half a kilometre away on the plateau. She waved at Mikael and jogged back to the sledge. "Do you want to ride?"

"Sure," Fenna said and sat down on the thwarts. She swung her legs into the centre of the sledge.

"Haw," Mikael called and guided the sledge to the left as Lucifer pulled the team around. Sunlight splintered the clouds and the wind brushed little more than a light layer of snow along the surface. The dogs picked up the pace, enjoying the break in the weather and the lighter sledge.

"Finally," Fenna said and leaned back against the sledge boxes containing the tent and basic provisions they would need if they were caught out on the ice. Mikael jogged around the left side of the sledge and leaped on. He squirmed his right foot between the boxes and the upright, standing at the rear of the sledge, like a buccaneer at the wheel of a corvette escaping the doldrums. Fenna fished a compact digital camera out of her jacket and took a shot of her partner, pearls of ice shining in his beard, the light reflecting in his eyes. "Now you're smiling," she said and took another photo. *That's one for Facebook*, she thought.

"Now we're sledging," Mikael said. He grinned and struck a pose worthy of a teenage selfie, framing his ice-matted beard within the apex of his finger and thumb. "Look," he said and pointed. "Lucifer has it now." The traces between each dog pinged tight as Lucifer picked up speed, homing in on the satellite half-buried in the snow before them.

"We should probably slow down," Fenna said and repositioned to a crouch on the sledge, ready to leap off and restrain the dogs.

"Wait until we get a bit closer." Mikael turned his body through a slow arc, searching the terrain in front of and behind the sledge. "I think we've got the place to ourselves."

"We're the only ones stupid enough to sledge through that storm," Fenna said and grinned. "Worth it."

"Yeah, okay rookie," Mikael said and shook his head at her teenage euphemism. "Get ready to get off." Mikael called out to the dogs to slow. He stepped off the sledge and jogged alongside until the team slowed to a stop. Fenna hopped off the sledge and walked the length of the team, securing Lucifer at the lead while Mikael organised the anchor line. He drove three ice anchors into the snow and secured a thin chain in a line between the metal plates. Fenna unclipped one dog at a time from the sledge traces and attached them by the collar to a length of chain branching out from the anchor line. Once the team was settled, Mikael and Fenna pushed the sledge closer to the satellite. Flurries of snow settled as the wind dropped. Beyond the satellite, and stretching across Greenland, ancient tongues of ice licked out from the Greenland Ice Sheet.

"I never thought to ask," Fenna started.

"What?"

"If it was radioactive."

"They probably wouldn't tell us if it was," Mikael said and walked around the satellite, noting the impact rings forming a circular perimeter in the snow interspersed with fragments of shrapnel. "It's relatively intact. What we can see of it." He took a step closer.

"I thought it would be round, like Sputnik," Fenna joined Mikael as he lifted the square panel out of the snow. It came off in his hands.

"Okay, not so intact."

"We'll need a sack, not a net, eh?"

"Looks that way."

"That looks important," Fenna said and reached into the shell of the satellite. She wiped a layer of snow from a panel of chips and circuitry. "No idea what it is, but it has a whole load of serial numbers." She turned it in the light, "and a name: Humble Technologies, Inc."

"That's the one Kjersing highlighted in the mission briefing."

"We'll need the screwdrivers to remove it," Fenna said and stood up. "I'll go get them."

ITTOQQORTOORMIIT, EAST GREENLAND

Fenna stopped speaking and waited as Petersen and Vestergaard exchanged a look. Vestergaard closed his notebook, pushed back his chair and stood up. He leaned against the cracked kitchen counter next to Petersen. The look they gave Fenna reminded her of wolves she had seen in a documentary on television, at the moment when they had run their quarry ragged and were regrouping to finish it off.

"Maybe I should see that letter," Fenna said. "The official one."

Fenna caught the faint smile teasing Petersen's lips before he looked away. She stared at Vestergaard. He took a long breath before reaching into his pocket and removing a packet of cigarettes.

"Do you smoke, Konstabel?" Vestergaard said as he tapped a cigarette into his hand.

"No, and I didn't think you did."

"That thing with the ashtray?" Vestergaard laughed. "I thought it would make you more comfortable to remove it."

"Comfortable?" Fenna looked around the kitchen and smirked.

"Yes," Vestergaard said and paused to light his cigarette. "It's cosy in here isn't it." He took a long drag. The tip of the cigarette glowed as he stared at Fenna. "Leave us for a moment, Sergent."

"All right," Petersen said. He shrugged and walked out of the kitchen. "I'll wait outside for Maratse."

"And go and find out if Burwardsley is done with his report," Vestergaard called after him. He turned to face Fenna, took another drag on the cigarette and then extinguished it with water from the tap above the kitchen sink. "Foul things," he said and tossed the cigarette into a bag of rubbish in the corner of the kitchen.

"Mikael preferred pipes," Fenna said. She watched Vestergaard as he washed his hands and returned to his seat at the table. "Although, I think it was a comfort thing considering the little he actually smoked."

"Yes." Vestergaard nodded. "Comfort." He opened his notebook and flipped through the pages from the beginning. "I can't imagine it was very comfortable on patrol."

"It had its moments."

"Like at the cabin?"

"Yes. Loch Fyne was a..."

"Was that the first time you heard the name Humble Technologies?"

Fenna frowned. "At the mission briefing? Yes."

"Have you heard of Richard Humble? In the media perhaps?"

"No." Fenna paused. *This is taking a new direction*, she thought. "Is he the owner of Humble Technologies?"

"A relation," Vestergaard said and continued. "What did you do with the component?" he said and pressed the nib of his pen on a fresh page in his notebook. "Where did you put it?"

"In the sledge bag that hangs from the uprights, we put all kinds of crap in there," she said and gauged the reaction on Vestergaard's face. To his credit, she mused, he practically ignored her, but for the smug dimples of satisfaction at the corners of his mouth.

Chapter 12

NORTHEAST GREENLAND NATIONAL PARK

Fenna unscrewed the part labelled Humble Technologies Inc. and gave it to Mikael.

"Put it in the sledge bag, together with any of the other smaller bits," Mikael said and laid the panel flat on the snow beside him. "We'll put the larger pieces in the net. Should be okay."

Fenna carried the circuit panel to the sledge, opened the flap of the canvas sledge bag looped between the uprights and dropped it inside. She walked to the rear of the sledge, gripped the uprights and pushed it over to Mikael. She teased the cargo net out from where it was wedged under the lengths of cord tied between the sledge thwarts and spread it out on the free area at the front of the sledge. Mikael pulled large sections of the satellite across the ice and laid them on top of the net.

"We'll have to dig the last part out. I'll do that while you box the area and see if we have everything. Better do that now, while the wind is favourable." He looked at Fenna and paused. "Better call it in on the satphone."

"I'll do that," she said and pulled the satellite phone from the sledge bag. Fenna called Daneborg while boxing the crash site. She scanned the ground three times in ever increasing boxes, finding nothing of interest. She walked back to Mikael as he placed the last parts of the satellite on the cargo net. "The guys at Daneborg say 'hi'."

"Okay. Thanks." Mikael pointed at the sledge. "I found the lens. That's probably the most important part."

"The most expensive," Fenna stared at the scrap metal lying on the sledge. "Not quite so glamorous anymore. Not worth Cisko."

Mikael walked to her side and let the shovel fall into the snow at his feet. "Somebody thinks so," he said and shrugged. "I think we have everything. If we leave now we can be back at the cabin in a couple of hours," he said and glanced up at the clouds. "The weather is holding. If all goes well, we can arrange a pick-up for tomorrow morning and save what's left of our patrol."

"Even without Cisko?"

"Yeah, I think so. We'll hit the books tonight in the cabin. Make a new plan."

"Sounds good." Fenna reached for the shovel. She slid it between the lines securing the boxes at the rear of the sledge. They worked from both sides, secured the cargo net, and added the smaller chunks of space debris to the bag before lashing the net tight to the sledge.

The mid-morning light burned through the clouds as the sun shone down on call-sign *Fever Dog*. Mikael and Fenna pulled off their outer layers and hooked the team up to the sledge. They stowed the anchor line and clicked their heels into their skis for the return journey. Picked clean of debris, the crash site disappeared with a fine dusting of snow blowing gently across the surface. With a last look to check they had everything, Mikael nodded to Fenna and gave the command for Lucifer to lead the team back along the tracks they had made.

They slowed at the crest of the long, shallow slope leading down to the cabin. Situated on the exposed shore fifty metres above the ice foot, the cabin overlooked the smooth sea ice covering the fjord. A thin, grey drift of smoke from the chimney twisted in the breeze. Fenna rubbed Lucifer's ears as she crouched in the snow by the side of the lead dog. She pinched the ice beading her eyelashes and turned as Mikael clumped through the snow to join her.

"What's up?" he said. The air creaked out of the snow as Mikael dropped to his knees.

"Smoke coming out of the chimney," Fenna said and pointed at the cabin.

"Who? I haven't heard any helicopters." He took a moment and scanned the snow around the cabin. "No dogs. We're way too far north of the Greenlanders' hunting grounds."

Fenna stroked Lucifer's nose as he wormed his head underneath her arm. "How do you want to play it?"

"If it wasn't for the satellite," Mikael glanced back at the sledge, "we would have been down there already."

"And now?"

"I don't know."

Fenna looked to the east across the flat expanse of ice covering the Greenland Sea. A shiver trembled across her shoulders. *This is it then*, she thought. *This is when life gets interesting.*

ITTOQQORTOORMIIT, EAST GREENLAND

Richard Humble. Fenna considered the name in her head. She remembered the manufacturer's name stencilled onto the satellite component, although she had no idea how it functioned or how secret it was, only that she and Mikael had been tasked to retrieve it. *During a hurricane.* She recalled the prick of ice on her cheeks and rubbed her fingers over the skin on either side of her nose. The sun had brought her freckles out, and the wind had burned her skin to a shade lighter than her hair. A sigh from Vestergaard brought her out of her thoughts and back into the close confines of the police kitchenette. Fenna decided to take a chance.

"Who is Humble?"

"We've already established that you don't know who he is," Vestergaard said and checked his mobile. "Still no signal."

"So, humour me," Fenna said.

"To what purpose?"

"Curiosity. We pushed through a storm for a piece of satellite with his name on it..."

"The name of his father's company," Vestergaard corrected her.

"Mikael died for it."

"Yes," Vestergaard said.

"Then people will kill for it, or him."

Vestergaard leaned back in his chair and studied Fenna's face. She felt his scrutiny pick at the peeled skin on her cheeks, peeling it back further and deeper as if he was searching for something. *If I'm lucky*, she thought, *he will think I'm just a dumb pawn in this game, and let something slip. Mikael died for something. I'm in the shit because of the same thing, and this guy Humble, he must...*

"Richard Humble is the third in a line of Richard Humbles. His father and his grandfather before him have run Humble Technologies Inc. successfully for the past forty years, under one name or another. The current Richard Humble maintains a more advisory role within the company – he became a lawyer. Humble and Lunk is a well-established law firm with a main office in Toronto. I read this in *Variety* magazine."

"The entertainment magazine?" Fenna said and frowned. "What does satellite technology have to do with entertainment?"

"Absolutely nothing, but the money," Vestergaard said and smiled, enjoying the topic. "Money and entertainment go hand in hand, and Richard Humble enjoys plenty of both."

"So we sledged after a piece of kit to save some millionaire's reputation?"

"No. You retrieved a sensitive component to stop it falling into the wrong hands."

"Whose?" Fenna said. "This is Greenland. There are fewer people in the entire country than there are in a small town in England. In the National Park, there is only a handful."

"And one of them is dead, Konstabel. I would say the *wrong hands* are obviously in this up to their necks. As are you," Vestergaard said and picked up his pen.

Bastard, Fenna thought. *And yet*, she realised, he had been relatively forthcoming with the information.

Fenna flicked her head towards the door as Petersen walked into the station. She noticed the sheet of paper in his hands, focusing on it as the Sergent handed it to Vestergaard. The light from the window highlighted a watermark in the centre of each of the two pages of printed writing. Fenna tilted her head and studied what looked like an image of a large ship sailing past an iceberg.

"What is *The Ice Star*?" she asked as she read the words around the logo. Vestergaard folded the papers to his chest and stared at Fenna. "It's written on the paper," she said.

"It's not important."

"No? Nothing I could read in a magazine?"

"Actually," Vestergaard said, and tucked the papers inside his jacket. "*The Ice Star* has been the subject of several articles."

"It's a ship?"

"A ship?" Vestergaard said and laughed. He turned to Petersen and gave the Sergent a look that made Fenna feel stupid. "Yes, Konstabel, you could say it was a ship."

"And Burwardsley works on it," she said and held her breath. It was a gamble.

Vestergaard's laugh died on his lips. "More coffee?" he said and waited for Petersen to take his mug.

"He wrote his notes on headed paper from the ship. Didn't he?" Fenna said and nodded towards the papers Vestergaard had inside his jacket. "His version of the story, written on the only paper he had available."

"You're quite the detective all of a sudden."

Petersen stopped pretending to make coffee and turned to listen.

Fenna pressed her hands together beneath the table and steeled herself to meet the Premierløjtnant's scrutiny.

"Yes," she said. "I have nothing to lose."

"All the same," Vestergaard said and pulled his mobile from his pocket. He thumbed the screen and then put it away, a slight fleck of irritation flickered in his eyes. "You shouldn't ask too many questions, Konstabel. It's not your place."

"So I can't ask about his side of the story? Burwardsley's?"

"No."

"Then I have nothing to go on."

"You suggested you were drugged..."

"Yes," Fenna said and stabbed her finger at the corner of the paper sticking out of Vestergaard's jacket pocket. "By him."

"Which he maintains was necessary, given your heightened level of anxiety. You were," he said and paused to remove the papers, "*...a danger to yourself and others.* Lieutenant Burwardsley administered a sedative as a precautionary measure prior to transporting you here, to Scoresbysund, where you could be both *treated and questioned regarding the death of your partner.*"

"Bullshit."

"And yet, that's what it says," said Vestergaard as he pocketed Burwardsley's report.

"This is a setup," Fenna said. She clasped her fingers together as they began to shake.

"Perhaps so. But if we don't get to the bottom of it, then the Lieutenant's report will be the only report that matters."

"What about my statement? Don't I get to write my version of what happened?"

Vestergaard tapped his notebook. "I have my notes. Petersen has... Well, he started making a shorthand reference. Perhaps you can resume once we have the proper facilities at our disposal?"

"Yes, Premierløjtnant," Petersen said and glanced at Fenna. "As soon as the *Knud Rasmussen* gets in."

"This is a sham."

"I beg your pardon, Konstabel? A sham?" Vestergaard said. "Whatever it might be, it only exists because of you. So, call it what you will."

Fenna pressed her palms to her eyes to shut out the light. *Think, Fenna, think.* The logo of the ship, *The Ice Star*, floated in her mind. A big ship. One Burwardsley works for – Vestergaard didn't deny that. But what was the connection? If *The Ice Star* was in the area, and it had to be for Burwardsley to be here, then it must have an ice class certification. It had to be able to operate without the need for an icebreaker to be this far north. *And it has to have a helipad*, she realised.

"You're doing a lot of thinking, Konstabel. Please, don't wear yourself out," Vestergaard said and tapped the nib of the pen on his notebook. "We need to continue."

Fenna rubbed her eyes one last time and lowered her hands. She blinked in the light. She took a long breath, lifted her heels and let her knees rock up and down as she bounced on her toes.

"I'm lost," she whispered.

"Then stick to the facts," Vestergaard said. "And let me help you."

"Okay," she said and nodded. "Okay."

"What happened next, Konstabel?"

Chapter 13

NORTHEAST GREENLAND NATIONAL PARK

Lucifer bit at the balls of ice frozen in the hairs between the pads of his feet. The rest of the team lay curled in the snow or flat on their bellies, their long forelegs stretched out before them. Fenna glanced at the team and then crawled back into position beside Mikael, the snow crunching beneath her elbows and knees.

"Well," he said, "Whoever they are, they have all our gear and supplies."

"I'll get on the phone." Fenna pushed Lucifer away and stood up. Mikael gripped her arm as she turned toward the sledge.

"This could be nothing. We might even have left something on the stove."

"You know we didn't."

"I know." Mikael glanced at the Glock holstered to Fenna's waist. "You ready to use that?"

"You have to ask?"

"This is different, Fenna. Euthanising dogs is one thing..."

"And when was the last time you pulled a gun on someone?"

"I haven't."

"So don't suggest this is any different for you than it is for me."

"I'm just saying we don't know what to expect and I want you to be ready for anything." He turned to glance at the satellite and Fenna caught a flash of concern in his eyes. "Okay?" he asked.

"Yes, okay," said Fenna.

Mikael pulled Lucifer by the harness and turned the team away from the crest of the slope, drawing them down below the lip and out of sight. The dogs waited as he secured the travelling anchor line in the snow. Fenna stood a few metres behind the sledge, trailing the antenna for the satellite telephone from the handheld unit. She pressed the buttons on the phone and dialled the Sirius base at Daneborg.

"Hello? Noa? This is Fenna. I need to speak to Kjersing," she said and waited for Noa's response. She shook her head at Mikael. "Kjersing's not in the office. He has to go look for him."

"Just give him the message and we can get down to the cabin," Mikael said. Fenna noticed the rifle slung on his shoulder. She nodded.

"Hey, Noa. Wait. Just give him this message." Fenna paused to look at Mikael.

"Tell him," Mikael stopped and held out his hand for the phone. "Hey, Noa, it's Mikael. Tell Kjersing that we think we have a guest at the cabin." He paused. "No, no-one we know and no sign of helicopters or dogs. A bit of a mystery really." Mikael paused again, nodding as Noa repeated his message. "Yep, we're going to go and take a look. We'll call you when we know more."

Mikael ended the call and handed the satphone to Fenna. She packed the antenna away and tucked the unit inside her jacket.

"You ready?" Mikael said with a flash of teeth beneath his beard.

"As much as I'll ever be," Fenna said. "Nothing like a bit of smoke from the chimney to get the heart racing, eh?"

"Yeah," Mikael laughed. "But remember," he said, "We're Special Forces."

"Oh, we're special all right."

"So very special." Mikael nodded. He took a breath and slipped the rifle from his shoulder and into his hands. "Be careful, Fenna."

"I will," she said and tugged her pistol from its holster. "I'll come in from the south."

"Sounds good." Mikael took a last look at the dogs and nodded. "I'll cover you from above as you go inside the cabin." He cuffed Fenna on the arm, turned and slipped over the crest of the slope.

Fenna watched Mikael as he boxed the cabin from the east, stretching out on the snow, the Lee Enfield rifle balanced on a smooth rock covering the cabin entrance. He waved at Fenna to advance. She held the Glock 20 in a double-handed grip and slid through the powder snow until the slope flattened on the southern, window-less side of the cabin. She reached the wooden wall and leaned on it. The wind whipped a polar devil of snow around her boots, the snow stuck to the ice clogging her laces. Fenna bit her lip.

"Okay," she breathed. "I'm going in."

The squeak of the door of the Morsø wood-burning stove broke the polar quiet surrounding the cabin. Fenna glanced in Mikael's direction. With her back against the wall, she shushed through the snow until she was leaning against the hinges of the door. She reached for the handle with her left hand, and, remembering it was designed with polar bears in mind, she turned it upwards. The stove door clanged shut. Fenna slammed the door against the wall, left palm flat against the wood, the Glock shaking slightly in her right hand, the iron sight wavering over the face of a young Greenlandic woman, her hazel eyes startled, darker, stronger than the coffee-cream skin of her face framed by long jet-black lengths of hair. The woman trembled but didn't move.

Fenna stared at the Greenlander. "You're wearing my jacket," she said, and lowered her pistol. Fenna stepped inside the cabin. "Are you alone?"

The woman squeezed her lips shut.

"Do you speak Danish?"

The woman nodded.

"Are you alone?"

Fenna caught the hint of a nod as Mikael called from the snow beyond the cabin.

"Fenna?"

She turned to wave to her partner. "It's a woman. A Greenlander." Fenna beckoned for Mikael to approach. "Sit down on the floor," she nodded at the space between the door and the stove. As the woman lowered herself to the stained floorboards, Fenna holstered her pistol. "I'm going to put this away. See?" She snapped the holster flap over the grip of the Glock and leaned back against the door. Mikael crunched through the snow to the cabin, the rifle slung over his shoulder,

"Is she alone?"

"I think so. We can ask her again."

The woman pointed at her lips. Opening her mouth she clucked guttural noises until Fenna stepped closer, crouched in front of her.

"Jesus Christ. She's missing her tongue."

"What?" he said and stepped into the room. He closed the cabin door behind him. "Let me see." The woman glanced at Mikael, opened her mouth wider. "Jesus." Mikael slipped the rifle from his shoulder and leaned it against the table by the side of the stove. "That's not from birth."

"No," Fenna stood up. "It looks recent." The woman tilted her head, glancing from one Dane to the other as they talked. "We still don't know if she is alone. I guess a hunter left her here while he went out on the ice."

"Then why is she wearing your jacket?"

Fenna turned back to the woman. She held out her hand and

helped her to her feet. "What are you wearing?" Fenna pulled at the woman's arm, turning her to one side. "You're wearing a cocktail dress?"

"Plus your extra jacket and my spare socks," Mikael said and wiped at the ice thawing in his beard. "I don't think she is with a hunter."

The woman made a sound in the back of her throat.

"What was that?" Fenna said and studied the woman's face.

The woman moved to crouch by the ragged mouth of the oil barrel, cut down to store wood, and traced letters in the dust with her finger.

"Dina," Fenna read aloud. "Your name is Dina?"

Dina nodded. Smoothing the dust into a new pile, she wrote the number two with her finger.

Mikael stepped closer. "Two people? You and one more?"

She shook her head and pointed at her chest, held up one finger.

"One person," Mikael said and waited as Dina nodded. She held up two fingers and pointed to the door of the cabin. "Two people outside?" Dina nodded. "Okay," he said and reached for the rifle. "I'll go and have a look outside."

"Take my Glock," Fenna pulled her pistol out of her holster and pressed it into Mikael's hand. "I'll take yours from the gear."

"All right." Mikael tucked Fenna's pistol into his belt. "You'll stay with her?"

"I'll find out what I can."

"See if she is injured, besides her mouth." Mikael looked at Dina. "And try to find out why the hell she is wearing a cocktail dress." He shook his head and walked to the door. "I'll have a look around. Be back in ten minutes."

"Fire off a shot if you need help."

Mikael paused in the doorway. "If it's all clear, I might just bring the dogs down with the sledge."

"I can help you."

"You could," Mikael said. "But I think one of us should keep an eye on our new friend. She's already been in our things, and she could use some help."

"I'll keep an eye on her. You be careful."

"Always." Mikael pulled the door handle up and pushed the door open. He stepped out into the snow and the eerie pink light of the polar evening.

ITTOQQORTOORMIIT, EAST GREENLAND

"And you never spoke to him again?" Vestergaard said as he leaned against the refrigerator, his pen poised over a fresh page in his notebook. Fenna shook her head. "Why did you give him your pistol?"

"It was colder. We try to keep one pistol inside and the other outside when on patrol. Stops them freezing up."

"But you had your Glock and Mikael the rifle, both of you were inside the cabin."

"Not for long, it was only a few minutes before Mikael left. I stayed with Dina."

"We will come to that," Vestergaard said and waved his pen at Fenna. "But you left Mikael's Glock in the cabin with the rest of your gear when you departed that morning."

"Yes."

"How many rounds did you fire from your Glock, Konstabel?"

"One, when I put Cisko down."

"Just the one?"

"Yes." Fenna watched Vestergaard make a note in his book.

"Do you know how many rounds were fired in total from your Glock?"

"No," Fenna shook her head. "There was a lot of shooting. I lost track of how many shots were fired, from any weapon."

"There was more than one weapon?"

"Yes."

Fenna looked up as Maratse appeared in the doorway. He plucked the cigarette out from the gap between his teeth and blew smoke into the kitchen. The policeman caught Fenna's eye and flicked his head towards Vestergaard and back again. She frowned at him as Vestergaard waved his hand at the smoke and moved to sit down at the table.

"So, let me check. Your unit had two pistols and a rifle."

"And the Webley," Fenna said.

"And where was that?"

"In Mikael's personal kit."

"Inside the cabin?"

"No. He had a satchel he carried inside the sledge bag. The

Glock won't stop a polar bear."

"But a handgun from World War II will?"

"Yes. It was the same age as the rifle."

"I suppose there are things I will never understand about the Arctic," Vestergaard said as he made another note. Fenna saw the elongated W at the beginning of the word Webley.

"Clearly," she said and glanced again at Maratse, but the policeman withdrew from the kitchen without another word.

Chapter 14

NORTHEAST GREENLAND NATIONAL PARK

Fenna pulled a spare pair of heavy cotton trousers and thermals from her pack. She pointed at the clothes as she pulled the satellite telephone from the cargo pocket of her trousers.

"You had better get more clothes on, and then we can talk," she said and turned on the satphone. Fenna paced around the room as she searched for a signal. Dina pulled the thermal bottoms over Mikael's thick socks. She shrugged off Fenna's jacket and pulled off her dress. Fenna stared at the lacerations on Dina's back. "What happened to you?"

Dina reached for the thermal top. She pulled it over her head and tugged it down her back, hiding the thin raised lines and welts. Fenna placed a hand on Dina's arm as she reached for the jacket.

"Are you hurt, Dina?" Dina shook her head and then pointed at her mouth. "Your mouth hurts?" Dina shook her head, no. She raised her hand and pinched a few centimetres of air between them. "A little then?" Dina nodded. "Okay, I'll see what we have in the medkit." Dina pulled on the jacket.

The report of the first shot echoed about the rock walls surrounding the cabin. Fenna looked up at the howl of a sledge dog and the *crack*, *crack* of two more shots.

"Wait here," Fenna said and tugged the sledge box containing Mikael's personal kit from beneath the pile of gear. She opened the lid, pulled out Mikael's pistol and stuffed it into her holster. A wave of adrenalin trembled through Fenna's body. Her hands shook as she picked up the spare magazine and slipped it into her jacket pocket. Fenna held her palm flat in front of her face, clenching her fist to stop it shaking. Dina grabbed Fenna's arm as she walked to the door. "It's okay," she said. "Just wait here while I go and look."

Dina pulled at Fenna's arm and shook her head; low guttural mewls fleeing from her mouth. She pointed at the cabin door, shook her hand and then pointed at the window in the rear wall of the cabin. Fenna jerked her arm free of Dina's grasp as three more shots echoed around the cabin. Dina crawled away from the door and hid behind the table and extra clothes and equipment littering the floor.

"That's good, just stay there," Fenna said and held up her palm. She stopped at the sound of her name drifting on the polar breeze across the snow, breaking on the walls of the cabin.

"Konstabel Brongaard? We have your partner. Come on out and we can talk."

Fenna flicked her head towards the door. *English? And how do they know my name?*

Dina stamped her feet. Fenna glanced at the Greenlander before reaching for the door handle. Another round of stamping caught Fenna's attention and she paused.

"It'll be okay. I'm just going outside."

Dina shook her head, her black hair whipping from one side of her face to the other. Tears caught the occasional strand, gluing them to her cheeks.

"You know them, don't you?"

Dina nodded.

"I'll see what they want. We'll be all right." Fenna turned her back on Dina's cries, unsnapped her holster and placed her hand on the grip of her pistol. She took a breath and opened the door.

Fenna had the door half open when Mikael was pushed onto his knees about twenty metres from the cabin entrance. She let go of the door handle as the man holding Mikael by the shoulder, pulled a pistol from his belt and shot her partner through the back of his skull. Fenna's breath caught in her throat as Mikael's body twisted, slumping into the snow in slow motion. She slammed the door shut and slid to the floor. With exaggerated gasps she fought to breathe.

"Konstabel? Fenna? Are you ready to come out?"

Fenna tugged the Glock from her holster and forced herself onto her knees. She shook as she slid over to the window and peered over the sill. Fenna watched as the taller of the two men kicked at Mikael's body. Her partner didn't move. The man adjusted the white ski mask, smoothed his hands down his Arctic camouflage smock and nodded at the second man. Fenna watched as the smaller man opened the tripod legs beneath the barrel of his weapon and slid into a prone position in the snow. She ducked as the man leaned into the weapon and shredded the door with three measured bursts of lead.

Fenna leaned over to the splintered door frame, pushed the muzzle of the Glock around the wood and loosed two 10mm rounds into the space in front of the cabin. Dina choked a long scream from where she hid at the back of the room. A fourth burst from the machine gun forced Fenna away from the door.

"Dina. Can you hear me?" she said and ducked beneath the window. Dina stared from behind the sledge boxes. "I need to know if you can drive a dog team." Dina stared at Fenna, waiting. "Can you drive dogs?" Dina nodded. Fenna took a breath. "Thank God for hunters' daughters," she said and bit her lip. "Okay. I'm going to get you out of here. Are you listening?" Fenna watched as Dina opened the box nearest to her, the Greenlander began stuffing snack bars into the pockets of Fenna's spare jacket. "Okay then. When you're ready, I want you to go out that window and wait until it's clear. When these guys come in here, you run for the top of the slope," Fenna pointed the Glock in the direction of the dog team. "There's a team of dogs and a sledge. You can get away," she said and slid the satellite phone across the floor to Dina, "far enough to use this. Have you used one of these before?" Dina nodded. "Good," Fenna let her head rest against the wall of the cabin. "This might just work." She turned back to Dina. "When you get a signal, dial the last number and just leave it on. Someone will come for you."

Dina searched among Mikael's personal items. Pulling a floppy mad bomber hat from the box, she held it out to Fenna.

"Take it," Fenna said as another bout of adrenalin shivered through her body.

Dina pulled the hat over her head, tucking loose strands of black hair beneath the rabbit fur. She looked at Fenna and stuck out her thumb.

"How old are you, Dina?" Dina flashed both palms twice, a single palm once. "Twenty-five, eh? Same age as me." Fenna shook her head. "What the hell are we doing?"

Dina stomped stocking feet on the floorboards. She pointed at her toes.

"In the box at the back," Fenna said and pointed.

"What's going on in there, Fenna?" The Englishman called from outside the cabin.

"No. The other one." Fenna waited until Dina found her spare boots. As Dina tugged them onto her feet, Fenna fired another round out of the cabin door. Dina stopped. "Keep going. Get them tied and get out of the window."

"Come on, Konstabel. That's no way to treat friends. We just want to talk."

Fenna pressed her head closer to the doorframe, listening as the men outside trampled the snow to either side of Mikael's body. "Dina, you ready?" Fenna pointed at the window. Dina moved to the window, opened it and unlocked the bolt holding the bear shutters in place. They swung open when she pushed them. Fenna blinked in the pink glow of the polar sky as Dina lifted one leg up and out of the window. Fenna nodded. "Go."

Dina climbed out of the window as Fenna fired three rounds out of the door, to the right of the cabin. She fired three more to the left. Two bursts of 5.56mm blistered the cabin walls. Fenna fired again. She looked back at the open window, a reflection in the square-framed glass revealed Dina moving away from the cabin. Fenna reached around the door and fired another two rounds. When she looked back, Dina was gone.

ITTOQQORTOORMIIT, EAST GREENLAND

The smoke from Maratse's cigarette still clouded the kitchen. Vestergaard coughed.

"I don't understand," he said and sighed. "How the hell does a twenty-five year old woman, wearing a…" Vestergaard checked his notes, "cocktail dress, escape from a remote cabin during a gunfight." He shook his head. "You expect us to believe this crap, Konstabel?"

"I'm sure Maratse does," Fenna said and nodded towards the policeman's office. She pictured him there, smoking beneath the portrait of the queen.

"Wearing a cocktail dress."

"She was wearing my spare clothes, Premierløjtnant."

"Sorry, yes of course. That makes it all the more plausible that a young woman leaps out the back of a cabin and makes her getaway on a sledge loaded with a top secret Canadian spy satellite," Vestergaard tossed his notebook onto the table. "Your words, Konstabel," he said and pointed the tip of his pen at her.

"You don't believe me?"

"I'm struggling, Konstabel, believe me."

"I'm the same age as Dina," Fenna said and crossed her arms over her chest.

"You've been trained by the military."

"And I grew up in a flat in Esbjerg. The most adventurous thing I did before Sirius was competing on groomed biathlon courses in Sweden and Norway. I cycled to school every day. When it was windy, my dad drove me. This was my life until I was finished with school and gymnasium." Fenna paused and gestured towards the tiny kitchen window. "Dina grew up here, wrangling sledge dog puppies as a toddler, she learned to throw stones at the big ones to keep them away. She grew up with dogs and ice and temperatures below forty. Do you hear what I'm saying?"

"Konstabel. Fenna," Vestergaard said and lifted his hand from his notes. "It's not that I don't believe she could get away. It's just highly improbable."

"For a Danish girl, sure. And yet here I am. But if we don't find her, before Burwardsley does, if we just sit on our arses, then Mikael..." Fenna gripped the table edge. "Mikael will have died for nothing."

"I understand that, Fenna."

"Then..."

"Wait a second. Let's agree that I believe you. Then you're right, we need to find Dina and retrieve the satellite, or what is left of it. But first," Vestergaard pulled out the chair. "I need to finish your debriefing. Petersen needs to get these recordings sent to the navy legal office and..."

"We're wasting time with all this protocol."

"Be that as it may, Konstabel. This protocol might just save your life. Now, continue, if you will, and tell me what happened next. Then, afterwards, we will find out what happened to Dina and get you to a safe place."

"A safe place?"

"Well, not here," Vestergaard looked out of the tiny kitchen window. "The fog is lifting. It's just a matter of time before helicopters can resume flying. The *Knud Rasmussen* is en route and as soon as we have communications again, I can hand the operation over to the navy."

"I thought you were the navy."

"I am," Vestergaard said with a look that Fenna couldn't interpret. "Now let's get this finished."

Chapter 15

NORTHEAST GREENLAND NATIONAL PARK

Fenna ejected the magazine from the Glock. She weighed the magazine in her hand and slid it back inside the pistol grip, flicking her head to the left at the sound of footsteps in the snow.

"Don't do anything stupid, Konstabel," said the Englishman as the short, black barrel of a bullpup rifle wormed its way around the door frame. Fenna squeezed her hand around the grip as the Glock shivered in her grasp. "Just drop the pistol."

"And if I don't?"

"It's your choice. Doesn't bother me either way. Although..." the barrel slid down the bruised wood as the man dropped to his knee. "You might want to look out the rear window." Fenna turned her head toward the back of the cabin. She grimaced as the Nepali waved from behind his rifle. "You understand now, eh? Just toss your Glock out through the doorway." Fenna turned the pistol in her hand and threw it outside. "Now get on your knees. Slowly. That's it. Place your hands behind your head..."

Fenna shuddered forward as a gloved hand gripped her fingers. She watched the shorter man climb through the window as her wrists were bound with a plastic tie. The tie snapped as it was pulled tight.

"Damn this fucking cold," the man said and gripped her fingers tighter. "Bad, come over here and help me."

The shorter man crossed the floor, slung his rifle and pulled a length of paracord from his pocket. He stood behind Fenna and wrapped the cord tight around her left wrist, pulled her arms behind her back and tied both wrists together.

"That'll do it. Now then," the tall man said and kicked Fenna onto the floor. "Let's have a little chat."

"Who are you?" Fenna turned her head to one side. The man with the ski mask shook his head.

"You're obviously new to this," he said and kicked Fenna in the stomach. "That isn't how this works." He squatted by Fenna's side, his breath misting out of the pores in his mask. "Where is the girl?"

"What girl?" Fenna said and coughed a spat of blood onto the floor.

"Seriously? You want to play rough? Bad," the man said and looked up at his partner. "Do you have any advice for this gal?"

"Yes, Saheb," Bad said and punched Fenna in the kidneys. Fenna grunted as she doubled over and swore in Danish.

"Speak English, love, or my friend will have to do that again and you will be pissing blood for a week, if you live that long." The masked man sat on the floor. "We'll try again, shall we? Where is the girl?"

"The Greenlander?"

"Yes, the fucking Greenlander. How many other girls have you seen wandering around this shithole?"

"She came with you?"

"More questions? Wait a minute, Bad," he said and held up his hand. "We'll give her that one. Yes, she came with us. A loose end, needing tidied up."

"Like my partner?"

"The Oversergent? Yes, you could say he was a loose end. If I had to choose between interrogating him or playing with you, well... it was a no-brainer, really."

"So you just killed him?" Fenna said and took a ragged breath.

"That's right, love. But it's a little more complicated than that," the man drew Fenna's Glock from his belt. "You killed him, actually. This is your Glock. This one is Gregersen's," the man pulled a second Glock from the belt at his back. He slid it over to his partner. "Wouldn't want to get them mixed up."

"Do you want the satellite? Is that what this is about?"

"You're a quick girl," he said and nodded. "Good guess. Where is it?"

"On the sledge."

"And the girl? The Greenlander?"

"Dina."

"Yes," the skin around at the corners of the man's eyes creased. "Dina."

"She escaped."

"Escaped? What, like she was your prisoner?"

"No. She escaped from you."

"No one escapes from us. Where is she going to go?"

"She has a sledge with a fully-rested team of Sirius dogs. She is going to get help."

Fenna watched the man's eyes flick to look at his partner before they turned back to her. He shook his head and laughed. "Damn, you are funny. You think your new friend is just going to disappear. Just like that."

"Yes."

The man lifted his head at the sound of rotor blades chopping the air from the east, nearing the cabin.

"I hope for your sake that she doesn't, or this is going to be a really long day for you. Get her up, Bad." He stuffed the Glock back into his belt and pushed himself to his feet. "That's our ride."

Snow blasted in through the cabin door as the AugustaWestland thundered into a hover, landing fifty metres away from Mikael's body. The men held Fenna inside the cabin as two crewmen from the aircraft dragged Mikael's body inside and began dousing the equipment and wood floors with aviation fuel.

"Get her on the chopper, Bad," Burwardsley said and handed him a syringe.

Fenna stumbled through the snow, the barrel of the man's rifle prodding her toward the aircraft. She turned as a wave of heat washed over her back. The masked man slipped a Zippo lighter into her jacket pocket as he passed. Fenna watched the cabin ignite, ducking as the rounds from Mikael's Glock started cooking off in the heat.

ITTOQQORTOORMIIT, EAST GREENLAND

"Well," Vestergaard leaned back in his chair. "That is quite a turn of events."

"That is what happened."

"Burwardsley paints a rather different picture, Konstabel."

"And you believe him?"

"He has a witness."

"Who shot my partner."

Vestergaard picked at a loose thread on his trousers. "So you say."

"Did I miss something? Have you switched sides all of a sudden?"

"I think you misunderstand, Konstabel. I was sent to debrief you, to discover the truth behind Oversergent Gregersen's death. I was never on your side."

"And Burwardsley?"

"The Lieutenant has been helping us with our enquiries.

Burwardsley and his Nepalese friend have been very cooperative."

"And I haven't?"

"Fenna," Vestergaard said and stood. "I'm sure you are tired. Perhaps it's best if we take a break and you take the opportunity to get some rest. Maratse? Please escort Konstabel Brongaard to her quarters."

Maratse smoothed the creases from the front of his uniform sweater. He nodded at Fenna, beckoned her to follow with a wave of his hand.

"My quarters, Premierløjtnant? I take it you mean my cell?" Fenna said. She pushed back her chair and stood up. "I guess I now know just how far the navy will go to protect its own."

"It's for your own good, Konstabel." Vestergaard picked the empty coffee mugs from the table and carried them to the sink. He turned around, leaned against the unit, and drummed his fingers on the work surface.

"You're not interested in what happened in the house, before you turned up?"

"It's not relevant to this stage of the investigation."

"And the satellite? Is that no longer relevant either?"

"I'm sure it's just a matter of time before your sledge and the satellite is retrieved. I'll be sure to wake you if I require any further assistance."

Fenna glared at Vestergaard. She resisted the urge to spit in his face, and followed Maratse into the cell.

"Shoes," Maratse held out his hands. "Belt," he pointed at the draw cord tied around Fenna's waist. Fenna kicked off her boots and slid them out through the door. She pulled the cord through the belt loops of her trousers, with one hand, holding her trousers up with the other. Maratse took the length of cord, wrapped it around the palm of his hand. Glancing over his shoulder toward the kitchen, the policeman leaned in close to Fenna. "*TELE* has repaired the connection. Mobiles are working." Maratse pulled his smartphone out of his pocket, swiped the screen with his thumb and presented an image of a man to Fenna.

"Who is he?" she whispered.

Maratse thumbed forward to the next photograph.

Fenna shook her head. "Who are they?"

"Dead. Danish," Maratse slipped the phone back into his pocket.

"In Kulusuk."

"Where the airport is?"

"*Iiji.*"

"Is everything all right?" Vestergaard said from the kitchen. "I thought I heard you talking."

Maratse lifted his hand with Fenna's makeshift belt. "She can keep this?"

"I don't think that is wise. No, you should probably keep that."

"Okay," Maratse said and leaned close to Fenna. "I'll be back soon," he whispered. The policeman stepped out of the cell and locked the door.

Fenna walked the short distance to the metal cot. She sat on the floor of the cell and leaned against it. She wrinkled her nose at the smell of urine drifting in from the toilet bucket next door, turned her head at the cries of children scrambling about the insulated pipes on the rocks outside the police station. Outside the cell, the sound of someone kicking sand and gravel from their shoes, reverberated from the wooden steps through the floorboards. Fenna shuffled closer to the door.

"Ah, Lieutenant," Vestergaard said. Fenna felt her stomach tighten. She tried to ignore it and pressed her ear to the door.

"She's still here?" Burwardsley's English accent slurred through the walls.

"Yes. In there," Vestergaard said and dragged a chair from the kitchen. "We can sit out here."

"She can hear us out here."

"That's the point. Isn't it?"

"Where's the policeman?" The chair creaked as Burwardsley sat on it.

"Maratse? He went out for a moment. He'll be back soon."

"Has he got any jurisdiction?"

"In this village? Yes. On this case? Absolutely none."

"I think we need to remind him of that."

"We?"

"It would be better coming from you. He seems to have taken a little too much interest in our girl in there," Burwardsley raised his voice and turned toward the door of the cell. "Can you hear me, love?"

Fenna pulled her knees to her chest. "Yes."

"Good." The legs of Burwardsley's chair scraped along the floor as the big lieutenant stood. He walked across the office floor and leaned against the cell door. "I hope you've been cooperative with your friend the Premierløjtnant."

"I think," Fenna said and took a breath, "he is more your friend than mine."

"Well, *love*. You have smartened up since we last met. Any more revelations you want to share?"

Fenna pushed herself to her feet and leaned into the door. "I think you had this planned from the start."

"That is possible," Burwardsley laughed. "More than you know."

"And you've covered your tracks well, getting rid of Mikael. Cutting out Dina's tongue…" Fenna waited. "You did cut out her tongue, didn't you Burwardsley?"

"Careful, Fenna," Vestergaard called out. "Don't say anything that can implicate you further."

"It's all right, Vestergaard," Burwardsley tapped the door with his knuckle. "Our little Sirius girl is hardly going to change anything from inside a cell."

Fenna tipped her head forward until it rested on the door. "What would Mikael do?"

"What's that, love? Couldn't hear you," Burwardsley said and laughed. "How about I come in there and keep you company?"

Fenna felt her heart begin to hammer inside her chest.

"We were so rudely interrupted last time we had a little chat." Burwardsley rapped the door again with his knuckles. "How about it, *love*? Shall we have a cosy chat? I'm sure Vestergaard won't mind."

"By all means, Lieutenant. Be my guest."

Fenna whirled around the cell, looking for a weapon as Burwardsley grasped the handle of the cell door. She held her breath as it rattled in his grasp.

"The key, Vestergaard?" Burwardsley said and kicked the door.

"I haven't got it. The policemen must have it."

Burwardsley swore and kicked the door a second time.

"Thank you, Maratse," Fenna breathed.

Chapter 16

Maratse's Toyota churned to a stop in the gravel outside. Fenna waited for the sound of the door closing once, twice, catching on the third go.

"There's one thing I want to ask you," Fenna said and took a step back from the door. She heard Maratse's footsteps as he kicked the grit from his boots at the door to the station.

"And that is?" Burwardsley said.

The door hinge squealed. Fenna leaned close to the gap between the cell door and the wooden frame. "Who are the dead Danes in Kulusuk?" she said and stepped back.

"Damn it, Vestergaard. I have to get in there," Burwardsley said and slammed his fist on the door.

"Not now, Mike," Vestergaard said and stepped closer to the lieutenant. "Not now." He paused as Maratse opened the door. "Officer Maratse. You remember the British lieutenant?"

"*Iiji*," Maratse said and tucked his hands into his gun belt.

"He was just helping with the investigation. Thank you, Lieutenant Burwardsley. I know where to find you if I have anything further."

"Sure. No problem." Burwardsley rapped the cell door on his way out. "I'll be seeing you, *love*."

Fenna moved to the tiny window at the rear of the cell. She stood on the edge of the bed and peered out, watching Burwardsley as he stomped past the children and pulled out his mobile. Fenna dropped down to the cell floor as Maratse unlocked the cell door.

"Time to go," he said and handed Fenna her boots.

"Where?" Fenna sat on the bed and tied her laces. She reached up to take the leather belt from Maratse's hand. "Yours?"

"*Iiji*." Maratse waited. "I'll take you to Kula."

"Where is Kula?"

"Not *where*," he said and laughed. "*Who*. Kula is a hunter."

"Wait just a minute, Maratse," Vestergaard said and pushed his way past the policeman and into the cell. "She's staying here."

Maratse placed his right hand on the grip of his service pistol and pulled his smartphone from his pocket. "Nikolaj Petersen," he said and pointed the screen towards Vestergaard. He thumbed forward to the next picture. "Klaus Vestergaard. Dead in Kulusuk." Maratse popped the quick release snap open with his middle finger and gripped his pistol. "She comes with me. You stay here." He nodded to Fenna. "Get out of the cell."

"Big mistake, Maratse," Vestergaard said and pointed at Fenna. "You side with her and I won't be able to help you."

"Like you helped Fenna?" Maratse said and pointed at Vestergaard's feet. "Shoes. Belt."

"You're kidding?"

"Shoes." Maratse tugged the pistol a few centimetres out of the holster. "Belt."

"It's no real wonder Greenland will never be independent," Vestergaard said and tugged his belt through the loops of his trousers. "Such a backward people. You're just not smart enough to make the right friends. Friends who can help you get out of this frozen shithole." Vestergaard pressed the toe of his shoe against the heel of the opposite foot, slipped his ankles out of his street shoes. "I could be a good friend to you, Maratse. Get you anything you want. Help you out of this mess and get you set up for life. Money. Flat screen television. Anything you want."

"I have a flat screen television. Fifty inch," Maratse said and took Vestergaard's belt. He stepped back to close the door.

"Wait," Fenna said and pushed past the policeman. "Who do you work for, Vestergaard?"

"You'll see," Vestergaard said and lay down on the bed. He crossed his arms behind his head and rested one foot over the other. "If you live that long." Vestergaard closed his eyes and smiled.

Maratse slammed the cell door and turned the key in the lock. "Open the gun safe," he said and pointed to his office. Fenna crossed the room, reached around the desk and grabbed the handle.

"Combination?"

"It's open," Maratse said and grabbed his jacket from the hook by the front door.

Fenna pulled open the door and found an M1 Carbine leaning against the back of the safe. She swept her hand around the dusty shelves and found an empty magazine and a small box of .30 calibre ammunition. She pocketed the smaller items, pulled the semi-automatic carbine out of the safe and joined Maratse at the door.

"Where did you get this? It's ancient."

"Standard issue," Maratse said and pushed half a cigarette into the gap between his teeth. "Kula is waiting." He held out his jacket and nodded for Fenna to put it on.

"Where?" Fenna switched the carbine from one hand to the other as she put on the policeman's jacket.

"On the ice."

"And where are we going?"

"To get Dina."

"They said she was dead?"

"Dina is not dead. You came by helicopter. Dina is north of here. She is coming by sledge."

"How do you know this?"

"Dina did not call Daneborg with your satellite phone. She called her grandfather."

"Kula?"

"Aap."

"How do we get to the ice?"

"We drive."

"Burwardsley is outside."

"We drive fast," Maratse said and shrugged. He reached beneath Fenna's arm and pulled a police issue wool hat from the pocket of the jacket. "Put this on. Hide your hair."

"It won't fool Burwardsley," Fenna said and pulled the hat over her hair, pushing the loose strands under the lip.

"Maybe not, but your hair won't get in the way when shooting." Maratse chuckled around the cigarette between his lips. "Ready?"

"You're enjoying this?"

"Better than picking up drunks on the weekend," he said and gripped the handle of the door. He pushed it open only to duck back inside the station as the first of Burwardsley's bullets thwacked into the door frame, the report of the *Browning Hi Power* ricocheting between the wooden buildings, echoing in the last clouds of fog. Maratse pulled his service pistol and loosed three rounds across the street at Burwardsley's position, the big lieutenant dropped to the ground and sought cover.

"Go." Maratse said and pushed Fenna toward the Toyota, the engine rumbling in the gravel.

Fenna pulled open the passenger door, hesitating at the sight of Petersen in the boot behind the rear passenger seat, his fingers curled around the square mesh of the dog guard.

"Don't worry about him," Maratse said as he jumped into the driver's seat.

"What's he doing there?"

Maratse threw the Toyota into reverse, gravel spewing from the front wheels, spattering the front of the station with stone shot. He reversed onto the street and shifted into first gear.

"He followed me," Maratse said as floored the accelerator. Fenna rocked into the policeman's shoulder. She gripped the carbine in her left hand, reached for the door and slammed it closed.

"You have to stop him, Fenna. He's breaking the law," Petersen said, his fingers gripping the dog guard.

"He's not the only one." Fenna shifted position to look out the rear window, flinching as the glass shattered and Petersen's head slammed into the guard, the crack of Burwardsley's Browning chasing the shot. She caught her breath at the sight of Petersen's blood, brain matter and bone fragments spattered across the plastic grille.

Maratse slewed the Toyota around the corner of the dirt street, sledge dog puppies and children scattering in front of the police car. He turned on the siren and the flashing blue light. A grin spread across the Greenlander's face. Fenna turned away from Petersen as the man's body slid into the rear and out of sight. She pulled on her seatbelt.

"Do we have a plan?" Fenna said and pushed her palm against the roof of the vehicle as Maratse bumped over an old sledge runner, shifted into fourth gear. "We're going to run out of road."

"No problem," Maratse said and pointed at the sea ice covering the fjord. "Lots of road there." He swung the Toyota into a right-hand turn, braked hard and wound down the window. Maratse pulled his service pistol and fired two rounds toward the red-striped yellow Hilux bearing down the dirt road. Fenna stared at the Nepali Sergeant behind the wheel.

"Where did they get a vehicle?"

"Stolen from the heliport," Maratse said and shifted gear. He stomped on the accelerator and slung the police car down the incline to the harbour. Fenna pushed one hand against the dashboard as Maratse bumped the Toyota up and over the ice foot. Once on the sea ice, Maratse shifted through the gears, surface melt-water spraying from the wheels, funnelling to each side of the car as he wound up the window. He turned to Fenna. "It's good? No?"

Fenna leaned into Maratse, tilting her head for a better view of the wing mirror. The yellow and red Hilux bumped over the ice foot, the rear end swerving left and right as Bahadur settled into pursuit. Burwardsley stood in the bed of the pickup, gripping the roll bar behind the cabin as he jostled the Nepali's SA80 onto the cab roof. Fenna watched as he leaned into the weapon and took aim.

The first burst from Burwardsley's SA80 raked the passenger side of the police Toyota. Maratse bounced up and down behind the steering wheel, cursing the ruts of the wheel tracks locking them in a straight line across the ice. He pushed the accelerator pedal flat to the floor, glancing at Fenna as the Toyota's engine growled - a mere thirty centimetres of ice between them and the Greenland Sea.

"We have to get out of this rut," Fenna said and banged her head on the window. She flinched at a second burst of lead to her right.

"Shoot back," Maratse shouted. "Crawl into the back seat."

Fenna threw the M1 Carbine onto the back seat, unclipped her seatbelt and squirmed between the seats into the back. She ducked behind the seat back and loaded the carbine, leaning her back against the passenger seat. Fenna poked the barrel of the carbine through the dog guard, resting the stock on top of the seat. She took aim.

Fenna's first bullet splintered the windshield, startling Bahadur into the same tracks they were caught in. With her target trapped in a static line of pursuit, Fenna took her time with each shot, anticipating the bumps and jolts in the ice road with well-placed rounds and the occasional near-miss. The Nepali slowed, the Hilux bumping further and further behind them.

"I made them cautious," Fenna called out as she peered along the sight.

"Maybe," Maratse said and adjusted the rear-view mirror. "Maybe not."

Fenna watched as Bahadur rolled the Hilux back and forth until the front wheel on the passenger side crept over the lip of the tyre tracks. The Hilux inched forward, bumped onto the surface of the ice and accelerated.

"They're coming back," Fenna said and pulled the M1 out of the grill. She slid over to the other side of the seat and took aim.

"Not long," Maratse called out.

"Until what?"

"Thin ice," he said and grinned at her in the rear view mirror.

Maratse shifted down through the gears and slowed the Toyota, rolling backwards and forwards until the police car bumped out of the tracks. With a volley of shots, Fenna pushed the Hilux to her left, further out to sea and wide of the Toyota. Burwardsley walked a long burst of 5.56mm into the ice and rear passenger window showering Fenna in a storm of glass.

"Maratse," Fenna yelled as she ducked.

"All okay," he said and accelerated, aquaplaning through a large puddle of surface meltwater. Maratse gripped the steering wheel as the Toyota spun one hundred and eighty degrees. When the Toyota stopped spinning the engine stalled.

The Ship

EAST GREENLAND

Chapter 17

"I'm getting out," Fenna said and slid across the seat. She opened the passenger door on the driver's side and dropped onto the ice. Fenna crouched by the rear wheel and took aim, firing single shots at the rapidly approaching Hilux.

The Toyota engine coughed and shuddered as Fenna ran back to the passenger door. The engine caught on Maratse's third attempt, exhaust fumes spattered the ice. Fenna climbed in behind Maratse as he shifted into first and spun the Toyota out of the puddle and in front of the Hilux just as Bahadur rammed the passenger side, crumpling the bonnet. Fenna fired blindly, emptying the carbine's magazine into the rear of the Hilux.

"Take this," Maratse ripped his pistol out of the holster and flung it onto the back seat. Fenna grabbed the Heckler and Koch 9mm USP Compact pistol, leaned into the back of the passenger seat and fired. Maratse flicked the finger at the Nepali as the police car and the Hilux roared alongside one another, alternating between jarring bumps and the *crack* and *thump* of incoming rounds.

"Shit," Maratse said and slammed on the brakes, spinning out to the left and away from the Hilux. He turned the Toyota toward the brown rocky coastline and accelerated away from a wide lead of black water splitting the ice in a long line before them. Fenna held her breath as Bahadur accelerated, throwing the Hilux over the lead and crashing into the sea ice on the other side, the rear wheels spinning, half on, and half off the ice. Burwardsley threw himself over the cab, sliding down the bonnet, spreading his weight over the front end of the vehicle. The Nepali turned the steering wheel back toward the ice, swerving toward the open water and back again, slinging the Hilux onto the safety of thicker ice. He accelerated in a course parallel to the police car. Burwardsley clambered back into the bed of the pick-up.

"We're going to run out of ice," Fenna said and crawled into the passenger seat beside Maratse. "It will be even thinner near the shore. The current around that point," she said and jabbed her fingers toward the granite coastline, where black lichen and bare rock peppered the snow above the ice foot. "It's bad there, isn't it?"

"*Iiji*," Maratse said and shifted to a higher gear.

"Then what?"

"Wait," he said. He jerked the Toyota into fifth and fished a crumpled packet of *Prince* cigarettes from his pocket. He tossed the packet into Fenna's lap.

"I don't smoke."

"I do," he said and pointed at his mouth.

Fenna pulled a cigarette from the packet and poked it between Maratse's lips. He rolled it into the gap between his teeth with his tongue and leaned forwards as Fenna lit the cigarette with the lighter tucked inside the packet.

"*Qujanaq*," he said. Maratse gripped the wheel with both hands and puffed at the cigarette.

Fenna turned to stare at the Hilux churning along the ice on the other side of the lead. Bahadur gripped the wheel. Burwardsley leaned against the roll bar, the stock of the bullpup rifle resting on his hip.

"What do we do about them?"

"Wait," Maratse said and swerved around a patch of thin ice. The Toyota buoyed as the pack ice bowed under the vibration of the wave building beneath the surface. Maratse slowed, driving in ever-widening curves around patches of ice too weak to hold the weight of the vehicle. "There," he said and pointed towards the shore.

"Where?" Fenna said and placed her hands on the dashboard. She leaned forward and scanned the coastline.

"Left of the point."

"A sledge," Fenna said and pointed. "I see it."

"Kula," Maratse said and grinned, smoke billowing out of the corners of his mouth.

"That's a big team." Fenna squinted, shading her eyes as the sun cut through the fog. A team of dogs running in fan formation pulled a long, broad sledge smartly across the ice. With an extra two metres of line, a small bitch led the team.

"Seventeen dogs," Maratse said and stabbed his chest with his thumb. "Seven of mine." He leaned over the wheel, staring at the ice as he accelerated.

Fenna twisted in her seat and looked across the lead of open water at the yellow and red-striped Hilux. She watched as Burwardsley banged his fist on the cab roof as he bent down to shout through the driver's window. The lieutenant pointed at the approaching sledge.

"Bad ice," Maratse said and pointed to the right as the Hilux slowed. "They won't make it."

"What's the plan?" Fenna said and rested the 9mm pistol on her thigh.

"You get on the sledge and go find Dina."

"With Kula?"

"*Iiji.*"

"What will you do?"

"Stop them," Maratse said and pointed at the Hilux crawling along the ice behind them. Fenna watched as Burwardsley jumped down from the vehicle and then walked ahead of it, directing Bahadur around the thin ice.

"You'll need this," Fenna said and slipped Maratse's pistol back into the policeman's holster.

Kula slowed his dog team to a stop. He leaped lightly from the sledge, curling the sealskin whip back and forth along the surface of the ice until the team dropped to their bellies. Maratse lifted his foot from the accelerator pedal, down-shifting and drifting to a stop by the side of the team.

"Out," Maratse said and nodded towards the sledge.

"Thank you," Fenna said and gripped the policeman's hand.

"Find Dina," he said and gave Fenna's hand a final squeeze.

"Be careful, Maratse."

"*Iiji.*"

Fenna stepped out of the Toyota as the policeman waved at Kula. Maratse stuck a new cigarette between his lips, lit it and crunched the Toyota into gear. He turned the vehicle through a slow circle on the ice as Fenna watched him leave.

"Fenna?" Kula said and pressed a firm hand upon her shoulder.

"Yes," she said and turned. The hunter cracked a smile in his weather-beaten almond-skinned face. His cheeks creased beneath bushy, black eyebrows.

"We must go," he said and hurried Fenna to the sledge and dogs.

The dogs stirred as she sat sideways towards the front of the sledge. Fenna zipped Maratse's jacket and pulled up the collar as Kula pressed the patrol's satellite telephone into Fenna's hand.

"The battery is dead," he said.

"Where did you get it?"

"From your sledge." Kula pointed to the mouth of the fjord to the east. "Around the point."

"Dina sledged all that way?"

"Maybe," he said. "I haven't found Dina, only your sledge and team. I'll take you to them." He glanced over his shoulder at the Toyota, cracked the whip on the ice and leaped onto the sledge, his thin legs hidden within the thick fur of polar bear skin trousers. Kula curled the whip along the ice, distracting the dogs from the alternating crack of 9mm and 5.56mm rounds as Maratse harassed Burwardsley and his Nepalese Sergeant. Fenna started at the noise of another round close by. Kula grinned, and snapped the whip a second time. The team tugged at the traces, blurring into a mass of fur and bushy tails pulling the sledge across the ice towards the open lead of black water.

"That's a big lead," Fenna said and clenched her fists.

"*Iiji*," Kula said and shrugged. "They're good dogs." He reached into a sledge bag hanging between the uprights and handed Fenna a pair of sealskin mittens. He nodded for her to put them on. The sealskin blocked the wind and Fenna's fingers prickled as they warmed.

She looked up as a long, low blast of a car horn cut across the ice. Maratse waved from beside the Toyota. The Hilux crawled along the ice towards them, Burwardsley leading on foot from the front.

Kula leaped from the sledge as the team slowed in front of the lead. Larger floes of ice bobbed in the water, and it dawned on Fenna that the hunter intended to use them. She waited for instruction as he encouraged the dogs with whip curls on the ice and soft words. Kula guided the lead dog over a smaller crack in the ice and towards the edge where a large floe bobbed two metres away in the dark seawater. The hunter ran to the sledge and picked up a length of rope.

"Hold this," he said and threw one end to Fenna. "Stand here." Kula pointed at the edge of the ice before the floe, in front of the dogs. He walked the length of the team to the rear of the sledge.

Fenna stuffed the mittens in her jacket pockets, gripped the rope and planted her feet squarely on the ice. She took a moment to study the hunter, the sealskin kamiks on his feet, the polar bear-skin trousers and the blue fishing smock pulled snugly over a thick wool sweater. *He is shorter than me*, she realised, *and three times my age. At least.* She held her breath as Kula, the whip in one hand and the end of the rope in the other, ran to the edge of the ice and leaped onto the floe.

Fenna gripped the rope as Kula scrabbled to his feet, the floe seesawing as the skin soles of his kamiks gripped the surface. He dropped the whip onto the ice and pulled the rope, hand over hand, tugging the floe to the ice. Fenna held on and laughed as the hunter grinned at her. He had fewer teeth than Maratse.

At Kula's command, the dogs pulled the sledge onto the floe. He picked up his whip and gestured for Fenna to get on the sledge. The next floe was smaller, but wedged against the opposite side of the lead. There was a metre of black water between the floes, and Kula tossed his lead dog by the harness over the water and onto the floe. The bitch skittered for balance, claws rasping on the ice. Kula leaped onto the floe and slipped. Fenna gasped as he gripped his lead dog by the leg and pulled himself into the centre of the floe. Kula kneeled on the ice, and, with a firm grip of the gangline, he pulled the floes together. The dogs shuffled on the ice, their paws spread and claws splayed for purchase on the slippery surface.

"I'm impressed," Fenna said and walked to the rear of the sledge. She gripped the uprights and prepared to push the sledge as Kula directed. As the floes crunched together in the water, he turned to leap onto the ice on the other side of the lead. His lead dog followed and the fan-shape of the team narrowed into a cornet as the dogs scrambled from one floe to the other and then onto the ice. Kula curled the whip behind them and nodded for Fenna to get back on the sledge. He ran for a few metres more before leaping on to the sledge and settling on the reindeer skins beside Fenna. Kula tucked the whip beneath the cord criss-crossed over the sledge, and let the end of the whip trail along the ice. He clasped his bare, nut-brown hands in his lap and watched as Fenna coiled the rope. The ice thickened and the runners shushed across the surface layer of snow and Fenna relaxed to the familiar sounds and rhythm of the sledge. She placed the rope on the thwarts beside her and slipped her hands inside the mittens.

"We made it," she said and smiled at the hunter. Kula nodded and turned to look over the rear of the sledge.

"They didn't," Kula said and laughed. He pointed at the Hilux sinking through the ice on the other side of the lead. The two British soldiers scrabbled to get clear. Fenna looked beyond the sinking vehicle and saw the familiar shape of the police Toyota as Maratse drove back towards the settlement. Kula nodded at the sky. "The fog is clearing. It will be a good day."

"Yes," Fenna said and looked up. "Good flying weather."

The dogs leaned into their traces, the lines taut, pulling the sledge across the sea ice to follow the coastline east toward the mouth of the fjord.

Chapter 18

The snow reflected the late morning sun and forced Fenna's eyes closed. She felt the warmth on her eyelids, lulling her into a sense of security at once familiar and dangerous. She blinked in the sunlight, the weight of her eyelids feeling heavy after the previous day's interrogation and escape. She slipped into the rhythm of the sledge, her chin tucked inside the collar of Maratse's jacket and her mittened hands clasped between her thighs. Fenna dozed as the dogs *shushed* the sledge along the ice, encouraged with a soft double clap of Kula's gnarled hands and an accompanying whistle.

They rounded the corner of the fjord in this way, Fenna's nose resting against the rim of the stiff collar, her breath freezing in tiny pearls upon her cheeks and bleaching the ends of her hair with a rime of frost, stiff and white. If she dreamed it was the soundless dream of fatigue, her body too tired to seek a more comfortable position, her mind too exhausted.

She woke at the jerk of the sledge as the dogs laboured up and over the ice foot that marked the boundary between the sea ice and the land. Diamond hard it was a minefield of sharp edges, crazy paving flipped vertical. The ice foot rose and fell with the tide. The tide was out and the dogs had to work to reach the safety of the hunter's winter camp. They whined as the sledge runners caught, and the lines tangled around the mini bergs barring their way. Kula worked the dogs back and forth, lifting the lines and lifting the dogs when they stumbled, confused within the labyrinth of ice, as if the sea was reluctant for them to leave and the land was too stubborn to receive them.

Fenna opened her eyes and stepped off the sledge, stamping her numb toes to life and clapping her hands, urging the blood into her fingers. Her cheeks, the prominent parts just below her eyes, were thick like putty. She removed a mitten and pressed her fingertip against each cheek, cursing at the stubby resistance – the early stages of frostbite, her penance for fifty minutes of rest. She walked to the rear of the sledge and helped guide it up and over the ice foot as Kula untangled the dogs and led them into camp.

They were met with a chorus of whines and the familiar half-bark of Greenlandic sledge dogs, tethered with short lengths of chain to bolts hammered into cracks in the rock. Fenna recognised their voices and felt a tear begin to freeze beneath her left eye as she recognised one canine voice in particular.

"Lucifer," she whispered and choked back another tear. The remaining dogs from call-sign *Fever Dog*, tugged at the chains and lifted their paws in the air, snapping at the new arrivals and howling at the sight of Fenna. She let go of the sledge and let Kula lead his team up to the dirty canvas tent another twenty metres from where her team was anchored. Fenna dropped to her knees in front of Lucifer and buried her nose in the fur around his neck as he wriggled within her grip and strained to bump noses.

"I've missed you," she said, her words lost in the lead dog's fur. Lucifer leaned against her side and Fenna felt the reassuring weight of his body and the tickle of sharp claws pressing through her trouser leg.

"Fenna," Kula called and she pulled away from the dog and looked up. The hunter beckoned for her to come and help secure his team. He tugged the bight of rope leading to all seventeen dogs and freed it from the line attaching it to the centre thwart between the sledge runners.

"You don't want to tie them individually?" Fenna said as she helped him haul the dogs to a large iron ring sealed in a crack of exposed rock with cement.

"*Eeqqi*," he said and flicked his eyes towards the blue sky. "Good flying weather. We might want to leave in a hurry."

Fenna nodded and helped Kula secure the dogs in the fan formation. She knew they would twist the lines, as they roamed, but was surprised when they flopped to the ground as one and lay quietly, gnawing at the ice and wind-packed snow.

"We'll feed them later," Kula said and gestured for Fenna to follow him.

Inside the tent, Kula pulled Fenna's sledge bag out from behind a packing crate. He let her rummage through it while he lit the wood-burning stove, peeling off his smock as the temperature inside the tent rose. He picked at the holes in his thermal top while Fenna arranged the items from the sledge bag on the flimsy cot beside the stove. She placed the spare battery for the satphone beside the antenna, spare ammunition for the Glock and a handful of bullets for the Webley. She pulled the pistol out and handed it to Kula. He turned it one way and then the next.

"Good for bears," he said, admiring it in the yellow light of the tent.

Fenna nodded and pulled spare clothes out of the bag, together with the component she had unscrewed from the satellite. She tossed it onto the cot and unzipped her jacket. Fenna turned her back to Kula as she peeled off Maratse's spare clothes and replaced them with her own thermal layers, olive drab windpants, thick socks and a Norwegian wool sweater. She paused before pulling the sweater over her head and turned to look at the hunter.

"Dina wore this," she said. Kula raised his eyebrows in silent affirmation. "Where is she?"

"I don't know."

"But the sledge? The gear?"

"I found the sledge and your dogs on the ice. Alone. They were tired," he said. "I brought them here and fed them. Then I went to look for Dina."

"You found nothing?"

Kula pointed at the satellite phone Fenna removed from Maratse's jacket. "I found that," he said. "On the ice."

"But no trace of Dina?" Fenna sat down on the cot as Kula set a black kettle on the rusty stove. "Kula," she said. "Do you think Dina is still alive?"

Kula fiddled with two enamel mugs, preparing a mug of strong tea with lots of sugar for both of them before he answered. "*Iiji*," he said. And then, "Maybe."

Fenna thought about the distance the dogs had travelled. Even with a light sledge, it was a long way. A few hundred kilometres. When the going was good, a Sirius patrol with a fully-loaded sledge averaged fifty kilometres a day. Dina had travelled four times that distance, perhaps stopping to feed the dogs, and to dump the satellite. *That's what I would have done. It's just dead weight.*

Kula handed Fenna a mug of sweet tea and fished inside a cardboard box for a packet of ship's biscuits – hard crackers full of fat. Fenna nibbled at one as she replaced the battery in the satphone. The cold had sapped it of energy, but there was just enough power to check the call history. She turned the display towards Kula and pointed at the last three numbers dialled.

"That's Daneborg," Fenna said and pointed at the last of the three numbers. "I made that call when we found the satellite." Kula nodded and pointed at the second number.

"Me," he said and took a sip of tea.

The last number was a long one that Fenna didn't recognise. "And this one?" she said.

Kula shook his head and brushed biscuit crumbs from between the hairs of his trousers.

Do I call it? Fenna wondered and rested the satphone in her lap. She powered off the phone and placed it on the cot. Kula handed her the Webley and she added it to her gear.

"What did Dina do for work?" she asked.

"She worked on a ship, as a guide."

"A guide," Fenna said and glanced at the satphone. *Then she would be familiar with satellite phones.* "Who did she work for?"

Kula shrugged and sipped his tea.

"She spoke Danish and English?"

"*Iiji*," he said. "and East Greenlandic."

"How long had she been a guide?"

"Three years," Kula said. He put down his empty mug and stood up. He reached behind the stove and plucked a faded photograph from its place on a wooden shelf tacked between two crates. He handed it to Fenna. "When she graduated school," he said. Fenna smiled at the glow of pride that flushed the hunter's wrinkled cheeks.

"She looks so young," Fenna said.

"1991."

"The year she graduated?" Fenna said and frowned.

"The year she was born."

"Okay," she said and handed the photograph to Kula. He smoothed a wrinkled corner with his thumb and returned it to the shelf.

"Dina," he whispered and sat down. On the cot opposite Fenna. She waited for him to speak, but Kula closed his eyes and took several breaths before he said another word. Fenna emptied the sledge bag while she waited. Other than the spare clothes and the Webley, the spare battery was the only other useful item. She slipped the pistol and phone into the bag and rolled it at her feet.

"Sorry," Fenna said as Kula opened his eyes. "I didn't mean to disturb you," she said and nodded at the bag.

"You didn't," he said and cocked his head to one side. "Listen."

Fenna listened as a breath of chill wind flapped at the tent door.

She shook her head and opened her mouth to speak, stopping as Kula raised his hand.

"Helicopter," he said. "From the south."

Fenna heard it then and picked up the sledge bag. She glanced at Kula and he nodded, pulling the smock over his head as he stood up. As an afterthought, Fenna picked up the satellite component and thrust it into the sledge bag, pausing briefly to scan the tent for useful items before following Kula outside.

The dogs pricked their ears at the sudden activity as Kula pulled Fenna behind the tent to where he had hidden the Sirius sledge. Kula ripped off the plastic tarpaulin and shoved the sledge past the tent, stopping for a moment as Fenna looped the sledge bag over the uprights and helped him slide it down to her team. They wrangled Fenna's dogs into harness and clipped them into the ganglines.

"There's nowhere to hide," Kula said and nodded towards the ice. "Best to keep moving."

"Where to?"

"Out there," he said and gestured into the distance. Fenna peered in the direction he pointed and squinted at the grey fog lapping at the ice to the east. "We can lose them in the fog."

"Okay," Fenna said and tugged Lucifer to the front of the team. Kula had arranged the lines in fan formation. *Or was it Dina?* Fenna wondered. Once they were through the ice foot maze, running in fan formation would be faster. *And speed*, Fenna realised, *was everything.* She turned at the click of a rifle bolt and watched as Kula slung it around his chest. It was a small calibre with a rusty barrel and a sling made of bailing twine, but Fenna didn't doubt the old man knew how to use it. Kula grinned and pointed two fingers at the sky, shaking his hands and spluttering like a machine gun.

"Yes," she said. "If only we had one of those." Fenna stopped as her stomach turned a somersault. She steadied herself with a hand on the uprights, before checking the sledge and walking the gangline to fuss the dogs.

"Fenna," Kula said as he joined her at the head of the team.

"Yes?"

"Go east, into the fog, all the way to the open sea."

"And then?"

"North, to Daneborg."

"Yes," Fenna nodded. It made sense to try to get to the Sirius base. "It's a long way."

"*Iiji*," Kula said. "And dangerous."

"Because of them?"

"*Eeqqi*," he said and wrinkled his brow. "Because of bears." He pointed at the sledge bag. "Keep the pistol close."

"I will."

"Good," he said and paused at a new sound whining beneath the *whop whop* of the helicopter. "Snowmobiles."

Fenna brushed her hair behind her ear and listened. "Two of them," she said.

"Go," Kula said and waved Fenna towards the ice. "I'll follow you."

Fenna watched as Kula jogged back to his own team. He slid the rifle from his shoulder and secured it between the cords criss-crossing the thwarts on his sledge. Kula pushed a plastic fish crate onto the sledge, fastened it and then heaved a clear plastic sack of dried fish into the crate.

He thinks of everything, Fenna mused before the whine of the snowmobiles forced her into action and she ran to the rear of the sledge.

"Come on boys," she yelled and pushed at the sledge uprights. Lucifer tugged at the harness and picked a route through the jagged barrier of the ice foot and down onto the sea ice. Fenna found her skis tucked beneath a cord on the sledge and clipped them into her boots as the dogs paused for direction. She turned to see Kula move his team through the ice to join her, and flicked her head to the south and west for sign of the snowmobiles. Fenna saw the helicopter first, the same one that had landed at the cabin. "Burwardsley," she said and suppressed a tremble through her body. She reached into the sledge bag and tucked the pistol into the waistband of her windpants. "This time, you British bastard," she said. "We'll see who owns the ice."

Kula whistled that he was ready and his sledge shushed past her. He tossed Fenna the sealskin mittens and clapped his hands for his team to pick up speed. Lucifer jerked Fenna's team into motion and she slipped behind the uprights as the helicopter worked its way overland towards Kula's camp. Fenna glanced over her shoulder as the snowmobiles whined around the point.

"Come on, boys," she yelled. "Let's go."

Chapter 19

The remnants of call-sign *Fever Dog* clawed at the ice. Nine dogs and one bitch raced after the hunter's team of ten lean dogs and Maratse's additional seven. The ice was smooth, with only the occasional ridge or bump to jar their progress. Fenna alternated from the left to the right-hand side of the sledge, correcting the team depending upon Kula's course towards the open sea.

The petrel grey fog licked at the ice in the distance and Fenna blinked at a cream blur ahead of the team. *Polar bear*, she wondered only to have Lucifer confirm it as the lead dog slowed to sniff the air, much like when the team had encountered the wolf. Kula's dogs had spotted it also, and the distance between the two sledges increased. The whine of the snowmobiles behind Fenna turned her head. The drivers hunkered behind the low plexiglas windshields and increased the throttle, leaping ahead and splitting up to flank the sledges, one on either side. Fenna reached for the pistol in her waistband, reassured by the weight. She tapped the butt and returned her hand to the upright as the snowmobiles closed the distance.

"Come on, boys," she shouted, her breath misting and freezing in front of her face, it pearled upon her sweater and froze on the fleece around her neck. She licked at the ice beading above her lip and cast another quick glance at the snowmobiles. Burwardsley, she observed, was on the one to her right, his large awkward frame instantly recognisable. She shuddered at the thought of what he would do when he caught up with her. But the fog, Fenna noticed, was thickening.

She scanned the horizon, twisting her neck to stare at the sky behind her, where the camp should be on the coastline. There was no sign of the helicopter and she couldn't hear the beat of its rotorblades above the grating of the runners on the ice and the incessant buzz of the snowmobiles. *And the bear,* she remembered and flicked her eyes to the horizon. *Where is it?*

Burwardsley was the first to draw his weapon, the snap of the bullet from his Browning caused Fenna to duck and ski to the other side of the sledge. She watched as Kula tugged his rifle free of the cords criss-crossing the thwarts. He dropped to one knee and leaned against the uprights, tracking the approach of the Gurkha on his snowmobile. Kula fired, chambered another round and fired again, forcing the Nepali to swerve out of range. Fenna reached for the Webley only to duck again as Burwardsley fired two shots in quick succession. The second splintered the right runner as it clipped the sledge and skittered across the ice.

"Fuck it," Fenna yelled and drew the Webley from her windpants. The handgun was heavy in her hand. She leaned into the left hand upright, curled her left arm around it, and straightened her right arm, pointing the Webley in the general direction of Burwardsley's snowmobile. She pulled the trigger and almost smiled at the reassuring boom, only to feel the shot go wild as her arm flicked with the recoil from the unsupported firing position. Lucifer skittered at the head of the team, but Fenna made her point and Burwardsley throttled down and swung further to the right. She thrust the pistol back into her waistband and swung to the right of the sledge, holding on to the uprights and yelling encouragement to the dogs.

"Come on, boys. Let's go."

In the confusion of the snowmobile chase and the exchange of bullets, the dogs had all but lost the scent of the polar bear. It came back with a vengeance as Lucifer changed direction, veering to the northeast, and the sledge surged ahead with renewed vigour. Fenna caught sight of the bear as she passed behind Kula's team. The hunter waved his arms into a cross above his head.

"I know," she shouted. "I can't slow them." She braked her skis into a vee only to feel the vibration rumble through the bindings and threaten to tear the skis from her boots. Fenna straightened them, placed them flat on the ice and held on.

Bahadur, she realised, had also seen the bear. He slowed his snowmobile to a stop and pulled the SA80 from the holster he had jury-rigged to the passenger seat. Fenna watched as he slipped off the snowmobile and stepped behind it, resting the assault rifle on the seat, tracking the bear as it loped across the ice. The Gurkha's first shot, however, lifted Fenna's wheel dog off the ice. It tumbled in its traces and slid across the surface as the team continued to chase the bear.

"Fuck," she said and drew the Webley. *He's going to take out my team.*

Bahadur's second shot clipped the end of the sledge, and Nansen, the second of the two wheel dogs, lost its footing, skidding to its knees and yelping as the rounded tip of the right sledge runner pressed into its back. The dog clawed at the ice and staggered into a running position as its running mate was dragged lifeless alongside it.

Fenna fired a random shot in Bahadur's direction. As the Nepali ducked she gritted her teeth, rested the pistol on the crossbar between the two uprights, and fired again. The satisfying crack of the bullet piercing the engine casing of the snowmobile brought a smile to her face. She turned away from Bahadur to scan the ice for Burwardsley. She found him, in front of her and to her right. He was trying to cut her off. Fenna looked for the bear and realised that Lucifer had pulled the team to within a few hundred metres.

If I can get in front of it, I can use it. Fenna let Lucifer lead the team as she worked her way along the sledge towards the sledge knife the hunter had secured just behind the runners. "Thank you, Kula," she whispered as she pressed her bottom onto the sledge thwarts and let the ice bump her skis. Fenna inched forwards until she could draw the knife and cut the dead wheel dog from its traces. The sledge rode up and over the dog's body with barely a missed beat. Fenna slid the knife back into its scabbard and searched the ice for Burwardsley.

The Royal Marine was behind her, easing down on the throttle and signalling to Bahadur to run to him. Fenna watched as Bahadur jogged across the ice to Burwardsley. Behind them, the helicopter blurred into view as it thundered towards them, just twenty metres above the ice.

Kula, Fenna realised, was gone, enveloped by the fog and the snow clouds that had rolled in behind it from the sea. Fenna's world turned grey and thunderous, as the visibility decreased only to be replaced by machine noise and the excited clamour of sledge dogs. She caught a whiff of something feral and watched the bear's flight turn into fight as it slid to a stop and turned to face Fenna and her team.

"Fuck," she said and drew the knife again. Fenna sawed through the gangline and released the dogs. Once free of the sledge, the team leaped towards the bear as the sledge ground to a stop. Fenna kicked off her skis and ran to the rear of the sledge. She tugged the sledge bag free of the uprights and thrust her arms through the loops. She ignored the dogs as they baited the bear with half-barks, bared teeth and feints. Fenna caught a last glimpse of Lucifer as the bear batted a giant paw at the lead dog, only to be attacked from behind by Betty and Ninja. Fenna ran across the ice in the direction she imagined Kula had driven his dogs, towards the open sea.

The whine of Burwardsley's snowmobile increased in pitch, louder than the helicopter as it escaped the thunderous chop of the aircraft and followed Fenna into the fog and snow. As the air thickened, Fenna caught the static crackle of radio chatter between Burwardsley and the pilot as the Lieutenant ordered the helicopter to stay close. Fenna smiled at Burwardsley's frustration as the rotor noise diminished and the helicopter retreated from the fog. The dogs, she realised, had also disappeared. Fenna slowed as the fog enveloped her and her visibility decreased to a mere handful of metres. She stopped and turned a slow circle as she listened for the sound of the snowmobile, the dogs, anything.

"Not good," she whispered and raised the pistol in her right hand. She clutched the knife in her left.

Fenna heard the distant whine of the snowmobile to her left. It increased in pitch but diminished as if Burwardsley was accelerating in the wrong direction. She held her breath and cocked her head towards the other sound, the soughing breath and the huff of something large padding across the ice towards her.

Snow tickled Fenna's cheeks as the flakes thickened and swirled around her body. She imagined the bear to be to her right, and caught a whiff of wet fur, not dissimilar to that of the dogs. The scent was stronger and suggested something bigger, more powerful, faster. Fenna whirled at the first sight of the bear, its black snout pointed down toward the ice, its tiny ears alert and those great paws – Fenna could see the claws, black, thick as two fingers, sharp as pitons.

"Go away," she shouted and levelled the pistol at the bear. At one hundred metres Fenna had thought the bear to be huge, at ten it was mountainous. Fenna pointed the Webley at the ice, a metre in front of the bear and pulled the trigger. The bear reeled at the explosion, amplified as it was by the fog. The 11.6mm bullet punctured the ice in front of the bear, and it faltered. Fenna fired again, half a metre closer and the bear staggered back as a small crater cracked just a paw's length in front of its snout. The empty Webley wobbled in Fenna's grasp as the bear twitched in front of her, turned and loped back in the direction it had come.

Fenna slumped onto the ice and let the Webley rest in her lap. The knife slipped out of her grip and Fenna tucked her hand beneath her armpit to stop it shaking.

She sat there until the cold penetrated the seat of her windpants and forced her to stand up. She bent down to pick up the knife and slipped the Webley back into her waistband. Fenna turned to sniff the air and felt a fresh breeze with a subtle tang blow in from her right. She turned to face it and hoped she was walking east, towards the sea, to Kula.

She stopped after five minutes to slip the Webley into the sledge bag. She looked at the knife and placed that inside the bag too. She remembered the satphone and pulled it out. The phone flickered into life with a power warning. Fenna dialled Daneborg and waited. The phone burred through the number; the dial tone sounded to Fenna like it was being bounced around the world.

"Noa?" she said when a familiar voice answered her call.

"No, this is Kommandør Kjersing. Who am I speaking to?"

"This is…" Fenna started. She paused as a beam of light captured the fog in a brilliant white triangle and staggered in increments toward her. "This is..." Fenna tried again, but then the light caught her and she was at once blind and dumb as the familiar sound of metal biting into ice was magnified, far more than the metal edge of her skis when she braked, greater than the sound of runners on black ice. This was bigger than that; the noise was monstrous. A behemoth of marine industry. As the ice protested, the smell of diesel engulfed Fenna, reeking of industry, power, and man.

"Fenna? Is that you?" Kjersing said but Fenna was silent. She stared up at the massive bright red bow of a ship as it pressed down on the edge of the sea ice. Fenna was pinned to the spot with a searchlight from the deck of *The Ice Star.*

Chapter 20

The power warning on the satellite phone beeped and ended the call. Fenna lowered her hand and held the phone by her side as two men in full Arctic gear clumped down the accommodation ladder, zigzagging down the hull of the ship and stepped onto the ice. She watched as they walked towards her. The second the men stepped inside the cone of light from the deck, their shadows flanked Fenna on either side. Compared to the men, Fenna was underdressed. In the time it took them to unzip their fur-lined parka hoods, lift their goggles and tug their fleece balaclavas below their chin to speak, Fenna had made her decision – she would ask them to take her onboard the ship. Kula was gone, Burwardsley would realise his error and change course – *he might have done so already*, she realised – and the polar bear could return at any moment. With her survival instincts adapting and reacting to every new scenario, Fenna spent less and less time reviewing each new development since her escape onto the ice in the police Toyota. *One step at a time*, she reminded herself. *Just stay ahead – always at least one step ahead, and adapt. And*, she thought as she recognised the name of the ship, *find Dina.*

"My name is Bose," said the shorter of the two men in Indian-style English. "I am the ship's purser, and this is our head of security, Charlie Watts."

"We received a distress call for two hunters in trouble on the ice," Watts said. "Are you in need of assistance?"

"Yes," Fenna said and nodded. "I need assistance."

"Where is your sledge?" Watts said.

"Back there." Fenna pointed over her shoulder. "But there's a bear," she said and added, "A big one. I frightened it off, but I think it will be back." Watts reached behind his back and drew a large Magnum pistol.

"Mr Bose," Watts said. "Time to get back on the ship."

"Yes," Bose gestured for Fenna to follow him. "Do you have any belongings?"

"No," she said and fell into step beside the purser. He twisted at the waist to look at her, tugging at his hood with thick-gloved fingers.

"It's a little odd to meet a woman, alone on the ice. We were told to expect two hunters."

"Life is full of surprises," Fenna said and winced at her own cynicism. "I was with my grandfather," she said.

"You are Danish?"

"Yes, but my grandfather is Greenlandic." Fenna smiled at the thought of Kula and enjoyed the little white lie.

"I see," Bose said and stopped at the first step on the accommodation ladder. Watts joined them and nodded for Bose to go first. He lifted his foot onto the first step and stopped. "This is a private vessel. We will need to process you through security before you are allowed to venture further inside the ship."

"All right," Fenna said. "But I don't have any form of identification on me."

"We'll figure something out," said Watts. "Let's just get onboard before the bear comes back, shall we?"

Fenna followed Bose up the ladder, to the right, left and right again as they worked their way to the lower deck on the port side of the ship. She turned as the searchlight flicked in sharp increments across the ice before being extinguished with a soft thump.

"Where is your grandfather?" Bose asked as he guided Fenna to the security desk and a custom-sized baggage x-ray machine. Fenna paused to look at the security officer with a metal detector wand in his hand and a pistol holstered at his hip.

Fenna hesitated for a moment. "He is on his way back to camp. I called him on the satphone," she said and held up the phone in her hand.

"He doesn't require assistance?"

"No."

"But he didn't come back to get you?"

"We were separated in the storm. I called him as soon as I saw your ship. I told him I was okay." Fenna took a breath and continued, "The storm looked like it was going to get worse. I wanted him to get home."

Watts stepped inside the door and instructed the crew to raise the accommodation ladder. He holstered the magnum, pulled down his hood and removed his gloves. Fenna's pulse increased as Watts studied her. As head of security, she knew she was ultimately his responsibility, but his predator eyes were unsettling nonetheless. She slipped the sledge bag off her shoulders and handed it to the security officer standing beside the x-ray machine.

"I have a gun and a knife," she said. Watts stirred but Fenna tried a smile. "For protection. From bears."

"That's not a gun," the x-ray officer said as he pulled the pistol out of Fenna's bag. "It's a relic."

"Oh, I know someone who would like that," Bose said as he leaned around Fenna's shoulder for a closer look at the Webley.

"Is it loaded?" Watts said.

"With empty shells," Fenna said. "I used them all on the bear."

"Fair enough," Watts said and nodded at the crewmen to close and lock the door. He stepped around Bose and lifted a handset from the wall. "Captain, this is Watts. We're good to go." He replaced the telephone and returned to his position against the wall as his men ran Fenna's bag through the x-ray machine and checked her body with the wand.

"What's this?" the baggage security officer asked as he turned the satellite component in his hands.

"A bit of old radio," Fenna said and shrugged. "It was in my grandfather's bag. He is always collecting junk from old machines. It's difficult to get parts in the Arctic," she added. The officer slipped it back inside the bag along with the satphone.

"We'll have to keep your weapons," he said. "There is a safe in the hold the next deck down. We'll keep them there and you can have them again when you leave the ship." He reached for a clipboard and pushed it across the desk to Fenna. "Sign here." Fenna signed her name, conscious of Watt's scrutiny. "That should do it," the officer said and returned the clipboard to a hook on the bulkhead behind him.

"And this is your ID card," Bose said and showed Fenna a plastic card with a V for visitor stencilled onto the front. He clipped it onto her sweater. "Keep it on you at all times."

"Okay."

"Now, before we go any further, there are rules," he said. Bose paused as a forty-something woman wearing a stone-coloured alpaca dress and brown Bedford coat stepped into the security lounge. She paused to look at Fenna before addressing Bose.

"Who is our new guest, Kabir?" she said.

"Mrs Marquez," Bose said with a discreet dip of his head. "This is..."

"Fenna Brongaard," Fenna said and held out her hand.

"Vienna," said the woman. She held Fenna's hand and studied

her fingers. "My dear," she said. "Have you been in battle?"

"Something like that," Fenna said and smiled. The woman's touch was feather-light and yet firmer than Fenna had imagined. She reached for Fenna's left hand and held them both under the light. "Your skin deserves more, Fenna," she said and looked up. "Did I pronounce your name correctly, dear?"

"Yes," Fenna said and caught her breath. The woman's eyes glittered like ice, as the corners twitched in a smile. Fenna restrained the impulse to flinch as Vienna let go of her hands, reached out and teased her hair into single strands.

"Just what *have* you been doing?"

"We found her on the ice, Ma'am," said Watts.

"Charlie," Vienna said as she studied Fenna's face. "You know how I detest that title."

"Yes, Mrs Marquez."

"And that one is hardly any better," she said and flicked her eyes at the head of security. "Mr Bose?" she said and turned away from Watts.

"Yes?"

"How long will Fenna be staying?"

"Ah, that is as yet..."

"Undecided? Good." Vienna took a step back and nodded at Fenna. "My husband is away, and you shall be my guest."

"Your guest?"

"Of course," Vienna said and plucked the visitor card from Fenna's sweater. "G for guest," she said and took Fenna by the arm. "Do you have any luggage?"

"Just my sledge bag," Fenna said.

"Bose will bring it to my apartment, while I show you around."

"Mrs Marquez," Watts said and took a step forwards. "With respect, this woman has not been vetted. Neither has she been briefed on ship protocol, or even dress code. I really don't think..."

"And I don't care, Mr Watts. You know what my husband does for a living."

"Yes," he said.

"Then you should know the types of *guest* I am familiar with. I think we can both agree that my current guest, despite her cosmetic needs, fits a rather different category than those I am accustomed to receiving in my home."

"I was just doing my job," Watts said and sighed.

"And you do it admirably," Vienna said. "And I trust you will continue to do so. If I require more assistance, and if my guest," she said and paused to squeeze Fenna's arm, "should prove to be troublesome, I trust you to do your job, Charlie, as per your contract."

"To the very letter, Mrs Marquez," Watts said and pressed his hands inside his belt. Fenna caught the look he shot at Bose as she was whisked out of security and into the reception lounge.

"Such bores," Vienna said as she pointed out the grand piano, waving to the pianist as he experimented with *Rachmaninoff Concerto No. 2*. "The pianist, however," Vienna said and pulled Fenna close, "is far more interesting. He only plays Rachmaninoff for me – it's my signature tune."

Vienna guided Fenna through the lobby and into a corridor lined with a few select shops. They paused in front of a window and Fenna marvelled at the jewellery on display.

"There's no price tag," she said.

"If you have to ask the price, my dear, then you simply can't afford it," Vienna said and gently pulled Fenna along the corridor past the delicatessen and the ship's general store. It reminded Fenna of *Meyer's Deli* in Copenhagen. "People are starting to stare," Vienna whispered as they passed two couples coming out of the store. "It must be your authentic rustic look," she said and giggled. "I couldn't care less, but chins will wag if we don't do something about it. We'll take the lift to my deck and you can relax while I find you something to wear."

"I don't want to trouble you," Fenna said as she tried to gently prise her arm free of Vienna's.

"Nonsense," Vienna said. "It's my pleasure. Besides, as long as you join me for dinner, then you will have repaid me a thousand times more than I can expect."

"Dinner?" said Fenna.

"Yes," Vienna said and sighed. "I have been summoned to dine with the ultimate of bores, his partner and their wives." Vienna stopped at the lift to press the button set in an elegant brass panel. "It seems that Richard thinks a woman is incapable of eating alone. It's the same thing every time Alejandro is away on business, I am summoned."

"By who exactly?" Fenna said as the door to the elevator slid open.

"By that bastard, Humble," Vienna said and stepped inside the elevator. Fenna's boots stuck to the floor, like sledge runners caught in a patch of meltwater freezing on the ice. "Well, come on, my dear. We can't keep the bastard waiting. And," she added, "I fear it will take more than a quick shower to rinse away the grime of battle." Vienna laughed and held out her hand. "Don't worry," she said as Fenna took her hand and let herself be pulled inside the elevator. "I won't let the bastard bite."

Fenna watched as the door closed and her reflection slid into view. She studied her face beside Vienna's and willed her cheek muscles into a smile. *Humble is here.* The thought crowded her mind as the elevator purred upwards through the decks.

Chapter 21

The elevator whispered open and Fenna paused before stepping out of the mirrored interior and into the plush-carpeted passageway. Everything about *The Ice Star* was plush, she realised. Plush and functional. It was also over-designed, sailing in a class of its own, the brainchild of a group of rich Norwegians looking to combine five star comfort with an insatiable lust for adventure. Few ships of its size could cope with the ice, fewer still could afford to. *Don't let yourself get sucked in*, thought Fenna as she followed Vienna to her cabin door. *Stay sharp.*

"Did you hear me, dear?" Vienna said as she slipped her keycard from her jacket pocket.

"No," Fenna said and shook her head. "I'm sorry. I was just trying to take it all in."

"All what? Oh," Vienna said with a nod to the passageway. She smiled. "My dear, you really have been in the wilds far too long if a bit of brass, a couple of oil paintings, and a thick carpet throws you for six." The door unlocked with a beep and Vienna closed her fingers around the handle. "Do you have a problem with dogs?" she said and waited for Fenna to answer.

"Dogs?" she said and peered through the gap in the door as Vienna opened it. "I'm fine with dogs," Fenna said and suppressed a laugh.

"Good for you," Vienna said and opened the door. The shrill bark of a small dog cut through the hum of the warm air conditioning as they stepped inside the cabin. "Personally," she said as she closed the door, "I can't stand them. The dulcet tones you can hear are from Alejandro's beast. I keep the little mongrel in the bathroom. Over there," she said and shut the cabin door. Fenna glanced behind her as the door locked with a beep.

Vienna took off her jacket and hung it on a wire-frame mannequin by the door. She ushered Fenna beyond the pine finish of the hallway and into the cabin proper. Fenna caught a gasp in her throat as she followed Vienna inside, her eyes flitting from the leather sofa to the mirrored wall, beyond the spacious kitchen and back to the black hardwood table facing the balcony. The cabin was twice the size of Fenna's family flat in Esbjerg. She took a few steps towards the sofa as Vienna walked into the kitchen and prepared two mugs of coffee. The polar bear rug beneath the glass and birch coffee table was the only item in the flat Fenna could identify with, that and the view of the thick fog pressing against the cabin window.

"The crew call us guests," Vienna said as she waited for the coffee machine to finish preparing the first mug.

"Guests?"

"Yes. Instead of passengers. Although, I rather like to think of myself as a resident," Vienna said as she placed Fenna's coffee on the kitchen counter. "I spend all my time here. It keeps me away from Alejandro and his dreadful business." She turned back to the machine.

"What business is that?" Fenna asked as she curled her fingers around the mug.

"Cocaine," Vienna said as she sipped at her coffee. She raised her eyebrows, and Fenna caught the twitch of a smile in the corners of her eyes.

"Seriously?"

"Fenna, my dear," Vienna said as she guided her into the lounge. "How else do you think I can afford to live here?" Fenna sat down in the corner of the sofa as Vienna shushed at the dog whining from the bathroom and then sat down opposite her. "I speak for myself, of course," she said. "Most of the residents aboard *The Ice Star* are thoroughly reputable. Incorrigible and ruthless, but reputable all the same. You seem surprised?"

"Yes, perhaps," Fenna said and put her mug down on the coffee table.

"Take off your boots, dear. You are stiffer than one of Alejandro's dead rivals."

Fenna paused as she reached down to untie her laces. Vienna wore that smile again, the one that threw a coal of warmth upon her ice-bright eyes. She undid her laces and hesitated before removing her boots.

"I'm not quite dressed for your apartment," she said.

"Nonsense. Take off your boots, my dear. Relax. I have too few guests to complain. You are my first since October. Alejandro comes once a month or so, just for a few days," she said as Fenna placed her boots behind the sofa and, at Vienna's urging, curled her feet beneath her legs and settled onto the cushions. "He never stays long. Always on the move. Of course, I make sure to feed up the dog before he comes."

Fenna lifted the mug of coffee to her lips and looked around the cabin as Vienna talked. She lingered over a painting hanging on the bulkhead to the right of the balcony.

"Monet?" she asked and pointed at the painting with her finger.

"Yes," said Vienna and kicked off her own boots. "Do you like it?"

"I recognise it," Fenna said. "I'm not sure what to make of art."

"It's a fake. Alejandro has the original at home, but wouldn't settle for a print, so he had a local artist make a copy." Vienna sighed. "It's all about the *look*, the *feel* of money and what it can buy. These clothes, for example," she said and tugged at the hem of her dress. "I am from Switzerland, but I dress like Katherine Ross."

"Who?"

"From *Butch Cassidy and the Sundance Kid*," Vienna said and smiled. "Before your time, I'm sure."

"Yes," Fenna said. She uncurled her legs and stood up. Vienna followed her to the balcony. The ship's engines thrummed through the floor, tingling Fenna's toes as she studied the fake oil painting.

"I even married a bandit," Vienna said as she stood beside Fenna. "Only he's from Colombia, not Bolivia." She waved her hand as Fenna frowned. "Don't mind me," she said. "More film references. I see far too much television. That and books are all that keeps me sane on this damned boat."

"Why do you stay?"

"Why? Ha," Vienna said. She walked around Fenna and placed her mug on the dining room table. "I don't stay, my dear, I am kept. I am an amusement," she said and glanced at the bathroom door. "Like the fucking dog."

"I'm sorry," Fenna said and raised her hands. "It's not my place."

"No, perhaps not, but..." Vienna paused as if to erase a shadow from her mind. Fenna watched as her host made a decision. "Yes," she said. "It was rash of me to invite you into Alejandro's den, but I'm so very lonely, Fenna. I don't know how long you will be aboard – as short a time as possible if it's up to Charlie – but let us relax this evening at least. Within these walls, we can tell each other secrets, and pretend that no-one is listening."

"Pretend?" Fenna said and looked around the cabin.

"Oh, no, silly me," Vienna said and placed her hand on Fenna's arm. “It's not bugged. There are no cameras. Believe me,” she said and let go of Fenna's arm. “I’ve had plenty of time to look. No, there are others onboard that like to film things.” She shuddered for a moment and then continued, “But Alejandro can't risk having anything on file. For obvious reasons.”

“I can imagine,” Fenna said and smiled.

“What the other guests do with their cameras, well, that's up to them. I’m sure that one day,” she said with a sneer that Fenna could feel as easily as she could see it, “those bastards will realise they made one film too many.”

“Is there anyone onboard that you like or is likeable?” Fenna asked.

“Oh, yes, I’m sure there is. I just don't mix with them, my dear. No, Alejandro has vetted my circle and that’s why we must suffer the likes of Richard Humble tonight.”

“Who is he?” Fenna forced herself to ask.

“Humble?” Vienna said and paused to tap her fingers on the table. “Richard is as Canadian as Alejandro is Columbian. Impeccable manners, polite and generous. He is a charmer. His only public flaw, the only chink in his armour, is his partner, Mark Lunk.” Vienna curled her fingers into a brief fist before smoothing her palms over her dress. “I don't know what it is that binds the one to the other. But Lunk is a pig with...” She stopped at the curl of her lips. “Excuse me,” she said. “That's enough for now. No matter the company, it does not do to speak ill of dinner guests before the meal. Let’s find something for you to wear, then I’ll let the dog out of the bathroom and you can relax and freshen up. You'll have the cabin to yourself,” Vienna said as she led Fenna to the bedroom. “I’ll take the mongrel upstairs.”

“Upstairs?”

“Yes,” Vienna said and nodded. “Alejandro has bought the cabin above. He’s hired a marine architect to draw up plans to put in a staircase, over there,” she pointed, “right where the coffee table is.”

Fenna pushed the image of a two-storied cabin out of her mind and waited as Vienna let the dog out of the bathroom. She caught a smile at the sight of the Pekingese as it yapped at her feet. The thought of a Colombian drug baron tickling the dog behind the ears made her laugh out loud, causing the dog to yap even louder.

“It is laughable, isn't it,” Vienna said and tried to call the dog to her. She gave up and fetched a treat for the dog from a ceramic pot on the kitchen counter. "Like its master it has a high opinion of itself," she said as she held out the treat and clipped a leash from her pocket into the dog's collar.

"When you breed the wolf into a dog that size," Fenna said, "You're asking for trouble."

"A wolf?" Vienna said as she stood up, tugging at the leash every time the dog barked.

"All dogs come from the wolf," Fenna said with a shrug. The thought of Betty and the wolf flashed through her mind, as did the image of her team as they raced towards the polar bear. *If they are smart*, she thought, *then they will follow the scent back to Kula's camp.*

"You look distracted, dear. Let me get rid of the dog, then you can clean up. We're about the same height," Vienna said as she glanced at Fenna. "And you are a size A?"

"As flat as they come, yes," Fenna said and glanced down at her chest.

Vienna laughed and tugged at the leash. "We're going to get along well, Fenna, my dear. I might just have to encourage the Captain take the long way back to the mainland." She pointed at the bathroom. "Fresh towels are on the rack. The maid was in earlier, but who knows what the dog has done since then. Watch your step."

"I will."

"I'll be down later to find something for you to wear." Vienna looked at her one last time and nodded as if she had already decided on Fenna's evening attire.

The dog erupted into a new round of shrill barks as a porter knocked at the door. Vienna fumbled with the leash as she opened the door and received Fenna's sledge bag. The porter nodded and retreated down the passageway towards the elevator as the dog nipped once at his heels.

"Damn this animal," Vienna said. She gripped the sledge bag as Fenna took the leash from her hand, reached down and flipped the dog onto its side. Fenna slipped her right hand over the dog's muzzle and held it firmly as the dog settled beneath her grip.

"I know dogs," she said and smiled up at Vienna. "I think that's mine." Fenna gestured towards the sledge bag.

"Yes," Vienna said and closed the door. "May I look inside?"

"Sure, go ahead," Fenna said. "There's not much."

"There's nothing at all," Vienna said as she reached inside the bag. "Oh, wait. There's a phone. That's all."

"That's all?" Fenna relaxed her grip on the dog as she did a quick mental inventory. The Webley and the knife were locked in the safe. Vienna had the phone. The muscles of Fenna's stomach tightened as she realised the satellite component was missing. She let go of the dog and checked the sledge bag, sweeping her fingers around the inside, and fighting another round of muscle cramps as she confirmed that it was gone.

"You look pale, dear. Is something missing?"

"Yes," Fenna said and took a step back. She held out her hand as Vienna gave her the satellite phone. She looked at it, bit her lip and nodded. *Next step*, she thought to herself. "Do you have a USB charger?"

"Now that," Vienna said, "is something I do have."

Fenna nodded as she glanced at the satphone. "Time to call for backup," she whispered as Vienna led the dog across the cabin floor in search of a charger. "But who do I call first?"

Chapter 22

Fenna's mind raced with questions. She showered, dressed in a robe and towelled her hair, then she walked into the lounge area of the apartment – she couldn't call it a cabin – and checked the battery level of the satellite phone. She frowned at the single solid black bar, one of five. *Not even enough to turn it on.* Fenna put the phone down, sat on the sofa and hugged her knees to her chest.

"*Think*," she said to herself, the single word lost in the upholstered interior. Fenna leaned back on the cushions and closed her eyes. She imagined Kula on the ice, running his dogs on the thinnest layer where the sea bit at the edge, where snowmobiles could not follow. She saw Burwardsley then, his face a mask of professional hatred, eyes piercing the fog, searching for Kula, for Fenna, for Dina. "Dina," Fenna said and opened her eyes. The room drifted into focus and she gripped the hem of her bath robe. She slipped her legs over the side of the sofa and checked the phone battery once more, shaking her head as she pushed it back onto the surface of the small table next to the power outlet. *Who did you call, Dina?* she wondered. *Who would you call after your grandfather?*

Fenna chewed on the thought and returned to the sofa. She closed her eyes again, thinking through what she knew, rejecting her best guesses. Her thoughts returned to the ship, and how it came to be there, at the edge of the ice, at the right moment. A blurred image of Burwardsley's handwritten note pressed its way into the fore of Fenna's mind. The logo, a ship. A ship with a name. *The Ice Star.* A ship for the rich and the infamous. A home from home at sea, beyond borders, beyond the law. *A haven*, she realised as her mind wandered and her thoughts drifted, merging with the incessant fog pressing at the windows.

Fenna woke at the sound of the lock beeping. She sat up as Vienna let herself in, the keycard in her right hand, a dress draped over her arm, and a pair of high heeled shoes in the other.

"Did I wake you, dear?" she said as she bumped the door closed with her hip. "You must be exhausted."

"No. I'm fine. Really."

"You sure you're up for dinner?"

"Yes," Fenna nodded. *I need to meet him.*

"Good," Vienna said. She hung the dress by its hanger from a shelf and held out the heels. “I hope we have the same size.”

Fenna slid along the sofa and took the heels, slipping the left one onto her foot. “They fit,” she said. “But I’ve no idea how I’ll walk in them.”

“I am sure your boots will be more comfortable, but there is a dress code, and you simply won't be allowed into the restaurant unless you are dressed for it.”

Fenna put on the right heel and stood up. She took a breath and walked around the sofa. “I haven't worn heels since gymnasium,” she said and laughed. It felt good to laugh, to be distracted.

“Try on the dress,” Vienna said. “I’ll fix us a drink.”

The heels left deep impressions in the carpet as Fenna willed her way across the floor of the cabin. She lifted the dress from the shelf and noticed the panties and bra folded over the inside of the hanger. Black, like the dress. Fenna took it into the bathroom. She put on the panties and bra and then pulled on the dress. After almost a year of olive drab cotton windpants, wool sweaters that scratched at her skin until she learned to ignore the itch, and the cling of week-old thermal layers, the dress slipped across her skin like spindrift. Fenna caught herself smiling in the mirror. She teased out her hair, curling a handful into a loose ponytail and letting the sides hang in bangs to frame her face, and hide the bite of the Arctic wind and the slap of a Nepalese fist. She twisted to the left and the right, enjoying the swish of the side panels and the tickle of rayon on her legs. With a last look in the mirror she stepped out of the bathroom. Vienna sighed as she walked into the lounge.

“Stunning,” she said and pressed a gin and tonic into Fenna's hand. “Truly, stunning. Do you like it?”

Fenna curled her fingers around the glass and nodded. “I do. Although the heels,” she said with a guilty glance to where they lay on the bathroom floor.

“You can kick them off under the table.”

“Yes.”

Vienna walked over to the kitchen and placed her glass on the counter. She returned with a pair of black elbow-length lace gloves. “The final touch, before make-up,” she said.

Fenna exchanged her glass for the gloves and slipped them over her frost-beaten fingers. She slid her thumb into the loop and tugged the gloves to her elbows. The thumb loop was at least familiar, but her mind raced with that which was not – the clothes, the apartment, the ship.

"Think of it as camouflage," Vienna said and took a sip from Fenna's glass. "You are simply getting ready for battle." She reached out and teased a few more strands of Fenna's hair, letting it fall across her cheeks. Fenna's stomach turned over as Vienna's fingers brushed her cheek. Vienna caught her eye and withdrew her hand. "Drink up," she said and gave Fenna her glass. "I'll change in my room and then we can go to dinner."

Fenna waited until Vienna had closed the bedroom door before putting down her drink and checking the battery level of the satellite phone. "Two bars," she whispered. She unplugged the charger and took the satellite phone to the window. The door was unlocked and Fenna stepped out onto the balcony. The chill wind tugged at the fine hairs on her skin as she powered up the phone and scrolled down to the second to last number, the one between her call to Daneborg and Dina's grandfather. She checked the signal, wrinkled her brow at the poor reception, and pressed the button to dial. Vienna's shadow flickered in the light from her bedroom window next to the balcony as the dial tone burred in Fenna's ear.

"Come on," she said, the fog beading her hair as the wind tugged at the strands. The dial tone ended and the sound of wind crashed through the earpiece.

"Dina?" said a man's voice. The single word clamped around Fenna's chest before the satellite phone beeped with the loss of signal.

"Fuck," Fenna said and lifted the phone from her ear. She held it above her head and looked up as if searching for the satellites through the fog, above the earth. The phone beeped as the call ended and the words NO SIGNAL flashed across the screen. A rumble that could have been rotor blades caught her attention before Fenna slipped back inside the cabin and pushed the charger into the micro USB port. She stepped away from the phone as Vienna walked out of her bedroom.

"Were you just outside?" she said. "I was sure I felt a draught."

"Yes, I needed some air." Fenna felt the blood rush to her cheeks. Her mind wandered back to the call. *Dina, whose voice was it?*

"What do you think, my dear? Will I do?" Vienna turned on the spot, the graphite ribs of her dress hugged her body above the waist, flaring above her knees.

"Stunning," Fenna said.

"That's my word, dear. You shall have to think of another over dinner, or there will be a forfeit. Now," she said as she joined Fenna in the lounge. "Make-up." She gave Fenna a tube of lipstick and a powder blush for her cheeks. Fenna stared at them. "May I?" Vienna asked and took a soft brush from the purse hanging from her arm.

"Yes," Fenna said and nodded. She held her breath as Vienna applied powder to her cheeks.

"You seem distracted, dear," Vienna said as she finished with Fenna's left cheek and dusted her right with the bristles of the brush.

"I'm fine, really," she said as Vienna stepped back to give Fenna a look.

"If you say so. Although, I must admit, you know rather more about me than I do about you."

"There's not much to tell," Fenna said. She stopped talking and closed her eyes as Vienna pressed the tip of the lipstick to her lips.

"No? The Captain came by while you were showering," Vienna said. Fenna flicked her eyes open. "He said it was highly unusual for a woman to be sledging on the ice, even more so that she should be alone. In fact," Vienna paused to roll the lipstick along Fenna's bottom lip, teasing at the vermilion borders. "He said that the only white women to sledge on the East Coast of Greenland were tourists or," she smiled as she smoothed an errant smudge of lipstick from Fenna's skin, "soldiers."

Fenna could feel the weight of the lipstick tugging at her lips. She stood, lips parted, her face barely two hand lengths away from Vienna's, close enough to catch the diamond scrutiny of her eyes and the crow's feet concealed beneath a dusting of powder.

"Do you trust me, Fenna?"

"No," she breathed.

"Good," Vienna said with an enigmatic nod. "Then we will be the perfect partners this evening."

"Why?"

Vienna closed the blush with a snap and stepped back to perch on the arm of the sofa. She slipped the make-up into her purse and tossed it onto the cushions.

"If Alejandro has taught me anything," she said and plucked at the edge of one of the ribs of her dress, "it is that partners must never trust one another. That way neither partner can be disappointed or surprised."

"I am a soldier," Fenna said.

"I know."

"A sailor, actually, with the Danish Navy."

"With the sledge patrol?"

"Yes."

"The Captain said as much," Vienna said and rested her hands in her lap. "Do you intend to steal from me?"

"No."

"Use me?"

Fenna paused for a beat. "If I can."

Vienna nodded. "An honest answer." She tugged at a hair tickling her eyebrow, pulled it from her head and twitched it out of her fingers onto the carpet. "Do you know Richard Humble?"

"I know of him, yes."

"And you've heard of *The Ice Star*?"

"Yes."

"But not of my husband?"

"I have no interest in your husband."

"That makes two of us," Vienna said. She chuckled as she stood up. She glanced at Fenna's hands. "I'm afraid no amount of cream or varnish will help those nails of yours. But then, in tonight's company, it might be appropriate to show a little of your wild side. Just to keep the bastards in check."

Fenna nodded towards the bathroom. "I'll get my shoes."

"Yes," Vienna said. She caught Fenna's wrist as she passed. "I won't pretend to know your plan, I'm not even sure you have one, but I will help you."

"Why?"

"Because if you came aboard this ship knowing the name Richard Humble, then you, my dear, are in a lot more trouble than I will ever be."

"Thank you," Fenna said, and nodded. She tugged her wrist free of Vienna's grip and pointed at the bathroom door. "My shoes."

"Of course," she said and let go.

When she walked out of the bathroom, Vienna gave her a keycard and a raisin coloured shawl. Vienna, she noticed, had an identical one wrapped around her shoulders.

"I bought two by mistake," she said and shrugged.

Fenna let Vienna wrap the shawl around her. She ran her hands over her hips, biting her lip at the lack of a weapon. *I have never felt so naked*, she thought, *not even when Mikael pulled me out of the ice*. She shivered at the memory as Vienna opened the door.

"Ready?"

"Yes," Fenna said and tucked the keycard inside the glove on her left arm. She stepped into the passageway and ignored the scrape of shoes on her heels. Vienna held out her arm and they walked to the elevator. Fenna smiled at the ship's guests, singles and couples, as they passed them in the passageway and squeezed beside them in the elevator. Vienna chatted and exchanged pleasantries as Fenna studied the ship's schematic hanging at numerous positions on their route to the restaurant. She let Vienna guide her through the lobby, the notes of the piano altering key as they passed, and then they were past the jewellery boutique and delicatessen. The glass doors of the bar were open and the restaurant, one of two onboard, was only a few metres away when Vienna stopped.

"Fenna?"

"Yes?"

"Do you see them?"

Fenna looked beyond the entrance to the restaurant and searched the tables for anyone that might resemble Humble and his partner.

"No," she said.

"There are three men and two women at the table furthest from the bar."

Fenna found the bar and looked to the right of it, towards the windows, and there, sitting beside two men and their wives, was Burwardsley. She faltered on her heels as he caught her eyes and glared at her.

"Bathroom," Fenna said and tugged at Vienna's arm.

"Here," she said and led Fenna out of the passageway and into the ladies' restroom. Fenna stumbled to the sink and retched.

Chapter 23

Fenna wiped her mouth with a cloth hand towel and checked her face in the mirror. To her amusement, her lipstick wasn't even smudged. Unlike my confidence, she mused. "Fuck," she said and stared at herself in the mirror. "He doesn't have the right to make me feel this way," she whispered. *But he does.*

"Do you want some water, dear?" Vienna said and filled a glass from the drinking fountain. She handed it to Fenna. "I thought you had never met Richard?"

"I haven't," Fenna said and sipped at the water. She set the glass by the sink and stood up straight. "I'm okay. Let's go," she said and nodded towards the door. She followed Vienna into the passageway and to the front desk of the restaurant. Fenna caught the name *Starlight* above the door and then her attention was consumed by the table the waiter led them to. He stopped as the men at the table stood as they approached. Vienna kissed each man on the cheek. She paused beside Burwardsley.

"Mike," she said. "I didn't know you would be joining us."

"Neither did I," he said and winked at Fenna.

"Mike just got in on the chopper," Humble said. Fenna studied him as he stepped around Vienna to pull Fenna's chair out from the table. The cut of his tailored suit matched his cologne, delicate but sharp. Fenna caught herself admiring his jawline and the way he wore his black hair, casual but neat. "I don't know any man that can slip into a tux faster than Mike Burwardsley," he said and gestured for Fenna to sit. "Richard Humble," he said and took her hand.

"Fenna," she said and caught the lump in her throat. She forced a smile upon her lips and made a point of looking at each of the guests seated at the table. Vienna waited for Humble to pull back her chair and Fenna realised he would be sitting next to her.

"So glad you could join us, Fenna," he said as he sat down. "When the ship stopped to pick you up we were intrigued, only to discover our luck that Vienna had taken you in." He glanced at Vienna as he poured Fenna a glass of wine. "How's that dog of yours?"

"You know perfectly well how he is," she said and held out her glass. Humble filled it, put down the bottle and picked up his own glass by the stem.

"To Vienna's dog," he said and raised his glass.

"Vienna's dog," the party chorused and then stilled as they drank. Fenna sipped at her wine and forced herself to look at Burwardsley. She tried to anticipate the rules of the game but was distracted as Humble interrupted her thoughts.

"Introductions," he said and placed his glass on the table. "To your left is my lovely wife, Stella." Humble waited for Stella to smile. "Mike has just been introduced," he said and gestured at Vienna sitting next to him. "Vienna you have met. And sitting beside her is Mark Lunk."

"Richard's partner," Lunk said and nodded at Fenna. She caught his gaze as it rested on her chest. The colour in his fat cheeks and his blatant stare suggested to Fenna that he was drunk, or doing his best to become so.

"Yes, for my sins," Humble said and flicked his hand to the woman sitting to Mark's right. "Madeleine, Mark's wife, completes the circle, and," he added, "no circle would be complete without her."

"Thank you, Richard," Madeleine said and blushed. Fenna imagined it was not the first time she had been the last to be introduced.

The waiter gave Fenna a moment to think as he returned to take their orders for starters. Humble ordered the same main dish for all of them, *something French*, she thought as she struggled with the unfamiliar words. Bread was served and Fenna forced herself to eat as the conversation returned to Vienna's dog and then to her guest.

"Of course," Stella said, "we're dying to know all about you."

"Me?" said Fenna and swallowed.

"Oh we know all about her already," Lunk said and reached for the bottle of wine. He frowned as Humble moved it away from him, emptying the last drops into his own glass. Fenna caught the look Humble shot at his partner as he set the bottle down on the table. Lunk's lips snarled as he turned to Fenna and said, "Jane fucking Bond herself."

"Mark," Humble said with a nod at Burwardsley.

"No, it's all right," Lunk said. "I'll explain." He lifted his palms and made a slowing sign towards Burwardsley. "I was just going to say that our guest is like a spy."

"A spy?" said Stella.

"That's right," he said. "I mean, who else turns up in the middle of fucking nowhere with a gun, a phone and a radio, eh?" He looked around the table. "Jane Bond," he said and thrust his arms across the table. Madeleine reached for her glass as he knocked it over, the wine stained the tablecloth. Lunk chuckled and took the napkin from his lap to dab at the wine.

"I'll do it," Madeleine said and brushed his hands away. Burwardsley suppressed a smile and took a long sip from his glass. He watched Fenna over the rim.

"Mark," said Humble.

"What?"

"Why don't you go and get a drink at the bar."

"You sending me away, partner?" Lunk said and lifted his finger to stab at the space between them. "You're starting to make a habit of that..."

"A habit I would dearly like to quit." Humble nodded at Burwardsley. "I think Mike might like a drink. It's thirsty work out on the ice." Burwardsley pushed back his chair, but Lunk lifted his hand.

"No," he said and wobbled to his feet. "I prefer to drink alone. Either that, or maybe I'll drink with that savage whore in the hold." He looked up and grinned. "Eh, Richard?"

Fenna held her breath as Humble smoothed his fingers on the tablecloth. Burwardsley stood and dropped his napkin onto his seat. He ignored Fenna and moved to stand right behind Lunk, his eyes focused on Humble, waiting for a nod.

"I really don't know why I put up with this," Humble said. Lunk stopped grinning, his face paled and he jerked his head around to look at Burwardsley.

"Hey, I'm sorry, Richard. Really," he said and pressed his knuckles on the tabletop. "I was out of line." He turned to his wife. "Out of line, *again*," he said. Madeleine turned away as Burwardsley placed his huge hands around Lunk's shoulders and guided him away from the table to the bar. Fenna turned in her chair to watch as Burwardsley found an empty stool for Lunk and slipped a tip to the waiter to keep an eye on him. He waited until Lunk ordered a coffee and then returned to the table.

"Madeleine," Humble said as Burwardsley picked up his napkin and sat down. "Would you like another glass of wine?" She nodded and Humble raised his hand to attract a waiter. He ordered two bottles of wine and more bread. Fenna looked at Burwardsley only to find his attention was fixed on Lunk as he sipped his coffee at the bar.

The savage whore in the hold? Dina? she wondered. Fenna turned to glance at Lunk and, forgetting for the moment the voice on the other end of the satphone, she made a decision. She looked up at a brush of toes on her legs. Vienna caught her eye and mouthed the word, *sorry*. Fenna shrugged and took a sip of wine as Stella made another attempt at conversation.

"I don't believe you are a spy," she said. "But do tell. Who are you and how did you come to be on the ice, so far from civilisation?"

"Civilisation?" Vienna said and laughed. "That is assuming that Greenland is civilised. Personally," she said and took a sip of wine. "I find that hard to believe."

"There is plenty of civilisation in Greenland," Burwardsley said without taking his eyes off Lunk. "The capital, Nuuk, has a concert hall, museums, cafés," he turned to look at Vienna. "They even have a court and a bank. Just how civilised do you want them to be? The population of Greenland is about the same size as Hereford, in England. But they are spread out over an island about nine times the size of Britain." Burwardsley turned to continue his observation of Humble's partner. He flicked his gaze towards Fenna for a moment and she thought she caught the briefest of smiles.

Conversation halted as the waiters brought the food to the table. Fenna studied Burwardsley as she turned his words over in her mind. She lifted her hands as the waiter placed a plate in front of her. As he arranged her cutlery, Burwardsley pushed back his chair to stand.

"Bugger," he said and moved around the waiter for a better view of the bar.

"Mike?" said Humble.

"He's gone. I can't see him."

"Really?" Humble said and twisted in his seat. "I shouldn't worry, Mike. He's probably gone to the restroom." Humble thanked the waiter as he turned back to the table. "He'll be back shortly. Sit down and enjoy your meal."

Fenna waited until Burwardsley sat down before excusing herself. She felt Burwardsley's eyes on her back as she walked to the restaurant entrance. She paused to wait for a group to walk through the door and then used them as cover to enter the men's restroom.

She slipped around the door and let it close softly behind her. She found Lunk at the sink, washing his hands. He looked up and caught her eye in the mirror.

"Mrs Bond, I presume," he said and grinned. "What brings you in here?"

Fenna walked to the centre of the bathroom, glanced at the stalls to her left, the urinals to the right and then back to Lunk as he turned around and leaned against the counter. She could see the sweat plastering his black hair to his forehead, smell the alcohol on his breath. She blotted out the image of the man and focused on Dina. *Find Dina. Get off the ship. Clear my name.* Fenna recalled Mikael's surprise at finding Dina in the cabin, a cocktail dress tucked beneath their spare clothes. She glanced down at her own dress and looked up to find Lunk staring at her breasts, his mouth drooping into a sadistic leer.

"You said something at the table," she said. "I want to hear you say it again."

"Say *what* again?" Lunk pulled his eyes from Fenna's chest and wiped spittle from his chin. He leered at Fenna and shook his head. "I'm a little drunk. Although," he said and pushed himself off the counter and took a step towards her. "Not *that* drunk."

Fenna slipped the shawl from her shoulders and wrapped the ends around her fists, pulling the shawl tight like a rope.

"Ooh, little girl wants to fight," Lunk said and feinted with a lurch to Fenna's right. Fenna wobbled on her heels and moved to kick them off just as Lunk launched himself at her chest and slammed her to the tiles. The air *whumphed* out of Fenna's body as she scrabbled for breath beneath Lunk's massive frame. Where Burwardsley was all muscle, Lunk's advantage was in the pounds of fat rolled around his belly, jowls and arms. He crushed Fenna with his weight and fumbled his right hand around her throat.

"You want to know about the whore, eh? The little savage? Well," he said and grunted. "Why don't I just show you what I did to her." Lunk gripped Fenna's throat as he pressed one knee after the other onto her thighs. Fenna clawed at Lunk's fingers, but her broken and battered nails left only the slightest impression. Lunk laughed as he grasped a fistful of Fenna's dress in his left hand and tugged it upwards. "Just let it happen like a good little Bond Girl," he said and tugged again, higher this time.

Fenna let go of Lunk's hand at her throat and stretched her arms to reach for the door of the closest stall, or the wall between the door and the urinals. Anything. Her left hand swished across the tiles, empty, but her right caught hold of her shoe and she turned it within her hand and slammed the point of the heel into Lunk's head.

"Fucking bitch," he said as he reeled under the impact. The drool of spit dripped from his chin as he renewed his grip on Fenna's throat. With her last breath Fenna hit him again, this time the heel entered Lunk's ear and he screamed, rolled onto his side and pulled the shoe out of her grasp. Fenna squirmed to her knees and slammed her lower arm onto the shoe before Lunk could remove it. Blood fantailed out of his ear and she slipped on it as she straddled Lunk's body and gripped the shoe in her hand.

"Where is she?" Fenna shouted. "Where's Dina?"

"Fuck," Lunk said and screamed as she turned the heel in her hand. His hands spasmed around Fenna's as he tried to wrench her hands free of the heel, but the pain kept him pinned helpless to the tiles, now bloody.

"Where is she?" Fenna lifted the heel slightly and then pressed it home again, squinting through another shriek of pain and a skeletal geyser of blood. Lunk trembled beneath her and Fenna realised his was not the only body that was shaking. She pushed herself off Lunk and trembled to her feet. The blood on her legs clung to the gauze panels of her dress. She turned to the mirror and pressed the bloody fingers of her right hand to her throat, staring at the red shadow of Lunk's grip. The door opened and Fenna looked into the mirror. Burwardsley stared back at her.

Chapter 24

Fenna watched Burwardsley in the mirror as he stepped into the restroom and walked across the floor to check on Lunk. He prodded the lawyer with his foot and nodded as he moaned. Not once did he look away from Fenna. She noticed the bulge at his hip and wondered why she hadn't seen it earlier. Burwardsley followed her gaze and opened his jacket just a little, enough to reveal the Browning and to ratchet the tension to the next level. He let his jacket fall, straightened his back and smoothed his hands down the front of his jacket.

"You had every opportunity," he said, "more than once, to end this. And now," he gestured at Lunk lying in the foetal position on the floor, bloody hands clasped to his ear.

Fenna shuddered as she opened her mouth to speak. The rush of adrenalin peaked with each breath, her body ready to fight, as her eyes flickered in the mirror, looking for an alternative, a way out.

"There's nowhere to go, *love*," Burwardsley said. He lingered over the last word and scratched the side of his nose, casually brutal. *A monster.*

"He mentioned a girl," Fenna said as she gripped the edge of the counter. "You know who he means, don't you?"

Burwardsley clasped his hands in front of his stomach. Fenna studied him through the mirror, not daring to turn, as if her back was a shield, a line he would not cross. So long as she held that position...

"That was before," he said. "Not now. I don't know about now."

"He spoke in the present tense. My English is pretty good, you know."

"He was drunk."

"Not that drunk," Fenna said and lifted her head to let the light shine on her neck. Burwardsley shrugged.

"He didn't know what he was saying."

"Humble didn't think so."

"Konstabel," Burwardsley said and sighed. "What do you think is going to happen here?"

"That depends on you."

Lunk moaned and mumbled something about help and a doctor. Burwardsley glanced down at him and took a step back as Lunk fumbled a bloody hand towards his shoes.

"How do you figure that?" he said. "You think I call the shots?"

"Maybe," Fenna said and hoped, just for a moment, to appeal to Burwardsley's human side – the one she glimpsed at the dinner table.

"Then you're just as stupid as this thick fuck," he said and pressed the sole of his shoe onto Lunk's outstretched hand. "Humble's the boss, love. I go where he points, do what he says."

"And you call me stupid?" Fenna said and gripped the counter again, harder now as the shivering rippled through her body.

Burwardsley turned at the sound of voices outside the door. He slid his hand to the Browning and slipped the holster further around his belt, almost behind his back. He let go of his jacket as Watts stalked into the restroom together with a man Fenna assumed to be the Captain, the chevrons on his shirt epaulettes suggested as much.

"You," the Captain said and stabbed his finger at Burwardsley. "I told you to get off my ship. You and your Nepali friend."

"His name is Bad," Burwardsley said.

"I don't care what his name is. You have no authority on this ship. Mr Watts is in charge of security."

"Hey, Charlie," Burwardsley said, ignoring the Captain. "How's things?"

"Fuck off, Mike," Charlie said and walked around the Captain to kneel beside Lunk. He lifted Lunk's hand from his ear and was rewarded with a moan and a string of curses. "He'll live," he said to the Captain. But he'll be deaf in one ear."

Fenna caught the disappointed look in Burwardsley's eye and turned to face the Captain.

"You're the one we picked off the ice?"

"Yes," Fenna said.

"You followed this man into the restroom?"

"Yes."

The Captain paused to look at Fenna's bloody knees. She flinched as he reached forward to lift her hair from her neck. "He did this?" Fenna nodded. "And you defended yourself?"

"Yes."

"With a shoe?"

Fenna said nothing. Burwardsley smirked.

"Charlie, get this man out of my sight and confine him to his quarters."

"Be seeing you, *love*," Burwardsley said as Charlie took his arm and led him out of the restroom.

"I'll need your pistol, Mike," she heard him say.

"Fuck off, Charlie."

The door closed with a snick of the lock behind them, leaving the Captain alone with Fenna and Lunk. The Captain walked to the door and locked it. He turned to face Fenna and gestured at Lunk as he moaned on the floor.

"I don't care for any of these men," he said. "They operate around my command, disobey my rules, and, together, they bring a bad name to a magnificent ship. If I had my way..." He stopped and took a breath. "I'll let the medics in, shortly. But before then," he said and glanced at Fenna, "before I have you locked in a cabin, I want you to do something for me."

"What can I possibly do for you?" Fenna said and frowned.

"One of the guests said he heard a woman shouting. It was you, wasn't it?" he said. Fenna nodded. "He said you were asking about a woman, wanting to know where she is. Is that right?"

"Yes," Fenna said and held her breath.

"Then before I lock you up, I want you to push past me and get down to the lower deck. Below that, the orlop deck, there is a compartment, a hold, towards the bow. It's on the port side. That's the..."

"The left," said Fenna. "I know."

The Captain sighed. "This voyage will be my last. Humble intends to kill my career. Dares to call me insubordinate..." Fenna watched as a tick worried at the Captain's left cheek, just below his eye. "I won't be able to help you very much. I can do little more than bark a few orders, but maybe you will find something down there. Or someone."

"Thank you," Fenna said and stepped around the Captain.

He shook his head and said just one word, "Go."

Fenna grasped the handle, unlocked and opened the door. She saw a gap in the crowd gathered in the passageway that ran from one side of the ship to the other. Fenna stepped over the lip of the doorway and shoved her way through the guests.

"Fenna," said a man. She recognised the voice as Humble's and kept going. The carpet was smooth beneath her feet and she ran to the nearest elevator and launched herself at the stairs going down to the lower decks. The rustle of jackets whispering down the passageway behind her warned Fenna of the security officers giving chase. Fenna saw a crewman coming up the stairs. She gripped the handrail and swung herself around the corner, kicking the man off balance as her feet crashed into his chest. She landed on the landing between the stairs and continued down to the next deck.

Beyond the carpeted stairs, the lower deck favoured form and function over comfort and style. Fenna raced down the wide passageway, weaving between bedding hampers and catering trolleys pushed by Filipino crew members. She ran past the crew canteen and ducked into the passageway leading to the bow of the ship. A metal ladder on the port side of the passageway led down to the orlop deck and Fenna ran towards it.

She paused at the sound of her name, turned and gripped the handrail for support as she recognised Burwardsley's Nepalese thug as he raced towards her, his kukri glinting in the overhead lights.

"Fuck," she said and stomped down the ladder, gritting her teeth as she pounded her soles on the metal. The orlop deck was darker, lined with lengths of spare cable, wires bunched and secured with plastic ties. Fenna ran forwards, past the dark workspaces of tool-pushers and modern day grease monkeys. The Gurkha's boots clattered down the ladder and Fenna ducked through a passageway. She crossed the ship to the starboard side, clambered over a coil of cables and squeezed into a body-sized crevice that even the Filipinos would struggle to fit inside. It wasn't a question of fitting, but surviving. Fenna waited until the ring of Bahadur's boots along the metal passageway had disappeared. She pressed her nose into a gap between the coils and turned her cheek to scan the passageway with her right eye. Bahadur came back, paused at the cable and ran to the ladder on the starboard side, the opposite of the one Fenna had used. Fenna waited until the ring of his boots had cleared the ladder and squirmed out of her hiding space.

She wiped a smear of blood from her cheek, a cut from a stray twist of cable, and padded along the passageway to the bow. She crossed to the port side of the ship and stopped at a door, closed and secured. The light flickered above the door – a loose connection or a failing bulb. Fenna grasped the wheel in the centre of the door and turned it, the dogs in each corner slid open and the door creaked as she opened it.

Fenna cupped her nose and mouth in her hand and hesitated

before stepping over the lip of the door. She waited for the light to filter through from the faulty bulb, and for her eyes to adjust to the darkness. A shudder of movement made her jump and Fenna took a breath of foetid air and fought to steady her pulse.

Her mind raced with warnings, as if her very nerves extended from her body, wrapped around the handrail by the door like a lifeline, ready to pull her back from the brink and into safety. Fenna took another step. She saw a flicker of movement to her left and pushed her bare feet ahead of her, testing the floor. She slid on a puddle of liquid and fell onto her knees by the side of a crate, and a body, the naked form of a woman with long hair glued to her skin in matted twists and knots.

"Dina?" Fenna whispered and held out her hand. "Dina, is that you?"

Fenna paused at the thought of how many kilometres she had sledged, how far she had run, fought and bled to get to this point, in a dank, black hole of the richest ship afloat, the hold where even the brightest star would never shine. She let her fingers brush against the woman's shoulder, smoothed her hand into a firm grip and crawled forwards to pull the woman into her arms.

"Dina," she said. "I found you."

Dina choked a response and flung her arms around Fenna, clucking and clicking the stub of her tongue at the back of her mouth as she squeezed with what little strength she had left.

"I won't let you go," Fenna said and smoothed her hands through Dina's hair to free her face. "I've got you," she said and kissed Dina's forehead. "Bloody hell, I've got you." The echo of Mikael's words jerked tears onto her cheeks and she pulled Dina closer still as the door to the hold squealed shut and the last of the light was extinguished. Fenna closed her eyes and let her tears mix with the Greenlander's. *They can do what they want with me now. I have found Dina.*

The deck vibrated as the Captain ordered more thrust from the *The Ice Star*'s engines as he turned the ship in a lazy curve away from Ittoqqortoormiit and set a course for the southernmost point of Greenland, Cape Farewell.

Chapter 25

The cold from the metal deck seeped into Fenna's body, pressing raised diamond shapes into her skin. She opened her eyes and moved her arm, only to have Dina clutch it once more. The Greenlander curled her naked and bruised body into Fenna's, her long black hair flowed in knotted strands and greasy twists across her back and was lost in the black fabric of Fenna's dress. The dogs on the door squealed as someone unlocked them and Dina shivered. Fenna closed her eyes, squinting through her lashes as Humble, Burwardsley and the vicious Nepali were framed briefly in the lowlight from the passageway before they stepped into the hold. Bahadur carried a chair for Humble. He moved around the two men and placed it just a few metres from where Fenna and Dina lay curled on the floor. Fenna closed her eyes and listened to Humble's voice as it drifted through the dark hold.

"The Captain played his part well," he said. "I'll give him that, although it will count very little towards his career." Fenna heard Burwardsley grunt a reply as Humble scraped the chair along the deck, and moved it closer to her. He sat down and she opened her eyes. "Konstabel," Humble said as Fenna blinked to focus. She kept her head low, behind Dina, until a pang of guilt reminded her that the Greenlander had been used enough. She prised her arm free of Dina's grip and sat up.

"I see you're just like him," Fenna said and nodded at Burwardsley.

"What? Oh," Humble said and made a show of looking around the hold. "You don't like your accommodation?"

Fenna said nothing. She flicked her eyes from Humble to the two men he used for muscle, and back again.

"What do you think, Mike?" he said. "She seems pretty quiet."

"She's learned when to keep her mouth shut."

"And yet, that's not enough, is it?"

"No, Mr Humble. Not nearly enough."

Humble clicked his fingers and Bahadur handed him an object. Fenna recognised it as he held it up and twisted it in the light. Humble tossed it onto the floor in front of her.

"Do you know what that is, Konstabel?"

"Part of a satellite, made by Humble Industries," she said. "Your company."

"You're right, in part," he said and gestured at the component. "My father's company did make it, but it's not from a satellite," he said, smirking. Humble turned to look at Burwardsley. "I've been looking forward to this."

"It should never have gotten this far," Burwardsley said.

"Oh, Mike, stop beating yourself up. A loose end is a loose end. Besides, she's here. They both are. All tied up, figuratively and," he laughed, "literally, in a little while anyway."

"Still," Burwardsley said and shuffled his feet. "It should have gone smoother."

"No matter," Humble said and turned back to Fenna. "In fact, I like it this way because I get to gloat."

Burwardsley bristled as Fenna shuffled forwards and picked up the piece of metal. She moved back to sit beside Dina and studied the component in the gloom. Dina kept her eyes shut, her knees tucked into her chest, and her elbows jammed into her thighs. Her skin goosebumped as Humble talked. He ignored her, but for a casual glance at her body. Fenna threw the component at Humble's feet.

"I don't understand," she said and waited for him to respond.

"What was your mission, Konstabel?"

"To retrieve that," she said and pointed at the component.

"What would you say if I told you it was a fake, that, in fact, the entire satellite was a fake, dropped out of a plane, a matter of hours before you were tasked to pick it up?"

Fenna felt a surge of adrenalin prickle through her body. It raised her pulse, pressed her heart against her chest, confused her lungs into thinking she needed more oxygen. "What plane?" she said, but she already knew. "The Chinese..."

"No," Humble said and laughed. "A stolen transponder on a charter plane, made to look like it was from China. You see," he said and rested his elbows on his knees. "The Danes aren't the only ones who can play games in the Arctic."

"I don't understand."

"Hans Island," he said. "In 2005 we sent our Minister of Defence, Bill Graham, with a bottle of whisky and a flag to that pathetic rock in the Nares Strait. The Danes responded with a delegation of their own, putting a battleship in the strait, and a bottle of booze beneath *their* flag."

"It's an island," Fenna said and shook her head. "I don't understand what it has to do with a fake satellite."

"Of course you don't." Humble paused to flex his fingers. "But it didn't stop with the island. Did it? It's not enough to mock the Canadian presence in the Arctic, now you want the fucking Pole."

"This is about the North Pole?" Fenna shook her head. "You're insane."

"No," Humble said and leaned back in his chair. "Not insane. Not even close to being slightly mad. You see, while you and your teammates are laughing it up over failed manoeuvres in the Canadian north – mocking our so-called Rangers – you are missing the bigger picture. The future economy. Hell, Konstabel, the Northeast and Northwest Passages are open, it's only a matter of years before the Pole itself is ice-free. And if you think for a minute that we're just going to sit back and let you take it..." Humble took a breath. "No," he said. "It's not going to happen. You've had your fun in the Arctic, Konstabel, you and your Sirius boys. Welcome to the real world of geopolitics. It's time to get serious, and for Denmark to realise it is seriously out of its depth."

Fenna snorted, "You *are* mad. Canada is our ally. We're not at war..."

"No? Like we're not at war with Russia? Or China?" Humble leaned forwards. "Understand this, if an independent group of patriots can drop a piece of junk from an aircraft and have your navy task a mission to pick it up, just imagine what we could do if we decided to bring some real resources into play. It's only a matter of time, Konstabel. Greenland is begging to be independent, free of its Imperial masters. What if Canada were to step in and offer it a way out? What if we were to create such a scandal that the whole world was forced to question Danish sovereignty and their competence as a ruling power in the Arctic? How long do you think it would take, how many years, before you were out and we were in? Denmark would be a very small country all of a sudden, wouldn't it?"

Fenna swallowed a rebuke, and focused on her breathing. Her head was beginning to spin and she felt small, as small as Denmark, just a pawn in a political game. "But Mikael…" she said.

"A piece of the puzzle," Humble said and turned to look at Burwardsley. "A counter to be moved around the board. A loose end."

"Like me," she said.

"Exactly like you, and the girl," said Burwardsley and nodded at Dina. "You were just unlucky – you were chosen to be in the right place, at the right time."

"And Kjersing?"

"Ah," Humble said and smiled. "Commander Kjersing. Our man in the Arctic."

"Your man?"

"Ours, yes. He was proving to be troublesome. I needed to test him, and this was the perfect test. If he could sweep this little incident under the rug then he would indeed prove his worth." Humble paused. "He failed, of course."

"You set him up," Fenna said and resisted the urge to shout. "You concocted all this as a test? For one man?"

"With the added benefit of creating a scandal if he couldn't resolve it. Yes, that's exactly what we did." Humble pushed back his chair and stood up. "I need Kjersing driving a desk at Arctic Command in Nuuk, not driving dogs in some East Greenland armpit. He's no good to me there."

Fenna looked up at Humble. She felt the energy and adrenalin drain from her body. "Who *are* you?"

"A good question," he said. "You can take it to the grave, Konstabel."

Fenna blocked Humble's words from her mind. *Not yet*, she said to herself. *I need to know.* "Vestergaard," she said. "What about him? He works for you?"

"Vestergaard?" Humble said and turned to Burwardsley.

"You know him as *The Magician*," Burwardsley said. Fenna recognised the look on his face, as if it was more information than he wanted her to know.

"Yes, yes. Now *he* proved his worth."

"But he's Danish?" said Fenna.

"Yes. So was Kjersing."

"Was?"

"Mike?" Humble said and looked at Burwardsley.

"Not yet," he said.

"Oh, come on, Mike."

"Mr Humble, sir," Burwardsley said and sighed. "What with her and the Greenlander..."

"Fine," said Humble. "I'm sure you'll get around to it."

Burwardsley nodded as if it was one more task on a very long list. Fenna watched him and then turned her attention to Bahadur as he shuffled closer, his hand grasped around something. Fenna squinted to see what it was but failed. She glanced at Dina. The Greenlander had not moved. She was completely locked down, as if Humble's presence had tripped a switch and short-circuited her body. Humble took a step to one side and cocked his head. Fenna looked up as she became aware of him staring at her. She met his gaze and placed her hand on Dina's leg.

"And her?" she said. "What about Dina?"

"What about her?" Humble said and shrugged. "She heard too much."

"So you cut out her tongue?"

"Christ no," he said. "She bit it off herself. Some foolish attempt at suicide."

"Why would she do that?"

"It's in the Greenland psyche…"

"You're a bastard. An evil piece of work," Fenna said and spat.

"All the same, Konstabel, Dina heard far more than was good for her, or you," Humble said as his lips curled into a smile Fenna wished she could erase from her memory. He leered at her, looked at Dina and then licked his top lip. "There are some rewards in this line of work, and I have certain needs, things I desire that I would not wish on my wife. Dina satisfied those needs," he said and Fenna shuddered at the matter-of-fact manner in which he said it.

"You're an animal."

"And she is a savage," he said and shrugged. "Your country treated them as savages for years, why shouldn't I?"

"She's a human being."

Humble shook his head and turned his back on Fenna. He walked across the deck to Burwardsley and nodded. "Drug her," he said. "The guests have forced a vote. Apparently they're tired of the east coast and want to go to the west. That suits me fine. I'll get a plane to pick me up once we get there. They can fly me over to Canada. You can reach me at the Toronto office if you need me."

Burwardsley nodded and clicked his fingers at Bahadur. Fenna watched as the Nepali opened his hand to reveal two syringes. She shuddered as he held them up to the light.

"Just the Dane, Bahadur," said Humble. "I have to talk to the Captain, but when I'm done," he said and nodded towards Dina. "I might have some appetite left." He turned towards Fenna and said, "They're no good if they're drugged. It's like having a limp fish on your cock." Humble slapped Burwardsley on the back and laughed as he walked towards the door of the hold.

"You bastard," Fenna shouted at his back. She scrambled to her feet as Burwardsley pulled a Taser gun from behind his back and fired. Two probes punctured Fenna's dress and knocked her to the floor as the electroshock incapacitated her. Burwardsley tossed the Taser onto the deck and kneeled down beside her.

"You haven't got much time left, Konstabel," he said. "There's been a bit too much drama these past few hours. The guests are all on edge and dumping two young women over the side will only make them nervous. They might be rich, but not all of them are stupid." He waited as Bahadur pressed the needle into Fenna's neck and depressed the plunger to pump the sedative into her body. Fenna's teeth chattered as she tried to focus her eyes on Burwardsley, Dina, anywhere.

"Done, *Saheb*," said Bahadur.

The Nepali moved to stand up but Burwardsley caught his arm. Fenna fought to focus on his words as he nodded in Dina's direction.

"Do me a favour, Bad," he said.

"*Saheb*?"

"Shoot her up too."

"But Mr Humble..."

"Fuck Humble," Burwardsley said and waved his finger in front of Fenna's eyes. She followed it as best she could. "You think I'm a monster, Konstabel," he said. "But even monsters have days off." Burwardsley stood up and shrank out of view, and the thrum of the ship's engines seeped into Fenna's mind as her body let go.

The Schoolhouse

WEST GREENLAND

Chapter 26

UUMMANNAQ, WEST GREENLAND

The light from the passageway tugged at Fenna's eyelids, pressing, insistent, painful. She rolled her tongue within her mouth, it flopped to one side and lay heavy in her cheek. She tried to open her eyes and caught a glimpse of a man with the head of an elephant, huge ears, before her lids failed and her eyes shut. Something kicked at her feet and she felt the deck beneath her legs as they were spread apart.

I must wake, the thought tumbled within her head. *Wake up, Fenna. Wake up.*

"Wake up," a voice said. "Open your eyes, bitch."

Fenna opened her eyes as the shadow of Lunk towered above her, extinguishing the light from the passageway, extinguishing hope.

"No," she said, the word mumbled from her lips.

"Oh, but I say yes," Lunk said and laughed. He moved his head and the light caught the elephantine bandage covering his left ear. Lunk unbuckled his belt and slipped it out of the loops of his trousers. He huffed for breath as he kneeled beside Fenna and bound her hands in front of her stomach. "Payback's a bitch, *bitch*," he said, his breath ragged with excitement.

Lunk gripped Fenna's jaw within his meaty hand and squeezed her mouth open. He spat in her face and lumbered into a standing position. The muscles in Fenna's face trembled into a limp grimace as her body fought the drugs.

Wake up, Fenna.

Lunk unzipped his trousers and reached inside the fly, pleasuring himself with one hand as he wiped a swathe of sweaty hair from his forehead. He leered at Fenna, the smile on his face dimpling his fat cheeks. He hawked and spat again, the spittle and phlegm landing squarely on Fenna's breast. Lunk twisted to free his penis from his trousers, sneering as the tip caught on the teeth of the zipper. He sighed as he stroked himself above Fenna, pleasure flooding his body, dulling all other senses, blinding him to the chair that crashed into the back of his head.

Fenna blinked as Dina raised the chair a second time, gutter noises clucking from her mouth as she hit Lunk again, and again. She turned as he lifted his right arm in defence. Dina slammed the chair into his bandage. Lunk screamed and collapsed to the deck. She hit him again and the chair bounced out of her grasp, it skittered across the deck as she leaped upon Lunk, curling the fingers of her right hand into a fist full of greasy hair as she punched his left ear. Fenna blinked at the vision of Dina, cat-like, her hair streaming like a banshee's, rising and falling as she lifted Lunk's head and hit him again and again.

"Dina," a man's voice shouted from the passageway. Dina hit Lunk again as the man leaped over the lip of the door and ran across the deck, the stomp of his boots echoing around the hold, drumming into Fenna's body. She lifted her head as the man turned and the dim light flickered across the face of *The Ice Star*'s head of security.

"Dina, stop," Watts said. He dropped the bundle of clothes and boots in his hands and wrestled Dina off Lunk's back. She screamed a gargle of abuse and fought back, pushing Watts to the floor. He tried to stand but Dina pressed her knee into his chest, fumbled for the pistol at his waist, ripped it from the holster and pointed it at Lunk's head. Fenna squirmed to one side, out of the line of fire.

"No, Dina," Watts said.

Dina flicked Watts a look through slitted eyes, turned to face Lunk and pulled the trigger. The report of the 9mm boomed through the hold as the bullet punctured the back of Lunk's head and pulped the left side of his face. Dina lowered the pistol, slipped off Watts' chest and kneeled on the floor.

"Fuck," Watts whispered as he pushed himself to his feet. He reached down and pulled the pistol from Dina's hands and holstered it. The echo of the shot lost momentum and faded into the depths of the hold as Watts ran a hand across his chin. He took a breath, nodded and crouched by the side of Dina.

The Greenlander's body trembled as Watts wiped the hair from her eyes and slipped a t-shirt over her head. He lifted Dina's limp arms and guided them through the holes. He did the same with a sweater then walked around her, slipped his arms beneath hers and lifted her to her feet.

"How are you doing, Konstabel?" he said as he helped Dina step into a pair of military trousers.

Fenna licked her lips and coughed a reply, "I am okay."

"Can you stand?"

"My hands," she said and lifted her wrists, Lunk's belt pinched the skin, the buckle digging into the back of her hand.

"Give me a minute," Watts said. He glanced towards the passageway as he lowered Dina to the deck, tugged socks over her toes and shoved boots onto her feet.

Fenna wriggled into a sitting position, wobbled onto her knees and stood up.

"All right, Dina. I am going to help the Konstabel now," Watts said as he tied the laces of Dina's boots. "Do you hear me?" Dina stared at the deck. Watts tied the last bow, cupped Dina's face in his hands and kissed her brow. He reached for the second set of clothes and boots, stepped over Lunk's body and nodded at Fenna. "Let's get that belt off," he said and dropped the clothes and boots onto the deck. He glanced for a second time at the doorway and then unbuckled the belt around Fenna's wrists.

"It was your voice on the satphone," she said as Watts freed her hands. "It was you Dina called, wasn't it?"

"Yes," Watts said and tossed the belt onto the deck. The dim light reflected the tears welling in his eyes as he tried to smile. "She is *my* ice star. Not this fucking ship. Not these people. I can't live without her. I won't live without her..." he wiped away a tear with his finger, then palmed it away with his hand. Fenna dressed as Watts recovered. "We met only a few months ago, when she first came onboard. I got to know her as she guided the guests. Then she got sucked in by Humble's charm, and the next thing I know, she is gone for days. I overheard one of the Filipinos say they saw Burwardsley dragging her into the chopper. I guess he was tying up a loose end. He was off the ship when she called me. I found her on the ice with a dog team," he said as Fenna fastened the buttons of her windpants. "They found her, of course, in my cabin." Watts clenched his fists. He looked away as she pulled the dress over her head and slipped her arms into the sleeves of her thermal top. She sighed as the sleeve caught on Vienna's gloves. Watts looked up and tugged the gloves free. He slipped the fold of the top over her breasts and pulled it down to her waist.

"Thanks," she said and took the sweater from his hands.

"We don't have much time," he said and glanced for a third time at the doorway. Fenna tugged her boots over her bare feet. "No socks," Watts said. "I couldn't find them. Sorry."

"It's fine," Fenna said. "You got all this from Vienna's cabin?"

"She gave me the key," he said and nodded. "I also have this."

Watts tugged the Webley from the waistband at the back of his trousers. "I even found a single bullet in the bottom of your sledge bag." Fenna fumbled the pistol as Watts handed it to her. "You sure you're okay?"

"I'll be fine," she said and pressed the pistol into her windpants. "Just a little groggy."

"Okay," he said and nodded towards the door. "We have to be going." Watts walked around Lunk's body and pulled Dina to her feet. "You've been out for four days. They gave you at least one more shot that I know about. Maybe two. You don't remember them feeding you?"

"No."

"Food and water. They even forced you to pee."

"Thorough," Fenna said as she blocked the image from her mind. "Where are we?" she asked as she followed Watts and Dina to the door.

"Uummannaq fjord. We're anchored just outside the harbour. It's a popular stop for tourists and the guests got tired of Humble planning their itinerary. He's rich, but not *that* rich," Watts said and smirked, but Fenna could see no amusement in his expression.

"So what happens now?"

Watts paused at the lip of the door. Her curled his arm around Dina and kissed her gently on the side of her head. "I have a Zodiac waiting to take you into town. You can trust the driver," he said as Fenna frowned. "He owes me a favour."

"And then what?"

"I called ahead to the hospital. It's the yellow building right on the water's edge. They are expecting you. I told them you were both in need of medical attention, and that they might want to inform the police."

"Okay," Fenna said as she processed the information. "Okay, let's get to the boat."

"You'll have to do that," Watts said and pressed Dina into Fenna's arms.

"You're not coming with us?"

Watts shook his head and tugged the pistol from its holster.

"He'll kill you." Fenna caught the edge of fear in her voice.

"Burwardsley? Maybe," he said and smoothed his hand through Dina's hair. "But I can't live with the knowledge of what they did to her," he paused to swallow, "on my watch."

"You're not responsible."

"Yes, Konstabel, I am," Watts said. "I practically delivered her to them." He let go of Dina and pressed his fingers into his shirt pocket. He pulled out a micro SD card in a tiny plastic case.

"What's this?" Fenna said as Watts placed the card in her palm.

"Humble likes to watch," he said and gave Fenna a grim smile. He closed her fingers over the card and nodded. "I'll get you off the ship. Just promise me you'll get the bastard. For Dina," he said and let go of her hand.

"I promise," Fenna said and zipped the card inside the chest pocket of her thermal top.

Watts stepped over the lip of the door and pointed to the ladder halfway down the length of the passageway. "Take the ladder to the next deck. The door is open and there is a ladder down to the Zodiacs. There will be a crowd," he said. "Guests going into town. Go past them and get on the last boat."

"Got it," said Fenna as she guided Dina through the door. She flexed her fingers and smiled as the feeling returned to the tips beneath her scratched and broken nails. She caught Watts' arm as he took a step down the passageway. "Vienna?" she said, "Is she with Humble?"

"I don't think so. She let me in to her cabin and helped me find your clothes," he said and shrugged. "She is also a prisoner aboard the ship. Just not Humble's."

Fenna took a breath and nodded. With one hand curled around Dina's back, her fingers gripping the waistband of the Greenlander's trousers, Fenna walked down the passageway behind Watts. He held his pistol low but ready, his index finger tapping the trigger guard.

Dina stumbled along beside Fenna, all the way to the ladder. Fenna took a step and tugged at Dina's trousers. Dina shook her head and looked at Watts.

"It's okay," he said. "Go with her. I'll find you later."

Dina stamped a foot on the deck.

"Dina," Watts said. "Go."

She stamped again and Fenna winced at the ring of her boots echoing down the passageway. Watts pressed his hand against Dina's cheek. He smoothed a strand of hair from her eye with his thumb. Dina's eyes glistened and a tear rolled onto Watts' thumb, seeping into the pores of his skin.

"Go," he said.

"Come on, Dina," Fenna said and took a step up the ladder. She pulled at the waistband of Dina's trousers, yanking the Greenlander up and onto the first step as Dina clawed at Watts' jacket. Dina choked and the guttural sounds of her cries were painful for Watts to hear. He took a step back, out of reach. Fenna yanked Dina onto the next step as the sound of someone jogging along the passageway from the stern of the ship forced Watts into a defensive stance. He held the pistol in a two-handed grip as Bahadur slowed to a walk and lowered the British SA80 rifle to a casual position.

"Charlie, Charlie, Charlie," said Burwardsley as he stepped out of a workspace between the hold and the ladder.

"Mike," said Watts as he glanced over his shoulder. Bahadur slipped behind a fire hose mounted on the bulkhead, his rifle raised as Watts flicked his attention away from Burwardsley, searching for the Gurkha. Fenna tugged Dina onto the next step.

"The Captain chose the right side," Burwardsley said. "Why couldn't you?"

"Oh, I don't know," Watts said as he stepped backwards around the base of the ladder and pressed his back against the side of the ship. "I guess I have principles."

"Principles?" Burwardsley said and laughed. "That's rich." He nodded at Bahadur and took a step towards Watts. "You sold out, just like the rest of us."

"Maybe I did, but..." Watts flicked his eyes from Burwardsley to Bahadur as the Gurkha inched forwards. Fenna pulled Dina up the ladder, just three steps from the deck above. She looked over Dina's shoulder just as Burwardsley drew the Browning, straightened his arm and fired.

The crack of the shot thundered along the passageway, drowning Dina's scream as Fenna dragged her up the last steps and onto the deck. Watts tumbled to the floor, raised his pistol and fired two shots in quick succession only to be silenced by a three-round burst of 5.56mm from the Gurkha's rifle. The impact flipped the security officer against the bulkhead. He slid onto the deck as Burwardsley leaped over him and ran up the ladder. Fenna shifted her grip to the front of Dina's waistband and dragged her into a stream of crewmen as they bustled about the passageway, heads bobbing around one another for a better view. Fenna crashed through the crowd, located the open door and pushed Dina out of the ship and down the ladder to the Zodiacs, squinting in the brilliant light, and stumbling past the guests and into the Zodiac at the end of the pontoon dock.

The Filipino driver clicked the Zodiac into gear and pressed the throttle lever as Fenna tumbled Dina over the rubber sides of the boat and grabbed the safety line. The wind flicked at her hair as she turned to see Burwardsley charging down the ladder only to be stopped by the throng of excited guests filling the pontoon. Fenna turned her head as she heard the *thunk thunk* of small chunks of ice hitting the rigid hull of the Zodiac, and she let the wind blow her hair free of her eyes. The heart-shaped mountain that gave Uummannaq its name towered above the yellow hospital. Fenna plucked a strand of hair from her mouth and dared to breathe.

Chapter 27

The driver of the Zodiac powered the inflatable craft in a wide arc around an ice floe, a sheet of ice that defied the warm sea temperatures. The bow waves of the small blue fishing trawlers chopped the water as they motored past. Fenna noticed the patches of blood on the floe, the remains of a hunt when the fjord was frozen. The island of Uummannaq, 650 kilometres above the Arctic Circle, had been locked in for the brief, unseasonable but increasingly common, winter. Fenna scanned the road and shivered in the cool breeze. She didn't have enough layers for sailing despite the warmer weather. The ice may have melted but it was still sub-zero.

She spotted a familiar blue police Toyota parked outside the hospital, a Rav4 minus the bullet holes. A policeman was leaning against the door, smoking and watching the Zodiac slip between the hunters' dinghies. Fenna held his gaze as the man finished his cigarette and walked down the road to the concrete slipway. The hull of the Zodiac crunched over a layer of ice as the Filipino driver cut the power and raised the outboard motor. Fenna waited for the boat to bump to a halt, then stood up and helped Dina to her feet. She nodded at the driver and stepped over the side of the boat, tugging Dina's sweater and encouraging her to follow. The policeman stopped at the top of the slipway and waited.

Fenna realised that Dina was walking with the weight of the dead, as each step took her further and further from Watts. She barely lifted her toes from the ground, sliding her feet forward, up the slipway, away from *The Ice Star*, away from the scene of so much horror. *And love*, Fenna thought as she remembered the security officer's tenderness, the light kisses he placed on Dina's forehead, the wet sheen to his eyes as he looked at her.

"It's going to be okay, Dina," she said and pulled her another few steps.

"Konstabel Brongaard?" the policeman said and pulled his hands out of his pockets.

"Yes," Fenna said and studied the man. She thought of Maratse and realised she would have preferred a Greenlander, but also that it was quite normal for the more senior ranks to be Danish. She stopped a half metre in front of him and circled her arm around Dina's waist.

"My name is Simonsen. I'll take you to the hospital."

"Okay," she said and glanced over her shoulder as the Filipino slipped over the bow of the Zodiac and pushed it back into the water. She waited for him to wave, but the man dipped his head low inside the high collar of his jacket, his breath misting over the lip as he lowered the outboard, started the motor and weaved between the dinghies on his return to *The Ice Star*.

We're on our own again, Fenna thought as she guided Dina along the road behind the policeman. Simonsen waited for them beside the Toyota, pausing as a second policeman, a Greenlander, walked out of the side door of the hospital and held it open.

"We'll go in the back way," Simonsen said and nodded towards the policeman. Fenna took a last look at the ship and the two Zodiacs heading towards the harbour. She relaxed when she couldn't see Burwardsley's massive frame; the Zodiacs were full of guests, six to each boat.

The policemen kicked the snow off their boots before entering the hospital. Fenna did the same, but Dina dragged each toe as if it was frozen to the floor, as if she had to break every step free before she could move on. The dim light of the corridor cast a yellow light on the white walls as they passed the tiny morgue and skirted around a gurney. Simonsen stopped as the mobile in his pocket rang. Fenna smiled as Europe's *The Final Countdown* rang louder and louder before he swiped the screen and nodded for his assistant to take them into the room off to the left.

"In here," the policeman said and opened the door to a small storage room with a chair in one corner. Fenna guided Dina between the packing cases and plastic storage boxes and helped her sit down. She turned to the policeman as he stepped out of the room and gripped the handle of the door.

"What are we doing in here?" she said. "I thought we were going to be seen by a doctor?"

"Maybe," he said and shrugged. He nodded towards Simonsen, out of sight but within earshot. Fenna strained to hear his voice as he continued to speak on the phone.

"Yes," he said. "I understand." Simonsen's mobile beeped as he ended the call. Fenna listened as his boots clumped along the corridor. The policeman let go of the door and took a step back, making way for his boss. Simonsen stepped inside the storage room, glanced at Dina and then fixed Fenna with a steel gaze.

"You're not going to help, are you?" she said.

Simonsen unzipped his jacket and wiped his sleeve across his brow, strands of thin grey hair caught in the Velcro at the wrist. He cocked his head to one side and called the policeman over.

"Danielsen," he said.

"Yes?"

"Stay here while I go back to the office. No-one comes in. Not even a nurse."

"Not even a nurse?" Fenna said and took a step forwards. Her elbow nudged a cardboard box and it crashed to the floor, spilling its contents of vacuum-packed needles capped in plastic.

"Settle down, Konstabel," Simonsen said. Fenna watched as the man's hands moved to the ready position. "I'll be back very soon, and we can sort all this out."

Fenna caught his arm as he turned. "Who was that on the mobile?" she said as he brushed her hand from his sleeve. "Who was it?"

Simonsen held up his palm and waited for Fenna to take a step backwards. She glanced at Dina and then back at Simonsen's hand. *I could snap his wrist*, she thought as she played out the move in her mind. *Snap it and pull the Webley, force him to give me his pistol. And then what?* She took another look at Dina and then a slow step backwards.

"That was your commanding officer," Simonsen said. "Kommandør..."

"Kjersing?" Fenna said and resisted the urge to spit. "He's crooked. Working for Canadian Intelligence," she said.

"Really?" Simonsen said as his mouth creased into a grin. Fenna saw the flecks of tobacco between his teeth as he laughed. "He said you might say something like that."

"It's true," Fenna said and glanced at Dina. She wished she would at least lift her head so that she could see her eyes, but Dina kept her face covered. Fenna flexed her fingers as Simonsen laughed. *As soon as I see my chance – we have to go*, she thought.

"I find it difficult to imagine that the leader of Sirius is a secret agent, Konstabel." Simonsen's last word cackled out of his mouth, his cough rasping and his chest rattling. Danielsen grinned behind Simonsen's back.

Fenna slipped her left hand behind her back and closed her

fingers around the handle of the Webley. *A metre and a half*, she calculated, *from me to Danielsen, through the laughing policeman. Down the corridor and... where?* She paused for a moment as Simonsen doubled over in a second bout of coughing. *The boats, and into the fjord.* She smiled as Simonsen caught her eye. Then she drew the Webley, changed her grip and pistol-whipped Uummannaq's Chief of Police on the side of his head. Fenna leaped over Simonsen as he crashed to the ground and threw herself into Danielsen's chest. She dropped the Webley and gripped the policeman around the throat with her right hand, slapping his hand away from his pistol with her left. Fenna changed her grip again, grabbing the policeman by the ears with both hands and slamming his head on the corridor floor as she wormed her knees onto his arms. Danielsen moaned until Fenna smacked his head for the fourth time. She felt his body go limp beneath her knees. Fenna let go and tugged the USP Compact, the same model as Maratse's pistol, from his holster, cursing at the spiral of plastic securing the pistol to his belt. She searched Danielsen's utility pockets and found a folding knife. Fenna flicked it open with her thumb and sawed through the plastic. She slipped the pistol into the side pocket of her windpants, stepped over Danielsen's body and picked up the Webley. Fenna whipped the butt of the handle into the side of the policeman's head and pushed the Webley into the waistband of her trousers. She found two spare magazines and shoved them into her pockets. Simonsen's pistol had no security loop so Fenna could pull it free of the holster and shove it into the front of her windpants, leaving the handle poking out of the waistband. She searched his belt and removed another spare magazine and fished his lighter out of his pocket. Fenna remembered how cold it had been on the water and unzipped Simonsen's jacket. She rolled his body from one side to the other and pulled the jacket free. She did the same with Danielsen as Dina lifted her head and stared at the two policemen.

"Put this on," Fenna said and gave her Danielsen's jacket. She slipped her arms into Simonsen's jacket, folded the knife and stuffed it into the pocket with the lighter. Fenna flicked her eyes upwards and mouthed a quick *thank you* as Dina zipped her jacket and tucked her hair inside the collar. Dina stamped her foot and pointed at Simonsen.

"I had to," Fenna said. "He got a call from Kjersing," she said and held up her hands. They trembled and she clenched her fists to suppress the adrenalin pumping through her system. *Not for the first time*, she realised. *And probably not the last. Not before this is over.*

Dina nodded and walked towards the door. She skirted around Fenna, stepped over the policeman and turned towards the door at the end of the corridor. Fenna followed her and pulled the pistol from her waistband. The grip was familiar in her hand and she slipped her finger alongside the trigger guard.

"Dina," she said. Fenna waited until Dina turned to look at her. "We have to finish this."

Fenna's chest ached as Dina took a step towards her, reached out and cupped her hands either side of Fenna's cheeks. She raised her eyebrows, *yes*.

"We can't keep running. You understand?"

Dina raised her eyebrows again. *Yes.*

"I don't know how it will end."

Dina shrugged and smoothed her thumbs on Fenna's cheeks. She nodded, let her hands slide down Fenna's face, onto her shoulders, along her arms and to her hands. Dina slipped the fingers of her right hand into Fenna's left and lifted her chin towards the door. She tugged Fenna along the corridor and Fenna let herself be guided to the end, realising as they walked towards the light filtering through the salt-stained window, that an end was all Dina wanted.

They stopped at the door and Dina moved to give Fenna space to look through the window. She lifted her hand but Dina did not let go. Beyond the Toyota the road wove to the right along the harbour towards the stone church and *Pilersuisoq*, the supermarket. To the left, Fenna remembered, was the slipway and a fleet of dinghies. She bit her lip and scanned the road once more. Fenna could see the bright red jackets and the slim lifejackets worn by the guests from *The Ice Star*. The tourists clumped in small groups along the road, and Fenna held her breath in anticipation of seeing Burwardsley or Bahadur among them. Dina stamped her foot and Fenna turned as a nurse entered the corridor at the opposite end of the hospital. The nurse cried out at the sight of the two policeman as Dina increased her grip on Fenna's hand, pushed the door open and pulled her outside.

The cold air caught Fenna's breath for a moment and then they were running and sliding, slipping the soles of their boots along the slick snow, which was compacted and ground into the road, all the way to the slipway. Fenna paused at a single shout. She turned towards the hospital and saw Burwardsley running towards them, one hand tucked beneath the parka he wore over his Arctic camouflage pants, the other waving at the Nepali in the Zodiac powering through the water towards the slipway. Fenna tugged her hand free of Dina's. She gave the Greenlander a short shove down the slipway and pointed at the dinghies. As Dina picked her way across the ice to the boats, Fenna gripped the pistol in two hands, fired two shots in Burwardsley's direction and then turned to empty the magazine into the pontoon of the Zodiac as Bahadur increased speed. The pontoon deflated with a violent gasp as Greenlanders nearby and the guests on the road began to scream and shout. Fenna changed the magazine and fired two more shots at Burwardsley as Dina tugged at the start cord on an outboard. The motor coughed to life and Fenna fired once more as Dina untied the dinghy and waved for Fenna to come quickly.

The *boom boom boom* of Burwardsley's Browning barrelled along the road as he walked the rounds across the ice-coated rocks, puncturing the dinghies between him and Fenna. Plastic jerrycans of fuel in adjacent dinghies popped and burst just a metre from Dina's back as she twisted the throttle arm and turned the bow of the greasy and blood-stained hunter's vessel into the fjord. Burwardsley cursed as he changed magazines and yelled for Bahadur to come and pick him up.

"Go, Dina," Fenna said and pointed towards the tip of an island in the middle of the fjord. Dina planed the dinghy to the left and right of the larger floes and growlers at the entrance to the harbour, lifting the bow of the dinghy as she increased speed and steered a course away from the island, away from *The Ice Star*, towards the end.

Chapter 28

UUMMANNATSIAQ, WEST GREENLAND

The outboard motor failed ten metres from the curved point of Ikerasak island. Dina gripped the throttle arm of the motor and used the remaining forward motion to steer the dinghy closer to the ice lining the shore. Fenna twisted in the seat at the bow, the pistol pointing at the deck in a loose grip. She looked over Dina's shoulder and scanned the fjord, searching for the black hulls of *The Ice Star*'s Zodiacs. She knew Burwardsley would follow just as soon as he got a replacement for the one she hoped she was lying on the sea floor in Uummannaq harbour, preferably with the bloody Gurkha inside it. She turned and faced forward as Dina bumped the dinghy into a flat growler grounded on the rocks just a few metres from the shore. Beyond the ice and rock of the coastline, Fenna could see wooden buildings, painted red and blue, sitting on granite foundations. She focused on a red building, the largest and furthest from the shore, across a wide open field of snow with little to obstruct a bullet, a killing ground should anyone wander into it. She nodded at Dina, tucked the pistol into her windpants and scrambled over the side of the dinghy, her feet sliding for purchase on the ice as she held the boat steady for Dina to climb out of it. As Dina clambered around her and onto the island, she kicked the boat free. *One way or another, we won't need it*, she reasoned. Fenna watched as the boat drifted out between the growlers of ice and into the fjord. The tide might take it deeper into the fjord, *if we're lucky*, she thought. She turned and followed Dina towards the red building.

It was a schoolhouse, with thick square rafters of dark hardwood in the roof space, long benches around broad tables, and bunks at the rear. Dina walked from the door into the kitchen and searched the cupboards, pulling tins and dried goods onto the counter. She found a tin of peaches and pulled open a drawer, rattling through the cutlery until she found a tin opener. She beamed at Fenna as they sat down opposite each other at the table closest to the kitchen. It was the first time she had seen Dina smile, Fenna realised. She watched as Dina chiselled her way into the lid of the tin and twisted it open, turning the tin with one hand at the base and cutting the lid with the blade and quick flicks of the tin opener. The syrup spilled onto Dina's hand and she smiled as she licked it from her fingers.

"Dina," Fenna said as the Greenlander prised back the lid and fished a peach slice out of the tin. "You're going to need this," she said and slid Simonsen's pistol across the table. Dina flicked her eyes at the pistol and shook her head. "Yes," Fenna said and placed one of the two extra magazines next to the pistol. Dina ignored Fenna and ate two more slices of peach. Syrup dribbled down her chin and dripped onto the tabletop.

Fenna sighed and made a play of wrestling the tin from Dina's grasp. She tried to smile, then slipped a slice of the preserved fruit into her mouth. Dina nodded and then grabbed the tin. They shared the last of the slices until there was only syrup remaining. Dina drank half of it and pushed the tin to Fenna.

"No," she said. "You finish it." Fenna waited until Dina had wiped the last drop of juice from her chin. The twenty-five year old woman grinned like a cheeky toddler and Fenna smiled at her. Then she placed her hand on the pistol and pushed it all the way to Dina's chest. "I can't do this alone," she said.

Dina's hair shook as she frowned and looked away from the pistol as Fenna wrestled with the image of Dina shooting Lunk in the head, only hours earlier.

"They are coming," she said. "You understand, don't you?" Fenna reached across the table and tugged at Dina's arm. "Don't you?" she said as Dina turned to face her.

Yes, Dina raised her eyebrows. She scowled and took the pistol and the extra magazine, pushed them into the voluminous pockets of her jacket. Dina lifted her right leg over the bench, stood and walked to the window. She picked at the sealskin cord of a dog whip hanging on the wall – there was another on the wall opposite – and stared out across the snow towards the fjord. Fenna joined her and realised she could just see the dinghy before it floated out of sight behind a large berg. The tide had cleared this area of the fjord, carrying the larger floes deeper into the black waters, around the peninsula and out to sea. Apart from the numerous bergs, the sea was clear and free for sailing. The sun was low in the blue sky, and the glaciers on the mountains were tinged with pink. If it wasn't for the drone of the outboard motor that drifted towards the schoolhouse on the wind, Fenna thought she might have enjoyed the view.

"I have no plan," she said to Dina as the Greenlander cupped her mouth and nose in her hands, staring through the window at the sea. "But I will finish this," she said. "For Mikael, for you..." Fenna stepped behind Dina, wrapped her arms around her and smoothed her hands through her long, black hair, tugging it free of the jacket collar and letting it flow down her back. "I will finish it for you, Dina," she said. "And Charlie," she whispered.

Dina trembled as Fenna stroked her hair. The pink glow of the late Arctic afternoon spread down the mountain and disappeared into a cold shadow, black like the water, black like the hull of the Zodiac that drifted around the corner, black like death. Dina turned away from the window and buried her head against Fenna's chest as the driver of the Zodiac cut the power and the hull bumped against the ice. Fenna recognised the four men who clambered out of the inflatable. She watched as Bahadur secured the Zodiac to the rocks with a length of rope. She recognised the two policemen. They wore non-regulation jackets and carried the same model of antiquated rifle that Fenna had fired from the back of Maratse's police car. The scowls on their faces and the bandages around their heads were new. Burwardsley, she noted, stood apart from the rest as he removed the magazine from the SA80 rifle he carried, checked it and slapped it home. Fenna shuddered as she heard the click, as if all her senses were wired to that one man. A second click caught her attention and she flicked her eyes from Burwardsley, scanning for his Sergeant, the merciless Nepali with the curved blade.

"These men," she whispered, "are the single most important men in my life." She watched as Bahadur nodded at Burwardsley and stalked towards a lip of rock, an elevated position above the schoolhouse to Fenna's left. "But it is *my* life," she said and sank below the window. She eased Dina to the floor to the right of the window, and took the pistol and magazine from Dina's pockets as she leaned her back against the wall. Fenna crouched. She moved to the door, keeping low, and opened it. She peered around the frame as the policemen stopped in the snow, five metres from the boat and just thirty to the schoolhouse. Burwardsley didn't move.

"Konstabel," said Simonsen. He coughed and spoke again in English for Burwardsley's benefit, raising his voice. "Fenna," he said. "Throw out your weapons and come out. There's nowhere to go," he added and gestured at the fjord with his left arm.

Fenna stood and pressed her body to the wall. She shouted through the open door, "Get rid of your friends and I might consider it." She glanced at Dina while she waited. The Greenlander looked at Fenna through the strands of her hair, as if she was peering through a blind in the jungle, shallow breathing, hoping the tigers would go away.

"I'm not going anywhere, Konstabel," Burwardsley said. "You know that."

Fenna took a breath and a firm grip of the pistol in her left hand. *I knew that*, she said to herself. With a quick glance at Bahadur's position, she snapped off a single shot at the Gurkha and ducked back inside the schoolhouse.

Dina clucked the remains of her tongue and pressed her hands to her ears. She looked at Fenna and then crawled the length of the table and hid at the end furthest from the door. Fenna leaned against the wall and listened as the policemen swore in Danish, thumping the snow from their trousers and jackets as they picked themselves up and moved into cover. Fenna smiled until she heard Burwardsley's laugh, deep and indulgent, as it broke against the schoolhouse wall, slamming into Fenna's gut like a boulder.

"We've been here before, *love*," he said. Fenna heard the snow crunch beneath his boots as he walked forwards.

"Get down, you fool," Simonsen shouted. Burwardsley ignored him and Fenna counted his strides. "She has two pistols."

"Yes," Burwardsley said. "Both of them yours."

Fenna imagined Bahadur settling into the stock of his gun and lining his sights on the door. *I'll give him ten strides*. "And then I will kill him," she said and shifted her position to the second of two windows, furthest from the door and closest to the kitchen. She counted five more strides, scooted a metre from the window, popped up and fired twice. The window shattered and she fired twice more at the British Lieutenant as he crashed to the ground and rolled to Fenna's right. She tracked him with the pistol, stepping to the left and firing again. Fenna felt the impact of her fifth round as if she controlled its flight with a wire, slamming into Burwardsley's right shoulder and spraying blood across the snow like a reckless painter.

"Bad," Burwardsley yelled as he switched his grip on his rifle. "Take her."

Fenna dropped to the floor and rolled into the kitchen unit as the Nepali shredded the exterior of the schoolhouse and the windows disintegrated under his sustained burst of fire. *This isn't for me*, Fenna realised and forced herself to move. She cut her hands and knees on the glass as she crawled to the door. "It's covering fire," she breathed and thrust the pistol around the door frame, firing blind and emptying the magazine as she sprayed the approach with lead.

"Fuck," Burwardsley shouted.

"You like that, eh?" Fenna shouted as she switched pistols, stuffing Simonsen's into her pocket.

"Laugh it up, *love*," Burwardsley shouted and opened up with three-round bursts that splintered the door frame and tore the door from its hinges. Fenna rolled onto her side as the door crashed onto the stone floor and fell against the remains of the frame. Another burst from Burwardsley's rifle splintered the door in the middle and it collapsed into two pieces, flat on the floor.

Fenna ignored the glass splinters in her hands and popped up behind the first window, firing two shots blind and sighting the third as she found Burwardsley, as close to the schoolhouse as he dared, too close for Fenna's liking. She aimed. Squeezed the trigger and then paused at a *whush* of air behind her and the sound of wood creaking and leather snapping like a whip on the ice. She turned as Dina's feet brushed the surface of the table, her neck noosed within a dog whip lashed by her own hands around the beam above her.

"No," Fenna screamed and clambered onto the table top. She gripped Dina's feet and pushed them upwards, trying to lift her body as the British rifles pulped the side of the schoolhouse. Fenna screamed again as a tornado of splinters cycloned around the room, piercing her cheeks, stabbing at her body, pricking Dina with jagged chips as her almond face paled into blue and she swung beneath the beam until a burst of bullets severed the sealskin cord and she fell onto the table and rolled onto the floor. Fenna dropped the pistol and scrambled after her, lifting her head and tearing at the cord around Dina's neck with bloody fingers. It was tight, cinched, she pinched Dina's skin as she tried to pull it free.

The whip was no ornament. Cut from the skin of a ring seal, it was cured, greased in blubber, finger-wide at the base, it fluted to the diameter of a square pencil at the end where it was bound tight around the Greenlander's neck. Fenna held Dina's head in her arms and then, as the splinters withered to the floor, she pulled Simonsen's pistol from her pocket and slipped the last magazine inside the grip. She let go of Dina and reached for the other pistol beneath the table.

She tapped the barrel into the floor to remove any stray splinters. With a pistol in each hand, Fenna stood up and walked to the door. The glass crunched beneath her feet, blood trickled from the cuts in her hands, from the ends of the splinters embedded in her cheeks, but her focus was elsewhere. Fenna raised the pistols and stepped over the remains of the door, pulling the trigger of each weapon alternately, first left, then right, searching for targets with a haphazard sense of apathetic justice, letting the bullets fall where they may. She was done. There was no more, and this was the end.

"Sergeant," Burwardsley shouted as Fenna cleared the schoolhouse.

"Yes, Saheb," Bahadur said and pulled the trigger.

Chapter 29

Fenna lay in the snow as the blood pulsed out of her left arm. The beat was stronger than the pain. The flesh of her right leg was clipped below her knee and a third shot from the Gurkha's rifle had broken at least three of her ribs. Glancing blows, all of them. Crippling but not mortal. She would recover, she realised, and that was the last thing she wanted. Fenna stared at the fading light above her as the sky turned from pale blue to bruised purple, fading to black, unlike her memory. In her mind's eye, Dina swung from the beam still as Burwardsley pressed his boot on Fenna's wrist, plucking the pistol from her right hand. He repeated the action for the one in her left. Fenna ignored him, staring past his face, and the blood staining the shoulder of his parka. She heard the policemen as they entered the schoolhouse and called out Dina's status.

"She's dead," Fenna said, speaking the words at the same time as Simonsen, as if they had rehearsed. But they hadn't. *It wasn't meant to be like this*, Fenna told herself, admonishing herself with another image of Dina swinging from the cord whipped around her neck. Dina swung back and forth, even as the snow crunched beneath the policemen's feet as they carried the Greenlander's body past Fenna to the Zodiac. As the sound of their boots and Simonsen's huffing and grunting receded, Fenna heard the Gurkha arrive, his light step revealed only by the slap of the rifle against his back as he slung the SA80 and stopped at her feet.

"Saheb?" he said and nodded at Fenna. "What we gonna do?"

Burwardsley stepped over Fenna and crouched beside her. He prodded her ribs with two stiff fingers, smirking as she winced, ignoring the pain in his own shoulder. He lifted his hand. Fenna watched as Bahadur pressed a field bandage into it. Burwardsley lifted Fenna's arm and, with Bahadur's help, he bound the wound, pressing the bloody sleeve of the jacket beneath the bandage. He bound her leg with a second bandage from Bahadur, flicking the Gurkha's hand away as he tried to plug the wound in Burwardsley's shoulder.

"It can wait," he said. "Like her ribs."

"Policemen coming back, Saheb," Bahadur said.

"Stall them. I need a minute with the Konstabel." Burwardsley reached down and turned Fenna's face towards him as Bahadur met the policemen and discussed when they would leave. Fenna stared past Burwardsley until he pressed her cheeks together, his finger and thumb squeezing between her teeth and forcing her lips to part. “Look at me, Konstabel,” he said. Fenna flicked her eyes past the swinging shadow of Dina's corpse and stared at Burwardsley. “That's better,” he said and relaxed his grip.

Burwardsley pulled the glove off his left hand and searched Fenna's body. She waited for him to violate her, to cup his hand around her breast, to grope between her legs, but Burwardsley was professional, thorough but fast. He dug the Webley out from beneath Fenna’s back and tossed it towards the policemen. His fingers lingered over the square of plastic tucked inside her thermal top. He unzipped the pocket and pulled out the SD card.

“Interesting,” he said and held it up in the last of the evening light. “Charlie give you this?”

“Yes,” Fenna breathed. Her eyes flickered from the card to Burwardsley's face, and then back to the image of Dina in her mind.

“Do you know what's on it?” he said. “Hey, Konstabel.” Burwardsley slapped her face with the back of his hand. “I said do you know what's on the card?”

Fenna flicked her eyes towards his. “I have an idea,” she said.

“Will you use it?”

“I don't understand...”

“Yes you do,” he said. “Will you use it?”

Fenna listened to the throb of her blood, pulsing past her temples and pressing at her wounds. She ignored Burwardsley until, a second slap later, and he had her attention.

“Yes or no, Konstabel.”

“Yes,” she said.

“Good.”

“Why?” Fenna said.

“Because I’m done,” he said and flicked the lapels of her jacket to the side. Burwardsley reached beneath her sweater and slid the card inside her pocket. He zipped the pocket halfway as Simonsen crunched through the snow. He removed his hand and stood up.

“Is she hurt?” Simonsen said and stared around Burwardsley at Fenna.

“She’ll live,” Burwardsley said. “What about the Greenlander?” he said and nodded towards the Zodiac. Bahadur helped Danielsen shove the boat off the ice and into the water. The policeman held the rope as Bahadur crawled over the side and started the motor.

"Hmm," Simonsen said and cast a glance at Fenna. "I'd love to pin it on her, but honestly don't know how she could have done it." He shook his head. "She was pretty intent on killing you."

"I have that effect on women," Burwardsley said. Fenna waited for him to laugh, and couldn't decide if she was surprised when he didn't.

"Lieutenant," Simonsen said and lowered his voice. He gestured for Burwardsley to step away from Fenna. "What happened here today, I need to write it up. If it hadn't been for the call from Premierløjtnant..."

Fenna stiffened, the throb of blood forgotten as she strained to hear what Simonsen was saying. Burwardsley turned his back to her and leaned in close to the policeman. He towered above the Dane and Fenna gave up on trying to hear what was said, the look on his face confirmed it. It was a done deal, she realised. Bulletproof. Fenna let her head flop back onto the snow. The back of her neck cooled and she looked up at the first stars, closed her eyes, and imagined Dina's face. The image of the Greenlander stayed with her as the policemen lifted her up, cuffed her, and marched her to the Zodiac.

Dina was her focus as Bahadur sailed across the fjord, weaving slowly around the ice, and steering past the bergs as they threatened, in all serenity, to crumble at a glance. Fenna crumbled each time the image of Dina in her mind was replaced with the sight of her slumped in the bow of the boat, a red welt around her throat, the sealskin whip hanging loose around her neck. The lights of the town flickered into her vision as the Zodiac idled at the slipway, long enough for the policemen to drag Dina's body out of the boat and into the back of the ambulance, long enough for them to return and march her into the Toyota waiting at the top of the slipway.

Burwardsley walked alongside the policemen, leaning on the door as they shoved her into the passenger seat. He waved Danielsen away as the policeman tried to shut the door.

"Give us a minute," he said and the policeman walked away to smoke quietly next to Simonsen. Burwardsley took a breath and Fenna watched as he favoured his left arm. She hoped the right hurt like a motherfucker. He followed her gaze and laughed. "Yes, love, you finally got me."

"I'm not your *love*," she said. "I never was."

"No," he said and glanced over the roof of the car at the mountain, its features snow-cut and stark in the distance. "It's a pretty country. Brutal and unforgiving but pretty. Don't you think so, Konstabel?" Burwardsley said and looked down at Fenna.

"I used to," she said as the bump of sledge runners in her mind forced her to think of Mikael, Dina...

"Listen, Konstabel, shit happens and jobs have to be done." Burwardsley shrugged. "Bahadur and I, we're just good at what we do. More or less. We were meant to gather all the loose ends at the cabin. Kjersing arranged for you to bring the satellite to us. We brought Dina. Only," he paused and winced at the wound in his shoulder, "things didn't go quite to plan."

The twinge of satisfaction Fenna felt at the obstacles she had overcome, how she had evaded the British Lieutenant, again and again, was banished by the guilt of Dina's death and Mikael's murder. "What did you mean when you asked me if I would use the card?"

Burwardsley glanced at the policemen as they finished their cigarettes and took a step towards the Toyota. He leaned inside the car and said, "Humble pays for everything, but the things he takes for free still have a price. The girl should never have been involved," he said and glanced at Fenna. "I'm not a complete monster. Use the card, Konstabel. Make the bastard pay." Burwardsley nodded once, turned and walked down the slipway to the Zodiac. Fenna watched as he slipped his long legs over the side of the boat and waved for Bahadur to take them back to the ship. Danielsen closed the door and Fenna pressed her face to the window, watching as Bahadur ploughed a course through a patch of brush ice towards *The Ice Star*. The ship stirred in the fjord, the navigation lights sparkling as the propellers maintained its position in the face of the tide. Fenna lost sight of the Zodiac as it disappeared in the black water and Simonsen backed the Toyota onto the road and drove the short distance to the hospital.

She let them drag her from the back of the car. She let them stand in the room as the nurse undid her bandages and stripped Fenna to her underwear, tossing her dirty, blood-stained clothes onto a chair in the corner of the room. Fenna sat on the bed at the nurse's instruction and lifted her arms for her to clean and bind the superficial wound in her chest where Bahadur's bullet had glanced her ribs. *He was surgical*, she realised. *And I got off lightly.* Unlike Dina down in the morgue. Danielsen and Simonsen stepped out of the room as the nurse undid Fenna's bra. She cleaned her skin and bound a fresh bandage over her arm before slipping a gown over her head. Fenna noticed that Simonsen had found a seat in the nurse's office in the adjacent room. He stared at her through the observation window, and Fenna realised she was in the island equivalent of Intensive Care, a pane of glass and a spit wad from the medical staff.

The nurse dumped Fenna's bloody bandages and her own surgical gloves into a yellow medical waste bag and helped Fenna onto the bed and beneath the sheets. Fenna lowered her head onto the pillow and stared up at the ceiling as Danielsen entered thc room, closed his fingers around her left wrist and cuffed her to the rail of the bed. He tugged at the chain once and then walked out of the room without a word. The nurse followed him and turned out the light. Darkness, Fenna realised, was not the friend she'd hoped for.

She tried to sleep, tried to force the image of Dina from her head, but she was trapped in the room with the ghost of the Greenlander. And when the image of Dina did fade, Mikael sledged into her mind, his red beard dark with blood, and the back of his scalp flapping as they crested the top of a gulley, or pushed the sledge over the ice foot and onto the frozen sea. The howl of the dogs kept her awake, as did the *crack crack* of 9mm rounds and the maniacal grin of the elephant man as he bled from his ears and pleasured himself, one stroke after another until Dina returned, swinging in front of Fenna through the long, dark polar night and into the morning. It was only the bustle of the nurses and breakfast that forced her to accept that sleep was gone and the nightmares were not confined to the night.

The lights came on and Fenna turned her head towards the nurse. The woman paused at the door, her short body half inside the room as she turned her head to talk to a policeman in the corridor. Fenna heard the nurse switch from Greenlandic to Danish and then tut to allow the policeman to enter the room. The tears that Fenna's nightmares had held at bay, welled in her eyes at the sight of Maratse. He grinned as the nurse scolded the unlit cigarette from between his lips and into his jacket pocket. Maratse stepped aside and let her pass, closing the door behind her with his foot.

"Konstabel," he said as he fished the cigarette from his pocket and pushed it into the space between his teeth. "I've come to take you home."

Fenna nodded and sniffed once before lifting her wrist and rattling the cuffs chaining her to the bed. Maratse grinned and fished a key from the pocket on his belt. He tossed it to Fenna and nodded at the clothes in the bag on the chair.

"Get dressed," he said. "We have to take Dina to the heliport."

And there she was, Dina, again, but this time Fenna wasn't alone.

Chapter 30

There was a crowd outside the hospital when Fenna walked out of the front door. She tugged the collar of Simonsen's jacket high around her neck and dipped her head, covering her face with her hair. Her leg was stiff but she was determined not to limp. Maratse opened the taxi door as Fenna slid her feet along the smooth surface of the snow. She noticed that Simonsen was sitting in the driver's seat of the police Toyota, watching her from where he was parked on the road, outside the light blue offices of Nukissiorfiit, Greenland's energy utility company. Maratse waited for Fenna to get inside the car and closed the rear passenger door. He sat down next to the driver and told him to wait on the road. Dina's body, Fenna had heard the nurse say, was sealed inside a zinc casket and loaded onto the back of a pickup. She saw the vehicle outside the side entrance to the hospital, the early morning sun reflecting on the shiny surface as the driver secured it with straps to the pickup's bed. Maratse nodded for the taxi driver to follow the pickup as it pulled out of the hospital parking area and onto the road. Simonsen followed in the Toyota.

The road to the heliport wound around the mountainside, cut into the rock. Wooden houses painted blue, red, green and yellow, leaned over the edges. They drove past the town scrap yard and an assortment of sledge dog houses, drying racks, snowmobile carcasses stripped for parts, and the ubiquitous plastic fish crates borrowed indefinitely from the Royal Greenland fish factory. Fenna took it all in, her face pressed to the passenger window as she avoided looking through the windscreen, avoided the thought of Dina, and tried to block out the shoot-out at the schoolhouse.

The taxi slowed as the pickup drove up the slight rise beside the heliport and through the gates onto the landing pad. The ground crew helped the driver unload the casket and secured it inside a net to be slung beneath the red Air Greenland Bell 212 helicopter. Maratse paid the driver and got out of the taxi. Fenna waited for him to open the door. He pressed a small backpack into Fenna's hands and waited for her to look inside.

"I can't take that on the plane," she said and opened the pack to show Maratse the Webley. He shrugged and fished a cigarette from the packet in his pocket.

"It's all you have," he said.

Fenna closed the backpack and slung it over her shoulder as Simonsen parked the Toyota beside the heliport building, stepped out of the car and bummed a cigarette from Maratse. He stared at Fenna's jacket as he lit the cigarette.

"Konstabel," he said and paused to blow out a lungful of smoke. "I don't pretend to understand what happened before you arrived in Uummannaq. All I know is I want you off this island. You are now in his custody," Simonsen said and nodded at Maratse. "He'll see you all the way to Kangerlussuaq. You'll fly to Denmark later today."

"That's it?" she said. "What about Kommandør Kjersing?"

"Dead," said Maratse.

"What?"

"Shot himself yesterday," he said and shrugged.

Fenna's shoulders sagged as she processed the information. The distant beat of rotors *whopped* through the air and she thought about Humble's *man in the Arctic* and the cost of the Canadian's test, the number of dead, and the potential implications for the Sirius Patrol should the story ever find its way into the papers.

"You are advised to keep your mouth shut, Konstabel," Simonsen said, raising his voice as the helicopter settled into a hover over the helipad, buffeting them with the wash of the rotors as it landed. "There are no journalists on the island," he said. "And, fortunately for you, no-one thought to film your gunfight outside the hospital. If someone had posted this on YouTube..." Simonsen shrugged and took a last drag on his cigarette. He flicked the butt into a snowdrift.

Maratse tugged at Fenna's elbow and nodded towards the helicopter. The ground crew had finished attaching the net to the bottom of the aircraft and the pilots were signalling that they were ready.

"You can keep the jacket," Simonsen said as he walked beside Fenna to the gate. "Consider it a souvenir, a reminder. I have mine," he said and smoothed his hand over the purple welt on the side of his head. Fenna nodded and followed Maratse through the gate and across the helipad. They ducked instinctively as they walked beneath the rotors and climbed into the helicopter. Fenna slid along the bench beside Maratse, dumped the backpack on the floor and buckled her seatbelt. Maratse handed her a pair of ear defenders and she tugged them over her ears. Simonsen waited by the gate until they were in the air before returning to the Toyota. Fenna watched him drive along the road as the helicopter lifted off the helipad and into a hover, settling the weight of the casket before gaining altitude and dipping the nose of the aircraft. The island was busy as people walked along the roads to the supermarket, glancing up at the helicopter as it chopped through the air above them.

The flight to the mainland took less than twenty minutes. Maratse was silent and Fenna closed her eyes. She immersed herself in the high pitch and tremor of the rotors, blocking out images of the schoolhouse, and focusing on Kjersing's abrupt death. She thought about Humble and pressed her hand against the pocket in her thermal top. She felt the card at the bottom of the pocket and pulled the zip closed. Maratse tapped her shoulder and pointed out of the window at a whale breaching the surface between the icebergs in the dark waters of the fjord below the helicopter. Fenna noticed the pilots exchanging gestures and felt the aircraft dip to the left as they angled for a better look. The pilots levelled the helicopter and raised the nose of the aircraft, losing speed and altitude as they settled above the gravel landing strip at Qaarsut airport. More ground crew guided Dina's casket to the ground before stepping back as the helicopter shifted position and landed. The rotors whined as the pilot powered down, reaching up to apply the rotor brake as the helicopter shuddered and the motor ticked cool. Fenna grabbed her backpack and followed Maratse out of the helicopter as the ground crew jarred the door open, sliding it alongside the fuselage. Dina waited to one side.

"I told Kula I would bring his granddaughter home," Maratse said. Fenna stood by his side as the ground crew removed the net and straps. They paused at the roar of the four-engined Dash-7 aircraft as it touched down on the gravel strip, air-braking all the way to the airport building. Maratse turned away from Dina's casket and stuck a cigarette in his mouth. He walked towards the building and Fenna fell in step beside him. The aircraft turned at the end of the strip and taxied to the terminal, a small wooden building with a tiny tower.

Fenna's bag was shoved in the hold with the other passengers' luggage. Maratse sorted her boarding pass and they waited in the small lounge as the crew removed several rows of seats inside the aircraft to make space for Dina. When they climbed onboard, Fenna was relieved to sit in the seats directly in front of the casket. While the first sight of the casket had troubled her, she now realised that Dina was finally at peace, and that no man could ever hurt her again. She smoothed her hand over her breast pocket, not for the last time, and imagined how she could use the card inside it.

What was it Burwardsley had said? She tried to remember as the aircraft taxied to the end of the strip, powered up and lifted into the air. The short take-off thrust Fenna back into her seat. *Toronto*, she recalled. *That's where Humble will be.* Fenna closed her eyes as Maratse fidgeted beside her. When the stewardess brought coffee, Fenna shifted her position and winced at the pain in her ribs. Maratse stared out of the window as they flew over Disco Island. Fenna tapped him on the arm and beckoned for him to lean in close.

"Vestergaard?" she said. "What happened to him?"

"Gone when I got back to the station," Maratse said.

"Where to?"

He shrugged and took a sip of coffee.

"And the dead Danes in Kulusuk?"

"Navy," he said and reached inside his jacket for a newspaper clipping. He unfolded it and presented it to Fenna. She read the headline and shook her head at the caption citing *an unfortunate boating accident* – the two men supposedly drowned when sailing in a hunter's dinghy from Kulusuk to Tasiilaq on the mainland. Fenna furrowed her brow and returned the clipping.

"Cover up," she said.

"*Iiji*," he said and stuffed the clipping inside his jacket. He sipped his coffee and then grinned.

"What?"

"Us," he said and finished his coffee. "They said it was an exercise."

"The gunfight on the ice?" Fenna said and laughed.

"*Iiji*," Maratse said and smiled. "The Chief of Police flew in from Nuuk. He said we had to be prepared to fight terrorists, even in Greenland."

"Terrorists? Really?" Fenna laughed again and felt her cheeks begin to ache.

"*The world is changing*," Maratse said. "*And Greenland with it.*"

"He said that?"

"*Iiji.*"

Fenna leaned back in her seat. She warmed her hands on the

paper cup and sipped at the coffee. The world was indeed changing. The Arctic, and Greenland, she realised, was, now more than ever, firmly in the spotlight. It had started with global warming, when hundreds of politicians and journalists had been encouraged to visit the glaciers calving in Ilulissat, to see climate change in progress. *And then came oil*, she mused, or the promise of it. And minerals. Tourism alone will never support an independent Greenland. *And everyone wants a slice of the pie. Before it's too late.*

The plane landed to pick up more passengers in Ilulissat, before touching down at Greenland's main hub: Kangerlussuaq. Maratse escorted Fenna out of the aircraft once all the passengers were gone. She lingered by the side of Dina's casket and turned to look at Maratse. He nodded.

"I will tell Kula what you did for Dina," he said.

"It wasn't enough."

Maratse shrugged and gestured towards the exit. Fenna smoothed her hand on the casket and then turned her back on Dina, nodding at the stewardess as they climbed down the steps and onto the layer of firm snow that covered the tarmac. The dense, inland cold bit at her lungs and she thrust her hands inside the pockets of her jacket, the tips of her ears prickling as she followed Maratse to the terminal. He waited by her side as airport security processed her, presented her with a boarding pass and queried her backpack.

"Evidence," Maratse said and waited as the officer inspected the Webley.

"It will have to go in a strong box," he said. "And then someone will have to sign for it in Copenhagen."

Fenna watched the man place the Webley inside an aluminium box, a strip of yellow warning signs blazed on the lid, and a combination padlock that secured it. *What was it Bose had said? 'I know someone who would be interested in that.'Humble*, she realised and then smiled at Mikael's words, mumbled in disgust inside the tent. *'Fuck eBay.'*

"I have to go," Maratse said as Fenna was shown to a secure waiting room. He shuffled his feet and Fenna saw the awkward flicker of his eyes.

"Thank you," she said and held out her hand. Maratse ignored it and pulled Fenna into a brief hug. She caught her breath as he managed to trap her arm and squeeze her ribs in his embrace, but the tears rolling down her cheeks were not from pain. She smiled as he let her go.

"I won't forget," she said.

Maratse nodded once, turned and walked away. Fenna watched as he walked through the security door and was lost in a sea of passengers. The sense of being alone clamped her stomach and she stumbled towards the nearest seat. The dead had departed, and now the living had abandoned her. She sucked at the air through her teeth and tapped her hands on her knees. It was going to be a long flight to Denmark.

The Office

TORONTO, CANADA

Chapter 31

KASTRUP AIRPORT - COPENHAGEN, DENMARK

Fenna woke at the light touch of the flight attendant on her shoulder. The woman left her hand there as Fenna blinked and fidgeted beneath the blanket. She nodded at the attendant that she was awake and squinted out of the window at the baggage handlers moving into position alongside *Norsaq*, Air Greenland's Airbus 330. The passengers bustled out of their seats as Fenna retrieved her temporary passport – a hastily printed official document – from the sleeve of the chair in front of her. She waited until the aircraft was all but empty, unfastened her seatbelt, slid out of the seat and into the aisle. Fenna smoothed her hand around the outline of the SD card in her shirt pocket, grabbed Simonsen's police jacket from the overhead locker and made her way out of the aircraft. The cleaners had already entered the aircraft to prepare it for the following day's flight to Kangerlussuaq.

Fenna winced at the bullet wound in her leg as she worked the pins and needles out of her system, picking up the pace along the jet bridge to the terminal. She ignored the passengers waiting at the gate, barely noticing the airport luggage trolleys as she weaved her way between them. Fenna blinked at the image in her mind of Dina swinging from the rafters of the schoolhouse, and every black-haired woman in the terminal thereafter wore the Greenlander's almond death mask. Fenna stopped and pressed her hand to her forehead, her temporary passport clutched between her fingers. She looked up and searched for a toilet. Fenna pushed through a group of aircrew and burst into the ladies' restroom. The cubicles were occupied. Fenna threw up in the hand basin.

"You all right, love?" Fenna whirled around at the word, fists clenched, only to glare at the face of a middle-aged British woman. Fenna unravelled her fists and did her best to ignore her. She wiped her mouth with a paper towel and waved her hand beneath the tap to rinse the sink. Fenna scrunched the towel into the wastepaper bin and walked out of the restroom.

"Feeling better, Konstabel?" said a man standing by a vending machine.

"Who are you?" Fenna said and wiped her cheek with her hand as she studied the man in the jeans and suit jacket. He wore a graphite wool sweater beneath the jacket and, Fenna noticed, a 9mm pistol in a shoulder holster rig on the left side of his body. *Old school*, she thought and almost laughed at the observation.

"My name is Per Jarnvig," he said and waved a hand towards the nearest café. "Can I buy you a coffee? You look like you need it."

"Sure," Fenna said as she scanned the crowd of passengers. "Let's go." She folded the passport and slipped it into the inside pocket of her jacket. Jarnvig nodded at the jacket and smiled.

"Souvenir?" he said as he led Fenna to an empty table near the huge windows overlooking the runway.

"Something like that." Fenna waited for Jarnvig to order two coffees. She decided to let him talk, and waited for him to flash his badge tucked inside a leather wallet. She recognised the logo of *Politiets Efterretningstjeneste*, the Danish Intelligence Service of the Police. "PET?" she said and sighed as the waitress returned with two black coffees.

"Yes," said Jarnvig and slipped his badge inside his jacket.

"Then you knew I was coming." Jarnvig nodded, and took a sip of coffee. "And you know everything that happened?"

"Most of it, although I am sure you can elaborate," he said and held up his hand as Fenna started to speak. "But that's not why I'm here."

"No?"

"No," he said and shook his head. "There's a lot about this case that needs investigating, and just as much that will be swept under the carpet. No," Jarnvig said and leaned back in his chair. "I'm much more interested in you."

Fenna warmed her hands around the coffee cup, turning it slowly within her fingers. She blinked an image of another coffee and another interrogation out of her mind and focused instead on Jarnvig and the man's forty-something stubble of white hair on his chin and the groomed cut of grey on his head. The butt of the 9mm peaked out of his jacket and Jarnvig adjusted his position to conceal it.

"What do you want?" she said.

"I'm just curious as to what you plan to do next," Jarnvig said and waited as Fenna turned the coffee one more revolution.

"What I really want," she said, "is a flight to Toronto."

"Canada? Are you sure that's a good idea?"

"You asked me what I want," Fenna said and looked up. "Can

you get me what I want?"

"Well," Jarnvig said and leaned forwards. "That all depends on you." Fenna lifted the paper coffee cup to her lips and waited for Jarnvig to explain. The hot coffee stung her broken lips. "I need a young woman with your expertise..."

"Expertise?" Fenna said and spluttered the coffee onto the table. "You think I am an expert?"

"I could have said *experience*," Jarnvig said and wiped the coffee from the table with a napkin.

"You know what happened?"

"Like I said, I know enough," he said and dropped the wet napkin onto the floor. "Konstabel," Jarnvig continued, "you're going to have a tough time adapting to life after Greenland." He held up his hand as Fenna opened her mouth. "Hear me out," he said. "You'll need a place to stay, money, a job – I can set you up with all these things."

"And a diplomatic pouch?"

"What?"

"One of those bags they won't open at the airport."

"I know what a diplomatic pouch is."

"I'll also need a ticket to Toronto, and one more thing."

"Fenna," he said and leaned over the table. "Forget Humble. He's untouchable."

"I think he'll listen to me," she said and pressed her hand against her shirt pocket.

Jarnvig rubbed his hand across the stubble on his chin. Fenna heard the rasp of hair on his fingers as he stared at her.

"What do you want a diplomatic pouch for?"

"That's for the other thing," Fenna said and took another sip of coffee. She swallowed. "You're recruiting me, aren't you?" She smiled at Jarnvig's curt nod of the head. "Then this is the price. Plus, the other things you mentioned."

Jarnvig tapped his fingertips on the table. Clipped and filed, Fenna noticed and looked at her own broken nails and scarred fingertips. Greenland was still ingrained in the pores of her skin. *I'll carry it forever*, she realised.

"All right," he said.

Fenna almost spilled her coffee for the second time. "All right?"

"Yes," Jarnvig said and shrugged.

"You do know what I am going to do?"

"I have a pretty good idea."

"Fuck," she said as the realisation of what he wanted in return sank in.

"Fenna," he said. "There's no going back after this. I'm willing to turn a blind eye to your business in Toronto..."

"Because your *business* is much worse? Is that right, Jarnvig?"

"There's that possibility."

Fenna turned her fingers within the light from the window. Gone were the icebergs and the harsh polar light, the sting of ice splinters on the wind, and the howl of the sledge dog beneath the pitch black winter canopy of the Arctic. *But there are things to be done*, she reminded herself. *Debts to be paid.* She looked up and nodded.

"I am twenty-four," she said. "My father is dead, my mother is an alcoholic and may as well be dead, and my sister probably hates me for leaving her to cope with our mother by herself." She looked at Jarnvig and sighed. "Everyone else I ever cared for, I lost in Greenland."

"Greenland has its price," Jarnvig said and nodded. "I've heard that before."

"And so does the rest of my life," Fenna said and stood up. "I need to pee."

Jarnvig's chair squealed as he pushed back from the table and stood up. He pulled a card from his pocket and handed it to Fenna. "When you're done, go to customer service and ask them to show you to this room. I'll have the things you need, a change of clothes, luggage..."

"And the other thing," Fenna said. "The Webley. It was sent with my personal effects on the same flight – addressed *care of* Airport Authorities. I think that means you."

Jarnvig shook his head. "That's not going to be possible."

"And yet, that's the price," she said and turned to walk towards the nearest toilet. Fenna smiled as she savoured the last look on Jarnvig's face, and her own renewed sense of strength and purpose.

PEARSON INT. AIRPORT - TORONTO, CANADA

Fenna shrugged her backpack higher onto her shoulder and waited for the Canadian Border Services Agency officer to return with her documents. The officer's shoes whispered along the airport carpet as she approached Fenna, a clipboard and several documents in her hand.

"Miss Brongaard?"

"Yes," Fenna said, ignoring the mispronunciation of her name.

"If you'll come with me?"

"Sure." Fenna followed the woman into a tiny room. She noticed her diplomatic pouch and the new duffel bag Jarnvig had bought for her on a table in the corner. Fenna waited for the officer to close the door before sitting at the table.

Another table, another interrogation, she mused. *This seems to be my lot in life.*

"So," the officer said. "This is just a formality."

"Okay."

"All your papers are in order, and I must admit, my supervisor and I are impressed at the speed at which they were prepared."

"The Danes can be quite efficient when they want to be," Fenna said and tried a smile. She regretted it as a fresh scab on her lip began to split. She reached into her pocket and smoothed some salve from a tube onto her bottom lip.

"So we can see," the officer said. "Your first stop?"

"Is the Consulate General," said Fenna. "Here in Toronto."

"All right." The officer checked her notes and placed the clipboard onto the table. She pressed her fingers together and took a breath. "We only have one question."

"Go ahead."

"More of a concern, really."

"Yes?" Fenna said and nodded. She had a feeling she knew what was coming.

"Your appearance worries us a little," the officer said and smiled in such a way that Fenna could feel the sympathy pouring out of her. "We don't have a lot of information about you, Miss Brongaard, but, if you need any assistance," she said and gestured at Fenna's face.

Fenna almost laughed. *My papers are in order, but they are worried if I am not?That's a first,* she mused and turned her head to look at her reflection in the glass. *Fair enough.*

"I can assure you I'm all right," she said. "It's not as bad as it looks."

"I don't know," the officer said and, testing, she added, "If my husband..."

"Husband," Fenna said and laughed. "If only." She took a breath, scratched a broken fingernail through her hair and looked at the officer. "I work for the Danish Navy. I have been on exercise and this," she said and nodded at the diplomatic pouch, "is a comfortable job they have given me while my body mends." *That sounded good – almost plausible.*

"I see," the officer said. Fenna could see that she didn't, but that her questions, for the moment at least, were satisfied. "How long are you planning to stay in Canada after you have visited the Consulate?"

"I'll be leaving tomorrow evening, on the first available flight," Fenna said. *All being well*, she thought.

"Then we're done. Thank you, Miss Brongaard." The officer stood and gestured at Fenna's luggage. "You'll find a taxi outside, unless the Consulate is sending a car?"

"A taxi will be fine," Fenna said. She walked around the desk to the table with her luggage, nodding at the weight of the diplomatic pouch as she picked it up. She slipped it inside her backpack and turned for the door.

"Your duffel bag, Miss Brongaard," the officer said. "Don't forget it."

"Right," said Fenna. She turned back for the duffel. "It's been a long flight." *Maybe I'll sleep on the return*, she wondered. *But then, that all depends on tomorrow.* Fenna thanked the woman and walked out of the room in search of a taxi.

Chapter 32

DOWNTOWN TORONTO, CANADA

The office building of Humble & Lunk was as space-age as the technology its parent company created. The huge glass plates reflected the summer sun, much like the icebergs off the coast of Greenland. Fenna pulled on her sunglasses and pressed the bridge against her nose. She shrugged the backpack onto her shoulder and climbed the marble steps in front of the building. She waited for two men and women in suits to walk out of the revolving doors before dipping her head to her chest and walking beneath the security camera and into the foyer of the lion's den. Like *The Ice Star*, the building reeked of money, all the way from the door to the mahogany reception desks and into the elevators. Fenna walked to the desk closest to her and gripped the strap of her backpack.

"I have an appointment," she said and fiddled with a lock of her hair as the receptionist checked the computer.

"Name?"

"Gregersen."

"And who are you here to see, Ms Gregersen?"

"Richard Humble," Fenna said and tapped her finger on the surface of the desk. "He is expecting me."

"Not according to his schedule," the woman said and looked up from the computer screen. "I suggest you wait while I contact his office." She pointed to the area of the foyer closest to the door, the sofas, Fenna realised, were longer than Sirius sledges.

"I'll wait," she said and turned towards the sofas. The receptionist picked up her phone and dialled through to Humble's office. Fenna heard the name *Gregersen* as she crossed the marble floor to the sofa. She sank onto the cushions and leaned back as the receptionist clicked her heels across the floor and looked down at Fenna.

"Rachael will be down to see you shortly," she said.

"Who's Rachael?"

"Mr Humble's secretary."

Fenna shifted position and pulled the backpack closer. "Is Mr Humble here today?"

"He is in the building, yes," the receptionist said and gestured at the coffee machine and water dispenser. "Please help yourself to coffee. Rachael will meet you here."

"Thank you," Fenna said and watched as the receptionist returned to her desk.

This will go one of two ways, she thought as her pulse quickened. Fenna looked around the foyer and flicked her eyes from the security man by the door to another by the elevator. *And then there's the Toronto Emergency Task Force. And everything that entails.*

But I got this far, she said to herself. *I just need to get a little further.*

The elevator door opened and Fenna turned her head to see a young woman, perhaps the same age as Fenna – chestnut hair and a flat chest. *My city double*, she laughed.

"Ms Gregersen?" the woman said as she approached. "I'm Rachael. Mr Humble's secretary."

"Mikaela," Fenna said as she stood. She shook Rachel's hand and pulled the backpack over her shoulder.

"Mr Humble was intrigued by your email," Rachael said as she led Fenna to the elevator. "It came quite out of the blue."

Because I wrote it last night at the hotel. Fenna pinched her thumbnails into her index fingers and nodded. "He is interested in the piece?"

"Oh, yes," Rachael said. "There are very few things that he would cancel a meeting for, but a handgun from The Great War is one of them. You're lucky he's in town. He has a flight scheduled for the afternoon. And then he will be flying on to meet his ship..."

"*The Ice Star*?"

"Yes," Rachael said and frowned as she stepped into the elevator. "You know of it?"

"In passing," Fenna said and felt the hairs on her neck rise as the elevator door whispered closed.

The security guard pressed the button for the twenty-eighth floor and clasped his hands in front of his waist. He stared at Fenna through floors two and ten until Rachael nodded that it was okay and he turned his attention to the control panel.

"You're from Europe?" she asked. "Your name, is it Norwegian?"

"Danish," said Fenna and smiled. She gestured at the control panel and said, "I thought Mr Humble would have an office on the top floor?"

"No," Rachael said and laughed. "He's always getting teased about that," she said and paused. "Mr Lunk used to say it was like going down to the basement, every time they held a meeting in Richard's office." The corners of Rachael's lips soured at the mention of Lunk's name. "Of course, after Mark's death..." At a look from the security guard, Rachael stopped talking and Fenna bit back a smile. The elevator slowed to a stop and the doors opened into a modest reception with two sofas identical to the ones in the foyer. Fenna followed Rachael through the doors and into the main office area of the twenty-eighth floor. She waited until the elevator doors had closed before opening her backpack.

"I'll just let Mr Humble know you're here," Rachael said as she walked to her desk.

"That won't be necessary," said Fenna as she pulled the Webley out of her backpack and pointed it at Rachael's head. Rachael's assistant screamed, but, to her credit, Fenna mused, Humble's receptionist stayed cool and nodded. "Which office?"

"That one," Rachael said and pointed at the double doors in the centre of the office space.

"Is he alone?"

"Yes."

"Okay," Fenna said and took a breath. "Let's do this." She nodded towards the doors and let Rachael lead the way. Fenna followed Rachael inside as she knocked and opened the door.

"Rachael," Humble said as he looked up from his desk. "And Konstabel Brongaard," he said. For a brief moment, Fenna enjoyed the lack of composure on the man's face, and then he was all business and she knew what she must do.

"Surprised?"

"Yes," he said. "I really thought you were dead." Humble leaned back in his chair. Fenna kicked the door closed. She waved the Webley at Rachael and nodded for her to stand beside Humble.

"Burwardsley finally choked on your money and had a change of heart," she said and pulled the SD card from her shirt pocket. She handed it to Rachael and nodded at the computer. "Put it in and let me show you who your boss really is."

"Fenna," Humble said as he removed his glasses and wiped them on his tie. "I see you brought the Webley."

"That's not all," she said as Rachael clicked on the folder icon on the computer to open the SD card.

"Really? You have something to show me?"

"Oh yes," Fenna said. "I remember how you like to watch." Humble paled and reached for the mouse. Rachael moved to one side only to pause at the click of the pistol's hammer as Fenna cocked it. "There's a movie file," she said. "Click on it."

"Burwardsley," Humble said and stammered. Sweat beaded on his brow and he pushed Rachael away from the computer.

"Yes," Fenna said. "Like I said, he finally got sick of your shit, just a few minutes after the woman you tortured hung herself from the rafters in the schoolhouse on that island."

"What is she talking about, Richard?" Rachael said and stepped away from the computer. Humble said nothing. He stared at Fenna as she centred the pistol on his face.

"Are you going to tell her?"

"Security has called the Emergency Task Force by now," Humble said and swallowed. "You know that?"

"I'm counting on it," Fenna said.

"In the time you've wasted on this," he said and gestured at the screen. "I could have bought the Webley and you could be safely on your way."

"This isn't about money."

"It's about the girl?"

"The girl, my partner, Oversergent..."

"Gregersen," Humble said and sighed. "I should have guessed at the name."

"You didn't know his name."

"No," Humble clicked his tongue. "You're right, I didn't."

"What about the girl? Do you remember *her* name?"

"Diana," Humble said and shrugged.

"Dina," Fenna shouted. "Her name was Dina, you fuck." Rachael backed away from the table and Fenna swung the Webley towards her. "Stay there. Open that movie file."

Rachael clicked the file and stared at the image on the screen. Her lips paled as the phone rang. Humble looked away from the screen and focused on Fenna.

"That's ETF," he said and reached for the phone.

"She answers it," Fenna said and walked to the side of the desk furthest from the window. Rachel picked up the phone. She held it to her ear, trembling as the grainy image of a woman chained to a pipe twisted on the screen, the only sound a whimper and the chatter of two men as they tore the clothes from her body with their hands. Humble flicked his eyes to the screen and back to Fenna.

"Keep watching," she said.

Stifled cries of pain wept out of the computer's speakers. The image on the screen blurred back and forth from the picture of a young woman, naked but for her own panties gagging and choking her. Tears streamed down her face, mixing with the saliva spooling out the corners of her mouth.

Rachael held out the phone and nodded at Fenna. "They want to speak to you, Richard."

Humble turned away from the screen.

"You will look, you bastard," Fenna slammed the Webley onto the table top, took two steps and gripped Humble's head between her hands, turning and pushing the lawyer until his head was a hand's width from the screen. "This is your boss, Rachael."

Rachael gasped as Dina screamed, the blurred motion of the camera focusing and refocusing on the face of the Greenlandic woman and the man penetrating her from behind, the sweating, heaving, grinning face of Richard Humble.

The metallic clack of weapons and the shuffle of feet on the other side of the door turned Fenna's head. She let go of Humble, paused the video and picked up the Webley. "Get back on the phone, Rachael." Fenna pointed the Webley at Humble's crotch. "It's time to negotiate."

"They really want to speak to Richard," Rachael said. The telephone trembled in her grasp.

"Tell them they can open the door," said Fenna.

"Wait," Humble said and looked up at Fenna. "Just wait a second."

"I'm waiting."

"Just wait. Rachael," Humble turned to his secretary. "Tell them we will be out in five minutes. She is here to negotiate," he said and turned to Fenna. "You want something in return for the video? Right?"

"Something like that," said Fenna.

"Then tell me what you want."

Fenna pointed at the image of Humble, mid-thrust, as he penetrated Dina's tied, torn and twisted body. "You can't bring her back. Can you, Richard?"

"No," Humble said and shook his head. "You know I can't."

"Oversergent Gregersen, then. Can you bring him back?"

"No."

"Then I don't know what you can give me," Fenna said and pressed the gun to Humble's head, the barrel depressing the skin beneath the lawyer's receding hairline.

"Ms Gregersen." Fenna turned at the shout from outside the office door. "We need to talk to Mr Humble."

"Your friends are impatient, that wasn't five minutes," Fenna said and lifted the Webley from Humble's forehead.

"Rachael," said Humble. "Set up a transfer of $1,000,000 to an account of the Konstabel's choice." Humble looked up at Fenna. "In return," he said, "I get all the copies of that video."

"That's what Dina's life is worth? And Mikael's? 1,000,000 Canadian dollars?"

"I can't give you their lives back, Fenna. I am buying my reputation. You know that."

"Yes, I do," Fenna said took a step back. "You pay and I walk?"

"Yes."

"Then make it $2,000,000 and you can have all the copies." Fenna turned to Rachael. "You'll find the account number in my original email with the title 'Webley'."

"There are two numbers here," she said.

"There are two families."

"And what about you, Konstabel?" said Humble. "What do you want?"

"Your assurance you won't press charges. That will be enough for me."

Humble nodded his head at the door. "You have my word," he said and reached for the mouse.

"Not for that," Fenna said as Humble closed the movie file. She took a step backwards, away from the desk. "For this," she said and pointed the Webley at Humble's crotch and fired.

Chapter 33

At the crash of the bullet and the combined scream from Humble and his secretary, Toronto's Emergency Task Force breached the door. Fenna closed her eyes and opened her mouth a second before the flash grenade rolled into the room, detonating in the centre of the office. Two ETF officers tackled Fenna to the ground, pulling the Webley from her grasp; they cuffed her and pressed her body to the floor with a knee in her spine. Two more officers assisted Rachael out of the office while a third attended to Humble's bleeding crotch. The tactical team leader stepped around Fenna. He pointed to the door with the gloved thumb of his right hand. The officers holding Fenna changed their grip and pulled her to her feet.

The team leader looked down at the medic cutting away Humble's trousers with medical shears. "How bad is he hurt?"

The medic looked up at Humble. He turned to the team leader. "The bullet has severed his penis and blown one of his testicles to mush, sir." Humble groaned.

"But he'll live?" said the team leader.

"Yes. I'll give him a shot of morphine," the medic said and looked up at Humble. "Are you allergic to morphine, sir?"

"No," Humble said and gritted his teeth. The medic pressed a needle into a phial from his pack and drew the clear liquid into the syringe. He jabbed the needle into Humble's thigh and depressed the plunger.

"Wait," said Humble. He gasped and pointed at Fenna. "Please, wait."

"What is it, sir?" the ETF team leader walked around Fenna and stood in front of Humble.

"She didn't do anything," said Humble, his chest rising and falling with rapid movements.

The team leader pointed at an ETF officer unloading and securing the Webley. "She shot you, sir. With that pistol."

"No," said Humble, his face contorted, his cheeks wet with sweat and tears. "It was an accident." He gritted his teeth and continued. "I wanted to see if it was in working order." Humble looked at Fenna. "It went off in her hands."

"You're saying she *accidentally* shot you with a loaded pistol?"

"Apparently," said Humble and took a ragged breath.

The team leader rubbed his face with his glove. "Okay, sir. Are you sure you want us to release this woman?" he said and pointed at Fenna.

"Yes," Humble said and twisted as the medic applied a large bandage over his crotch. Humble glanced at the medic's hands as he packed the wound and then averted his eyes. "I have already bought the pistol. It is mine. Ask my secretary."

"All right then, sir. We'll get you to a hospital and she..." the team leader said and shook his head. "She walks free." Fenna stared at Humble.

"Thank you, officer," said Humble.

"Ms Gregersen. If you'll come with us."

Fenna's body shook within the ETF officers' grasp as the rush of adrenalin in her body dispersed. She sagged within their grip and the men pulled her to her feet and marched her towards the door. She willed her legs to hold her as she stopped and turned to face Humble. He stared at her, biting back a spasm of pain as the medic bound his groin.

Fenna took a breath and let the men lead her from the room. The irony of being captive in the hands of men once again, was not lost on her. As they neared the door she heard Humble begin to choke. The ETF officers paused and Fenna turned as they did to see Humble start to convulse in his chair. The medic pressed his hands to Humble's shoulders and nodded for the team leader to help him.

"It must be an allergic reaction," he said.

The team leader shook his head. "But he said..."

"I know what he said." The medic's voice faltered. "Shit. We're going to lose him."

The team leader turned and waved at the men guarding Fenna. "Get her out of here," he said.

The officers pulled Fenna from the room as she twisted for one last look at Humble, his face turning a shade of blue, a stark contrast to the white froth bubbling at his mouth. The image of Humble's last minutes flickered across Fenna's mind as she was escorted into the elevator. Fenna suppressed a smile as the elevator descended to the ground floor and the men escorted her through the lobby. A cordon of police cars blocked the street and a plain clothes man met them at the door.

"Inspector Mitchell," he said and flashed his badge. "I'll take her from here. RCMP," he said when the ETF officers frowned at him.

"We have our orders," said the senior officer.

"And so do I," Mitchell said. "Now, we can wait for your team leader if you want, and then *he* can explain to the Danish Consular General why ETF has a Danish national in custody. Or," he said and slipped his badge into his pocket, "I can get the ball rolling and let your team leader deal with the other pressing matter – the death of a prominent Canadian lawyer on his watch." Fenna felt the officers relax their grip on her arms. "It's all over the radio," Mitchell said.

"Take her then," the senior officer said and shoved Fenna towards Mitchell.

"Wise choice," he said and pulled Fenna down the steps of the building towards a black SUV parked on the curb. He opened the passenger door and pushed Fenna inside. She watched as he jogged around the hood of the SUV, opened the door and climbed behind the wheel.

"RCMP?" Fenna said, as Mitchell pulled away from the curb and drove around the police cordon. She realised the motor had been running the whole time.

"Not exactly," he said and manoeuvred into traffic. He leaned across Fenna and opened the glove compartment. "There's some keys to your cuffs in there."

Fenna lifted the user's manual. She found the keys next to a phial of morphine. Fenna smiled as she slipped the keys into her hand. She fiddled with the cuffs as Mitchell stopped at a red light.

"There's a phial of morphine in the glove compartment," she said.

Mitchell glanced at her and then turned back to study the road ahead. He shrugged. "A mutual friend sends his regards," he said, "and requests that you get the fuck back to Denmark as soon as possible."

"Jarnvig," Fenna said and unlocked the cuffs. She tossed them into the glove compartment, took one last look at the morphine and closed the lid. "I should have guessed."

"Yes, and you should have maybe thought too."

"Meaning?"

"We've had our eye on Humble for a while. Did you really think he would let you live considering everything you know?"

"You mean the video?"

"Fuck, Brongaard," Mitchell said and accelerated as the light changed. "The video? Really? How about espionage and government-sanctioned acts of terror." Mitchell sighed as he turned, following the signs for the airport. "Humble had to go, one way or the other. But you tipped our hand, and we had to act. Hell, my cover is blown, that's for sure. I'll be recalled to Denmark any day now." Mitchell paused to glance at Fenna. He stuck out his hand. "Nicklas Fischer," he said.

"Is that your real name?"

"For the moment, yes."

"And you work for Jarnvig?"

"Let's just say we know each other and leave it at that."

The traffic on the highway was steady all the way to the airport. Jarnvig's man escorted Fenna through security and all the way to the boarding gate.

"Good luck, Konstabel," he said and walked away. Fenna watched him leave.

She found a seat close to the gate and waited, replaying the scene of Humble's death. The beginnings of a smile tickled the corners of her mouth. Fenna bit her lip to suppress a giggle. It was done. No more games. He was dead. The bastard was dead.

The Beach

BLÅVAND, DENMARK

Chapter 34

BLÅVAND BEACH, DENMARK

The sand dusted across the beach, settling on Fenna's jeans and filling her pockets. She picked up the dismembered pincer of a crab, pressed the tips of her fingers against the spines and lifted it to her nose to sniff at the meat rotting inside the claw. It smelled of the sea. It took her back to the summer ice-free waters of Greenland, on a rocky beach just down from the dog yard at Daneborg. A Labrador splashed into the surf in front of her, its owner apologising as Fenna brushed at the spots of salt water staining her jeans.

"It's not a problem," she said and wished the man a good day as she watched him hurl a tennis ball into the sea. The Labrador splashed after it, and Fenna smiled; her first of the day.

Once the dog and its owner had retreated along the beach and out of sight, she dug her hands into the sand and hid them there, feeling the cool sand beneath her palms, and the brush of the grains on the backs of her hands. She wriggled her toes into the sand and closed her eyes. She filtered out the chatter of the tourists on the beach, the flap and flutter of kites, focusing instead on the crash of the waves as they spilled onto the long, broad beach of Denmark's west coast.

She felt the soft tremor of city shoes in the sand before she heard the man's approach. Fenna had an idea of who it might be and opened her eyes, blinking at Per Jarnvig's face as he stared down at her.

"Konstabel," he said. "All well?"

"Yes," Fenna said and dug her fingers and toes deeper into the sand, like tiny anchors.

"Still wearing the policeman's jacket, I see," he said. "Having difficulty letting go?"

"Yes."

"Good."

Jarnvig made a show of enjoying the sea air, smiling at a group of Germans as they walked past, the tiny dog at their heels paused to investigate what Fenna had buried in the sand. It scurried away as the children in the group called to the puppy.

"How's the house?" Jarnvig said when they were alone.

"It's nice," Fenna said and glanced over her shoulder at the beach house tucked behind the dunes. The tiles of the roof glittered in the sun. "Bit posh for a Sirius girl," she said.

"Hmm. About that." Jarnvig turned his head in the direction of the lighthouse to the north of where Fenna sat. "Walk with me," he said.

Fenna dusted the sand from her hands. She curled her fingers into the ankle loops of her boots and carried them, one in each hand, as she walked alongside Jarnvig.

"You've stopped limping then. How are your ribs?"

"They're fine. I'm fine."

"Physically, yes, I'm sure you are. But how are you really doing?"

"Do you care?" Fenna asked and double-stepped to avoid a sharp swathe of shells beneath her feet.

"Actually," Jarnvig said and lifted the manila folder he carried in his left hand. Fenna hadn't noticed it. "Your mental well-being is more important to me than the shape your body is in." Fenna laughed. "You stirred the pot in Canada, Fenna," he continued. "But you also sent a message. The Canadian Security Intelligence Service will never recognise any association with Richard Humble, nor will they admit to knowing anything about covert operations in Greenland. You understand this, don't you?"

Fenna nodded, biting her lip at the mention of Humble.

"What happened in Toronto," he said and paused. "Let's just say we gained some ground and lost some. Fischer has been recalled, but Humble has been neutralised. I mention this freely as you and I have an agreement, Konstabel. You work for me now." Jarnvig lifted the folder in his hand and used it to point to the path between the dunes that led to the beach house.

Fenna followed his lead and felt the itch of the straw and grass beneath her feet, laid along the surface of the path to protect the dunes. They didn't speak until they reached the house. Jarnvig waited for Fenna to unlock the door, brush her feet on the mat and invite him inside. He placed the folder on the table as Fenna filled the coffee machine with water.

"What about my rank?" she asked as she heaped coffee grounds into the filter paper. The machine beeped as she turned it on.

"You'll keep your rank," Jarnvig said and sat down at the table. "But it will be more of a codename, than a title," he said.

"A bit like *The Magician*," she said.

"He's not your concern, Konstabel."

"No?"

"No," Jarnvig said and gestured for Fenna to sit at the table. The chair legs squeaked across the tiles as she pulled it out and sat down.

"Whose *concern* will he be?" she said and tried to look Jarnvig in the eye. He was good at avoiding eye contact, she realised and gave up.

"We will deal with him if and when he turns up, not before."

"Then what do I do in the meantime?" Fenna said and reached for the folder.

"You," Jarnvig said and pushed the folder towards her, "are going back to school."

"University?" she said and frowned.

"Not that kind of school."

Fenna opened the folder and skimmed the first page.

"Tradecraft?" she said and looked up.

"It's jargon for communication skills and the practical application of..."

"Explosives?" Fenna said and tapped her finger on the page.

"That too. Yes."

"I thought I was going to be trained as an investigator?"

"You are," Jarnvig said and smiled. "But I like my investigators to be able to act, when the occasion calls for it." He let Fenna read and stood up to get two mugs from the kitchen. He poured them both a coffee and returned to the table.

"Your Arctic skills and knowledge of Greenland are invaluable, Fenna. That will be your area of operations, and your focus. But your training," he said and paused to take a sip of coffee. "Let's just say, there are things you can get away with in the desert that we just can't do here in Denmark."

"You're sending me to the Middle East?" Fenna said and looked up.

"Almost," he said. "Konstabel, I am sending you to Arizona."

Fenna closed the folder and leaned back in her chair. The sun glittered through the blinds and she squinted in the glare. *Arizona? That's a long way from Greenland.*

"One more thing," Jarnvig said. "Do you speak Chinese?"

"No," Fenna said and laughed. She studied Jarnvig's face and stopped laughing. "Not yet, I guess."

"Good," he said and stood up. Jarnvig picked up the folder, tapped it once on the table to settle the papers and slipped it under his arm. "You leave on Tuesday. I'll have someone pick you up and bring you some more suitable clothing."

"So there's a mission or an assignment?" she said and looked up at Jarnvig.

"Your assignment is to get top marks at school. Your mission, well," he paused, "there's something I want you to investigate."

"Where?"

Jarnvig smiled and said, "Somewhere north. In the shadow of a mountain."

THE END

A GREENLANDIC GLOSSARY

The characters of Maratse, Kula, and Dina in *The Ice Star* are from the east coast of Greenland. East Greenlandic is a dialect of Greenlandic. There is, to date, no real written record of the language and children in East Greenland are required to learn West Greenlandic. For Dina to learn English, she would have had to learn West Greenlandic, then Danish and English as her fourth language. There are no foreign language dictionaries translating East Greenlandic words to English. English is predominantly taught through Danish, with all explanations and points of grammar written in Danish. Dina, however, is unremarkable in the sense that many East Greenlanders learn English, and work in the tourist industry. But it is far from easy.

Here is a very brief glossary of the few East Greenlandic words used in *The Ice Star*, and the English equivalents.

East Greenlandic / West Greenlandic / English
iiji / aap / yes
eeqqi / naamik / no
qujanaq/qujanaraali / qujanaq / thank you

ACKNOWLEDGEMENTS

The Ice Star has had a lot of help over the years since I first started writing it. It began life in 2013 as a project for my Master of Arts in Professional Writing at Falmouth University, England. A number of my peers critiqued the first few incarnations of the manuscript, and I would like to thank Ramon James and Erik Poirier for their "gloves off" feedback. Sarah Acton knows more about *The Ice Star* than I do, and has contributed to the development of many aspects, not least the main character. Isabel Dennis-Muir, also from the MA, has provided invaluable editing skills and feedback on the later drafts of the manuscript. Of the different supervisors involved in the project, I would like to thank Tom Bromley who saw the project through to its completion, with lots of valuable feedback and plot revisions along the way.

Research was a vital part of the project, and I would like to thank SIRIUS Sledge Patrolman Per Jessen, and Anders Kjærgaard, leader of the SIRIUS Sledge Patrol (2015-16), for their patience and insight. Both Per and Anders helped give the manuscript the authenticity I was looking for. However, I take full responsibility for all deviations from standard operating procedure and the dramatic license I have taken with the story. It is a thriller after all.

I spent seven years in Greenland – four on the island of Uummannaq, and my seventh year in the capital of Nuuk. I met many exceptional Greenlanders, professionals, and friends, but I would particularly like to thank Akisooq Vestergaard-Jessen for year six in Qaanaaq, and Stephen Pax Leonard, a Brit from the Scott Polar Research Institute, studying the Qaanaaq dialect, for year five. I must also thank Jes Lynning Harfeld for introducing me to a whole new world aboard a very special ship.

I had a sledge team of my own while living in Uummannaq, much to the amusement of my Greenlandic neighbours. While they will never know, it makes sense to thank the members of my own dog team: Kassassuk, Vitus, Trip, Piska, Simba, Hidalgo, Balto, Ninja, and Nansen. They taught me more than I could ever learn from a book, and I would like to think that by year three, we could finally call ourselves a team.

And to my wife, Jane Petersen – thank you.

A lot of people contributed to *The Ice Star*, but the mistakes and inaccuracies are all my own.

Chris

January 2017
Denmark

IN THE SHADOW OF THE MOUNTAIN

Book 2 in *The Greenland Trilogy*

AUTHOR'S NOTE

As our climate changes and the sea ice around the North Pole diminishes, the question of who owns the North Pole becomes increasingly relevant. While no country can claim the North Pole, coastal states surrounding it have the sovereign right to exploit the natural resources of the continental shelf connected to their territory to a distance of 200 nautical miles*. Claims beyond that distance - a so-called *extended continental shelf* - must be filed with the Commission on the Limits of the Continental Shelf (CLCS), in accordance with the United Nations Convention on the Law of the Sea (UNCLOS), *article 76. Claims must be supported with data "describing the depth, shape, and geophysical characteristics of the seabed and sub-sea floor" (The Arctic Institute, 2017).

In the Shadow of the Mountain has been inspired by the 2012 LOMROG III Expedition to collect data in support of the Danish claim to the Lomonosov Ridge - the extended continental shelf that reaches beneath the North Pole. While the expedition was real, the characters and events in the following story are all fictitious, and are not to be construed as real in any way.

The fictional actions and adventures of Konstabel Fenna Brongaard are intended to encourage the reader to think about the Arctic, to consider its future, and to draw a little more attention to an area of the world that is often forgotten, and yet is becoming increasingly important in light of the changing climate on Earth. The North Pole may seem awfully far away for the average reader, but its reach is global.

In the Shadow of the Mountain is written in British English and makes use of several Danish and Greenlandic words.

The Desert

ARIZONA, USA

Chapter 1

YUMA PROVING GROUNDS, ARIZONA, USA

Fenna ignored the soft needle feet of the insect trespassing across her skin and pressed her forehead to the rubber lip of the Schmidt & Bender high magnification scope attached to the rail of her PGM 338 rifle. The dust in the bed of the canyon swirled behind the battered Jeep Cherokee. Her instructions were to look out for a 1999 model off-roader and the Cherokee matched for age, custom outfitting, and colour. Fenna made a note with a light brush of the pencil on the pad she had wedged into the dirt beside the PGM's trigger guard. She had placed it, as instructed, in the exact position her hand would fall when she let go of the trigger. Everything about her position was exact, precise, calculated, only her camouflage net was random, like a blanket it offered her a greater sense of security than a ghillie suit.

She had moved into position two nights earlier, using water from her hydration pack and dirt from the desert floor to disguise the netting that would cover her observation position.

The Jeep slowed to a stop, dust billowing in its wake and two men got out of the rear of the vehicle and peed by the side of the road. The driver stepped out for a smoke. Fenna watched the tip of his cigarette glow in the evening gloom and calculated the distance as if she was going to take the shot. Comments from the briefing rolled through her mind as the man smoked long after his companions had returned to the vehicle. He blew out another lungful and Fenna felt her own lungs swell with a rush of something, a charge of energy. A stream of sweat wet her armpits, her breasts, and slicked her short blonde hair to her forehead. Any stray thoughts of pasting and teasing hair dye into her hair in the bathroom of the summer house in Denmark were forgotten as she revelled in the security of watching without being seen. She lifted her right hand, slowly, from the pad, pressed her palm around the grip and tickled the trigger with her index finger.

The PGM sat heavy in the dirt as Fenna rested her cheek against the tubular stock. She had waited two cold nights and almost two scorching days for this moment. The instructor had told her to watch and wait. With no radio communication, Fenna would have to decide when and if to shoot. She was on her own, he had said. Fenna thought back to the last training session before deployment.

"If the conditions are less than perfect, don't shoot."

She nodded, wiping her sweaty fringe.

"And stop doing that," he said. "The slightest movement will get you killed."

"Okay," she said and tucked her hands in the pockets of her cargo pants.

"You are using live rounds, and I know you can shoot, but the metal plates we have set up are proportionately small. They are about the size of a human head, but they are smaller than you think." The instructor looked up from his position beside a prone sniper student. "If in doubt, don't shoot."

The instructor patted the student on the shoulder and moved out of the way to allow the young man's sniper-observer to slide into position. Fenna listened to the observer, a Marine like his partner, as he called out the ranges and talked the sniper onto the target. She flinched at the report of the rifle as the sniper fired, the three men standing behind her snickered. The tiny hairs on her arms stiffened despite the heat.

The instructor was watching her, "Everything all right, Konstabel?"

"Yes," she said and took a breath of hot desert air. "I'm fine."

The memory of the second and third reports of the Marine sniper's rifle jogged a succession of images through her mind as she relived the shoot-out at the Arctic schoolhouse, right up to the moment when the whip had cinched tight around the Greenlander's throat, and Dina had broken her neck with a snap.

Thoughts of Greenland and the pre-deployment training receded and she let her finger slide from the trigger. Her cheek slid down the stock as the driver flicked the butt of his cigarette into the scrub beside the road and positioned himself behind the wheel. The door closed with a metallic thud and the Cherokee accelerated along the road.

"Fuck," she said, as the vehicle disappeared and the rush of adrenalin in her veins dispersed and was gone, right when she needed it the most. The click of a stone behind her, to the right, made Fenna turn her head. It was the last movement she made before a pair of size sixteen desert boots pounded into her back and her forehead crunched into the dirt.

"Hello, Blondie," the Gunnery Sergeant said, his voice rasping like the desert. "Having fun?"

Fenna bit back a remark as the man shifted his position and twisted her body beneath his, pinning her arms with his knees. She spat dirt from her mouth and watched the big man grimace as he struggled to pull plastic ties from his back pocket, relaxing the pressure on her arms. She managed to worm one arm free, the desert floor cutting into her flesh. He turned, just as she gripped a rock in her hand and slammed it into the side of his head.

"Fuck you, Gunney," she said, as he tumbled off her body. Fenna scrabbled to her feet and kicked him in the groin. He moaned, she kicked him again in the head, and then, a third time, planting the sole of her size five desert boots in the centre of his chest. She ignored the Gunnery Sergeant and collected her equipment, slipping her arms through the straps of the empty hydration pack, closing her notepad and stuffing it into the cargo pocket of her trousers, before pushing the rubber caps over the ends of the scope and slinging the rifle over her shoulder. The evening chill descended quickly, cooling the sweat on her back. She tugged a buff from her trouser pocket and slipped it over her neck. She took one last look at the Gunnery Sergeant and took a breath. It was time to move.

After just three paces she lowered the rifle and carried it in the ready position. She had no secondary weapon, choosing to travel light, and relying on her experiences in the Arctic to help her through the chilly nights. The heat of the day was the problem, but now she had been compromised, she needed to move.

The escape route she had originally planned to use was too predictable. *If the Gunney could find my position*, she mused, he would have figured out her escape route too. Counter-sniper teams at the Desert Training Center worked in groups of four on the ground, with a drone in the air. *That's how they found me*, Fenna realised. She filed that thought for later; she would tell the instructor, away from the other students. The gravel slipped, giving way under her feet, slowing her descent of the ridge. There was movement in the valley below, so she slid to a crouch behind a spiny bush.

The voices of the men below her chattered up the side of the canyon. *No noise discipline. Why?* A bullet snapped above her head and she realised why the men were so undisciplined.

A distraction, she thought and pushed off along a tiny game trail to her right. Another snap of a suppressed shot made her duck and she pushed harder, racing down the track, the heavy tube gun tugging at her arms. Two more snaps and a crack of an unsuppressed rifle forced Fenna behind a boulder. She raised her rifle and rested it on the flattest part of the desert rock. She pressed the soft flesh of her shoulder into the butt, and sighted on the military vehicle in the canyon below, aiming for the hood of the engine. Compared to the tiny metal plates she practised on, the Humvee was a massive target. She focused and pulled the trigger. The report was loud and the recoil satisfying. Fenna smiled as she pulled back the bolt and chambered another round. The empty shell casing tumbled onto the path and down the side of the canyon. *Another item lost*, another penalty point against her.

She rested the barrel of the PGM in the crook of her left arm, pulling it to her chest as she traversed the slope, following the track, stumbling only once, before she slid to a stop. The shadow of a man moved in from her right and levelled a short-stocked M4 carbine at her chest.

"Fenna," said the man holding the assault rifle.

She frowned and let the weight of the rifle tug at her arms. "We..." she started.

"We're not supposed to use names?" The man laughed. He took a step onto the track and shifted his position into a firmer combat stance. "Having fun in the desert, Konstabel?" he said.

"Yes," she said and turned at the sound of men grunting as they scrabbled up the canyon side.

"We haven't got much time."

"No." Fenna felt the pinch of her frown as she tried to remember where she had met the man.

"Don't."

"Don't what?" she said and squinted in the gloom at the man's face. The desert paint he wore was mixed with dust and obscured his features, but his voice was measured, smooth, familiar. "Toronto?"

"Yes."

"Nicklas Fischer?"

"Yes," he said and Fenna caught the flash of a smile.

"When did you..."

"No questions," he said, looking past Fenna. She caught the frown on his face, followed by the full impact of the Gunney's fist as she looked behind her.

"Blonde bitch," the Gunnery Sergeant said, and he hit her again.

Chapter 2

The Cherokee returned, its headlights flickering back and forth as it bounced up the gravel track and crunched to a stop behind the Humvee. The rear of the military vehicle cut the Cherokee's light in half, illuminating Fenna where she knelt, wrists bound and the Gunney's fingers gripping her hair in a fist. He jerked Fenna's head back, greeting the Cherokee's passengers with his prize as they exited the vehicle. The driver lit another cigarette and watched her through the smoke as he exhaled.

"What's wrong with the Humvee?" the shorter of the two passengers asked. His companion stared at Fenna.

"Bitch put a bullet through the engine block," said the Gunney.

"Why?"

"Fuck'd if I know."

The man bent down in front of Fenna and gripped her chin in his hand. "Konstabel, isn't it?"

"Yes."

"You realise this is an exercise?"

"Yes."

"Then why did you destroy US Army property?"

Fenna jerked her chin out of the man's grip and looked up, squinting in the glare of the headlights. She recognised his hair from her observations through the rifle scope and idly wondered if he had washed his hands since pissing in the desert.

"Konstabel?"

"I was being pursued. It felt like the right thing to do."

"Oh, that's rich," the man said and laughed. "The Major is going to love you."

"The Major is back?" the Gunney asked.

"Yep, and the barracks to the east are now off limits. Make sure your people stay clear." The man scuffed his shoes in the dirt as he stepped away from Fenna. He paused and looked at her once more. Fenna caught his eye and the curious angle at which he cocked his head. "You know," he said, "we get all kinds here. Soldiers, sailors, even airmen. *Men* – all of whom understand the chain of command, and obey the rules. Yuma is a privilege. Officers get sent here before promotion, operatives before a mission, assets before an operation. You're in a category all your own, Konstabel, a foreign national with a phoney rank and a fake hair colour."

"Thorough though," the Gunney said and tugged at Fenna's hair. "Either way, you're still a piece of ass in Uncle Sam's backyard." He spat on the ground. "Let's see what the Major makes of you. I'd like to see how you're going to settle the bill for that," he said, pointing at the Humvee.

The man nodded to his companion. They walked past the Cherokee and stood to one side of the gravel road. The Gunnery Sergeant tugged Fenna to her feet with a firm grip of her hair, and marched her to the back of the vehicle as the driver flicked the butt of his cigarette into the scrub and climbed in behind the wheel. Fenna banged her head as the Gunney pushed her into the rear of the vehicle.

"It'll be the *Sonoran Shuffle* for you, if the Major has his way. I'll make sure to find you the right partner," he said and slammed the door shut.

"All set?" said the driver, as he looked at Fenna through the rear-view mirror.

"I guess," she said and squirmed into a sitting position. She caught a glimpse of Nicklas as he passed in front of the vehicle, the light flickered across the dusty webbing cinched and strapped across his body. Fenna thought he paused to nod in her direction. *A flash of sympathy, perhaps?* But then he was gone and the driver shifted the Cherokee into gear and backed down the slope. He used the side mirrors, and she watched as he corrected the vehicle's course with small adjustments of the wheel.

"What's the *Sonoran Shuffle*?" she asked, as the Cherokee bounced up and over the lip of the desert road leading back to base.

"We had a bunch of Brits here once," the driver said. "A while back. Paratroopers, I think. They introduced us to *Milling* – sixty seconds of controlled aggression." Fenna caught his eye in the mirror. He continued. "Sure, we had our own version, but the boss, back then, was the son of an engineer, and he liked the idea of the milling process – grinding and shaping something with a rotating tool. The *Sonoran Shuffle* is Yuma's name for a minute's worth of shit-kicking." She could tell he was smiling. "Of course, it's officially frowned upon, and therefore fully endorsed by the Army. It's also, usually, same sex, but for you, I think the Major will make an exception."

"Great." Fenna leaned back on the seat, arching her back to make room for her bound wrists.

"How heavy are you?"

Fenna glanced down at her body. The year with the Sirius Sledge Patrol in Greenland, the 10k runs along the beach in Denmark, and the first two weeks of orientation at Yuma had trimmed whatever fat she might once have had. Her curves were curbed and her breasts and bottom were firm to non-existent. "Fifty kilos?" she said and shrugged.

"What's that in English?"

"Oh, about 110 pounds, give or take."

"Christ," the driver said and whistled. "Well, at least I know where to put my money. Good luck, Konstabel."

He was quiet for the remainder of the journey back to base, just flashing his headlights as two Humvees passed on the road to pick up the rest of the team.

"This is where you get out," he said, pulling to a stop outside the office block.

"Can you open the door?" Fenna asked. She watched as he shrugged out of the driver's seat and helped her out of the vehicle. "Maybe take these off?" she said, turning to show him her wrists.

"Better not," he said before shutting the rear passenger door. "The light's on. Just go right in."

Fenna waited until the driver had pulled away in the Cherokee. She stared at the light shining in the Major's office and wondered why the base was run by a Major and not someone with a higher rank? She stepped onto the deck, walked to the door, and pushed it with her shoulder. It opened with a creak and she stepped inside.

The Major's aide turned away from the wall-mounted television and the CNN report questioning the latest in a long line of military budget cuts. He looked up at Fenna and nodded for her to enter. *Another man*, Fenna noted. The Desert Training Center at Yuma was, it seemed, practically off-limits to women. She knocked on the door and walked in.

The Major pressed his fingers on the loose pages on his desk as Fenna closed the door behind her. He said nothing, and Fenna remembered she should probably salute. With her wrists bound all she could do was shrug her shoulders. The Major sneered and shook his head. He looked down at his papers and rearranged them.

"You're the Dane?" he said.

"Yes, sir."

"Sir?" The Major looked up. "I suppose I should give you credit for remembering that little formality." He shuffled the papers into the top drawer of his desk and sat down on his chair. Fenna noticed a manila folder beneath the Major's battered briefcase. He smiled when he realised she had seen it. "That's you," he said and lifted his briefcase to pick up the folder. "Do you know what it says about you?"

"No, sir," Fenna said and watched as he opened it.

"Nothing," he said and let a single piece of paper flutter to the desk. Fenna studied the man's hands as he picked up the paper. His hands were gnarled and scarred, like his chin and the left side of his face. She guessed he was a veteran who had been in combat, although the lack of decoration or photographs on the walls suggested he didn't crow about it.

A soldier's Major, she realised. *They'll do anything for him*. She turned her attention to the paper in his hands as the Major began to read aloud.

"Konstabel Fenna Brongaard," he began and then stopped to slip the paper back inside the folder. "That," he said and tapped the folder with a stubby finger, "is my warrant to do whatever I want to you, short of having you killed." He waited for Fenna to speak. She noticed a tic of irritation pinch his scarred cheek as she remained silent. "Something I find very difficult to understand." He stood up and walked around the office, circling Fenna as he spoke. "How tall are you?"

"Five and a half feet."

"Weight?"

"About 110 lbs."

"Unit?"

"I can't say, sir."

"Can't?"

"Under orders..."

"Fuck your orders, Konstabel," he said and stopped in front of her. The Major stabbed Fenna's breastbone with a bent knuckle.

"I don't like spies," he said, emphasising each word with a stab to Fenna's chest. She tried not to gasp. "Christ, I could drop you onto the floor with my finger." He took a step back. "What are you being trained to infiltrate? An orphanage? Hah," he said and forced a second laugh before leaning against his desk. "You know Jarnvig? Personally?"

"Yes, sir," Fenna said and remembered the day at the summer house, on the beach in Denmark, when he had ordered her to the desert.

"He obviously thinks highly of you. This is only the second time a Dane has been sent here, and the first time it's a woman."

"You don't like women, sir?" Fenna asked and then bit her tongue. Her body stiffened as he tensed. She waited for him to stab her again with his knuckle, but, instead, he laughed and she relaxed as his shoulders shook.

"Do I like women?" he said and shook his head. "Yes, Konstabel, I like women. And, I have to admit, I like looking at you, even though a few extra pounds wouldn't go amiss. What I don't like," he said and scowled, "is when women fuck around with my camp and my equipment. You," he said, jabbing his finger toward Fenna, "fucked up a perfectly good Humvee. And now," he said, as he slid off the desk, walked around it, and yanked open the top drawer. "I have another fucking woman – Miss Fucking Anonymous Beauty Pageant drop-out. Apparently, she needs a whole fucking wing of the base to herself."

Fenna caught the frown wrinkling her forehead and tried to relax as the Major tossed the papers in front of Fenna, including a large colour photo of the woman. He paused as he looked at the photo.

"Pretty, eh?"

"Yes, sir."

"And now I have two pretty girls distracting my men." He picked up the folder and gestured with it toward the door. Fenna walked beside the Major as he escorted her out of his office. "Of course, the difference is," he said and shoved the folder beneath Fenna's arm, "I can do whatever the fuck I want with you."

Fenna clamped the folder to her side and stumbled into the centre of the outer office as the aide stood to attention.

"Dowd," the Major said.

"Yes, sir?"

"Do we have any Brass visiting at the moment?"

"No, sir."

"Good," he said and nodded at Fenna. "Schedule a *Shuffle* for midnight tonight." The Major snorted at Fenna, turned and walked into his office. The building shook a little as he slammed the door and the aide sat down at his desk.

Fenna waited for a moment and then realised she was dismissed. She ignored the aide and walked out of the outer office and onto the deck. She let the door close behind her and then stepped onto the road leading to her quarters.

A figure slipped out of the shadows by the side of the office and jogged to catch up with her. She turned, recognising Nicklas; the moonlight catching the crusts of the camouflage paint flaking on his cheeks and forehead.

"You met the Major then?" he said and cut the ties around her wrists with a pocket knife.

"Yeah, he's a real gentleman," Fenna said. She realised she had been creasing the folder. She relaxed her grip and rubbed her wrists.

"Your orders?"

"My death warrant."

"From Jarnvig then?" Nicklas said and reached for the folder. He let out a short whistle as he read the letter inside.

"Bad?"

"Let's just say you should be pleased your time here is limited."

"Why? What do you know?"

"Not so much. Only that you're to leave in two weeks," he said. "That's why I'm here."

"To keep an eye on me?" she said and laughed.

"To keep you alive," he said and nodded at the letter. "Jarnvig has written one of his *no special treatment* letters."

"You've seen them before?"

"I've *had* one before."

"Nicklas," Fenna said. She stopped as a black SUV drove through the gates, slowing as it drove past the office and Fenna heard the driver tell the passenger behind him to wind up the window. As the smoke glass purred upward and obscured the interior, Fenna caught a glimpse of blonde hair, short, like her own. She waved and was rewarded with a brief smile from the beauty pageant drop-out.

"Cut it out," Nicklas said and pressed Fenna's arm to her side with a firm hand.

"What?" she said, as the SUV continued past them.

"Forget about it."

"Forget what?" Fenna took an irritated step away from him.

"Forget about the girl," he said and tugged Fenna in the direction of the barracks.

Chapter 3

Nicklas guided Fenna from one shadow to the next as he led the way to her barracks. *He knows this place*, she realised and caught his arm as he paused at the passing of another Humvee. He frowned as Fenna let go.

"What?"

"The Major said I was only the second Dane to train at Yuma, and yet you walk around this place as if you've been here before."

"Three times," he said. "This is my fourth."

"But you're Danish."

"I was, but they think I'm Canadian, at least my mother is," he said and gestured for Fenna to follow. "Come on. They'll be looking for you soon."

She followed Nicklas across the main road dissecting the base and onto the deck of the barracks reserved for women stationed at Yuma. Before the arrival of the blonde in the SUV, she had been the only one. Fenna stepped around Nicklas and pressed her palm against the door.

"Listen," he said, "about the *Shuffle*."

"I've been beaten before," Fenna said. "I'm not worried."

"But this isn't about being beaten, this is a test, the kind used to determine combat suitability, showing your team that you can turn on the aggression when needed, and give it all you've got."

"No-one is on my team here, Nicklas. I won't be fighting alongside any of them."

Nicklas paused to look at Fenna as the light from a passing vehicle caught her cheek and she blinked in the glare. "One day you might."

Fenna shrugged. "I got the distinct impression that Jarnvig plans to send me to places on my own."

"Even more reason to prove that you're one of them, to give them a reason to want to come and get you." Nicklas paused. "Operators making it to this level work within a fairly small community. You will meet some of these guys again. You don't want to piss them off with stupid stunts." Fenna caught the edge in Nicklas' voice and stiffened.

"Stupid stunts?"

"The Humvee," he said. "It was reckless. Your shot could have gone wide, hit one of the men."

"But it didn't," she said and pushed the door open.

"I'll see you after the *Shuffle*," Nicklas said as Fenna walked into the barracks. "I have a secure, online briefing scheduled with Jarnvig in an hour. I'll have more information for you then."

Fenna let the door swing to a close and waited until she could hear Nicklas' footsteps in the gravel, just a metre or so beyond the thin barrack walls. She clenched her small fists and pressed the base of her palms into her eyes.

"Fucking men," she whispered, and then, louder, "Fuck all men. All of them." She let her fists drop to her sides, spun around and tilted her head to study the metal locker pressed against the wall. She reached out and yanked it onto one of the four corners and it spun onto the floor. She imagined Nicklas pausing at the crash and she grinned, running her tongue across the film of grime on her teeth. She hadn't brushed them in days.

She spent the next hour sitting on the edge of her bunk, tracing the rough knots of the wool blanket with her fingertips. A bulb began to flicker at the far end of the barracks and Fenna lifted her head to look at it. It blinked twice with a *pling* before settling into a dull glow. She tapped her fingers on her head to the rhythm of each blink and pling until the filament finally gave up and that end of the barracks was lost to the shadows. It was there, in the dark frame of the doorway, that Fenna saw the figure of a young Greenlandic woman swing from a cord lashed around her neck.

"Stop, Dina," Fenna said. "I can't deal with you right now."

The Greenlander twisted in the doorframe. The fingers of her hands splayed away from her body. They were thin, delicate. Fenna remembered clutching them in her own as she dragged Dina away from the men, away from Burwardsley.

Fenna took a breath and forced herself to stare at Dina, to draw her back inside her mind, from one dark place to another. Dina's hair whispered in the desert wind that coiled around the base, blowing through the barracks from the open door at the opposite end of the long room. Fenna looked up and away from Dina, and into the fierce eyes of the Gunnery Sergeant as he pushed a large plug of tobacco into his mouth, positioning it between his gum and top lip with his thumb.

"Busy?" he said and strode into the barracks. The thud of his boots drilled along the wooden slats of the floor. "Only, there's a dance tonight, and you're invited." He stopped a metre from Fenna and sucked at the tobacco. Fenna watched the Gunney as he spat a leaf-flecked brown gob of saliva onto her right boot. "Shall we dance?" he said and grabbed her arm.

"Get your fucking hands off me," Fenna said and slipped free with a jerk of her arm as she stood.

"Whatever you say, bitch," he said and pressed his face into hers. Fenna wrinkled her nose at the sweet smell of tobacco that brushed against her face as he spoke. "But come the end of the night, you'll be too fucked to fuck. The Major and I agreed that you get to dance twice, maybe even three times tonight. That's the going price for a Humvee," he said and shoved Fenna in front of him. He stayed there, just two paces behind her, all the way to the door of an old warehouse. The outside lights were smashed; the glass bowls of the lamps were cracked and filmed with desert dust. A blue light filtered through the gaps between the boards in the walls, and Fenna caught herself, fascinated for a moment by the striped building, and then the image was lost as the Gunney yanked open the door and shoved her into the neon blue hell.

Fenna found herself in a den of dust, drink and wide-eyed devils. They whooped as the Gunney pushed her all the way to the ring in the centre of the den. He lifted the slack hawser rope looped around each of the four oil drums, one in each corner, and shoved Fenna forward. She stumbled and the devils cheered. Fenna caught single words cast into the ring, lifted her chin and searched the men's faces, chasing the words as they were nudged around the spectators.

"Bitch."

"Cunt."

"Pussy."

They laughed at that one, spluttering cheekfuls of light beer over each other, pressing grimy dollar bills into the bookie's hands, and jostling for a better view in the four-deep throng of military men.

"Men," Fenna mouthed and shook her head. She took a breath of fetid, sweaty air and scanned the faces once more, lingering over Nicklas' as he lifted a bottle of beer to his mouth and stared at her. His eyes focused, intense, oblivious of the men around him, and the bookie tugging at his arm and spilling his beer. Fenna watched as Nicklas wiped his chin and pushed the man away.

"It's your loss," the bookie said, with a flick of his head in Fenna's direction. "But then I wouldn't bet on her either."

Fenna caught the movement of Nicklas' eyes as they flicked away from her and focused on the arrival of two men. She watched the Major enter the den, his aide one step behind him. The Gunney raised his arm and the men hushed.

The attention of the men diverted away from Fenna to centre on the Major. She realised they didn't just respect him, they revered him. She faced him as he nodded at them and smiled.

"Where's my beer?" he said and the men whooped and raised the beers in their hands as his aide thrust a dew-budded *Budweiser* into the Major's hand. He took a long slow slug of beer and raised his bottle. "Yuma," he cried and they roared back at him.

"Yuma."

"Gunney," the Major said, when the men were finished. "Are we going to dance tonight, or what?"

"Yes sir," the Gunney said and raised his hands for quiet. The men hushed as the bookies tugged dollar bills from the last show of hands and folded them into their notebooks. A man belched and tossed his empty bottle at Fenna, only to be pulled out of the den by two large men, Military Police that had been lurking at the rear of the crowd. Fenna relaxed for a second at the sight of them, until the largest of them returned and unbuttoned his shirt. He handed it to his partner and stepped over the rope and into the ring.

"Our first dancer," the Gunney said.

"Are you sure, Gunney?" the Major said and made a point of gesturing toward the difference in height between the MP and Fenna. "I thought we agreed on three dances for our Little Mermaid."

"Yes, sir," the Gunney nodded as the MP winked at Fenna. "I suggested the Sergeant start with a light Tango, sir."

"Very well," the Major said. "When you're ready, Gunnery Sergeant."

The hush that descended around the ring tugged at Fenna's resolve and she remembered Burwardsley with the kukri blade pressed into her back in Greenland, Bahadur's backhand, and the weight of the fat lawyer, Lunk, as he forced the air from her lungs with his body on the bathroom floor of *The Ice Star*.

The spectators pressed their bodies against the rope between each of the four oil drums. She was trapped inside a ring of sweaty desert fatigues and the leers and jeers of men of differing ages, races, and ranks, united in the ecstasy and promise of a one-sided fight with a defenceless girl. *Me*, Fenna realised and shuddered at the realisation that these men didn't baulk at beating girls or, better still, seeing one getting a beating.

The Gunney raised his hand once more, and Fenna caught a glimpse of Nicklas as he took a step back from the wall of men, his eyes lasered to her face. He nodded, once, but it was enough. Fenna dropped her shoulders and bent at the knees, just a touch, as she squirmed her boots in the dirt and faced her opponent.

"Let the dance begin," the Gunney shouted, and Fenna caught the single ring of a bell before the MP thrust his fist at her chest.

Lazy, Fenna thought as she stepped away from the MP's attack and let his own momentum propel his body past her. *He thinks he's fighting a girl*, she mused and aimed a kick at the side of the man's knee. She felt her boot connect and then leapt back as he buckled. The MP grimaced as he spun around, reeling a little to one side, enough for Fenna to land a punch to his head and kick the man in the groin. He groaned and she stepped back again, only to have a man wrap his arm around her chest and butt her in the back of the head.

"Fists only, bitch," the man said and shoved her back into the centre of the ring. Fenna's face took the full brunt of the MP's fist as he ploughed his knuckles into her nose and she felt the pump of blood as it cascaded onto her chin and chest. The men roared and the MP pulled back his fist and punched Fenna a second time.

The monkeys chattered and whooped as Fenna fell from the jungle canopy, through the upper and mid layer of branches, past fluorescent-scaled snakes coiled around thick mossy trunks, past the fingers and vines of tree monsters tugging at her hair, until she landed on the fetid floor of the jungle with a thump, the air emptying from her body like a jet exhaust, as a troop of monkeys pummelled her body with hairy fists and squealed in her ears. Squealing for blood, beer, and money.

Fenna ratcheted the jungle air into her lungs, arched her back and pressed her shoulders into the floor. She waved at the monkeys, slapping her hands at their faces, teeth and claws until the jungle fell silent, and the desert air returned. The blue light was replaced with a brilliant pin-prick of white, as rough fingers prised her eyelids apart, first her right, and then her left. The light disappeared with a click and she felt the fingers wipe her mouth and nose free of slime. And then she remembered, it wasn't slime, it was blood. The dirt encrusted in the blood from her nose scratched at her skin as the hands, as gentle as they were rough, cleared her nostrils so that she could breathe. Fenna opened her eyes and blinked to focus on Nicklas' face.

"Hello, Konstabel," he said.

Fenna closed her eyes and licked at the dry blood on her lips.

"Water?"

"Beer," Nicklas said and she felt the glass mouth of a bottle rest against her bottom lip. She let the first mouthful dribble over her lips and chin. She rinsed her mouth with the second and swallowed the third. Then she sat up and groaned.

"I hate men."

"I know," Nicklas said and pulled her to her feet. "Let's get you home."

"Home?"

"Well, your bunk for starters. You have a long day ahead of you."

"It's Saturday tomorrow."

"Yes."

"I have the day off."

"You did, yes. But, not anymore," Nicklas said and gripped Fenna around the waist, as he walked her toward the door. "Jarnvig wants me to brief you on your mission."

"Tomorrow?"

"Yes."

"But..."

"Yes, I know," Nicklas said and pushed the door open with his foot. "It's your day off."

Chapter 4

The jungle was silent but for the soft pummel of drums behind Fenna's eyelids. The desert air, dry and warm, blew in through the open window, and she felt the blood crust as it dried inside her nose. Saturday's light was harsh and she was not inclined to open her eyes for any man, beast, or God. No one was going to force her to face the world, but then the mattress of her cot shifted as someone sat down, and she knew that Nicklas had arrived to ruin her day. He was gentle, as he pressed his hand around her arm to wake her, but he was persistent, oblivious to her pain, *the bastard*. Fenna tried to roll away from him, but the drumming on her eyelids increased and she lay back down and forced her eyes open, the rheumy sleep sticking to her lashes and requiring more effort than she felt she had.

"Fenna," Nicklas said. "It's time."

She grunted and pulled free of his grip. Fenna blinked in the light and tried to ignore the drums and the image of the jungle from the night before. Nicklas laughed and she focused on his face. The camouflage paint was gone, and the combination of a clean shave and the sharp morning sun accentuated his jawline.

"You laughed?"

"Your eyes," he said.

"Like two piss holes in the snow? I can imagine," she said and lifted one hand to her nose. She pressed her finger to her cheeks and explored her swollen nose.

"Don't," Nicklas said, "best to leave it."

"You're probably right." Fenna let her hand fall to her side and pushed herself into a sitting position. The drums beat again, as she squirmed on the cot and she felt a stream of fresh blood trickle from her nose and onto her lip. "Tissues," she said, pointing at a pile of napkins on the desk.

"*Taco Bell*?" he said, as he stood up and picked up a wad of napkins. He pressed them into her hand.

"Can't a girl have secrets?" Fenna said and wiped the blood from her nose.

"Yes, but not today." Nicklas dragged a chair from the desk to the side of Fenna's cot and sat down, opening a folder as he crossed his legs. "I got this from Jarnvig. It's your mission," he said and looked at Fenna. "At least, part of it. I'm still waiting for more details."

"So you're my handler?"

"Sort of," Nicklas said and shrugged.

"And the Major doesn't know?"

"Doesn't need to know either. You've been through the basics already. The DTC specialises in insertion and extraction, weapons, sniping, spotting and communications." Nicklas flipped through the contents of the folder. "Jarnvig wants you to take a tracking course at the end of next week, but you're to start your specialist training on Monday."

"Dancing lessons?" Fenna said and tossed the bloody napkin onto the floor.

"No," Nicklas said and laughed. "Although, I thought I would give you a few hints later."

"Great." Fenna sighed and inspected the napkin for blood. Nicklas laughed again and she shot him a look. "What?"

"I never thought *panda eyes* could be so sexy."

"That's a line if ever I heard one."

"It's not a line, Konstabel," Nicklas said. Fenna caught his gaze and snorted a fresh trickle of blood onto her upper lip. She considered telling him to fuck off, but then she remembered the same intense look on his face right before the military policeman knocked her out with a second punch to her face. She returned Nicklas' look until he looked away. He coughed, shifted his position and read aloud from the folder in his hands. "Investigation techniques, criminal and covert. Oh, and Chinese."

"I prefer *Taco Bell*, but thanks for the invitation."

"Funny," he said and shook his head. "You start Chinese lessons Monday evening."

"On the base?"

"No, actually," Nicklas said and flicked the pages back and forth. "Off base for some reason. It doesn't say."

"I'll find out."

"You'll need a driver. It's in Phoenix."

"That's a long drive for a Chinese lesson," Fenna said and frowned.

"Two hours each night for the next week. You're going to be busy."

"Apparently." Fenna swung her legs around and placed her bare feet on the wooden floor. They were pale compared to her bronzed arms, neck, and face. She glanced at her boots, spotted with blood and dusty from the two days and nights in the desert. She looked at Nicklas. "Can we look at that over breakfast?"

"Sure," Nicklas said and stood up. "We'll drive into Yuma."

"You have a car?"

"I have a Humvee," he said and smiled. "It goes with my rank."

"Captain?" Fenna said, as she noticed the brass crown pinned to Nicklas' collar.

"Inspector," he said. "I almost lost it after your stunt with Humble."

"Stunt?" Fenna said and laughed. She pressed her palms to her eyes for a moment as the drummers picked up the tempo. "I didn't kill him, *Inspector*. I haven't killed anyone."

"No," Nicklas said. He tucked the folder under his arm and pointed at Fenna's boots. "Put them on. We can talk about Humble another time. Let's get some breakfast."

Fenna padded across the floor and tugged her boots over her bare feet. She wrinkled her nose as she bent down and took a careful sniff of her armpits, the blood caked in the lining of her nostrils was not enough to disguise the rigours of the past few days in the desert and the stench of the *Sonoran Shuffle*. "I stink," she said.

"Do you want to take a shower?"

Fenna finished tying the laces and stood up. She laughed, softly this time, and looked at Nicklas. "Breakfast first."

"Come on," Nicklas said. "I know a place. You'll fit right in."

Nicklas bumped the Humvee up a narrow track and over a low rise; *Freddy's Diner* was a rusted airstream camper nestled, within the brush at the end of the track, on the banks of the *Gila River*. Fenna cranked open the passenger door and waited. She watched Nicklas as he approached her, noting the casual cut of his fatigues, his shirt tight around his biceps.

Get it together, Fenna, she scolded herself. *He's not the first man you've worked closely with.* She stopped mid-thought as the image of Oversergent Mikael Gregersen flickered into her mind, the ice hanging from his red beard, a stark contrast to the desert heat. Fenna pushed Mikael's image away, hoping that Dina's would also stay hidden, silent, but then she was always silent, and would remain so, forever. *Just let me enjoy breakfast*, she pleaded to her demons. *After that, you can plague me all you want.*

"Everything all right?" Nicklas asked.

"I'm fine," she said. "Let's eat."

Nicklas led the way through the spiny scrub and across a wide deck of desert-bleached wood, splintering beneath the first of two steps into the diner. A man greeted Nicklas as they entered and tipped his *Diamondbacks* cap in the direction of the table at the window at the front end of the airstream. The heat inside the trailer was even more intense than outside. Nicklas wiped his neck with his hand and waited for Fenna to sit before sliding onto the seat opposite her.

"Freddy," he said, with a nod towards the man in the grimy baseball cap, "spends any spare cash on trips to see his wife in Phoenix. He can barely afford the medication, so…"

"No air conditioning."

"That's right. But what Freddy's lacks in comfort, it makes up for in privacy." Nicklas placed the folder on the table. "We won't be disturbed, and Freddy doesn't speak Danish."

"All right," Fenna said, as Freddy shuffled over to their table.

"What'll it be?" he said.

"Two burgers and cokes," Nicklas said before Fenna could respond. "Coffee to follow."

"You want pie?" Freddy glanced at Fenna. "It's good."

"We want pie then," she said.

"Could use some fat on those bones." He studied her eyes for a moment and then nodded at Nicklas. "He did that?"

"No," Fenna said and smiled.

Freddy leaned forward, closer to Fenna. "But could he have stopped it, eh? That's the question."

"Well…"

"Well, nothin', miss. I'll make sure he pays," he said and paused to squeeze Nicklas' shoulder. Fenna heard him whisper, "Thanks for the help the other day, son."

"You're welcome, Freddy. You only have to ask."

"I know," Freddy said and gave Nicklas' shoulder another squeeze. Fenna watched the old man shuffle back to the counter and disappear into the kitchen area. At the sound of a knob of fat sizzling on the hot plate, Nicklas opened the folder and started speaking in

Danish.

"You're going back to Greenland. Flying into the capital, Nuuk, three weeks from now."

"What will I be doing?" Fenna said and savoured the words. It had been a long time since she last spoke Danish.

"That," said Nicklas with a frown, "is where it gets complicated. I can tell you what I know." He shuffled the papers inside the folder to find the one he wanted. "You will be acting as a company representative, on a fact-finding mission attached to a Chinese delegation currently in talks with Tunstall Mining Consolidated."

"Sounds English," said Fenna.

"It is, but they have Chinese investors. A man called Hong Wei is the leader of the delegation. You will be accompanying him and his liaison from the Greenland Self Rule government and the Department of Natural Resources in Nuuk."

"That all sounds great, Nicklas, but I know nothing about mining…"

"Hence the crash course in geology in Copenhagen the week before you fly out," he said.

Fenna shook her head. "Great. Jarnvig thinks of everything."

"He says you're a fast learner, wrote as much in your profile."

"And so what if I am?" Fenna said. "Why am I going to be a go-between for the Chinese and the Greenlandic government?"

"Because," Nicklas flicked to the last few pages in the folder, "there is another matter." He slid them across the table to Fenna and tapped his finger on the letters highlighted in bold.

"LOMROG?" Fenna said and frowned.

"It's the acronym for a research expedition exploring the *Lomonosov Ridge off Greenland*, a joint scientific venture with an international crew of Swedes, Danes, Norwegians, and Canadians. I have the field report for you to read back at the base."

"Have you read it?"

"Skimmed it. The report is relatively recent, the expedition vessel returned to Sweden late last summer." Nicklas paused. "The sea ice conditions were poor – or good, depending on how you look at it. There was plenty of open water and so they could have stayed out longer."

"Where were they?"

"About 100 miles from the Pole."

"And why did they come back?"

"Something about equipment malfunction, and a dead crewman."

At the sound of Freddy arriving with their food, Nicklas collected the papers inside the folder and placed it on the seat next to him. Freddy served their meal and winked at Fenna as she smiled at the tulip-shaped tomato beside her burger.

"Enjoy," he said. "I'll be out on the stoop if you need me."

"Sure, Freddy," said Nicklas. "Thanks."

"You're welcome," he said and left them alone. Nicklas took a sip of coke.

"What were they researching?" Fenna asked.

Nicklas swallowed and set his glass down on the table. "The continental shelf. You must have heard about this when working with Sirius?"

"Yes," Fenna reached for her burger. "If Denmark can prove the shelf extends from Greenland to the North Pole, then we can claim it," she said and took a bite. "This is good."

"I know," Nicklas said and smiled. "UNCLOS – another acronym – the *United Nations Convention on the Law of the Sea* gives a claimant, in this case Denmark, a period of fourteen years to prove they have a claim on the Pole. With the current thinning of the ice, and the retreating coverage…"

"Whoever owns the Pole can control sea lanes and navigation routes," Fenna said and paused. "It hurts when I chew," she said.

"Take smaller bites," Nicklas said and picked up the folder. Fenna watched as he pulled out the last paper. "There is a hearing scheduled for the end of June. The research from the LOMROG expedition is going to be a central part of the evidence in proving that Greenland is not connected to the Pole, and that Denmark has no more right to the sea lanes around it than, say, Russia."

"Or Canada," said Fenna and remembered the extent to which Humble's splinter group had tried to humiliate the Danish sovereignty mission in Greenland.

"It's not Canada we need to worry about, not at the moment."

"Who then? The Chinese?"

"The Chinese have a delegation on the Arctic Council. They are observers only, but have a growing interest in the Arctic, not least for oil and minerals."

"And Danish agents posing as mining company reps."

"Exactly," Nicklas said and grinned. "For a nation with no geographical ties to the Arctic, they are committed, with one ice breaker…"

"The *Xue Long*," Fenna said.

"And the *Haibing*, which is under construction," Nicklas said, with a quick flick through the papers. "The Chinese are very interested, and are already negotiating the building of a mineral mine in the mountains north of Nuuk, in Godthåb Fjord."

"The Tunstall mine?"

"Yes."

"And that's where I'm going?"

"Yes, but your brief is more specific." Nicklas paused. "The Field Report suggests that data was spoiled by a member of the expedition, and that the results are inconclusive."

"So they can't be used."

"No, not unless the nature of the spoiled data can be re-evaluated."

"I don't follow?" Fenna said. "Is Greenland connected to the Pole or not?"

"The data says it's not."

Nicklas turned his head at the swing of the screen door as Freddy came back in and prepared a fresh pot of coffee. Fenna took a small bite of her burger and waited for him to continue.

"Jarnvig thinks the data is fake, that the so-called malfunction of the machine is fake."

"And he thinks the Chinese are behind it?"

"That's the theory," Nicklas said and nodded.

Fenna mused over the implications, and the memory of the *Xue Long* entering Canadian waters unannounced several years ago. That incident alone had forced the Canadians into an escalation of military activities and patrols in their Arctic territories; it had also culminated in the death of her patrol partner, and Dina. *And it was almost the death of me*, she thought as she swallowed. A Chinese foothold in Greenland could be used as leverage for a greater Chinese role in the Arctic, she realised.

"And Jarnvig wants me to find out the truth?" she asked.

"Not exactly," Nicklas said and lowered his voice as Freddy approached with their coffees and pie. "He wants you to find the researcher who falsified the data, before the hearing." He paused and leaned forward. "Jarnvig thinks the Chinese have turned someone on our side," he said. "There's a traitor among us, Fenna, and your job is to expose him."

Chapter 5

Fenna wound down the Humvee window and let the warm air scour the grime from her face. She enjoyed the flick of her hair against her skin, and ran her hand through her fringe. Nicklas was silent and Fenna thought she caught a glimpse of him looking at her, but when she turned, he was focused on the road. The glimpse was gone, but she slid her fingers through her hair one more time, laughing at herself when she saw her reflection in the Humvee's mirror. *Get over yourself, Fenna*, she thought. *These are hardly come-to-bed eyes.* She smiled again as the thought flushed her cheeks and she tried to remember the last time she had lusted for a man.

"Too long," she said, as Nicklas turned his head toward her.

"What is?"

"Nothing," Fenna pressed the heel of her right boot against the solid wheel arch in front of her. She closed her eyes and let her mind wander in the desert as they continued along Highway 95 towards the base.

Nicklas slowed the Humvee as they approached the entrance to the DTC. He flashed his ID card and leaned back so Fenna could do the same. The guard nodded for them to pass. Nicklas drove beneath the raised barrier and onto the base. Fenna took a moment to prepare herself for going back to the barracks, but Nicklas continued past them, slowing to a stop by the side of a dishevelled warehouse. Fenna recognised it, even without the blue light leaking out between the wood panels.

"Why are we here?" she asked.

"Dancing lessons," Nicklas said and got out of the Humvee. Fenna stared at him as he shut the Humvee's door and waited for her to get out. She climbed out of the vehicle and slammed the door.

"I'm hardly ready for this," she said and scowled.

"But you need it," he said and signalled for Fenna to go inside.

The wind licked tiny clouds of dust from the heels of her boots as Fenna walked up to the door and yanked it open. She squinted into the dim interior, stepped inside and waited. She watched as Nicklas found a length of wood to prop against the door.

"The lock's broken," he said. "Come on."

"I don't like this place," Fenna said, as she followed him to the dusty ring in the centre of the warehouse. She remembered the screech of the monkeys, the fetid taste of sweat and testosterone as she ducked under the rope and stood opposite Nicklas. He grinned and pulled his shirt off.

Fenna's eyes adjusted to the soft desert light creeping in through the holes in the tin roof. She watched the dust motes as they filtered down on shafts of light to settle on Nicklas' body. She traced the shadows that cut his body into muscle, ribs, a scar here, a patch of burned skin there. The drumming behind her eyes was lost as her heart beat faster, thudding against her chest.

"Forget about this area," Nicklas said and traced his finger around the muscles on his flat belly. "Fat or muscle, you won't get the effect you're looking for with a punch to the stomach. Not with a soldier, not with these guys." Nicklas tapped his breastbone with his knuckle. "Here. This is where you want to hit. Maximum effort," he said and let his hands fall to his sides. "Now," he said and squared his feet in the dirt.

"You want me to hit you?"

"I want you to try."

"All right," Fenna said and took a step forward. She made a fist with her right hand and extended the knuckle of her middle finger. Nicklas stepped to one side, turned sharply and caught Fenna's arm in the crook of his own. He closed his left hand around her fist and started to bend it back on itself.

"Fuck," Fenna said and jerked to her right.

"Kidneys," Nicklas said. "Ignore thc pain. Go for the kidneys."

Fenna grimaced and slammed her left fist into Nicklas' back.

"Lower," he said and grunted when she made contact. He bent her hand again. Fenna's wrist consumed her focus and she twisted in his grip. "Again."

Fenna ignored the pain in her wrist and slammed her fist into Nicklas' back, lower this time. He grunted and twisted his back away from her. Fenna bent her left leg and kneed him in small of his back.

"Better," Nicklas said with another grunt. "Keep going."

She tried but the pain in her wrist overwhelmed her. He spun her onto the ground and her body went limp. Dust pillowed from the floor as she slammed onto it. He let go of her and slapped at her hands as he sat astride her chest.

"You're always going to be weaker," he said. "You're never going to win a fight if you let them get close. Keep your opponent at a distance. Always."

Fenna spat dirt from her mouth, squirmed her heels into the dirt and arched her back, trying to propel him away. She glared at Nicklas.

"Forget it, Konstabel. I'm at least 50lbs heavier than you. You're pinned."

"Then what do you suggest?" Fenna said. She felt a fresh trickle of blood leak from her nose. With her arms trapped beneath Nicklas' knees, the blood trickled down her left cheek.

Nicklas lifted one hand and wiped the blood away with his thumb. The scratch of his skin was familiar. His eyes, brown – almost black in the dim light – settled on hers. Fenna felt his knees lift from her arms, as he positioned them on either side of her body, and Fenna, silent, her blue eyes locked on his, arched her back, her hips brushing against his inner thighs.

"Konstabel," Nicklas said, his voice hoarse.

Fenna said nothing. She arched her back again and he pressed down into her. She spread her arms at right angles and pressed her fingers into the dirt. Fenna ignored the pain in her eyes, her nose. She heard her breaths rasp in and out of her mouth as she arched her body again and he matched her movement. Fenna licked her wind-chapped lips and sniffed at the air. It was hot. Moist. She was on the floor of the jungle again, and she succumbed to its feral nature as he unzipped his cargo pants and Fenna reached down to unbutton and squirm out of hers.

The dust of the ring clung to their skin as sweat beaded their faces, glued Fenna's hair to her cheeks, and ran in spasmodic streams as Nicklas thrust his way inside Fenna and she pushed to feel him deep inside her. Fenna purged the violent and dominant images of man from her mind and lost herself in Nicklas, in the fusty dirt of the ring. *The dancing lessons are over,* she thought as she caught him mid thrust, cupped his balls and rolled him onto his back. Fenna straddled him until he closed his eyes and groaned. She felt the jungle, smelled it as it enveloped her, the vines curling around her legs, her arms, her ribs, constricting her breathing, until the jungle withdrew and she let herself slip onto his chest, content, for the moment, and Nicklas opened his eyes.

Fenna felt another stream of blood trickle onto her chin and she wiped it with the back of her hand. Nicklas took her hand, her blood smearing into the cracks in his rough skin. Fenna sat back on his thighs as he lay down in the dirt. She felt him inside her, limp but warm, and smiled.

"You're pretty," he said. "But…"

"But?" Fenna said and dug her knuckles into his stomach.

"But beautiful when you smile."

"Hah," she said and moved as if to roll off him.

"Stay," he said, and moved his hands to her hips.

"Can't," she said with a glance toward the door.

"No-one's coming, Konstabel."

"How do you know, *Inspector*?" Fenna shook her head and laughed.

"I don't … care," he said and reached up to caress her cheek. Fenna turned her face and took his finger between her lips. "I wouldn't," he said and pulled his finger out of her mouth. "Not clean."

"I don't care," she said and closed her teeth around his finger, biting until he complained. Fenna released him and Nicklas slipped his hand to her breast, smoothing his palm over her dusty thermal top, searching for her nipples. "They're tiny," she said, as he rubbed her nipple to a hard bud.

"I don't care."

"You're my handler," she said. "Aren't you?"

Nicklas nodded and said, "And do you like the way I *handle* you, Konstabel?"

"Yes," Fenna said and slipped onto Nicklas' chest. She felt him slide out of her as she kissed him. Her eyes hurt, and she closed them. Her nose ran and she ignored it. Her heart hammered and she felt it. Nicklas stirred beneath her and she anticipated it. The jungle enveloped Fenna once more and she lost herself in the wild beat of its drum.

The canteen was empty when Fenna entered. She had revelled in the shower that gave her a chance to scrub the stubborn desert grime from her body and now she was ready to eat. Nicklas was gone for the evening, and she realised she didn't even know where he slept. The thought amused her as she helped herself to a meal from the fridge and took her tray into a corner, choosing to eat in the shadows. The anchor of a late night talk show on the television was berating the President for his short-sightedness on defence job cuts, and the need for a strong, capable military in an increasingly volatile world. Fenna was almost finished when the door opened and the beauty queen walked in. Two sturdy men accompanied her, one on either side. They studied the rows of empty tables and chairs and Fenna shrank deeper into the shadows. The men nodded for the girl to help herself and walked out of the canteen to wait outside. Fenna watched her walk to the fridge, and, when she was looking for a seat, she whispered to her, "Hi."

The girl was startled, but Fenna continued.

"Sorry. Come and join me." She beckoned to the girl, who took one step and stopped.

"I'm not supposed to," she said and glanced at the door.

"How long do you have?"

"They usually give me fifteen minutes."

"Then I'll be gone in ten," she said. "Sit with me."

The girl took one more look at the door and then, with a breath, walked over to Fenna's table. She slid her tray onto the table and sat down. Fenna smiled and studied her face. She was a natural blonde. They shared the same glacial-blue eyes.

"Fenna," she said and held out her hand.

"Alice," the girl said.

"We're the only two girls on the base. How old are you?"

"Nineteen."

"I'm twenty-four," said Fenna. "They keeping you busy?" she said, looking toward the door.

"I'm really not supposed to talk about it."

"I understand," Fenna paused as Alice started to whisper.

"They want me to do something, and I'm pretty sure it's bad, but they won't tell me what it is."

"You don't have any idea?" Fenna said and leaned forward. Alice shook her head and slipped her pale arms either side of the tray. Fenna noticed that her hands were trembling and she placed hers on top of them and squeezed. "It'll be all right," she said.

"No," said Alice. "I don't think it will."

Chapter 6

The base was quiet when Fenna slipped out of the kitchen. Alice intrigued her. The way she constantly checked towards her minders, encouraging Fenna to leave after only seven minutes, during which time she had said little, only stared at Fenna's eyes, and taken tiny bites of the sandwich on her plate. She had flinched when Fenna leaned across the table to smooth a lock of her hair from her face.

"It's okay," Fenna had said. "I won't hurt you."

"You won't?"

"No, I promise," she said, "us girls have to look out for each other."

"And you'll look out for me?"

"Yes," Fenna said and clasped Alice's hand. "Do you eat at the same time each night?"

"Yes."

"Then I'll be here, in the shadows."

"Okay," Alice said and Fenna caught the beginnings of a smile.

"I'll see you tomorrow night," Fenna said. She squeezed Alice's hand, and then slipped out from behind the bench and into the kitchen. Fenna looked back from the doorway, but Alice turned away, chewing small mouthfuls of sandwich as she stared at the door. Fenna left through the back entrance.

The two of them shared a similar build, but where Fenna's skin was tanned and tight, Alice's was pale and smooth. *Cute*, Fenna realised. *Pretty and innocent. The kind older men go for,* she thought and felt sick at the thought of Richard Humble.

A cascade of thoughts plagued Fenna as she crossed the grounds of the base. She half expected to see Dina hanging in the doorway, or Mikael grinning from behind the uprights of the Sirius sledge, the dogs wagging their tails, anxious, anticipating his commands. Fenna pushed each image aside, spinning through the cruel carousel in her mind before it settled on one image, Dina. *Always Dina.* Fenna, her hand on the screen door, closed her eyes and tried to push the carousel on to the next image, Maratse, his cigarette rolled into the gap between his teeth, but Dina's face remained.

"I'm sorry," Fenna whispered, as she let the door close behind her. It clapped against the wooden frame and Fenna sank to her knees. She opened her eyes and blinked. There was Dina, twisting from the beam above Fenna's bunk, and, for a moment, the Greenlander's almond face paled, her cheeks swelled a fraction and her eyes opened, changing from black to brilliant blue. It wasn't Dina's long black hair she saw, but short hair, curled into a blonde fringe. Fenna gasped when she realised it was not her own face staring back at her, but another – Alice. Then Dina returned, twisting silently three full turns before Fenna turned the carousel in her mind, stopping it on a single image, an iceberg locked into the ice, extending from the coastline and far into the Greenland Sea. She stared at it until the white surface of the berg consumed her and everything and everyone was gone. Fenna was alone.

She stood up and dragged her pack to her bunk, tugging the LOMROG report out from the back of the pack. She flicked through the first few pages, familiarising herself with the Swedish author's name, Lars Johansson and his Danish colleague Karl Lorentzen. She crawled beneath the blanket and folded her pillow in half, lay on her side and drew her knees toward her chest. She skimmed over the academic descriptions detailing the remit of the expedition, and focused instead on the opening sentences of the report. Johansson was wasted as a scientist, surely his true calling was writing. She absorbed his descriptions of patchwork plates of ice, hinged with elastic tongues of black water, desperate to freeze, thwarted by the movement of the plates, and the curved bow of the icebreaker rising up over the ice and cracking it beneath its monstrous displacement. Fenna forgot the desert, the pain behind her eyes, only to wake as the report slipped from between her fingers and slapped onto the barrack floor. She set the alarm and pulled the blanket up and over her head. She needed to sleep.

The canteen at breakfast reminded Fenna of the jungle floor of the ring. The taint of testosterone hung heavy over the tables of men, who were sweating and coated in dust from a morning run through the desert. She recognised some of the faces as they looked up from their meal, elbowing each other in the ribs, nodding and sneering in her direction as she passed. The counter-sniper team sat at one end of the table closest to the serving area. Fenna stopped as the Gunnery Sergeant extricated himself from the bench and made his way toward her, the tread of his boots heavy on the floor. Fenna picked up a tray and faced him.

"Konstabel," he said and stopped in front of her. The men at the table behind him leaned around each other to watch. He gave them a threatening look and they turned away.

"*Konstabel*?" Fenna said, as he looked at her. She tilted her head. "Not *bitch*, or *pussy*? What about *cunt*?"

The Gunney laughed. "Save it for the ring," he said and nodded at the soldiers queuing at the serving counter. "Major wants to see you after breakfast," the Gunney said, as he walked away. Fenna let out a breath and joined the line.

She ate alone at the same corner table she had sat at the previous evening. She looked up from her meal and scanned the soldiers for a glimpse of Alice, chiding herself for even hoping she might see her. She twisted around as the bench creaked beneath the weight of someone sitting down.

"She's not here," Nicklas said, as he opened his carton of milk and drank from it.

"I know," Fenna said and sighed. She pushed her spoon around the muesli in her bowl. "Where did you sleep last night?"

"The same place I always do. Why?"

"It occurred to me," she said, "that I don't know where that is."

"And that bothers you?"

"No," Fenna said and smiled. "I'd just like to know. That's all."

"So you can make a booty call?" Nicklas said and laughed.

"God," she said and caught herself in the act of slapping him on his arm. Fenna let her hand drop to her lap. "No," she said. "I don't do booty calls."

"Shame," said Nicklas. "If you did, I might be more inclined to tell you where I slept."

Fenna hid her smile behind a spoonful of muesli, chewing over the thoughts that tickled her mind.

"I have to see the Major," she said, as Nicklas finished his milk. "Should I be worried?"

"No. He's just going to give you a car, and a driver."

"Chinese lessons?"

"Tomorrow night, yes. But before that, you'll need to get over to the quartermaster and draw some more kit."

"It's Sunday."

"He'll be open."

"And what do I need?"

"Here's a list," Nicklas said and tugged a slip of paper from his pocket. He handed it to Fenna, pausing as he caught the eyes of the counter-sniper team watching them.

"We've become an object of interest," Fenna said and took the paper.

"You were the moment you arrived."

"And you?"

"I'm Canadian, remember? We're never interesting, just polite. No," he said, shoveling egg onto his French Toast, "you're the item of interest, and they are hungry. Watch yourself, Fenna."

"I'll be fine," she said and slipped the list into her pocket.

"You're not going to read it?"

"After I've seen the Major." Fenna stood up and picked up her tray. "I'll see you later?"

"No," he said and shook his head. "I have to leave for a few days."

"Jarnvig's orders?"

"No, Toronto's. I'm lucky enough to have two masters. I'll see you when I get back."

"Okay," she said.

"Fenna?"

"What?"

"You're getting better, but I think more dancing lessons might be in order," Nicklas said. He grinned and stabbed his fork into the toast. Fenna caught the smile on her face and wrangled it into a frown.

"I'm not so sure about that, Inspector," she said and smirked at the flash of insecurity in Nicklas' eyes. She walked away from the table, conscious of the eyes following her all the way to the door. She knew Nicklas' gaze was among them, and the thought lifted her step all the way to the Major's office.

The woman sitting on the chair against the wall of the outer office was older than Fenna, her clothes tighter, her perfume sweeter. She caught Fenna's eye before the aide stepped out from Major's office and closed the door. Fenna caught a glimpse of a man talking with the Major and recognised him. It was the same man that had confronted her in the dirt beside the Humvee in the desert, the one that had warned the Gunney and his men to stay away from eastern barracks.

"That's three women on my base," Fenna heard the Major bark through the thin wall. "And damn it, this one is a fucking hooker."

"Exotic dancer," the woman said, as Fenna looked over at her. "I'm not a hooker."

Fenna shrugged and walked over to the aide's desk as he called to her.

"Konstabel."

"Yes?"

"The Major has arranged a car and a driver. You'll be picked up at 18:00 hours each night from Monday. The car will wait for you at the main gate. You're to be back by midnight. If not, the guards have been instructed to hold you at the gate."

"Really?"

"Yes," the aide said and smiled. "Really."

Fenna nodded and turned to leave.

"Just one more thing, Konstabel."

"Yes?" she said and looked at the aide. She noticed the smile on his face as it broadened into a smug grin that filled his cheeks.

"The Major instructed me to remind you that you are invited to a second dance this evening." Fenna's stomach churned as the aide's grin widened. "He hopes you will come suitably dressed."

"Hey," said the woman. "I thought I was the only one dancing?" She moved to one side to look around Fenna at the aide. "Nobody said nothing about dancing with a partner." She paused and made a point of appraising Fenna's body. "No offence, honey, but your body and," she spun her finger around her face, "those black eyes n'all. I just don't do no kinky stuff."

"Don't worry," Fenna said and took a step toward the door. "I dance alone."

Fenna pulled the crumpled slip of paper from her pocket as she walked to quartermaster's store. She listened to the woman protesting as she was ushered into the back of a black SUV. Fenna watched for a moment and then focused her attention back to the paper – Jarnvig's shopping list.

"Interesting," she said and smiled as she scanned the different items.

The quartermaster didn't smile when she handed him the list. He whistled and scratched at flakes of skin on his parched head. He caught Fenna's look and explained, "Had a barbecue yesterday. Forgot my cap."

"Okay," Fenna said and placed her hands on the counter between them.

"This will take a while," he said. "Some of these things… Well, we have them, but they haven't been used in I don't know how long. You might want to take a seat."

Fenna nodded and sat down on the bench opposite the counter. The quartermaster whistled for a second time and then looked at Fenna, deep wrinkles furrowing his brow.

"I'm probably not supposed to ask," he said.

"But?"

"But," he said and nodded. "Why would you need an M1 Carbine? Those things are ancient. I mean, we have a couple, but…"

"It's a Greenland thing," Fenna said and smiled. The carousel in her mind clicked and there was Maratse, grinning behind the wheel of a Police Toyota Rav4 as it sped across the ice. Fenna let the image linger as the quartermaster disappeared into the strip light interior of the stores to rummage around the lockers and shelves. She found an empty chair and pulled the LOMROG report out of her pack, losing herself once more in Johansson's lyrical description of the Arctic, and his unhurried detailing of life on board the Swedish research vessel *Odin*.

The quartermaster returned faster than he had anticipated, forcing Fenna to tuck the report back inside her pack, and to find room for the various items he had assembled from her list.

"You'll have to sign for all of it," he said. Fenna nodded. "And," he said as she picked up the pen, "that makes you responsible for it."

"So if I break it...

"You bought it," he said and shrugged. "I don't make the rules."

"That's okay," Fenna said, as she shouldered her pack and picked up the carbine. "I don't often follow them." She turned away before the quartermaster could respond, smiling as she stepped out of the stores and into the afternoon heat. *It would be dark soon*, she realised as she walked toward her barracks, anticipating with pleasure a little feminine contact. *Alice*, she thought. *I wonder what you have learned today?*

Chapter 7

The base was dark and quiet but for the muffled beat of rock music coming from the barracks beyond the canteen. Fenna put down the LOMROG report and checked the equipment that she had arranged on her desk and bunk. She had spent most of the evening cleaning the carbine. *The quartermaster was right*, she had mused, *it was a relic.* But neither the carbine nor the scientist's field report held her interest. It was getting late, and the canteen would be empty. Fenna checked her watch. The dance, she imagined, would start at midnight. She tugged on her boots and slipped out of the barracks.

Fenna entered the canteen through the kitchen door. The emergency exit sign cast a green glow above the doors and she saw the familiar shadows of Alice's protection detail. She pressed her palms against the swing door and pushed it open a crack. Alice was at the table, a half-empty glass of milk in her hand as she nibbled at a sandwich. Fenna slipped inside and padded over to her.

"I thought you weren't going to come," Alice said, as Fenna sat down.

"Sorry. I lost track of time."

"It's okay."

"How was your day?" Fenna asked.

"Actually," Alice said and smiled. "It was a lot of fun."

"Fun?" Fenna said and tilted her head. The wry smile that tugged at Alice's lips caught her attention.

"Kinda naughty."

"Now I'm interested." Fenna leaned forward. "Tell me."

"Well," Alice said and placed her sandwich on the table. She licked a crumb from her lips, glanced at the door and then whispered, "This woman came. She was older than you. A dancer." Fenna nodded, she knew exactly who the woman was.

"And?"

"She taught me to lap dance. You know? Like in a strip joint?"

"Yes, I know," Fenna said and frowned. "Did they say why?"

"No," Alice said, "that's the thing. They haven't told me anything. They just give me classes in different stuff and expect me to do it."

"What kind of classes? Apart from lap dancing, I mean."

"There's gym, for one. They have me out running a lot."

"In the desert?"

"Yeah," Alice said and shrugged. "I like it. It's the only time they let me outside in the daylight. Although we're up so early…"

"You don't meet anyone."

"That's right. But it reminds me of the dawn at my daddy's favourite place, in Washington state," she said. "In the Cascades."

"He has a cabin there?"

"Kind of. He was a mountaineer. He got sick – cancer – and he'd spend every night talking about this cabin, way up on the top of a mountain – an old lookout hut on top of the North Cascades." Fenna listened as Alice continued. "When I was seventeen, daddy got better for a little bit – even the doctors were surprised. So we went up there."

"To the lookout?"

"Sure," Alice said and grinned. "Scariest thing I ever did in my life. There's all these ladders, and you climb through the clouds..." Fenna lifted a finger to Alice's lips and she lowered her voice. "The ladders go all the way to the top, some 7,000 feet high. Then there's this amazing cabin – it looks like it's going to fall apart, but people look after it, and it's still there. You can see all around it, for miles." Alice sighed. "The climb nearly killed him. He wasn't ready. And when we came down, well, he died, just a few weeks later. I held his hand, right at the end, describing the cabin over and over, until he stopped breathing. Until his body just stopped."

"It sounds like an amazing place," Fenna said and took Alice's hands. She squeezed them, smiling as Alice squeezed back.

Alice slipped her left hand free of Fenna's and wiped a tear from her cheek. She glanced at the door. "They'll come in soon."

"I'll go," Fenna said. She reached out and smoothed Alice's cheek. "You're okay though?"

"Better now. I still don't know what I'm doing. They tell me nothing. There's no TV. They took my Smartphone the day they picked me up."

"I know the feeling. They took mine too. You're cut off from the world."

"Pretty much."

"Okay," Fenna said, as Alice pulled away. "I'll see you tomorrow night."

"I hope so," Alice said and smiled. Fenna slid back on the bench and melted into the shadow of the corner, as Alice emptied her tray at the counter and walked toward the door. One of the men opened it for her and she walked past him. She didn't look back.

Fenna waited several minutes, mulling over the strange classes Alice was taking, before standing up and making her way to the kitchen. She padded past the stoves and hotplates and opened the door. A warm draft of desert air tousled her hair as she stepped out into the night, only to be replaced by a cloth sack pulled over her head that blotted out the stars and, when the opening was tightened around her neck, threatened to turn that breath of warm wind into her last. Fenna struggled and was rewarded with a knee in her stomach. She doubled over and sprawled onto the deck as rough hands bound her arms behind her back and she heard the all-too-familiar snick of plastic ties as they locked her hands together.

"Get her in the truck," said a man, and then she felt more hands on her body. They clamped around her ankles, jammed into her armpits and lifted her. Fenna was weightless for a brief moment before her chin cracked on the metal bed of a pick-up and the metal gate hit the soles of her boots as it was slammed shut. Doors opened on both sides of the vehicle and it rocked as the men got in. The engine coughed into life and Fenna slid across the metal bed as the vehicle roared off the base and onto what she imagined was a side road, her knees and elbows jarred as the pickup bumped up the track.

Fenna fought to calm her breathing and tried not to retch as the oily cloth pressed against her lips and teeth with each breath. Dark scenarios raced through her mind.

She struggled onto her knees and half slid, half rolled to the gate at the rear of the pickup. It pressed into her back when the vehicle crunched through another pit. As the driver accelerated out of the hole, Fenna arched her back, straightened her legs and pitched backward out of the bed of the pickup. She landed on her shoulder, gritting her teeth at the crack of bone on the compacted grit and rock of the track. The vehicle continued and Fenna scrabbled to her feet.

"Move," she breathed and stumbled to one side. She continued in the same direction until the ground disappeared beneath her, she then fell a metre and a half. She laughed as she landed on her feet. Grit and dirt tumbled onto her fingers and she explored the earth wall behind her back and leaned into it. Fenna twisted her head for sounds of the vehicle and thought she heard the muffled shouts of men searching both sides of the track.

"Fuck," said a man. His voice was pitched higher than the others. Fenna didn't recognise it. But a second voice caused her stomach to tighten.

"She won't get far." Fenna recognised the southern drawl of the Gunnery Sergeant. She held her breath and leaned into the earth, willing it to envelop her. "Let's get back."

"Gunney?" said another man. "We can't leave her out here. What if she talks?"

"About what, dick wad? She knows nothing, there's nothing to tell," the Gunney said. Fenna could almost feel the tremor of his boots as he walked around the vehicle. He raised his voice. "Konstabel," he said. "Do yourself a favour. Stay the fuck away from the girl."

Fenna held her breath and tilted her head to listen, willing her heart to slow down, and for the pulse of blood in her ears to quieten. At the sound of doors slamming she let out one ragged breath after another. As the pickup bumped and grinded through a four-point turn and then accelerated down the track, Fenna became aware of her bladder. She waited until the vehicle was gone and flexed her wrists within the plastic ties. She almost laughed at how loose they were. *The plastic is too thick for small wrists*, she thought as she wormed her left hand free of the loop. She closed her eyes and was, for once, grateful of her skinny frame and low body fat.

I might have a flat chest, but being skinny has its advantages, she mused, ignoring the taste of motor oil inside the black cloth sack, she raised her hands, brushed the dirt from the skin, and felt for the plastic tie around her neck. With all the movement, from bouncing around the bed of the pickup and tumbling over the gate and off the track, the cloth skirt at the opening of the sack was loose. She pulled it off, tossing it to one side as she took a gulp of air. Fenna took two more long, deep, breaths before running her hands over her body to check that the bumps and scratches were nothing more than superficial.

"I got off lightly," she whispered and sighed.

"That," said a voice with an unmistakeable lengthening of the letter A, "is a matter of opinion, Konstabel." The shadow of the Gunnery Sergeant grew as he left his concealed position behind a boulder and took a single step closer to Fenna. She held her breath as he scuffed the toe of his boots in the dirt. "What do you say, *bitch*?"

Fenna didn't trust her voice to carry over the first wave of tremors rippling through her body. She clenched her fists and let her arms fall to her sides. She took another breath when she realised the Gunnery Sergeant had not moved since he startled her.

"You didn't go back in the truck," she said.

The Gunney shook his head. The white of the moon glistened in his eyes, his pupils huge, round, and predatory.

"Smart."

"I've been around the block," he said. "I know a few things."

"Enough to send your buddies back to base."

"No witnesses."

Fenna nodded, slowly. *I've been here before*, she reminded herself. *But last time I had a gun.* She let out an even breath and the Gunney caught her staring at his waist. He made a point of turning on the spot before facing her again, his hands folded in front of his crotch.

"I'm not armed, Konstabel," he said.

"I can see that," she said. "I'll be missed."

"Accidents happen."

"But I'm not American. My country would start an inquiry, ask questions."

"You don't have accidents in Denmark?" the Gunney laughed. "I find that hard to believe."

Fenna tried a new tack. "But there are people at the base," she said, looking in the direction of the arc lights blazing in the distance. Cones of light pointed inward, outward, but nowhere near Fenna. She was in the dark, again.

"Oh, that's right," he said and took a single step forward. He stopped when Fenna flinched. The Gunney smiled. "Your friend. The *Canadian*?"

"Yes," said Fenna.

"I know a lot of Canadians," he said. "I go hunting there a couple times a year."

Fenna waited. She worked on her breathing as the Gunnery Sergeant took another small step toward her. She reached one hand behind her back and felt the earth wall just centimetres away. She took a handful of dirt and slid her hand to her side.

"He's been recalled."

"Fuck," Fenna breathed.

"Seems they… the real Canadians… have some issues with

double agents. Just like we do."

"I don't understand?"

"You don't? Then you're not here to spy on us? It's just a coincidence then?"

"Coincidence?"

"You meeting with the girl, late at night, in the canteen."

"Alice..."

"Shit, Konstabel," the Gunney ran his hand through the tight stubble that was his hair. "Don't they teach you anything at Danish Spy School?" He lowered his hand and slipped it inside his pocket. When he pulled it out, his fingers were wrapped around a short blade with a thick metal ring, like a trigger guard, protecting his index finger. "Let's imagine that this," he said and waved the knife at the desert scrub surrounding them. "This is Spy School and Rule One is..." he paused. "Well, it's gotta be the most important fucking rule there is."

"Okay," Fenna forced herself to focus on both of the Gunney's hands, his stance, and the look in his eyes, and not be distracted by the knife flashing in the moonlight. "Rule One," she said, as she leaned forward, changing the balance of her weight from her heels to her toes.

"Rule One is never give information voluntarily, and never ever *after* you've just been told that your enemy knows you are alone."

"Are you my enemy, Gunnery Sergeant?" Fenna asked, her voice level, despite the thunder in her chest.

"Hah," he snorted. Fenna noticed that the knife sank as he shifted on his feet. "What do *you* think, Konstabel?"

"I think," Fenna tightened her fingers around the dirt in her right hand. "We've moved beyond dancing."

"Yeah," the Gunney drawled, "that's about right."

He lunged forward and Fenna released a cloud of grit into his face.

Chapter 8

The Gunnery Sergeant spat as the desert dirt clung to his lips and caked his eyes, blinding him for a brief moment, long enough to piss him off, and just long enough for Fenna to strike. She pushed off the earth wall behind her and let the momentum carry her left fist, middle knuckle extended, between the Gunney's arms and into his solar plexus. Fenna cried out as she felt her knuckle crack. She caught her breath as he faltered onto his heels. Fenna ignored the pain in her hand, bent her arm, and swung her elbow up, screaming as it caught the top of his chin, the impact snapping his head up and back. She reeled and stopped to regain her balance as her opponent stumbled one more step, and then a second, away from her.

Press your advantage, Fenna imagined Nicklas would say, and she did, slamming the toe of her boot into the Gunney's crotch as she cradled her left hand in her right. The Gunnery Sergeant grunted but only for a moment. He twisted his knife hand, palm upward, extended his reach and slashed at Fenna's calf muscle as she withdrew her foot. The knife nicked at her skin and caught on the collar of her desert boot, startling her. The Gunney recovered his stance, shifted his weight onto the balls of his feet, and lurched toward her. Fenna moved backward only to catch her feet in the exposed roots of desert scrub and sprawl to the ground. She cried out in pain as she broke her fall with her injured hand.

Fenna gritted her teeth and rolled toward the earth wall as the Gunney pounced. He cursed when he landed on the ground and not on Fenna's back as he had planned. Fenna scrabbled to her feet, ducking to the right as the Gunney slammed his knife hand toward her, burying the blade in the earth. She wondered at his aim and, after a quick glance at his face, she realised his eyes were still smarting and the fine desert dust was clogging his vision.

You'll always be weaker than your opponent, Nicklas' voice reminded her. *Be smart*, *Fenna*, she added. Fenna spun around the Gunney's back as he worried the knife out of the earth wall. She pummelled his kidneys with her right fist, and, in a move that was as surprising as it was savage, she butted him in the left eye with her forehead as he twisted toward her.

"Bitch," he said, and then she butted him again, and a third time until her head began to throb and the blood from the tear in his skin above his eye blinded him once more. The Gunney pushed at Fenna with a blind sweep of his left arm as he jabbed the knife where he thought her body should be. Fenna moved around him and punched him in the kidneys again, the thunder of her heart and roar of the blood through her temple lost in a funnel of intensity that guided her hand and purpose. *Put him down*, she mouthed, again and again until the Gunnery Sergeant sank to his knees.

Keep going, Fenna. Nicklas' voice said from somewhere in the desert, off to her left, maybe her right – she resisted the urge to look. *He's down. Keep him down.* Fenna bit back the pain and shoved the Gunney's head down with her left hand. The stubble of his hair rasped against her palm. She curled the fingers of her right hand into a fist and punched the base of his neck. She did it again, her left hand creeping down the Gunney's forehead and curling beneath his brows to keep his head up as she hit him one more time. The big man slumped to the floor and Fenna took a breath.

She took a step backward and flicked her hair from her eyes. Striped with blood, sweat, and desert dust, her fringe clung to her forehead and she wiped it to one side. Her fingers trembled and she clasped them together only to realise it wasn't just her fingers, but her whole body. She felt her knees, twitching to an unfamiliar rhythm, the pulse of the desert, of battle, and her first real *Sonoran Shuffle.*

You know what you have to do, Fenna, Nicklas' voice chided her.

"I know."

He would have done the same to you.

"Yes," she said, and then, angrily, "I know."

Then do it.

Fenna took a single breath and held it as she stomped forward. Her knees thumped into the dirt beside the Gunnery Sergeant. Fenna exhaled as she reached across his body and yanked at the knife looped around his index finger. She swore as the trigger ring caught on his knuckle, forcing her to lean across him and use both hands to pull it free. She pushed off him and swallowed as he let out a single groan.

Hurry, Fenna.

"Fuck off, Nicklas," she waved her hand in the dark space behind her.

Get it done.

"I know," she said as she sank onto her heels. Fenna could feel the grip of her desert boots as they gnawed at the thin layer of fat in the flesh of her bottom. She wiped a tear from her cheek with the back of her left hand and cursed at the pain of the forgotten knuckle.

Fenna.

"Yes," she said and reached for the Gunney's shoulder.

Kill him.

"Yes," Fenna heaved the Gunnery Sergeant onto his back. She curled the finger into the trigger guard of the knife and thrust her right hand forward. The tip of the blade slipped into the Gunney's windpipe and Fenna gasped at the burst of air that slipped out as she withdrew it. The Gunney's eyes opened. Fenna pressed her left hand over them and jabbed the knife into his throat until his chest was bloody, his lungs were empty, and the desert was still but for the soft sobs that tumbled out of her body.

Good, Fenna, Nicklas' voice said. *Good. It is done.*

Fenna half imagined Dina to drift through the night and arrive on a desert wind to admonish her, but the Greenlander was silent and unseen, for once. Mikael was absent too. Her demons, it seemed, had decided to leave her alone with her thoughts. Only Nicklas was determined to plague her, and he wasn't even dead.

Fenna, his voice said. *You need to move.*

"I know," she curled her arms around her knees, her bottom cooling on the desert floor. The knife, sticky and sweetened with blood, dangled from the crook in her finger. "Give me a moment. Please."

A moment then. No more.

Fenna let the desert's breath lap at her face and twist the fringe of her hair. The blood dried as she let one moment pass into another. She moved her chin up and down her right knee with exaggerated movements of her jaw, as if the silent shapes she formed might become words and tell her what to do.

"I killed a man," she said, as her stomach spasmed and she retched on the desert floor. Fenna wiped her mouth with the back of her hand and flicked her eyes toward the Gunney's bloody body. Now the act of burying him forced her into action. She pushed his body tight against the earth wall, clawing at it until he was buried in a thin layer of desert. She rubbed the last of the dirt from her palms onto her bloody fatigues and slipped the Gunney's knife inside her belt. The handle pressed into the small of Fenna's back as she walked and she was surprised how reassuring it was.

You have a plan then?

Nicklas again. Fenna ignored him until she was back on the road and headed in the direction of the base. It shone like a beacon before her. She preferred the shadows.

Fenna?

"Yes, I have a plan, Nicklas," she said aloud. Her voice fragmented on the wind. It was stronger now, flicking at her fringe. It felt good.

And what is it?

If Fenna had wondered at the personification of her thoughts, she didn't let it show. Her face was set, and determined. She picked idly at a patch of blood drying on her cheek. Her left hand dangled by her side, as she adjusted her step to the throbbing in her knuckle.

It's not broken, you know.

"What?"

Your finger. The knuckle is dislocated. That's all.

"Oh," Fenna said and stopped. She wrapped her right hand around her middle digit, gnawed her bottom lip into a bight of flesh and bit down as she pulled and straightened her finger.

Better?

Fenna imagined Nicklas smiling as she stifled a stream of curses. She tasted blood on her lip, spat on the ground.

"Nicklas," she said.

Yes?

"Fuck off."

He was silent then and Fenna's thoughts were her own. She needed to plan her entry onto the base so that she could collect her gear. The carbine could be a problem.

It's too big, she thought. *I can't conceal it, and I can't fly out of here with it.*

Flying. The thought of getting away unnoticed was her primary goal. Flying out of the States was a distant and luxurious dream.

"Jarnvig, he'll get me out. He needs me."

That thought occupied Fenna the last hundred metres to the perimeter of the base. She crouched behind a patch of thick desert scrub at the first rise of the track she had been bumped along only a few hours earlier. She wondered where the Gunney's soldiers might be, but a quick scan of the immediate area revealed no sign of the pickup. There was little activity beyond the blue glow of a monitor projected onto the far wall of the guard's office. She selected her route and counted the paces she would have to take, using the shadow patches beneath the eaves of the offices, the canteen, and the barracks. She took a breath, stood up, and moved.

The first patch of open ground would be dangerous. The glare of the lights threw her shadow in a slow arc on the ground as she moved out of one light sphere and into another. She ran, her breath escaping from her lungs through pursed lips as she reached the deck of her barracks. The first of the bruised boards creaked, she waited three heartbeats, and then opened the screen door and walked inside.

Her gear was still strewn across her bed, the rifle rucking the blanket into ridges, the spotting scope and sight still in their cases. She padded across to the desk, opened the top drawer and pulled out the LOMROG field report. She tucked it inside the desert-ravaged daypack that was hanging by dusty straps from the back of the chair. She put several items into the pack, pausing at sounds beyond the walls. First, the yip of a desert fox, then the slap of the desert wind as it toyed with a loose shutter on the barrack opposite her own. She crossed to the bed and slipped the sight and scope inside the pack, the leather was warm beneath her fingertips.

She lingered over the M1 carbine, her fingers brushing the folding metal stock. A slow smile tugged at the corner of her mouth as she remembered Maratse and their wild dash across the sea ice, the policeman grinning behind the wheel, revelling in the madness of it all.

She packed spare clothes, together with energy bars and a bottle of water. She carried the pack around the bed, knelt in front of her footlocker and spun the combination lock. She rested the lid against the foot of the bed and tucked her personal effects, passport and wallet inside the pack. The memory of the handle of the Gunney's knife pressing into her back made her pause for a moment, her forehead resting in the crook of her arm as she gripped the locker lid. She took a breath and closed it. Then, closing the buckles of the pack she slipped it over her shoulders. She took one last look at the carbine on the bed before tightening the laces of her boots and walking toward the door.

The desert night welcomed her with a flick of dust that brushed her trouser legs and deposited another layer of Yuma dirt on her boots. She looked beyond the administration block of the DTC and squinted at the gate in the distance. She shook her head, tightened the straps of her pack and looked toward the track she had walked in on, the one with the body she had buried halfway along it.

Her first kill.

"But maybe not my last," she said, quietly, tasting the desert on her tongue. It was time to leave the States, it was time to go north.

Chapter 9

Shadows grew in the pre-dawn light, the personnel on the base would soon wake. There was no sign of the Gunney's thugs as she stepped onto the deck. She gave a moment's thought to Alice, picturing her briefly before tossing the image aside.

"Get it together, Fenna," she whispered, her words blown away by the desert wind. Another step and she was at the edge of the deck. She scanned the buildings and roads around her for sign of the black SUVs, synonymous with the young girl and the mystery surrounding her education and training.

Fenna's backpack pressed the handle of the knife into her back. She slipped her hand beneath the pack, removed it, curled her finger into the circular guard beneath the blade and took a breath; the surface of the knife and the handle still tacky with blood.

The sound of the knife plunging in and out of the Gunney's throat festered in Fenna's mind, the soft cut of flesh, the rasp of air as it raspberried out of the man's lungs. *They will be looking for him soon*, she reminded herself.

A second voice pushed the image of her first kill out of her mind.

Time to go, Fenna.

"I know," she said, with a slight nod. "But the girl…"

Was never your concern.

Fenna shook her head and gripped the knife in her right hand, she could feel the layer of blood pressing into the creases of her palm.

And neither was Dina. You have to let them go. Save yourself.

"For the good of the mission? Hah," she said, her voice low. "That's Jarnvig talking."

And what if it is? You need to move, Fenna. Now.

The sky lightened, the shadows lengthened, and Fenna stepped off the deck and slipped between the barracks toward the track. She skirted the offices and, ducking between the shafts of light she left the base. She stopped at the first rise and looked back.

"I'm sorry, Alice," she said, closing her eyes for a moment before tightening the straps of her pack and walking off the track and onto a game trail. It had been widened by the passage of soft desert boots, the kind preferred by snipers and spotters, the same as the ones she wore. She knew it led over the mountain, and that two more – one twisting east, and the second west – would lead to the road. Fenna had already decided on Phoenix, but a payphone at a truck stop or diner was her priority. She slipped the knife into the space between her belt and her cargo trousers and picked up the pace heading west.

As the gradient increased she relaxed, her breathing easing into a familiar rhythm. She let the rigor of the trail free her mind, suppressing her thoughts and the chiding from Nicklas, focusing instead on the desert and the potential for ambush and capture. She spotted the dust of the first roving patrol – four men, lightly armed, returning to base – and altered her course, using the contours of the slope and the tracks of desert predators to box the patrol and slip past them unnoticed. They seemed relaxed, she reasoned, and guessed that the Gunney had yet to be missed. Fenna turned west and glimpsed the highway, as she crested one rise before dipping into a gully.

She paused in a patch of dense scrub and removed her pack. She pulled out the water bottle and took a sip, her eyes scanning the desert. Her boots were dusty, blotched with dark patches of blood. She knelt down to smear dirt over the evidence of her kill, wrinkling her nose as she smelt her stale sweat. Fenna lifted her hand and studied the dirt and blood beneath her nails. She spared a little water to rinse the tips of her fingers, sucking the stubborn blood from her thumbnail.

Time, Fenna.

"I know," she whispered.

Sun's almost up.

Fenna screwed the cap of her water bottle and shoved it inside the pack. She took out the spotting scope and placed it on the ground, shrugging the pack onto her shoulders and tightening the straps. Then, as she bent down for the scope, there was a sound of stones trickling down the side of the slope, about four metres from her position. She sank to the ground, one hand on the scope, the other reaching for the knife in her belt.

She peered into the scrub, her heart pumping, her breathing shallow. She willed her body to still. At the sound of a second trickle of stones, Fenna held her breath, her eyes lasered on the area immediately in front of her.

A small black nose pressed out of the scrub, followed by the sleek contoured cheeks of the desert fox. Fenna kept still but for the twitch of a smile on her lips. The fox, one paw in the air, stared at her and she was rewarded with a moment of wild curiosity wrapped in lupine eyes that reminded her of her sledge team, of Lucifer, Betty and the wolf. The wind dusted down the side of the slope and flicked the blonde fringe from her forehead. The fox bolted and Fenna let out her breath. She checked the periphery, relaxed her grip on the handle of the knife and slowly straightened into a standing position. The sounds of the fox receded and she picked her way up the slope, settling into a prone position to study the highway below her.

She scanned the highway through the scope, following the path of an old and bruised Ford Bronco, as it turned into a diner roughly one kilometre north of her position. *I can be there before he finishes his coffee*, she reckoned, and pressed the rubber caps onto the ends of the scope.

Be smart, Fenna.

She checked her surroundings before picking a route to the highway, leaving her concealed position and moving swiftly down the slope, small clouds of dust billowing up from beneath her heels, like cobras rearing for a strike. The clouds dissipated, the dust twitching into the wind, invisible to all but the sniper team the Gunney had ordered to watch the road before he had bundled Fenna into the bed of the pickup. She didn't see them, nor think to look for them as her goal shifted, and time trumped caution. She let the terrain determine her speed and raced down the desert hill and ran parallel to the highway.

She was in the sniper's sights as she crossed the highway and settled into a jog toward the diner, the spotter calling out the ranges as she closed on the dusty parking lot. A Greyhound bus saved her, throwing up dust and grit as it passed. She squinted through the bus's wake and pressed on as the sniper lifted his finger from the trigger and waited for his spotter to call it in. She slowed to a brisk walk past the Bronco. The sniper watched as she smoothed the worst of the desert from clothes, slapping the dust from her palms before she reached for the door and entered the diner.

You can't stay long. You have to keep moving.

"I know," she mouthed, as she walked inside. She smiled at the waitress and looked around the tables, nodding at the man she presumed to be driver of the Bronco, his cap, shirt and jeans as ragged as his car, his face as dirty as her own.

"You're up early," the waitress said. "Coffee before you look at the menu?"

"Sure," Fenna said, as she dropped her pack from her back and slipped onto a seat at the table nearest the door. She brushed her hair from her forehead with one hand as she picked up the menu with the other.

"I'll be right back," the waitress said and walked to the counter. Fenna was tempted by the thought of breakfast, but a glance at her watch reminded her she needed to keep moving.

"So," the waitress placed a large mug in front of Fenna and filled it half full of coffee. She reached into her apron and tumbled tubes of sugar and creamer onto the table. "Anything else?"

"Um, what's fast?"

"Fast? You in a hurry, darlin'?" she peered at Fenna's face. "Some fella comin' after you?" The waitress flicked her eyes at the parking area beyond the smoke-hazed glass behind Fenna.

"Maybe," Fenna said and shrugged.

"The chef has eggs on toast, ready to go. How about that?"

"Yes. That'll be fine." Fenna cupped her hands around the mug, sipping at the coffee as the waitress scribbled a note on her pad. When she walked away Fenna turned her attention to the driver. She noticed he had finished his breakfast. *Damn*, she thought, only to relax when he lifted his hand for more coffee. He nodded in her direction as the waitress wove between the empty Formica tables to give him a refill.

As Fenna turned to look out of the window, a blur of movement in the distance on the highway caught her eye. She recognised the familiar shape of the black SUVs she had seen on the base and tapped her fingers on the table. The driver coughed as her drumming increased to match the tempo of her heartbeat.

"Hey," he said, but Fenna ignored him. She scanned the room, the parking lot, the desert to either side of the highway. Her head flicked from side to side, oblivious to the man until she noticed him standing beside her, the mug of coffee in his hand, a frown on his forehead, and, to Fenna's delight, his car keys held loosely between wrinkled fingers. "You okay?" he said and leaned down toward Fenna.

Fenna looked up and studied the man for a second.

"Your eggs are ready," the waitress called out, making her way over to the table.

Fenna turned her attention back to the driver, grabbed the top loop of her pack and swiped the man's keys. "Sorry," she said, as she twisted out of his reach. The waitress stumbled as Fenna charged past her, through the door and onto the parking lot. She could hear the man give chase as she sprinted to the Bronco. Fenna wrenched the door open and tossed her pack onto the passenger seat. She slammed the door shut and thrust the key into the ignition, grateful as the engine caught on the first turn.

"Hey, what the hell do you think you are doing?" the man shouted, as he reached for the door handle. Fenna looked straight ahead, shoved the gearstick into drive and slammed her foot on the accelerator. The Bronco lurched forward as its owner banged on the side of the vehicle. Fenna glanced at him in the mirror as he gave chase, stopping and wheezing at the entrance to the parking lot. She accelerated onto the highway and bumped the Bronco over the central reservation and onto the northbound lane.

She straightened the vehicle and willed it to go faster than the SUVs she could see in the rear-view mirror. While the Bronco lurched from gear to gear, the SUVs seemed to glide along the tarmac, the wheels barely kissing the surface. Fenna spared one second for a wistful thought of the carbine lying on her bed in the barracks before tightening her grip on the wheel and wrenching it to the right. The Bronco protested as she slammed on the brakes and skidded onto a track leading deep into the desert.

"Come on," she screamed, as the Bronco juddered over the first twenty metres. She glanced down at the gearstick, shifted it into first and whooped as the old Ford remembered its purpose and bit into the track with chunky tyres and an automobile heart that was part combustion engine part warhorse.

Fenna prayed that the SUVs were as unsuited to off-roading as they were suited to the highway. She whooped again and pushed the Bronco through second and into third, the gravel pebbling the underside and panels reminding her of bullets. Then the rear window shattered beneath a long burst of automatic weapons fire.

Chapter 10

Fenna grabbed the steering wheel and ducked as safety glass plastered the back of the seats, scratched at her neck and lodged in the tangled strands of her dirty hair. She took a breath, recovered, and stomped on the accelerator, the Bronco lurched forward and Fenna swung the aging off-roader around a sharp bend to the right. A second burst of 9mm blistered the desert to the left of the vehicle, dirt and dust pluming under the impact. The track dropped beneath the wheels and Fenna guided the Bronco in a mad descent to the bottom of a shallow gulley. It handled well despite its age and Fenna spared a thought for the owner, only to forget him again as the lead SUV loomed large in the rear-view mirror and Fenna heard the growl of its engine beneath its massive hood. She risked a glance over her shoulder and through the shattered window but the windows of the SUV were smoked and the driver remained anonymous. *But no less lethal*, she surmised and willed the Bronco to go faster.

"Come on, girl," she yelled and leaned into the steering wheel.

The back end of the Bronco reared as the SUV rammed into it. Fenna yelled a second time as the Bronco threatened to flip, the rear wheels spinning free in the air almost a metre higher than the hood. She felt a twinge in her back as the Bronco touched down and the worn suspension failed to compensate. Fenna recovered, gritted her teeth and shuffled the sole of her boot back onto the accelerator pedal and knuckled down, riding the Bronco as it bucked down the track.

Fenna.

The voice caught her by surprise and she flicked her eyes to her right as if Nicklas was in the passenger seat beside her. She imagined him to be nonchalant, the epitome of calm, a true inspector of the Royal Canadian Mounted Police. And then she remembered he was a spy, a PET agent like herself. She flipped him a mental finger and ignored him.

Fenna. The road.

"Fuck off, Nicklas. I'm busy," she said and gripped the wheel. A quick glance in the rear-view mirror confirmed what she already knew – the SUV was still there, black and ominous. She spared an idle thought as to who might be behind the wheel. *Was it the Gunney's men, or Alice's minders?* And then Nicklas' voice punctured the thought and captured her attention.

End of the road, Fenna.

"What?" Fenna said and looked up. "Oh."

Fenna eased up on the accelerator. The receding growl of the SUVs motor confirmed that her pursuers knew she was cornered, trapped – again. She scanned the track as the Bronco sped down the last five hundred metres. There was a wooden building, shanty-like, on either side of the track, and a larger structure – a tired and worn plywood cabin – in the centre. It marked the end of the road. Fenna thought for a second, gripped the wheel and accelerated toward it.

What are you doing, Fenna?

"I could ask myself the same question," she said. "But somehow I think I already did."

And?

Fenna grinned, and, in that moment, for one joyous second, she forgot the wake of dead in her near and distant past, she ignored the chiding of her subconscious. In that brief moment, and for however long she had left before the end, Fenna chose to live.

"I'm tired of running."

But the cabin?

"Tired of being chased by men," she flicked her eyes to the mirror. The lead SUV had pulled back, the second had stopped, blocked the track and disgorged men with long rifles from its interior. Now all her focus was on the track and the cabin at the end of it.

You're not going to…

"Yes," she said. "And you had better get with the programme or get the fuck out." Fenna accelerated, squeezing the last, the richest, and the most precious drops of power from the Bronco's combustion engine – a gas-guzzling product of the eighties. "C'mon, girl," Fenna said and slapped the steering wheel with her palm. "Let's see what you've got."

Grit blasted the side panels of the Bronco. The motor roared. The cabin loomed. Fenna yelled.

"Do it," she screamed and shut her eyes as the front wheels of the Bronco bumped up and over the shallow deck with a crunch of desert-husked wood. The timber walls imploded in a cloud of splinters and dust. Nails, embedded in the panels and freed from the structure, clawed at the Bronco, as it careened through the one-roomed hovel, carrying the prospector's bed clinched beneath the bumper. Fenna opened her eyes a second before the Bronco burst through the rear of the structure and bounced onto a narrow ledge of flat ground. The bed crumpled under the front wheels, a blanket wrapped around the left wheel, its tattered tail twisting and slapping at the driver's door.

"Fuck," Fenna said, as the desert dropped from under the front of the Bronco and she was airborne again, her foot pounding on the brake pedal, her head slamming the top of the steering wheel as the old Ford bounced down a boulder-strewn slope and into a dry river bed. Fenna screamed the whole way down, biting her tongue and tasting blood as the Bronco's hood concertinaed upon impact with the dry bank of the river. The engine stalled and she slumped back in the seat. She blew the air from her lungs until the pressure in her chest told her she was alive and that she needed to breathe.

"Okay then," she said, after a long breath of dust-drenched air. She opened the door and slid out onto the river bed, leaning against the side of the vehicle until her legs stopped trembling. Fenna looked up at the splintered remains of the cabin, cursing at the sight of two men scrambling down the slope, rifles bobbing in their grasp. "Time to go," she said and climbed back into the Bronco and slammed the door.

The engine caught on the second turn of the key and Fenna blessed the ground its owner walked on. She shifted into reverse, cringing at the sound of the suspension grinding on the axle. With a last glance at the men behind her, she shifted into first and tickled the accelerator with her boot. The Bronco limped forward under protest, the screech and grind of metal on metal increasing in tempo and pitch as Fenna willed her bloody and beaten charge forward, drifting to the centre of the river bed. The Bronco bled oil in a spattered and broken line behind it, an easy trail to follow, but Fenna dismissed the thought in favour of the lone house on the horizon.

"They must have a phone," she said and shifted into second gear. The Bronco responded with a reluctant judder and the hiss of water boiling out of a burst radiator. Oil purged from the motor as Fenna accelerated into third. She ignored the crack of rounds as the men behind her punctured the tail gate with well-placed shots designed to intimidate her and remind her that they had not given up, whoever they were. She dipped her head to look up at the house at the top of the slope, in the bend of the dry river.

Fenna drove the Bronco as far as she could before it died, parched of oil and water, another desiccated husk of life succumbed to the desert. She pulled her pack from where it was lodged in front of the passenger seat and considered her own fate, preferring the thought of a quick cold death to a dry, hot one.

"Thanks, girl," she said as she climbed out of the Bronco. She tugged her pack onto her shoulders and jogged to the base of the slope before picking her way up and around the boulders to the house. The phone lines strung from the roof were a good sign. She opened the screen door and broke the lock of the main door with a kick. Once inside, she squinted in the gloom of what she imagined was a seldom-used office belonging to the highway maintenance company, the heavy jackets and dusty boots confirmed as much. Fenna found the phone on the desk and lifted the receiver. She dialled zero for an outside line and punched in the number she had memorised so many months earlier. The line crackled and buzzed, as if protesting the distance of the call, and then she heard a familiar voice answer with the flat guttural tone of Danish. For that moment it was the most beautiful voice Fenna could ever remember hearing.

"Jarnvig?" she said and waited.

"Yes?"

"It's Fenna."

Jarnvig grunted and Fenna imagined him shifting position. She glanced at her watch and realised, with the time difference, he was likely finishing his shift. It would be early evening in Denmark.

"I thought we agreed you would never call this number."

"We did."

"And yet?" he said and added a silent rebuke in the weight and length of his pause. "What do you need?"

"Help. A ticket out of here. Safe passage…"

"Stop, Fenna," he paused again as Fenna took a breath. "Where are you?"

"In a house, north of the base."

"Why?"

"I killed someone," she said, tapping her hand and flicking her gaze from one window to the other as she waited for Jarnvig to process the information.

"Anyone important?" he said.

"You're not going to ask why?"

"I would say *who* is more important right now. If I know who, then I might be able to help."

"Might? Fuck, Jarnvig…"

"Who was it, Konstabel?"

Fenna told him. "It was me or him," she added.

"Which begs me to ask the question *why*?"

"Because of the girl, Al…"

"I don't need to know her name." Jarnvig cut her off. "I thought I ordered you to leave her alone?"

"Nicklas said…"

"He was relaying my orders. Damn it, Fenna…"

Fenna whirled at the sound of gravel crunching beneath what she imagined were large military boots outside the house.

"I don't have much time," she said.

"And neither do I," Jarnvig said and cursed. "I need you in Nuuk, not some American Black Site in the middle of the fucking desert."

"Jarnvig," Fenna said and stared at the window.

"What?"

"They're here."

A tall man, his biceps larger than Fenna's neck, steadied his M4 carbine in one hand as he waved his finger at Fenna, motioning for her to hang up.

"Stall them. I need time."

"I can't," Fenna said, as the man's partner entered from the door at the front of the house. Fenna turned in a slow circle to face him. He stalked around the furniture toward her.

"I'll get someone to you, Konstabel. Just hang in there. Keep breathing."

Breathing was fast becoming an art form. The man yanked the phone from her hand and pulled a black hood from his belt.

"Put it on," he said, as he tossed it at Fenna. She caught it and held it in front of her. "Now," he said as the man with the M4 walked in.

"We could talk about this," Fenna said and twisted the hood between her fingers.

"Tell that to the Gunney," the man said.

"He's here?" Fenna said and arched her eyebrow.

"Funny," the man said and drew his pistol from the holster

attached to his chest rig. "Now put on the fucking hood, Konstabel, before I put a bullet through your pretty little skull."

"Do it," his partner said and jabbed the barrel of his M4 into Fenna's shoulder. Fenna resisted the temptation to twist and grab the carbine, favouring instead the brief moment of calm before the inevitable storm.

"All right," she said and lifted the hood to her head. Nicklas, she mused, was silent for a change, and it was then that she realised he had always been silent, and that she truly was alone. The man behind her tugged her pack from her back as soon as her head was covered. Fenna stumbled forward and into the butt of her captor's pistol, as she fell into another kind of blackness, one that she knew only too well.

Chapter 11

The thick hood muffled the sounds of activity inside the SUV, but Fenna knew the men were rifling through her gear as the driver drove off the gravel strip in front of the house and onto the highway. Fenna toyed with the ends of the plastic strips the men had used to bind her wrists. She had lost count of the number of times she had been bound in this way. It was almost laughable.

"Laugh it up, Princess. We'll see how funny you think it is when we start your interrogation."

"You don't have to interrogate me. I'll talk."

"Sure you will, but we want to have a little fun first," the man said. Fenna recognised his voice and pictured the man with the M4, the one who had poked her with the barrel.

"Perks of the job," said the other man. Fenna heard him grunt and flick through the pages of the LOMROG report. "What's this?"

"Bedtime reading," she said, and tensed in anticipation of the man striking her, but he seemed more interested in the report than her sarcasm. Fenna realised that they had yet to lay a hand on her. The thought festered in her mind beneath the hood, occupying her thoughts and distracting her from the driver's curses as he slammed on the brakes. Fenna's head pounded into the passenger seat, as the men opened doors and leapt out onto the highway. She could hear the click and clack of weapons being readied and the concise and confident commands the men exchanged.

"What's going on?" she asked, only to realise that the SUV was empty. The engine growled and she twisted her head to the left to hear the growl of the second SUV just a few metres away.

"Behind us," a voice said. Fenna assumed it was one of the men from the second SUV. Fenna dipped her head, pinched the hood between her palms and tugged it off. She blinked in the noon-day sun and scanned her environment in all directions.

The SUVs were blocked by three white SUVs in front and two vans behind. Her captors were outnumbered at least two to one, and the desert air was heavy with the taint of testosterone and tension. Fenna slipped out of the SUV and leaned against the side.

"Get back in the vehicle, Princess. This will all be over in a heartbeat." The man Fenna realised was the leader didn't even look at her, his finger feathering the trigger of his M4 carbine as he leaned into the hinges of the passenger door. The driver assumed a similar position on the opposite side of the vehicle.

"Who are they?" she asked.

"Unknown, but I'm guessing they're not friendly," he said.

"Not to you anyway." Fenna looked beyond the roadblock and noticed a police patrol car slowing traffic to a stop a few hundred metres further up the highway. A quick glance behind her confirmed that they had done the same in both directions. The operation had a surgical Scandinavian feel about it, *or Canadian*, she realised as she scanned the men for a glimpse of Nicklas. They were wearing masks and helmets, but she recognised the stance of one man, the way he held his automatic rifle as he approached the SUVs.

"That's far enough," the leader said. "Unless you want lead for lunch?"

"Just want to talk," the man said and Fenna smiled as she recognised his voice.

"So talk," the leader said, before quietening his voice and addressing the driver. "If this fool so much as breathes wrong…"

"Got it, boss."

Fenna watched as Nicklas tugged his mask down to his neck, slung his rifle and removed his helmet. He waved and indicated that he intended to approach.

"You ditch your weapon, you can come closer."

"All right," Nicklas said and lowered his rifle to the ground. "But I'm keeping my sidearm."

"Sure you are. All buttoned up and snug in that fancy holster." The leader slung his weapon over his shoulder and rested his arms on the sill of the open window. "What do you want to talk about?"

"The girl," Nicklas said and nodded at Fenna.

"Okay."

"Both of them."

The leader tensed. Fenna watched as he straightened his back. He moved one hand from the window to the pistol strapped in a holster around his right thigh. "You might want to reconsider that, Inspector."

"So you know who I am? That's good," he said and took another step closer. Fenna couldn't see the leader's face, but she doubted he returned Nicklas' smile. He unsnapped the holster and closed his fingers around the pistol grip. Fenna shuffled forward, closer, but a voice behind her whispered for her to stop.

"Let my boss talk, unhindered," the man with the M4 said, "and I might just let you live." Fenna nodded. "Good. Now let's hear what your boyfriend has to say."

"Let's hear it, RCMP, before I lose my sense of bipartisanship." Fenna noted the man's hand did not stray from his pistol.

"My friend, the Konstabel," Nicklas said, with a gesture toward Fenna, "is too curious for her own good."

"On that we agree."

"But she knows nothing. I can promise you that."

"Promises? Shit, Inspector, promises mean nothing to me."

"That's right, of course," Nicklas said and nodded. He looked up at a glint of metal high up in the sky. "Are they with you?"

"Unlikely." The leader glanced at the drone circling above them. He looked at Nicklas. "We're wasting time. Get to it."

"The Konstabel is important to us, to the group I represent. She is needed in the north."

"And?"

"And I have been instructed to inform you that, when the time comes, you have our support."

"Really?"

"Yes."

"We have your support?"

"Yes," Nicklas said and crossed his hands in front of the buckle on his webbing belt.

"You can confirm that?" said the leader, as the man guarding Fenna fidgeted. The tension ratcheted up another notch and the leader slipped the pistol from his holster.

"You're going to get a call. Any second now."

"Boss?" Fenna's guard said, as the leader's mobile phone burred in his pocket. Fenna watched as he used his left hand to answer the call, holstering the pistol as he listened and nodded.

"Let's go," the leader said, as he pocketed his mobile and slid into the passenger seat. The man behind Fenna shoved her away from the SUV, reached inside, and threw her pack onto the highway. The wheels were moving as he tossed the LOMROG report out of the window. Nicklas' men made a hole in the roadblock as the SUVs roared past him and disappeared in the direction of the DTC. Fenna shook her head and frowned as Nicklas picked up his rifle, tucked his helmet under his arm and walked toward her.

"Fenna," he said, as he cut the ties around her wrists with a folding knife from his belt.

She glared at him. "What the fuck was all that about?"

"I could ask you the same thing. Jarnvig certainly wants to know."

"Jarnvig?"

"You called him."

"And you were pretty quick to get here," Fenna said, pulling her arm away as Nicklas guided her to the side of the road, away from the traffic released by the police behind them. "I thought you had been called away. Far away."

"Far enough," Nicklas said and shrugged. "Besides," he said and grinned. "You passed the test."

"The test? What fucking test?"

"Your first kill."

"What?" Fenna clenched her fist and raised it. Nicklas dropped his right hand to the grip of his pistol.

"Stand down, Konstabel."

"Stand down?" Fenna spat in his face. She took two steps toward the desert before wheeling, and jabbing her finger at Nicklas. "I killed a man."

"Yes," Nicklas said and wiped his face with his hand.

"With a knife…"

"Yes. A knife. You're operational now. Congratulations."

"Congratulations?" Fenna gripped her hair in her fists. She yelled as she tore out two chunks of dirty blonde hair. "Would you have congratulated him, the Gunney, if he had killed me? Would you?" she said and cast the hair into the wind. Several strands caught in the Velcro of Nicklas' vest and he plucked them free, twisting Fenna's hair between his finger and thumb as he answered.

"No," he said and sighed. He let his hand drop, the hair still pinched between his fingers.

"He could have killed me."

"Yes."

Fenna trembled as she took a step closer to Nicklas. He let his right hand fall from his pistol. Her hair twisted in the wake of the cars speeding past them, the wind buffeting her body.

"What about us? Was that a test too?"

"No."

"So you fuck on your own time, Inspector? How convenient," she said, her bottom lip quivered.

"Fenna…"

"No, Nicklas," she said and shook her head. "No." Fenna walked past him, picked up her pack and the report and strode into the desert.

"Fenna," he called after her.

"Stay out of my head, Nicklas," she said and continued walking. Sooner or later, she realised, she would have to stop, or they would force her to. Her mission was waiting. But right now, *right fucking now, they can wait*, she told herself. Fenna let the wind dry her tears as they streaked down her cheek.

"A test," she said. "It was a fucking test." Fenna stopped and looked back at Nicklas. "And what about Alice?" she said, but either the wind took her words or Nicklas had been ordered not to hear them.

Fenna found a flat boulder and sat down. She let the pack fall onto the ground between her dusty boots. She kicked at the straps, flicking them into a straight line pointing toward the highway. She untied her laces and removed her boots. Her bare feet were blotched with dust and dirt, her toes black beneath the nails. She bent forward to pick at the dirt with her fingers, rubbing her toes until they were red, raw, and warm to the touch. They stung, but Fenna rubbed them one more time, then stood and squirmed the soles of her tiny feet in the sand, the dead and dry skin rasping from her feet and into the dirt. *My DNA*, she mused, *part of the desert now.*

She looked up as Nicklas picked his way around the boulders toward her. She placed her hands in her lap and watched him as he approached. "Come to take me away?" she said, as he stopped in front of her.

"Those are my orders."

"From whom? Jarnvig?"

"Amongst others, yes," he said and let his hands fall to his sides.

The wind carried a wisp of red dust between them, coating his boots and tickling her skin.

"Fenna," he said.

"What?"

"What happened in the boxing ring, that wasn't Jarnvig…"

"I know," she said.

"It was me," he said, his voice rasping like the sand across her feet.

Fenna looked up at the gleam of metal, circling, droning above them.

"Did you hear me?" Nicklas said.

"Yes," she said. She got up and shouldered her pack, nodding toward the men waiting for them on the highway. "I'm ready now."

The City

COPENHAGEN, DENMARK

Chapter 12

BRITISH AIRWAYS TRANSATLANTIC FLIGHT

Fenna braced her hands, palms flat, against the sides of the space; she had to bend her elbows. The walls thrummed beneath her fingers and the sensation of movement, erratic, undisciplined, and violent, tugged at her stomach. She looked up at an insistent knock at the door.

"The seatbelt sign is on," said a voice, muffled, on the other side of the door. "You must return to your seat."

Fenna ignored the woman. She slid her palms up the walls and stood up. She held onto the sink, glancing at herself in the mirror and focusing, of all things, on the chestnut roots of her hair pushing the blonde strands further from her scalp.

I'll have to colour it again, she thought.

Fenna averted her eyes from the reflection. She didn't want to confront the killer she had become. *I passed the test.* The thought flickered through her mind as the flight attendant thumped her fist on the door.

"I'm going to have to open the door if you don't return to your seat."

Fenna sat down on the toilet seat and waited.

Her memories of the chatter and bustle of two American airports, the smell of coffee and food stalls, restaurants and terminal cafés competing for customers turned her stomach once more as the Boeing 777 aircraft, a *British Airways* transatlantic flight, was buffeted by another bout of turbulence. *It's like sledging*, she mused. *Long stretches of smooth, rapid ice, followed by short, intense sections of challenging geography – the shifting peaks of the ice foot along the coastline, a steep gulley, a wolf.* Fenna's thoughts centred on the wolf, and, for a few precious moments, she forgot her nausea, sidelined her murderous thoughts, and pictured the lanky gait of the white Arctic Wolf, its black eyes reminiscent of the polar bear – two obsidian orbs pressed into a white furry face. The wolf's face was lean, like its body, a stark contrast to the bulk of the bear. Fenna considered her own body, the tight muscles pressing at her skeleton-hugging skin. She was the wolf, loping alongside the bear, her boots secured in the bindings of her skis, Mikael towering above her to her right, the wind abrading their faces with snow needles.

I'm going back, she thought as the flight attendant unlocked the door and scolded her with official-sounding words that Fenna chose not to understand.

"In future," the woman said, as she escorted Fenna to her seat. "When the seatbelt sign is on…"

Fenna ignored her as she squirmed past the passenger sitting by the aisle, lifted the belt buckle and flopped onto the seat. The flight attendant tutted and wove her way back to her seat by the exit. If Fenna had been bothered she might have withered under the woman's glare, instead she wiped her hand across her face, buckled the belt across her lap, and reached for the bottle of water she had tucked into the mesh pocket in front of her.

"You don't fly well?" said the passenger on her left, the teenage girl on Fenna's right was hidden beneath a blanket, and Fenna envied the girl's indifference to the turbulence and the activity around her.

"Sorry?" she said, facing him, an African American she imagined to be in his sixties.

"Flying," he said. "You don't like it?"

"It's okay," Fenna said and shrugged. "I'm not usually bothered by it. I've just had a rough time lately."

The man turned in his seat and held out his hand in greeting. "Solomon," he said and shook Fenna's hand. He frowned as she let go. "That's a strong grip for a pretty child such as yourself."

"Yes," Fenna said and smiled.

"You have a name to go with that grip?" he said and made a show of massaging his hand.

"Yes." She laughed. "Fenna," she said and paused to smile at the look on Solomon's face. "I'm from Denmark."

"Well," he said and relaxed back in his seat. "I never met nobody from Denmark before."

"Now you have," Fenna said and took a sip of water.

"And what do you do, child?" he said with a glance at Fenna's clothes and a nod at her hands. "I'm thinking you don't work in no convenience store."

"No. I'm in the military," Fenna said. *I can't hide it*, she realised.

"Ah," he said. Solomon closed his eyes for a moment and Fenna stared at the husks of white whiskers, the salt in his peppery stubble. The corner of her mouth twitched and she hid her smile behind the lip of the bottle as Solomon opened his eyes.

"My son," he said. "He was in the military. He sent me letters all the time. Then," Solomon said and reached for Fenna's hand, "he stop. You know, child? From the one day, to the next. The letters just stop." Fenna squeezed Solomon's hand. He took a breath and looked at her as he spoke. "They sent me his things, what he had left, in his locker or some such. There was one last letter. He stay writing, right up to the end." Solomon chewed at his lip. Fenna squeezed his hand one more time. "He done good by his family, my son."

"What was his name?"

"Jesse," Solomon said. The wrinkles around his eyes spread, splayed like slender toes as he smiled. "Jesse Solomon Patrick Owens."

"Patrick?"

"Yup. Mama, my Mary, she stay Catholic all this time. Even now, still Catholic."

"Why isn't she with you?" Fenna asked as Solomon squeezed her hand and let go. He gripped the ends of the seat rests as if he was about to stand.

"Oh, she don't travel too well. Besides," he said and turned to Fenna, "my family said said it was best I go alone."

"Go where?"

"Germany," he said. "My son died in Germany." Solomon chuckled for a moment. "You was thinking Afghanistan, wasn't you?"

"Yes."

"You ain't the first. But no, he died in a training accident. He was drivin' a tank somewhere east of Germany. Estonia, or some such." Solomon leaned back in his seat. "The whole world is squaring their shoulders, getting' ready for a spittin' competition, and my son died for it."

"I'm sorry," Fenna said and pressed her hand against Solomon's arm as he nodded.

"I know you are, child," he said and turned his head to the side. He smiled at Fenna, flicking his eyes once at the seatbelt sign as it disappeared with a low ping. "Family is never more important than when there is none. I just wish I knew that before. I might have taken this trip before he died." Solomon shook his head and sighed as he pushed himself out of his seat. He stopped in the aisle, resting his hands on the seat backs for balance. "My turn to visit the tiny John," he said and winked.

She watched him go, tugged the in-flight magazine from the mesh pocket, and, now that the turbulence had disappeared, made herself comfortable. Fenna flipped through the magazine, stopping to read the article predicting the beginning of the end for the American President's administration. According to the article, his popularity was falling further than predicted, even among his staunch supporters and members of his own party. *Defence cuts*, Fenna thought as she closed the magazine. *There's one place I wouldn't miss if he cut it from the budget.* She looked out of the window, but the vast stretch of sea below looked uncannily like sand, and the desert, and her actions in it, occupied her for the remainder of the flight.

HEATHROW AIRPORT, ENGLAND

Fenna bought Solomon a coffee while they waited for a connecting flight from Heathrow Airport. She lost herself in the details of his family, picturing the pranks he and his brothers played as children, smiling at the scolding they had received from his mother, wincing at the slipper his father had used later that same night. *Family.* The thought lingered in her mind, as she remembered her father, and the time they had spent together before he died, in Afghanistan.

Fenna enjoyed another hour of Solomon's company and then he had to leave to catch his flight. She hugged him when he left. She had no choice. The big African American wrapped his arms around her slight frame and pulled her close.

"I don't know where you is heading, child, but be safe."

"I will," she said. "And thanks."

"For what?" he said, as he let go of her and extended the handle on his walk-on baggage.

"For our conversation," Fenna said. "About family."

"Conversation?" Solomon laughed. "Child, a *conversation* requires two people to talk. I done all the talkin'. But you a good listener, and it's me that should be a thanking you." He winked and tipped his baggage onto the back wheels. "You take care now, child. And if you're ever in Washington State," he said. "Well, there ain't too many Solomon Owens in the phone book. You be sure to look me up."

"I will," said Fenna as Solomon waved and walked away. She sat down as he turned the corner and took a sip of coffee. She tipped the paper cup to drain it. She sat for another five minutes and thought about her extraction from Arizona, and her re-entry to Denmark. *If there is a watch list for agents going off the reservation*, she mused. *I don't seem to be on it.* Fenna slid her pack out from under the table, shouldered it, and made her way to the departure gate.

KASTRUP AIRPORT, DENMARK

The flight from London to Copenhagen was too short for Fenna to see the new Jason Bourne movie to the end, but she watched it anyway. *The CIA doesn't need a foreign state to fight*, she thought and shook her head, *they're too busy fighting themselves.* Analysing the movie helped Fenna distance herself from the close-quarters fighting, the quiet grunts and gasps from the combatants, the hiss of air leaking from a punctured throat. Fenna gripped the armrests and, closing her eyes, she forced the image of the Gunney from her mind as the aircraft began its descent. She opened her eyes again as the wheels kissed the runway and the pilot taxied to the gate.

Per Jarnvig was waiting for her as she got off the plane. He guided her around and through passport control without a word. He ushered Fenna into a small office in the customs area, closed the door, and gestured for her to sit at the table.

"This room is secure," he said and plunged Fenna back into the world from which she had escaped with Solomon. She waited for him to sit down.

"I just want to say…" she said and stopped as Jarnvig lifted his hand.

"Don't," he said. "It's done. You passed the test."

"A man died. I killed him."

"Yes," Jarnvig nodded. "And passed the test." He smoothed his hands on the table. "It's time to move on, Konstabel. I need you to move on. I need you in Greenland."

"So I can kill another man?"

"If necessary," he said and shrugged. "Yes."

"I thought you were going to train me as an investigator. That's what I signed up for."

"No," Jarnvig said and shook his head. "The minute you decided to board that plane to Toronto, and pull the trigger on Humble, you agreed to do whatever job I deemed necessary." Jarnvig tapped a finger on the table. Fenna focused for a moment on his groomed nails, so different from her own. "You showed real grit in Greenland," he said. "I call it potential, and when I recognise that in a person, I'm compelled to do something useful with it. Your career with the Navy is over, Konstabel. You could never have returned to the Sirius Patrol, not after Mikael's death."

"I didn't kill him," Fenna said and jabbed her finger at Jarnvig.

"We have established that, and I believe you. But let's get something straight, Konstabel. When I tell you to do something, you do it, to the letter. If I tell you to kill someone, or if the situation requires it, you do it. Without pause. Without question. Do you understand, Konstabel?" Fenna leaned back in her chair and splayed her hands on the surface of the table. "Because if you don't…"

"I understand," Fenna said and stared at Jarnvig.

"Good," he said and rested his hands in his lap. "Now, tell me what you know about the LOMROG expedition."

Chapter 13

Per Jarnvig was a thorough man. During the first two hours of her briefing in the tiny customs office Jarnvig focused on tiny details buried within the LOMROG report, as if he was teasing threads from a shirt, only to push them back in, one millimetre at a time, until the garment was still a shirt, but essentially rewoven. The configuration was the same, but the layered meaning and significance of each thread was known and its place in the garment understood. Fenna knew it was for her benefit, but she wished the process would go faster.

"Tell me again about Dr Johansson," Jarnvig said. He paused at a knock on the door. Fenna brightened at the smell of the fresh coffee and breakfast rolls a customs officer brought in on a tray. "Thank you." Jarnvig waited for the man to place the tray on the table, gesturing for Fenna to help herself. He started talking again once the man had left and closed the door. "Dr Johansson?" he said and reached for his coffee.

"He was enthusiastic," Fenna said, wiping butter from her lips with the back of her hand. "His report is optimistic. It's part field report, part nature book…"

"And another part mystery suspense."

"Yes. About halfway through the expedition."

"The report was originally intended to be posted online in the public domain," Jarnvig said and reached for a roll. The crusty exterior cracked into jagged flakes as he cut into it with the serrated teeth of the thin plastic knife; Fenna was reminded of sea ice breaking up in June along Greenland's east coast. "Obviously, his superior…"

"Dr Peters. The Canadian," said Fenna.

"Yes," Jarnvig said, "she put a stop to that." He put down the knife and peeled a greasy square of cheese from a paper plate on the tray. Fenna noted that he used no butter and realised she was hungry. She took a second breakfast roll from the tray and waited for Jarnvig to continue. "Johansson's report took on a different character after the midway point of the expedition, when the first data started to come in. What is your take on that?" Fenna tried to recall the particular section of the report and reached for her pack. Jarnvig stopped her with a raised hand. "Let's see what you can remember, shall we?"

"Is this a test?" Fenna said, as she sat back in her seat. Jarnvig took a bite of his roll. "All right," she said. "Johansson was convinced that someone had tampered with the instruments." She paused, waiting for Jarnvig. He took another bite. "The Kongsberg EM 122 multibeam echo sounder in particular."

"Go on."

"As Johansson explains, the data is recorded within a known reliable range. The report was very clear about the margin of error, but…"

"The readings were way beyond that."

"Yes. Johansson believed the machine needed to be recalibrated."

"And he approached Dr Lorentzen."

"Because he is the so-called authority on the MBES," Fenna said and smiled. She realised she was enjoying the step-by-step process of analysing the details of the report. She had, she remembered, been impressed by Johansson's style of writing, his descriptions of standing at the bow of the *Odin* as it broke through the ice, plying the northern waters, heading for the pole. When his style had changed, she found the reading less interesting, reminding her more of the science texts at Gymnasium. But then the report shifted character again, beyond the initial documentation of the problems with the MBES, to a series of speculations and deductions, as Johansson focused on his conviction that the instrument had been tampered with. She forgot about her jetlag, brushed a flake of bread from her chin and cupped her hands around the paper cup of coffee. She leaned over the table and grinned. "Lorentzen went from scientist to suspect," she said.

"Over the course of three days."

"By which time they were approaching the most northerly boundary of the operating area."

"You mean the pole."

"Yes."

"So?" Jarnvig said and took a sip of coffee.

Fenna looked away for a moment. She tried to recall the next sequence of events, enjoying the test for what it was, enjoying the lack of testosterone and sweat. This was the kind of investigating she had assumed Jarnvig wanted her to do. *And I could be good at it*, she thought as she faced Jarnvig.

"Johansson was convinced that, even with the margin of error, the data would reveal that Greenland's continental shelf was connected to the North Pole. So were his colleagues."

"What do we know about Johansson?"

"He is Swedish. In his forties. Married with three kids. A career scientist, mortgaged beyond belief," Fenna said and grinned. "I'm sure his wife despairs, but loves him for it."

"I am sure she does," Jarnvig said and allowed a faint smile to creep across his lips. "And Lorentzen?"

"Dr Karl Lorentzen. Danish. Unmarried." *Attractive*, she remembered.

"And highly respected in the community. Lorentzen has been the so-called expert on the continental shelf for the past five years. He is an established scientist, and a regular publisher of articles for the Danish Polar Center." Fenna sipped her coffee as Jarnvig continued. "I met Lorentzen on two occasions, although I doubt he will remember me. He is popular at functions, and has an attractive personality to match those good looks of his." He paused and looked at Fenna. "You read his profile?"

"And saw the picture," Fenna said, smiling at the memory.

"Good," Jarnvig said and leaned back in his chair. He waited for Fenna to finish her coffee. "He is based in Nuuk, seconded to the Department for Natural Resources. He has an office there. He divides his time between the office, holding talks at Katuaq, the cultural centre, and giving lucrative lectures to tourists on the cruise ships visiting the capital." Jarnvig paused as Fenna sat up straight in her chair. "I have checked the location of *The Ice Star*, Konstabel." He smiled as Fenna relaxed. "It is currently in the Bahamas."

"It wouldn't have mattered," she said, as she pushed the paper cup between her fingers.

"We both know it would," Jarnvig said.

Yes, Fenna thought, *it would have.* She remembered the dank hold and the cold metal deck as Dina, beaten, bruised, and bloody, had pressed her naked body into Fenna for warmth. She remembered the elephantine image of Lunk, the bandage ballooning the side of his head as it covered the ear she had perforated for him when he had tried to rape her on the bathroom floor, and, finally, the boom of the shot that killed him as it reverberated around the hold, the gun steady in Dina's hand. Fenna gripped the paper cup, crushed it in one hand and nodded at Jarnvig. "Good," she said and nodded for him to continue.

"When Lorentzen is not charming tourists and politicians," Jarnvig said, as he appraised Fenna with a casual glance, "he acts as an advisor to the Chinese representatives, currently in talks with Tunstall Mining Consolidated."

"The Chinese are in the process of buying Tunstall?" Fenna said and smiled. *I'm okay now*, she thought. *Back on track.*

"Yes, Tunstall carried out the original geological surveys, at great expense."

"But they can't afford to begin operations."

"Few private companies can," Jarnvig said and tapped the table. "The standard operating procedure is to make a good show of it and deplete the company funds to show a maximum level of commitment…"

"And hope to be bought out by a larger company?"

"Or country."

"China."

"Exactly." Jarnvig gestured at Fenna's wrinkled paper cup. "More coffee?"

"Yes," Fenna said and waited as Jarnvig sent a text on his mobile. The LOMROG report was the only reading material she had while she was in the desert. She looked at the mobile in Jarnvig's hand and wondered if she had been deprived her own for security reasons, or to keep her in the dark and pique her curiosity. *If it was the latter*, she mused, *it had worked.* Her mind swirled with the different threads she and Jarnvig had teased out of the story. *I'm in. I'm invested. So let's cut to the chase and get started.* Fenna felt the fatigue of flying lift from her shoulders and she straightened her back. Jarnvig looked up. When Fenna smiled, so did he.

"Konstabel?" he said and pocketed his mobile.

"I was thinking about the Chinese, and the mining site."

"Isukasia," said Jarnvig. "There has been some confusion around the name, but the proposed site for the iron mine is on the edge of the ice sheet, north of Nuuk, in the mountains at the top of Nuuk fjord."

Fenna frowned and shook her head. "I'm not familiar with it."

"And why should you be? Sirius patrols in Northeast Greenland.

Beyond looking for new breeding stock amongst the sledge dogs on the west coast, Sirius have no business in Nuuk."

"But the headquarters for Arctic Command are in Nuuk," Fenna said.

"Yes, and I want you to avoid them at all costs."

"Then what exactly do you want me to do?"

Jarnvig turned at a knock on the door. Fenna recognised the routine, and waited until the customs officer had exchanged the empty tray for a new one with fresh coffee. Jarnvig continued once the officer had left the room.

"China was afforded observer status on the Arctic Council in 2013. There is no doubt that China is paving a road to the Arctic. They have recognised the wealth of raw material in Greenland, and they are in a position to fund operations, such as Tunstall. The quest for oil might have dipped out of the media spotlight – it's too expensive and technically challenging for limited rewards, but the Chinese plans to invest in Greenland have stirred up the Greenlandic government, and the environmentalists - including a lot of Danes, I might add. The Chinese plan includes wild propositions of a new harbour, a new airport, and a new city for the Chinese workers. There will be few jobs for Greenlanders, but, potentially, a lot of investment, and likely benefits for the Greenlandic elite. If anything comes of this, it will put Greenland on the map and confirm China as a major player in the Arctic."

"I can see that, but where do I fit in?"

Jarnvig paused for a moment to pull a thin folder from his briefcase and place it on the table. "The LOMROG expedition, as you know, was funded as a means of confirming, once and for all, who owns the North Pole. The Russians have claimed it, but the evidence is weak. LOMROG should have put an end to that. Two weeks from now, a representative of the Danish Government will present the findings of the LOMROG report to the UNCLOS hearing, convened to satisfy the Danish claim to the Pole. We believe…"

"We? Who's *we*?"

"Konstabel?"

"Sorry," Fenna raised her hands in apology.

"It is believed," Jarnvig said and continued, "that the Danish representative will present the LOMROG findings as they are, currently, with no mention of any discrepancies, or appeal for more time to launch a new expedition."

"So," Fenna said, "effectively giving up Denmark's claim to the Pole?"

"Yes," said Jarnvig. "Now, whereas that might be attractive in some circles – maintaining sovereignty over Northeast Greenland is a challenge at best, but doing the same as far as the Pole will require a serious amount of funding…"

"But the potential financial rewards through shipping routes…" Fenna suppressed a shiver as she recalled Humble's words and his motivations aboard *The Ice Star.*

"Given the current warming of the climate and the retreat of the sea ice," Jarnvig said and nodded. "Yes, there is potential there, which is why we are convinced that our Danish representative, unbeknown to him, is being influenced by a foreign power."

"The Chinese."

"Most likely, but unconfirmed. That's where you come in."

A jolt of adrenalin surged through her at the prospect of a new mission. A real investigation, she realised, was just what she had been looking for. *A chance to prove myself, on a level playing field for once.*

"As you already know, you are going to join Lorentzen, as a representative from Tunstall Mining Consolidated."

"Hah," Fenna snorted. "I'll be exposed in a heartbeat."

"Hence the intensive geology course tomorrow."

"Yes, Nicklas mentioned that. And afterward?"

"You must find evidence to support Johansson's theory that the instruments were tampered with. You have to prove the link between the Chinese and the representative at the UNCLOS hearing."

"Is that all?" Fenna said. She suppressed a wry smile, as she wondered where to start.

"No. Not quite," said Jarnvig. Fenna waited as he opened the folder and pushed it across the table toward Fenna. She studied the grainy image of a man sprawled on the deck of a ship. There was blood on the deck. "If you recall the notes at the end of the LOMROG report, you'll remember that the report never did get posted online."

"Yes," Fenna said as she studied the photo. "I guessed it was something to do with Johansson's accusations." She moved closer to examine the photograph and tapped the image with her finger. "The metal object sticking out of the chest." She looked up. "Is that the tip of an ice axe?"

"It is." Jarnvig said, and added, "The rest of the axe, the shaft and the adze, is hidden beneath the body. It was written up as a freak accident, but it is clear that the axe penetrated the man's body from behind, with enough force to puncture his sternum." Jarnvig waited as Fenna looked up. "You'll recall, from the report, that it was published posthumously."

"Posthumously? I missed that."

"Yes," Jarnvig said as he leaned forward to tap the centre of the photograph. "You're looking at the body of Johansson. About twenty minutes after his death."

Fenna studied the photograph as Jarnvig removed his finger. She noticed the striations of blood frozen to the deck, the look of anguish pasted to the man's face, and the impression of a boot, the ridges of its sole preserved on the deck, frozen for all to see.

"Find Johansson's killer, Konstabel. Bring me substantial evidence…" Jarnvig said, his voice faltering for a moment, "and I will put Lorentzen away for good."

"You think it is him?"

"I have my suspicions," Jarnvig said. "Do it quickly, and I'll get the Pole for Denmark."

"For Greenland," Fenna said, her voice a whisper, as she studied the dead Swede. *Another body on another ship*, she said to herself. *It's like* The Ice Star *all over again*. The thought lingered as Jarnvig pulled the folder from beneath her fingers and closed it. *Here we go again.*

Chapter 14

COPENHAGEN, DENMARK

Copenhagen in spring buzzed like any other major European city. Fenna tried to ignore the bustle on the street beneath her hotel window, choosing instead to enjoy the lazy day ahead of her, before her meeting with the geology professor later in the evening. She curled her leg over the duvet, trapping the thick quilt between her knees. The traffic continued to tease her with the occasional hiss of a large vehicle – a bus or a lorry – interspersed with the wail of a two-tone siren and the single ring of a bicycle bell. She smiled at the bell, and the next one, imagining a street twisting with steams of confused tourists, and a steady stream of Danes plying the international waters, armed with shrill bells and sharp tongues. Fenna had never liked the city, but from her hotel room overlooking the train station and Tivoli Gardens, she revelled in a sense of familiar comfort and let the twinges of patriotism tug her out of bed. She wrapped a sheet around her body, her elbows pressing the thin material into sharp angles as she padded barefoot across the carpet, pulled back the curtains and looked out onto the activity below her. The coffee machine with a built-in clock alarm filled the room with Radio P3's playlist, insignificant banter, and the smell of coffee.

"I could get used to this," she said and smiled. "Better than a barrack in the desert."

She thought about Jarnvig's methods as the coffee brewed, the way he sent her into the desert, to train, fight, and kill. *To kill*, as if she was a real secret agent, an assassin, being hazed, hounded, and herded, funnelled into the nastiest and narrowest phase of her training, squeezed into a tight corner and expected to kill or be killed. *Well*, she mused, *I killed. And now I'm here.*

The coffee machine beeped and she let the sheet slip to the floor as she walked into the kitchen area of the room. Fenna used the same cup from the night before and filled it to the brim. She eyed the plastic *Matas* shopping bag on the counter and smiled as she took her first sip of coffee. She pulled down one corner of the bag and chuckled at the result of Jarnvig's shopping expedition. The bag contained hair dye and an assortment of make-up. She put down her cup, picked up one of the boxes of dye and walked into the bathroom, but the headlines of the hourly news made her stop.

"Strong criticism of the American President continues, as more military bases are marked for closure in the White House's unprecedented budget reforms, the first ever to target American military spending to such a degree under a Republican President."

Fenna closed the bathroom door, turned on the shower, and drowned out the radio broadcast with a deluge of hot water.

Once she was showered and towelled dry, she waited for the mirror to demist enough to see her reflection and apply the hair colour. She opened the packet while she waited, pulled out the product and stopped.

"Black?" Fenna sighed and looked in the mirror. "I'm going to have to do it all," she said, with a glance down the length of her body. She recalled the folder Jarnvig had given her on leaving the airport, her profile and the physical description of her new alias. She must have glossed over the part that said she had black hair, and suddenly it made sense that Jarnvig needed a new photograph for her passport, something he had requested as he dropped her off at the hotel. Fenna shrugged, read the instructions and applied the product to her hair. When she was done, she used the scissors from the complementary sewing kit to tidy up her fringe.

Jarnvig had left a new suitcase in the hotel room. It contained a selection of clothes fit for a young geologist, jeans, t-shirt, and a figure-hugging fleece. The worn-in boots surprised her; she wondered who might have the same size feet to break in her boots.

"And the rest of my outfit," she said, as she took a closer look at her clothes. Jarnvig, it seemed, was a stickler for details and was leaving nothing to chance. She tied her boot laces, grabbed her pack and her copy of the LOMROG report, pulled the key card from the unit by the door and left the room. Two minutes later and she was on the street among the tourists, and walking past the entrance to Tivoli and the Hard Rock Café. Fenna drank in the air of the city and found she preferred it, for the moment at least, to the dry air of the Arizona desert. She spared a brief thought for Nicklas, and then pushed him out of her mind and into a mental compartment labelled: Jarnvig's Puppets. There was room in that headspace for more than one, she realised, and was suddenly conscious of her new hair colour, her newly fashioned clothes, and her new mission. The thoughts occupied her all the way to the University of Copenhagen's Department of Geosciences and Natural Resource Management, on

Rolighedsvej. She stopped a couple of students and asked for directions to the main lecture theatre, nodded her thanks, and set off for her evening class. Fenna paused to use a passport photo machine, slipping the photos for Jarnvig inside her pack before hurrying to class.

The students moved differently to the tourists, with an almost imperceptible balance between purpose and procrastination. Fenna bumped past the students in the corridor outside the main lecture hall for the natural sciences, waited for a line of students to exit, before slipping past them and hovering by the door as she scanned the room. She recognised her tutor from the description Jarnvig had given her. She knew he was at least twice her twenty-four years, but he seemed to be in good physical shape, and, given she knew his specialist area of study, Fenna imagined she knew why.

Greenland did that, she thought, as she made her way between the rows of seats all the way to the lecture stage and pulpit. The man looked up as she sat down on a seat in the front row.

"So you're the reason my wife is cooking for the kids tonight?" he said and grinned.

"Is that a bad thing?"

"They'll survive, and Carina will appreciate the extra cash." He walked forward and extended his hand. "Anders Nielsen," he said, as he greeted her.

"Fenna."

"Do you have a second name?"

"Yes," she said and stood up. "When do we start?"

"All right," Anders said and scratched at the stubble on his cheek. He frowned for a moment and then said, "What do you know?"

"About geology?"

"About Greenland."

"I know more about ice than rocks."

"That's a start, a good one, considering that the one has significantly shaped the other." He paused. "I understand that this is a rush job, like cramming for an exam."

"Yes."

"Then why don't you tell me what you need to know, specifically, and I can help you from there."

Fenna returned to her seat and pulled a notebook from her pack.

"Tell me about mining in Greenland."

"Specifically?"

"Everything," Fenna said and opened her notebook. She scribbled notes as the geologist talked, stopping when he stopped, pausing to clarify a point before he rambled on to the next topic. There were slides, and Fenna stood up when the projector froze and needed to be restarted. The last image before the screen went blank was of the mountains to the north of Nuuk Fjord. Fenna stared at it and realised how much she missed Greenland. Anders fiddled with the remote control and the image disappeared. Fenna suppressed a sigh.

I'll see it again, she thought. *Soon.*

"This will take a moment," Anders said. He gestured with the remote to his right. "There's a coffee machine at the end of the corridor," he said. "Be sure to press the plus symbol for extra strength, otherwise it tastes like dishwater."

On the way back from the coffee machine, a paper cup in each hand, Fenna studied the students loitering in the corridor after class. *I could be any one of them*, she mused, as she passed couples and small groups. She imagined a life of academia, the occasional field trip, and the little she knew of things like peer-review and publication, remembering stories she had overheard between lecturers at her old Gymnasium, and the snobbish ways of academics. She opened the door to the auditorium with her shoulder and smirked at the thought of working in the field alongside any one of the students she had passed in the corridor. She could feel the muscles in her arms, her thighs, the strength in her fingers, the ones she had used to kill a man. Academia, all of a sudden, didn't seem so bad. She walked down the shallow steps and handed one of the cups to Anders just as he clicked the next slide into focus.

"Isukasia," she said, as she recognised the shadow of mountains, the contours, and the proximity of the ice sheet beyond it.

"That's right," Anders said and frowned as he looked at her. "You've been there?"

"No," Fenna shook her head. "Tell me about it."

"It's a hot subject right now," he said, as he walked away from the projector and onto the low stage beneath the large image. He straightened his arm and pointed, clicking the remote with his other hand. "Granite, mostly, like the majority of rock formations and features in Greenland. The difference here," he said, is what you can't see, the story told in the geology of the land, beneath the surface." Fenna listened as he told her about the millions of years required to create the ore that, if mined, could be forged into iron, and then steel, the building materials of a nation with ambition, a superpower for the twenty-first century. "It's interesting," he said, after he had finished flicking through the slides, "when you consider the activities of the current leader of China."

"What do you mean?"

"The way he's courting the Arctic countries at the moment. He visited Alaska recently." Anders paused to laugh. "I mean, Alaska. No politicians ever visit Alaska, not since the gold rush, back in the age of the frontier."

"Greenland is the new frontier," Fenna said, setting her empty cup down on the seat next to her.

"You believe that?"

"Yes."

Anders nodded, "So do I." He walked off the stage and sat next to Fenna. "So, tell me," he said. "Why all the urgency?"

"I don't know what you mean?" she said and fought to control the buzz of adrenalin his words induced. "I'm studying for an exam, and if I pass…"

"You'll get your promotion. Yes," Anders said and waved his hand. "I remember your boss explaining it to me." He stared at Fenna as he finished his coffee. She waited as he turned the empty cup between his hands. "My wife Carina, is also a geologist," he said.

Here it comes, Fenna mused, as he smiled and studied her face. *That clever moment when he thinks he has figured it all out. Should I put him out of his misery or…*

"She said you're not interested in iron and you're certainly not cramming for a promotion."

"Oh?" Fenna said and smirked.

"She said it would be about oil, and that you are here to sound me out and to get my professional opinion for a reduced consultancy fee."

"Is that a problem? I thought you said your wife would appreciate the extra cash?"

"I did, and it's not, but now that I have met you," Anders said and paused. He turned to point the remote at the projector and clicked forward one more slide. Fenna flicked her eyes to the screen, taking a moment to pause as she processed the image of a man standing in front of an orderly ridge of white triangular tents, pitched in a line close to a small helicopter and a row of fuel barrels, ubiquitous to the Arctic, the waste product of one geology expedition after another. The man in the foreground, standing with his arm around Anders Nielsen's shoulder, could not have looked more comfortable with his surroundings, the pink glow of the late Arctic sun flushing his bronze complexion as he grinned through the swathe of mosquitoes at the camera. Fenna recognised Lorentzen from the profile photograph Jarnvig had given her and she turned her attention back to the geologist.

"Oil is a dead end for the time being," said Anders. "But if you want to get your promotion, you should be talking to that man, not me."

"But I'm talking to you," Fenna said.

"Yes, and that's what I tried to tell Carina."

"What?"

"The real reason you are meeting with me, late in the evening, the night before you fly to Greenland."

Fenna took a breath and raised her hands in a clueless gesture. "You're going to have to spell it out," she said.

"I've known Karl Lorentzen since University. We graduated in the same year, and have been on three major expeditions together. I even led one of them." Anders paused to smile. "Your boss knows that much, even if you don't."

"So tell me what it is I want, and we can stop guessing," Fenna said and shrugged. "You seem to know that I'm getting on a flight tomorrow – something I didn't. What else do you know?"

"I know that without an endorsement from me, you're never going to get a meeting with him, let alone the chance to be his chaperone when he visits Isukasia at the end of the week." Anders smiled, as Fenna worked hard to disguise the surprise threatening to encompass her whole face. "We're a small community of geologists who specialise in Greenland," he said. "As much as I like and even admire Karl, he is still a pompous ass with an inflated ego."

Fenna laughed, relaxing and letting her hands fall into her lap. "So," she said, "if I wanted your endorsement, would you give it to me?"

"Yes, and something else, for free."

"And that is?"

"A friendly warning," he said and took a moment to study Fenna's face. She blushed as his eyes drifted down her body before returning to her face. "Karl is an incorrigible man in his early fifties. His looks have probably accelerated his career just as much as his knowledge. You should be careful, Fenna *with-no-last-name*, Karl has a reputation for destroying the careers of peers and competitors, and there is a wake of pretty women in his past, all of them young, all of them who have changed course and career." Anders stood up. "Karl uses people he finds useful, and takes advantage of those who can satisfy his career needs, or his sexual ones. He is a cautious and calculating man," Anders said and shrugged. "I'm sorry to say this, but I hope you are stronger than you look, because he is going to eat you alive."

Fenna paused for a beat and hoped the surprise she revealed earlier was enough to hide the spark of excitement she felt pricking beneath the surface of her eyes. She nodded once and cleared her throat. "Thank you," she said and stood up.

"You're welcome," Anders said, as Fenna shook his hand, shouldered her pack and brushed past him. He called after her just as she reached the door. "You never asked if I will do it," he said.

"Do what?" Fenna said and turned to face him.

"Endorse you."

Fenna felt a rush of energy through her body and embraced it, smiling as she looked down at the professor standing by the projector. She prepared her voice, searching for just the right tone of attitude and assertion.

"I think, professor, I'm my own endorsement."

Fenna left whatever geology she had gleaned from her private session with the professor in the auditorium. She knew how she would tackle Lorentzen, how she would approach the investigation, and how she would root out the agent sabotaging the Danish polar agenda. What pissed her off, she realised as she walked off the University campus and entered the steam of early evening tourists, was the thought that Jarnvig had set her up, in the desert, in the lecture hall, even in the airport when he practically gave her his blessing to go to Toronto with a loaded gun in her luggage. What pissed her off was that she had been accomplice to all his machinations, he had played her, and she had let him. She was still fuming when the kiss of rubber on the curb caused a bubble of tourists to burst around her, as a black BMW parked beside her. The rear window rolled down and Jarnvig waved from the seat.

"Get in, Konstabel."

Chapter 15

The driver stepped out of the car and opened the passenger door. Fenna ducked inside and stuffed her backpack in the space between her feet. She buckled her seatbelt as the driver got back in the car, checked the side-view mirror and pulled out into the evening traffic. Fenna turned to face Jarnvig.

"Do you have the photos?"

"Yes," she said and pulled the thin contact sheet from the front pocket of her backpack. She handed them to Jarnvig and leaned back in her seat.

"You're quiet," he said, as he glanced at the photos. "Something on your mind?"

"You," she said and smirked.

"Care to elaborate?"

Fenna considered for a moment the consequences of exposing her understanding of Jarnvig's manipulations, and then she realised that although he might have been responsible for everything since Greenland, he had no part in what happened prior to Mikael and Dina's deaths. *And, very nearly, my own*, she mused. Without Jarnvig's intervention she could be dead, detained, or, at the very least, destitute. *I have a job*, she thought. *I have an income*, although details surrounding her bank account eluded her for the moment. *And I'm going back to Greenland.* She forgot all about Jarnvig, choosing instead to think about Maratse, the policeman, and Kula, the hunter. She thought about her unprecedented contact with the Greenlanders. *Most Sirius patrollers never meet actual Greenlanders in Greenland*, she remembered, *they operate too far north. But, neither do they have high-speed car chases on the sea ice, escape from sadists on cruise ships, or have gun battles with private armies.* Fenna smiled. *Unreal*, she thought and turned to look at Jarnvig.

"I don't know how much I learned from the professor," she said. "But he has *endorsed* me."

"Good," said Jarnvig.

"Mostly for my looks, of course," Fenna said and waited for Jarnvig to comment.

He sighed and tapped the corner of the photos on his knee. "Do you remember when we first met?"

"In Kastrup airport? Yes."

"I said I needed a young woman with your expertise, and I meant it."

"Because of Lorentzen?"

"He has been on my radar for a while, yes."

"Yours or PET's?"

"When it comes to Greenland and the Arctic I am PET," Jarnvig said. He leaned forward and spoke to the driver. "Remember we have one stop before the airport."

"Yes, boss."

Jarnvig straightened his jacket as he leaned back on the seat. "We need to get your passport updated. You and I will stay in the car and discuss the mission while Møller," he said with a nod toward the driver, "sorts out your passport." Fenna opened her mouth to speak and then closed it again. "What is it, Konstabel?"

"Lorentzen," she said. "You said you have been watching him for some time."

"I said he has been on my radar."

"But not under surveillance?"

"Not officially."

Fenna was quiet as she processed the information. She was beginning to put things into order, a timeline of events as it were. *There must be an overlap*, she realised. *A time when Jarnvig became aware of me, and realised…* Fenna paused. She swallowed at the taste of bile in her throat. She felt her cheeks flush. She dug her fingernails into her palms as she clenched her fists. Small as they were, *they can still do damage.* She turned in her seat and fought to control her breathing, measuring out her words, one at a time, for fear of spillage, losing her message, losing control.

"Konstabel?" Jarnvig said. Fenna flicked her eyes to the 9mm pistol he wore in a shoulder rig hanging on the left side of his body. She saw him glance at the driver, and the look that Møller returned in the rear-view mirror.

"You knew," Fenna said.

"Knew what?" Jarnvig shifted in his seat and Fenna felt the car slow as it neared a traffic light at a crossroad. She could see the airport in the distance, but Møller signalled that he intended to turn left onto Saltværksvej. The *tock tock* of the signal light repeated loud in her ears and caught in her throat, she forced her words around it.

"You had Humble under surveillance," she said and waited.

"Yes," Jarnvig said, slowly, with another glance at Møller. Fenna thought she saw Møller shift his position, moving his right hand into his lap as if he was drawing a gun from his own shoulder rig. She pursed her lips and breathed out, raising her hands so that Møller could see them, and then shuffling further back into her seat. The traffic light was still red. Fenna positioned her body so that she could slip her hand around the handle of the door. She turned her attention back to Jarnvig.

"You knew about Kjersing, Humble's man in Sirius."

"I had my suspicions."

"And Burwardsley?"

"The Marine Lieutenant? Yes," Jarnvig said and smoothed a wrinkle from his jeans. "I knew he was in Greenland, aboard *The Ice Star*."

Fenna flicked her eyes toward the traffic light. It was still red, but the movements of the drivers in the cars either side of them suggested it would change soon. She took a breath and turned once more to face Jarnvig.

"Then you knew what Humble was doing, how he was manipulating Kjersing, and…" Fenna almost choked on the next word, a name. "Mikael," she said and felt tears well in her eyes. "You fucking knew what Humble was going to do."

Jarnvig drew a breath as the traffic light changed to amber. He parted his lips to speak, but Fenna had already opened the passenger door. "Fenna," he shouted as the cars behind and to both sides of the BMW blasted their horns, the drivers waving their arms as Fenna wove her way between them, slinging her backpack over her shoulder as she swerved around a cyclist and pounded down the pavement. She ignored the sound of the passenger door slamming and the screech of rubber on the tarmac as Møller swung the BMW around in a U-turn and roared down the street toward her. Fenna ducked down a side street, stopped beside a door and kicked at it until it opened. She put her shoulder to it and burst inside a stairwell leading to the roof of a small warehouse. She pounded up the stairs, barely hearing the BMW braking to a stop in the side street, and Jarnvig's commands as he exited the vehicle, slammed the door, and followed her inside the building. Fenna stopped at the door to the roof, kicked it open, and stepped out into the evening air. Copenhagen hummed with activity, but it was nothing to the rage of emotions buzzing through Fenna's skull. She pressed her hands to her temples as she cut a path around the vents and antennas on the roof, like growths on the canopy layer of the urban jungle.

She stopped and turned at her name as Jarnvig stepped onto the roof. His right hand, she noted, was tucked inside his jacket. He let it fall to his side and straightened his back as he walked toward her.

"Konstabel," he said. "Fenna…"

"You knew they would kill Mikael," she said and pushed her fingers through her black hair. She tightened her grip, as if entwining her fingers in her hair might stop her from beating her handler to death with her fists. That's what he was, she realised, her handler. Not Nicklas, but the real one, the one who called the shots. *And he has been handling me from the very beginning.*

"There was a risk…"

"No," she said, working her jaw as she took a breath, and then, "it was a certainty. You knew the outcome, knew what they would do. There was no risk…"

"The risk, Fenna," Jarnvig said, as he took a small step closer to her, "was losing you."

"Me?"

"Yes," he said. "You."

Fenna let her hands fall to her sides. She shrank to the floor, pushing herself against a vent, the base of her backpack resting on top of it, the straps suspended above her shoulders. Fenna tucked her knees to her chest and wrapped her arms around them as Jarnvig sat down beside her.

"I didn't know about Dina," he said and waited for Fenna to react. She shuffled her feet closer to her bottom, the heels of her boots scraping across the rough surface of bitumen. Jarnvig continued, "Arctic sovereignty is complicated, and expensive. There are many players and, while it might have cooled down for a few decades," he paused to smirk at his own joke, "all eyes are now firmly on Greenland and the lands around the pole. It's like the Great Game of Central Asia in the 1800s, but further north, with more nations involved."

"It's not that I don't understand the bigger picture," Fenna said and lifted her head. "But at my level, sea level, on the ice, with the dogs, with Mikael, it was so much less complicated."

"I know."

"All that changed," she said and looked at Jarnvig. "I'm just trying to find out why."

"I can tell you why, but before I do, I need to know if you are onboard? If I can trust you. If my judgement was correct." Fenna lifted her chin and stared at Jarnvig. He continued, "*The Ice Star* was a good cover for Humble. It gave him legitimate access with very little fall out. But it also made him careless."

"Dina," Fenna said and waited for her to appear, but she was alone on the rooftop with Jarnvig.

"Yes," he said. "But all the while Humble was working to discredit the Danish military presence in Greenland, preparations for the LOMROG expedition were already in motion, and the Chinese were posturing in the capital, seeking a foothold, securing their Arctic future. Mikael and you, your patrol, were tiny pawns on a huge chessboard. But as soon as Mikael was killed and you put Dina on your sledge, you moved up in that game, and…" Jarnvig paused.

"And *what*?"

"That's when I saw a possibility, a big one, to make some moves and to put some new pieces into play."

"Me?"

"Yes." Jarnvig shifted his position and sat opposite Fenna. He bent his knees and rested his forearms on top of them. "I knew Mikael would be killed, that it was a possibility at least." Fenna glared at him, dipping her eyes as he continued. "I knew of you, but only really became interested when I learned that you were not dead."

"And how did you hear about that?"

"From a mutual friend," Jarnvig said and laughed. "Maratse," he said.

"Maratse?" Fenna looked up and, as she lifted her head, the weight of Jarnvig's revelations ebbed for a moment at the mention of the Greenlandic policeman's name.

"He was quite popular for a while. After your high-profile gun battle on the sea ice… Well, let's just say that the Chief of Police in Greenland reached out, and the man he reached out to was me."

"Your story was that it was an anti-terror exercise?" Fenna could feel the skin of her lips tighten.

"Lame, I know," Jarnvig said and laughed with her. "It was the best I could do. You didn't give me much to work with."

"No…"

"But you certainly caught my attention. The way you reacted, kept your cool. You had a future, if only I could get to you before they did."

"Yeah," she said. "You failed and Dina died."

"Yes, she did."

Fenna flicked a tear from her cheek and listened to the hum of life in the city as Copenhagen pulsed all around them. Seagulls drifted past from the docks, and she followed their flight until they were gone, out of sight, and she was back on the roof, with her future, and possibly Greenland's in her hands.

"So what happens now?"

"That all depends on you," Jarnvig said and picked up a pebble of bitumen from the rooftop. "I'm already invested, and I would be lying if I'm just going to let you walk away from this mission. I've pleaded your case and defended your actions to too many of my superiors, and too many committees, to walk away now. We have a window of opportunity. Lorentzen is on his way back to Nuuk. He is meeting with the Chinese, and all this just two weeks before the UNCLOS hearing. If ever we needed to act it is now. And right now, this very evening, he is in Copenhagen."

"But he'll know that. Lorentzen, if he is half as clever as you think he is, he will already know that."

"True," Jarnvig said and tossed the bitumen to one side. "But he has his Achilles heel." He paused. "For all his fame, and despite his academic reputation, he is a lonely man, Konstabel, and that is our advantage."

"You want me to fuck him? Is that what you want me to do?" Fenna said and snorted. "Jesus."

"Listen to me," Jarnvig said and pointed at her. "If I wanted to entrap or blackmail Lorentzen, if that's all I wanted to do, I could get a hooker to do that for less than the price of a meal at Noma."

"You're calling me a hooker now? Finally. Now we get to it…"

"Would you shut up for just a minute, Konstabel," Jarnvig said. Fenna looked up as she recognised the edge in his voice.

"Talk," she said and stared at him.

"I meant what I said when I needed a young woman with your expertise. Yes, your looks are a key feature that figure heavily in my plan…"

"And Lorentzen prefers girls with black hair, eh?"

"Yes," Jarnvig said and blustered, "but listen. Your resourcefulness, and, damn it, even your stubbornness, gives you the edge, it keeps you sharp, and I need you to be sharp. Always."

He paused to look away for a moment. Fenna watched him, waited for him to face her. When he did, she could almost read the conflict that had played out in his mind. She waited for him to speak.

"Others have tried to train naïve young women with physical attributes to do a specific job," Jarnvig said. He caught the quizzical look in Fenna's eye and continued before she could explore it. "They have met with various results, few with any measure of success, and most ending in some political debacle."

"But I'm different? I'm not a naïve woman?" Fenna said and shook her head.

"That's not what I said," Jarnvig said, as he recovered, "but you're not the first woman to be recruited from the military. What you do have, something I admire, is an investment."

"An investment?"

"Yes. You are *invested* in Greenland," Jarnvig said and smiled. "Maybe it's the time you spent in the far north. Maybe it's a little of Mikael rubbing off on you… His record said it all – the environment came before any inkling of patriotism. But you," Jarnvig said, noticing the smile creeping across Fenna's face, the glint of cold fire burning in her ice-blue eyes. "You actually care about the people, not just the country."

"I think I found something there," she said, sighing as she looked up. "Despite it all, I think I found peace."

"And would you fight for that, Konstabel? Would you fight for Greenland?"

"Yes," she said. "I would." *I really would*, she thought.

"Good," Jarnvig said as he stood. "Then let's get down to the street. I sent Møller after your passport. He should be finished soon. Then we'll get you to your flight."

"I thought I was leaving tomorrow?"

"You are, but, as I said, Lorentzen is in Copenhagen. There is a meeting at the Clarion Hotel tonight, in one of the airport suites, a kind of reception. Lorentzen is the keynote speaker and you're going to be there."

Chapter 16

The bathroom of the suite at the Clarion Hotel Copenhagen Airport was larger than the combined area of the kitchen and living room of Fenna's family flat in Esbjerg. She ran the taps for the bath and listened to Jarnvig's and Møller's low voices on the other side of the door. Møller, it seemed, was to be Fenna's chaperone at the function of International Geologists, scheduled to begin in the late evening in the *Ellehammer* conference room. He had proved to have more than a passing interest in geology when they were properly introduced after Fenna and Jarnvig had finished talking on the Copenhagen rooftop. *He knows more than I do*, Fenna realised, and was relieved to discover that Jarnvig had fine-tuned her cover story. Tunstall Mining, while too busy to send any senior employees to Copenhagen, did not want to miss anything of interest.

"They are sending you," Jarnvig had explained as he presented her with her evening wear, "to be their eyes and ears at the function. Your cover is safe, Konstabel."

"And my name?" she said. "It's my real name on the passport."

"Few people know what went on in Greenland. I made sure of that. Until you are comfortable with aliases, your real name is safer. Trust me. Now," he said and indicated the bathroom. "If you'll get ready, I will go over the last details with Møller."

Fenna tested the temperature of the water with her hand and tugged off her *geologist disguise,* smiling at the effort Jarnvig had put into weathering her clothes. She stopped laughing when she caught her reflection in the mirror. She wore the trials of physical training in swathes across her skin. Her panda eyes were, with a little makeup, much harder to distinguish than earlier, but if anyone was to see her naked, they would find it difficult to believe she was just a company representative.

"More like a malnourished sex slave smuggled out of Eastern Europe," she said and traced the bruises and the lacerations, the cuts and the abrasions with a finger. But beneath the blemishes on the surface, Fenna knew she possessed a physique to rival even her biathlon days. Patrolling with Sirius, pulling her weight and wrangling forty kilo sledge dogs through unforgiving terrain, had changed her lithe skiing and shooting form into a hardy, wiry body that could take as many punches as it could give. She pictured Nicklas in her mind and remembered the sparring, the kidney punches, and then the sex, in the dust of the desert boxing ring. She switched her attention to the bath before any images of the Gunney, or Dina, slipped past her mental safeguards. Fenna bathed, longer than she imagined Jarnvig would approve. She picked up the reading material he had left by the sink and flipped through the pages, enjoying the thought of him checking his watch and stressing outside the door. *It's time to take control*, she mused and slipped her head beneath the surface of the water.

When her skin was thoroughly pruned, she dried and dressed. When she opened the bathroom door and stepped into the suite, she knew that she had successfully shrugged off one disguise and assumed another. Jarnvig and Møller revealed as much in their expressions. She joined them on the sofa, perching on the edge with her legs pressed together to avoid wrinkling the black cocktail dress Jarnvig had bought for her.

"It's a little loose," she said when he asked.

"Where?" said Møller. Fenna laughed and dropped the façade long enough to confirm she was the same woman who had walked into the bathroom, irrespective of how she looked when she came out.

"Makeup?" asked Jarnvig, as he focused once again on the details.

"No," Fenna said and shook her head, the wet ends of her short hair clung to her cheeks. "That's not what he's looking for."

"Who?"

"Lorentzen," she said and nodded at the folder on the table between them. "Your surveillance report included photos of the women he had contact with. They are, almost without exception, young, skinny, dark haired, flat-chested…" Fenna paused and made a show of gesticulating at her own tiny breasts. "And," she added, "all of them favoured the natural look, with little or no makeup. I have, I'll admit, added some colour around my eyes to hide the last of my desert souvenirs. Otherwise…"

"You look amazing, Konstabel," Jarnvig said and held her gaze for a moment, long enough for Fenna to glimpse a sense of admiration, perhaps even longing. She pushed the thought from her mind and picked up the report. She flicked through it as Møller excused himself to use the toilet.

"Sorry," she said, as he stood up. "I took my time."

"Not a problem," he said, as he walked around the sofa. She watched him as he entered the bathroom, turning her attention back to Jarnvig at the sound of the door locking.

"He seems all right," she said. "Is he PET, or something else, like Nicklas?"

"Nicklas?" Jarnvig said. He reeled for a second as if caught off guard. "Nicklas is more of a liaison to PET than a direct employee."

"And yet, you seem to have full control over him?"

"With the blessing of the RCMP, yes."

"And what am I?" she asked. "Am I an agent?"

"A PET agent, yes," Jarnvig said and reached for a bottle of water on the sofa table. "HUMINT," he said. "Human Intelligence. Not everything can be discovered through electronic eavesdropping. Intelligence agencies still need boots on the ground."

"Or heels," Fenna said and lifted her foot.

"Yes, heels," Jarnvig said and laughed and then went quiet.

"What?"

Jarnvig twisted the cap of the bottle backward and forward. "Fenna," he said. "I read something recently. Heard it, actually, an audiobook, a dramatization of one of John le Carré's books. Have you read any?"

"No." Fenna said.

"He writes spy books – the thinking man's James Bond. There's a passage in the book when the men training a man to go over the wall in Berlin, after the war, talk about giving him a gun, to make him feel safe. They make him carry it all the time – to the pub, on the street. They even have him place it under his pillow."

"And?" Fenna said and shrugged. She felt the strap of her dress slip from her shoulder and pulled it back into place as Jarnvig wrestled his eyes from the dress strap to her face.

"The night of the operation, when the man, the agent, is being sent behind enemy lines, they tell him he can't take his gun."

"Why?" Fenna said and frowned.

"To put him on edge," Jarnvig said and stared at Fenna. He caught her eye and held it. "To keep him sharp."

"To scare the crap out of him more like."

"If that's what it took," Jarnvig said and looked away. He leaned back, tugging the thought with him until Fenna grasped it.

"So," she said. "You're not giving me a gun."

"No," he said. "I'm not."

Møller opened the bathroom door, pausing to look from Fenna to Jarnvig. He walked to the sofa and stood to one side. Fenna ignored him. Jarnvig focused on Fenna.

"I'm ready," Møller said. "Whenever you…"

"If that's the case," Fenna said, cutting him off with a glance, "then you can leave the gorilla in the suite." She stood up, tossed the folder onto the sofa table and walked toward the door.

"Konstabel," Jarnvig stood up, lifting a finger to silence Møller, and then stepping around the sofa to follow Fenna. She had her hand on the door when he slammed the palm of his left hand against it. "You will listen to me."

"Let go of the fucking door, Jarnvig."

"Not before you listen to me."

"No," Fenna said, turning within the space cordoned off by Jarnvig's body. She knuckled him in the sternum, just enough to put him off balance as she pulled the 9mm from his shoulder rig, turned it for a better grip, and shoved the muzzle into the side of his head. "I'm done listening to men," she said and tapped the pistol against his temple. Jarnvig staggered back and she shifted position, depriving Møller of a clear shot as he levelled his own pistol at her.

"Fenna," Jarnvig said.

"Now it's *Fenna*?" she said and took a breath. "You use *Konstabel* to order me around. *Fenna* when you want to appeal to my conscience, or my emotions. Well, I'm done with that. You have a problem," Fenna said, "a big fucking problem."

"And what is that, Konstabel?" Jarnvig said, as he rubbed his chest.

"You are my handler, but I won't be handled."

"Just remember," he said, "who got you out of Toronto, and out of the desert, Konstabel. Remember that."

"I don't have to," she said. "You did. And you'll do it again, because the thing is…" Fenna paused to lower the gun. "You need me. And right now, I'm the best option you have of gathering intelligence. You said it yourself, Jarnvig. You recruited me, in part, for my stubbornness. And now you have to deal with that." She pointed at Møller. "You send me in there with him, and you may as well flash a sign saying *secret agent in training*, and Lorentzen will be gone. But if I go in alone, with Nielsen's endorsement, this dress, the bobbed black hair, and my body – for what it's worth, and I guarantee I'll have him on the hook before midnight." Fenna stopped to lift the straps of her dress and slide them back onto her shoulders. She looked at Jarnvig, daring him to disagree.

"Okay," he said and waved at Møller to stand down. "You've made your point."

"Good."

"But, damn it, Fenna. You are every handler's worst nightmare." Jarnvig sighed.

"You better believe it," she said and tossed him the 9mm.

"Konstabel," Jarnvig called out, as she turned toward the door.

"Yes?"

"Be smart. Be safe, and be back here by midnight."

"And if I'm not?"

"I'll make sure Møller is sitting in the bar."

"All right," she said. "I'll agree to that."

Jarnvig slipped the 9mm into his shoulder holster. "Good luck, Konstabel," he said. Fenna nodded as she opened the door and stepped into the corridor.

Fenna's adrenalin cooled as she walked toward the lifts. The carpet and the heels she was wearing reminded her of another corridor and another lift, another time and place. She thought of Vienna, trapped as she was in her luxurious lifestyle aboard *The Ice Star. I'm trapped too,* she realised and pushed the thought to the back of her mind as she approached the elevator. The suite was on the top floor of the hotel, giving Fenna time to rein in her heartbeat and prepare herself for first contact with her target. *The last time,* she remembered, *I wasn't prepared for Humble. This time is different.*

"Just keep telling yourself that, *love,*" she said aloud, adding the chill of Burwardsley's familiar moniker to chide herself into action. The elevator slowed to a stop on the ground floor and Fenna took a breath as the doors opened with a soft rumble.

She stepped out into the foyer, found her feet and settled into her walk across the tiled floor. The clack of her heels gave her a cadence to work with, and, despite its unfamiliarity, she realised she enjoyed the extra height they gave her, and the looks she drew from the men, seated at the tables in the foyer, pausing in their banter as she passed.

I don't need a gun, she thought as she followed the signs to the *Ellehammer* conference room. *I'm already lethal.*

Chapter 17

The clock on the wall above the stage at the far end of the room showed Fenna she had less than an hour to make an impression on Lorentzen. So far, the only thing the professor's endorsement had given her was a seat at one of the tables furthest from the stage, together with an octogenarian with halitosis and his portly young assistant with roving eyes and a highly inflated ego, based on some obscure geology expedition to which he had been accepted. The drinks, at least, were included in the admission fee.

She saw him the moment he entered the room. A collective hush alerted her to his arrival, and Fenna turned, along with the majority of people in the room, to see the famed geologist and keynote speaker for the evening. She could see how he charmed his way into the beds of women half his age, into the most exclusive clubs, and onto high profile executive boards eager for the chance to share the same space as Lorentzen and to profit by association.

And yet, Fenna mused as he ignored her on the way to the podium, *you are languishing on assignment in Nuuk. Bored. Or is that just a front?* She pushed the thoughts away and listened as he began to speak.

Lorentzen had obviously studied the art of public speaking, Fenna realised, stopping herself for a moment as she, like those around her, leaned forward, ever so slightly, in anticipation of his next word, the punch line, or the lessons learned from his various anecdotes. It was clear that he had been chosen to speak on a variety of subjects dear to the audience's heart. He was among friends, and many of them had shared more than one of his adventures. He made a pointed at and referenced each of them as his speech progressed. It was his last story that sealed her interest in Lorentzen, especially as she knew the source material intimately. There was even a moment when she imagined that he might confess to the murder of Johansson, and her mission would be over. Of course, he did not, but Fenna's inside knowledge, and her appreciation of sea ice and the north, ensured that he had her full and undivided attention. A fact which, even from the podium at the other end of the room, he noticed, pausing to take a sip of water as he did so.

"He's a bit full of himself," the young geologist whispered.

"Shh," said Fenna, as Lorentzen put down his glass and

continued with the story.

"The mist was thick with ice when they found the body of my dear colleague, Dr Johansson. His body was layered in a quilt of crystals, they shone in the midnight sun, and I remember being moved, beyond the tragic nature of his death, to imagine a serenity in the scene that, although wholly inappropriate, I chose to focus on, to remember him, in that moment, as I hope you will do now." Lorentzen picked up the glass of wine beside his water and raised it. "To Dr Johansson," he said.

"Dr Johansson," the audience of geologists, journalists and one PET agent chorused.

Lorentzen put down his glass and signalled to the host of the symposium that he was ready to answer a few questions. The first, as Fenna had predicted, concerned the identity of Johansson's killer.

"Something we all want to know, not least his wife and children," Lorentzen said and placed his hands on the sides of the podium. "The circumstances of his death suggest that it was no accident, and, when you consider the goals of the expedition," he paused to gesticulate. "It begs the question, will people kill for the North Pole? Will countries?"

Clever, Fenna thought as the audience murmured in response. Lorentzen had fuelled the conspiracy theorists among them, and she heard the word *Russians* as it filtered down from one table to another, toward the back of the hall.

Lorentzen answered two more questions before thanking the hosts, the Royal Danish Geological Society, and wishing everyone a pleasant evening. He made his way down from the podium to mingle with the geologists standing and clapping as he stepped off the stage.

He was still pressing flesh and charming his way between tables as Fenna, standing at the bar, finished her second glass of wine. She had already dismissed three offers of something stronger to drink when she saw Lorentzen walk toward her, only to be stopped, just a table away, by two geologists and a journalist Fenna recognised from one of the reports Jarnvig had forced her to read while in the bath. Standing next to the journalist was a tall Chinese man. Fenna noted the way he nodded at Lorentzen as he approached, and the grim but civil expression he wore.

"Karl," said the older of the two geologists. "Terrible business on the LOMROG expedition."

"Yes," Lorentzen said, as he shook his hand. "Still, I'm sure we agree that the outcome is much worse, Dr Villadsen? Wouldn't you say?"

"You mean losing the Pole to the Russians?"

"I mean losing the Pole to anyone." Lorentzen looked up as Fenna made her way to the periphery of the table. The men turned to see what had caught his attention, dismissing Fenna with a mixture of bored stares and raised eyebrows. Dr Villadsen ensured Lorentzen ignored Fenna by adding a follow-up question.

"Forget about the Pole for a minute," he said. "What do you make of the Canadians upping their presence in the north? Their Rangers have skidoos and automatic weapons, you know. It's time we upped our ante and showed them a bit of muscle, not just a few young fellas from the Sirius Patrol with a bunch of dogs and an antiquated rifle. What do you say to that?"

"I'd say..." Lorentzen said, pausing as Fenna chose her moment to make an impression.

"That skidoos will never replace dogs and men," she said, as she stepped between the chairs and joined the men standing in the space between two tables. "That's what you'd say," she said, "if you knew what you were talking about." Fenna winked and took a sip of wine, amazed at her own boldness and praying that the thump of her heart could not be seen trembling the skin between her breasts and the low cut of her dress.

"Ridiculous," said Villadsen, as he scowled at Fenna. "I don't care how many dogs you hook up to a sledge, they simply can't cover the distance that a skidoo can, nor can they pull the kind of loads required to sustain a patrol in the high Arctic. Isn't that right, Karl?"

"Well…"

"A single team of dogs can pull enough supplies to last them a month," Fenna said and took a step forward. "That month can be extended with seal meat caught on patrol, food and fuel for both men and dogs. Tell me," Fenna said and paused to read the man's nametag, "Dr Villadsen, how much fuel can a skidoo carry?"

"I don't know, I would imagine…"

"Imagining won't cut it in the high Arctic. There's no room for miscalculation, nor is there any room for mechanical breakdowns or repairs. If a sledge breaks, the team has the skills and the materials to fix it. If a harness rips, they sew a new one. If a dog is injured in a fight, they sew it up. Same with a teammate. If he gets a tooth infection, his partner pulls it."

Villadsen looked from Lorentzen to the geologist smirking beside him. "I…"

"Don't know? No," said Fenna, "it appears that you don't. But the next time you scowl at a woman as if she is as intelligent as the cushion you pressed your chauvinistic arse on this past hour," she said, with a nod at the man's chair, "you might remember our little chat." Fenna lifted her glass to her lips and drained it. "Cheers," she said and turned toward the bar.

Fenna heard the journalist chuckle as she reached the bar, and the soft voice of the Chinese man as he spoke in English, suggesting that he had understood what she had said, despite not knowing a single word of Danish. She ordered another glass of wine, her third of the evening, and waited for Lorentzen to join her. She didn't have to wait long.

"Do you always do that at parties?" he said as he leaned against the bar and ordered a whisky.

"This isn't a party," she said, facing him.

"Fenna," he said, as he read her nametag. "My name is Karl."

"I know who you are," she said and shook his hand. Fenna nodded toward the stage. "Keynote speaker, Dr Karl Lorentzen. It's on the poster."

"Yes," he said. He thanked the bartender for the whisky and turned his attention back to Fenna. "Shall we find somewhere to sit, and you can tell me who you are?"

"I can tell you here," she said and waved her glass of wine. "It's closer to the bar."

"That's because it *is* the bar," he said and laughed.

"It is?" Fenna said and laughed. "I've been here longer than I thought."

"Or not long enough." Lorentzen raised his glass to his lips. He finished it in one and waggled the glass at the bartender.

"Another *Laphroaig*?"

"As long as it's on the house, why not." He looked at Fenna. "Do you drink whisky?"

"No. I get into enough trouble with wine."

"I see," he said. "Do you know who you just insulted?"

"Insulted? I put him in his place," Fenna said, leaning back against the bar. She let her elbow touch his, and, despite the alcohol in her system, she knew he could feel it, just as she knew he was staring at the straps hanging from her bare shoulders whenever he thought she wasn't looking.

"When you reach his age, it's the same thing."

"Good," she said and took another sip of wine. "But he's not the interesting one. Who is the Chinese man talking with the journalist from *Politiken*?"

"You know Henning?"

Fuck. Careful Fenna, she thought. "Oh, I read something of his recently, something about Greenland."

"Yes, he did write a good piece in Sunday's paper," Lorentzen said with another glance at Fenna's shoulder. "Henning is talking to Hong Wei, a representative of the Chinese government. He's here to…"

"Assess the mine at Isukasia?" Fenna said and smiled at the look on his face.

"Okay," he said, as he pushed himself away from the bar. Lorentzen straightened his jacket and stood in front of Fenna. With a quick glance over his shoulder he turned back to face her. "You officially have my attention. Who *are* you?"

"I'm glad I have your attention," Fenna said, a smile played across her lips.

"So tell me."

"You don't know?"

"I don't," he said, and for a moment, Fenna was almost lost in the boyish flicker of failure that settled on his face. Perhaps it was the wine, the satisfaction of putting a pompous old man in his place, or the realisation that she was on the job and off the leash. Investigating, *finally*, and loving every minute of it. "You're going to have to tell me," he said and reached for his glass.

Fenna caught his hand as he rested his arm on the counter. She smoothed her fingers over his skin, hesitated for a second, and then squeezed his hand in hers. He looked at her, and at the glass in her hand.

"I know," she said. "It probably is the wine, but I really wanted to meet you tonight."

"You did?" Lorentzen said with a raised eyebrow.

"Yes," Fenna said. She removed her hand and caught a little thrill as she recognised the look on his face as he displayed his disappointment. "My name is Fenna Brongaard, and I represent..."

"Tunstall Mining," he said. "Of course."

"Yes," she said and pushed the straps of her dress back onto her shoulders.

"Obviously," Lorentzen said. "It makes sense now. I got the email a few weeks ago, and then Anders' call earlier this evening. I should have put it all together. You'll be accompanying me to Isukasia. Right?"

"That's right," Fenna said, hiding the feeling of irritation that she didn't have any more information for him to tease out of her. "I'm flying to Greenland tomorrow."

"Tomorrow? Then we are on the same flight. You're flying *Nanok Class*? Business?"

"No," she said and frowned. "I'm pretty sure Tunstall Mining want to keep their costs at a minimum on this venture."

"Well, I'll have to see what I can do about that," he said. "I have some good connections at *Air Greenland*. I'll make some enquiries, get you a seat next to me, and Hong Wei," he said, with a glance over his shoulder.

Fenna was surprised at the thrill the name of the airline elicited in her. It had been a long time, but she was returning to Greenland. *Just a few hours from now*, she added and placed her glass, half-full, on the counter.

"You're leaving," he said and gestured at her glass.

"It's a long flight."

"It's not, actually. It's the wait in Kangerlussuaq that usually takes time."

"Not *Søndre Strømfjord*?" she said. "You used the Greenlandic name."

"Yes," he said and frowned. "And from what you know of the Sirius Patrol, back there, I imagine you to be a Greenland aficionado. Am I right?" he said and pointed in the direction of Villadsen's table.

"I know a few things," Fenna said. "From what I have read, mostly."

"You've never been?"

Fenna paused for a moment as she recalled the cover story Jarnvig had pressed upon her in another folder, also to be read and memorised while she bathed. "Once, when I was a teenager. My daddy arranged it." Fenna almost choked on the word, but realised the girly term might endear her even more to her mark.

"What did he do? Your father?"

What did *he do?* Fenna recalled her real father, the soldier in the Danish *Jægerkorps*, Special Forces. She wondered if he would be proud of her, honey-trapping a Danish national on behalf of *Politiets Efterretningstjeneste.* Her training kicked in and she said, "He fixed photocopying machines, would you believe?"

"I would," Lorentzen said and took a sip of whisky. "You can make a career of fixing anything in the Arctic, photocopying machines included."

"That's what my daddy said."

"Your *daddy*?" he said and grinned. Fenna smiled as he finished his whisky. "I'm guessing he is about my age?"

"I wouldn't know," she said and lifted her chin. "How old are you?"

"Guess," he said.

"Forty?" Fenna said, and then, "Forty-two?" She bit her bottom lip as if she was thinking. If she got too close, she knew, his suspicions might be aroused. And yet, she could tell he was already aroused. She watched as Lorentzen slipped his hands in his pockets. *A casual move*, she thought, *if it wasn't intended to hide his arousal.*

"I'm fifty-one. But," he said and shrugged, "Greenland…"

"Keeps you in shape?" Fenna said. "I've heard that before."

"It's a physical place. You have to be active if you want to do anything, go anywhere."

"I look forward to seeing it again."

"And I look forward to showing it to you."

"Tomorrow, then," Fenna said and removed her nametag. She placed it on the bar, laughing as he stared at it. "It's not my hotel key card," she said.

"I never thought…"

"Yes you did," she said. "And maybe you were even right to do so. But I have a flight to catch tomorrow, and I don't intend to miss it."

"You are a mystery, Fenna Brongaard."

"Yes," she said and turned and walked away.

Fenna knew his eyes followed her across the room. She felt a surge of adrenalin and a flood of different emotions, wondering just how far she would have gone. She was pleased with herself for reaching out and making physical contact. *My fingers on his hand*, she mused. *Electric. And yet those same fingers*, she recalled, *killed a man.* Fenna stopped in the corridor outside the conference room. *Am I going to have to kill him?* Jarnvig's words filtered through her own as she made her way to the hotel bar.

"Whatever it takes," he had said, and she wondered if she could.

Fenna spotted Møller sitting at a table in the corner of the room. She walked past the bar and sat down opposite him.

"Well?" he said.

"You can tell Jarnvig," she said. "That Lorentzen is on the hook and the mission is on."

The Mine

SERMERSOOQ, GREENLAND

Chapter 18

Lorentzen's influence had, in some circles at least, a limited reach. Fenna travelled in economy class from Kastrup Airport to the old American runway at Kangerlussuaq, the hub of almost all air traffic to and from Greenland. She sat next to the window, grateful for the lack of turbulence, and dozed as they flew over Iceland, only to wake as the *Airbus 330-200* turned feet-dry over Greenland's east coast. She pressed her nose to the glass, looking for familiar landmarks, knowing they were too far south for her to see anything resembling the coastline she had patrolled with Oversergent Mikael Gregersen, or the settlement of Ittoqqortoormiit where she had been deceived, detained, and interrogated about his death. *A sideshow*, she thought. *Just another move of another piece on the chessboard in the Great Arctic Game – a game that I'm a part of.*

The steward disturbed her with the offer of a drink, the last chance before landing in Kangerlussuaq. Fenna asked for coffee, nodded her thanks as she cupped her hands around the paper cup and stared at the ice sheet. She sipped her coffee and thought of the hundreds of people who had skied across the ice, from east to west, since Fridtjof Nansen led the Greenland Expedition, reaching Nuuk, then Godthåb, in October 1888.

Why ski when you can sledge? she thought and smiled as the steam from the coffee settled on the window. She was sitting uncomfortably close to the cool panel of the plane's interior, and yet, she was unwilling to distance herself from the comfort of the ice. She adjusted her position and the passenger beside her snapped the sheets of his newspaper and grunted something about flying *monkey class*. Fenna ignored him and pressed her nose to the glass once more.

There was little comfort to be found in the thoughts that pressed to the fore of her mind as she lost herself in the stark, white surface of the ice, it was a blank slate upon which memories of the settlement of Ittoqqortoormiit were served. *The Magician* appeared as she remembered him in the guise of Premierløjtnant Vestergaard – first name *Klaus*. Jarnvig had said, prior to her leaving for Arizona, that *The Magician* was not her concern.

Whose concern is he, if not mine? she thought and leaned back in her seat.

Another piece on the board. Another puzzle. Fenna wondered

just how many demons her return to Greenland would invoke. *And how many can I resist?*

The Magician's role in the Canadian plot to sabotage the credibility of the Danish sovereignty mission in Greenland had been both clever and thorough. Fenna considered what she knew of Lorentzen and his involvement in the subterfuge at the Pole, and who was pulling *his* strings. *The Magician*? It wasn't the most ridiculous idea she had ever had. Fenna smiled at the thought and pulled at the thread, teasing her theory into a thin length of cotton, too thin to sew with, but just enough to feel if she was to rub it between her finger and thumb. She finished her coffee, glancing at the man beside her as he grunted again. When she pulled on the different threads she had assembled in her mind, when she tied knots, only to see them unravel, even *when* they unravelled, Fenna discovered a sense of purpose that she did not experience in the dust of the desert, or the sweat of the Sonoran boxing ring. Thinking, investigating, she realised, was delicious, a tangible mental kick that she could easily become addicted to. Whoever she had been on patrol, on the ice, that girl, that young woman – fighting for a place in a man's world – had now found a niche, a seat at the table, stakes in the game. *And what a game*, she thought. *Perhaps Jarnvig had been right to test her. Perhaps, now, she was ready*. She certainly felt ready, and as the *Airbus* began its descent into the canyon on the last stages of the approach onto the runway at Kangerlussuaq, Fenna felt, for the first time, that the job was not just something she could do, that she was trained for, but that she *wanted* to do it, that she *needed* it. The thought buoyed her through the landing, out of her seat, and across the tarmac into the arrivals building of Kangerlussuaq International Airport. It lightened the load, slipped her through security with nothing more than a cursory glance at her fake passport, all the way into the lounge, where she would wait for her connecting flight. It was a rough male voice and a string of words that shattered her confidence and threatened to start a cascade reaction, a shutting down of all systems.

"Nice to see you again, *love*."

Fenna froze for a second, until her training kicked in. It took all her reserve not to strike first. Instead, she tightened her grip on her North Face holdall and turned, slowly, to face the British Marine Lieutenant, the man who had tried so hard to kill her, the man who ordered her partner killed, on his knees, in the snow.

"Burwardsley," she said.

"Hello, Konstabel," Burwardsley grinned, as she stared up at him. His bulk blocked her view of the nearest exit. *All of them*, she realised. She flicked her eyes to the left and right of his shoulders, stopping when he laughed.

"He's not here," he said. "I left Bad in Britain. I'm all alone."

"Somehow I doubt it," Fenna said and steeled herself to look in his eyes. She studied them, searching for clues, anticipating a reaction, waiting for a strike.

"Honestly, I am here by myself. Sightseeing," he said and grinned. "I always wanted to see Greenland in the summer." Burwardsley shrugged. "Here I am."

"Here you are," Fenna said and tensed. She looked to Burwardsley's right as Lorentzen approached together with Hong Wei.

"Friends of yours?" Burwardsley asked.

"You don't know me," she said and bit her bottom lip.

"It's a bit late for that. They've seen us talking."

"Shut up," she said, drumming her fingers on her thigh. "You're a tourist…"

"As I have been trying to tell you. Christ, you're not very good at this." Burwardsley shook his head and tugged the backpack over his right shoulder higher up his back.

"No, I'm not," Fenna said, as Lorentzen noticed her and waved. She waved back. "But until I figure things out, you're a fucking tourist who mistook me for a guide."

"Whatever you say, *love*," Burwardsley said, and grinned as he dragged out the last word.

"Hi," Fenna said as Lorentzen and Hong Wei stopped beside her.

"I'm sorry I could not find you a seat with Wei and me in Business Class," said Lorentzen. She held her breath as she noticed Burwardsley raise his eyebrow. "I'm sure you would have made an uneventful flight more interesting."

"Interesting?" Burwardsley mouthed.

Fenna ignored him and forced herself to remember the role she was playing – this life versus her old life. *Even though the one is a direct result of the other*, she mused. The thought slipped from her mind as she smiled and said something about not having slept much and needing to recover on the flight. She almost didn't hear Lorentzen's response, tuning in at the last second as she composed herself and did her best to ignore Burwardsley.

"… Air Greenland has to move the chopper to Nuuk for our benefit anyway," he said, and switching to English, "but I'm not sure there is room for your friend."

"My friend?" Fenna said and realised he was looking at Burwardsley.

"Oh, we're not friends," Burwardsley said and repositioned his backpack. "I thought…" he paused as if to remember her name. "Fenna, is it?"

"Yes," she said and lifted her chin, turning her attention from Lorentzen to Burwardsley.

"I thought she was my guide," he said. "I booked a hiking trip and I'm waiting for someone from…" Burwardsley glanced at a carousel of brochures. "Arctic Adventure." Fenna let out her breath as Burwardsley smiled at her. He shook her hand, holding her grip for a second longer than she liked before he excused himself and walked out of the main lobby area in the direction of the cafeteria.

"You were saying something about a helicopter?" Fenna said, as she watched Burwardsley leave.

"Yes, with a female pilot. A Greenlander," Lorentzen said, as he gestured toward the lounge. "She is waiting for us in there. Let me introduce you."

Fenna felt Lorentzen's hand on her shoulder as he guided her and Hong Wei to the lounge. A tall Greenlandic woman, her jet-black hair pulled back and tied in a neat ponytail, stood up as they entered. Fenna caught her breath as she looked beyond the pilot's dark flight suit – an ultra thin drysuit designed to keep her warm long enough for a rescue should they ditch in the sea – and studied her face. *Dina* – the thought flashed into her mind and Fenna's demons were alive again. A slight wrinkle creased the pilot's frown as she stepped forward to greet them. She greeted Fenna first, and it was all Fenna could do to avoid saying Dina's name. They could have been twins – sharing the same soft caramel skin colour, the same burnt chocolate eyes – and yet, the pilot, Panninguaq Korneliussen, could not have been more different, Fenna realised, especially when she introduced them to her son.

"I'd like you to meet Anguteq. He is seven," she said, as the small boy curled his arms around her left leg."

"Anguteq?" Lorentzen said, twisting his tongue around the boy's name as he knelt to greet him. Anguteq shrank behind his mother and Panninguaq, speaking in Greenlandic, said something that made him reach forward for a second to shake the tip of Lorentzen's outstretched hand. The boy looked at the frown on Hong Wei's face and then retreated behind his mother's legs.

"He is shy," said Panninguaq. "His father and I broke up a few months ago and he is…" she paused. "Struggling a bit."

"I'm sorry," said Lorentzen as he stood up.

"I hope you don't mind, but I need to bring Anguteq with us to Nuuk," she said and glanced at Fenna. "I didn't know there would be three of you."

"Oh, I can find another flight…" Fenna said, stopping as Panninguaq shook her head.

"It's not a problem. The service technicians have already installed luggage pods on the skids. There is plenty of room inside the helicopter. Plenty of fuel too," she said, as she appraised Fenna for a moment. "We're about the same weight."

"Yes," Fenna said and smiled at Anguteq. He grinned and hid behind his mother, only to peek once more when Fenna waved at him.

Panninguaq gestured toward a door to the rear of the lounge and encouraged Anguteq to collect his things with a few words in Greenlandic and a pat on the bottom. Fenna caught her smile, as Panninguaq watched her son struggle into the arms of an oversized *Spiderman* backpack. *Not Dina*, Fenna reminded herself as Panninguaq caught her eye.

"We'll be flying in a Eurocopter AS350," said Panninguaq, as she led them along a corridor. Anguteq ran ahead of them, stopping at a security door, pushing and straining against it in mock exasperation until his mother swiped her card through the door lock and interface. Fenna watched as he pushed the door open. They all blinked as they stepped through the door, into the glare of the bright polar sun and onto the tarmac, following the yellow dashes painted onto the surface all the way to the helicopter. It was parked on a large, square trolley, with a tow hitch angled down to the landing pad. Panninguaq nodded at one of the ground crew as he placed a metal step in front of the trolley, took their bags, and helped them up and into the aircraft.

Panninguaq guided Fenna into the co-pilot's seat and smiled as she handed her a set of headphones.

"So we can talk," she said.

"Thanks," said Fenna, as she strapped herself in. She turned in the seat to smile at Lorentzen and Hong Wei, as they settled onto the bench seat behind her. Anguteq made a show of helping them fasten their seatbelts, laughing as Lorentzen high-fived him.

Fenna settled into her seat, making a point of keeping her feet off the pedals and her hands off the control stick.

"Don't worry about them," Panninguaq said, as she buckled in beside Fenna. "They will move. Just ignore them. Unless," she said and brushed a loose wisp of black hair behind her ear.

"Unless what?"

Panninguaq grinned, as she pulled on her helmet. She pulled a stick of gum from the top pocket of her flight suit, pushed the microphone out of the way and popped it in her mouth. She repositioned the microphone and tapped it with her finger, indicating that Fenna put on her headset.

"Unless I fall asleep," Panninguaq said, her voice sudden and intimate in Fenna's ear. Fenna heard the Greenlander's light laugh and decided she liked her.

"Thanks," she said and shook her head.

"I thought you needed a laugh. You looked a little preoccupied back in the lounge. You afraid of flying?"

"What? Oh," said Fenna, as she realised the cloud of Burwardsley's sudden appearance had followed her further and for longer than she had thought. "No," she said and smiled. "I'm not actually afraid of anything." *Not any* thing *at least,* she added. *But people. People can still scare the crap out of me.*

Fenna heard Panninguaq laugh, talking to her son in Greenlandic as she flicked through the start-up sequence and talked to the tower. The rotors of the Eurocopterwhined out of slumber and a touch of obstinacy into a roar of motion. Fenna felt the vibrations through her feet, as Panninguaq waited for the helicopter to warm up and the engine to settle into a steady rhythm. The pilot spoke to the tower, twisted the collective and lifted the aircraft into a hover above the trolley with a smooth grasp of the control stick. Fenna spared a glance at Anguteq who was fidgeting between the two men on the back seat. He lifted his hands and stuck out his thumbs, jogging them up and down as his mother pointed the bright red nose of the Eurocopterin the direction of Nuuk.

There's no going back, Fenna realised. The aircraft picked up speed and Fenna settled in her seat.

Chapter 19

Sermitsiaq lies to the north of Nuuk. The mountain's flat angular crown listing to the west, piques the interest and captures the hearts of locals and visitors, not least with a pinched triangular peak focusing its granite energy into a single point. Its shadow does not reach Nuuk, and yet its reach is global, figuring prominently as it does on corporate and media logos and thousands of social media websites and galleries. Fenna studied the mountain, as Panninguaq called in her approach to the tiny provincial airport of Greenland's capital. Sermitsiaq, she noticed, resembled a wedge with the lower ridge curving around the mountain's base. *I've seen better mountains*, she decided, as the Eurocopter settled on the tarmac beside a Bombadier Dash 8 airplane. The bright red and white spotted liveries of both aircraft were a stark contrast to the large patches of brilliant snow covering the landscape surrounding Nuuk and crowning Sermitsiaq in gold, as the sun captured the higher of the two ridges. The rotors of the helicopter slowed from a thunderous chop to a slow protest, as the edges and tips bit at the cold, damp air until Panninguaq applied the rotor brake and the ground crew approached the aircraft.

"Welcome to Nuuk," she said and removed her flight helmet.

Fenna tugged the headset from her head and slipped it over a hook in front of her. She turned to watch Hong Wei and Lorentzen do the same. Anguteq bounced his calves on the seat, as he waited for the men to exit the cabin. He high-fived one of the ground crew before shouldering his backpack and racing across the tarmac to the airport building, launching into the legs of an elderly Greenlander that Fenna assumed was the boy's grandfather.

"He is pleased to be home, eh?" Lorentzen said, as he picked up his own pack and carry-on suitcase.

"Home?" said Panninguaq. "Home is further north. Nuuk is just where we live."

Fenna caught the look on Lorentzen's face, and, for a moment, his guard was down and she thought she recognised a longing for the north, something they each seemed to share. Hong Wei collected his luggage without comment, following the boy's path around the parked aircraft, head down and focused on placing each foot as securely on the slippery surface as possible.

"He's quiet," Fenna said and gripped her holdall.

"I think efficient is the word," Lorentzen said and gestured for Fenna to walk alongside him. "What little I know of Hong Wei suggests that he is a cautious man who appraises each situation economically, stripping away the flesh and cutting to the bone. He is a details man, with no interest in cosmetics." Lorentzen paused for a moment as he slipped, regained his footing and continued. "The Chinese chose their man carefully, and they trust him implicitly. If he signs off on the mine, then they will invest heavily, but ruthlessly. You can be sure they will maximise their profits with little or no thought extended to the Greenlanders. That's why I'm here."

"You?" said Fenna. "You're a negotiator?"

"No," he said and laughed. "That would be a mistake. My job is to do the field research and provide the details, including the cosmetic ones that Hong Wei will ignore. Isukasia is deep in Nuuk fjord, at the very end of it, in the mountains," Lorentzen said and pointed to the north east, his arm pointing straight between the airport building and the hangars. "But the traffic, tugs, barges and aircraft, will impact the wildlife and the environment between here and there in a way unprecedented in this part of Greenland."

"You're an environmentalist?" Fenna said and frowned. *Not what I imagined.*

"A tree-hugger? Me?" Lorentzen laughed again "God no, and," he said, "don't mention Greenpeace here in Nuuk. They are not welcome, not since their campaign against seal hunting. Those images of seals being clubbed in Canada in the 70s have haunted the Greenlanders for decades now. No, I'm not an environmentalist. I'm a pragmatist. It's about what the environment can cope with, before permanent damage results. The added challenge in Isukasia is the strain that a mine of that scale will place on Nuuk. Remember, there are only 15,000 people in Nuuk. The last figures for the mine suggested there might be as many as 7,000 workers, all of them Chinese, working in, around, or for the mine. They will need their own town, their own hospital." Lorentzen paused as they reached the airport building. "The politics of this project are splitting the country," he said and pushed the door open.

Panninguaq raised her eyebrow and said, "Like I said. Welcome to Nuuk."

Fenna followed Lorentzen inside, nodding at the policeman standing by the door to the waiting area and check-in desks. The sight of the policeman's dark blue jacket stalled Fenna for a second, her eyes drifting to the Heckler & Koch USP Compact pistol holstered at his hip. Fenna caught the policeman's eye; the thought of Maratse, and his boyish appreciation of a good gun battle, made her smile.

Hong Wei was waiting by the exit. He picked up his bag as they approached and waited as Lorentzen agreed to meet Panninguaq at the airport the following day.

"We'll be three, again," he said.

"No problem. You've chartered the chopper," she said. "I fly where you tell me to."

"Great," Lorentzen said and turned to Fenna. "Where are you staying? Hotel Hans Egede?"

"Yes," she said.

"So is Hong Wei. Let's get a taxi." Lorentzen shook hands with Panninguaq. "Until tomorrow."

Fenna went to follow him, but Panninguaq caught her arm.

"You seem familiar," she said. "Have we met?"

"No, I don't think so."

"Never been in Greenland before?"

"A long time ago," Fenna said and hiked her thumb toward Lorentzen. "I'd better be going."

"All right. I was just sure that…"

"Yes?"

"Last year there was…" Panninguaq paused and studied Fenna's face.

Come on, Fenna thought. *I don't need this.*

"No," she said. "I must be mistaken. I'll see you tomorrow."

"Okay," Fenna said and smiled. "Thanks for the flight." She walked out of the airport, her breath misting a cloud of smoke as passengers waited, cigarettes clamped between their lips and their eyes focused on the approaching snow clouds with the air of experienced travellers.

"We got in just in time," Lorentzen said, as he hurried Fenna to the taxi. The driver took her bag and tossed it into the boot. Fenna climbed into the back beside Hong Wei as Lorentzen got in the front. He turned in his seat as the driver pulled away from the airport, accelerating along the road running parallel to the runway. "It should clear up later," he said and pointed at the clouds. "But I have the feeling our pilot can cope with a little snow."

"A little, maybe," said Fenna. She caught the look on Lorentzen's face, his raised eyebrow, and realised, not for the first time, that she was struggling to find the balance between ignorance and showing an interest. *I'm not very good at this*, she thought. *Not yet.* "What?" she said as Lorentzen continued to look at her.

"There's something about you," he said. "I'm not sure what it is. Something familiar."

"You're mistaking me with another woman," she said and forced a laugh.

"No," he said. "I don't think so. Besides, I heard the pilot say as much. There's more to you, *Fenna*, than meets the eye."

Fenna wrestled with her thoughts and the façade she needed to maintain during the ten-minute drive into Nuuk. The lights of passing cars caught the twist of heavy flakes of snow as they tumbled to the ground. Ravens picked at the trash and fishing gear abandoned beneath the hulls of small boats and skiffs grounded for the winter. She spared a brief thought to the ravens teasing sledge dog puppies in Ittoqqortoormiit, only to be reminded at the first sight of Nuuk's housing blocks, that there was a world of difference between the settlements of Greenland and its capital. *And I need to remember that*, she mused. *I need to keep the two Greenlands separate – and the two Fennas.*

The bustle on the street outside the hotel snapped her attention back to the moment, as did the cold air entering the cab as Hong Wei opened the door to get out. Lorentzen paid the driver and Hong Wei collected his luggage. Fenna stepped out onto the street, orientated herself for a moment, taking in the activity around the entrance to the *Brugsen* supermarket, the buses, taxis and pedestrians, before grabbing her holdall and following the men inside.

"I'll see you in the morning," Lorentzen said, as he helped Hong Wei check in at the main desk. The Chinese man picked up his bags and made his way to the elevator. Fenna checked in, tapping her finger on the desk as she waited.

"You'll find the Internet is hellishly expensive," Lorentzen said, as the clerk handed Fenna her key card. "We got broadband a few years ago, but you get more gigabytes for less money with a mobile phone in Denmark than a cable connection here."

"I'll stay off the net," Fenna said. *He wants something*, she thought as Lorentzen glanced at his backpack leaning against the desk.

"We haven't established your role," he said. "And how Tunstall Mining just happens to have a Danish representative on their books."

"They are international," Fenna said. She felt her cheeks begin to flush and waved the key card in her hand. "I had better find my room."

"There's a bar. On the top floor."

"Okay." Fenna picked up her holdall and took a step toward the elevator.

"Maybe later?" he said. "To get to know you, and find out more about your remit?"

"Sure," she said and glanced at her watch.

"It's four hours earlier than you think."

"Right," Fenna said, "I forgot."

"Easy mistake. How about I meet you in the bar at six?"

"Okay. I'll see you then." Fenna walked to the elevator, pressed the button and waited for the door to open. She walked in, conscious of the proximity of Lorentzen as he waited in the lobby, watching her as the door closed. When it did, Fenna leaned back against the side and breathed.

"Damn," she said. She closed her eyes for a moment and then opened them at a ping as the elevator stopped on her floor, the fourth. She found her room, entered and tossed her holdall on the bed. She closed and locked the door, changed her watch to the local time, and looked down on the snowy street. Snow clung to the light blue of the supermarket, the warm glow of its lights like a beacon in the grey gloom of the storm. Fenna took a moment by the window to get her bearings, picking out the Bank of Greenland building, the tallest building on the horizon. Then she pulled off her jacket and flopped on the bed.

Panninguaq's curiosity and Lorentzen's suspicions cantered through her mind and she wondered if the mission was compromised, if it was nothing less than a monumental mistake to return to Greenland.

"In a country with just over 50,000 people, everyone knows someone, and that someone..." she sighed and closed her eyes. "That someone knows me."

Fenna propped herself up on her elbows and looked around the room, stopping to focus on the small kettle and the complimentary coffee and tea. She swung her legs over the side of the bed and pulled off her boots and socks. She padded across the carpet, filled the kettle with water from the bathroom, and prepared a cup of coffee. She dug the LOMROG report out of her holdall and made space on the small desk beneath the flat screen television hanging on the wall. Fenna flicked to the profile of Lorentzen, tucked in at the back of the report.

"You're a lonely guy, Dr Lorentzen," she said, as she looked through the report. "Why? What did I miss?" Fenna paused and traced her fingers over a few lines of scribbled notes in the margin. They were feint – *a bad photocopy*, she thought. Fenna read the lines, and then again, aloud, she processed the new information. "Parents died in car crash. Lorentzen, aged seven, pulled out of the car by firemen…" Fenna stopped reading. "I wonder," she said, remembering information gleaned from the profile during her first reading. "A history of short-lasting relationships, problems with attachment. And no wonder. Christ, if…"

She looked up at the sound of knocking on her door.

"Just a minute," she said and closed the report. She stuffed it into her holdall and zipped the bag shut. Fenna glanced around the room and took a few slow breaths before walking to the door. "I thought you said six o'clock," she said as she opened it.

"Now when did we agree that, *love*?" Burwardsley said and pushed her inside the room with the flat of his hand.

Chapter 20

Whether it was her training or the survival impulse she had been nurturing Fenna didn't know, but when Burwardsley's palm pushed against her chest, she let the momentum carry her into the room toward the desk. She grabbed the lamp and swung it at him. The two-pronged plug caught in the socket tightening the short electric cable with a soft snap and whipping the lamp out of her hand just as it connected with the side of his head.

"Fenna. Stop," said Burwardsley as he batted the lamp away from his face. She kicked at his right shin, and swung her left fist at his chin. She cried out as her knuckles connected with the Englishman's bone, her hand rasping against the stubble protruding through his skin. "Jesus. Fenna. You'll have hotel security her in a second."

Fenna leapt up onto the bed and swung her foot, aiming a kick at Burwardsley's head. He blocked her kick with his forearm, wrapped her leg within the crook of his arm and slapped his hand into her chest. Fenna crashed onto the bed and Burwardsley followed her down, his weight crushing her body as she struggled beneath him, stuttering short breaths as she spasmed for air.

"For fuck's sake," Burwardsley said. "Calm down and I'll let you go."

Fenna flicked her eyes at his and fought to increase the pause between each of her breaths until her chest stopped heaving and her heart adopted a rhythm that approximated that of strenuous exercise and not the feral beat of fight and flight. She trembled as she looked Burwardsley in the eye.

"Better?"

She nodded.

"I'm going to let go," he said and loosened his grip on her leg. Fenna flexed her fingers and Burwardsley paused, raising one eyebrow as he looked at her. "Konstabel?" She relaxed and he let go, shifting his weight as he pushed himself off Fenna and off the bed. She watched him as he walked to the door, closed and locked it, he picked the lamp up off the floor and put it on the desk. He fiddled for a moment with the lampshade, bending it back into shape between his fingers, turning the side with the dent in toward the wall. He pulled the chair out from beneath the desk, placed it in the space between the door and Fenna and sat down to face her.

Fenna lay flat on the bed. Her left leg hanging over the edge as if she had yet to reconnect with it. It was remote, detached, spent of energy, useless. A strand of hair was trapped within the lashes of Fenna's left eye, but she ignored it, peering through the hair, ignoring the irritation as she stared at Burwardsley. He stared back, dwarfing the chair beneath him, his hands resting on his knees, pale against the dark blue denim of his jeans. His arms were locked, elbows pointing to each side. Fenna flicked her eyes past him toward the door, her only escape route, blocked. She looked out of the window, listening to the faint buzz of the street below, the occasional shout and drunken slur, four floors below her. She turned her head back to Burwardsley as he coughed.

"You wouldn't make it," he said and nodded toward the window.

Fenna said nothing.

Burwardsley looked at Fenna's face and she felt his gaze blister her skin. "Black suits you," he said. "Although I liked it before." He paused and Fenna watched as his eyes softened and his cheeks relaxed. He wiped one large hand across his stubbled face. Fenna heard the tiny hairs scratch against his palm. "I never told you," he said. "How hard it was for me to hunt you."

Fenna closed a mental hand around her heart, willing it to stay within her chest, fearing her sternum plate, the cradle of her ribs, could not contain it. She had to get out, but her heart was the only part of her body not paralysed by Burwardsley's presence, his words. She wrestled her mind free of his grip, wrangled her thoughts into play and began to think.

What does he want? And why can I never beat him, this man, my *Achilles?*

"Of course," he said and placed his hand on his knee. "I thought it was all over, that you were gone and what happened on the island, onboard the ship ... I really thought it was all over. And yet…" He paused again and leaned forward. "Why are you back in Greenland, Konstabel?"

"Why are you?" she said, her eyes twitching, surprised at the sound of her own voice.

"That," he said, and sighed, "is a longer story."

"But you're not sightseeing, are you?"

"You never believed I was."

"No."

Burwardsley stood up and Fenna watched as he found the kettle and made coffee. As the water boiled she shifted position, pushing herself up against the headboard of the bed, drawing her knees into her chest. She wrapped her arms around her legs, and, for a brief moment, her wrists itched with the memory of rusted dog chain leashing her to the wooden wall of a distant cabin, the site of her first interrogation at the brutal hands of the man now serving her coffee in a paper cup on the opposite coast of the country. *That was the other Greenland*, she thought, *the other Fenna.* She took the coffee and waited until Burwardsley sat down before taking a sip. The chair creaked beneath his massive frame.

"I'm not sightseeing," he said and blew on the surface of his coffee. "This is personal."

"What is?"

"A good question." Burwardsley turned the cup in his hands. "I said I didn't like hunting you."

"You could have fooled me," she said and remembered the buzz of the skidoo and the exchange of lead as they shot at each other across the ice, the thunder of the helicopter changing pitch as it banked away from the clouds of snow obscuring Fenna, confusing the hunters, providing shelter and reprieve, only to deliver her into the hands of Humble and introduce her to the dark bowels of terror on the lower decks of *The Ice Star.*

"I'm a professional," he said and shrugged. "I happen to be very good at what I do, and people pay me well for it."

"A gun-thug for hire," Fenna said and sneered.

Burwardsley lifted the cup to his lips and stared at Fenna as he drank. He put the empty cup down on the desk. Fenna counted a full two minutes before he said anything.

"I heard about what you did to Humble," he said, a smile curled across his lips. "What I didn't hear was how you got away with it."

"I was lucky."

"No," he said and shook his head. "You had help."

"Yes."

"It's good to have friends like that, people who can get you out of a tight spot. Of course, that kind of help usually comes with a hefty price tag."

Fenna caught a scent of the desert, burnt sand, blood and sweat.

I know, she thought. *And he knows too.*

"Piece of advice," he said. "There'll come a time when the price is too high, and you're forced to do things that don't sit well, things that keep you up at night."

He's talking about Dina, Fenna realised. She lowered her knees, tilted her head to one side. "You see her too," she said. "You see Dina."

Burwardsley scratched his face again. Fenna leaned forward, searching his eyes. Her breath caught in her throat as he looked at her and she saw it, a flash of white, a reflection, the tip of the iceberg. She knew that following it would lead to the frigid depths below, where the demons floated dark beneath the surface, where Dina was.

"Yeah," he said. "I see Dina. She's naked, her skin pale, smeared in all kinds of shit. She's shivering, but not from the cold." Burwardsley paused. He looked at Fenna. "I'm here on my own dollar," he said. "You started something and… Shit. Would you believe I'm actually ashamed that it was you who finished things? A skinny Danish girl, with tiny tits and tiny fists?" He laughed and, despite herself, Fenna laughed too.

"I've learned how to use them," she said. When Burwardsley raised his eyebrow she added, "Really, I have." *Just not with you.*

"Well, that's good, I guess. But Dina," he said and they both stopped laughing. "Dina killed Lunk. You and your Danish friends got rid of Humble. Now there is only one guy left."

Fenna sat up. "You're going after Vestergaard? *The Magician*?"

"I have a lead," he said. "In my previous, more reputable life, I did a stint in the Arctic Cadre of the Royal Marines. I met a couple of Danes when on exercise in Norway. We used to sell whisky to the Norwegians, and, after a particularly good night, this Dane and I..." Burwardsley laughed. "Let's just say he owes me one."

"And he's here? In Nuuk?"

"Yep, he's at your Arctic Command Headquarters. But I wonder, are they even *yours* anymore, Konstabel? You went dark after Toronto," he said.

"And how do you know about that?"

"Perhaps we have a mutual friend?"

Fenna thought for a moment. *Nicklas*, she wondered. And then he was gone as she shifted gear, processing what Burwardsley had said, and wrestling with this new side, the new Burwardsley. *And yet, not so new after all.* She had seen the first signs when he had searched her outside the cabin at Ummannatsiaq. The cabin where Dina had died, taken her own life.

"Perhaps," she said. "But why do you think he is in Nuuk?"

"Vestergaard? Maybe. I don't know for sure. A man like that will be where you least expect it. Pulling strings, creating small pockets of chaos."

"So why are you here?"

"Because this is where the trail ends, and I intend to pick it up again."

Her stomach turned, as if someone had gripped it, squeezed it, tugging it in another direction, another course than the one she was already following. She pushed away images of Dina that threatened to overcome her. *Let him have them, for the moment at least.* But she couldn't stop the feelings of guilt and betrayal. And then the chair creaked and Burwardsley stood up.

"Where are you going?"

"To my hotel." Burwardsley paused by the desk to write something on the notepad. "My mobile number," he said.

"I want to help," she said and swung her legs off the bed and stood up.

"There's nothing you can do. Not yet," he said and shrugged. "Besides, you have your own mission."

"Yes."

"I'll be in touch when I know more. Who knows, perhaps you can help me in the end."

Burwardsley walked to the door, the tread of his boots pressing into the carpet. Fenna followed his tracks. She reached out and tugged at his fleece jacket, pulling back in an awkward recoil as he turned to look at her.

"Listen," she said.

"What?"

"I just want to say that…" Fenna ran her fingers through her hair, gripping two tiny fistfuls as she searched for the words. *Christ, my mind is a mess.*

"Fenna?"

"It's just that, well, I appreciate what you said. I've been having those same dreams. Maybe not the same, exactly, *my* Dina, she twists at the end of that whip, and I'm trying to cut her down, but she's too heavy, and the room, the fucking room is splinters and bullets, and I'm there in the middle of it all…" Fenna loosened her fingers and let her hands fall to her sides. "I'm there," she said, softly, her eyes glistening. "And you're there, and she's dying, killing herself, and I didn't do anything to stop it. I let her die, and Dina, she's…" Fenna's last words caught on her lips.

"You did what you could." Burwardsley took a step toward the door and reached out for the handle. "I'll be in touch," he said and opened the door. Fenna waited as he turned in the corridor. He paused for a moment and then looked at her. "You did the right thing," he said. "You did all you could. It was me who chased her there. It was me who pulled that whip around her neck."

"No," Fenna said. "Humble did that. And that monster, Lunk."

"Sometimes, I tell myself that," he said. "But at the end of the day, love, no matter how small a part we played, you can always find a way to make yourself responsible. Whether you're responsible for doing something, or responsible for *not* doing something. It's all the same. Given your new career, you might want to remember that." Burwardsley nodded. "I'll be in touch."

Fenna listened to his footsteps as he walked along the corridor to the elevator. She heard the soft rumble as the doors opened, and again when they closed. His words caught in her mind as she closed and locked the door. She tried the lamp on the desk, blinking in the glare of the bulb before turning it off again. She tidied the top cover of the bed, rearranged the pillows, tossed the paper cups into the waste paper basket, until there were no more signs of the man she had hated until now. She looked at her watch and realised any thoughts about Burwardsley and Dina would have to wait.

She walked into the bathroom, stopped in front of the mirror and clicked the mental switch she had discovered since her experience in the desert. "And until then," she said, as she smoothed a wet finger over her eyebrow. "I have a job to do."

Fenna fetched her holdall from the room. She stripped, glancing at the bruises healing slowly on her body, as she picked out a black bra and panties from among her clothes. Fenna pulled on her jeans, and applied a little make-up to cover the stubborn traces of her panda eyes, before tugging a tight-fitting t-shirt over her head. She ruffled her hair with her fingers and leaned in toward the mirror.

"You, girl," she said, "are seriously messed up. But with a little luck, you might just get through this. And yet…" Fenna felt the words extinguish on her tongue. The life of an investigator, a PET agent, one of Jarnvig's pawns, she realised, was far from straight forward. "But I'm in the game now," she said, as she pulled her boots over her bare feet. "And it's time for the next round."

Chapter 21

The Skyline Bar on the top floor of Hotel Hans Egede was busier than Fenna expected it to be, so early in the evening. She found Lorentzen at a table furthest from the piano on the small stage opposite the bar. He stood up to greet her, but she didn't recognise the man sitting next to him.

"Fenna," Lorentzen said as he gave her a hug and kissed her cheek. Fenna twitched at the familiarity, and then leaned in to the kiss, playing her role as she imagined she should. She sat down and looked at the man opposite her. "This is Kaptajn Christian Bertelsen. He's with Arctic Command, here in Nuuk," Lorentzen said, as he sat down.

"Hello," said Fenna, as Lorentzen caught the eye of a waiter and ordered her a beer. *I'm not supposed to meet anyone from Arctic Command*, she thought, and prayed that her basic disguise held up to the Kaptajn's scrutiny.

"Christian hasn't been in Greenland long," Lorentzen said as the waiter arrived with Fenna's beer. "But new faces soon become old friends this far north," he said and Fenna wondered how many beers Lorentzen had had already.

"What is it you do, exactly?" Fenna said and took a sip of beer.

"Well, I…"

"He's got an interesting story to tell, actually," Lorentzen said and leaned forward in his chair. "You remember that man you didn't know at the airport?"

"What man?" Fenna said, glancing from Bertelsen to Lorentzen and back. *Careful, Fenna.*

"The one who thought you were a guide?"

"Yes," she said, and placed her glass on the table. The chill of the beer had made the glass slippery and, given the nature of Lorentzen's story, she didn't want it to slip out of her hand.

"It turns out he's not just another tourist after all." Lorentzen pointed at Bertelsen. "You tell her," he said as he leaned back in his chair and studied Fenna.

He's not as drunk as I thought.

"His name is Mike Burwardsley, I knew him back when I was on exercise in Norway."

"Yes?" Fenna said and glanced at Lorentzen. He was still

watching her.

"Mike's name popped up on a watch list. I can't tell you too much, but I think you should keep an eye out, and let me know if you see him again."

"I don't know the man," Fenna said and frowned at Lorentzen. "Did you tell him that I did?"

Lorentzen shrugged. "It looked like you were talking…"

"He thought I was a guide."

"It looked like more than that," he said and stared at Fenna.

"Why do I suddenly feel that I'm the one you want to keep an eye on?" She looked at Bertelsen. "What do you know about me?" She waited for him to react and then said, "No. Don't look at him. What do you know about me, Kaptajn?" Fenna waited for five seconds before standing up and saying, "Fine. You've given me my answer." She turned to Lorentzen. "I'll see you at the airport in the morning. I think Panninguaq said we should be there at seven. I'll be early." She moved toward the entrance, stopped and said, "Thanks for the drink."

Fenna reached the elevator before she heard the sound of her name. She pressed the button to go down.

"Fenna, wait," Lorentzen said, as he walked past the leather sofa outside the bar and joined her in front of the elevator.

"So many questions," Fenna said and pushed the button again.

"Questions I had to ask."

"Is that why you asked me to join you for a drink? To ask questions? Is that why you brought your friend?"

"Hey, listen," he said, as the elevator doors opened. "These are interesting times. I vet everyone I meet."

"Good for you," Fenna said, as she brushed past the guest coming out. It wasn't difficult to play the role of the offended and affronted young woman, she realised, it was a good mask for the tumult of thoughts and apprehensions that were spinning through her mind. *Don't blow this*, she told herself. *Not now.*

"Fenna," Lorentzen said, as reached his arm inside the elevator to stop the doors from closing.

"Goodnight, Karl," Fenna said. She crossed her arms and waited for him to leave. The doors closed and she relaxed as the look on his face suggested he might have miscalculated. She spent the thirty second descent from the top floor to her own wondering at the turn of events, wondering about the watch list that Burwardsley had been put on, and if he knew that his so-called friend at Arctic Command had him under surveillance. *And if they saw him come into my hotel room?*

Fenna laid on the bed fully-dressed. She watched the flickering carpet of green Northern Lights swathing across the night sky as she tried to sleep, all the time anticipating a knock at the door. Would it be Burwardsley, the police, or a team of heavies from Arctic Command? The thought kept her awake and it wasn't just the bruises she needed to cover up around her eyes the next morning.

Two cups of coffee later, and Fenna ordered a taxi at the front desk. She thought she had seen Hong Wei at the breakfast bar, but chose to ignore him, deciding instead to travel alone to the airport. Nuuk airport was quiet, with just one member of Air Greenland's staff opening one of two check-in desks. The café was open, and Fenna bought a cinnamon pastry, found a chair facing the door and waited for Lorentzen and the Chinaman to arrive. Just as she finished her pastry Hong Wei walked through the door. He sat down next to her without a word, focusing instead on the Smartphone in his hand, his thumbs blurring in a flurry of texts. Lorentzen arrived a few minutes later, wearing a flat smile on his face as he approached Fenna's table.

"I'm sorry about last night," he said, as he pulled out a chair. He sat down opposite Fenna. She stared at him, took in the practical clothes he had chosen to wear, and realised that, apart from the duvet jacket she had put on, and the spare clothes in her daypack, she was wearing the exact same clothes as the night before.

"Don't mention it," she said, as Panninguaq opened the door to the baggage reclaim area and beckoned for them to follow her.

"Sorry," she said as she shook hands to greet them. "But we need to get going if we are going to beat the weather. Spring in Greenland is changeable at best," she said, as she pointed through the window at the dark clouds forming in the distance. "It should clear up again this afternoon, but if we don't take off in the next ten minutes, we'll be grounded most of the day."

"Let's get going then," said Lorentzen. He gestured for Hong Wei to follow them out of the baggage area and onto the tarmac. He slipped and Panninguaq caught his arm, guiding him to the helicopter. She showed him to passenger seat next to her, but Hong Wei pointed instead at the back seat and she helped him buckle in.

"I'll sit in the back," Lorentzen said and walked around the aircraft. Fenna climbed in beside Panninguaq and listened as she talked the ground crew through her pre-flight checks. It might have been easy banter, but, in Greenlandic, it sounded guttural and exotic. *Almost feral*, Fenna thought. Fenna tuned-in to Panninguaq's chatter, starting at the sudden switch to Danish as the pilot lifted the Eurocopter into a hover and taxied to the runway, the helicopter's nose dipping slightly, as she feathered the control sticks and pedals.

When they were clear of the airport and Nuuk lay behind them, with Sermitsiaq to their left, Fenna asked Panninguaq what she thought of the mine.

"What do I think of it?"

"Yes, you know, in terms of Greenland," Fenna said, hoping that Lorentzen was listening, as she played her role of fact-gathering mining representative.

"It's ugly, environmentally unfriendly, and expensive," Panninguaq said, her voice shushing in Fenna's ear through the headset.

"So you're against it?"

"I didn't say that."

"Then what do you mean?"

"It's complicated," Panninguaq said and gestured at the stark mountains, prominent in their coating of snow, spotted and patched with ice. The Greenland ice sheet shone white in the distance, and Panninguaq adjusted course toward it. "You see this," she said.

"The mountains?"

"The mountains, the sea, the ice, all of it. It's beautiful. It's my home, my country. But we have a lot of it. If the mine opens, and even with all the implications that has for the country, and the environment, it will still be just a small part of Greenland."

"So, you're saying you're for the mine?"

"No," Panninguaq said and paused. "And yes." The rotors whined above her and the airframe juddered as she lowered the nose to increase speed. Fenna felt the vibrations through her seat and the soles of her boots. "If Greenland is ever going to be truly independent, it needs money, and the only thing we have is our natural resources – in the sea and in the ground. We need to invest in tourism and we need to start mining or drilling if we want to be economically free of Denmark." She dipped her head toward the back seat. "Your Chinese friend knows this, and so do his politicians."

"Which makes it even more important to make the right decision," Lorentzen's voice chattered through the background hiss of Fenna's headset. *So, he* is *listening*, she thought.

"You're right," said Panninguaq. "But they should be decisions for Greenland to make. Even if they are environmentally wrong ones. It is still *our*environment."

Panninguaq stopped talking and concentrated on flying up the length of Nuuk fjord and into the mountains. The mine site popped out of the landscape with orange and red fuel barrels, white tents, two large timber-framed administration buildings with white pine sidings, and a larger mess hall painted red. Panninguaq slowed the aircraft into a slow, low orbit of the camp as Hong Wei took a rapid series of photographs with his Smartphone. Fenna spotted small digging machines, their yellow plates a stark contrast to the dark granite and dirt-speckled snow on the ground.

"Everything has to be flown in," Panninguaq said. "Although there is talk of a road."

"They fly it in from Nuuk?"

"No. They ship it up the fjord, and then charter a helicopter to lift it from the deck of the ship to the camp. It takes time."

At a nod from Hong Wei, Panninguaq flew the helicopter to the landing pad – a square of snow marked by white-striped fuel barrels, one in each corner. She landed, shut down the engine and slowed the rotors to a stop with the handbrake above her head. Lorentzen was the first to step out of the helicopter. He helped Hong Wei onto the skids and onto the ground. A tall, bearded Dane in a grimy wool sweater approached them, and Lorentzen introduced him as the leader of the camp. Hong Wei shook the man's hand, and then greeted three of his own countrymen as they approached. Fenna hid a smile when she noticed they were wearing alpine duvet suits. She was still smiling when Lorentzen tapped her on the shoulder.

"This is Bjørn Eskelsen," he said. "Veteran geologist and administrator for Isukasia."

"Such as it is," Eskelsen said. "And who are you?"

"I'm with Tunstall Mining. I'm here to have a look around."

Eskelsen glanced at Lorentzen. "The Chinese are backing the mine. What does Tunstall want?"

"A potential piece of the action or a buy-out. Who knows?" said Lorentzen. "But if the rest of the company are as pretty as she is, the more the merrier, I say."

That didn't take long, Fenna thought, *men treating women like playthings*, as she followed them toward the camp. She waved at Panninguaq as the pilot prepped the aircraft in case of strong winds and snow flurries. Panninguaq flashed the fingers of her right hand twice and continued working.

Ten minutes. Fenna waved again. She continued along the track, catching Eskelsen's comments as they drifted toward her on the wind blowing in from the southwest.

"… a skeleton crew. I've just sent most of the men into town for the weekend. There's nothing much more to be done here before people start making some decisions."

"So how many men are here?" Lorentzen asked.

"You, me, the Chinese, and the two ladies," he said and glanced over his shoulder.

"And there's a storm coming. Should be cosy."

"It might not come to anything," Eskelsen said. "But…"

"This is Greenland," they said together and laughed.

This is *Greenland*, Fenna thought, as she followed the men. She watched as they ducked into the first of the two administration buildings. She could see the Chinese men were already inside and decided to check on the mess hall, figuring it would be less crowded.

The mess hall, the size of a large rectangular cabin, reminded Fenna of the hunting cabins the Sirius teams used when on patrol. The walls were bare but for a single geological map, and a nude pin-up. She spotted the ubiquitous bookshelf and traced her finger along the cracked spines and mildewed pages. The heat from the wood-burning stove radiated as far as the ring of chairs arranged around it. Fenna paused at the sight of a black jacket hanging from the back of one of the chairs. The dull yellow emblem caught her eye. The emblem depicted three lions beneath the Danish crown, embroidered on a dark green patch. She walked over to it and smoothed her hand over the material, glancing over her shoulder as if the owner – a Greenlandic policeman – might walk in any minute.

Fenna smiled at the feel of the fabric, remembering the one man in uniform that had shown her any sense of kindness or understanding since Mikael had been killed and she had been framed for his murder.

"Maratse," she whispered. "Where are you now?"

On impulse, Fenna knelt down and slipped her hands inside the pockets. She found a packet of cigarettes, almost empty but for two whole cigarettes and a foul-smelling half-smoked one. She frowned and pushed the packet back inside the pocket. In the opposite pocket she found a couple of rusted metal clasps and a swivel, the kind used to anchor sledge dogs on a chain to the rocks. *There are no sledge dogs in Nuuk*. Fenna slipped the piece of rusty metal back into the pocket and checked inside the jacket. Fenna's fingers caught the leather edge of a thin wallet. She pulled it out and opened a police identification card. Fenna smiled at the flood of emotion she felt on seeing the picture of David Maratse, his bushy black eyebrows and his walnut skin, bronzed in the sun and glare of the ice.

"Maratse," she said and then frowned. "What the hell are you doing here?" Then she recalled Eskelsen and the tally of men he had related to Lorentzen. "But you wouldn't leave your jacket behind," Fenna said and closed Maratse's ID card. "Why didn't he say you were here?"

There was a tramp of feet in the snow outside the mess hall. Fenna slipped Maratse's card inside his jacket and scanned the cabin for a way out. She saw the window, prayed it could be opened, and ran toward it, just as the person coming into the mess hall banged the snow from his boots on the step outside the door.

Chapter 22

The window creaked open a few centimetres and started to vibrate in the wind; the snowstorm had caught up with them. Fenna leaned into the frame, slipping one leg over the sill before dropping to the ground. The strap of her daypack caught on the window latch. Fenna twisted beneath it, trying to tug herself free as the tramp of boots on the planks of the mess hall floor suggested more than one person had entered. She heard the men's voices and then Panninguaq's soft laugh.

"Come on, Fenna," she said, the words chased from her lips in a flurry of snow. Fenna felt the flakes tickle her cheeks, catch in her hair, as she pressed her toes into the ground and pushed upward, freeing the strap from the latch. She bent her knees and ducked beneath the frame of the window. She heard a man grunt and close it, the latch fastening with a stubborn squeal of metal that had seen too many winters, or one very long one. Fenna looked beyond the row of tents, and spied a path; the snow trudged and flattened beneath a hundred boot prints. She ducked around thc side of the mess hall and followed the path just to the left of a long, low granite ridge. The snow thickened, gusting in flurries like airborne steams of tiny fish, darting in large clouds one way, only to be spun in the other. In the absence of predators, the wind played the role of the hunter, chasing the snow at whim, swirling the flakes around Fenna's feet and plastering her hair with cold, wet clumps. It was heavier, denser, wetter snow than the dry, light crystals of the far north of Greenland. Fenna felt the cold faster too, much like Greenlanders complained at how cold winters in Copenhagen were, compared to the north. Fenna tucked her hands into her pockets and followed the path in anticipation of finding some kind of shelter. *Why else would there be a path?*

Her hunch was right. At the base of a large, smooth rock face, Fenna spied a shipping container, its doors dogged closed. She grasped the handle, flinching in anticipation of the freeze-burn of cold metal on warm skin. The air temperature was high enough that Fenna felt only the dull cold of the metal – its bark was worse than its bite, as the handle squealed all the way into the open position. Snow licked at the rubber lip insulating the edge of the door as Fenna opened it. The grey light of the snowstorm lit the first few metres of the interior, just enough to reveal the heel of a boot and to elicit a moan from someone inside the container. She opened the door wider and the light fell on the bloodied face of Sergent David Maratse of the Greenland police.

"Maratse," Fenna said, as she stepped inside the container, the hollow ring of her boots echoing around the space until she knelt beside the policeman, the cardboard packaging of the supplies between which he was bound absorbed the last echo of her steps.

She cleared his airway first, removing the dirty rag that filled his mouth. Maratse gasped for breath, as the snow settled on his tongue and dissolved. Fenna checked the pulse in his neck, untied his hands and began to search the policeman's body for wounds and bleeding. Maratse, his eyes closed, protested with soft moans and weak waves of his right hand. His left hand, Fenna noticed, was still, and lay flat on the floor. A first glance revealed that it was dark with bruises. Two of the fingernails were split and bloody, the nail prised from the skin by several millimetres. Fenna didn't touch them. She cupped her hand to Maratse's cheek and waited for him to open his eyes.

"Maratse. It's Fenna. Look at me," she said, as she shuffled closer to him.

"Fenna?" he said and groaned. "You shouldn't be here."

"Neither should you." Fenna laughed and Maratse joined her, coughing as he tried to sit up. "Don't," she said. "Stay still."

"*Iiji.*"

"What happened?"

"Chinese," he said and coughed.

"Why?"

"Ask them," he said and chuckled. "Cigarette?"

"No," Fenna said and smoothed Maratse's fringe from his forehead. She felt the sweat on his brow and wondered if he was bleeding internally. "I need to get you out of here."

"*Iiji.*"

The snow was thickening. *We're not flying in that, even if I could get Panninguaq away from the Chinese. Must be another way*, she thought and then turned to look at Maratse. *Stabilise him first. Make him comfortable.* She smiled.

"What?" said Maratse. His eyes followed Fenna as she smoothed her hands down each of his legs, worrying her fingers inside the lip of his boots, checking the temperature of his skin with her finger, checking for blood.

"Nothing. I'm going to look after you."

"Good," he said. And then, "Cigarette?"

"Nope," Fenna said and knelt by his side. "Best if you don't anyway." She looked outside. "The snow is going to slow things down. I'm not sure when and how I'm going to get you out." She took his right hand in her own. "Where does it hurt?"

"Stomach," he said and flicked his eyes down his body. Fenna tugged at the black wool sweater, and then the light blue police shirt beneath it. Even in the low light of the snowstorm, Fenna could see that Maratse's stomach was black with bruises, swollen and – she pressed her fingers against his skin – hard to the touch. Maratse grimaced and pushed her hand away.

"Cross-fit? You've been working out," she said and laughed, her voice softened by the snow.

"*Iiji*," he said and fidgeted. Fenna helped him into a sitting position as he shuffled backwards to lean against the boxed supplies.

"So tell me again, why are you here, and why did they do this?"

"Ittoqqortoormiit."

"Yes?"

"A research ship came into port."

"*Odin*?"

"*Iiji*. The crew came ashore. They had a body with them. A scientist."

"Johansson," Fenna said and nodded. "He was murdered."

"Accident, they said. Not murdered," Maratse said. He squinted at Fenna in the gloom. "How did you know?"

"I'm here because of the same ship," she said. "I will tell you later. Keep going."

"There was another man. He wanted to tell me something. But he was killed in a bar fight."

"By one of the crew?"

"*Naamik*," Maratse said and wrinkled his brow. "By Samuel, my brother-in-law."

"Why?"

"Paid to do it, he said. I came here to Nuuk to find out."

"Why here?"

"You met the man with the beard?"

"Bjørn Eskelsen? The camp leader? Yes, I met him."

"*Bjørn*," Maratse said and laughed. "The *bear*."

"Yes."

"Strong. He was also on the ship. He paid Samuel."

Fenna sat on the floor of the container and crossed her legs. "You know this for sure?"

"*Iiji*. Samuel is a drunk, but not a liar." Maratse looked at Fenna, his eyes glistened in the grey light. "Life can be difficult," he said. "Money, even a little bit, can make a difference. That's why he did it. That's why Samuel killed the man from the ship. I just need to make it right. Maybe keep him in jail, in Greenland."

Because killers are sent to Denmark, she remembered. *A double sentence.*

Maratse coughed and Fenna studied his face, remembering the smile that creased his cheeks when they had fled across the ice, windows shattering from Burwardsley's bullets. He looked different without the cigarette between his lips, parked in the gap between his teeth. Fenna wished she smoked, or that she had brought his jacket at least.

"Fenna," he said, "why are you here?"

"I'm here because of the ship, and the dead man you carried off it."

"And what are you doing?" Maratse paused to cough. He wiped his mouth with the back of his hand, and Fenna saw the blood smeared on his skin.

"Don't worry about that. I have to get you out of here."

"*Iiji*," Maratse said and shrugged. "Maybe."

Fenna stood up. She tugged at the hem of her jacket and tightened the straps of her pack. "Wait here," she said and laughed and then added, "Don't move."

"I'll be here," Maratse said and smiled as Fenna stepped toward the door. "Konstabel," he said.

"Yes?"

"Cigarette," he said and pointed at his mouth.

"Sure," she said and slipped out of the container. Fenna pushed the door closed, leaving a gap the width of her hand for air and light. She squinted into the snow and scanned the path for tracks. There were none. *And why should there be? Everyone will be inside*. And she knew exactly where. *Huddled around the stove, in the mess hall*. Fenna leaned into the wind and jogged down the path to the camp.

She almost ran into the row of tents, the white fabric lost in the snow. A loose guy snapped in the wind and she followed the sound as the snow thickened. The mess hall loomed to her left, but Fenna jogged around it and back on the path toward the makeshift helicopter pad. Panninguaq had plugged the air intakes with bulky baffles. The rotors were weighted, the shrouds securing them taut when Fenna tested them. *We're going nowhere*, she realised.

On the far side of the helicopter Fenna spotted a wooden stake, flashed at the top with fluorescent orange paint. She followed it, ignoring the snow as the ground sloped beneath her feet, shuffling her way across hidden patches of ice, from one marker to the next. The wind dropped as Fenna entered a narrow gulley. She peered through the snow and tried to remember the terrain they had flown over, how far the fjord was from the camp, and how on earth she was ever going to get Maratse down the path.

"And even if I do," she said, licking at the snow settling on her lip. "All the boats have left for Nuuk." *A skeleton crew*, Eskelsen had said.

A tap of rock behind her, to her left, caught Fenna's attention and she froze, resisting the urge to duck and move into cover. She called out instead.

"I guess it's too late to hide?" she said, looking back up the path in the direction of the helicopter.

"That depends," said a man's voice. Fenna's breath caught in her throat as the man stepped into view, a rifle held in his mittened hands, the barrel levelled at Fenna's chest. His beard, heavy with snow, reminded Fenna of Mikael. *The Yeti*, she thought and smiled. "You're amused?" Bjørn Eskelsen said as he took a step toward her. "I didn't expect that."

Fenna turned her hands at her sides, palms outward. "Not amused. Just at a disadvantage," she said and shrugged. "What's a girl to do?"

"Ordinarily, I wouldn't know. But then you're not quite an ordinary girl, are you?"

"No," she said. "I guess not."

Eskelsen slung the rifle over his shoulder. He lifted his leg and set his foot on a boulder. "You found the policeman," he said and jerked a mittened thumb over his shoulder. "Didn't you?"

"Yes."

"You know him?"

Fenna nodded. "Yes."

"You know why he's here?"

Fenna lowered her hands and waited for Eskelsen to speak. She watched as he lifted his foot and took another step toward her. She studied him as he moved, listing to one side, like a stricken ship. He paused mid-step as he noticed her watching him.

"What's wrong with your leg?"

"Mining accident," he said and shrugged. "Why? What's your interest?"

Fenna said nothing. She pressed the tips of her fingers into her legs, felt the beginnings of the familiar surge of adrenalin. *Control it, Fenna*, she thought. *Use it.*

"How is he?" Eskelsen said. "Your friend. The policeman."

"My friend?"

"Yes, Konstabel," said a second voice. Fenna flicked her head to her right as Lorentzen manoeuvred around a boulder above her. "It's Konstabel Brongaard, isn't it?" he said, as he joined Eskelsen on the path in front of her.

"How long have you known?"

"About an hour. Bjørn told me," he said, looking at Eskelsen. "Your friend mentioned you in an earlier chat."

"The Chinese have a way of making people talk," Eskelsen said. "It's not my thing, but they are useful when suitably invested."

"Apparently," said Lorentzen, "the Chinese, are more interested in you than they are in the mine. Your friend followed Bjørn to Nuuk, and, Greenland being the small country that it is…" Lorentzen paused to chuckle. "Well, when Bjørn told the Chinese about his little problem, they became quite animated at the prospect of chatting with officer Maratse. Isn't that right, Bjørn?"

"It is," he said. "And now they are even more excited to talk to you, Konstabel."

"Which presents us with a bit of a dilemma," said Lorentzen.

"Such as?" Fenna said, as she tasted the adrenalin pulsing through her veins.

"Whether we should let them."

Chapter 23

The fjord, Fenna remembered, was to the southwest. She could just see the black water if she squinted through the snow flurries thickening around her and the two men. A glance at Lorentzen suggested that he was getting cold, in spite of his experience in the field. Eskelsen, Fenna noted, was hardened to the elements, a sign that, despite the limp, he was comfortable with the environment and used to long periods in camp. *Leading the camp*, she remembered. *He is here because he understands the terrain.* The thought lingered as her gaze shifted to the rifle in his grasp.

Lorentzen clapped his hands and Fenna looked up. "Our friends will be wondering where we got to," he said and took another step closer to Fenna. "Hong Wei might be a quiet fellow, but I can assure you he is quite the chatterbox when you get to know him. And I have decided that you *should* get to know him," Lorentzen said with a quick nod at Eskelsen. "Intimately," he added. He wiped a swathe of snow from his forehead and brushed the thick flakes from his fingers. Fenna watched him and took a step along the path as Eskelsen levelled the barrel of the rifle at her chest. "It's a shame, really," he said.

"What is?" said Fenna as she passed Eskelsen, navigating between the snow-frosted boulders in the path leading toward the landing pad.

"I'm curious to get to know you, I think we might have had fun together."

"You don't think this is fun?" she said and cast a glance over her shoulder. Eskelsen was close behind her, the end of the barrel within a metre of her back. *And he has a gammy leg*, she thought.

"As much as I love Greenland," Lorentzen said, peering through the snow as he picked his way around the boulders. "I have grown accustomed to certain luxuries."

"It's your age then," Fenna said and smiled at the pause her words gave the geologist. "Or is it just one too many society functions?" Fenna ignored the scowl on Eskelsen's face and stared at Lorentzen. "You've grown soft, in here," she said and tapped the side of her head with a finger. "It'll be your belly next, and what pretty young thing will have you then? When the grey hair on your temple isn't rakish, just retired." She turned her back as Lorentzen opened his mouth to retort. Eskelsen, she saw, was smiling. Fenna slid her heels along the patches of old ice as Lorentzen stumbled to catch up.

"You think I fell for you, Konstabel? Is that it?"

"Your profile says you like black hair."

"My profile? Hah," he said and snorted. Fenna heard the tumble of loose granite beneath his boots. "My profile is phoney."

"So's my hair," she said. *Let him come*, she thought at the sound of more grit being ground into the path.

"I admit, I'm intrigued, Konstabel," he said as he stumbled into step alongside Eskelsen. "What else do I like?"

"Let it go," Eskelsen said as Lorentzen brushed past him.

"My tits," Fenna said as she reeled him in, step by step. "You don't like more than a handful. All the breasts of all the women you have ever been with," she said, "could fit in the palm of your hand." Lorentzen stopped in front of Fenna. "Am I wrong?" she said and gestured at her chest. As his gaze dropped she kicked his right knee and scraped the thick tread of her boot down his shin.

"Move," Eskelsen said as he limped to one side of his colleague.

"Fuck," Lorentzen said, as he twisted and reached for his knee. Fenna moved with him, using his body as a shield between her and the barrel of Eskelsen's rifle. Eskelsen pressed the barrel over Lorentzen's shoulder as Fenna leaned into the geologist and slammed her elbow up to catch his chin, whipping his head back toward Eskelsen. She curled her left fist into Lorentzen's sternum as he cried out, and then silenced him with her right in his stomach. The wind from his lungs brushed her fringe as Fenna shoved his body into Eskelsen, closed her left hand around the barrel of the rifle and yanked it free as Eskelsen caught Lorentzen before they tumbled onto the path. Fenna changed her grip and slammed the butt into Eskelsen's forehead. She held the rifle in the ready position, poised like a hunter waiting with a harpoon above a seal's breathing hole in the ice, until Eskelsen's head lolled to one side. Fenna slung the rifle on her back and then jammed two fingers inside Lorentzen's nostrils.

"Up."

"Fuck. Stop," he said, as he pushed himself onto his feet only to have Fenna fell him again with a kick. Lorentzen crumpled beneath her and Fenna let his head crack against a boulder. He groaned and cupped the back of his head in his hands. Fenna ignored the blood staining the snow clinging to his skin.

"Your profile," she said, "suggested you were bored in Nuuk. So how's this for excitement?" Fenna took a handful of Lorentzen's hair and forced him to crawl away from the path and down the side of the mountain toward the fjord. Lorentzen cried out as he scrabbled across the rocks to keep up with her. Fenna noticed he was favouring his left knee, protecting his right.

She stopped on a small plateau about twenty metres from the path. Eskelsen's body was just visible when she squinted through the snow. Fenna let Lorentzen catch his breath as she slipped the rifle from her shoulder and chambered a round.

"I have a dilemma," she said, as Lorentzen looked up at her. "The mission or the man?"

"What man?" Lorentzen said, his words absorbed by the snow as the air thickened around them.

"The policeman, my friend. He needs a hospital." Fenna glanced toward the path, relaxing her shoulders as she identified the outline of Eskelsen's knee. "But the mission…" she said and paused. Eskelsen was still there. *But, did he move?*

"What mission?"

Fenna blinked in the snow and focused on Lorentzen. "The Pole," she said. "Why did you sell out?"

"I don't know what you mean," he said and pressed his hands around his knee. Fenna kicked it and he wailed.

"You fiddled with the instruments, and changed the results. Now some politician is about to present the findings to UNCLOS and Greenland loses the Pole."

"Denmark," he said through gritted teeth. "Denmark loses the Pole, or did you forget who you are working for, Konstabel?"

Fenna shrugged and took a step back. She lifted the rifle and aimed it at Lorentzen's chest. "My friend chased Eskelsen all the way here to this camp. Eskelsen had a man killed in a bar in Ittoqqortoormiit – probably the only bar – and I'm guessing that was to cover for you. Am I right?" she said with a glance toward the path. She frowned and took a step to the right, squinting through the snow.

"You think Eskelsen is covering for me?" Lorentzen started to laugh. "That's rich. I can't wait to tell him."

"Tell him what?" Fenna said and shifted her attention back to Lorentzen. *He's still lying there, Eskelsen. Isn't he?*

"Tell him your little theory. Really, girl," Lorentzen said and sneered. "You are just a very *little* girl in a very big game." Fenna paused and took another small step away from Lorentzen. She flicked her eyes from him to the path and back again. *I can still see his knee…*

"Keep talking."

"If I must, but really, *girl*, you haven't been sent here to find out the truth."

"No?" she said and gripped the rifle in one hand as she brushed the snow from her eyes.

"No," Lorentzen said and laughed. "You've been sent to cover it up."

"What?" Fenna said and frowned at Lorentzen. He spoke but she didn't hear his words as she realised it wasn't Ekselsen's knee she had been staring at. *It was a fucking rock.*

Fenna ducked into a squatting position and scanned the terrain to either side of Lorentzen. He turned his head as Fenna stood and followed a shadow of movement, as it lumbered through the snow. She lifted the rifle and tugged the butt of the stock into her shoulder, but the shadow was gone. *And too far away*, she thought. *Damn, Fenna. Stupid.*

"And now you have a problem," said Lorentzen.

"What's that?"

"The policeman just got upgraded from friend to bargaining chip. At least he will live for a little while longer, until you get him to a hospital, or Eskelsen puts you both in the morgue."

"Not today," Fenna said, her voice low as she considered her options. She bit her lip and looked down at Lorentzen. "You said I was sent to cover up the truth?"

"You were listening?"

"I was, and now you better start talking."

"And yet," he said. "Every minute you spend with me is another minute Eskelsen has to reach the camp, and your friend."

"You're right," Fenna said. She took three quick steps backward, raised the rifle, and pulled the trigger. Lorentzen screamed as the bullet tore through the flesh, ligament, and bone of his left knee.

Fenna ignored Lorentzen's screams as she ran, chambering another round into the rifle, skirting around large boulders, leaping over flat ones, as she charged up the path toward the camp. She tried to focus, but could not ignore Lorentzen's words. *I'm covering up the truth? But for whom, and to what purpose?*

She slowed as she reached the helicopter, the sight of the snow layering the rotor blades twisting at her stomach as she realised they were not flying out of camp. *Not anytime soon.* The crack of a small calibre saloon rifle forced her into cover as she ducked behind an empty oil drum marking one of the four corners of the makeshift landing pad. Fenna pressed her body into the rusted metal surface as two more rounds snapped through the air above her head.

"Stop shooting," Eskelsen said, his English scarred at the edges with a blend of barroom accents. Fenna imagined he had picked up the varied inflections on his travels in the north. "You'll hit the bloody helicopter."

Fenna nodded a quick *thank you* at the bright red Eurocopter. "At least they want to get home," she said and took a breath. "Let's see how much." She stood up and raised her rifle, searching for targets as she took slow steps toward the helicopter. Eskelsen's Chinese associates were almost comical in their puffy down suits. Fenna spotted one of them through the rifle sights as he ran from one side of the path to the other. She tracked him, leading the rifle in front of his body, firing before he reached a large boulder. The man's suit deflated, expelling a puff of bloody feathers as Fenna chambered another round. "Two men down," she said and searched for another target. "Just four more to go."

Snow drifted around the tubular skids of Fenna's protecting angel. She squinted around the flurry of flakes, searching for her next target. *Another puffed-up Chinaman or…* Fenna swore and lowered her rifle as Panninguaq stumbled onto the path with Eskelsen's hand around her throat and Maratse's service pistol pressed to the side of her head. She heard Panninguaq whimper as Eskelsen shoved her down the path, toward the helicopter.

"No," Fenna breathed. "Not again."

"Drop your rifle, Konstabel," Eskelsen said, as he manoeuvred Panninguaq to the perimeter of the landing pad. "It all ends here."

"For you, maybe," she said and let the rifle slip from her grasp and into the snow at her feet. *For me*, she thought as she fought the urge to retch, *it is just beginning.*

Eskelsen shoved Panninguaq to the side and lumbered across the snow, the USP pistol aimed at Fenna's chest, as he bent down to pick up the rifle. Fenna noted the bloody gash on his forehead with a smile. He nodded for her to walk past him. Panninguaq was shivering, her eyes flickering from Eskelsen to the helicopter.

"Prep it," he said. "I want to be able to fly as soon as the storm lifts." Fenna looked up at the sky, her gaze resting on a whiter patch of grey before Eskelsen pushed her forward with the barrel of the rifle. As they passed the dead Chinese man Eskelsen spoke in English, ordering the dead man's colleagues to go down the path to find Lorentzen.

"I didn't kill Lorentzen," Fenna said.

"Perhaps you should have," he said and pointed. "First tent, on the left."

The last few metres were the longest Fenna had ever known. She rubbed her wrists and thought of Burwardsley and Bahadur – the Gurkha with the wicked blade – and the last time she had been interrogated. *But I've changed since then,* she thought as Burwardsley's image was replaced with that of the Gunney. Her first kill. The Chinaman, her second. *Number two was easier*, she realised before her stomach contradicted her and she doubled up and retched onto the snow.

"Not so tough now," Eskelsen said. He slung the rifle over his shoulder, gripped Fenna by the hair and pressed the pistol into her neck. He pushed her through the door of the canvas walled tent, grunting that she should go inside. "I wouldn't worry though," he said as they entered and Fenna sniffed at the warm air and the coppery stench of blood – a lot of blood. "We're not going to hurt you. Not to begin with anyway."

Fenna blinked in the glare and heat of halogen worklights as the judder of a diesel generator changed pitch as Hong Wei pressed metal paddles onto Maratse's bare and bloody skin. The lights flickered, Maratse screamed, and Fenna retched.

Chapter 24

Hong Wei let go of the paddles when the wooden handles began to smoke. The lights went out and the tent descended into a grey pallor as Maratse's scream receded in a long, slow, wail. Fenna wiped spots of bile from her lips with the back of her hand and took a step toward the policeman.

"Don't," said Eskelsen and motioned with the pistol that she should sit in a folding chair to her left. Fenna looked at Maratse as she sat down, holding his gaze for as long as she could before looking away.

"The generator," said Hong Wei as he pulled off a pair of thick rubber gloves. "Has stopped."

"I'll fix it," Eskelsen said, his English less accented than the Chinese man's. He pressed the pistol into Hong Wei's hand as he walked past him to open a flap in the corner of the tent. The floorboards creaked as he limped across them. Fenna watched him leave and then faced the Chinese man as Hong Wei leaned against the desk to the right of Maratse. They watched each other as Eskelsen fiddled with the generator.

"This is unfortunate," Hong Wei said.

"The generator?" Fenna said, stumbling over the words as she glanced at Maratse.

"No," he said. "This." Hong Wei waved his hands around the tent. "You and me, here. This man. His pain. All most unfortunate."

"You're the one hurting him."

"Me? No," he said and shook his head. Hong Wei pointed his finger at Fenna. "You. You are the one hurting him."

Fenna swallowed as Hong Wei stood up and walked the two steps to the chair in which Maratse was sprawled and bound, the thin copper wire cutting into the skin of his wrists and ankles. She stood up when Hong Wei pressed his finger into Maratse's bruised and swollen stomach.

"Hey," she said and took a step forward.

"Sit down, Konstabel," Hong Wei said and pointed the pistol at her face. "This man is unwell. He does not have time for us to discuss things. So, you must tell me what I want to know, and quickly. Maybe then, there will be time for your friend."

With another glance at Maratse, Fenna sat down as the generator lurched into life with a shudder and a belch of blue smoke. It settled into a steady rhythm as Eskelsen released the choke and entered the tent. The barrel of the rifle caught on the flap. Fenna watched as he fiddled it loose, unslung the rifle, and placed it on the desk. Eskelsen took the pistol from Hong Wei as the Chinese man reached for the rubber gloves he had thrown onto the floor.

"Wait," said Fenna. "You don't need to do that."

"Do what?" Hong Wei said, as he pulled on the gloves. Eskelsen stood behind Maratse.

"That," she said and nodded at the paddles on the floor, the insulation tape wrapped around the base of the handles was melted, the cables snaked with sticky streams of Maratse's blood.

"You will tell me everything?"

"Yes," she said. "I'll tell you anything," she added as she slumped into the chair.

"No, Konstabel, not just *anything*," Hong Wei said and pressed his finger into Maratse's blistered skin." Fenna held her breath as the policeman moaned. "You will be specific. Do you understand?"

"Yes," she said, her eyes fixed on Maratse.

"Good," Hong Wei said and picked up the paddles. Fenna watched as he hung them from the back of Maratse's chair. He kept the gloves on, she noticed. "First," he said. "Tell me what you know about Lorentzen? Why are you so interested in him?"

Fenna thought for a moment. *The mission or the man? What would Nicklas do? What would Jarnvig want me to do?* Then she thought of Greenland and Lorentzen's words about securing the Pole for Denmark, not Greenland. *When did I become such a Greenlandophile?* She wondered and then looked at Maratse. *When he saved me, and when Dina died. That's when.* Fenna made her decision.

"We think Lorentzen fiddled with the instruments on the LOMROG expedition," she said and glanced at Eskelsen. "But maybe we were wrong."

"Maybe you were," said Hong Wei. "But what does it matter?"

"If the results are wrong they cannot prove that the continental shelf of Greenland is attached to the geographical North Pole."

"Yes. And?"

Fenna shrugged and said, "Denmark wants the Pole."

"So do a lot of countries. Russia," said Hong Wei, "has already claimed it."

"They claim a lot of things. Usually by force," she said, as she flicked her eyes toward the paddles on the desk.

Hong Wei smiled as he considered Fenna's response. "How do you know the results are false?" he said and paused to scratch at his ear, frowning at the stubby tips of the gloves. "How do you know?"

"There was a log, kept by one of the scientists on the expedition. It says as much, before he was killed," she said and turned her attention back to Eskelsen.

"Strange things happen at sea," he said and shrugged. "Lorentzen asked me to meet him in Ittoqqortoormiit."

"Where you tried to cover up Johansson's death with another one," she said and looked over at Maratse. "That's why he is here."

"Some policeman follows me all the way from the east coast of Greenland, that's his problem," said Eskelsen.

"But," Hong Wei said and held up his hand. "No matter. The results are interesting," he said and pointed at Fenna. "What she knows is not important. *Who* sent her – *that* is important. She must tell us now." Hong Wei picked up the paddles. "Tell us," he said, as he flicked the switch for current and pressed the paddles into Maratse's chest.

"Stop," Fenna shouted as Maratse screamed. A bloody mist steamed from the policeman's chest, dissipating as the generator stopped and the camp was quiet. "I can tell you," Fenna said in the hush.

"I know you will," Hong Wei said. He grimaced as the paddles came free of Maratse's skin with a sucking sound. Maratse fainted, his head lolling back on the seat, hanging over the edge toward Eskelsen. Hong Wei tossed the sticky paddles onto the desk beside the rifle and removed his gloves for the second time; Fenna hoped it would be the last.

And I just have to give him a name. That's all.

The smell of charred flesh and fresh blood pricked at her nostrils and her conscience. Fenna thought for a moment as she considered what she knew, what it might mean, and, ultimately, the consequences of doing so. *We're never getting out of here*, she thought. *Not without something to whet their interest, something to suggest that this game is bigger than even they thought.* She pressed her hands to her cheeks, feeling the rough skin of her fingers on her lips. "*The Magician* sent me," she said and looked at Hong Wei.

"A magician?" said Hong Wei. "Like a wizard? Hah," he said and picked up his gloves.

"Wait," said Fenna and waved her hands for him to stop.

"Sit down," Eskelsen said and pointed the pistol in her direction. "And tell him what he wants to know."

"I *am* telling him."

"No, Konstabel," said Hong Wei. "You are wasting my time, and his," he said and nodded at Maratse. "There is no proof of anything. We can kill you both without a trace. There are many accidents in Greenland, and a fire at a remote mining camp is very difficult to stop."

"You kill us," Fenna said and stood up, "then you will never find out who is working against you." Fenna faced Eskelsen as he lowered the pistol, the wrinkles on his brow tugging a fresh stream of blood from the open wound she had given him.

"Talk," he said.

Okay, she thought. *Make it good.* Fenna sat down and rested her arms on the chair. She curled her fingers around the ends. "Do you know who I am?" she said and waited.

"An agent with the Danish government," said Hong Wei.

"PET," said Eskelsen.

"And before that?" she said and watched as Hong Wei glanced at Eskelsen. The Dane shook his head.

"No," Hong Wei said.

"Then you've never heard of *The Ice Star*?"

"Should we?"

"It's a ship," she said. "A luxury adventure cruise ship with an ice class that makes it relatively independent."

"Why is this important?" Hong Wei said. He paused at the distant sound of rotors beginning to turn.

"That'll be the pilot," said Eskelsen. "I told her to be ready to fly as soon as the weather lifted."

Hong Wei turned back to Fenna. "Talk faster."

Fenna thought of the two remaining Chinese men that were likely with Panninguaq, making sure she didn't leave. She took a breath and started, "I was onboard that ship, together with men working for *The Magician*."

"What men?" said Hong Wei. Fenna enjoyed the tic of irritation pulsing in his right cheek.

He's used to knowing everything. He takes pride in it, she thought as she considered what to tell him next, and what to leave out. "There are other countries playing this game," she said. "China is only an observer, the *real* players," Fenna said with a nod toward Eskelsen, "control men like him, women like me, and others…" she paused. "Like you."

"You are saying this *Magician* is a player?"

"Yes," Fenna said, "with a seat at the main table." She waited as Hong Wei seemed to process her words. Maratse groaned, his head lolling to one side as he opened one eye. Fenna's heart skipped a beat. *He's alive.*

"You have access to this man?"

"You want to meet him? I can…"

"That is not what I asked," he said and shook his head. He turned to Eskelsen. "Give the gun to me." Hong Wei looked at Fenna as he held out his hand for the gun. "Do you know who I am?"

"An advisor to the Chinese. High up in government. Probably something to do with intelligence," Fenna said and shrugged as Hong Wei took the gun from Eskelsen. She watched as he tested the weight in his grasp. "You weren't mentioned in my file."

"No? Interesting," he said. "Perhaps, later, I can tell you why, Konstabel. But, first, tell me more of this *Magician*."

"He orchestrated a plot to humiliate the Danish sovereignty mission. I was on that mission."

"And you put a stop to it? The humiliation?"

"In a way," Fenna said and snapped her head toward Eskelsen as he snorted.

"You're the one? The woman who killed her partner? Jesus."

"I didn't kill Mikael," Fenna said. *How many times am I going to have to repeat that?*

"This is public knowledge?" Hong Wei said.

"Only if you know the right people," Eskelsen said and shrugged. "I have met a few guys from the Sirius Patrol. She," he said with a nod at Fenna, "is the first *girl* to get selected."

Girl, Fenna thought. *Like it is a bad thing, a plaything*. She took a long breath. She noticed the light inside the tent was less grey, brighter, and the snow no longer scratched on the canvas. Even Maratse's blood seemed to have stopped pooling on the floor.

Optimism will be the death of me, she thought and gauged the distance between her and Hong Wei. *Too far.*

"And *The Magician*? How was he involved?" said Hong Wei, as he turned his attention back to Fenna.

"Behind the scenes, pulling strings, but he was there in the beginning. I met him. I just didn't know who he was. But I found out that he was working for the Canadians."

Hong Wei said nothing. The floorboards creaked as Eskelsen shuffled on his feet, searching for a more comfortable position for his leg. Maratse lifted his head until Fenna cautioned him to let it fall again with a flash of her hand. The policeman winked at her and mouthed the word cigarette, and if Fenna had had one, she would have taken a bullet just to put it in his mouth and light it, to give him that one last smoke. Instead, she hid her smile and waited.

"Do you know how important the Pole is?" Hong Wei said.

"I have an idea."

"The money from shipping alone will make control of the sea routes around Greenland and across the Arctic very expensive, and very lucrative." Hong Wei paused to walk across the tent to stand at the wall to the right of Maratse and Eskelsen. He held the pistol in his left hand, smoothing his right on the canvas wall. "If there is oil in Greenland, it will take years before it can be extracted. If Greenland is to make money, it needs to make it now. If Greenland owns the Pole, it can make that money, but not without Denmark."

"No," said Fenna. "Greenland could never patrol the sea. It has no navy."

"No military forces whatsoever," said Hong Wei. "China needs that sea route, and it needs it to be cheap." Fenna waited as Hong Wei took a step away from the wall of the tent. "This mine," he said and gestured with his right hand, "will never earn enough money to pay for itself. It would be cheaper to buy the country…"

And finance its independence, Fenna thought. *Patrol the coast. The Arctic sea lanes.*

"…which is what we are doing," he said. "One harbour and one airport at a time. You have seen the plans, Konstabel?"

"Yes," Fenna said and remembered the artist's impression of a new Nuuk, a capital city the Greenlanders could be proud of, one that would catapult them onto the world's scene.

"And you approve?"

"They are ambitious."

"Futures are built on ambition," Hong Wei said. "Which is why the results of the LOMROG expedition were never falsified, just hidden."

"Hidden?" said Fenna as she leaned forward.

"What?" said Eskelsen.

"Yes," Hong Wei said. "The results were hidden. Not falsified. Lorentzen did not tamper with the machine, he used another machine."

"You can't hide that kind of equipment on a ship," Eskelsen said and tugged at his beard with his hand.

"There was another ship."

"The *Xue Long*," said Fenna.

"Yes. On a parallel course, but a week later."

"I had a man killed for him," Eskelsen said, his voice low as he looked at the back of the tent in the direction of the landing pad.

And I was sent to cover the truth, Fenna thought, as she remembered Lorentzen's words. "*The Magician*?" she said.

"I need to meet him," Hong Wei said. "I will need an introduction. Can you arrange that?"

"I know a man who can," Fenna said and nodded at Maratse. "If you will help him."

"Yes, of course. We will put him on the helicopter."

"The helicopter?" Eskelsen said and took a step forward. "No-one is getting on that bird before I say so. I'm the camp administrator."

"You were," said Hong Wei as he raised the pistol and fired.

Maratse started at the crack of the gunshot as Eskelsen crumpled to the ground, and then Fenna was at his side, untwisting the wires around his wrists and ankles, releasing him from the chair and buttoning the tatters of cloth that used to be his shirt.

"Cigarette," he said and coughed.

"I don't have one."

"My jacket. Over there," he said and pointed a bloody finger at a wooden chest on the far side of the tent. "They collected my things," he said as Fenna picked up Maratse's jacket and fished the crumpled packet of smokes from the inside pocket. She slipped half a cigarette between the policeman's bloody lips and lit it with the lighter stuffed inside the packet. Maratse rolled the cigarette into the gap in his teeth and coughed a cloud of smoke into the air above his face.

"You're going to be all right," Fenna said and covered his chest with the jacket.

"*Iiji*," he said and grinned.

"Still better than picking up drunks?"

Maratse smiled and closed his eyes. "*Iiji*. Much better."

Fenna stood up and watched the blood pool beneath Eskelsen's head as Hong Wei rifled the dead man's pockets, throwing his wallet and identification badge onto the wooden floor. Fenna glanced at the rifle on the desk and took a step toward it.

"Konstabel," said Hong Wei, as he pointed the pistol at her. "Don't."

"Okay," said Fenna and stepped closer to Maratse. "What do we do now?"

"Now," Hong Wei said and stood up. "We start a fire that is very difficult to put out."

Chapter 25

The fire licked at the walls of the tent as Fenna dragged Maratse along the path to the helicopter. Blood dripped from his wrists into the cuffs of his jacket as he smoked the last cigarette from the packet. Fenna tugged the policeman closer to her body, curling her arm around his waist to grab his belt. She pulled his left arm around her shoulder as she encouraged him to take one slow step after another until they reached the helicopter. The two Chinese men wearing puffer jackets lapped them several times with crates and gear that Hong Wei wanted to be flown out. Then they dowsed the other tents and equipment with aviation fuel and lit them. Fenna wrinkled her nose at the acrid stink and blinked through the thick smoke as the wind curled it down the path and enveloped them. She stopped at the first barrel that marked the corner of the landing pad and let Maratse rest as she walked toward the helicopter. Panninguaq sat in the pilot's seat, her face hidden behind large aviator glasses and her hair. Fenna took a step toward the cockpit window only to stop when she noticed Lorentzen finishing the knot on a fresh bandage around his knee.

"You didn't believe me, did you?" he said, as Fenna stopped to face him.

"About what?" she said.

"Cleaning up. Eskelsen is dead, isn't he?"

"Yes."

"As I said, you're here to clean up."

"I came here to find out the truth. To see if you had falsified the LOMROG data."

"I didn't. Not in so many words."

"No. But you still withheld it," Fenna said and paused. "How much did they pay you?"

"The Chinese? Enough," he said and tossed the empty bandage packet onto the ground. "How much are they paying *you*?"

"I don't take bribes to shit on my own country."

"Ah, and which country is that, Konstabel? Because it seems to me that you are becoming less and less Danish in your actions. You might want to watch that. Your boss, Jarnvig, doesn't appreciate disloyalty," Lorentzen reached for the flask of water by his side and waved at the smoke drifting down from the camp. "We're not so different," he said and took a swig of water. "We could even have been friends."

"You don't have friends," Fenna said. "You sold Eskelsen out in a heartbeat."

"Bjørn? He knew the risks. The minute the Chinese got involved, well… it was only a matter of time before this happened."

"This?"

"The cleaning up. You think the Chinese want the world to know how deeply they are grubbing in the Arctic? They have observer status on the Arctic Council, Konstabel. They are courting Finland, and the Alaskans. Do you think they want anyone to discover the other activities they are engaged in?"

"No," Fenna said and waited.

"Then you might want to consider how long you've got before it's your body burning in some conveniently remote location."

Fenna opened her mouth to speak and then stopped at the sound of rotors thudding through the air from the south, from Nuuk.

"Not so remote," she said and ran back to Maratse. "Come on. Let's get you out of here." Fenna heaved Maratse onto his feet and pulled him across the landing pad. "Panninguaq," she yelled, waving with her left arm. "Get out of the chopper."

Panninguaq opened the door a fraction and pulled the headset to one side, strands of her hair twisting in the wind as she freed her left ear. "What?"

"Get out," Fenna said. "There's another helicopter coming. We need to move. To get away from Hong Wei."

The crack of Maratse's pistol and the snap of the bullet in the air above the helicopter confirmed what Fenna already knew. It was too late. The Chinese intelligence operative had finished overseeing the destruction of the camp and was ready to leave.

"Start the helicopter," Hong Wei shouted as he marched toward them, the snow sticking to his heels and the toes of his boots. "Get in," he said to Fenna. "Bring your friend."

Fenna opened the passenger door as Panninguaq checked the instruments. She helped Maratse onto the backseat and then looked at Lorentzen as he held up his hand.

"I could do with a lift," he said, as Fenna reached down to help him.

"No," said Hong Wei. "I will help him. Get inside, Konstabel."

Fenna nodded and closed the door. She walked around the nose of the aircraft and opened the rear passenger door as the rotors began to turn. She stepped onto the skids and paused at the sound of one shot being fired from the pistol, and then a second. She turned as Hong Wei followed her path in the snow and gestured for her to get inside with a wave of the gun. Fenna climbed in and closed the door. She leaned over Maratse and looked down at the entry wound in Lorentzen's head and the stain of blood on the front of his jacket. She leaned back on the seat and watched as Hong Wei got in beside Panninguaq. He put on a spare headset and motioned for Fenna to do the same.

"I have some friends on the way," he said and pointed to the south. "They will pick up my associates and clean up the rest of the mess. Now," Hong Wei said, as he fastened his seatbelt, "keep quiet and enjoy the ride." Fenna noticed he kept the pistol trained on Panninguaq.

As Panninguaq twisted the collective and pulled back on the stick, the Eurocopter lifted off the pad in a tornado of snow, a whiteout that reminded Fenna of the documentaries she had seen of troops being lifted out of the dustbowl of Afghanistan. She thought of her father, bit her lip, and buckled Maratse's belt before fastening her own.

Dad, she thought, *you were Special Forces. You pushed me in this direction.* Fenna thought of the conversation she had had with Solomon on the flight across the Atlantic, how he stressed the importance of family. *And yet*, she thought and looked at Maratse as he gritted his teeth beside her. *Sometimes sharing the same blood isn't enough, you have to spill it together too.*

As they flew down the fjord Fenna considered her next move and wondered if Burwardsley had made any progress in finding *The Magician*. The irony was not lost on her, that the very man she and Maratse had fled from across the sea ice in a bullet-ridden police Toyota was now the only man who might be able to save her and the policeman she had become so fond of and now felt responsible for. *I have a tendency to do that*, she thought, *to feel responsible for people*. Now she needed to plan as best she could, with the limited resources she had, and the dubious allies she could muster.

She put her thoughts on pause as Panninguaq flew past Sermitsiaq, and the shadow of the mountain seemed to reach out and pluck at Fenna's arms. She wished it could, that the mountain might swallow her and end this – *all of it.* But they were soon beyond the mountain's reach and Fenna suddenly realised why Hong Wei had remained so calm – there were friends waiting for him in the harbour. He tapped Panninguaq's leg as she vectored in towards the airport.

"Land there," he said and pointed toward the helicopter pad at the stern of a massive red-hulled and white-decked icebreaker, dwarfing the cruise ships and naval patrol boats as it loitered in the sheltered bay to the east of the commercial dock. Fenna tried not to be impressed, but when Maratse fidgeted by her side for a better look, she exchanged a smile and raised her eyebrows as Panninguaq circled the Chinese icebreaker, the *MV Xue Long*, and hovered above the deck to land. "You are impressed," Hong Wei said, as he turned in his seat to look at Fenna. "Just wait until you get on board."

I am impressed, she thought. *We have nothing like this. And yet…* Fenna pushed thoughts of the impressive ship and the equally impressive commitment China, a non-Arctic nation, was making to polar research. *They are building a second*, she remembered, as the helicopter touched down on the landing pad. And then her thoughts were racing as the efficiency of the Chinese Arctic Research Mission took over. Fenna watched as Maratse was lifted onto a stretcher and wheeled across the deck and into a lift. She walked after him only to have Hong Wei catch her by the arm and point her in the direction of a door leading inside the main structure.

"What about Panninguaq?"

"She stays," he said and nodded at the deckhands securing the aircraft.

"As a hostage?"

"As a guest."

"And what am I?

"An asset, for the moment. Come with me."

A tall man with a jagged scar on his chin met them at the door. Hong Wei handed him Maratse's pistol and gave a few short commands in Chinese before leading Fenna inside.

"The northeast passage," he said, "cuts 4,000 miles off the shipping distance from Shanghai to Hamburg." Hong Wei paused to let a group of crewmen scurry past. "Even ice-free, the waters in the Arctic are still dangerous. We will need ships like the *Xue Long* to escort our container ships. Expensive, but time is money, and if we save time, we save money."

"She looks like a container ship," Fenna said, as she followed Hong Wei down a stairwell to the next deck and into a cabin.

"She used to be," he said as he shut the door. "But then my country bought it and refitted it. A bit like what we are going to do with you."

"I'm not going to work for the Chinese," she said and clenched her fists at her sides.

"But your mission is over. Cleaned up. I cleaned it up for you, and now you work for me."

"I work for the Danish government."

"Of course." Hong Wei poured two mugs of coffee from a pot at the end of the small cabin. He gestured at the table and placed Fenna's coffee in front of her as she sat down. "It has been a long day," he said and sipped at his coffee. "It can be difficult to keep track of the time when the sun does not go down."

"Or when it doesn't come up."

"I would not know. I have never experienced an Arctic winter." Hong Wei took another sip and studied Fenna. "You did not react when I shot Eskelsen. He was your countryman."

"He was going to kill me."

"And Lorentzen? He was not going to kill you, but still, no reaction when I shot him."

"I've seen a lot of death recently," Fenna said and sighed. "I'm getting better at dealing with it." A brief image of Dina challenged her words as the Greenlander twisted beneath the dog whip in her mind's eye, but Fenna ignored it, pushed her away. *Save the living*, she thought. *There's nothing I can do for the dead.*

Hong Wei put his mug down and leaned on the counter. "I have never heard of you, and this troubles me. I'm the head of intelligence for all things pertaining to the Arctic. I should have heard of you."

"Are you trying to impress me?" Fenna said. "Because I'm just too tired."

"I'm merely paying you a professional compliment, or should I just pass it on to your boss, Per Jarnvig?" Fenna looked up and Hong Wei smiled. "Some things I *do* know, but this *Magician*. Perhaps he has another name, because that one I have never heard. Tell me more about him, and then we will approach your contact."

"He is Danish," said Fenna, "as far as I know. His accent and mannerisms were perfect when he interrogated me."

"When?"

"Actually," Fenna said and paused as she realised it was true, "just a few months ago. It was in March, this year."

"You have been busy."

You have no idea, Fenna thought and scanned the room with a quick twist of her head from right to left. It was spartan, efficient. She had the feeling that *efficient* was the official motto of the *Xue Long*. Something she was not, she realised, as she considered the wake of bodies and destruction she left in her path, on her quest for the truth. *The truth*, she wondered. *What truth? What am I searching for?* And then she remembered. She recalled how she could cope with being in close proximity to Burwardsley, the one man who scared her, because they shared a common goal, to finish things, not for themselves, but for Dina.

"You seem lost in your thoughts, Konstabel," Hong Wei said. His words jogged Fenna out of her mind and into the present.

Just lost, she thought and stood up. "We need to find a Royal Marine Lieutenant called Burwardsley. He has been tracking *The Magician* since March."

"And where is this Marine?"

"He is here, in Nuuk."

"Because the man we seek is here?"

"Perhaps. I don't know. But this is where the trail led Burwardsley."

Hong Wei shook his head. "Perhaps our little chat over coffee has confused you, Konstabel. Perhaps you have forgotten just what I will do to discover the things I need to know, to find the people I need to talk to. Your story about a wizard intrigues me as I have heard similar stories of a man, perhaps even an organisation that is manipulating events in the Arctic faster than the Arctic states can react. But, be smart, Konstabel, because I will not hesitate to visit our friend in the ship's medical bay if you need the slightest help in remembering why you are here, still alive, and not blistering in a flaming tent in the mountains. Do you understand?"

"I do," Fenna said and stuck out her chin. "More than you think."

"Then are you ready to make contact with Burwardsley?" Hong Wei said and Fenna almost smiled at the difficulty he had in pronouncing the Lieutenant's name.

"I need a phone," she said and held out her hand as Hong Wei fished a mobile from his pocket. Fenna pulled a crumpled note from her pocket and dialled the number Burwardsley had given her. She looked at Hong Wei, choosing to focus on him and what he might do to Maratse, instead of thinking about what Burwardsley had done to her. The dial tone stopped and Burwardsley answered. "It's Fenna," she said. Hong Wei took the mobile from her hand and turned on the speaker. He put it on the table between them.

"Nice timing, *love*," Burwardsley said. "Where are you?"

"In the bay. On a ship. We need to meet."

"That could be difficult."

"Why?"

"I have some new friends, and they seem keen for me to stay put."

"Then I'll come to you."

"Hah," Burwardsley laughed. "You'll need a small army."

"Mr Burwardsley," Hong Wei said, as he leaned over the mobile.

"Fenna? What the fuck. Who's this?"

"Who I am is not important. What is important is that I happen to have a small army. You said that you needed one. Can I be of assistance?"

Burwardsley was quiet for a moment and Fenna pictured him thinking it through.

"Yeah, all right," he said. "Bring your army."

"Very well. We will see you very soon."

"Wait," said Burwardsley. "Fenna, can we trust this guy?"

"No," she said and finished the call.

The Sea

NORTH ATLANTIC OCEAN, GREENLAND

Chapter 26

Fenna followed Hong Wei out of the cabin and along the deck toward the mudroom where the scientists don their survival suits and gear ready for the field. He stopped at the doorway and gestured for Fenna to wait as he spoke to the same tall Chinese crewman who met them on arrival. Hong Wei beckoned for her to join him as the man left.

"The Air Greenland pilot…"

"Panninguaq."

"Yes. She will fly you to the airport from where you will take a taxi to your contact's location," Hong Wei said and paused for a moment to study Fenna's face. "You work for me now. Do you understand?"

"You think you've turned me?"

"I don't need to. You'll work for me of your own accord because I have something of yours."

The mission or the man, thought Fenna. *Now the mission* is *the man*. "I will need proof. Constant updates, and," she said. "I'll need a phone. They took mine in the desert. I haven't had one since."

"I will provide you with a phone, and I will send reports…"

"Video."

"… of the policeman's progress. Believe me, he is receiving the very best care."

"Because of what you did to him," Fenna said through gritted teeth.

"And I can do it again," he said and waited for Fenna to relax. "Now, do you understand what is required of you?"

"You mentioned something about an army?"

"Yes," Hong Wei said and laughed. It was the first time Fenna could recall she had heard him laugh. She shivered at the harsh tones, as unfamiliar to him as they were to her. "In my official capacity as a representative of the People's Republic of China, I visited one of the schools in Nuuk. The new one, in the new part of town. As a gesture, the school has taken a Chinese teacher on exchange. Chen is one of mine. The small army I mentioned is her class. I think you will find that children are the best means of diffusing a tense situation, especially *en masse*. You are in luck. They are cooking seal meat at the school tonight – a fundraiser. Chen has her class. She will bring them to the location of your contact on the pretence of collecting something. You will accompany them."

"You've thought this through," Fenna said.

"It is my job."

"And after that? You will get Burwardsley and me back on the ship?"

"Yes, of course." Fenna studied Hong Wei's face as he reached inside his jacket for a mobile, thinner and smaller than the one she had used earlier. "This," he said, "is what the American's call a *burner.*"

But who is burning whom? Fenna wondered as she took the mobile. She slipped it inside her pocket. Her thin fingers trembled, catching on the hem of the pocket. *Treason*, she thought, *makes me nervous*. And then she thought of Maratse in the medical wing, and Hong Wei's personal interest in his well-being.

"I'll need a weapon," she said.

"I don't think so," Hong Wei said and gestured toward the door at the far end of the mudroom. "Up the stairs and onto the deck. Your helicopter is waiting."

Fenna walked past Hong Wei. She paused at the door and looked back. "Just to be clear. I give you information about *The Magician*, and you let Maratse go."

"We are agreed."

"And what about me?"

"We'll see how useful you are this evening. Perhaps I will have need of further information."

"But you will let Maratse go for this one piece of information?"

"Yes," Hong Wei said and Fenna really wanted to believe him. "Are we clear?"

"Yes," she said and opened the door. Fenna heard the rotors of the Eurocopter whine as she jogged up the stairs, through a second door, and onto the open deck. She felt the mobile vibrate in her pocket and took it out. Hong Wei's text gave her the time and location of her meet with Chen. She had twenty minutes.

Panninguaq was quiet as Fenna slid into the passenger seat. Fenna slipped the spare headset over her head and heard her talk to the tower at Nuuk airport, confirming her approach and landing permission. Panninguaq lifted the Eurocopter off the deck and into the air, hovering into a slow turn before dipping the nose to gain speed and then climbing above and around the city. Fenna could see the high rises of Qinngorput, the new part of the town, and the long, straight road sloping down to the school. She imagined Burwardsley watching the helicopter from the balcony of one of the apartments and her stomach twisted at the thought. The old cliché, the enemy of my enemy is my friend, distracted her from the view and Panninguaq's voice coming through the headset.

"This for my son," she said and Fenna looked at her.

"What?"

"Anguteq. He is the only reason I'm doing this."

"Doing what?" said Fenna. She recognised the tremor in Panninguaq's voice, the roar of the rotors couldn't hide it.

"Keeping my mouth shut."

"About what happened at the mine?"

"Yes, *what happened at the mine*," Panninguaq said and whipped her head to one side, staring at Fenna, her hair caught in the seatbelt and in a strip of old Velcro on the headset. She yanked it free and glared at Fenna. "That man, he…"

"Killed someone," said Fenna. "Yes."

"He sent someone to talk to me."

"Who?"

"I don't know his name. A man. Tall…"

"With a scar on his chin? Yes, I've seen him."

"He said that if I wanted to see my son again, that I had better keep my mouth shut. That there were people everywhere," she said and took a ragged breath. Fenna listened as Panninguaq fought with the next sentence. "They even have someone at the school, he said."

"I know," said Fenna.

"You know? How do you *know*?"

"Panninguaq…"

"No. Don't tell me. I'm leaving. Tonight. I will fly to Kangerlussuaq. I'll take Anguteq to Denmark tomorrow morning."

"They will have people in Denmark too," Fenna said, but Panninguaq ignored her and the airport loomed in the near distance. Panninguaq said nothing more to Fenna, sparing words for the tower only as she talked through her approach and set the aircraft down on a square trolley close to the two main hangers. Panninguaq shut down the engine, applied the rotor brake and then glanced at Fenna.

"I don't want to see you again," she said and waited for Fenna to leave.

Fenna took off her headset and stepped out of the helicopter. She took a last look at Panninguaq and then walked across the tarmac to the gate, slipping outside and around the arrivals, enjoying the anonymity of an internal charter flight.

It was Hong Wei's men at the mine, she thought as she caught the last available taxi. *So Lorentzen won't be missed yet. I have a little time at least. Before the shit hits the fan.* Fenna gave the address to the driver of the taxi and settled into the back seat. The road looped around the runway and Fenna wasted a few seconds looking at Sermitsiaq, its summit lit by the evening sun, as bright as midday in Denmark. *It's growing on me*, she thought. *That's something.* But the sight of the mountain, the fjord, the small patches of cotton growing along the road, the brightly painted houses – bigger than those in the settlements, but just as colourful – couldn't distract her from Burwardsley. Someone she had hated yet now, *I need him*, she thought, *if I am going to save Maratse.*

The driver turned left at the T-junction and Fenna could see the *Xue Long* – Chinese for *Snow Dragon*, sitting in the bay and the arrival of the navy's *Knud Rasmussen*, grey and insignificant beside the red hull and white decks of the Chinese icebreaker. Fenna stared at the vessel until it disappeared behind the new high rises of Qinngorput.

"The school," said the driver and slowed at a roundabout, the wheels slushing through the puddles of melting snow, as they drained into the ditches either side of the road.

"Yes," said Fenna. "Wait," she said, as she looked to the right and saw a small army of children striding up the long road leading up to the row of five towers looking out to the bay. "Up there. Take me all the way to the top."

"*Aap*," said the driver as he drove past the school and past the group of children. The children's clothes were tidier and cleaner than those of the children Fenna had seen in Ittoqqortoormiit, but the faces were the same, only some were paler. *No glare from the ice*, she realised as the taxi slowed to a stop at the top of the hill. Fenna paid the driver and got out.

"Wait for me," she said and gave him an extra one hundred Danish kroner.

"Where do you want to go?"

"Back to the airport," she said and closed the door.

She spotted the first surveillance team within a few seconds of getting out of the car. A discreet black SUV, but with two men wearing light blue shirts sitting in the front. Fenna kept an eye on them as she took out her mobile and the scrap of paper with Burwardsley's number on it. The policeman looked at her as she dialled.

"Yes?" Burwardsley said after two rings.

"I'm outside," said Fenna. "Which building?"

"Number three," he said. "You're coming up?"

"I have friends." Fenna waved at the Chinese exchange teacher and her Greenlandic colleague. She flashed three fingers and waited for the class to pass her before tagging along behind them.

"Christ. You have kids with you."

"You can see me?" Fenna said and looked up.

"I'm on the balcony, fifth floor, facing the bay. Can you see the men below me?"

"Yes. Third floor."

"Exactly. They are the ones we need to get past. Get the kids to stop outside their door."

"Fine," Fenna said and jogged to catch up with the teachers at the head of the class. "Hi," she said in English as she slowed to walk beside them. "You're here to pick something up?"

"Yes," said Chen before her colleague could answer.

"Great. It's the second flat on the third floor. They might not be expecting you, but just go right in."

"Okay," she said and ushered the class inside the building. Fenna got into the lift and watched the children as they climbed the stairs, pleased that Anguteq was not among them. She hoped they would provide the necessary distraction.

The lift stopped at the fifth floor. Fenna jumped as the doors opened and Burwardsley slid between them. He pushed the button for the ground floor. She pressed herself against the glass wall of the lift and stared at him.

Burwardsley glanced at her as the lift started to move and said, "You're going to have to get over that if we're going to work together, love."

"I know," she said. "It's just…"

"I get it. I do. You just can't dwell on it. Dina's gone. Humble's dead. Move on."

"I can't."

"Why not?" he said, pausing as the lift neared the third floor and the excited chatter of children and deep male voices filtered through the thin doors of the elevator.

"They have Maratse."

"The policeman? Fuck. What the hell is he doing here?"

"It's a long story and…" Fenna froze as Burwardsley towered over her, grabbed her arms and twisted her to one side. Fenna held her breath as he leaned in close to kiss her.

"Just pretend. I don't want them to see you."

"They already have," she said, as two men, wearing the classic black uniforms and tactical vests of a counter terrorist unit, disappeared inside the apartment, shoving the children to one side, only to reappear with helmets and Heckler & Koch MP5s. Fenna slipped out from beneath Burwardsley and nodded at the door of the elevator. "There will be two cops in a car at the far end of the parking area."

"And beyond that?"

"A taxi. He's waiting for me."

"Well, this is going to spook the shit out of him."

"Yeah," Fenna said and felt her cheeks crease for a second.

"Having fun all of a sudden, Konstabel?"

"Maybe," she said and grinned. "It's the adrenalin."

"Just keep telling yourself that." Burwardsley took a breath as the lift stopped and the door started to open. "We go fast and hard," he said. "I want you on my right. Driver's side."

"Okay," Fenna said, noticing the sound of boots tramping down the stairwell.

"Forget them," Burwardsley said. "Take out the driver. Take his weapon if you can. Get in the taxi."

Fenna started to nod only to feel her head whip back as Burwardsley yanked her out of the lift and propelled her at the glass doors at the building's entrance. She lifted her arms as Burwardsley shoved her toward the right-hand door, battering through it – one hand slamming into the glass pane, the other into Fenna's back. As they cleared the steps and the door recoiled with a snap of hinges, he pushed Fenna to the right as the policemen in the car opened the doors of the vehicle.

He's fast, Fenna noted as Burwardsley outstripped her, his legs pounding the surface of the car park, she could almost feel the vibrations, and then he was at the car and kicking the door into the policeman, grabbing the man's pistol with his left hand as he backhanded him in the face with his right.

"Move it, Konstabel," Burwardsley shouted, as Fenna reached the driver's door. The policeman was already outside of the car and drawing his weapon. Fenna barrelled into his chest and butted him in the head. The policeman staggered and Fenna followed him down onto the ground, straddling his chest and punching him once in the face, and a second time in the breastbone.

"Stop fucking about, Fenna." Burwardsley wrenched the passenger door open and pulled the policeman toward him, locking the man's neck within the crook of his left arm. Burwardsley fired two shots in the air and then placed the pistol to the policeman's head.

"What are you doing?" Fenna yelled at Burwardsley, as she pulled the driver's pistol from his holster. She swore as the pistol jerked to a stop at the end of the safety wire. It took another few seconds to find the policeman's multitool on his utility belt and cut the pistol free, and then she was up, on her feet and running for the taxi.

Fenna glanced over her shoulder and saw the two Danish soldiers – *Frømandskorpset*, she guessed – as they sought cover behind two vehicles, one man talking on the radio clipped to his vest as the other aimed at Burwardsley. *They'll block the road*, Fenna thought, slowing as she realised they were never going to get to the airport.

"Just keep going," Burwardsley said, the policeman's heels dragging across the tarmac as he jogged to the taxi.

"No," the taxi driver said as he got out of the car.

"Get in," Fenna yelled. "Get in the fucking car."

"*Naamik*," he said, as he stumbled and ran down the road.

"Drive," Burwardsley said, as he opened the back door and stuffed the policeman onto the backseat. Fenna climbed behind the wheel, tossed her pistol onto the dashboard and slammed the door. "Just go," Burwardsley said, as he knelt on the edge of the backseat and fumbled with the cuffs on the policeman's belt. "Fuck," he said, as Fenna spun the car in reverse and the tips of his boots scraped the surface of the road.

"Are you getting in?" she said and crunched into first gear.

"Drive for fuck's sake," he said and grabbed the headrest behind Fenna's head, catching a handful of Fenna's hair beneath his fingers. Fenna tugged her head free and accelerated around the top of the road, threw the car into second and stomped on the accelerator. The car jerked as she caught third gear halfway down the hill.

"Are they behind us?" she shouted as she accelerated into fourth.

"Stop shouting, Konstabel," Burwardsley said, as he snapped the cuffs around the policeman's wrists, forced his massive body through several contortions Houdini would have been proud of, and closed the passenger door. "We're all right. Relax. Drive."

"Relax?" Fenna said. "How the fuck can I relax?" She caught herself for a moment, her heart hammering in her chest, pulsing at her throat, thudding in her ears. She glanced in the rear-view mirror. "We just kidnapped a policeman."

"And the night is still so young," Burwardsley said and laughed as he checked the pistol in his grip.

Chapter 27

The taxi squealed around the roundabout as Fenna braked into third gear and accelerated past the school, the smell of fresh seal smoked across the road and through the window Burwardsley had opened. Fenna swallowed the saliva that seemed to ignore the adrenalin flooding her body to remind her that, at some point soon, she really should eat.

"I'm starving," she said, as she threw the taxi into a tight right turn and pressed her foot down on the accelerator pedal.

"Then you're in luck," Burwardsley said. "Gotta love police utility belts," he said and held up two magazines. "Extra ammo, cuffs, and…" He paused. "A Mars bar."

"Share it?" Fenna said and blasted the horn at a gaggle of kids on bikes.

"It's yours," he said and peeled the chocolate out of its wrapper. Burwardsley broke it in half, reached around the driver's seat, and pushed it into Fenna's open mouth. "Now that your stomach is satisfied. Let's talk."

"All right," Fenna said, her words chunky and rich with chocolate.

"What the fuck are you doing with the Chinese?"

"They've got Maratse?"

"Who's *they*?"

"Hong Wei. Chinese intelligence. On the ship in the bay."

"Okay," Burwardsley said and looked at his watch. "You're going to hit a roadblock after the pass, before the turn for the airport, in about forty seconds."

"You know this?"

"It's what I would do."

"Fair enough," Fenna said and accelerated into fifth gear.

"Keep it in fourth," Burwardsley said and shoved the second half of the Mars bar into Fenna's mouth. The engine protested as Fenna dropped down a gear.

"What about you? Why were you being watched?"

Burwardsley looked through the back window before answering. "Seems my mate at Arctic Command doesn't remember the old days as fondly as I do."

"Not when he puts a Counter Terrorist unit on you."

"That's who they were? I thought they were a bit more pro than the usual goons."

"Why didn't they pick you up?"

"Waiting for you, I guess." Burwardsley grabbed the back of the passenger seat with his left hand and said, "Keep driving, Konstabel."

"Why? What are you going to…" And then she saw it, the roadblock, just as Burwardsley fired three shots through the windscreen. "Fuck," Fenna shouted as the glass shattered and the crack of the pistol cuffed her ears.

"They won't shoot back because of our guest," Burwardsley said with another glance behind him. "The two behind us are gaining," he said and turned around. "Look to the right of the roadblock, there's a patch of gravel. Bump the car over the curb and gun it."

"Okay," Fenna said and tugged at the seatbelt.

"Forget the fucking belt, Fenna. Just drive."

Fenna ignored the spinning blue lights of the police Toyotas blocking the road. She dropped the taxi into third and accelerated, pushing the needle of the rev counter into the red. Fenna yelled louder than the engine and floored the accelerator as she swung the taxi at the curb.

"To the right," Burwardsley shouted and slapped at Fenna's arm. "Gravel – piled up like a ramp. Use it, Konstabel."

With both hands on the wheel, Fenna slurred the car to the right, up the gravel, and bumped the car up the curb and onto the rough open surface in front of a small supermarket. She swerved to avoid a child running after a dog, swerved again to avoid the dog and then slammed into the side of a Volkswagen. The engine stalled as the taxi continued rolling toward the smooth surface of the road, the tyres slick with melting snow.

"What the fuck?"

"I know, I know," Fenna yelled and prayed the car would start as she turned the key in the ignition. Burwardsley leaned out of the passenger window and fired at the counter terrorist team speeding toward them in a black SUV. The engine stuttered into life and she shifted into first gear and accelerated onto the road.

"Go."

Fenna shifted from first through third, flicking her gaze from the road to the police roadblock as it unfurled into a column of vehicles flashing after them.

"Just fucking drive, Konstabel," Burwardsley shouted between taking pot shots at the pursuing vehicles. He stopped to change magazines. Fenna breathed in the lull, her stomach cramped and her mouth dry.

"Fuck," she said and laughed.

"What's the plan, Konstabel?" Burwardsley said, as he slapped a new magazine into the butt of the pistol. "How are we getting out?"

"Hong Wei said he would pick us up."

"He lied."

"Yeah, I know," Fenna said and smoothed the car into fourth gear. She looked to the right at the runway, craning her neck to better see the bright red Bell Huey helicopter sitting on the tarmac. It looked like it was being prepped for launch.

"So? New plan?"

"Working on it."

"All right," Burwardsley said, as the taxi lurched forward. The policeman lifted his head and groaned. Burwardsley pressed the man's face into the seat and changed position to sit on his back. "Our friend is getting restless."

"Okay," Fenna said, as she braked into the corner. A quick glance in the mirror stung her eyes with the flash of blue lights. She blinked and accelerated. As the taxi approached the airport she pointed through the shattered windscreen and said, "See the helicopter?"

"The Huey?" Burwardsley said, as he looked between the seats. "Yeah, I see it, *love*. You can't fly, can you?"

"No, but it's being prepped. The rotors are spinning."

"Then we're out of time."

"Not yet," Fenna said and floored the accelerator.

The image of another high-speed chase in another part of the country flashed across Fenna's mind. She grinned at the memory, of emptying the magazine of Maratse's M1 rifle through the back of the police Toyota, the exact replica of the ones chasing them to the airport. *Except this time*, she thought, *I'm driving.*

"Hold on to something," Fenna yelled, as she accelerated toward the gate between the runway and the airport building.

"Do it," Burwardsley shouted as he lay flat on the policeman. Fenna crashed the taxi through the airport gate. The vehicle spun to the left, the wheels chewing on the gate in a shower of sparks, as they careened toward a Dash 8 aircraft, parked in front of the arrivals lounge. Fenna shouted again as the taxi slammed into the landing gear beneath the starboard wing of the aircraft. The taxi stopped and Burwardsley pushed himself off the policeman, opened the passenger door on the driver's side and crawled out. Fenna joined him on the tarmac, pausing to reach inside and grab her pistol from where it had fallen into the passenger foot well.

"We've got one chance," Burwardsley said, as he grabbed Fenna by the shoulder and ran across the tarmac. He lifted the pistol and pointed it at the pilot in the helicopter, ignoring the wail of sirens and the bark of commands through loudspeakers behind them. Burwardsley thrust Fenna toward the rear sliding door and yanked open the door to the co-pilot's seat. He climbed in and thrust the pistol at the pilot. "Fly," he said, with a quick glance at Fenna as she scrambled into the aircraft and slammed the door shut.

Fenna pushed her hand against the floor to lift herself up, frowning as she pressed against something soft, a backpack, with Spiderman sprawled across it. She looked up into the wide brown eyes of a young boy, buckled into the backseat as his mother lifted the helicopter into the air and away from the crash and chaos of men and equipment below them.

"Anguteq?" Fenna said and tried to smile. The boy said nothing. Fenna crawled onto the seat beside him and sat down. She buckled the seatbelt across her lap and looked at the pilot. She wasn't surprised to see the long black hair beneath the helmet, nor the patient rage of a mother waiting for the moment to fight for her son. Fenna grabbed a headset from the hook on the bulkhead and slipped it on. "Panninguaq," she said, "listen to me."

Panninguaq flew out toward the bay, her lips tight, her knuckles the colour of snow. Burwardsley pointed at the *Xue Long* as it made its way out of the bay and Panninguaq followed his directions, her eyes flicking from the pistol in his lap to the horizon and back again.

"Panninguaq, it's going to be all right. I'm going to fix this," Fenna said. She tried another smile with Anguteq, but the boy just stared at her.

"How?" Panninguaq said, her voice low but defiant.

"Your friend is leaving, love" Burwardsley said. "What's the plan?"

Fenna ignored him and continued speaking in Danish. "I've been set up," she said. "But if you get me on that ship, me and my friend, we will fix this, and then you won't have to worry about Anguteq, you can stay in Greenland, in Nuuk…"

"If I get you on that ship?"

"Yes."

"You'll fix this?"

"Yes," Fenna said.

"I don't believe you."

Burwardsley coughed and cut through the silence as Fenna thought about what to say next. He turned in his seat, flicked his eyes at the boy and then waved his pistol at Fenna. "We're not going to achieve much with these," he said. "Your friends are going to be all tooled-up."

"We'll make do."

"Sure, and we're just going to land on the deck?"

"No," she said. "We'll jump onto it."

"Great," he said and faced forward as Panninguaq flew the Bell Huey 212 past the harbour and over the sea in the wake of the Chinese icebreaker. Burwardsley looked down at the bay beneath them. "It looks like your old friends are joining the party," he said and pointed at the grey hull of the *Knud Rasmussen*, and the sea frothing at the stern of the naval patrol vessel.

"Then we'll have to be quick," Fenna said and slumped back in the seat. Anguteq shifted his wide eyes from the gun in her hand to her face. Fenna wiped a strand of hair from her eye and tried for the third time to elicit a smile from him. She stuck out her tongue and, after a moment, Anguteq did the same. *Small steps*, she told herself. *Get on the ship. Get to Maratse. Wait for the navy. We're going to be all right.*

She looked up as Anguteq curled his tiny brown hand around her little finger. He tugged at it, and she smiled. A moment of reprieve. The quiet before the storm. Fenna tugged her finger free and held Anguteq's hand as Burwardsley directed Panninguaq toward the stern of the ship. She listened as he gave the commands in English, his northern accent punching through the chop of the rotor blades with practised authority. Anguteq's hand was warm, hot almost, and Fenna felt the sweat bead between their skin. She sighed and expelled all the breath from her lungs, wanting the next lungful to capture at least some of the calm the boy provided, in the still of the moment, the one that always preceded action of the most violent sort. She felt the vibration of the helicopter change in pitch, noticed the attitude was more angled, more aggressive, and then the helicopter was flaring, nose up, above the landing deck, and the rush of Arctic sea air goosebumped her skin and whipped at her hair, as Burwardsley crawled into the back, slid the passenger door open, and stepped out onto the skids.

Fenna let go of Anguteq, tugged the headset off her head, and unbuckled her belt. She played the canvas belt through her fingers as she joined Burwardsley on the skids. The tips of her hair stung her eyes as she leapt after the big Marine Lieutenant to land hard on the deck of the *Xue Long*. And then Anguteq's soft brown eyes were gone, lost in the flash of gunfire.

"Suppressing fire," Burwardsley yelled, as he tossed Fenna his spare magazine and rushed the first of the Chinese guards to step onto the deck, starboard side. With a slap to the man's chest, Burwardsley ripped the Changfeng 9mm submachine gun out of the man's hands and sprayed the port side with a long burst of lead.

Fenna gripped her pistol in two hands, aiming up at the gantry running along the deck above the landing pad. She fired two rounds, moved forward, firing another two rounds until the magazine was empty and she was crouching beside Burwardsley as he prepared to enter the mudroom.

"You ready?" he said, as Fenna slapped a fresh magazine into the grip of her pistol.

"Yes," she said and remembered to breathe. It was automatic now. Burwardsley was the lead. She was his second. Fenna had his back. One room after the other. One stairwell at a time. Until they had Maratse, or they were dead. *But I am not ready to die*, she thought and allowed herself a last glimpse of Anguteq's eyes, of Dina's playful smile, peach juice dribbling from her chin, of Mikael's ice-beard, of dancing lessons with Nicklas', of…

"Fenna?" Burwardsley said.

"I'm ready," she said and shook her head. "Let's go."

"Because, if you're not…"

"Hong Wei sold us out. I'm ready. Let's do this."

And the memories were gone, and it was one volley of lead after another as Burwardsley cleared the way with short controlled bursts. Fenna followed behind him, covering the corners, the shadows, suppressing her demons, looking for dragons – *snow dragons*, the

Chinese kind.

Burwardsley scavenged magazines from the crewmen bleeding at his feet, tugging them from their belts as he stepped over their bodies. After the initial resistance, the crew of the *Xue Long* withered into a retreat before the hail of bullets from the Royal Marine Lieutenant with one last goal in sight and little to lose. Fenna tapped his shoulder and pointed at the stairwell.

"Down one deck," she said. "Second room on the port side of the ship."

They smelled the medical bay before they saw it, a wave of antiseptic splashing down the corridor. Burwardsley stopped at the door and nodded for Fenna to stack up – positioning herself ready for a dynamic entry.

"Ready?" he whispered.

"Yes."

"And when we're in?"

"We wait for the navy."

"And a prison cell," Burwardsley said and snorted.

"Yes."

"So long as we're together, *love*," he said and winked.

Fenna almost laughed, but then he nodded, a single dip of his stubbled chin, before he peeled into the medical bay, and Fenna followed him.

Chapter 28

Fenna pressed her left palm against Burwardsley's shoulder, herpistol steady in her right hand. As Burwardsley moved she moved with him, only to stop when he stopped, and to lower the pistol when he lowered the submachine gun. Maratse was bleeding, and the ship's doctor had his hands inside the policeman's stomach as his assistant passed him swabs and forceps to save the Greenlander's life. *We're too late*, Fenna thought, and then she saw Hong Wei. He nodded toward Maratse and flicked his head toward the crewman in the corner – the one with the jagged scar on his chin.

"Impressive," Hong Wei said, looking at Burwardsley. "I ordered six men to stop you, and now I have six bodies, two more than the ship's morgue can accommodate." He gestured with his hand at Maratse. "This man, at least, can be repatriated before his body begins to rot."

"He's not dead," said Fenna.

"Not yet."

Fenna let the pistol hang by her side, her fingers loosely wrapped around the handle as she took a step closer to the operating table around which the *Xue Long*'s medical staff exchanged brief commands and updates.

"Careful," Burwardsley said and Fenna heard the metallic clack of the sling bevel screwed into the stock as he shifted his grip on the weapon.

"As you can see," said Hong Wei. "The doctor and his team are doing their very best to save your friend's life." Fenna could indeed see – more than she wanted to. The skin of Maratse's stomach peeled away from his gut like the petals of a viscous flower. Gone was the bruised blue skin, to be replaced by swollen organs peeping through a steady stream of dark red blood pooling around coagulated lumps of black blood, old and stubborn. "Of course," Hong Wei continued, "they will stop whenever I order them to do so."

Fenna looked up to meet the Chinaman's eyes. "I thought you were going to pick us up," she said, "as agreed."

"Ah," he said and straightened his back – Burwardsley and Hong Wei's bodyguard tensed, and, for a moment, the smell of antiseptic and blood was lost in a tense flood of adrenalin. Fenna recognised it, caught a whiff of her own sweat as the same chemicals surged through her body. She swallowed and whispered to Burwardsley to stand down.

"The navy will be here soon," she said.

"Then I suggest we get down to business," Hong Wei said with a glance at Burwardsley. "This is your associate? The one with the information about the mysterious *Magician*?"

"Yes."

"And what do you have for me?" Hong Wei said.

"How about your *associate* lower his weapon and then we can talk," said Burwardsley, with a look toward the scarred man holding his machine pistol tight to his body, the folding stock creasing the shoulder of the thermal top he wore beneath the contours of his slim-fitting body armour. At a nod from Hong Wei, the man lowered the pistol. Fenna noticed the doctor's shoulders sag for a moment as the man sighed behind the mask covering his mouth and nose. Burwardsley lowered his weapon, and the only sounds were the doctor's hushed commands and the soft, wet, sucking noises of soft tissue being squeezed between bent forceps and gloved fingers.

Hong Wei spoke as the first distant whops of the navy's Lynxhelicopter reverberated through the open doors and down the corridors of the *Xue Long*. "I was promised information," he said.

"I have the number of a man trusted by *The Magician*," Burwardsley said.

"A Greenlandic number?"

"No," he said and shook his head. "International. Area code forty-five."

"Denmark," said Fenna.

"And the rest of the number?" said Hong Wei. "What is it?"

"Listen, mate," Burwardsley said, looking over at Maratse, unconscious on the table. "I need some assurances, because…" he paused to glance at Fenna. "He is not going to make it."

"It is doubtful," said Hong Wei. "I agree."

"Assurances then…"

Fenna turned her head at the sound of soft footfalls in the corridor outside. *Just a few men*, she thought, *or several moving very quietly*. If Burwardsley or the Chinese had heard the arrival of the Danish Counter Terrorism Unit they did not show it. Fenna took a breath as she imagined them stacking-up on either side of the door. She opened her mouth and closed her eyes in anticipation of the flashbang grenades they would use. *Maratse would probably enjoy the excitement*, she thought as her lips creased into a thin smile. *He'll be pissed to hear he missed it.* She breathed out as the first of two stun grenades was tossed into the room, grateful for a second that the wet sounds from within the policeman's stomach were lost in a brilliant flash of white and two explosions that made her ears ring and her head spin. Fenna dropped to the floor as rough-gloved fingers shoved her head toward the deck and kicked the pistol from her grip. She imagined Burwardsley dropping to the deck beside her, the heavy thud and English expletives suggested as much, and then the hood was pulled over her head and cinched tight at her throat. She was cuffed, punched, and dragged by her elbows out of the medical bay and along the corridor, her heels bumping on the steps, her shins scraping the lip of the Lynx' door as she was stuffed inside it, her nose bleeding as her head was pressed onto the metal floor. Fenna caught a stale breath of air, the hood billowing into her mouth as she breathed in, and heard the grunt of the men stuffing Burwardsley inside the helicopter alongside her.

"Fucking outrageous," he said and Fenna almost smiled, and then the doors were closed and the rotor noise increased in pitch. She closed her eyes and tried to think as the helicopter lifted off the deck of the *Xue Long* and made the short flight back to the *Knud Rasmussen*. Thoughts of the grey navy patrol ship lingered in her mind, and the prick of a needle in the left cheek of her bottom was almost too quick to notice. Fenna lifted her head only to lose control of her muscles and then it was black, and all trace of the world beyond the hood was gone.

Few twenty-four year old women have seen as many prison cells, or variations of the same, in such a short space of time as Konstabel Fenna Brongaard. The grey walls, smooth but for the chunky angular bolts and button-head rivets, staggered around her as she opened her eyes. The weight around her wrists and ankles suggested it was useless to try to move, but the cold metal chair goose-bumping her flesh surprised her, and, when she blinked the rheumy pus from her eyes, she realised she was naked, and so was the man chained to the chair opposite her. He grinned and blew at his blond hair tickling his eyes. Fenna started at the sudden noise and at his voice.

"Hello, *love*," Burwardsley said. "Sleep well?"

"Fuck off," she said.

"I'd love to, but…" Burwardsley said and rattled the chains at his wrists.

Fenna shook her head and laughed. She turned away from the scars on Burwardsley's chest and the muscles ribbing his stomach. She scanned the room and tried to sense the movement of the ship through the soles of her bare feet.

"We're not on a ship."

"No," she said and frowned.

Burwardsley made a show of nodding at the cameras in the four corners of the square room. "Black site," he said and shrugged.

"But the Danes don't…"

"Who says it's the Danes?" Burwardsley raised his eyebrow and said, "We could be anywhere."

Fenna thought for a moment as the antiseptic and blood smells of earlier were replaced with a scent of Sonoran wind. *No,* she thought. "We're not in the desert."

"The desert?" said Burwardsley. "Shit, they must have given you more than me. We haven't been out long enough for them to get us out of the country. We're just not anywhere official."

"How would you know?" Fenna said and caught herself staring at the scars on Burwardsley's chest. "Is that why?" she said.

He followed her gaze and looked down at his body, nodded once and looked up. "Wait 'til you see my back."

"What happened?"

"Afghanistan," he said and shrugged.

Fenna swallowed and said, "Is that where you met Bahadur? Was he with you?"

"The little runt saved me," he said and was quiet for a moment. "Yes. Afghanistan is where I met Bad." Burwardsley's eyes misted for a second, and Fenna was suddenly impressed with the sense of loyalty, perhaps love, that fighting men might share with one another. But it was a feeling she could not know. *Not yet at least. It might be the same world,* she mused, *but the sex,* my *sex, always gets in the way.*

She turned away from Burwardsley's scars and looked for the door. It took a long minute before she found it, a feint shadow of dark grey grooved into the wall, outlining a square door. She scanned the room again, noted the corrugated effect of the far wall, the rectangular shape of the room, the sturdy metal beams in each corner. "This isn't a room in a building," she said. "We're inside a shipping container."

Burwardsley studied the room. "Like I said. A black site."

"You've been in one before?"

"Not as nice as this," he said and then, "It's different when you're working."

"For the British?"

"The British, the Yanks, the French," Burwardsley said and shrugged. "Hell, even the Aussies sent some people our way."

Fenna thought back to the wooden house in Ittoqqortoormiit where Burwardsley and Bahadur had stretched her, the thin puppy chain around her wrists pressing rusted teeth into her flesh, and the sharp nick of the Gurkha's kukri blade as Burwardsley had pierced her skin as he stripped the sweater from her back. *And now I am naked*, she thought and shivered, her arms flinching in an attempt to cover her breasts. Her movement caught Burwardsley's eye and he stared at her body and then looked Fenna in the eye.

"You won't understand," he said. "But I've seen too much skin to be aroused at just another pretty young thing."

"What does that mean?" Fenna said, as the cuffs rattled with another bout of shivering. She noticed Burwardsley's skin was paling and looked around the room for some kind of vent. Burwardsley talked as she twisted her head back and forth, scanning the room.

"It means I had a wife, I have a daughter, I'm not the thug you think I am, I'm just damn good at what I do."

"And Dina?" Fenna said, the words chattering from her lips, the Greenlander's name heavy, laden with cold, all comfort frozen out of it. Her breath misted before her face.

"Dina…" Burwardsley said. He licked at his blue lips. Fenna watched as he trembled, pressed the soles of his feet together, tried to rub them. "I couldn't help Dina."

"Couldn't?"

"There were other things at stake," he said. "Greater things."

"Greater than her life?"

"Not fair, Konstabel," Burwardsley said, his words slurring as he spoke. "You know that's why I'm here." He stared at a point directly above her head. "There. Right above you."

Fenna tipped her head back, caught a glimpse of the white-frosted tips of her hair, and saw the vent. "Shit," she said. "It's colder than…"

"The Arctic?" Burwardsley said and laughed. "We're trained for this, love. Remember that."

"But why are they…" Fenna's lips trembled over the words as her body began to shake. The metal chair sapped her heat and she felt her skin begin to stick to it. She lifted her bottom, tried to reposition herself on the chair. A fan began to blow. Fenna listened to the blades chopping through the frigid air as her hair tickled her face, her nipples budded upon her breasts, and her skin tightened, the tiny hairs on her arms and legs standing on end.

"Listen," said Burwardsley as Fenna lowered her head and tucked her chin to her chest. "Konstabel," he said, louder this time.

"What?"

"This is just the beginning. You have to be strong."

"But I don't know anything."

"You'd be surprised," he said. "It's not always what you think they want to know. It could be something else entirely."

Fenna didn't hear Burwardsley stumble over the *t* in *entirely*. She stopped listening to his words, could only hear her teeth chattering between frosted images of her treading water in the dark Greenland sea, the fingers of her hands stiffening around the collars of two sledge dogs. *Pyro*, she remembered, *and… and Hidalgo*. The lead dog's name had taken longer to remember, but she could see Mikael's face, the ice on his beard, his breath misting in the lamplight as he tossed the braided loop of rope at her and barked at her to, "Forget the fucking dogs and grab the line." She let go of the dogs. Fenna let go. Mikael's voice was lost in the black polar night as it folded upon her.

It was dark.

It was cold.

She supposed she was drowning, and then a warm wave washed across her shoulders.

A blanket? Fenna didn't know.

A mug was thrust between her thin frigid fingers. Fenna's nose tickled at the steam of cocoa, or something sweet at least. She heard a voice encouraging her to sip the drink, helping her with smooth firm hands, lifting the mug to her lips and telling her to do it again, to take another sip. The blanket scratched at her skin and Fenna felt the prickles of heat throb into warm waves of pain in her extremities. She felt her chest relax, her nipples soften, and her hair fall wet upon her cheeks. She looked up into the eyes of Per Jarnvig as he smiled at her.

"Welcome back, Konstabel," he said and walked around the desk between them and sat down. "You've had quite the adventure."

"Where am I?" Fenna said, as she lowered the mug from her lips and pressed her fingers around it. "What did you do? Why?"

"Lots of questions," Jarnvig said. "But I have one for you."

Fenna held the mug with one hand and tugged at the blanket. It slipped from her shoulder and revealed her left breast. Jarnvig stared as she put down the mug and gripped the blanket in both hands, pulled it around her shoulders and looked up at him. "What do you want to know?"

"Tell me about the girl," he said.

"What girl?"

Jarnvig opened a drawer and removed a remote control. He turned around and pointed it at a modest flat screen television mounted on the wall behind him. The screen brightened and Jarnvig muted the noise with a quick stab of a button on the remote. Fenna watched as the anchor of MSNBC cycled through a news story under the banner of *President Assassinated*, and a rapid ticker of information at the bottom of the screen moving too fast for Fenna to process. Jarnvig stood up. He walked the few steps to the screen and stood to one side of it. Fenna saw the familiar bulge of the 9mm pistol holstered in the shoulder rig beneath his jacket, she flicked her eyes back to the screen when Jarnvig clicked his fingers and pointed at a closed-circuit television screen capture of a blonde-haired young woman moving through a crowd at a bus station. Fenna caught her breath for a moment and looked from Jarnvig to Alice and back again.

"That one, Konstabel," said Jarnvig. "Who is she?"

Chapter 29

The fibres of the blanket scratched at Fenna's skin as Jarnvig turned off the television and returned to his chair. He tumbled the remote into the drawer, placed his elbows on the desk and laced his fingers together. Fenna waited as he took a long breath and then opened his mouth to speak.

"Just a minute," she said.

"What?"

"Lorentzen," Fenna said and shrugged. "Don't you want to know about him?"

"He's dead. Isn't he?"

"Yes," she said and frowned. "You've talked to Hong Wei?"

"And avoided an international incident. Yes, I've talked to him."

"And that's it? What about UNCLOS? The hearing?"

Jarnvig gestured at the screen behind him. "The Americans are preoccupied at the moment and the UNCLOS hearing has been postponed."

"But the Pole?"

"Will be there tomorrow. It can wait."

Fenna leaned back in her chair. It creaked beneath her. She tugged again at the blanket and wondered where they could have found one so small. "You tortured me," she said.

"I cooled you down. God knows you needed it. Since you were given this mission, I have had to clean up one incident after another." Jarnvig lifted his left hand and began counting the fingers, pressing each one with the tip of his right index finger. He started with the smallest. "The fire at the camp," he said and moved onto the next finger. "Assisting in the escape of a person of interest…"

"Burwardsley," Fenna said.

"… and the attack on two Greenlandic policemen – something you have a history of."

"When necessary," Fenna said.

"Don't be cute," Jarnvig said. He continued, "A shootout and a car chase, the hijacking of a helicopter…" He switched hands. "Attacking a foreign ship, resulting in the deaths of six Chinese nationals…"

"To save a Greenlandic policeman…"

"Now in an artificial coma at Queen Ingrid's Hospital in Nuuk."

So he's alive, Fenna thought and felt a brief flood of warmth through her body.

Jarnvig checked Fenna's relief with a warning, "The doctors say it is touch and go. There is some concern that he had been tortured."

"*Concern*? He *was* tortured. I was there. I saw it. He was electrocuted by Hong Wei, the same guy now crying International Incident because Burwardsley and I busted onto his ship."

"And killed six of his men."

Fenna threw up her hands. "God, you are impossible," she said and then bent down to pick up the blanket.

Jarnvig smiled and then said, quietly, "I'm not, God, Konstabel, but with the right cooperation, I can work miracles. You do remember Toronto?"

"Yes," Fenna said and sighed. "I don't believe you will ever let me forget."

"No. Probably not, but I also got you out of the desert."

Out of one shit storm and into the next, she thought. "Yes, you got me out of the desert, but I thought I was going after the Pole, at least to secure it."

"And you are, but…" he paused to nod once more at the television. "Things change. This is a dynamic world we live in, Konstabel. And," he added, "it comes with a price. Are you listening?"

"Yes. I'm listening."

Jarnvig opened the drawer to his left and pulled out a folder. Fenna saw the screen-capture of Alice clipped to the first of a thin sheath of papers. "The Americans want to know who she is," Jarnvig said and stared at Fenna. "I told them you could tell them."

"Then you lied," she said. "I was warned away from her. Nicklas warned me away from her." Fenna frowned. "They were your orders," she said. "You know who she is."

"Perhaps," Jarnvig said and turned the folder around to face Fenna. He lifted the photo of Alice and tapped the first line of a heavily redacted email, the broad black lines obscured almost everything but the date; it was the same day Fenna had arrived at the Desert Training Center. Jarnvig leaned back in his chair and folded his hands in his lap. "There is talk of a deep state in America. A group of powerful, strategically placed individuals…"

"Men," Fenna said and scoffed.

"And not a few women," Jarnvig said and continued. "There have been growing concerns that started in first term of the President's administration, and again during the recent campaign for re-election. These concerns accelerated last November, and a plan was put into action, one that played on the President's weakness for attractive young women."

Fenna shivered at the thought of her own actions when approaching Lorentzen, to gain his trust, in order to elicit information from him. *For what?* she thought. *Nothing. That particular mess has been cleaned up. I helped do it, and now…* Jarnvig's next words slapped her out of her thoughts as sharply as if he had back-handed her across the table.

"You might be surprised to know this, Konstabel, but you were under consideration, as a potential agent provocateur, a honey trap, a gartered assassin."

"What?" she said and clutched at the blanket.

"But," Jarnvig said and waved a hand in the air. "They soon discovered you were too impulsive, too tenacious, too tough, believe it or not."

"They were watching me?"

"Yes," he said and returned his hands to his lap.

"But you sent me there."

"I did."

"For training."

"Yes."

"And…" Fenna paused and collected her thoughts. She looked up at Jarnvig. "Did Nicklas know?"

"Yes," he said. "It was Nicklas who suggested you were not suitable. And so they brought in the girl."

"Alice."

Jarnvig nodded. "Yes. Alice."

"For fuck's sake, Jarnvig, she's just nineteen."

"I didn't recruit her, Konstabel."

"No? You just sent me instead."

"Not to recruit her. You're confusing things. I was approached by the Americans. They were looking for a young female who could be trained for a difficult and sensitive mission." He laughed. "Sensitive. I think we both know that subtlety is not your speciality. Anyway," he said, "as it turns out, they went with a naïve young girl, who could be moulded to their needs."

"So you knew who they were? This *deep state*."

"Far from it," Jarnvig said and shifted in his seat. "However, it is not unusual for intelligence agencies to reach out to one another, on occasion, when a job requires a specific profile or set of skills."

Fenna listened with half an ear as Jarnvig mentioned something about past understandings and periods of co-operation with different agencies under different administrations. She looked at the picture of Alice, recognised the fear in the young woman's eyes. *A girl, really*, she thought. *Alone in the world. Pursued by men.* Fenna nodded at the thought, and Jarnvig interpreted it as a sign to continue. She let his words wash over her and considered where Alice might be, and then recalled one of their conversations in the canteen. Alice had said she had a special place she had visited once. One that no-one knew about – not even her minders, the men shadowing her every move. *Men like the Gunney*, Fenna remembered and trembled again at the memory of his blood spilling across her fingers. *Did I clean up in Arizona, too?* she wondered. She almost laughed. *I'm a cleaner. That is my role in this game, to clean things up. Well*, she thought and nodded again, *I'm not done cleaning.* She looked up into the barrel of Jarnvig's 9mm and realised that neither was he.

"What are you doing?" she said.

"This is when it gets interesting," he said and tightened his grip on the trigger. "Do you remember the woman you met in the Major's office?"

"Yes?" Fenna said and swallowed as he nodded at the folder.

"Next page, the next sheet of paper."

Fenna turned the page and found a paper clipping from a local newspaper in Arizona. It was a short piece about the disappearance of an exotic dancer.

"Page three," he said.

The next page was another redacted email with details and names rendered unreadable, but for the number of Special Forces soldiers, the Gunney's men, killed in a helicopter crash overseas. Fenna didn't remember hearing about the crash, but… She tested the thickness of the stack of pages with a broken and blunt fingernail. There was one left.

"Go on," said Jarnvig.

"I don't need to," she said, her voice faltering. Fenna cleared her throat and stared at Jarnvig. "It's Nicklas, isn't it?"

"Page four," Jarnvig said.

Fenna placed her hands flat on the table, one on each side of the folder. "Where's Burwardsley?"

"Turn the page, Konstabel."

"Is he still being *cooled down*?"

Jarnvig said nothing. He shifted his grip on the pistol.

Fenna continued, "Did he tell you he had a mobile number? It belongs to a man trusted by *The Magician*. Do you remember him?"

"I remember telling you that he was no concern of yours," Jarnvig said. "Read the next page, Konstabel."

"I have an idea, that if I called that number…"

"If you had a mobile…"

"If I called it," Fenna said and straightened her back. She let the blanket fall from her shoulders. "I think I know who might answer it."

"Just," Jarnvig said and shook his head. He glanced away from her breasts and then back again, flicking his eyes from her lightly-weathered skin, the slim bulge of muscle in her arms, the fine hairs standing on end on her forearms, to her eyes, to her hair... "You would have been perfect for the job," he said.

"Alice's job?" Fenna said and lifted her chin. "Do you think I am pretty, Jarnvig? Do you?"

"Yes," he said, his words whispering out of his mouth. His cheeks flushing beneath the finely manicured stubble.

"You like my hair, don't you?"

"Yes."

"My face," she said and smoothed her hand along her jaw. Jarnvig nodded. She reached out and took his free hand. Fenna leaned toward him, her small breasts hanging above the desk like tiny pyramids, firm, pointed. She lifted his hand, turned it palm upwards, and cupped her breast in the curve of his hand. "You want me?"

"Yes," Jarnvig breathed. "I have wanted you since…"

"Since we met first met at the airport? Before Toronto," she said and pressed his hand hard against her breast.

"Yes," he said.

Fenna nodded and climbed onto the desk. She repositioned his hand on her right thigh, arching her back to brush the hair from her forehead. She smiled at him, glanced at the pistol and pressed it with a delicate touch to the surface of the desk. Jarnvig put his hand flat on the table, his fingers still wrapped around the pistol grip. When he looked up at Fenna she lifted her left knee and pressed it down upon Jarnvig's gun hand. He frowned for a second and then tugged at the pistol as Fenna slammed the heel of her left hand into his forehead and curled her right fist into his throat. Jarnvig choked, gasping for air as he released his grip on the pistol and slumped into the chair. Fenna moved into a crouch and used the lip of the desk to press down on Jarnvig as the chair tipped beneath him and they crashed to the floor. Fenna gripped Jarnvig's forehead and punched him twice more in the throat before spinning around to grab the pistol. The door had barely opened before Fenna had fired the first two shots through the wooden door and into the chest of the PET man guarding the entrance. She leapt over the desk and put another bullet through the opening and into the man's head.

Fenna burst through the door and into the carpeted corridor of what looked and smelled like the administration floor of an office complex. The shared reception at the end of the corridor was framed in an open plan room surrounded by rented office spaces, each with its own window and door. All the doors were closed, Fenna noted, and, apart from the dead man at her feet, the place was empty. Fenna ran down the corridor and stared out of the windows and into the sunlight lingering over Nuuk, enticing the capital of Greenland into a new day. She paused at the familiar sight of Nuuk's main street, the blue façade of the supermarket and the ubiquitous containers littering the building site beneath her.

I'm in the bank, she realised as she recalled the cityscape she had seen from the hotel. She moved to the window and looked down at the containers, pressing her fists against the glass as she scanned them, looking for one in particular – the refrigerated kind, the one with the police car parked by the side of it.

"Think, Fenna," she said.

She ran back to Jarnvig's office, her feet padding along the carpet, the fibres soft on her hard soles. She stopped by the side of the man and tugged the boots from his feet, discarding them after measuring them against her own. She unbuckled his belt and tugged his jeans off.

"Thank God for short men," she said and pulled on the man's jeans. She cinched the belt tight and worked a new hole into the leather with the buckle. The man's shirt was bloody. Fenna ignored it and went back inside the office. She walked around the table and stared down at Jarnvig's blue cheeks and his collapsed windpipe. She nodded once and then bent down to remove his suit jacket. Fenna buttoned both buttons and slipped the 9mm pistol into the waistband of the jeans; the weight of it tugged the belt towards her slim bottom and the grip pressed into her back. "Time to move," she said and grabbed the pages from the folder, stuffing them into the inside pocket of the jacket as she ran out of the office. The clock on the wall encouraged Fenna with a time uncivilised for most people. *And yet*, she remembered, *it's spring in Greenland. It's light. Everyone will be up.* When she stepped out onto the street after a short ride in the elevator, she was disappointed to know she was right.

Fenna skirted around the couples, kids and drunks as they stared at her bare feet, and climbed over the metal fence sealing the entry to the building site. She pulled the pistol from her waistband and crouched behind a cement mixer; the cold container was two car-lengths away.

I hope you're in there, Burwardsley, Fenna thought. *Because I seem to be all out of friends.* She bit her lip at the thought of Nicklas.

Fenna ducked at the sight of a policeman, a tall Dane, as he opened the door to the Toyota and lit a cigarette. Fenna scanned the car, allowing herself a brief smile when she realised he was alone. The man walked as he smoked, stopping to pick up a broken shovel handle. He banged the side of the container and laughed, and Fenna laughed with him.

You're alive, you British bastard, she thought and smiled. *He wouldn't do that if you weren't.* Fenna waited until the policeman tossed the shovel handle to one side and turned his back on her. She raced across the fractured earth and rubble, twisting the pistol in her grip as she closed on the policeman. If he hadn't turned, Fenna might have hit him in the back of the head. As it was, he caught the full brunt of her assault in the face, the blood spattering from his nose across her cheeks as he slumped to the ground. Fenna took the policeman's keys from his belt and moved on, running around the container to the door. She rushed inside and coughed at the chill air as she peered through the mist of her breath to see Burwardsley cuffed to the same metal chair in the middle of the refrigerated space. Fenna unlocked the cuffs with the keys as he cracked the ice beading his eyes and looked at her.

"Thought you left me," he said, his voice rasping over his blue lips.

"Thought about it," Fenna said and pulled the Marine Lieutenant to his feet. "Can you walk?"

"Yeah, I can walk," he said. "Daft buggers thawed me out every forty minutes. But…" Burwardsley paused to hold up his fingers. "I might lose these."

Fenna inspected the tips of Burwardsley's fingers and recognised the frostbitten flesh. "You might," she said and pulled him toward the door. "Let's get you some clothes."

She dragged Burwardsley to the car and jogged back to the policeman. He was, she realised, only slightly shorter than Burwardsley. *It's me that will need a change of clothes*, she thought as she stripped the policeman and bundled his jacket, shirt and trousers beneath her arm. She carried the boots in her hand, dumping the clothes at Burwardsley's feet. She waited until he was dressed, helping him with buttons, buckles and zips as his own fingers failed him.

"We need a new plan," he said, as Fenna zipped the fly of his trousers and buckled the belt. She knelt down to tie his laces.

"Then it's lucky I have one," she said and stood up.

"Care to tell me?"

"After we have been to the hospital." Fenna opened the passenger door and pushed Burwardsley onto the seat.

"Hospital?"

"I want to see Maratse," she said, as she climbed in behind the wheel. And I need some different clothes."

"Whose are those?" Burwardsley said and frowned.

"The jacket belonged to my boss."

"Belonged?"

"Yep. He's dead," Fenna said and turned the key in the ignition. "Any more questions?"

"I guess not," Burwardsley said. He switched on the heating as Fenna bumped the Toyota through the gate and onto the street. "You might want to wipe that blood off your face before you go inside," he said.

"It's not mine."

"I didn't say it was."

Fenna reached up to angle the rear-view mirror toward her head, wiping away the blood with the back of her hand as she studied her face. She looked beyond the blood, beyond the dirt of the mining camp and the grease and grime of ships and helicopters. Fenna looked into her own eyes and saw the eyes of a killer. She stopped the car.

"What are you doing?" Burwardsley said and opened his eyes as Fenna opened the driver's door.

"Throwing up," she said and retched. The small puddle of bile on the road reminded her once again that she needed something to eat. She slammed the door shut and drove in the direction of the hospital.

"Are you going to do that a lot?"

"That depends," she said, as she parked behind the hospital.

"On what?"

"How many people I kill before this is over."

"Hah," Burwardsley said and laughed.

"You think it's funny I throw up every time I kill someone?"

"No," Burwardsley said, as Fenna turned off the engine. "I think it is funny you think one day this might be over."

One day it might be, she thought as she stared at Burwardsley. *One way or another*. Fenna took a breath, opened the door, and stepped out of the car. She looked up at the red and yellow beams of wood decorating the floors of the building, just a few stories high.

"Maratse," she whispered and shut the door. The mission had become the man, Fenna realised, but with each step she took toward the hospital entrance, she realised that the mission had always been about a man, and, perhaps, a girl.

The New Frontier

NUUK, GREENLAND

Chapter 30

Fenna ducked her head as she walked past the reception desk, conscious of her ill-fitting and unusual choice of clothes. With a quick glance at the building plan screwed into the corridor wall, Fenna located the stairwell and went down to the basement and the laundry room. She picked her way through the folded piles of trousers and smocks until she found the best fit for her small, wiry frame. *It's a long time since I worried about underwear*, she mused, smiling as she tied the draw cord at the waist of the trousers. Fenna found socks and clogs on a rack beneath the clean clothes. She pulled them on and dumped her clothes in the trash, folding a towel around the 9mm she returned to the stairs and made her way to the first floor.

She followed the signs for Intensive Care, pausing at the door to the small ward before walking inside. The Greenlandic nurse sitting at a small desk by the door frowned as she walked in.

"Can I help you?"

"Yes," said Fenna. "I'm just getting my bearings. I'm the new temp. Came in yesterday."

"Yesterday?" the nurse said and shook her head. "We're not expecting anyone."

Fenna pulled out the gun and let the towel drop to the floor. The nurse, to Fenna's surprise, took a gulp of air and thrust her hands above her head.

"Okay," said Fenna. She fought the smile creasing her lips and said, "You have a policeman here. Where is he?" The nurse nodded and dipped her head toward the end of the ward. Fenna laughed and lowered the gun. "You need to breathe." The nurse nodded again, her cheeks blossoming as her eyes bulged. "Really. Breathe. Now," Fenna said and let the gun fall to her side. The nurse exhaled with a rush of air and collapsed into the chair, lowering her arms like a clockwork drummer unwinding.

"Sorry," she gasped as she recovered.

"You did fine," Fenna said and nodded toward the last bed. She spied the familiar black of Maratse's jacket hanging on the back of a chair beside his bed. "How is he?"

"He's not well," the nurse said. "He's in a coma. The doctors…"

"Will he recover?"

"*Aap*. But he might have problems."

"What kind?"

"Motor control," the nurse said. She studied Fenna's wrinkled brow and added, "He will have difficulty walking."

Fenna took a step toward Maratse. "Can I see him?"

"*Aap*. Come." The nurse stood up and Fenna realised she was tiny. She followed her to Maratse's bed and stopped at his feet. Fenna reached out and smoothed her hand over the policeman's foot, the blanket rough beneath her fingers.

"I'm sorry," she said, sensing a tear well up and run down her cheek. The nurse reached out and took her hand.

"He's going to be all right," she said and squeezed Fenna's fingers. "I will look after him."

"Thank you," Fenna said.

"What about you?" she said. "Are you all right?"

"I'm fine. Maybe a little hungry."

"I have food," the nurse said. "Come." She led Fenna away from Maratse and into a small kitchen area. She gestured for Fenna to sit at the round table, opposite the door. Fenna could see Maratse, could hear the rise and fall of his chest and the lungs of the machine helping him breathe. She placed the gun on the table and looked up as the nurse placed a plastic food container between them, the smell of fish wrinkled Fenna's nose as the nurse removed the lid. "*Ammassat*," she said and snapped a small dried fish from a clump and handed it to Fenna.

"Capelin," Fenna said, as she recognised the fish. "Thank you." The nurse studied Fenna's face as she ate. Fenna nodded and took another fish as the nurse smiled and poured her a glass of water. "They're good."

The nurse raised her thick black eyebrows and said, "My father dried them on a rock, in the sea, away from the dogs. Then my sister brought them on the plane last month. Ten kilos." She nodded at the box. "These are the last."

"They're good."

"*Aap*." The nurse pulled her mobile from her pocket and swiped her hand across the screen. She turned the mobile toward Fenna. "The dayshift starts soon," she said.

"Okay," Fenna said and stood up. She tucked the pistol into the waistband of the trousers, pulling it out again as the weight of it strained the draw cord. She held it in her hand and smiled. "Thank you for the fish."

"You're welcome."

"And thank you for looking after my friend." The nurse raised her eyebrows again – a Greenlandic *yes*. "When he wakes up, will you tell him Fenna was here?"

"*Aap*."

"And tell him that I'm sorry."

"I will tell him."

"*Qujanaq*," Fenna said, her tongue tripping over the unfamiliar assembly of Inuit syllables. The nurse's eyes widened and she reached out to pat Fenna's hand. Fenna turned to leave. She paused for one last look at Maratse, his puffy eyes and swollen cheeks, the small tube inside his nose taped in place, a larger one secured with a mask to his mouth. The machine pressed air in and out of his lungs with a soft clap and hiss. Fenna lost herself for a moment in the serenity of Maratse's recovery, then forced herself to walk away, to turn her back on the one man she knew she could trust.

But he can't help me now, she thought as she picked up the towel by the desk and hid the gun on her way out of the ward. She stopped at the sound of a cart being pushed by an orderly making his way to the ward with breakfast.

"Do you need anything?" he asked, as he stopped in front of the door to Intensive Care.

Fenna glanced at the breakfast rolls and cartons of juice. She tucked the towel beneath her arm and took two rolls and a couple of drinks. "It's been a long night," she said and thanked him.

"It's going to be a beautiful day," he said, as she walked away.

For you, maybe, Fenna thought as she walked toward the main entrance. *For me... well, I'm not so sure.* Fenna waved at Burwardsley as he watched her approach the police car. He opened the driver door and Fenna climbed in behind the wheel.

"You're a nurse now?" he said as she gave him the rolls and juice.

"I'm full of surprises," Fenna said and turned the key in the ignition. The Toyota's engine rumbled into life and Fenna placed her hand on the gearstick. She turned to Burwardsley and sighed. "So," she said. "We need a plan."

"We do."

"And we should move."

"Where are we going to go? There's maybe twenty kilometres of road in Nuuk, and that includes the runway."

"Then we should park somewhere."

"We are parked."

"Somewhere discreet."

"Konstabel," Burwardsley said and sighed. "You don't *do* discreet," he said and laughed.

"No," Fenna said and grinned. "I really don't."

"You really don't, love."

Fenna switched off the engine and leaned back in the driver's seat. "But we still need a plan."

Burwardsley licked crumbs of bread from his lips and wiped the rest off the front of the police jacket he was wearing. Fenna watched as he fumbled with the straw of the orange juice carton. He swore and passed it her.

"I can't bloody open it."

"But can you still shoot?" she asked, as she pressed the sharp tip of the straw through the plastic sleeve and jabbed it through the circle of foil in the top of the carton. She handed it to Burwardsley.

"Too bloody right I can," he said.

Fenna studied the white tips of his fingers and remembered the cold bite of the north that threatened her own fingers when patrolling with Sirius. She thought of Mikael, how he chided her to remember her gloves, before the man sucking orange juice through a straw beside her killed him.

"Why did Mikael have to die?"

Burwardsley tossed the empty carton onto the floor. He took a breath and looked at Fenna. "Don't," he said. "The future is going to be difficult enough without worrying about the past, love. You're going to have to move on."

"Like you have," she said and thought of Dina.

"Hey, killing your pal was one thing, but what Humble did to that girl. Well, it's just not right. It didn't sit well with me. Not with Bad either."

"You can't worry about the past," Fenna said and snorted. She wiped a thin stream of snot from her nose with the back of her hand.

"You can't bring it back either."

Fenna looked up as a raven landed on the roof of the police car and clawed its way down the windshield. She watched as it stalked back and forth in front of them, the scratch of its claws on the bonnet the only sound as Burwardsley watched with her. She remembered the ravens teasing the sledge dogs in the north. They knew the length of the dogs' chains. When the dogs were fed, one raven would tease the dog, hopping just out of reach as it thundered toward it, while another would steal in beneath the taught chain and carry the fish head to safety. The ravens heckled the dogs with throaty caws between tearing at the dried fish with black beaks. *A simple distraction,* she mused. *To get what we want, what we need, to change our future.*

"I know what we need to do," she said and pointed at the raven.

"I'm listening."

"We need an ally."

"We do."

"My government wants the Pole, and I can give it to them. All I need is proof that the data from the machine used in the LOMROG expedition is false."

"So you need the machine?"

"It's not that simple," Fenna said. She paused for a moment as the raven squirted a stream of white shit onto the bonnet and took off. "Data collected by the Chinese contradicts Lorentzen's data. If we can get that from Hong Wei…"

"Never gonna happen, love," Burwardsley said and shook his head. "Forget about it."

"He'll give it to me."

"Because?"

"I have something he wants. Something bigger than the Pole, at least for the moment."

"And that is?" Burwardsley said and turned in his seat.

Fenna pressed the palms of her hands against her eyes and rubbed. "Shit," she said. "It's all so fucked up."

"Fenna?"

Fenna took a long breath and stretched her hands, curling her fingers around the steering wheel, squeezing until her knuckles turned white. She exhaled and said, "I know who killed the President of the United States."

"What?"

"I know who did it," she said and turned to Burwardsley.

"How the fuck can you know that?"

"I was in the desert. Jarnvig sent me to some secret training facility in Arizona."

"You were at Fort Huachuca?"

"Like I said…" Fenna laughed. "Secret." She went quiet as an image of Nicklas threatened her resolve. She bit back on her tears.

"You're going to have to learn to trust me," Burwardsley said.

"I know." Fenna let go of the steering wheel and folded her hands in her lap. She picked at the cotton trousers and said, "There was a girl. Nineteen years old. She had no reason to be there. It was weird. I was getting messed around, hounded by Special Forces thugs…"

"I know the type."

"Yeah," Fenna said and looked at him. "I'm sure you do. But while these guys had no problem beating the fuck out me, she was untouchable. Under twenty-four hour guard, apart from about fifteen minutes in the canteen every night."

"Where you were?"

"Once I knew she was there, yes. We met a couple of times before we were discovered." Fenna paused as thoughts of the Gunney and his crew – all of them dead, all traces of their existence covered, deleted, just like Nicklas. *And Jarnvig,* she thought. *Don't forget him.*

"And you know she did it? Assassinated the President?"

"She was being groomed. The whole thing orchestrated by some *deep state*." Fenna looked at Burwardsley, expecting to see a smile on his face, surprised when she didn't. "You believe me?"

"Why shouldn't I?" he said and shrugged. "Look at us, love. We're sitting in a stolen police car, wearing borrowed clothes, outside a hospital where a man was nearly tortured to death, after *we* were tortured… I mean, come on. Tell me the rest."

"Okay," Fenna said and lifted her hand. She pushed her fingers through her hair and said, "Jarnvig said the Americans were looking for a female agent, that I was a candidate, but I was too tough."

"Hah," Burwardsley sad and laughed. "I could have told them that."

"Well, they found Alice instead."

"That's her real name?"

"As far as I know."

"And how do you know she did it?"

"Because they have her picture plastered over the news."

"Then she doesn't have long to live."

"Nope," said Fenna. "They are cleaning up."

Burwardsley shifted in his seat as a police car drove past the car park. He watched as it drove out of sight. "Start the car," he said.

Fenna pulled her seatbelt on and started the engine. She peered around Burwardsley as the police car nosed around the corner and stopped, the driver and his partner staring at them through the driver's window.

"Just supposing Hong Wei gives you the data," Burwardsley said, as he stared at the policemen. "Are you going to give him the girl's name?"

"Yes," Fenna said and shifted the Toyota into first gear. She kept her foot on the clutch.

"It won't be enough."

"I know," she said and released the handbrake. "That's why I'm going to tell him where to find her."

"You know where she is?"

"Yes," Fenna said. The word caught on her lips as the driver of the police car turned on the blue emergency lights.

"And you're going to give her up?" Burwardsley said. He ignored the police car as it pulled into the car park and turned to look at Fenna. "That's not like you."

"No," she said. "It's not. But…" Fenna gripped the steering wheel with her left hand and the gearstick with her right. "You and me…"

"What about us?" Burwardsley said and frowned.

"We're going to be the ones to go and get her."

"Christ. You've got it all figured out."

"Not all of it. But we needed a plan. Now we have one." Fenna held her breath as the police car rolled towards them. She could almost hear the gravel tickling beneath the wheels. "The Pole," she said, "is all about leverage. The Chinese need leverage to force their agenda in the Arctic, and I can give it to them."

"That's great, Konstabel. Really, it is. But," he said with a nod toward the police car, "*they* don't know the plan."

"No," she said and lifted the clutch, "they really don't." Burwardsley's head thumped into the headrest as Fenna floored the accelerator and rammed police car. She yelled as the driver's door buckled under the impact. Fenna kept her foot on the accelerator, pushing the police car in a slow circle as Burwardsley braced against the dashboard and the policemen in the harried Toyota fumbled for the pistols in their belts.

"They're going for their guns," Burwardsley said, cringing at the screech of metal and the scream of the fan belt, as Fenna gripped the steering wheel and pressed her foot to the floor.

Chapter 31

Burwardsley pressed the blunt white tips of his fingers against the plastic dash as Fenna shoved the police car into a large American pickup – an import almost twice the size of the Toyota. As Burwardsley jolted forward in his seat, she shifted into reverse, backed up two metres, and then accelerated into the police car a second time. The policemen raised their hands and Fenna gritted her teeth and suppressed a smile as she reversed once more. The bumper of the Toyota peeled off with one end jammed inside the wing panel of the police car, the other wobbling on the gravel car park as Fenna continued backing away until she stopped, threw the Toyota into first and accelerated past the police car and onto the road.

"You're enjoying this?" Burwardsley said, as he tugged the seatbelt around his chest and fumbled with the buckle.

"Yes," said Fenna as she pulled the latch plate from Burwardsley's fingers and secured it. "Can't a girl have a little fun?" Burwardsley stared at her as Fenna weaved her way between two cars, drifted onto the wrong side of the road and accelerated toward a bus. "What?"

"Discretion, love, is the better part of valour."

"Really?" Fenna said, as she swung the Toyota out of the path of the bus and roared down the main street, barely glancing at the Hotel Hans Egede.

"Henry IV," he said. "The result of a private education. But no amount of Shakespeare rammed down my throat was ever going to clean my gullet of a real Manc accent."

"What?"

"Like right now," Burwardsley said and grinned at Fenna. "I'm buzzin' for this."

"So you're getting a kick out of it?" she said and slowed for the T-junction at the end of the road.

"It means I'm happy. Extremely happy."

"Well, all right then," Fenna said and braked into the corner. "We're going back to the airport. Are you happy about that?"

"Extremely," Burwardsley said and leaned around the seat to look through the rear windscreen.

"How many?"

"Two police Toyotas and a..." Burwardsley paused. "A black

SUV," he said and faced forward. "Your pals from the navy are back again."

"Then we can't disappoint them, can we?" Fenna smiled and accelerated up the street. At the base of a low rise she dropped into third and powered up the incline as the road dissected the rock, throwing up a sheer wall on both sides. "If we make enough noise," she said, "if we attract enough attention, then Hong Wei will hear of it."

"And you think he will just waltz in and pick us up? He's out of his jurisdiction. I think your plan is flawed."

"We'll see," Fenna said and shifted into fourth at the crest of the hill. She powered down the road, braking at a small roundabout before roaring up the hill leading toward the airport. The SUV, she noticed, had pulled away from the police and was gaining on them.

Burwardsley pressed his blunt fingers into a series of buttons on the dash between them, grinning as the siren wailed and the flash of the emergency lights reflected in the windows of the apartments on each side of the road.

"Should've done that earlier," he said and leaned back. "Where's the gun?"

"At my feet," Fenna said and shook her head. "Leave it. We don't want to get shot."

"Fair enough." Burwardsley dipped his head and pointed at a crossing ahead. "Watch the kid on her bike."

"Fuck." Fenna hit the brakes, slewing the Toyota to the left and then correcting it to stop just before the roundabout, as a Greenlandic girl crossed the road. Fenna gripped the wheel and took a series of deep breaths, her heart pounding as the girl, her black hair twisting beneath her helmet in the wind, stopped on the pavement and waved.

"Close one," Burwardsley said.

"Yes," Fenna said. She nodded at the girl and lifted her foot off the brake just as the SUV slammed into the rear of the car and punted the Toyota into the middle of the roundabout. Fenna swore as she fought to wrestle the car back onto the road. Burwardsley turned in his seat and called out as the SUV careered toward them. Fenna threw the car into first and accelerated.

"Go left," Burwardsley shouted.

"No," she said and continued straight. "It's a residential area. I'm taking us out to the airport."

"Then this ride will be over real soon."

"It wasn't meant to last forever. Just long enough to…

"Make some noise. Sure, I get it. But that was before you killed a PET officer," Burwardsley said and shrugged as Fenna swung the car to the left and onto the road to the airport. The Toyota's tyres crunched through the glass leftovers of the roadblock that had been set up in the same position the day before.

I know what I'm doing, Fenna thought and accelerated. When the rear window disintegrated under the first burst of 9mm bullets, she questioned herself, and then willed the car to go faster.

"We're reaching the end game, love. We might need the gun."

"No," Fenna said and shook her head. "We need to stay alive. For Alice."

"For Alice? Come on. That's a long shot. I'm doing this for Dina."

"She's dead, and we can't save the dead," Fenna said and spat blood from her mouth.

"Are you hit?" Burwardsley said. He pressed his hand around the back of her head. Pushed his fingers through her hair, checking for blood.

"Get your hands off me," Fenna said. "I bit my tongue. That's all." She jerked her head to one side as another burst of lead raked the driver's side of the Toyota.

"Calm down."

"It's okay," she said, staring straight ahead. She could see the curve in the road at the end of the runway. "There's a gravel road straight ahead. I don't know how far it goes. That's where this ends."

"Sure. Okay."

"I just need to know you are with me on this," Fenna said and slowed to drop down a gear.

"All the way."

"Really? Because a moment ago you said…"

"I take it back. You're right. Dina's gone. I can't redeem myself, can't make amends. If I'm going to hell," he said and grinned at Fenna, "I'd rather go with a pretty girl…"

"Fuck off, Burwardsley."

"Sure, all right," he said and laughed. "Now don't hit me. I'm going for the gun."

Fenna bounced the Toyota over the lip of the road and onto a track. Stones raked the chassis as Burwardsley reached down between Fenna's legs and pulled the gun out from behind her feet. He sat up and smoothed his hands over the weapon as Fenna slipped the Toyota into four-wheel drive and accelerated off the track and onto a wide path leading down to the fjord. She looked up and smiled at the sight of the mountain as the sun reflected on the last stubborn patch of winter snow and Sermitsiaq cast her shadow on the slopes below the summit. She switched off the siren.

"It's funny," she said and nodded toward the mountain. "It's one of the most boring peaks, but it's growing on me."

"What? That mountain?"

"Yes," Fenna said, as she wrestled the Toyota up and over a flat granite slab. She grimaced at the wrenching sound coming from the axles as she dropped the Toyota over the lip of the boulder and bumped onto the path. "During all this time, through all this drama, it's just been sitting there."

"It's a mountain. That's what they do."

"I know," Fenna said and sighed. "I *do* know." She looked up at the sound of a helicopter approaching and slowed the Toyota to a stop.

"Here?" Burwardsley said.

Fenna nodded. "Here," she said and looked out of the window. "In the shadow of the mountain."

Burwardsley watched as the police leapt out of their vehicles and set up a perimeter. The Counter Terrorism unit exited the SUV, checking their MP5s with a casual professionalism that brought a grim smile to Burwardsley's face.

"I'm sorry about your partner," he said without turning around. "I'm sure he was a good bloke."

"He was," Fenna said and turned in her seat. She released their belts. "Everyone I know is dead or about to die," she said.

"Speak for yourself, love," Burwardsley said, facing her. He rested his head against the headrest and studied Fenna's face. "You think we are going to die?"

"You said we were going to hell. If we step out of the car…" Fenna's words shrank beneath the *whop whop* of the helicopter as the Navy Lynx settled on a patch of rough grass fifty metres in front of the Toyota.

"I said we were going to hell. I didn't say we were going to die."

"There's a difference?"

"With all that you have been through?" Burwardsley laughed. "I thought you'd know."

Fenna raised her eyebrows and shrugged as the roar of the helicopter receded and she imagined the pilot powering down. A quiet wind rolled all sound into a bundle and spun it out of the valley toward the town of Nuuk. Fenna could hear the scratch of the stubble on Burwardsley's cheek against the fabric of the chair as he breathed, his chest swelling and falling in a steady rhythm. Fenna smiled and reached out to take his hand.

"You didn't kill Mikael," she said.

"Thanks, love. But you know I did. I gave the order."

"You didn't pull the trigger."

"I may as well have. But," he said and smiled, "thanks."

Fenna flicked her eyes away from Burwardsley as five men exited the helicopter. Her body stiffened and Burwardsley looked in the direction she was staring.

"Bloody hell," he said and shifted his grip on the pistol.

"No, Mike," Fenna said and squeezed his hand.

"But you know who that is? Right?"

"Yes," Fenna said and took a breath. "It's Vestergaard."

The five men, four of them carrying MP5s trained on the Toyota, walked across the grass, sidestepping boulders, and stopping within ten metres of Fenna and Burwardsley. The unarmed man at the head of the group took a step forwards, and the four men shifted position, as if they were one, covering him from all angles, fingers on the triggers, the submachine guns an extension of their bodies. Vestergaard made a show of removing his glasses, wiping them with a handkerchief and peering into the car.

"Lieutenant Burwardsley?" he said, "Mike, is that you?"

"Yeah," he said. "It's me."

"And who have you got beside you?" he said and took a step to the right. His men moved with him. "Konstabel Brongaard? What a surprise." Vestergaard looked at his men and smiled. "I know them," he said, "I know them very well indeed." The men kept their eyes on the Toyota, their weapons on Fenna and Burwardsley.

"Put the gun away," Fenna whispered.

"I could take him," Burwardsley said, "right now. Redemption."

"No, Mike. You couldn't." Fenna smoothed her hand out of Burwardsley's and reached forward for the pistol. "Give it to me."

"Fuck off, Konstabel. I'm going to end it."

"No," she said. "Not like this. I won't watch you die."

"You won't have to," he said. "I'm pretty sure that, after I drop that bastard, they'll kill us both."

"And they will have won. Again."

"We're never going to win, love. So long as he is alive…"

"That's quite the discussion you're having in there," said Vestergaard. "Why don't you both come out and we can talk. Together. Just like old times, eh?"

"You're a traitor, Vestergaard, and I don't talk with traitors," Fenna shouted.

"Traitor?" he said and laughed. "Tell me, Konstabel, how many Danes did you kill this time?"

"Just the one," she said. "Your pal, Jarnvig."

"That's right. Per Jarnvig. We found his body about an hour ago. But," he said and took another step toward them. "I'm willing to let that go."

Fenna pressed her hand to her chest as if the pressure alone might slow her heart to a normal rhythm. *How does he do it?* she wondered and looked at Burwardsley. *How does he stay so calm?*

"Will you come out?"

"If we get out," Burwardsley said, "we're dead."

"No," Fenna said and opened the door. "I don't believe that."

"Fuck. Fenna, wait." Burwardsley twisted to grab her but she was already out of the door. Two of Vestergaard's men covered Fenna while the other two took an aggressive step toward the Toyota, closing the distance between them and Burwardsley to five metres. Fenna turned her palms at her sides, waited for Vestergaard to nod, and then walked around the Toyota to within two metres of the man who had interrogated her only half a year earlier – the man who had accused her of killing her partner.

"Konstabel," he said and smiled.

"Premierløjtnant," she said and nodded. "But I could perhaps call you *The Magician*?"

"*Magician*? Yes, I like that. But there are no magicians in Greenland, Konstabel. Although if you know where to look, I'm sure you can still find a shaman or two," Vestergaard said, "I happen to know where to look."

"Of course you do," Fenna said and took a step closer. "What about the Chinese? Do you know where to find them too?"

"Ah, you were expecting Hong Wei. That surprises me," he said and frowned. "After what he did to your friend, the policeman."

"There was no-one else left," she said and shrugged. "At least he was consistent. I knew he was evil. He wasn't pretending to be nice, to be on my side."

"And now that you know who I am. Are you willing to talk to me?"

"Yes," Fenna said. The wind tickled the hair from her brow and she looked over her shoulder at the mountain. She turned back to Vestergaard, lifted her chin and stared at him. "I have something you can use."

"The name of the girl who killed the President?"

"Better than that. I know where she is."

"Now that," Vestergaard said and lifted his finger, "that *is* interesting." He paused for a moment to study Fenna. "What do you want?"

"There is some data…"

"Forget the Pole, Konstabel," Vestergaard said and sighed.

"I won't. Not if there is a chance to do something, for Greenland."

"For Greenland? Jesus wept, you are a very confused patriot."

"Yes, I am. But that was my mission," she said. "I want to complete it."

Vestergaard turned his head as the Counter Terrorist team closed on the rear of the vehicle. Burwardsley made a show of lifting the pistol by the barrel and tossing it out of the passenger window. Vestergaard nodded and the men moved in to drag Burwardsley out of the Toyota. He absorbed the first blow to his back with barely a stumble. It took two more before the men had the Royal Marine on his knees and his hands cinched within a plastic strip behind his back. Burwardsley grinned at Fenna.

"I guess it was my turn," he said and twisted to show her the strips pinching his wrists.

"Leave him," Vestergaard said, as one of the navy men raised the butt of his MP5. "We were partners once. Weren't we, Mike."

"You could say that," Burwardsley said with a nod, "but I'm with the Konstabel now."

"Really? I must say," Vestergaard said and turned to Fenna. "This is all very interesting."

"I'm glad you're amused," she said. "Now, here's what I want."

"I'm listening."

"The real data from the LOMROG expedition, the Chinese research, and the proof to back it all up."

"To complete your mission?"

"Yes."

"Done," Vestergaard said, "and you'll give me the location of the girl?"

"No," Fenna said and shook her head.

"No?"

"You get us into America and we'll get the girl."

"We?" he said and frowned. "Oh, you mean the two of you?" Vestergaard laughed. "If you don't mind me saying – and it's more of an observation, really – but it seems that the two of you have some unfinished business."

"We do."

"Dina," Vestergaard said and paused to look at both of them in turn, "is dead. Humble is also dead. Even the swine that raped her is dead. She – the Greenlander – killed him. You need to understand, there are no more loose ends. Apart from the two of you," he said and shrugged.

"Three," Fenna said.

She watched as the frown on Vestergaard's brow deepened for a moment, and then the creases in his cheeks replaced the frown with a laugh. His eyes brightened as he looked at Fenna.

"Yes," he said, "of course. I'm still alive. I'm a loose end."

"You are."

"And you want to kill me?" Vestergaard said and motioned with his hands for his men to stand down as they pressed into a tight defensive ring around him.

"I do," Fenna said. "Just to clean things up."

"Very well," Vestergaard said, "I understand." He took a moment to regain his composure and said, "You'll bring the girl to me?"

"Yes."

"And I'll give you the data."

"No," she said. "You need to sort that out first. The UNCLOS hearing has been postponed, not cancelled. The Americans will be back on their feet soon enough, and the Chinese have lost their leverage. I want to read about it in the papers, because if I give you the girl…"

"Then the Americans owe me, and I have leverage. Yes, I understand, Konstabel." Vestergaard took off his glasses and wiped the dust from the lenses. "What I don't understand is what you will do once you have given the girl to me." He put his glasses on and tucked the handkerchief in his pocket.

"That's simple," Fenna said. "I'm going to kill you."

Vestergaard paused for a moment. He looked at his men. He looked at Burwardsley. "What do you think, Mike? Will she do it?"

Burwardsley looked at Fenna. "Yeah, she'll do it."

"Very well," Vestergaard said and signalled for his men to move in. "I will arrange for you both to enter the United States, and I'll clear up this mess in Greenland."

Fenna stared at Vestergaard as his men surrounded her. She tilted her head. "Just one more thing," she said.

Vestergaard raised his hand and the men paused, the barrels of their MP5s just inches from Fenna's chest and head. "Go on," he said.

"Lorentzen."

"Yes?"

"Did he work for you?"

"A lot of people work for me."

"But I was sent to look for a traitor," Fenna said and looked at Vestergaard.

"No, Konstabel, you were sent to tidy things up," he said, "and now that you killed Jarnvig, it's left to me to clean up after you, again."

"But if Lorentzen worked for you…"

"Go on," Vestergaard said and waited for Fenna. The man closest to her pulled a black cloth hood from his belt.

"If everyone works for you…"

"I can see you are struggling to comprehend all this," he said and smiled. "Let me help you to understand." Vestergaard took a step closer to Fenna and gestured for his men to cuff her around the wrists. "There are times when governments lack the political will to get things done for the greater good. Public opinion can be so trying, and it is during those times that governments and other organisations, turn to men like me. Men who can get the job done."

"Men," said Fenna, "like you."

"That's right."

Fenna grunted as the man holding her kicked her legs and dropped her onto her knees. She caught her breath and looked at Vestergaard.

"I tend to have a problem with men."

"Something I am very aware of, Konstabel," Vestergaard said and laughed. "Of course, if controlled or manipulated correctly, a problem like that can be useful."

"You think you can control me?" Fenna said through gritted teeth.

"Yes," Vestergaard said, "I do."

"We'll see," Fenna said, as she was pinned to the ground and the man pulled the rough hood over her head. She closed her eyes and took a breath of fetid air. *We'll see.*

THE END

ACKNOWLEDGEMENTS

I would like to thank Isabel Dennis-Muir for her invaluable editing skills and feedback on the manuscript, and Jes Lynning Harfeld and Sarah Acton for their assistance in translating *Isblink*.

Once again, while several people have contributed to *In the Shadow of the Mountain*, the mistakes and inaccuracies are all my own.

Chris

July 2017
Denmark

THE SHAMAN'S HOUSE

Book 3 in *The Greenland Trilogy*

AUTHOR'S NOTE

The settlement of Nuugaatsiaq in the Uummannaq fjord region of Greenland was all but washed away by a tsunami during the night of June 20th, 2017. The settlement was devastated, buildings and homes were destroyed, lives were lost, and the community relocated.

I spent a memorable weekend in Nuugaatsiaq at the end of the summer of 2008. Even though I lived in the area for four years, I never returned, but the memory of the people and the spirit of their ancestors buried in cairns on the mountain has remained with me always.

I chose to return to Nuugaatsiaq in the pages of *The Shaman's House* long before the tragedy struck in the summer of 2017. I hope, therefore, that the descriptions of Nuugaatsiaq within the pages of this book, serve in some small way to preserve the memory of a very special place, and a very special community.

The Shaman's House is written in British English and makes use of several Danish and Greenlandic words.

Chris
December 2017
Denmark

The Settlement

NUUGAATSIAQ, GREENLAND

Chapter 1

NUUGAATSIAQ, GREENLAND

At the first crunch of gravel outside his house, the shaman hid the tupilaq in the top drawer of his work desk. He closed the drawer with his thumbs and brushed the loose hair, fur, bone, and seaweed to one side. He picked the last of the stubborn dog hair from the front of his cornflower-blue smock, twisted it between his palms into a long strand, and hid it in his trouser pocket. The visitors knocked at the door just a few seconds later. The shaman walked to the door, opened it, and welcomed his guests into the kitchen. He stood to one side as they jostled up the three wooden steps and inside the house, rubbing the straps of their deflated lifejackets against the walls as they made space for their guide, a middle-aged Australian, twice the shaman's height, half his age, three times as loud. The guide cleared his throat to get the group's attention and gestured at the shaman.

"This is Tulugaq, a good friend of mine," the guide said. The shaman shook the guide's hand just as he had been briefed. The guests – passengers or *PAX* from the adventure cruise ship in the fjord – smiled and greeted the shaman. "Tulugaq means raven in Greenlandic." The guide smiled and waited for the shaman to nod. He placed one hand on the Greenlander's shoulder and gestured with the other at the shelves covering the walls of the tiny kitchen. They were lined with figures carved in bone, each one more gruesome than the next. The figures leered at the PAX with assorted bulbous eyes, sharp teeth, exquisite fingers, and typically large phalluses. Some of the younger PAX giggled, the older ones stared, sizing up each figure for the display case in their dens back home in North America, Western Europe, and Australasia. "I've made a deal with Tulugaq," the guide said. "He has agreed to a buy two, get one free arrangement, but remember to buy only the tupilaq that are legal under the CITES agreement. So, only buy those that are…"

"Made from reindeer bone," said a large passenger as he crossed the kitchen floor to study a particular figure that had caught his eye. "It's a shame," he said as he inspected a small figurine polished to the colour of cream. "The narwhal figures are so intricate."

"And illegal to export," said the guide.

"I know, but…"

The shaman slipped into the living room and stood by his desk.

Two of the PAX followed him, beckoning to the guide to take their picture with Tulugaq.

"Do you mind?" they asked.

The shaman shook his head. He posed between the two women as the guide took photos with their digital cameras and iPhones. The shaman waited for the cameras to be returned, took a step backward and paused as a tall man entered the kitchen. The shaman's brow furrowed as he studied the man, noting that he wore no lifejacket, and that his jacket was black, unlike the red and yellow cruise ship jackets provided for all PAX. The man caught the shaman's eye at the same time that the guide noticed him.

"Sorry, mate, this is a private viewing," the guide said. "If you wouldn't mind waiting outside until we're finished."

"I can wait," the man said. He removed his glasses and wiped them with a cloth from his pocket.

"Outside, if you please."

The PAX paused to listen as the man cleared his throat, nodded at the shaman, and said, "I'll be outside."

"Thank you," the guide said as the man left. The shaman walked to a window and watched the man as he walked across the gravel to stand beside two tall men dressed in black fatigues. The men wore pistols in holsters clipped to broad belts. "Do you know them?" the guide said, as he leaned around the shaman.

"*Naamik*," the shaman said.

"Ah, and that means?"

"No. I don't know them."

The guide stepped back to answer queries from several of the PAX. There were twelve of them, and they spilled out of the kitchen and into the lounge. The shaman posed for more photos, and received handfuls of Danish kroner, as the PAX bought all of the figures made from the antlers, bones, and skulls of the reindeer. Once the shelves had been stripped of tupilaq fit for export, the PAX and their guide left, and the shaman was alone for the time it took them to walk back to the zodiac inflatables waiting to take them back to the ship. He stuffed the money in a second drawer in his desk and stared at the men outside, until the man with the glasses walked up to the kitchen door, knocked and entered.

"Tea?" the man said in Danish.

"Just for you?"

"For you and me. My men will wait outside."

The shaman filled a pan of water from a plastic container and put it on the stove to boil. The man studied the remaining figures on the shelves.

"Do you use a drill?" he said.

"Sometimes."

"So, that's how you get them so smooth." The man lifted a figure made of narwhal. He rubbed his thumb across the surface.

"Are you a collector?"

"Me? No." He laughed. "At least not these. I am only interested in tupilaq."

"These are tupilaq," the shaman said. He frowned through the steam as the water boiled.

"They might think so," said the man, with a nod to the retreating blight of yellow and red PAX as they boarded the zodiacs. "But I think you and I know the difference. Don't we?"

The shaman put a tea bag inside a dirty mug, added the water, and a generous helping of sugar. He removed the bag and handed the mug to the man.

"Thank you."

"You're welcome," the shaman said, as he prepared another mug of tea.

"Now," said the man, "how about you show me the real tupilaq. The ones you don't find in display cases, nooks, and dens. Eh?" He took a step into the living room. "Are they in here?"

"Wait," said the shaman. He left his mug on the kitchen counter and followed the man. He stopped as the man put his mug on the desk and picked at the loose strands of fur and seaweed on the work surface. The shaman watched as the man sorted them with his fingers, plucking a hair from the tangled mess and holding it up to the light.

"Human?"

"*Aap.*"

"Female?" The man teased the hair into one strand the length of his arm.

The shaman raised his eyebrows, *yes.*

"Whose?"

"I cannot say."

"Fair enough," the man said, as he laid the hair back on the desk.

"But you use it to bind the tupilaq. Am I right?"

"*Aap.*"

"Show me."

The man stepped to one side as the shaman opened the drawer in his desk. He curled his fingers around a rough figure and held it in the light. The man nodded as the shaman opened his palm.

"Yes," he said. "Just as I thought. You have used the woman's hair to bind the seaweed around the bone." He cocked his head to one side. "A human bone?"

"*Tuttu.* Reindeer."

"And this?" The man used the nail of his little finger to tease the arms of the figure.

"Wood, from the sea."

"Of course," he said, and lowered his hand, "and when it is finished, will you cum on it?" The shaman frowned, and the man made a jerking motion with his hand. "Will you cum on it?"

"*Aap.*"

"I read that somewhere. But why?"

The shaman placed the figure back in the drawer and said, "For energy. For the magic."

"Ah, magic," the man said. He picked up the mug of tea and walked across the floor to the couch, the cushions sighed as he sat down. "I know a thing or two about magic."

The shaman turned the chair at his desk to face the man and sat down. They stared at each other as the man sipped his tea.

"Do you want to buy a tupilaq?" the shaman said. "A real one?"

"Perhaps." The man leaned forward to place his mug on the floor. "Tell me," he said, "what can it do? What can *that* one do?"

"That one will keep a child safe."

"How?"

"I will throw it in the sea."

"After you have charged it with your energy?"

"*Aap.*"

"Why?"

"There is a girl travelling to Uummannaq. She is going alone. Her mother wants her to be safe."

"And so she paid you to make a tupilaq?"

"*Aap.*"

"I see," the man said. He stood up and walked over to the wall.

He stopped in front of a photo and tapped his finger on the frame. "Is this your family?"

The shaman nodded. He rested his hands in his lap. He waited.

"And where are they?"

"Nuuk."

"Why?"

The shaman wrinkled his nose and shrugged. "They don't like Nuugaatsiaq."

"They don't like this village?" The man removed his glasses and cleaned them. "That's strange," he said. "It's such a beautiful place."

"No jobs."

"That's true," he said and stuffed the cloth in his pocket. He put on his glasses and gestured in the direction of the cruise ship. "But you do all right."

"In the summer."

"And the rest of the year?"

"I hunt." The shaman pointed his thumb at his desk. "I help people."

"Yes," the man said, "about that." He crossed the floor and stood next to the shaman, "I want you to help me."

"You want me to make a tupilaq?"

"Yes."

"It can be dangerous."

"How?"

The shaman took the figure from the drawer. He pointed at the different elements as he explained. "If the girl finds this, she can take the magic. She can ruin it, turn it against herself."

"I don't understand."

"This tupilaq will guard her from the sea. If she takes it from the sea, it cannot help her." He paused. "She might drown."

The man looked out of the window, and waved at the two armed men waiting outside the house. The taller of the two tapped his watch, and the man nodded. He looked at the shaman. "Go on."

"This tupilaq is made to protect a person, but if I make a tupilaq to hurt someone the opposite is true. If I put something of a person inside and that person finds it, they can use it against you, if their magic is stronger than yours."

The man frowned. "How do you know I want to use a tupilaq against a person?"

"Them," the shaman said and pointed at the men outside the house.

"Alright. Suppose I do." The man reached inside his pocket and removed a length of black hair twisted around a pencil stub. "I want you to use this."

The shaman took the hair and held it closer to the window. He turned the stub in his fingers and rubbed a loose end of the hair. He sniffed it and said, "This is not real?"

"The hair is real."

"But the colour."

"No," the man said, "she has a habit of changing that." He leaned against the wall. "Can you still use it?"

"*Aap*. But maybe it will lose some power."

"Then maybe you will have to charge it twice," the man said. He shook his head as he laughed. "The very thought."

"You laugh."

"Yes."

"But this is not funny."

"No," the man said. The smile on his lips faded. "It is deadly serious."

"What should your tupilaq do?"

"It must kill." The man held the shaman's gaze and said, "Can you do that?"

"*Aap*," he whispered. "I can do that. But the hair…"

"I will settle for wounding or maiming the girl."

"Girl?"

"In her twenties. She is quite resourceful."

"And she is coming here?"

The man pushed off the wall, walked around the small living room and stopped at the window. He wiped a smear of grime from the glass with his thumb, leaned close to the clean spot of window and stared at the oil tank to the right of the general store. It was cordoned with a chain link fence, but the door was open, and the man smiled. Beyond the tank was a narrow beach leading to the water. The sand was littered with clumps and boulders of ice, debris from the icebergs in the fjord. He turned to the shaman and nodded.

"Yes," he said, "she will come here, eventually."

"When?"

"Oh, I don't know. Perhaps at the beginning of winter?" He

moved away from the window. "Which reminds me," he said, "I am going to need your house." He waved at the men outside and waited as they hurried to the door and into the kitchen. The shaman stood as they entered the living room.

"Don't move, grandpa," said the tall one. His hand strayed to the pistol at his hip. His partner moved into the room and took a position by the side of the couch.

"Who are you?" the shaman said. He looked at the man.

"You can call me Vestergaard, or you can call me *the Magician*. A lot of people do."

The shaman flicked his gaze from one face to the next, returning to the man in the middle of the room, the one calling himself a magician. "Then you know magic?" he said.

"I can make things happen, or people disappear, in my own way, yes."

"Then you don't need me," the shaman said and moved to throw the pencil stub of hair into the middle of the room. He stopped when Vestergaard raised his hand.

"You will make me a tupilaq, the most powerful you have ever made," he said, "and you will allow me to use your house, as and when I need to."

"What if I don't want to?"

Vestergaard clicked his fingers and pointed at the picture on the wall. The tall man walked to the wall and tugged the picture from beneath the tacks pinning it in place. The corners ripped and the shaman twitched, fists clenched.

"Careful, grandpa," the tall man said. He took a long look at the photo before folding it in half and stuffing it inside his jacket.

"You will do what I say, because I have friends in Nuuk," said Vestergaard.

"I have no choice?"

"None."

The shaman relaxed his fingers and smoothed his palms on his thighs. "I need a name," he said. "A real one."

"Why?"

"For the tupilaq."

"Alright." Vestergaard sat down on the couch. He leaned back and crossed his legs. "Her name is Konstabel Fenna Brongaard."

"Konstabel?"

"She was in the Sirius Patrol," Vestergaard said. He waved a hand in the air. "It's not important, but she still uses the title."

"Boss," said the tall man. "Should you be telling him all this?"

Vestergaard looked at the shaman. Studied him for a moment, and then said, "It's alright. I believe we understand one another." The shaman raised his eyebrows in agreement and waited for Vestergaard to continue. "Besides, it might come to nothing. We still don't know if our favourite Konstabel will complete her mission."

"And if she does, boss?"

"Then she will need a safe house," Vestergaard said and looked at the shaman. "This one."

The Mountain

NORTH CASCADES, WASHINGTON, USA

Chapter 2

SEATTLE TACOMA AIRPORT, WASHINGTON, USA

It should have been simple, but like most conversations Konstabel Fenna Brongaard had with men in uniform, it quickly turned into an interrogation, and then the border patrol officer called his supervisor. Fenna saw his hand as he slid it under the table and pressed what she imagined to be the emergency button, signalling that he required assistance. Burwardsley, she noticed, had been processed through the Seattle Tacoma Airport without any problems. *What is it about me*, she wondered, *that makes everything so complicated?* The supervisor approached the desk and stared at Fenna before signalling to his colleague to join him for a moment. Fenna watched as they whispered back and forth. She tapped her fingers on the counter. She stopped when she saw her nails. There was blood in the corners, the stubborn kind that soap could not remove. She traced the small scratches and tiny scars from her nails to her knuckles, shrugged and smiled as she decided that maybe the customs guy had a point. She saw her reflection in the glass of the booth and dipped her head so that her fringe might hide the bruising on her cheek, the graze beneath her eye.

"Yeah," she whispered. "I guess I was crazy to think this might work." She stopped speaking as the supervisor approached the glass and sat down, the officer stood behind him, and Fenna noticed his hand resting on the grip of the Beretta at his hip.

"Fenna Brongaard?" the supervisor said.

"Yes."

"Arriving from?"

"Reykjavik," she said. "Originally, anyway. There was a layover..."

"In Amsterdam. Yes, we have you there too."

"What does that mean?"

The supervisor studied her passport, giving Fenna a moment to take stock of the security crowding the entrance to the United States of America. She looked up when he started to speak.

"You're aware of the situation in America right now? You heard about the assassination?"

"Yes." Fenna held her breath for a moment, and thought, *more than you think.*

"Then you can appreciate us being interested in a young woman of your height, hair colour," he paused, his eyes lingering over Fenna's face, "facial description."

"You're saying you are looking for someone matching my description?"

"It was all over the news," the man said and stared at Fenna. "You must have seen the pictures?"

"Sure." Fenna frowned. "But if that's all this is..."

"It's a pretty big deal."

"I understand, but if I was that person, do you really think I would be trying to get *into* the country? You don't think I'd be trying to get out?" The supervisor stiffened, and the officer curled his finger around the grip of his pistol. "Sorry," Fenna said and raised her hands for a moment. "I'm just tired after the flight. I am sure the situation is tense." She glanced at the security officers as they talked into their microphones. "Very tense," she said.

The supervisor stood and gestured for his colleague to sit in the chair. He gave the officer Fenna's passport as the man sat down. "You're right, the situation is tense. We need to be thorough." He tapped the officer on the shoulder. "You filed ESTA, a tourist VISA. My co-worker will process you now." He took a step backward, lingering just a metre from the glass.

"What's the purpose of your visit, Miss?" the officer asked.

"Recreation."

"Specifically?"

"Backpacking."

The officer lifted his head and peered over the counter. Fenna smiled as he scrutinised her trekking trousers and hiking boots.

"The rest of my gear was in the hold," she said.

"You're hiking alone?"

"I can take care of myself." Fenna held her breath as the man shifted his gaze to her face. She tried a smile, but he ignored her.

"Just process her, Richard," the supervisor said. He nodded at the line behind Fenna as the officer looked at him."It's going to be a long day. We can't hold her just because she looks like someone – regardless of the circumstances."

The officer handed Fenna her passport, pinching it in his grip as she took it.

"What?" she said.

"Just one more thing. Where will you be staying?"

"Motels and camping."

"No contacts in Seattle?"

"Maybe."

"Who?"

Fenna thought about the hour she spent with an American at Heathrow Airport. "Solomon Owens," she said. "He's a friend of the family."

"Richard," the supervisor said.

"Alright," said the officer. He let go of Fenna's passport. "We're done here."

Fenna waited for a moment, tucked her passport into the pocket of her hiking jacket and looked from one man to the other. She walked away as the supervisor turned his back to her. *Don't push it, Fenna.* She nodded at the officer and walked through the border inspection area, following the signage to the baggage reclaim section of Arrivals.

Burwardsley met her at the conveyor belt for the flight from Amsterdam, as he did his best to blend in with the shorter travellers – mostly Chinese – waiting for their luggage. He stood close to Fenna, but, from a distance, observers would have struggled to connect the two.

"You took your time," he whispered.

"Mistaken identity," she said, her voice low, lips hardly moving.

"I'll pick up the car. Meet me out front."

Burwardsley walked to the belt and picked up his military Bergan. He slung it over one shoulder and walked toward the exit. Fenna waited for her backpack to roll around the belt before grabbing it. She used the bathroom, and then walked through the exit, orientating herself with a quick glance at the signs.

It had taken the best part of a week to set up what Fenna considered the rescue operation, to find Alice – America's most wanted – and to get her out of the country. The young assassin was going to be the world's greatest bargaining chip, and Fenna had sold her to the highest bidder. *I know where she is*, she had said to Vestergaard when he had cornered her at the end of the road just north of the landing strip of Nuuk International Airport in Greenland's capital. Now, the million-dollar question was if she had been right.

When Fenna met Alice on the military base in Yuma, Arizona, they had bonded, in secret, as the only women on a base populated by arrogant A-type special forces soldiers. *Men with more testosterone than sense*, she remembered. *Apart from the smart ones, and they were the most dangerous. Men like Burwardsley.* Fenna looked up as a Jeep rumbled past. It looked like the kind of car he would hire, and she wondered at just how much trust she had placed in him – *the man who had my partner killed.* She hadn't slept on the flight, not least for the conflicting thoughts battling in her mind, thoughts that included her closest ally, who, just a few months earlier, had not only been responsible for ending her Sirius partner's life, but had done his best to end hers too. *And yet, he's the one with the contacts all of a sudden.* She sighed. *I need him.*

A string of cars stopped in front of the entrance, loading and unloading travellers, friends, and loved ones. Fenna waited, long enough for drivers in the next line of cars to switch on their lights as the twilight became dusk. She blinked as the driver of a small Prius flashed its lights. Fenna shouldered her pack and walked over to it. The driver popped the trunk as she reached the car, and Fenna dumped her pack before opening the passenger door and sliding onto the seat.

"You took your time," she said.

"Tell me about it," Burwardsley said. He waited for Fenna to fasten her seatbelt before pulling away and into the stream of traffic heading toward the city.

"This is cosy," she said, looking around the interior of the car.

"But less conspicuous."

Fenna looked at Burwardsley hunched behind the steering wheel and laughed. "Yeah, about that."

"You want to drive?"

"I don't know where we're going."

"Exactly," he said and accelerated onto the highway. "So shut the fuck up."

"Touchy."

"Just tired." Burwardsley took one hand off the wheel and pressed his thumbnail into one of his fingers, just beneath the nail.

"Still can't feel anything, eh?"

"Just tingling. But better than before."

Fenna remembered pulling Burwardsley out of the refrigerated container on the building site in Nuuk – a convenient Black Site, operated by one of several likely agencies. *But which one?*

"How about you?" he said. "Tired?"

"A little. But we have to keep going, right?"

"Right. Just one stop, to pick up some gear, guns, and ammo." Burwardsley smiled. "Any preferences?"

Fenna leaned back, lifted her foot onto the edge of the seat and tugged off one hiking boot, and then the other. She bent her knees to her chest, squirmed her toes on the dashboard, and said, "I can shoot, but I don't really give a shit what I shoot with."

"You should," Burwardsley said and slapped at her feet.

"What?" Fenna sneered as she lowered her feet to the foot well.

"They smell."

"They've smelled worse," she said, and then, "*I've* smelled worse."

"I know."

"Yeah, I tend to forget that." Fenna chewed at her lip for a moment, glancing at Burwardsley when she thought his attention was focused on the road. "We never talked about it," she said, as he slipped the Prius into the outer lane. "When you and that Nepali bastard..."

"Bahadur."

"Right, when you had me stretched between you, when you sliced my clothes off with that fucking sword of his."

"Fenna..."

"How far were you going to go?"

"Come on, Konstabel."

"How far?"

Burwardsley looked at Fenna, held her gaze for a second, and then said, "As far as I needed to."

Fenna nodded and looked away. "I thought so."

"I'm a professional, Fenna. We both are. Right now we are on a job – your job. So, wind your neck in, and get with the programme."

"Right."

"I mean it," he said and slowed as they approached an off ramp. "Now, what preference do you have?" He slowed the car to a stop at the end of the ramp.

"Short-stock carbine. Can your friend do that?"

"Sure. What else?"

"Nine millimetre back-up."

"Glock? I'm not sure he can do Austrian."

"No preference. Just small, with a large mag."

Fenna looked out of the passenger window. The street lights and neon signage reflected on her cheeks and caught in her eyes. She saw her reflection in the side mirror and smiled at the thought of what a little colour could do to her cheeks, how she had used it on a ship and at a conference, to grab the attention of her mark, her assignment, usually some bastard who would die shortly after meeting her. *I'm getting good at this. Perhaps too good.* She nodded when Burwardsley said they should have a couple of grenades each.

The neon sign of the *Subway* at the junction caught Fenna's attention. She sat up and said, "Wait."

"What?"

"Food."

Burwardsley pulled into the parking lot of the *Subway* once the lights changed. Fenna tugged on her boots and they got out. She lifted her chin and flicked her eyes at the police patrol car parked outside and Burwardsley nodded.

"Won't be a problem. We're not on any watch list."

"No?" she said. "Why do you think it took me so long at passport control?"

Burwardsley stopped at the door, his massive frame blocked the light from the restaurant, throwing Fenna into shadow.

"Hey, I can't help it if I look like her."

"You look like Alice?"

"A few years older, otherwise..."

"Great," he said and pulled open the door. Fenna followed him inside. He nodded at the policeman eating at a table by the window, and approached the counter. The young Chinese man behind the counter pulled on a fresh pair of plastic gloves and waited for their order. Burwardsley ordered for both of them. Fenna said nothing.

"Go sit down," he whispered. "I'll bring it over."

Fenna sat at the table closest to the counter, her back to the policeman. She saw his image reflected in the glass, he was staring at her back. Burwardsley sat down and handed her a wrapped sandwich.

"We're eating here?" she said.

"Still waiting on my sandwich."

Fenna leaned across the table. "Fine," she said. "But it looks like you're dining with public enemy number one."

"Something you failed to mention back in Greenland," he said and stared at her.

"They had guns, you fuck. It was the end of the line."

Burwardsley's lips parted, and a barely-suppressed tremor rippled across his shoulders.

"You think this is funny?"

"No," he said, and laughed.

"We haven't even been in the States for more than..." she looked at her watch.

"A couple of hours, and we're about to be busted by Policeman Plod over there."

"What?" Fenna glanced over her shoulder. "Shit. He's coming over."

"Just relax."

Burwardsley shuffled his seat away from the table and placed his hands on his thighs. Fenna took a breath and followed his lead. She leaned back in her seat and placed her sandwich on the table. She closed her eyes for a moment and pictured the layout of the restaurant – the counter with the Chinese man preparing their food, the policeman, and no other guests. *He can take cover behind the counter*, she thought with a glance at the young Chinese man. She caught Burwardsley's eye. *He'll take out the cop while I get the car.* Fenna willed her hands to be still, and, with a quick plan in place, she felt that familiar calm that came just before the storm of action. She was ready, not for the first time, and definitely not the last. The policeman stopped at their table, his thumbs tucked into the front of his belt, just behind the buckle.

"Evening," he said.

"Hi," said Burwardsley. Fenna smiled. "Can we help you?"

"Maybe," the policeman said. "Your accent? British?"

"You got me there. It's a difficult one to hide, especially over here."

"It sure is. And what about you, Miss?" he said. "Where are you from?"

"Denmark," Fenna said, grateful all of a sudden for her own accent. She added a little more for effect. "West coast. I'm from Esbjerg."

"Really?" The policeman relaxed his grip on his belt, and Fenna imagined she saw the tension ease out of the man's shoulders. "My family is from Norway, originally."

"Really? Have you visited?"

"On my pay?" the man laughed. Fenna smiled, noticing for the first time his grey moustache and the wrinkles around his eyes. "Maybe as a retirement gift, for me and the wife."

"Norway's beautiful," Fenna said. "You agree, Mike?"

"Oh yes," Burwardsley said and smiled. He looked up as the Chinese man brought his sandwich. "And we'd better be going," he said and stood up.

"Nice to meet you," Fenna said. She picked up her sandwich and the two drinks from the tray. The policeman took a step back for her to pass and she followed Burwardsley to the exit.

The policeman coughed and called out just as she reached the door. "Just a second, Miss," he said and pulled his mobile from his belt.

Fenna glanced at Burwardsley, caught the slight shake of his head. She turned to the policeman and waited.

"Something wrong?"

"Well, you might be from Denmark, and I don't doubt your friend here is from England..."

"But?"

"But... you look real familiar." He held up his mobile and turned the screen toward them. "See what I mean?" he said and let his free hand slide to his gun.

"Yeah," Fenna said. "I see what you mean."

Chapter 3

Burwardsley let go of the door and it closed with a quiet snick. He nudged Fenna and took the drinks and sandwich from her hands, leaning in close to whisper in her ear, “He's all yours.”

The policeman turned the Smartphone in his hand and studied the screen, flicking his eyes from Fenna to the mobile and back again. The young man retreated from the counter, edging his way to the storage room opposite the cash register. Fenna followed his movement before turning back to the policeman. She felt the second kick of adrenaline since entering the restaurant, flexed her fingers, and curbed the rush of energy. She gauged the distance between them, made the calculations, factoring in the policeman's height, reach, build, age, his likely speed, his dexterity. She lifted her chin and took a step forward. The policeman tightened his grip around the pistol. He lowered the mobile.

“What are the odds,” Fenna said, “of you catching the President's assassin?”

“Then you know who that is?”

“Yes,” she said and sighed. “This is the second time today I've been stopped because of her.”

“And the first time?”

“At the airport.”

“And they let you in.” He let his hand slide from the pistol.

Fenna waited. The hum of the air conditioning unit filled the space between them, with a steady drone punctuated suddenly by a loud slurp. She turned as Burwardsley swallowed and let the drinking straw slip from his lips.

“What?” he said.

“You're enjoying this?” Fenna whispered.

“We're on holiday.” Burwardsley looked at the policeman. “A vacation. We've been planning this for months.” He shrugged. “It's not every day your girlfriend gets mistaken for an assassin.”

“I guess not,” the policeman said. He shrugged at Fenna. “Sorry, Miss, but the whole country is pretty keyed-up right now.”

“So,” she said, “maybe I should wear a hat?”

“Maybe.”

Fenna laughed. She could feel the adrenaline flushing out of her system. She relaxed, looked the policeman in the eye and said, “Did you just agree that I should wear a disguise?"

"I guess I did," he said and slipped the mobile into his trouser pocket.

Burwardsley took another slurp of cola. The *Subway* employee stepped out of the storage room and shuffled a selection of cookies onto the counter.

"They're on me," he said.

"Thanks." Burwardsley pressed his cola into Fenna's hand and grabbed the cookies from the counter. He winked at the policeman and walked to the door. "Time to hit the road, baby," he said and walked out of the restaurant. Fenna smiled at the policeman and followed Burwardsley into the parking lot. The light from the restaurant reflected on the rain beading on the car.

"Baby?" she said. "Really?" Fenna licked at a drop of rain on her lip.

"It seemed like the thing to say," Burwardsley said. He placed the food on the roof of the car and opened the door. Fenna did the same. They looked at each other for a moment, laughing as they picked up the food and slipped inside.

"We don't need that again," Fenna said and pressed the drinks into the plastic holders.

"Maybe you should buy a hat?" Burwardsley said, backing the car out of the parking space, as Fenna pulled on her seatbelt.

Fenna curled a fist into his ribs and suppressed a smile. "Just drive," she said.

Burwardsley pulled out of the parking lot and followed the road east, beyond a row of cheap motels and into a small industrial area. There was an open lot with a small concrete building framed by trash cans and dumpsters on either side. Burwardsley pulled around the back of the building, stopped the car and turned off the engine.

"Eat your sandwich," he said. "I'll let my guy know we are here."

Fenna ate as she watched Burwardsley climb out from behind the wheel and walk over to the building. There was a metal box screwed into the concrete wall by the side of a rusted metal door. Burwardsley opened the box and pulled out a handset. He held it to his ear and waited. Fenna heard him grunt a few words before he returned to the car, squeezed his massive frame into the driver's seat and unwrapped his sandwich. He left the door open and hooked his left leg out of the car.

"We just wait?" Fenna said, taking the last bite of hers and wiping her hands on her trousers.

"We do," he said.

She opened the glove compartment and shuffled through the papers until her fingers caught on something a little sturdier. "*Rand McNally*," she said and pulled out a map of the State. "Totally old school." Fenna unfolded the map on her lap and traced a route to the North Cascades Mountain Range to the east, close to the Canadian Border.

"So why did the girl…"

"Alice."

"Right," Burwardsley said. "Why did she choose this particular cabin?" He pressed the empty sandwich wrapper into a ball and tossed it onto the back seat.

"It's personal," Fenna said.

"How?"

She looked at Burwardsley. "It's the last place she and her dad visited, before he died."

"The lookout cabin?"

"He was a climber," Fenna said.

Burwardsley sipped at the cola. He pulled his leg inside the car as the rain increased, spreading from beads to damp patches on his cargo trousers.

"My old man was a banker. An arrogant sod at that. We didn't talk much, and he parcelled me off to boarding school when my mother got sick. We haven't talked since she died."

Fenna turned her head. "Not at all?"

"Nope." Burwardsley finished the cola and tossed the empty cup into the back. "It was my aunt who came to both my graduations – school and the Marines. She's the only link to my old man, and his money."

"Any brothers? Sisters?"

"Nope. Just my aunt."

Fenna thought of her sister looking after their alcoholic mother in Esbjerg. She stifled a pang of guilt, consoling herself with the thought that their lives were so far removed, they wouldn't have anything to talk about, nothing to connect them, not since her father died.

"What about you?" Burwardsley said. "What about your old

man?"

"He was in the Jægerkorps, killed in Afghanistan."

"Hunter Force? Yeah, I know them. They're about the only unit that can give us a run for our money. How did he die?"

Fenna took a breath. "I don't know."

"Classified?"

"Maybe. I never asked, and no-one told me." *Perhaps one day*, she thought.

Burwardsley slapped Fenna's arm, as a taxi stopped on the street and an African American woman got out. She walked around the cab, tottering as she found her balance. Her high heels, Fenna noticed as the woman approached, were like meat skewers, pressed into thick ankles.

"I thought you said it was a guy?"

"Just wait," Burwardsley said, a grin spreading across his face.

The woman stopped at the door to the building, nodded at Burwardsley, and then unlocked it with a key attached to a long chain. There was a metal tube dangling from the end. It reminded Fenna of a policeman's nightstick, just shorter.

"Let's go," Burwardsley said, as the woman opened the door. Fenna followed him out of the car. They picked their way between the trash until they stepped inside a dark space, the size of a closet, just wide enough for them to stand side by side. Burwardsley's upper arm pressed against Fenna's shoulder, and he cocked his head to one side of a naked bulb screwed into a plastic light fitting in the ceiling. They blinked as it was switched on, revealing a small armoury that filled the building space beyond the thick metal grille. Burwardsley squeezed around Fenna to close and lock the door behind them. He pressed against her as he turned to face the woman leaning against the counter behind the grille. Fenna looked at the stiletto heels the woman placed on the counter, and caught her eye.

"Them fuckers gonna kill me," the woman said. Fenna frowned at the deep boom of her voice. She looked at Burwardsley and said, "What you want, babe? What you need?"

"Two M4 carbines," he said. The woman pulled two purple tickets from a wire suspended beneath the counter. She placed them on the surface, tapping them with thick nails glued onto stubby scarred fingers.

"And?"

"Couple of pistols. One 9 mil."

"American?"

"Austrian," said Fenna. "If you've got one?"

"Listen child," she said and put a green ticket beside the purple ones. "There ain't nothing I don't got." She cocked her head and stared at Fenna. "What kind of Glock?"

"I don't mind."

"You should, child. How about a 20?"

"Sure. Why not?" Fenna caught herself from commenting as the woman sighed.

"And you, B? You don't want some Austrian shit, do you."

"You know what I want, Charlie."

"Yeah, babe," Charlie said. She flashed her white teeth at Burwardsley and placed a thick brown ticket on the counter. "A Browning Fighting Pistol," she said, forcing a mock shiver from her shoulders to her large, masculine behind. "Such a sexy weapon for my sexy friend."

"Alright, Charlie," Burwardsley said. "Take it down a notch."

"But, babe..."

"I mean it."

Fenna caught the edge in Burwardsley's voice. She glanced at his face and saw the steel in his eyes. She had seen it before. From Charlie's reaction, she had too. *Before or after he became a she?* Fenna wondered. Charlie placed her palms on the counter and lowered her eyes. Fenna studied her nails, broken, chipped, false. The rest of Charlie's ensemble was just as cheap, and yet, Fenna was beginning to see the merits of such a disguise, if that was what it was, for what must be the most well-stocked illegal arms store in Washington State. She nodded, and risked a smile for Charlie.

"What?" she said.

"Nothing. I'm just impressed. That's all."

Charlie stared at Fenna and then laughed. "Sure, honey. Be impressed. I don't mind. Charlie has the best stock..."

"In the wettest State of America," said Burwardsley. "I know, but we are on a tight schedule. We need to get going."

Charlie smoothed her hands off the counter and plucked at the plastic tickets suspended from the rail. "Okay, B. I'm all yours. Ready and ..." She closed her mouth at another look from Burwardsley.

"Eight grenades."

"HE or my friend, William Peter?"

"What's that?" said Fenna.

"White phosphorous," said Burwardsley. He waved a hand around the store. "There's a lot Vietnam surplus here."

"And white phosphorous?"

"Sticks on the skin and burns, child," said Charlie.

"It could be useful," Burwardsley said. "They certainly won't expect it. Okay," he said and nodded. "Add another M4 and one more Glock. As back-up," he said, when Fenna frowned.

Charlie swept the tickets off the counter into her large palm. She closed her fist around the tickets and said, "How many rounds?"

"Five magazines each for the carbines. Another three for the pistols."

Charlie nodded and walked away from the counter. She stopped when Burwardsley called out her name.

"You forget something, B?"

"No, but maybe you did." He took a step closer to the grille and said, "My special order?"

"Right," Charlie said and nodded. "For our mutual friend."

"That's right," Burwardsley said. He leaned against the grille as Charlie weaved her way between the racks of weapons, piling them into a shopping trolley as if she was picking groceries from the aisles in the local Kmart.

"What's that about?" said Fenna. "What special order? Who's the mutual friend?"

"You don't need to know everything, Konstabel."

"I think I do. It's my op."

"No," Burwardsley said. "It's Vestergaard's, for as long as we let him think it is. But if we are going to get out of this alive, we need to play an ace or two. I have an ace, and I intend to play it."

"You going to tell me what it is?"

"I won't need to. You'll find out soon enough." Burwardsley turned around as Charlie bumped the trolley full of guns and ammunition into the counter.

"It's all reconditioned, with the serials sanded off. Apart from the grenades. But," she said and laughed, "they're so old, no-one is ever going to trace them."

"It's all good, Charlie. Thanks."

"Don't thank me before you paid for it, honey."

"PayPal?"

"You know it."

Fenna pressed her hand on Burwardsley's arm. "How are we paying?"

"PayPal," Burwardsley said. He laughed at Fenna's wrinkled brow and said, "Don't worry about it. Charlie sends a mail to another mutual friend, and we make a transaction. See," he said and pointed at Charlie as she tapped the tip of a broken nail on the keypad on her Smartphone.

"Okay," Fenna said. "That answers that, but the other thing... the special order?"

Charlie slipped her Smartphone onto the counter and reached into the shopping trolley. Wedged between the crate of grenades and wooden box of magazines for the carbines and pistols, was a long blade wrapped in a leather cloth. Fenna's breath caught in her throat as she recognised the handle, and the curve of the blade as Charlie pulled it out of the cloth and flashed it in front of them. She made swooshing noises as the blade caught the light. Fenna felt her skin contract into bumps on her arms, as she followed the arc of the kukri blade, back and forth, followed by one false swoosh after another. She forgot about the mission. She was no longer wedged into a cubicle inside a secret arms store. Fenna was back on the ice, outside a cabin in Greenland's Northeast National Park, as a small Nepali man in Arctic camouflage pressed her Glock to the back of her partner's head and pulled the trigger.

"That's a Gurkha blade," she said, the words whispering over her lips as Charlie brought the blade to a stop, at the end of a mock attack aimed at Fenna's head.

"It sure is, child. You seen one before?"

"Yes," Fenna whispered. "I have." She looked at Burwardsley, glared at him as she clenched her fists to her sides. She pressed her knuckles into her trousers. She imagined the red marks beneath blooming on her skin stretched over tight muscle. Fenna opened her mouth to speak, but Burwardsley shushed her.

"You want to get the girl?"

"Yes," she breathed.

"And you want to live?"

"Yes."

"Then we need an ace."

"But not him." Fenna shook her head, "not the Nepali."

Chapter 4

Fenna forgot all about Charlie's eccentricities and barely registered the scrape and clang of the heavy iron door in the concrete wall beneath the counter, as Burwardsley received the weapons, followed by the crate of grenades, pistols, and ammunition. The kukri was in the crate. Fenna was consumed by the thought of it as she carried the carbines into the night, stashing them to one side of the trunk of the Prius, as Burwardsley found space for the crate. She got into the car without a word or a backward glance at Charlie's covert arms store. She was aware that Burwardsley was gone for a moment, aware that he closed the rusty door, crossed in front of the car, and climbed in behind the wheel. Fenna felt the car rock as he shut the door, she even answered him when he confirmed the road they wanted. It led north and east, out of the city, into the wilds, into the mountains. *Where he is*, she thought. *The Nepali.*

It was irrational, Fenna knew, to project her combined fear and hate onto a tiny man from the Himalayas. He was only following orders. Burwardsley's orders. But there was something about the Nepali's cold professionalism that was ingrained in Fenna's mind. The man was a killer, just like Burwardsley, but there was something more. Where Burwardsley was tall, muscular, the epitome of a Lieutenant in the British Royal Marines, his Gurkha partner seemed oddly built to be a killer, *and that's what frightens me.*

"You need to understand something about Bahadur," Burwardsley said, as he pulled out of the industrial lot and onto the road. "Where he comes from, his village in Nepal, it's a matter of honour to be recruited for the Gurkhas. The men that don't get selected – boys really – a lot of them don't go home. They throw themselves from the first bridge out of the village selected to host the recruiters. Better that than face the shame of returning to their home village."

Fenna listened to Burwardsley, but she didn't respond. The lights of the highway washed over the windscreen in waves, and she let the rhythm lull her into a kind of trance. The white light became a reflection from the ice, and the occasional thump of the tyres as Burwardsley changed lanes was a pistol shot, the same one each time, followed by the last sigh of Oversergent Mikael Gregersen's body as his body slumped onto the snow in front of the cabin. The only consolation she could find, was that he died in the terrain that he loved, in the country that he had adopted as his own, much like Fenna had done. *But I went one step further, I fell in love with the people too.*

It was the people, the Greenlanders, who helped Fenna forgive Burwardsley for his part in Mikael's death, for she knew he loved them too. *Love – too strong, perhaps.* He respected them, respected their harsh way of life in a wholly unforgiving environment. She had first noticed it aboard *The Ice Star*, before she had stabbed one of the men truly responsible for Mikael's death in the ear, on the bathroom floor. Burwardsley had ignored the fat lawyer's bloody ear and pitiful moans, focused as he was on Fenna. But in the hold, where the lawyer's partner, Richard Humble, had kept Dina like a filthy pet, naked in the bowels of the ship – it was there that Fenna had seen that even the consummate professional, the gun thug that was Burwardsley, had a human streak. He actually felt responsible for Dina in the end, as she twisted beneath the eaves of the cabin in Uummannatsiaq, a length of dog whip cinched around her neck. It was the death of the young Greenlandic woman that had driven Burwardsley to find the man truly responsible for everything that had happened on the ice, and it was the life of another young woman that had put Fenna and him in the same car heading north east to the North Cascades of Washington State.

"We're going into the mountains," Burwardsley said. "We need a man who understands them."

"And it has to be him?"

"I trust him with my life."

Fenna looked at Burwardsley, the corners of her eyes narrowing as she said, "But I don't."

"That, Konstabel, is something you are going to have to deal with."

"The back-up weapons. They're for him, aren't they?"

"Yep."

Fenna turned away, leaned back in her seat, and forced herself to focus on the plan. *Plan*, she laughed, *it's a hare-brained scheme at best.* She needed Alice, America's most-wanted assassin, as a bargaining chip. The girl was the only thing keeping Fenna and Burwardsley alive. Fenna laughed again.

"Something funny?" Burwardsley said as he fidgeted behind the steering wheel. "Or is the thought of Bad so unbearable you have opted for insanity?"

"Bad?"

"Sergeant Bahadur. Your mate."

"Fuck off, Burwardsley."

"Sometimes, love, I really wish I could. But one way or another, you and I are going to see this through to the end."

"It was the thought that we have a plan that made me laugh."

"Tell me about it."

Fenna leaned her head against the window and ignored him.

"I mean it, Fenna." Burwardsley yawned. "It's been a long trip. I need you to talk. Need you to keep me awake. Tell me about the plan."

"Okay," Fenna said. She pushed herself into a more upright position. She reached for the *Subway* cup and took a sip of cola. "If Alice is in the cabin..."

"She is."

"What?" Fenna's hair caught in her eyelashes as she flicked her head around and stared at Burwardsley. "You know she's there?"

"Listen, love, you think I would fly all this way, shove a load of guns and ammo into the back of a pissy little Prius and head into the hills on a hunch? I put Bad on the case."

"He's with Alice?"

"Relax, Konstabel. He knows nothing more than he needs to. I gave him the location of the cabin, and told him to keep an eye on it, and to keep me updated."

"You mean he just scrambles up and down the mountain with a situation report?"

"You've never been to the Himalayas, have you?"

"No."

"Well," Burwardsley shrugged, "there's a reason the British hand pick Gurkhas from the mountains."

"You never thought to share this information?"

"You never asked. You've been pretty cagey with any information up to now, pretty quiet too – preoccupied is another word for it. I just took over."

Fenna slumped into her seat. She pushed the cup into the drinks holder and nodded. "You're right. I've been preoccupied."

"And I've been busy."

"Yes."

"Hey, Konstabel." Burwardsley thumped Fenna's thigh. "We want the same thing, and we're working toward it."

"Vestergaard."

"Right. And this girl, she's our ticket. He wants her, and we are going to give her to him. And that's what you're struggling with."

"Yes."

"Well stop, 'cos we're not going to let anything happen to her. We need her."

"To kill him?"

"As leverage, yes. Then we send that motherfucker into oblivion." Burwardsley gripped the wheel and accelerated. Fenna glanced around the road. She spotted a police car in the distance and pointed at it. Burwardsley lifted his foot off the accelerator and slowed the Prius to within the speed limit. "Tell me more about the plan," he said. "I've just made the preparations, it's time you give me more to work with."

"There's a flight out of Iqaluit."

"Nunavut? Okay," he said. "So we're going to Canada."

"The flight is chartered. It's an evangelical flight direct to Qaanaaq."

"Greenland."

"Yes."

"And we're on that flight? With a load of evangelicals?"

"We will be. Provided we can get to it."

"And how do you think we are going to do that? How are we even going to get across the border into Canada?"

"That's where Vestergaard comes in. He wants Alice, alive. He needs her for whatever leverage he is trying to create with the Americans. His name will get us across the border. I just don't know how. Not yet."

Burwardsley yawned and held out his hand for Fenna's cola. She gave it to him, waited until he had finished it, and then pushed it back into the drinks holder. He scratched his head, yawned a second time and pressed the button to roll the window down a few centimetres.

"There's a good chance he is following our every move," he said.

"I'm counting on it."

"Then what's to stop him taking the girl any time from now until Greenland?"

"He won't."

"No? You're sure about that?"

"Vestergaard wants us as much as he wants the girl. And he wants us in a country he can control. There are too many variables in the US and Canada. Too many actors and agencies. No," she said, and ran a hand through her hair, "he wants us in Greenland. He wants to finish things there."

"Finish us you mean."

"Yes."

"But until then?"

"We keep her alive. At all costs."

Burwardsley rolled the window up and tapped the steering wheel. He snorted and said, "You're projecting an awful lot of Dina onto this girl..."

"Alice."

"Right. You know that, don't you."

"Alice is alive. You said it yourself. Dina's gone. We can't bring back the dead."

"But this girl – Alice – she is toxic. America wants her head on a plate."

"And it was America – some Deep State at least – that created her."

"And yet, you feel responsible?"

It was Fenna's turn to snort. "You wouldn't understand."

"Whatever it is, I am about to die for it, so try me."

"You're not a woman."

"No, love, I'm not."

"Until you can put yourself in my shoes, you'll never understand."

"Charlie tried," Burwardsley said and laughed. "And you saw where that got him."

"Yes." Fenna shook her head. She felt her cheeks dimple and she allowed herself a smile. "But a gun-dealing drag queen isn't quite the same."

"I never said it was."

"No. You didn't." Fenna closed her eyes. *There's no place for equality in the world of men*, she thought. *At least not this world, the world of guns, death, and power. Not unless you carve that place for yourself.* She pictured the kukri in the crate in the trunk of the car. *It's time to make this happen. It's time to even the odds. And*, she realised, *the Nepali might just be the ace that we need.*

Burwardsley slowed as he pulled onto an off-ramp. Fenna focused on her thoughts as he stopped at a tank station. He turned off the engine and switched off the lights.

"Coffee?" he said.

"No."

"Okay."

"Wait," she said, as Burwardsley opened the door. "I've thought about it. I understand why we need him. Why we need the Nepali."

Burwardsley nodded. "That's good."

"But I don't have to like it."

"I never said anything about that."

"Then you'll keep him away from me?"

"Jesus, Fenna. He killed your partner. Believe it or not, he said the same thing to me." Burwardsley shrugged and got out of the car. Fenna heard him mutter, "It's like I'm some kind of god-damned nursery teacher." He shut the door and Fenna smiled.

The plan then. Fenna pulled the map out of the glove compartment and studied the approach to the National Park. Once they were in she figured they would abandon the car, maybe even before the parking area and campsites. They would hike in under the cover of night, find somewhere to wait until the following evening, and then make the climb – mostly exposed ladders – and then get Alice out of the cabin, off the mountain, and into Canada. She took some solace in the fact that Bahadur had been keeping an eye on Alice, and that he would do whatever Burwardsley ordered him to. Loyalty, she realised, was going to be crucial to the success of the mission. Beyond getting Alice off the mountain, Fenna also realised that the plan was raw and full of holes. First they needed to get to Iqaluit, the Inuit governed territory of Canada, then Qaanaaq, in Greenland, then south from there. Fenna knew their ultimate destination. Vestergaard had even hinted at the location of a safe house – the shaman's house, in a tiny settlement ringed by glaciers. They would get there, of course, but the how and when were just a little obscure.

She forgot all about the details when she saw Burwardsley stride out of the tank station, two cups of coffee in a paper tray in one hand, his mobile in the other. He tripped before the car, and Fenna would have laughed if it wasn't for the look on his face.

"We have to go," he said, as he got in the car and thrust the coffees at Fenna.

"What's going on?"

"Text from Bad. There's movement on the mountain."

"Movement?"

"A team, well, he says it's a team."

"How many?"

"Two for the moment. A couple, posing as hikers."

"How does he know they're not actual hikers?"

Burwardsley started the car. He backed out of the parking space and accelerated out of the lot and onto the highway. The rain had lifted, and the first grey of dawn was stretching across the horizon. He held out his hand for a coffee.

"Tell me what you know?" Fenna said and pressed the paper cup into his hand. Burwardsley took a sip, stared straight ahead, as if willing the miles to be shorter, the distance less. There was an urgency in his grip, his frostbite long forgotten, and the look of imminent action that Fenna recognised.

"Bad recognised the guy. An Australian named Rhys Thomas. We've done some jobs together in the past. There's no way he's on the mountain for any other reason than Alice."

"No coincidence?"

"None."

Fenna took the lid off the coffee. She pictured dawn breaking between the peaks. A blood red dawn, and a very frightened young woman – *a girl*, she reminded herself. *A girl I am responsible for.* She looked at Burwardsley. *For better or worse, this is the mission.* She took a sip of coffee, squashed the lid around the rim, and stared straight ahead. Burwardsley steered, sipped, and stared in the same direction, toward the mountains, where there was no such thing as coincidence.

"Just so we are straight," he said, as he handed Fenna his empty cup. "We are about to mix it up with foreign nationals in what could be a pretty good gunfight."

"We're clear on that."

"Good," he said. "Because the consequences..."

"We're clear," Fenna said. "Now just get us there. We'll figure things out along the way."

"That's a bad habit, you know?"

"Yeah, and a hard one to break." Fenna sipped at her coffee, occupied, all of a sudden, with angles of attack, high rates of rounds per minute, and the shadow of gun battles, on and off the ice. She nodded and whispered through the steam of coffee, "Just hold on, Alice. We're coming."

Chapter 5

NORTH CASCADES NAT. PARK, WASHINGTON, USA

Fenna didn't say a word until they passed Everett and Burwardsley drove off I5 and onto the Mountain Loop Highway, heading east into the North Cascades National Park. He pulled his mobile from his pocket and tossed it into her lap.

"You must be the only twenty-something I know that doesn't have a Smartphone."

"Twenty-four, single and friendless," she said. Fenna swiped the screen and waited for Burwardsley to give her the pin code. The screen glowed with a limited number of apps and no history that Fenna could see. "Besides, it's not like you are drowning in social engagements." Fenna turned the screen toward Burwardsley and he shrugged at the lack of messages in the feed.

"It's a registered with a fake account." He slowed as they passed a tank station, turned around and stopped beside one of four empty pumps. The grey light of dawn lit the sky like pale smoke. Burwardsley turned off the engine. "Time to fill the tank. Do a search for this lookout of yours. Bad said something about turning off the highway and onto a forest road."

Fenna nodded as Burwardsley got out of the car. He left the door open and the smell of gasoline tugged at her nostrils. She curled a finger through her hair and teased the ends between her fingertips as she searched. Burwardsley leaned into the car and held out his hand for the trash.

"Want anything?" he said.

"We need food for a few days at least."

"My Bergan is full of MREs – meals ready to eat. We have plenty of food. I'm talking about snacks and coffee."

"Sure. Whatever you find."

"Alright."

Fenna finished her search, as Burwardsley paid. She enlarged the map on the screen and showed it to Burwardsley when he got back in the car.

"There," she said. "That's where we leave the highway. About forty minutes' drive."

Burwardsley looked at the mobile and nodded. He handed Fenna a coffee and a bag of doughnuts and then shut the door. "It's light now. We want to be on the trail as soon as possible, before any hikers."

"It's not that kind of hike," Fenna said. "It's not that popular – too strenuous for the casual hiker. We'll need to rope up before the climb to the lookout, depending on the conditions."

"I have rope." Burwardsley started the car and pulled onto the highway. "We have to decide what to do with the car. Depending on your girl, our best bet is to yomp over the border."

"Yomp?"

"Royal Marine for carrying heavy shit a long way. Heard it a lot when they talked about the Falklands."

"Okay, that's the second thing I have no clue about. The Falklands?"

"The war in 1982."

Fenna looked at Burwardsley and frowned. "Not your war?"

"Fuck off," he said. "How old do you think I am?"

"Thirty-five, single …"

"… and friendless. Yep, I get it. Burwardsley no-mates. We're a fine pair, Konstabel."

Fenna said nothing, concentrating instead on the twinge of her lips at the corners of her mouth. The mountain was forgotten for a moment, along with the mission, the girl, even Bahadur and the wicked curve of his kukri. She waited for Burwardsley to turn his head and said, "So? How old?"

"Thirty-seven," he said. Fenna's lips twitched and he continued, "I've been knocked about a bit, seen some shit, done a whole lot more."

"And yet," Fenna said, as she lost the battle over her smile. "You've aged so well."

"Jesus wept." Burwardsley sighed and gripped the wheel. He looked at Fenna, rolled his eyes, and stared at the road ahead. "I'm not forty yet, love. Still got a full head of blond hair."

"Mixed with a bit of grey," she said and reached out to tease at the short-cropped hair on the side of Burwardsley's head. He slapped at her hand and she giggled, laughed, and choked for the better part of a kilometre.

"Don't die, Konstabel. I'm not doing this alone."

"I won't," she said. "Not yet. But it's good to laugh. It's been a long time." She turned sideways in her seat and looked at

Burwardsley. "Since I applied to Sirius, my life…"

"Hasn't been your own? I know. Been there. I joined at eighteen, direct entry to officer training after A levels. That's the same as gymnasium in your country." Burwardsley smiled.

"High school in America."

"Right."

"And then you went to war?" Fenna blew a strand of hair from her lips and tucked it behind her ear.

"The first time, yep. That's where I met Bad. We were fighting alongside the Gurkhas."

Fenna felt her stomach churn as Burwardsley reminded her of the Nepali, but then the words tumbled from his mouth, as if he needed to speak all of a sudden, and the mission was lost once again as Fenna listened and Burwardsley drove.

We met on the ice, she mused as he spoke, *tried to kill each other, and yet, this man is about the only friend I have.* The image of Nicklas Fischer – the RCMP Inspector turned double agent – and the time they spent together at the Desert Training Center in Yuma, flashed before her, and then it was gone – *he* was gone, faded and dead, just as Jarnvig had said. *Dead, like Jarnvig.* Fenna turned back to the living, listened to Burwardsley's deep voice as he opened up, sharing from his past. She almost stopped him, almost reached out to touch his arm and shake her head. *The more he tells me*, she realised, *the more I might actually begin to care about him, despite our past, and because of it.* Instead, she clasped her hand between her thighs and listened, swapping images of snow for dirt, ice for dust, lots of dust, caked in the pores of Burwardsley's skin, crusting the bloody wounds on his body.

"We were trapped in the open, between these fucking lines of chalk in the dirt."

"Chalk?"

"Marking a path clear of Improvised Explosive Devices," Burwardsley said. "Of course, some bastard Taliban with a detonator triggered an IED just as we walked past. Cunningham, a corpsman, caught most of it in the chest. Saved the rest of the squad. At least to begin with." He paused for a sip of coffee. Fenna waited. "That was the first of three remote detonations. I was losing men left and right, the TACP was busy, so many contacts in the area, he was put on hold, like we could just wait. That's when the Taliban opened up with AKs and a .50 in the scrub, and from the compounds. We were surrounded. There was shit kicking off all around us," he said and waved a hand in the air. "This one kid, Nicholls – I think his name was, he was on the GPMG, it jammed, he screamed, and then lost his head from a burst of fire from the bushes. We were going to die there. I knew it. The TACP said he had an A10 circling above, ready to let rip with thirty millimetre. You've never heard the like, until you have, if you know what I mean, love."

Fenna shifted position as Burwardsley took another sip of coffee. He didn't look at her, just stared at the road, steered, followed the curves of the Mountain Loop Highway, but his thoughts, she knew, were in a field of dirt, under fire, near death.

"I told the TACP to call it, to put those rounds in Danger Close, right on fucking top of us. This big fucking beauty of a bird screams in and lets rip with a burr of bullets – big fucking bullets – and the ground, ahead of us, right? It's like it's pulverized into some kind of dirt cloud, and I'm up, kicking the guys up, and we're running. There's another rip, more clouds, more dirt, thick in your teeth. That's when this fucking trigger man detonates another IED, and the guy I'm dragging goes down. We both do."

Burwardsley slowed to a stop, bumping the Prius onto a patch of dirt on the side of the highway, letting the engine idle until it stalled, and it was quiet. Fenna unbuckled her seatbelt. She placed her hand on Burwardsley's arm, turned and listened.

"There was so much shit in the air," he said. "Dust so thick. You couldn't see anything. But I looked down, and there's these fucking lines in the dirt. Chalk lines, and I'm on the wrong side of them. I just lie there, right. Nicholls – I think it was him – he's half over the line. His legs are gone, and his blood is all over me. I thought it was mine. And then I hear them. Once the A10 has fucked off, and the field is quiet, orange with dust. I'm in this cloud and I can hear the fucking Taliban creeping toward me, all sides, and I … Fuck, Fenna, I thought that was it."

"But it wasn't."

"No," Burwardsley said and shook his head. "This one guy – a rag around his head and mouth – he comes out of the cloud and sticks his AK in my face. That's when I heard chatter on one of our radios. Guys asking for help, calling in air support – Troops in Contact – all that shit. And these Taliban, they're just laughing. There were four of them. And that guy with the AK in my face, I just knew he was the trigger man, and I started screaming and yelling at him, and he just keeps on laughing. Laughing and pointing, right up to the moment when his chest explodes and I have to turn away for all the blood that spatters across my face. Then there's more rounds, full auto, and this tiny little fuck in full British battle gear, he comes charging out of the dust, and I remember shouting at him to watch those chalk lines, and he just grins at me, fires his SA80 from the hip until the mag is empty, reaches behind his back and pulls out this fucking sword. He leaps over me, goes to work on the last of the Taliban, and then he comes back, grabs my webbing and pulls me to my feet. The little fuck carried me across the field to a compound we had secured. He dumps me against the wall, rocks back onto his heels, cracks a cheesy grin and hands me a bottle of water. Never saw anything like it." Burwardsley looked at Fenna and she leaned back. She squeezed his arm and Burwardsley shrugged. "Bahadur was just following orders," he said. "He got the order to rescue me, and he did it. I gave him the order to kill your partner, and he did it. If I tell him to get the girl onto the plane to Greenland …"

"He'll do it," Fenna said. She swallowed. "I know he will."

"That's good, love, because in about twenty minutes from now, you're gonna have to face him, and I just want you to know, I need you to know, that he's not a threat to you, and neither am I. Not anymore."

"We have a common enemy," she said and slipped back onto the passenger seat.

"And the enemy of the enemy is…"

"My friend. I understand." Fenna reached for the bag of doughnuts. "Breakfast," she said and handed him the bag.

They ate in silence and the light changed from grey to cream, the cloud base low, beneath the peaks and high mountain trails of the Cascades. Fenna rinsed the sugar from her teeth with the last of her coffee. She leaned against the door, propping her feet on the side of Burwardsley's seat. *The memory drained him*, she realized, as she studied the Royal Marine's face. He looked old, all of a sudden, and yet there was a young man just beneath the surface, a man who had seen too much, and been asked to do too much, just like the young men before him, *and now*, thought Fenna, *young women too*. She had once met a Danish female Tactical Air Control Party called Ida – embedded with and coordinating air support for troops on the ground, serving in the Danish Army. They had swapped stories over drinks, stories about training and men. Both of them single and serving in demanding environments, typically reserved for men. Fenna remembered being in awe of what Ida was required to do. She smiled at the memory of Ida's comments about what Fenna and her partner would be forced to do to while away the hours on patrol in the middle of nowhere.

"It won't be like that." Fenna had assured her.

"Right."

"Seriously."

And it wasn't. It had been nothing like that. Whatever Fenna might have felt for Mikael, whatever thoughts they might have entertained, they were just thoughts, and now he was dead, and his death had not been the last.

"I'm going to drive," Fenna said. She swung her feet into the foot well and tied her laces.

"Alright." Burwardsley got out of the car and Fenna clambered over the handbrake to sit behind the wheel. She reached beneath the seat and slid it forward so that she could reach the pedals. Burwardsley paused to open the trunk. When he got into the car, Fenna saw he was carrying two pistols.

"If Bad is right about Thomas," he said, "then we may as well get tooled-up before we get out of the car."

"And ditch it at the end of the fire road?"

"We have to." Burwardsley slid a magazine into Fenna's Glock and handed it to her. She tucked it beneath her thigh. "Bad knows we are coming. He'll meet us at the end of the road. We'll hear what he has to say, and decide whether or not to go for the lookout today, or once it gets dark."

Fenna started the car. She shut the driver door and pulled onto the highway. Burwardsley fiddled with the large Browning pistol he favoured, and Fenna let her thoughts drift to think of Alice. She was five years younger than Fenna, not even twenty, and she had been recruited to assassinate the hardest possible target: the President of the United States. Somehow, she had done it. Somehow, she had survived. *They let her go*, Fenna realised. To create chaos, a distraction, to allow them, the Deep State, to avoid attention, and to begin the work of influencing and rebuilding the government in a time of uncertainty, suspicion, and grief. *Shock tactics*, straight from the shock doctrine playbook.

Fenna pulled off the highway and onto Forest Road 41, two large telephone poles placed close together marked the turn. Burwardsley pointed them out. Grit from the road peppered the sides of the Prius as Fenna accelerated up each incline and steered around the bends. Burwardsley tapped the dashboard and pointed as they neared a bridge.

"It's damaged," he said. "According to a local trails site. We'll leave the car here."

Fenna pulled into the side of the road and stopped. She turned off the engine and got out, grabbing the Glock from the seat and tucking it into the waistband of her hiking trousers.

"You going to call him?" she said, the words masking the churning in her stomach.

"No need," Burwardsley said and waved in the direction of the bridge. "There he is."

The low cloud beaded their clothes with spots of rain, but it was the sight of the tiny Nepali man that bumped the skin on Fenna's arms. She forced herself to look at him, realised that they needed him, and focused instead on Alice.

He'll get you on the plane to Greenland, she thought as Burwardsley and the Gurkha embraced in an awkward man-hug made difficult by the extreme difference in height between the two British soldiers. "But if he makes one wrong move," she muttered, nodding at Bahadur when he looked at her, "I'll kill him."

Chapter 6

Fenna spread the *Rand McNally* road map on the bonnet of the Prius and pointed at their location with the tip of a folding knife. Bahadur leaned over the map and used the end of a twig to show the location of the lookout hut, followed by the location of Thomas' tent. A quick look at Burwardsley's mobile showed that the tent was above the tree line, pitched on a ridge in a meadow called Goat Flats, before the trail continued to Tin Can Gap. Fenna allowed herself to smile at the names. It helped ease the tension between her and Bahadur. They hadn't spoken, choosing instead to communicate through Burwardsley.

"You're sure it's him, Bad? Sure it's Thomas?"

"Yes, *Saheb*."

Burwardsley grunted. "And he's got a woman with him?"

"Yes."

"Long weapons?"

"No weapons. Maybe pistols in backpacks. I not see." Bahadur glanced at Fenna. He tapped the map with the twig when she looked up. "Your friend in cabin. All safe."

"For how long?" said Burwardsley.

"I see her one week. But maybe she be there longer. I only be here one week."

Bahadur ran his hand over his head releasing a shower of rain from his thick black hair. *Like a Greenlander's*, Fenna thought. She forced a smile and said, "Thanks."

"No problem," he said, and then, "she look like you."

"We know," Burwardsley said.

"Maybe not so tough," Bahadur said and then he punched Burwardsley on the arm. "You got my present, Mike?"

"Maybe."

"Maybe? What *maybe*?" Bahadur's face creased and he stared at Burwardsley. "I been on fucking mountain, one fucking week, *Saheb*. All rain. All fucking days."

"Calm down, you little runt," Burwardsley said. He grinned as Fenna looked from one man to the other.

"Rice and rain, all fucking days. I want a burger. Want my present. Special order you say."

"I might have."

"No fucking might. You say *special order.* I special. I want present."

While the thought of reuniting the Gurkha with his kukri gave Fenna the chills, she couldn't help but smile at Bahadur's vocabulary. *Endearing, almost*, she thought. If it wasn't for the fact that he was a stone-cold killer. *And*, she realised, *shorter than me.*

Burwardsley pushed his mobile toward the centre of the map and stood up. He shoved his hands in his pockets and ignored Bahadur. "The Gurkhas usually have a British commanding officer."

"Usually?"

"Historically," Burwardsley said and shrugged. "Anyway, there was this Taliban leader we wanted. We knew where he was, the intel was good, we just needed a unit mad enough to go in and get him."

"No, Mike," Bahadur said. He crossed his arms over his chest. "That not me."

"So, we sent his lot. Partly 'cos we knew they could get the job done, partly 'cos we knew they would scare the crap out of the Taliban." He paused to nod at Bahadur. "The CO wanted proof of death, once they took out the target."

"Not fair. Not me."

Burwardsley laughed. "They brought back the guy's head. It was all over the papers."

"Jesus," Fenna said. She looked at Bahadur, caught his eye. He was quiet for a moment before he cocked his head and shrugged.

"They wanted proof. They got proof."

Burwardsley reached for his mobile and waved it at Bahadur. "You could have taken a photo."

"Not me, I say."

The rain fell harder and Fenna shook the map before folding it. She tucked it into her jacket pocket as Burwardsley pointed at the Prius. "It's in the boot, Bad."

Bahadur nodded and jogged around Burwardsley. He opened the boot and pulled the kukri blade from the crate, tossing the leather wrap to one side as he twisted the grip within his hand. A second later it was gone, as he slipped it into an empty scabbard at the back of the broad belt around his waist. Fenna could see the change in the Nepali's demeanour, he seemed whole all of a sudden. Taller too. She noticed then the small pack on his back, the light grey fleece tube around his neck, and the jacket, cinched tight at the waist above trousers with cargo pockets bulging at the sides. His black boots came up above his ankles. They looked comfortable, as if they were painted onto his feet. Her own gear was bought, not customised. She was caught off-guard with a brief thought of how Bahadur might teach her a thing or too, but the moment was gone as he pulled a Glock from the crate, felt the weight in his hand, and looked over the iron sight, pointing downwards, execution style. *It's the same man*, she reminded herself. *The one who killed Mikael. And yet…* She looked at Burwardsley, thought about how she had overcome the paralysis she felt when he had forced his way into her hotel room in Nuuk.

"The enemy of my enemy is my friend," she whispered. Fenna lifted her collar and zipped it to her chin. She ran her hands through her hair and tugged a hair band from her wrist to hold it in place. Her chestnut roots were pushing through, but she was still mostly black. She felt a few strands of hair fall onto her cheeks and ignored them. She took a breath and said, "We need a plan."

Burwardsley nodded at Bahadur as the Nepali checked the M4 carbines and slapped a magazine into each of them and then turned to Fenna. "You okay?"

She shrugged and said, "The stories help."

"Good."

"And he's been looking out for Alice."

"Yep."

"We need him."

"Glad you feel that way. Now," Burwardsley said and nodded at the grip of the Glock peeking out from beneath the hem of Fenna's jacket. "You're gonna have to stow that so it can't be seen. We'll sling the carbines over our backs and pull the packs over them. They should be hidden, from a distance at least."

"And when we get close to your friend?"

"Thomas? Yeah, I don't know what his game is."

"Is he connected? To Vestergaard, I mean."

"Shouldn't be. I knew him before I got the gig on *The Ice Star*. But who the hell knows anymore."

Burwardsley looked up as Bahadur approached and handed them both an M4. He slung it over his shoulder and head so that it hung at an angle down his back. Bahadur took a step and adjusted the sling so that the carbine hung straight down, the muzzle pointing to the ground. He did the same for Fenna, and she bit her lip when she felt his fingers on her back. Then, as he moved away, she relaxed, thanked him, and looked at Burwardsley.

"Whatever Thomas' intentions, we may as well push on to the lookout," she said and looked up at the ridge. "We're close. I need to see her now."

"And we will." Burwardsley pointed at the boot of the car. "Share out the MREs, Bad, and pull out my rope. I'll sling it around my chest for the hike up."

"Yes, *Saheb*." Bahadur jogged to the car and Fenna turned to follow him. Burwardsley grabbed her arm.

"Listen…"

"What?"

"Thomas. Whatever his game is, we may need to take him out."

"I know."

"And, the woman with him."

"Yes?"

"Fenna…"

"Christ, it's like code or something." Fenna shook her arm out of Burwardsley's grip. "Every time some man calls me *Fenna* instead of *Konstabel*, they are preparing me for something difficult, as if killing Jarnvig, and the Gunnery Sergeant in the desert…"

"What Gunnery Sergeant?"

"My first test," she said, "and don't change the subject." She pushed a knuckle into Burwardsley's chest. "When the time comes, I'll pull the trigger. You don't have to worry about that. Alright?"

"Sure. Okay," he said and stabbed his finger into her shoulder. "And if this is just a coincidence?" He stabbed again, rocking Fenna onto her heels. "Konstabel. If the woman is some young thing, his fiancé?" He stabbed her again. "Innocent." Stab. "Young." Stab. "If she's just…"

Fenna slapped Burwardsley's arm to one side and slammed her forearm into his collarbone, a blocking action. She curled her fist toward his head, over her arm, stopping just a few centimetres from his jawbone. Burwardsley flicked his eyes to her fist, and stepped backward.

"We off them, both of them," she said. "Innocent or not. They're just collateral."

"That's harsh, love."

"Life is harsh," she said and lowered her guard. Fenna turned at the sound of Bahadur closing the boot. She saw her backpack and pulled it on. The straps were too tight and she loosened them until the sharp angles of the carbine pressing into her back were bearable. She pulled the Glock out from her waistband, tucked it under her arm, and fastened the buckle above her belt. Her jacket had a map pocket on each side of the zip, and she zipped the Glock in the pocket on the left. Bahadur handed her two spare magazines and she stuffed them into the other pocket.

"Everything okay?" he said.

Fenna ignored him and marched in the direction of the bridge. As she passed Burwardsley she said, "I'll lead."

"Sure," he said and waited for her to walk past him. Fenna heard him say something to Bahadur about letting her cool down, which only made her angrier.

"I'll pull the fucking trigger myself," she said, her words low, edged, and laced with venom. Fenna spat, crossed the bridge damaged by flood water, and continued along the trail through the forest toward the meadow on the ridge. A glance over her shoulder confirmed that the two men were following her. Burwardsley was one hundred metres behind her, Bahadur brought up the rear.

Fenna's anger churned the muddy trail beneath her feet. She slipped in the mud, cursing until the trees thinned and the ridge loomed above her. The trail steepened, and Fenna felt the familiar shortness of breath and the tight tug of the muscles in her thighs, as her body adapted to the trail. She cursed the stab of the rifle in her back between breaths, cursed the two men behind her, and the world of men they belonged to. She thought of Alice, and, finally, the waves of anger receded. She pictured the girl hugging her knees beside a gas stove in a corner of the lookout, preparing for one more uncertain night, and the challenge of another sunrise where, despite the beauty above the clouds, there were no solutions, only the solace that this was her father's favourite place. As long as Alice was close to his spirit, Fenna imagined, as long as she could talk to him, then she might put off the only option she might have considered: getting off the peak without using the ladders.

"I won't let you do that," Fenna said, pausing as the trail levelled out before the meadow. "I'm here to give you an option, to give you a life, the one that Dina can't have, that I couldn't give to her." She lifted her head and looked in the direction of Three Finger Lookout and said, "Just hang on, Alice. Just a little longer."

"Fenna."

She barely heard his whisper, but Fenna turned to see Burwardsley crouched by the side of the second row of trees inside the tree line. He waved her into a crouch, and she saw that his carbine was in his hands and his Bergan on the ground. Fenna searched for Bahadur, but could not see him. She moved slowly to the tree line and crouched beside Burwardsley.

"You didn't hear me?"

"When?" she said.

"Before the ridge."

"Been busy. Thinking. Cursing."

"Fuck, Fenna. Get it together."

Fenna shrugged out of her pack and peeled the rifle sling from her sweaty back. She wrapped the end of the sling closest to the muzzle twice around her left hand and held the carbine tight around the grip.

"Ready," she said.

Burwardsley nodded and pointed toward the beginning of the trail to Tin Can Gap. There was a small dome tent with a green flysheet tucked beneath rocky crags on the side of the trail.

"Bad is moving in from above. He'll let us know if anybody is home."

"Won't Thomas have thought of that?"

"Counter measures? Sure, he might have put in a few. If he has, then we'll know."

"What?"

"If this is a coincidence or if it's game on."

Fenna frowned, and said, "And if he deliberately *didn't*, in order to make it look innocent?"

"Don't over think it, Konstabel."

Fenna stood up. She rested the carbine against a tree and pulled on her pack. Once she had buckled the belt she picked up the M4 and tucked it into a fighting position.

"What the fuck?"

"Either way," she said, "your old pal is a dead man walking. We may as well plug him and keep going."

"Wait a minute." Burwardsley stood up. "Is this how it's going to be? You charging in half-cocked, guns blazing?"

"No-one put you in charge. You don't like it. You can fuck off."

"Fenna," Burwardsley said. He shook his head as she scowled. "Konstabel, fuck … whatever you want me to call you, just think. Just for a minute."

Fenna felt the rain pool into a blister above her hairline. When it was heavy enough the water bubbled through her hair and ran down her nose to slip onto her top lip. She let it roll into the crease between her lips. It seeped between them and she tasted the sweet water before she licked her lips and wiped more rain from her hair.

"Okay," she said. "Sorry."

"You're thinking now?"

"For a minute, sure. I'm thinking."

"Then we'll do this my way. We'll let Bad do a recce, and then we'll move in."

"Sure."

"Fenna?"

"Yes. We'll do it your way." She looked over her shoulder at the tent, and then dropped to one knee.

"Good," Burwardsley said. "Thank you."

"Don't mention it," Fenna whispered.

"What?"

"It's just we're close now, and there's always something or someone in the way."

"You thought it would be easy?"

"I hoped it would be easier. Just for once. Just for a change."

Burwardsley shifted into position behind a tree opposite Fenna. "It doesn't get easier, Fenna, never. You just stop caring how difficult it is."

Fenna thought about that, as the rain dripped from her hair and down her neck. She felt it merge with the sweat on her back and wished she wore a neckie like Bahadur's. The rain was slick on her hands, and she thought about wearing gloves. She thought about the things she could change, things that might make a difference, might make it easier. *To do what? To kill someone?*

Fenna ignored the questioning look Burwardsley cast, and pointed instead to the figure of a small man moving out of concealment and closer to the tent.

"Got him," Burwardsley said, switching the selector off the safety setting and into single shot mode. Fenna did the same.

A scream from inside the tent clipped its way across the meadow before the wind picked up and hurled it away, over the ridge and down to the plains below. The scream was followed by the sound of a tent zip opening and the curses of a man as he tumbled out of the tent wearing nothing more than a t-shirt.

"That's him," said Burwardsley with a grin. "I'd recognise those cheeks anywhere." He stood up and grabbed his Bergan, tossing it over one shoulder in anticipation of an easy stroll to the tent.

The pistol shots that followed the man's exit surprised both of them. Fenna and Burwardsley crouched on the trail as the flysheet was ripped to shreds by projectiles from a large calibre handgun.

"Fuck," Burwardsley said. "It's game on." He ditched his Bergan and ran down the trail. Fenna followed at an angle, increasing speed to cover more distance as the shooter inside the tent changed magazines.

Chapter 7

The rain splashed across Fenna's face as she pounded across the grassy surface, swerving around boulders and leaping over small rocky outcrops. She gripped the M4 in one hand as she unbuckled her waist belt and shrugged out of her pack. It thumped onto the ground behind her and she picked up the pace, gaining on the Australian and the white flash of his cheeks beneath his t-shirt. He glanced over his shoulder as she closed the distance to just a few metres, his eyes caught the dull outline of Fenna's carbine and he frowned for a second before increasing speed. Fenna might have admired his attempt to outrun her, if it wasn't for the spectacular way he twisted on a tuft of mountain grass and pitched forward onto his face. He sprawled on the grass, sliding for a metre or so until he stopped and tried to get back on his feet. That was when Fenna leaped, landing on his back, knees bent. She grabbed the back of his head and thrust his nose into the grass, pressed the muzzle of her M4 into his neck and yelled, "Keep your fucking head down."

"Alright, alright. I'm down."

"Thomas? Is that your name?"

"Do I know you?" He twisted his head. Fenna grabbed a handful of his hair, yanked his head up, and slammed his forehead into the ground.

"Is that your name?" she said, pausing between each word.

"Yes," he said, his voice grassy and muffled. She lifted his head, and he said, "Yeah, I'm Thomas."

"So, tell me, Thomas, what are you doing on the mountain?"

"Who wants to know?"

Fenna dug the muzzle of the carbine into his neck. She heard a scream, a curse from Burwardsley, and something like a cackle of laughter. *That's Bad*, she thought. She forced the image from her mind and focused on the Australian sprawled beneath her.

Perhaps it was the commotion at the tent that distracted her, or that she had underestimated Thomas, but he must have felt a change in the pressure of her knees, a shift in the muzzle pressed into his neck. Thomas bucked, freed one arm, and threw an elbow into Fenna's ribs, shoved his palm into her face. Fenna flinched and then he was on his feet, his penis dangling in front of her face, as he slammed a knee into her chest.

"Do I know you?" he shouted as Fenna slumped onto her back. She choked. Fumbled her grip on the carbine, caught the flat of Thomas' foot in a kick to her head. "I don't know you." He sidestepped around her. She turned, moved the carbine to grip it with both hands, but he kicked it out of her grasp.

Come on, Fenna. Fucking move.

Fenna took a second to focus. She caught a flicker of movement as Thomas opened up with another kick. She blocked it, twisted her arm around his ankle and gripped it beneath her armpit. Fenna yanked Thomas' leg toward her to slam a knuckle into his chest. She hit him again, her left hand pistoning back and forth into his breastbone, until he gasped and she kicked his leg out from beneath him, and they tumbled to the ground.

Fenna's hand got caught in Thomas' t-shirt and she fumbled it free. She released his leg, slapped at it and kneed him in the groin, pressing his penis beneath her knee as she hit him twice on the side of the head. Thomas groaned and tried to raise his hands. Fenna slapped at them, and punched his nose until it bled.

"Jesus," he said, blood spluttering from his mouth.

"Fenna," said a voice. It was distant. She ignored it, until she heard, "Konstabel." Closer this time, louder.

She looked up and saw Burwardsley striding toward her. He held his carbine in a loose grip around the magazine. She rolled off Thomas and stood up, scanning the ground for her own weapon. She found it, picked it up, and waited for Burwardsley. Thomas groaned at her feet.

Burwardsley chuckled as he crouched beside Thomas. He gripped the Australian under his arm and pulled him into a sitting position.

"Mike?" Thomas said, his voice gubby with blood. "S'that you?"

"Yep."

Thomas looked at Fenna. "Who's the fuckin' Pitbull?"

"That is Konstabel Fenna Brongaard."

"She with you?"

"'Fraid so."

Fenna said nothing, concentrating instead on her breathing, ratcheting her breaths into a steady rhythm.

"She's fucking insane, mate."

"She's passionate," said Burwardsley. "I'll give you that." He looked at Fenna, smiled and shook his head.

"What?" she said.

"Used to be me you looked at like that."

"And?"

Burwardsley kicked Thomas' leg. "I'm just pleased it's him. Pleased you've moved on."

Fenna said nothing. She checked the safety on the carbine, and glared at Thomas.

"What's going on at the tent?" she asked.

"Bad's on top of it, or on top of her. It seems Thomas' American squeeze didn't take too kindly to his advances," Burwardsley said and cocked his head to stare at Thomas. "Still can't shake those old perversions, eh, mate?"

"Fuck you, Mike."

"Anyway, Bad collapsed the tent with her inside it. He's got her pinned down. Literally. So, we," he said and stood up, "can have a more intimate chat with our friend, here."

Fenna looked up at the glacier. She could just make out the path leading up to the lookout tower.

"Just be quick about it," she said. "We have to move."

Burwardsley slung his carbine over his shoulder and pulled a knife from his belt. He opened it and locked the blade in place. Thomas watched him through bloody fingers. He gripped his nose and lifted his head up. *He should keep it down*, Fenna thought, *let it flow until it clots*. She smiled at the observation, then studied the Australian, the muscles on his calves, his bruised manhood, and the khaki camouflage shirt he wore over his muscled torso. There was a logo stencilled on the t-shirt above his left breast. He had the same logo tattooed on his forearm, a winged dagger.

"How's life, Rhys?" Burwardsley said and crouched beside Thomas.

"Peachy, mate. Yourself?"

"Bit hectic at the moment, to be honest." He pointed the tip of the blade at Fenna. "Pitbull over here drives like the devil."

"Thought you liked that kind of thing?"

"A few years ago, maybe. Getting on a bit now."

"Thinking of settling down then?"

"Like you and the missus?" Burwardsley nodded in the direction of the tent.

"I thought about it." Thomas looked at his hands. He pressed the length of his finger under his nose and checked for blood. He looked at Fenna. "You're a feisty one, that's for sure."

"You shouldn't have run."

"Hey, I didn't see you, alright? I was running from Sally. We had a disagreement. She found my pistol."

"And why do you have a pistol on you?" said Burwardsley. "I thought this was a romantic holiday."

"It is, and, well, old habits and that."

"So, you're not here for any other reason?" Fenna asked.

Thomas repositioned his legs, wincing as he moved them. "Nah, it's all good. I'm here for a little R&R. Nothing more."

"You just happened to be on this mountain, when we came along?" Burwardsley shuffled closer to Thomas. The blade flashed in his hand.

"Mike," Thomas said and sighed. "If you're gonna cut me, mate, stop fucking about and just… ow. Fuck." Thomas flinched as Burwardsley slashed the knife across his thigh.

"I don't believe in coincidences," Burwardsley said. He looked at Fenna. "What about you, Konstabel?"

"I think," Fenna said, "with all that's going on in the States right now, the chances of an Aussie special forces operator just happening to be on the same mountain as us, are far from coincidental."

She nodded at Burwardsley and dropped onto her knees, pinning Thomas' ankles to the ground. Burwardsley shoved a massive palm into the Australian's chest, pushed his body to the ground and stabbed the blade of the knife into Thomas' thigh, all the way to the hilt. Thomas gritted his teeth and suppressed a scream. Blood leaked out of his nose, as his nostrils flared and he snorted for air. *What am I doing?* Fenna resisted the urge to stand up, to back off and let the man go. *But we need to know*, she thought, steeling herself. *For Alice, to keep her alive.* She looked at Burwardsley. He gripped the shaft of the knife between his finger and thumb, and twisted it.

"Fuck," Thomas shouted. He gulped air into his lungs, his neck muscles straining as he bit back the pain and glared at Burwardsley. "I'm on my own, for fuck's sake. This isn't an op."

"No?" Burwardsley said, as he twisted the knife again. He pressed his knee onto Thomas' chest. "If you're sure? Otherwise, I could just swap with Bad. Let him give you the old Gurkha treatment."

"Fuck, no," Thomas said.

"I didn't think so." Burwardsley moved his knee off Thomas and sat beside the man's thigh. He tapped bloody fingers on the knife shaft.

"Mate," Thomas said, as he sat up. "Please?"

Burwardsley let go of the knife. He slipped the carbine into his hands, and pointed the muzzle at Thomas. "We'll just leave the knife there for the moment, eh?"

"Sure," he said, and grimaced. "Whatever, mate. I'm not going anywhere." Thomas looked at Fenna. "What's so special about the mountain?"

Fenna wiped the rain from her face. It had lessened, but she could feel the patches on her jacket that needed waterproofing. Her shoulders were soaked.

"Nothing that need concern you," she said.

"Ha," Thomas said. He wiped a bloody palm across his mouth. "You're both in the shit, aren't you? This is some Hail Mary, some private op to even up the odds. Am I right, Mike?"

"Keep talking," Burwardsley said, he glanced at the knife in Thomas' thigh.

"Right, well, I don't know all that much," he said, "but I can tell you that there's another team in the woods back there."

"What?" Fenna lifted her head and stared at the trail leading to Tin Can Gap.

"You won't see them. They're dug in real well. Of course," he said, "then there's the girl in the cabin." Thomas' brow creased as he smiled. "Your sister? Maybe?" he said with a glance at Fenna. "Funny thing is, she looks just like the girl on TV. The one they say killed the President." Burwardsley reached for the knife, and Thomas waved his hands. "No, mate, wait. Let me speak."

"I think you probably should," Burwardsley said.

Thomas took a breath and rested his palms on the grass either side of his body. "There's a bounty on this girl's head," he said. "That's why I'm here."

"How did you know to come here?" Fenna said. "To this mountain?"

"Ah, that would be secret, wouldn't it?" Thomas stared at Burwardsley as he reached for the knife. "A secret I would be happy to share."

"Go on."

"Whoever trained the girl, set her up to be caught. Only, they wanted to be sure that the right people caught her. Not an American. So, they left a trail of breadcrumbs, see? Snippets of information here and there, including a tiny bit about her dad being a climber, and how close they were."

"And that led you here?" Fenna frowned.

"No, that led me to the climbing fraternity, of which Sally there is a member."

"And you just used your charm to ask where would-be assassins might hide in the mountains?" Burwardsley laughed. "Give me a break."

"You can laugh, mate, but those breadcrumbs included a bit of family information, including the girl's home state."

"Washington," Fenna said.

"Right."

Fenna listened with just half an ear as Thomas told Burwardsley how he had used some shared contacts to meet climbers in the area, how he had created a contact within the community, and how he had narrowed down the likely possibilities.

"I mean," he said, "she's found a well-defended position, with great visibility, and at a height that puts off most visitors. Not to mention a great view. The only problem is, she can't exactly leave, not once everyone figures out where she is. The only way she is getting off the mountain is if she jumps."

And I won't let that happen. Fenna stood up and nodded at the trees. "Who's in there?" she said.

"I've no idea."

"But you know there's a team in there. How?"

"They rotate at night."

"Are they guarding her, or waiting for her?" Burwardsley said.

"At a guess," Thomas said, "a bit of both."

Fenna walked around Thomas. She stared at the trail leading into the woods, idly fingering the selector switch from safe through full auto as she studied the terrain. *If there's a bounty*, she mused, *then someone is counting on people coming after Alice. But who, and why?* She clicked the switch to the centre position, semi-automatic. The rain intensified. She licked the drops from her lips, lifted her chin and nodded.

"Right," Burwardsley said. "Brace yourself." Thomas yelled as Burwardsley pulled the knife from the Australian's thigh and stood up. He tugged a bandage from his pocket, tossed it onto Thomas' lap, and walked over to Fenna.

"I've figured it out," she said. "There isn't a bounty on Alice's head."

"There isn't? That makes no sense."

"It does if you think about it."

"And you have?"

"Yes."

Burwardsley bent down to clean the knife on the mountain grass. He closed the blade and waited for Fenna to speak. When she didn't, he said, "You're going to have to enlighten me, love."

"The bounty is for us."

"Us?"

"Yes," she said and laughed.

"What's so funny?"

"You don't get it?"

"No."

"They're covering their tracks," she said. Fenna sighed at the confused look on Burwardsley's face. "Alice was the instrument they used to kill the President."

"Yes."

"So, why would you want to catch her?" Fenna didn't wait for Burwardsley to answer. She nodded, and said, "It's brilliant, really."

"What is?"

"They set us up." Fenna swore. "That team over there in the woods, and others like them, they're waiting to catch the team sent to pick up Alice. They'll try to kill us, of course. Then they'll parade our bodies on TV as the agents that orchestrated the assassination."

"That's pretty thin, Konstabel. They've got no proof. No way to tie us to the President."

"They won't need to. Once we're dead, they can tie us to anyone they want to. Shit, he's done it again."

"Who? Vestergaard?"

"Exactly. *The Magician* has been pulling strings again, and we're dangling at the end of them."

Chapter 8

The meadow was above the tree line. It was rocky and exposed, below the glacier, and with little cover suitable for an ambush. *So, they are more of a blocking force then*, Fenna thought as she considered the role the team was playing. *They'll take us on the way down, block our escape.* She scanned the terrain as Burwardsley pulled a second field dressing from his cargo pocket and dressed Thomas' wound. She looked in the direction of the tent and saw Bahadur wandering around it, the carbine held loosely in his grip.

"Done," Burwardsley said and stood up. "Let's get back to the tent."

"That's it?" Thomas said. "We're just going to wander back up the hill as if nothing has happened?"

"You've been played, mate," Burwardsley said. "The bounty notice was selective. You never thought to ask if anyone else was in the loop?"

"No." Thomas shrugged. "You know me, Mike. I'm a man of few talents. I don't see the bigger picture. I just track. That's what I'm good at."

"And that's what they used you for," Fenna said, as they walked toward the tent. "You sure about your girlfriend? Sure she's innocent?"

"Yeah," Thomas said. "Poor girl. I used her. That's all." He looked at Burwardsley. "Catch and release? Can we do that at least?"

Burwardsley nodded and said, "We left the keys to our hire car on the wheel. It's down by the bridge. She can drive it out."

"And what about me?" Thomas said. Fenna swapped a look with Burwardsley. She looked down at the tree line. Thomas saw the direction she was looking and said, "There's five of the bastards down there, and a sixth up at the cabin."

"Six men, eh?" said Burwardsley, as Fenna flicked her eyes to Thomas. Her grip tightened on the carbine.

"One of them is in the cabin?" she said.

"He walked up there early this morning."

"Did you see him? What did he look like?"

"Yeah, I saw him. Kind of athletic. Good looking fella."

Fenna didn't need any more details. She imagined she knew just what he looked like, how he walked, moved under fire, how he spoke, his touch, the taste of his lips. Jarnvig had shown her a file back in Nuuk, just before she had killed him. But, like everything else in this game, there were so many threads, so many loose ends, and those that were tied off, could easily be unravelled, if they had ever been tied at all. Fenna realised that Vestergaard would have to minimise the number of people in the know in order to protect himself. She knew who he trusted, and with Jarnvig gone, there was only one person left who could be trusted enough to deliver Fenna and Alice, and he was supposed to be dead.

"Fuck," she said. Fenna stopped walking, signalling to Burwardsley that they needed to talk.

"What's up, love?"

Fenna waited until Thomas was out of earshot and said, "I know who's in the cabin with Alice."

"Who?"

"Nicklas Fischer," she said and swallowed.

"Who is he?"

"He's one of Jarnvig's men, so he works for Vestergaard. He got me out of Toronto, tidied up after I shot Humble." Fenna paused to swear.

"And?"

"He was at Yuma, watching out for me – maybe for me and Alice. After I killed the sergeant in the desert, he got me out. Shit, I remember him saying something now, something about being on the same side as the men who picked me up."

"You're not making much sense, Konstabel. Who is this guy?"

"He's an Inspector with the RCMP."

"He's a cop? Fuck me," Burwardsley said and laughed.

"He's not just a cop, he's anti-terror." Fenna punched Burwardsley on the arm, as he laughed again. "He's an operator, like you. Like me."

"So, the Mountie is a threat. Is that what you are trying to tell me?"

"Yes."

Burwardsley shrugged. "Let's just add him to the list, eh? Come on." He tugged her arm and starting walking toward the tent. Fenna walked beside him, thoughts about Nicklas momentarily put on hold as she saw Bahadur pull the tent pegs out of the ground as a dark-haired woman flew out from beneath the flysheet like a pheasant from a coop. She ran past Bahadur and didn't stop to look back. Thomas called after her, something about a car, the keys, and an apology of sorts. Fenna paid little attention, and once the woman had disappeared out of sight, she forgot all about her. She stopped to one side of the tent as Thomas pulled at the flysheet to find his pants, trekking trousers, and gear. He dressed as Burwardsley teased Bahadur.

"Thomas says there's a team in the woods," Burwardsley said.

"I no see anyone."

"That's the point, Bad. You missed a whole fucking team."

"No fair, Mike. He fucking tracker," Bahadur said and pointed at Thomas. "Not me."

"Too fucking right, mate," Thomas said and winked at Fenna. Bahadur leaped across the collapsed tent skin and drew the kukri from his belt. Thomas raised his hands and stumbled, partly dressed, onto the ground. He clutched his leg and groaned, waving at Bahadur to stop with his free hand. "Easy, Bad. Easy. I was joking."

"You fucking joking? I carve you up, you joking. See who laugh, eh?" Bahadur raised the kukri above his head. Fenna tightened her grip on the carbine and moved the butt slowly into her shoulder.

"Stand down, Bad," Burwardsley said.

"He the tracker, sure," Bahadur said, as he took a step away from Thomas. "But he no fighter. Girl beat him," he said and pointed the tip of the blade at Fenna before sheathing it in the scabbard behind his back. Fenna lowered her carbine and flicked the selector switch to safe.

"Everyone alright?" Burwardsley said. He made a point of looking each of them in the eye. Fenna nodded, her thoughts racing. She flicked her eyes more than once in the direction of the glacier, and the lookout cabin she knew was perched on the rocky summit.

We have to move, she thought. *We don't have time for this.*

"Get dressed." Burwardsley tossed a pair of boots at the Australian's feet. Thomas pulled the socks out from inside each boot, and pulled them on. Burwardsley looked at Bad and said, "He is the tracker, you're right, Bad. And now he's working for us."

Thomas stopped lacing his boots and looked up. "I am?"

"Yep, just like old times."

"I'm confused, Mike," Thomas said. He grimaced as he stood up. "You stick a knife in me, chase my lady down the mountain, and expect me to just join your crew?"

"Pretty much." Burwardsley tugged the Browning from the waistband of his trousers. "Do you have a problem with that?"

"I guess not," Thomas said. He smiled and looked at Bahadur. "No hard feelings, Bad."

"You the tracker," Bahadur said. "Not me."

"Sure." Thomas looked at Fenna. "You don't say much."

Since landing in Seattle, driving the three hours into the mountains, and discovering that her one-time lover is still alive, and preparing to deliver her straight to Vestergaard – *all things considered*, she thought, *it's no wonder I'm lost for words*.

"You're a tracker," she said. "Can you avoid people, too?"

"Like those guys in the woods?"

Fenna shook her head. "Not them. We're going to kill them," she said and looked at Burwardsley for confirmation.

"Yep," he said.

"I need to know if you can get us around law enforcement, and get us across the border."

"The Canadian border, you mean?"

"Yes."

Thomas scratched behind his ear and said, "What's in it for me? Seeing as there's no bounty anymore."

The rain splashed on the tent fly, but not enough to disguise the click of the selector switch as Fenna shifted her grip on the carbine. "Do I need to say more?" she said.

"No, mate," Thomas said. "I think we're clear."

"Good." Fenna nodded at the tent. "Take what you need. Bahadur will give you your gun." She took a step away from the tent and turned her back on the three men. She heard Burwardsley approach, waited for him to speak. When he did, it was a whisper.

"Take a breath, love," he said. "You're holding on too tight."

Fenna lifted her chin, as she felt tears well in her eyes. She let the rain wash them down her cheeks. "I've been played from the start," she said. "Ever since Sirius."

"Yep, I guess you have."

"Jarnvig said as much. He told me, back then, that he recognised certain abilities that I had, gave me some bullshit story about having the qualities of an agent." Fenna waited for Burwardsley to speak, and then continued when he did little more than grunt in understanding. "They sent me to the desert to create a timeline, to put me in the right places at all the right times. Which makes me wonder," she said, as she looked at Burwardsley, "what's your role in all this? Are you really doing this for us, for Dina, for some sense of rough justice, or…" She stretched her finger across the trigger guard.

Burwardsley looked at her and nodded. "Yes," he said, "for Dina."

"Really?"

"Yes."

Fenna tapped the trigger guard with her finger. "Can I trust you?"

"Yes," he said. He sighed and then shrugged his shoulders. "But, fuck, Fenna, I would understand if you didn't."

"What about him?" she said.

"Bahadur?"

"There's no question, he does what you do. I might not like him, but I know where I have him." She flicked her eyes at Thomas. "*Him.* The tracker."

Burwardsley smiled and said, "As far as the border, I would guess, no further."

"That far?"

"Hey, he needs to get out of the country just as much as we do."

Thomas caught Fenna's eye as he changed magazines in his pistol, and filled the empty one with rounds from a box in his pack. Fenna watched him until he looked away.

"And when that time comes, Mike, will you take care of him?"

"One way or the other, yes."

"Good." Fenna wiped the rain from her face and nodded in the direction of the trail they had walked in on. "I'll get my pack," she said and walked away.

The walk back for her pack gave Fenna the space and time she needed to think, to prepare for the coming action. She slung the carbine over her shoulder and smiled at the thought of how much she had changed. From the ice of Greenland, approaching the cabin door, heart thumping, Mikael covering her from afar with the bolt action rifle, before bursting in on Dina, scaring each other half to death with a cocktail of nerves and adrenaline. It had gotten easier. She had Burwardsley to thank for that. *And, I guess, Jarnvig and Vestergaard. Mikael. Nicklas.* All the men in Fenna's life, all the way back to her father, had encouraged her, trained, shaped, and forced her toward a life of action. *Dad*, she mused, *what the hell would you think of me now?* The thought had crossed her mind before, when her traitorous actions had likely caused her father to turn in his shallow grave, somewhere in Afghanistan. The casket they had buried in Denmark had been empty. She knew that. It hadn't bothered Fenna that her father's remains had remained on the battlefield, the location hostile, remote, classified; it was different for her sister. Fenna's acceptance of that fact had driven her sister and her apart. *And now she's caring for my mother, and I'm about to wage a private war in a foreign country. If I die*, she thought, *they probably won't even allow my body to be buried in Denmark*. The thought made her stop, and she saw her pack just a metre or so in the grass ahead of her. Fenna bent down to pick it up, wishing the traitorous thoughts out of her mind as she slung the pack over one shoulder.

She used the walk back to clear her mind, processing thoughts of each previous encounter through her mind as she settled on the one redeeming feature of her immediate and future actions: saving a life.

"I couldn't save Dina," she said aloud. "But I will save Alice." *Or die trying.*

Fenna heard the men talking as she approached, their words shivering on the chill wind blowing down from the glacier. They fell silent as she stopped in front of them. She suppressed a smile, as she studied them, Burwardsley towering above them all on the right, a climbing rope coiled around his chest, the carbine small in his large hands. Bahadur was tiny in the middle, his hair slick in the rain, the neckie loose around his thin neck. He had removed the sling from the carbine, wrapping it instead around the strap of his small pack, through which he stuffed a flashlight, the American kind with the lamp at right angles to the handle. Fenna recognised the type as surplus from the Vietnam war. She looked at Thomas last, surprised at his change in demeanour, and the professional care which he seemed to have taken over each tuck and crease of his gear. She doubted he would make any noise, there was nothing that could flap or twitch in even the strongest of winds.

"Ready, Konstabel?" Burwardsley asked.

Fenna leaned her carbine against her leg as she adjusted her pack and fastened the belt around her waist. She picked up the carbine and nodded.

"You're with Bad." Burwardsley paused, anticipating a reaction, but Fenna was silent. "Once we've engaged, he'll get you up the mountain, all the way to the lookout cabin. Thomas and I will keep the bastards busy, kill them all if possible."

"See, that's the part of the plan I'm less wild about, mate. You do realise, they know we're coming?"

"Yes."

"And that doesn't worry you?"

"No," said Burwardsley. "Should it?"

"Too bloody right it should, mate. There's six of them. All tooled up and spoiling for a chance to get it on."

"Five," said Burwardsley. "There's only five down here. That's what you said."

"I know, but that other fella, the one up top? He's the one you need to be worried about." Thomas looked at Fenna. "I might not have seen much in the way of features, but even in the gloom, and from a distance, anyone with an ounce of military training could see he was a fella who knows what he's doing. And we're sending her and Bad up to the cabin, alone, where he has a perfect field of fire. Christ, you won't get within a hundred yards before he fucks the both of you with a couple of high calibre bullets."

"That's why it has to be me that goes up there," Fenna said.

"And why is that?" Thomas said. He folded his arms across his chest and stared at her.

"Because the last person he fucked was me." Burwardsley laughed, as Fenna pushed past Thomas on her way to the head of the trail to Tin Can Gap. She saw shadows in the tree line and tightened her grip on the carbine. She took a deep breath. It was going to be a long day.

Chapter 9

They were good. Fenna knew as soon as they opened up with short suppressed bursts of 5.56mm rounds, shredding the trees with angles of fire that shepherded Burwardsley and Thomas into what appeared to be a prepared location. Burwardsley had just enough space to crouch, but not enough cover to fire without exposing himself to well-placed rounds, determined to pin him down and encourage him to surrender. Thomas hadn't fared much better. If he had been just a little taller, a little more muscular, he would have had difficulty taking cover at all.

They planned this from the start, Fenna realised. They obviously knew the direction Fenna and her team would arrive from, but the attention to detail surprised her. *Nicklas*. She knew it was him. *What other surprises has he prepared?*

Fenna fidgeted beside Bahadur. She tried to raise her body, to lift more than her head, but the Gurkha pressed her down with a small but firm hand on her back. She whispered, "Okay," and bit her lip as she watched the ambush unfold.

Each time Burwardsley tried to squirm into a better position, the blocking force opened up with another volley of lead. In the vacuum following each salvo, as the mountains absorbed the splinter of twigs and the chatter of bullets blasting through silenced assault rifles, Fenna heard Burwardsley curse. He was pissed off, she could see it in the hunch of his shoulders, the way he slapped the carbine on the carpet of pine needles beneath him.

"No," Bahadur said, as Fenna fidgeted one more time. "Wait and watch."

Fenna thought she heard the scratch of static and a series of clicks from a radio. She imagined the team to be radioing Nicklas with situation reports. She thought she could make out the voice of the leader in the trees, and words that might have been *affirmative* and *momentarily*, and a sentence that sounded like, *no sign of the girl yet.*

No, thought Fenna, *because the bloody Nepali won't let me join the fight.* She turned her head and gave Bahadur a hard stare. He ignored her.

A sudden shift in Bahadur's attention forced Fenna to look at Burwardsley. She heard him whistle to Thomas. He tossed a round object at the tracker, followed by one more. Burwardsley held up his hand, his fingers splayed, counting down, folding each finger over his thumb until there were none left. Thomas nodded, and the two men curled their fingers through the ring pull of the grenades in their hands and tossed them.

The shouts of alarm confirmed that the men in the trees had not expected grenades. At the first flash and shoosh of white hot phosphorous, the men broke out of cover, rolling out of range of the thermite explosions to the right and left of their position. Just as Burwardsley and Thomas had been herded into a specific spot, the two men did the same to the blocking force as they tossed two more grenades before rushing out of cover and emptying a magazine each in the direction of Nicklas' men. Thomas yelled, "Changing mag," and Fenna heard the loud bangs of Burwardsley's Browning as he covered the Australian. Then it was Thomas' turn to cover Burwardsley as he changed magazines. They threw two more grenades and moved forward.

"Now," Bahadur said and dragged Fenna to her feet. He raced toward the trailhead leading to Tin Can Gap and the glacier, Burwardsley's rope slung around his chest and bouncing on his knees as he ran. Fenna followed, amazed at the Gurkha's speed, and more than a little impressed at the way Burwardsley and Thomas had turned the ambush back on the blocking force, and given them the break they needed to push for the lookout tower.

They kept up the pace all the way to the edge of the glacier, the tongue extending into the valley far below them. Bahadur pulled off the rope as they caught their breath. Fenna felt the cold from the ice as she dragged it into her lungs. She smiled and allowed herself a brief laugh. On impulse, she slapped Bahadur on the arm.

"It's good to be back," she said and pointed at the ice. The rain had stopped, and the light in the sky was stronger, blue behind the grey clouds. They were going to climb in good weather, and Fenna felt her spirits lift. She smiled again and Bahadur nodded.

"Mountains and ice. Like home," he said.

"Like Greenland too."

"Greenland too flat," Bahadur said, his brow wrinkled.

"Flat?" Fenna shook her head, and then she remembered where the small man called home. "Yeah, okay. I understand," she said and tied the end of the rope around her waist. They had agreed that Bahadur would lead when they talked down in the meadow. The climb wasn't difficult, but it made sense to take precautions. *Besides,* she thought, *if Nicklas decides to make things interesting…* The thought tailed off as Fenna considered how Nicklas might react and what he might do.

Thoughts of Nicklas plagued her as they set out across the ice in the direction of the ladders that Bahadur had confirmed would lead them all the way to the lookout tower, over 2,000 metres above sea level. Fenna pushed any sentimental feelings she might once have had for Nicklas to the back of her mind. When Jarnvig had suggested Nicklas was dead, all traces connecting him to the operations he and Vestergaard were running cleaned away, she had buried those same thoughts, choosing to act instead. Killing Jarnvig and the guard outside the door, freeing Burwardsley and the chase that followed, had pushed any possibility of grieving to the back of her mind. Now she had to face the first man that had shown any kindness toward her since Bahadur had killed her partner. Fenna shook her head, tired of the threads twisting in her mind. *Remember the real villain*, she reminded herself, *the man who spins all these threads and pulls all the strings: the Magician. Vestergaard.* Fenna spat on the ice and kept going.

The ladders were fixed in place. The robust rungs were thick and square, the sides worn, smooth but fibrous to the touch. Fenna felt connected to the climbers and hikers who had scrambled up each rung before them, as she climbed up after Bahadur. He tugged the rope each time he was ready for her to follow, as the sunshine broke through the clouds, Fenna allowed herself to forget the firefight in the tree line below the glacier, to forget her hate for the man who killed her partner, and to enjoy the fresh air as it thinned, just a little, with each rung she climbed. She smiled the whole length of the second ladder from the top, stopping only when Bahadur placed his rough finger on her lips and nodded toward the last ladder, the shortest one yet, leading to the rounded summit and the Three Fingers Lookout Tower, the cabin with the greatest view of the Cascade Mountain Range.

"I stay here," Bahadur whispered. He held out his hand for Fenna's carbine, and exchanged it for two spare magazines for the Glock pistol she had in her jacket pocket.

"Where will you be?" Fenna asked.

"I go around," he said. He made a walking motion with two fingers.

Fenna looked in the direction he indicated and said, "But there's no ladder."

Bahadur grinned. "I am mountain man. Not some stupid tracker. I go around."

"Alright. But don't move in unless you need to."

"Why everyone think I am stupid?" Bahadur slapped his hand against Fenna's arm. "Go," he said, "before Mike call us on radio."

"What radio?"

"His," Bahadur said and nodded in the direction of the cabin. He flashed a smile at Fenna before scrabbling around the rock and out of sight.

Fenna untied the rope around her waist and looped it through the coil at the base of the ladder. She was stalling and she knew it, but she realised she wasn't prepared for what to expect in the cabin. It made no sense to keep Alice alive, and yet she hoped that was exactly what Nicklas had done. If Alice was dead, there would be nothing to stop Fenna killing him. *Nothing at all.*

The rungs on the last ladder were just as old and just as worn as the ladders below, but they felt tacky somehow, as if each successive rung was more difficult to let go of than the last. Fenna forced herself to reach for the next rung. She moved onward, upward, stopping only when she could see the roof of the cabin, the storm shutters clasped to each side of the window, and the glass, reflecting the sun, spoiling her view of the cabin's interior. Fenna finished her climb, raised her hands and shouted.

"Nicklas Fischer."

She kept her hands in the air as the light wind carried the sound of movement from inside the cabin to where she stood beside the top of the ladder. She saw him as he stood. Heard the scrape of something like a chair leg across a wood floor, as he walked to the window. Fenna held her breath, her hands trembling above her head, and then she laughed, a release, for there was Alice, beautiful Alice. She was alive, she seemed unhurt, and she was here, just four metres and one short-barrelled submachine gun away from Fenna. *It might as well be four kilometres*, she thought, as she stared at the weapon slung around Nicklas' chest and her smile faded. I'll never reach her. *Not before he can put an end to us both*. But then Nicklas did something that made Fenna at once hopeful and wary. He pulled the sling of the submachine gun over his head, removed the magazine, and rested the weapon in the corner of the window where Fenna could see it.

"I'm coming out," he shouted. And then, quieter, "Stay here, Alice."

Fenna lowered her hands as Nicklas opened the cabin door and stepped out. She glanced at Alice, and was relieved to see her smile. Alice pressed her hand against the window and splayed her fingers against the glass. Fenna took a breath and smiled. She turned back to Nicklas, and he stopped just two metres away.

"What now, Fenna? Shall we sit down?"

"Yes, okay," she said. He sat first, crossing his legs as he waited for Fenna to do the same.

"Not too cold for you?" he said.

"No."

He turned to look at the sun and said, "It finally cleared up. It's been rotten weather the past few days, I was thinking…"

"What do you want, Nicklas?"

"Want?" he said and looked at her.

"You want something. You wouldn't put a team in the woods for nothing."

"It's not me," he said, and Fenna thought she caught a flicker of sadness in his eyes. "I never wanted this. Never wanted the Yuma assignment."

"But you took it."

"I took it. Christ," he said and rubbed his hand across the stubble on his chin. Fenna waited. Nicklas rested his hands on his knees and said, "It's not like I had a choice. I was groomed from the start."

"There's always a choice," Fenna said.

"Really, Fenna. You of all people believe that?" Nicklas shook his head. "They teased me, you know? They had these intriguing stories, rumours of special operations, an elite fraternity, an exotic life." He paused to sigh, and Fenna noted the way he scratched at his knees with restless fingers. "It was exciting. I was fast-tracked into the RCMP anti-terror unit. Vestergaard came later. He recruited me with the full cooperation of my superiors. They could all see I had certain talents, and only one real flaw – I couldn't turn it off. I couldn't distract myself wholly from each assignment, had a tendency to get too engaged. Vestergaard said he could help. Promised he could fix me, and he did, to a point. Until you." Nicklas flattened his fingers against his thighs and looked at Fenna. He shrugged and looked away, blinking into the sun. "You were meant to be disposable, a patsy for the real assassin, the girl," he said and gestured at the cabin, "but you have real grit, Fenna, and I fell for that. I fell for the way you took a punch. Clean hair and make-up were furthest from your mind, but…" Nicklas looked at her and smiled. "I've seen the photos. You clean up good, but you'll always be that girl in the boxing ring for me. I can still smell your sweat, feel the grit beneath your fingers, the dust in your hair." He stared at her, and Fenna saw his eyes glaze, his pupils widen, just a little, despite the sun. "You were my assignment, Fenna, but not everything I did was for Vestergaard. Some things I did for me."

Fenna bit her lip, and said, "I was told you were dead."

"I probably should be."

"It was Jarnvig who told me. You were dead, the Gunney's team was dead – all of them, even the pole dancer they brought onto the base to teach Alice…"

"It's true. They are all dead."

"But not you."

"No." Nicklas ran his hand through his hair. "Would it be easier if I was?"

"Maybe," said Fenna. She unzipped her jacket pocket and pulled out the Glock. Nicklas just nodded as she pointed it at him. "I've come for Alice. She's all I want."

"I know," he said.

"Are you going to let me take her?" Fenna glanced at the cabin, reassuring herself that Alice was free to move, that she wasn't chained to the wall. *Like I was once, back in the beginning.*

"I want to, Fenna. You believe me, don't you?"

She knew, as soon as he said it, that she didn't. Fenna curled her finger inside the trigger guard, and applied the first squeeze of pressure. She felt the centre blade of the safe action trigger beneath her finger, followed by the flood of adrenaline as she tried to clear her mind, to ignore what Nicklas had said, how he had said it. *I need to be clear. Focused. I can't let him confuse me. Can't let him play on any emotions – his or mine. This is about Alice, it's for Dina, it ends with Vestergaard. But it starts with him.* Fenna raised the pistol, controlled her breathing, cleared her mind of conflicts, until Nicklas lifted his hand and pointed at the breast pocket of his fleece.

"I have something in here. You'll want to see it. Before you pull that trigger."

"What is it?"

"You'll let me take it out?"

"Yes," Fenna said. She frowned as he slipped two fingers inside the pocket and pulled out a thin piece of plastic. "Is that a remote?"

"Yes."

"Fuck." Fenna shook her head and lowered the Glock. "It's wired. Isn't it?"

"The whole cabin," Nicklas said. "Yes. And," he said, turning the remote in his hands. Fenna could see two slim buttons. "The top button will trigger the detonator. And the second button…" Nicklas looked at his watch.

"Pauses the timer?" Fenna looked away, swearing under her breath.

"Exactly." Nicklas stood up. "It's a little cold out here. Will you come inside?" He waited for Fenna to stand, took the Glock from her hand and led her inside the cabin.

Chapter 10

The sun lanced through the clouds as Fenna stepped inside the lookout cabin. The floorboards creaked beneath her boots and she blinked in the sunlight, as Alice flung her arms around her neck. Fenna leaned into the younger woman's embrace, pulling her close to her body, ignoring Nicklas and the pistol he pressed into her back to push her further inside the cabin. Alice's tears were warm on Fenna's skin, her sobs muffled. Despite the situation, because of it even, Fenna smiled, choked, and cried, her own tears splashing on Alice's hair. The world shrank all of a sudden, and the combined cares and concerns of the two young women were forgotten. No longer were they alone in the world of men, for once they outnumbered them, in that tiny cabin in the Cascades.

"They want me dead," Alice said, her voice hoarse, the words splintered with tears.

"If they did, then you would already be dead," Fenna said. "I won't let that happen."

Alice looked up. She wiped the tears from her face with one hand, clung to Fenna with the other. Her eyes misted, her pupils widened, and she gripped Fenna's jacket with both hands. Fenna wrapped her arms around her and pulled her tight, so tight she heard Alice gasp, but she didn't let go.

"Us girls," she said, "We have to stick together."

"For sure," Alice said.

Nicklas moved around them. He scraped the legs of a chair along the floorboards and sat down. Fenna heard the dull thud of her Glock as he placed it on the table. She lifted her head and looked at him. The lines of stress on his face, small fractures in his skin highlighted by several days of exposure to the sun, were new. She studied them, studied him, searching for the old Nicklas, the one who had protected her in the desert, the one who might resurface in spite of his orders. *But he's not there*, she realised. *That Nicklas is buried deep.* He shifted, fidgeting under her gaze, reached for the pistol, let it go, stared back at her.

"I have my orders," he said. Fenna noticed the remote was still in his hand. "But I'm not a monster. No matter what you might think."

"I've met my fair share of monsters," Fenna said, as dark thoughts of a fetid hold in the bowels of *The Ice Star* pricked at her, the image sharp, painful.

"I know," he said.

"You helped me get rid of the last one," she said, and replaced the image of the hold with that of Humble bleeding in his Toronto office.

"I did."

"Then help me again."

Fenna felt Alice relax in her arms. She smoothed Alice's hair from her cheeks and guided her to a chair against the wall opposite Nicklas. The sun lit Alice's face and Fenna was relieved to see there were no scars, no visible signs of trauma or weakness. *Don't be fooled*, she chided herself. *Her pain will be on the inside, and will run deep*. Once Alice was seated she turned back to Nicklas, calculating the distance between them to be about a metre and a half. *Too far*. Nicklas placed the remote beside the Glock and pressed his palm flat on the table.

"What are you up to, Fenna? Why did you come here?"

"I didn't have much choice. Your boss had me surrounded."

"Vestergaard?"

"Who else?"

"Jarnvig was my handler."

"Jarnvig is dead."

Nicklas pinched the bridge of his nose and said, "I thought so."

"But you didn't know?"

"Vestergaard works on a need to know basis. He gave me this assignment personally. He didn't mention Jarnvig."

"But you figured it out?"

"I figured it would go one of two ways, and, if you were involved, well…" He snorted. "You have a knack for getting out of tight situations."

Fenna let that sink in for a moment. She smiled and dipped her head, using the movement to scan the cabin, taking in the bookshelf, the desk, the deep window sills, the guest book and pencil on the table by the Glock and the remote. She saw the shelves of tinned food, and the makeshift kitchen area that Alice and Nicklas had used. There was an empty mug stained with dregs of filter coffee. Fenna swallowed at the sight of it. *But where are the explosives? The walls are too thin*, and she didn't remember seeing anything in the space beneath the cabin, between the wooden supports and the bare rock. *He's bluffing.*

"You're going after Vestergaard," Nicklas said. "That's why you came for the girl?"

"That's one reason, but it seems he already knew where she would be."

"Yes," he said and glanced at Alice. "We knew everything."

"And you played me from day one."

"That depends on when you started counting."

"In Copenhagen, when I met Jarnvig."

Nicklas nodded. "That fits," he said, "pieces were being moved into position. You were one of them."

Fenna gestured at the wall to the right of Nicklas and took a step toward it. She rested her bottom on the lip of the window sill, and stuffed her hands in her jacket pockets. Alice watched her every move. So did Nicklas.

"Who?" she said.

"Who *what*?"

"Who moved…" She corrected herself with a sigh. "Who is *moving* the pieces? I don't believe it is just Vestergaard."

"Ah," Nicklas said, "you think there is a deep state at play in America?"

"You suggested as much, when you pulled me away from the special forces operators in Arizona."

"I did." Nicklas tapped his finger on the table and looked at Fenna. She recognised the look, it was the same one he had used before, just before disclosing mission-sensitive information. "What if I were to tell you that Vestergaard is a freelancer? Would you believe me?"

"To a point. Maybe." Fenna frowned.

"But you think it is unlikely. How can one man wield so much power without the resources of a state backing him?"

"Yes."

"And what country serves to gain from turmoil in the United States?"

Fenna laughed. "That's a long list."

"Narrow it down," he said.

"In light of recent events?" she said and shrugged her shoulders. "I don't know. China?"

"That's one for starters."

"You only asked for one."

"To make you think." Nicklas rested his elbows on his knees and leaned forward, his head less than a metre from Fenna. He looked at her, waited for her to speak.

"Okay, more than one country..."

"Operating independently? They've tried that."

"So they need to coordinate their efforts."

"They can't. They won't, not publicly, not face to face. We're talking about rogue states and countries that are tired of America's domination, its meddling."

"You're saying they need a broker?"

"Exactly."

"Vestergaard?"

"They wouldn't call him *the Magician* if he couldn't work a little magic."

"Coordinating the efforts of several countries at once..."

"Magic."

"...to destabilise the United States?"

Nicklas leaned back and Fenna realised she had missed her first opportunity to strike, that she would have to wait for another. *If he gives me the chance.*

"So, the deep state," she said, "is really more than one?"

"And each state thinking they are the only one."

"And if they were to find out?"

"They won't."

"But if they did?"

Nicklas picked up the remote. He smoothed his thumb lightly over the two buttons. "They won't," he said.

Fenna took a deep breath. She felt the sun warm her face as she breathed out, her eyes on the remote, as she processed the information, coupled it together with what she knew of Nicklas, his professionalism. She wondered if Vestergaard had finally broken his Achilles heel, had taught Nicklas to overcome the flaw that prevented him from distancing himself completely from the mission. And then she understood that it was exactly that flaw Vestergaard was exploiting when he tasked Nicklas with the mission in the cabin at the top of the Cascades. *The blocking force*, she realised, *they're not just here for us, they're here for him too.*

Nicklas smoothed his thumb once more across the remote. He looked at Alice and said, "It'll be over soon."

"No," said Fenna, as Alice began to tremble. "You don't have to do this. I'm not alone. The men in the tree line… we've eliminated them."

"There's more than one team."

"Then we'll take care of them, too," she said and pulled her hands from her pockets.

"I'm too involved, Fenna. Vestergaard made sure of that."

"Then we'll work together. We'll change that."

"You don't understand."

"I do. Really." Fenna took a step toward Nicklas. He stood up and pushed her away. He raised the remote above his head.

"Stop," he said.

"You stop," she said. "We can stop this together."

"And do what? Tell the world? Forget it, Fenna. The world doesn't want it to be known. If we don't die here, we'll die somewhere else. We'll be pursued until it's over. They'll send one team after another." He pointed at Alice. "Ask her. She knows what it is like to be America's most wanted. How about the world's most wanted?"

"Not if we kill him first. Not if we stop him."

Nicklas shook his head. "You don't understand. It's already begun. It's over, Fenna."

Alice screamed as the first bullet from the M4 carbine shattered the window, showering her in shards of glass, as it tore through Nicklas' wrist. He dropped the remote and Fenna lunged for it, kicking at Nicklas' injured hand as he swore and scrabbled after the remote. She heard the light pounding of boots on the rock outside the cabin, followed by the splinter of wood as Bahadur kicked at the door and burst inside the cabin.

"No," she screamed, as Bahadur tucked the carbine into his shoulder and punctured Nicklas' chest with a burst of three rounds. Nicklas crumpled to the floor, his blood pooling onto the floorboards and seeping into Fenna's trousers and jacket as she cradled his head on her knees and pressed her hands on the entry wounds in his chest. He looked at her, blood spilling from his lips as he raised his shattered hand to her cheek.

"You were real for me," he said, his words wet with blood. He spluttered, coughed, and said, "You were real."

"I know," she said. Fenna pressed his hand to her cheek, her tears mixing with his blood as they splashed onto his fingers. He closed his eyes and she felt his hand slip from hers. She held on, ignoring the clump of the Gurkha's boots as he ordered Alice out of the cabin. Fenna looked away from Nicklas' face and saw the remote on the floor. She picked it up, considered, just for a moment, ending it all. *It would be so much easier*, she thought. *So simple. To end it here, on the mountaintop.* She recalled Nicklas' last words, about being wanted across the world, never being safe.

"Fenna?" Alice said. Her feet shuffled on the floorboards as she pushed past Bahadur and reached out to touch Fenna's shoulder. "This man says we should go. But I'm not leaving without you."

The remote was warm within Fenna's fingers. She traced the swell of the detonator button with her thumb, looked at Alice. *So simple.*

"Fenna? Won't you come?"

Nicklas' lungs expelled his last breath as his body slipped from Fenna's knees and onto the floor. She laid his hand across his chest, bent down to his face and kissed his lips. *He's gone.* She looked up, saw Alice by her side, Bahadur in the doorway. *And it's time we were gone too.* Fenna stood up. She took Alice's hand in hers and squeezed it.

"Give me a second."

"Sure," said Alice, "but only a second." Her body trembled. "The man…" she nodded at Bahadur, "he said we can't wait."

"I know. I just need…" Fenna let go of Alice. "I just need a second."

"Okay." Alice retreated to the door.

Fenna looked down at Nicklas. She held the remote in her palm, wiped the tears from her cheek with a bloody hand.

"You taught me to fight dirty," she said, choking on a laugh as she remembered the dancing lessons in the dusty boxing ring in the desert warehouse. "I won't forget. I'll never forget. How about that? Is that enough? I mean, can I just leave you here?" Fenna looked out of the window, squinting as the sun broke through another swathe of cloud and lit the cabin with a soft pink light. It filtered onto Nicklas' face, and then she realised that he was at peace. *Someone will find his body*, she thought. *And I have to go. He would want me to go.*

Fenna looked at the remote in her palm. She tapped the detonator button with her nail, and then pressed the button below it to pause the timer. She frowned, turned the remote between her fingers and slid the battery case from the back of the remote and swore. It was empty. Fenna bit her lip, pinching the skin between her teeth until she tasted the first drop of blood. She licked the blood from her lips and leaned down to slip the remote inside Nicklas' short pocket.

"Vestergaard never did erase that flaw, did he?" she said, wiping her tears from his cheek, her voice soft, a whisper. "I'll get him," she said. "I'll finish this." She smoothed Nicklas' hair from his brow and stood up.

Bahadur was waiting at the entrance to the cabin. Fenna picked up her Glock from the table and stuffed it inside her jacket pocket. She nodded at Bahadur, brushing past him as she walked out of the cabin to join Alice on the rock above the first ladder.

"He told me you would come," she said and took Fenna's hand. "I recognised him from the camp in the desert. He said you were friends."

"We were."

"He said you were tough, and that you would protect me."

"I will," Fenna said and looked at Alice, "if I can."

"I believe you." Alice smiled.

"And do you trust me?"

Alice nodded. "Yes."

"Good. Because this isn't going to be easy."

Fenna fell quiet as Bahadur joined them He tied the end of the rope around Alice's waist and nodded for her to climb down the ladder. Alice hesitated. She gripped Fenna's hand.

"Come on," Bahadur said. "We go. Now."

"Fenna?"

"It's okay," Fenna said. "You can trust him."

Bahadur looked at Fenna, his brow wrinkled as he studied her face.

"Yes," she said. "I mean it. I trust you. I have to."

The Gurkha smiled and gripped the rope, feeding it through his small hands as Alice let go of Fenna and began to climb down the ladder. Fenna looked back at the cabin, took one step toward it and then stopped. There was a shout from the ice below the ladders. She ignored it. As the cold pinched her cheek she realised that Nicklas was at peace.

"And if I want the same," she said, "I am going to have to fight for it."

Fenna turned her back on the cabin and walked to the ladder. She waved down at Alice and lifted her arms as Bahadur tied a bight of rope around her waist. Fenna stepped onto the top rung of the ladder and climbed down it as Bahadur fed the rope between his fingers. Alice took a step away from the ladder and Fenna felt the rope tug at her body. *We're connected*, she thought, and smiled. *And we'll stay that way, all the way to the end.*

Chapter 11

Burwardsley was waiting at the foot of the last ladder when Fenna started her descent. He tugged her to one side as she stepped off the last rung and untied the bight of rope around her waist. Bahadur climbed down the ladder and Burwardsley handed him the rope to coil. Alice was already free of the rope. She reached out and Fenna clasped her hand for a moment before following Burwardsley to the boundary between rock and ice, the carbine slung across his chest. Fenna pointed at blood coming from a long cut across his brow.

"A branch," he said. "What about you? What happened up there?"

"We're all fine."

"I didn't ask about the others. I asked about you."

Fenna frowned at the tone in Burwardsley's voice. *He cares*, she thought.

"Yeah, okay, Konstabel. I care," he said and fiddled with the sling. "It's a weakness, apparently. But tell me, what happened up top?"

Fenna waited a second and then said, "Nicklas was there. He had Alice in the cabin, captive, one way or the other. I think he had been there several days. But she looks fine. Doesn't seem to be concerned about anything he might have done, only what she did."

"And what is that, exactly?"

"I don't know yet," Fenna said with a glance at Alice. The young woman waved before resuming her conversation with Bahadur. The Gurkha seemed to be on his best behaviour, and, she noticed, he had a winning smile that seemed to please Alice. "Nicklas suggested the cabin was wired."

"Suggested?" Burwardsley said. He reached out to touch Fenna's arm and she turned to face him.

"There were no batteries in the remote. But…"

"What?"

"Bahadur shot him anyway."

"Yeah, that's on me, love. I told him to be vigilant and fast."

"He was." Fenna took a breath. "Shit, Mike, he did what he had to do. I don't hold a grudge, and, truth be told, I think Nicklas wanted out, and that was the only way."

The sun disappeared behind a cloud and Burwardsley looked at his watch. He wiped a smear of blood and dirt from the face and tapped the glass above the hour hand.

"We have to move," he said. "We need to get off the glacier and back on the trail before dark, before more teams show up."

"They will," Fenna said. "Nicklas said there would be more. I think they intended to trap us all up in the cabin, him included."

"Vestergaard tidying up again, eh?"

"I think so," she said, and paused. "Mike?"

"Yep?"

"How did you get involved with Vestergaard?"

"We can talk about this later, but now we really need to move."

Fenna studied Burwardsley's face for a moment, searching for signs of evasion, or lies, she found only guilt and something far worse – a worried expression that she had never seen before.

"What is it?" she said.

Burwardsley whistled for Bahadur to bring the girl. He clapped his hand on Fenna's shoulder, encouraging her forward along the path they had struck across the ice.

"Tell me."

Burwardsley peeled the sling over his head and shifted his grip on the carbine. He checked the magazine, slapping it home with a soft metallic thud.

"The team in the woods was good. Well trained," he said, as Fenna increased speed to match the pace he set with his long legs. She glanced over her shoulder to see Bahadur at the rear of their tiny column. Alice was a few steps ahead. Fenna looked at her hair as the setting sun highlighted Alice's natural blonde colour, pushing up from the roots. She made a mental note that they should dye it, and soon. Burwardsley sighed and said, "The grenades shook them up a bit. They weren't expecting that. But they rallied quickly. Thomas caught one in the arm and another in the leg – shattered his tibia. He's going to slow us down."

Fenna thought about that for a second, and then she said, "But you got them? All of them?"

"Yep, all five. Dead."

"But you're worried."

"Yes, love. I am. These guys were better coordinated than the majority of goons we meet – even in this line of work." Burwardsley slipped suddenly, skidded for a second and regained his balance.

Fenna saw a spot of blood on the ice. She grabbed his arm. "It's alright," he said, "just another scratch. I'll fix it later."

"You're sure?"

"Yep." He nodded, but Fenna caught the grimace of pain he bit back. She started to speak, but he interrupted her. "You remember the guys Vestergaard had in Nuuk? His protection detail. The ones in the chopper."

"Yes."

"They reminded me of them. Meaning, they're not some home-grown local types. He put these guys into play."

"I'm not following, Mike."

Burwardsley stopped, glancing around Fenna to gauge the distance between them and Alice. "If I'm right, then Vestergaard is putting his best men into the field, which means he is trying to cover this up as fast and as efficiently as possible."

"We knew that," Fenna said and frowned.

"I know, but at this stage in the game, well, I think he is scared."

"Good." Fenna turned at the sound of Alice and Bahadur catching up. Burwardsley gripped her arm.

"No, Fenna. Not good. It means he's dangerous, unpredictable."

Burwardsley stopped talking as Alice stopped beside Fenna. He nodded at her before moving past the two women to talk to Bahadur. Fenna watched him for a moment, thinking about what he said, before slipping her arm around Alice's and continuing down the icy path in the direction of the rocky trail below them. She could see Thomas resting beside their packs and she waved.

"Who's that?" said Alice.

"An Australian. He's with us."

Alice laughed. "We couldn't be any more international if we tried."

"You're right. You know I'm from Denmark? I can't remember if I ever told you."

"I don't remember either." Alice paused and Fenna wondered if she was thinking back to the canteen on the desert base where they met. "I never thought you'd come to get me."

"I promised myself that I would."

"Thank you," Alice said and slipped her fingers into Fenna's hand. "He was nice."

"Who? Nicklas?"

"It was him who said you would come. It's like he was waiting for you. How well did you know him?"

"Well enough, I suppose." Fenna felt a tremor pass through Alice's body. "You've never seen a man killed, have you?"

"No."

Fenna slowed as they neared the trail. She lowered her voice, and said, "Not even the President?"

"Not even him. I just…" Alice's voice faltered and Fenna pulled her close.

"It's okay. You can tell me some other time."

"Yeah, but…" she said and stopped.

Fenna took Alice's free hand and smiled. "What is it?"

"I didn't kill him. Not really. They just wanted me to dance for him. To show him a good time. They said the President chose me. They said if I was going to be close to him I had to have special training."

"He chose you?"

"Yeah, from some catalogue or other. I danced a bit at High School. I was on TV. But I never danced like that woman showed me." Alice's lips twitched and she whispered, "I think she was a stripper."

"I think you're right."

"Anyway. They said the President was real tired, that he never had a chance to relax, and that he really needed to, that the job was getting to him. I like the President, I mean liked. I even voted for him – I was just old enough."

Burwardsley passed them. He tapped Fenna on the shoulder and held up his hand, fingers splayed. *Five minutes*, she thought, and nodded that she understood. Bahadur remained on the ice, a few metres away, scanning the tree line.

"Sorry," Fenna said. "Tell me more. If you want to."

"Sure," Alice said. She let go of Fenna's hand and ran her fingers through her hair. She gripped her hair just above her ears, as Fenna might have done. "They said I should dye my hair, that he liked girls with black hair."

Fenna nodded and thought about how they really were meant to look like one another. *It was all in the details*, she thought. She looked up as Alice took a long breath.

"They told me I should put it in his drink," she said, clenching her hair in her fists. "They said it was a relaxant."

"But it wasn't?"

"I don't know. He was pretty relaxed." Alice shook her head. She let go of her hair and crossed her hands across her chest. Fenna noticed her right foot as it began to tap on the ice. "I danced. I even took my shirt off. They told me he might ask me to."

"Where were you?"

"Some hotel in New York. It was pretty fancy. They snuck me in through the kitchen."

"They?"

"The same men from the desert. Oh, and this other guy."

"Nicklas?"

"No. This one had a funny accent." Alice's brow wrinkled as she looked at Fenna. "Come to think of it, he said some words the same way you do."

"He spoke to you?"

"Just a little. Then they took me up in a service lift. I was already in the room before the President arrived. Just waiting on the couch. I was real nervous."

"Fenna," Burwardsley called. He waved his hand when she looked at him.

"One second," she said and looked at Alice. "What happened next?"

"The President walked in, and I was so nervous. I think I shook his hand. I think I apologised for being so sweaty. He said something sweet like *not to worry*, and I *couldn't guess how many sweaty hands he had shaken,* and how mine were the softest. He was really, really sweet. And I thought about all the things he had to do, and how difficult it must be, how stressful and…" Alice took a breath. "It sounds crazy, but, I just felt right there, that if I could give him a break, make him happy, just for an hour, then I would, and that I would maybe, in my own way, make a difference. You know? Do something for my country. Does that sound crazy?" She didn't wait for Fenna to respond. Alice continued, "and the stuff they said I should put in his drink. They said his doctor prescribed it. I mean… Why shouldn't I believe them?"

"You had no reason not to."

"For sure. And anyway, he was so sweet, and he just kinda started to doze off right after I took off my shirt. He said something about how pretty my bra was and I remember giggling like I hadn't done for a while. And all that time I'd spent in the desert, it kind of made sense. I had a job to do, for the President. For my country."

Alice tapped her foot and Fenna saw the tears on her cheeks. She hugged her, stepped back, wiped the tears from her cheeks with her thumb, and said, "What happened next?"

Alice bit her bottom lip and Fenna reached up to curl a lock of Alice's hair behind her ear.

"They told me I should wait until they came to get me. That the President would leave first. They said he would probably sleep after I put the powder in his drink. That it was normal. Well, it didn't look normal, and I got scared. I put my shirt on and I just wanted to leave, but there was a guard on the door. We had music on – real low – but enough so they couldn't hear us. I opened the door to the balcony." Alice surprised herself with a smile. She laughed at the memory, and Fenna saw a spark in her eyes. "I told you my dad was a climber, right?"

"Yes. You did."

"He taught me good. I climbed up onto the balcony on the floor above, and I promised my dad that if I got away I would come here. This is where he wanted to be at the end. I figured if this was the end of my life, then at least we would be together. You know, our spirits. Is that crazy?"

"No, it's not."

"You're sure? I think it's crazy. Anyway, climbing up one floor, and then another. That *was* crazy. That's how I got away. Once I got to the street I ran so fast. I got to a bus station – that's where they must have taken the photo of me, 'cos I was more careful after that. I started wearing a beanie. And I got some climbing gear, food – I had some money. They had paid me up front. Then I just came here. As fast as possible. I was here about a week before Nicklas showed up. I saw no-one else. The weather has been crappy. Until today." Alice smiled. "It must be because you came. You brought it with you."

"I'd like to think so," Fenna said. She pulled Alice into a tight hug as Burwardsley called out one more time. Fenna whispered in her ear, "I'm going to take you somewhere safe."

"Okay."

"You're going to have to trust me."

"I do."

"And do whatever I say."

"I will."

Fenna felt Alice's body shake as she began to cry.

"These men, they are my friends. They are going to help us."

Fenna turned her head as Bahadur coughed softly beside her.

"We go now. Mike say so."

Bahadur walked past them and Fenna let go of Alice. She held her hand as they followed the Gurkha to the beginning of the trail. The sun started to sink behind the peaks and Burwardsley looked at his watch. He picked up a spare German Heckler & Koch G36 assault rifle. The stock was folded and he snapped it into place before handing it to Fenna.

"You alright with this one, Konstabel?" he said, as he handed her two spare magazines.

"Yes."

"Konstabel?" Alice said. She stared at the rifle as Fenna did a quick physical check of the weapon.

"That's right," she said, "although I think rogue agent is what they prefer to call me now."

"Who?"

"The same men who put you in that hotel room."

"You know them?" Alice said. The look on her face suggested she found that hard to believe.

"You could say that," Fenna said and laughed. Her lips flattened into a tight smile. She picked up her pack from the pile at Thomas' feet, nodded at the Australian and slipped her arms through the shoulder straps. Fenna tightened the straps and fastened the waist belt before tucking the rifle against her chest. She nodded that she was ready.

"Okay," Burwardsley said. "Thomas, you've got the rear."

"For as long as I can, mate."

"Understood. Bad?"

"Yes, *Saheb*?"

"I want you on point. Keep a good pace, with a break every twenty minutes. Don't let us fall more than two hundred yards behind. Fenna, I want you and Alice in front of me."

"Where are we going?" Alice asked, as Burwardsley directed her onto the trail.

"Canada," he said.

"And then? What happens after we cross the border?"

"One step at a time," Fenna said. She would have said more, but the flick of Thomas' head in the direction of the meadows caught her attention.

"What is it?" Burwardsley whispered.

"Movement on the trail." Thomas paused. He cocked his head to one side and closed his eyes. "Four men, heavily armed."

"Okay." Burwardsley pressed his hand on Thomas' shoulder. "You know what to do."

"Yeah, mate. I know." Thomas reached into his pocket. He pulled out part of a map, folded in half, and pressed it into Burwardsley's hand. "I had some time while you were playing on the mountain."

"Alright," Burwardsley said. He glanced at Thomas' handwriting on the map and slipped it into his pocket. "I'll make sure your family gets it."

"Thanks, mate," Thomas said. "Now fuck off before I change my mind."

Bahadur and Thomas exchanged a brief look before the Gurkha turned and began to jog along the trail. Fenna followed with Alice right behind her. Burwardsley waited for a moment, and Fenna thought she heard him say a few more words to Thomas before the heavy tread of his boots on the trail confirmed that he was following them. She swallowed and surprised herself at how the thought of Burwardsley behind her, and Bahadur in front reassured her. *We met on the ice as enemies*, she mused, *and now we're heading back there. But as what? Friends? Allies?* The thought occupied her for the first few hundred metres, until the familiar bark of Thomas' M4 carbine ricocheted around the mountain walls, and along the trail behind them.

Chapter 12

The trail widened just before they reached the tree line, descending into the valley several kilometres from the border. Bahadur had increased the pace twice, and they had barely stopped since the first exchange of bullets behind them. Burwardsley had halted once, when Fenna paused to speak with him, only to be pushed on.

"Stay with the girl. Keep up with Bad."

"And Thomas? What about him?"

It was too dark to see Burwardsley's expression, but Fenna could *feel* his response, hear the way he breathed, the soft click of the fire selector switch as he flicked it to full automatic.

"Stay with Bad," Burwardsley said. He jogged down the trail in the direction they had come. Fenna watched him for a moment. She turned and caught up with Alice, pushing her on with short, soft words of encouragement.

They were well inside the tree line when the first burst of Burwardsley's M4 caught Fenna's attention. She slowed, unslung her assault rifle and took a step in the Royal Marine's direction.

"No," Bahadur said, his voice a whisper. Fenna flinched, amazed he had arrived so quickly, so quietly. "Mike say we go for border. I take you there now. Mike come later."

"You don't know that," Fenna said.

"Yes. I do. Mike say." Bahadur gripped Fenna's arm and pulled her down the trail. He let go when they found Alice leaning against a tree. "The border is close. Come."

Fenna's hair flicked across her cheeks as she nodded. She looked up when Alice took her hand. "It's okay," she said.

"You said you wouldn't leave me."

"And I won't. I just…"

"You want to go back for your friend?"

Friend. The word tumbled inside Fenna's head. In the darkness beneath the thick pine needle canopy, she shut out the dark images of Burwardsley, picturing instead the more recent memories in Greenland's capital, exchanging banter and bullets as they did their best to escape and evade her countrymen. "Yes," she said as she recalled the moment of their capture. "I suppose he is."

"What?"

"A friend."

Alice tugged at Fenna's hand. "I understand if you want to go back. But I'm scared, Fenna. I want to get out of here."

"I know." Fenna slung the assault rifle over her shoulder and squeezed Alice's hand. "Run," she said. "I'll be right behind you." Another short burst of automatic weapons fire gave her pause, but Fenna shut it out, released Alice and followed her down the path through the trees. *If Burwardsley makes it*, she thought, *when he makes it, I'll tell him…* Fenna stubbed the toe of her boot on a tree root. She stumbled, her feet thudding on the trail, arms flailing, until she found her balance, righted herself, and kept going. Another burst of weapons fire – an exchange this time – ricocheted around her mind as she processed her priorities. *The girl, it had to be the girl. That's what we agreed.* Fenna ran, bringing up the rear, surprised at Bahadur's speed, pleased that Alice could keep up.

Bahadur pushed them on, stopping after two hours at the rotten door of a small moss-clad cabin. He rested, his carbine held loosely in the crook of his arm. He grinned when Fenna slowed to a stop beside him, her chest heaving. She considered removing her pack, but thought better of it. Alice, she noticed, seemed to be in better shape that she was. It started to rain once more, and Fenna looked up at the canopy in anticipation of a few drops of relief splashing onto her face.

"Mike is okay," Bahadur said.

"You can't possibly know that," Fenna said.

"Yes. He tell me he will be okay."

"I'm sure he did, but…"

"No." Bahadur said. He shook his head and she caught the shadow of movement between the trees. "He is okay. We keep going. Meet him at the road, and cross the border."

We are never going to get across the border, Fenna thought. *It will be guarded, from the highway and into the hills*. She looked at Alice. *And I will have failed her. Failed another young woman. For what? Some twisted sense of…*

"What are you thinking?" Alice said.

Fenna bit her lip, said nothing. She flicked her gaze from Bahadur and back to Alice.

"You're thinking about something."

"Yes," she said.

"It's the border, isn't it?"

"Yes."

"You don't know how we will cross it?"

"That's right."

Alice smiled. She lifted a finger and pointed in a north-westerly direction. "We'll go that way. Once the trail widens into a road, we'll cut through the trees to the west, then north and over the border." She lowered her hand and searched in her pockets for a pair of thin gloves. She pulled them on and said, "Dad had a thing for Smarties."

"What?"

"The chocolate? They're like M&Ms."

"I know," said Fenna, "we have them in Denmark."

"Well, they don't in the US, so dad used to sneak across the border after a climbing trip, just to stock up. There's a gas station a few miles after the fire road. He would buy Smarties to last a month." Alice laughed. "Of course, they lasted about a week. He ate most of them walking back into the Cascades."

"And you can find the fire road?"

"Sure."

"At night?"

"Is there a better time to cross the border?"

"No," Fenna said. She laughed and looked at Bahadur. "What do you think?"

"Good plan."

"What about your friend?" Alice asked. "He won't know where to find us."

"He find us," Bahadur said. "Thomas not the only tracker I know. And, I leave sign. Show him way."

"Okay. Alice, we'll follow you." Fenna slipped the assault rifle from her shoulder, readjusted her pack and carried the weapon in her hands. She followed Alice, just a few steps behind her, as Bahadur moved to the rear. She could hardly hear his footsteps. Nor could she hear Alice's. *Just my own*, she mused. Fenna smiled in the darkness, amusing herself with thoughts of being *the only elephant in a herd of gazelle*. She shook the thought from her mind and concentrated on following Alice, and staying alert to any threats on the trail ahead of them. When Alice paused to find her bearings, Bahadur caught up. Fenna watched as he plucked three stones of equal size from the path and positioned them in a line indicating the direction Alice was about to lead them.

"What if it's not Burwardsley who finds them?" she whispered.

"If not, Mike, then it not matter. We all dead."

"Right," she said. Fenna took one last look at the stones and then followed Alice off the path and into the trees.

The lower branches of the pines caught in Fenna's hair, scratched her cheeks, and slapped at her body and pack. There are no trees in Greenland. The climate ensures that shrubs don't extend their reach beyond what is required for mere survival. *A bit like me*, Fenna thought. She remembered missing trees during the first few months with the Sirius Sledge Patrol, but then she grew accustomed to the wide-open surroundings of the stark Arctic landscape, the long fetch of wind across the sea ice, hurling snow needles into her face, the scale of the mountains on the land, the bergs in the sea. Everything was bigger, open, an agoraphobic's nightmare. Even in the desert, where she had first met Alice, the trees were just arrogant shrubs, too stubborn to remain close to the surface like their Arctic cousins, yet too parched to do more than twist in the desert wind a few metres higher than the dirt. Fenna had seen decades-old saplings clenched between rocks in Arizona and the Arctic, both deserts of a sort, with extremes that tested every living thing. Only the dead would outlive the living, as the extreme conditions parched skin, desiccated bones, and preserved the last rigors of the body for all to see, once the ravens and foxes had picked the bones clean of nourishment. Yet here, in the valley below the high peaks of the Cascade Mountain Range, in the lush, wet forest, Fenna felt claustrophobic all of a sudden, and wished for a break in the trees, no matter how exposed they would be, she just wanted to breathe.

"Hey," Alice said, and Fenna felt her hand on her cheek.

"Huh?" There was something tugging at Fenna's head. She reached up and brushed at a thin spiny branch twisted into her hair and slipped.

"Let me." Alice pinched Fenna's wet hair and pulled the branch out of it, showering Fenna's face with a thin storm of old, brown needles. "There," she said and knelt in front of Fenna. "You keeled over. You alright?"

"Yes," Fenna said. She brushed at a pine needle on her lip. "I must be tired. We haven't stopped since we boarded the plane." Fenna adjusted her grip on the assault rifle in her lap, the sling had caught in the belt of her pack. "Where's Bahadur?"

"Over there," Alice said, and pointed in the direction they had come. "Although, I can't see him."

"Okay." Fenna used the rifle butt to get off the floor. It sank a few centimetres into the loam before pressing against something firm. *Tree roots*, Fenna imagined, as she stood. Alice reached out to support her as she swayed.

"I can take your pack," she said. "I left mine in the cabin. She unclipped the clasp at Fenna's waist. Fenna shrugged the pack from her shoulders and Alice put it on the ground.

"Wait." Fenna opened the lid of the pack and dug around inside for a bottle of water and a bundle of energy bars taped together. She passed the bars to Alice and drank from the bottle. Bahadur joined them and Alice split the energy bars between them.

"It's quiet," he whispered, between mouthfuls. He took the bottle from Fenna's hand and drank.

Fenna scanned the area as they ate. She noted a line of boulders, *a good firing position*, to the right of the path they were forging, and a shallow ditch to the left. Given the darkness, the dense configuration of the trees, it was the best ambush position they might find all night, and the best place to wait. She took the bottle from Bahadur and offered it to Alice. "Finish it," she said, "so it doesn't slosh when you move."

Alice emptied the bottle, screwed the lid on tight, and stuffed it inside the pack. She collected the wrappers from each of them and zipped them inside the top pocket, smiling as she did so. "Reminds me of dad," she said, "always thinking of the environment." She closed the lid and lifted the pack onto one shoulder.

"We're going to wait," Fenna said, and put a hand on Alice's arm. "See those boulders? I want you to tuck in behind them. I'll be there in a second."

"You're sure? The road is real close. Maybe just forty minutes away."

"I'm sure. We're going to wait for Mike."

"No," Bahadur said. "Mike say keep going. He say…"

"He said some things about you, too," Fenna said, and Bahadur stopped speaking. "He told me about when you carried him away from the Taliban."

"Okay, maybe I do that."

"You did. And now we're going to wait."

"But Mike my boss."

"And he's not here. So, you do what I say. We wait."

"Lady," Bahadur said, "you not my boss."

"No, I'm not, but you killed *my* boss. Remember?"

Bahadur fiddled with the carbine in his hands. He looked away before staring straight at Fenna. "It was my job," he said. Alice took a step backward, toward the rocks.

"And this is mine," Fenna said and pointed at Alice, "to get her out of the US and somewhere safe. It's your job too, ever since Mike called you, and put you on the mountain. Now you do what I say, you little shit, because when you said yes to Mike, you said yes to me. My job. My orders. You understand?"

Bahadur let the carbine rest in the sling, and folded his arms across his chest. He spat to one side and glared at Fenna. "Mike say you one tough bitch. He also say you save him from freezer."

What freezer? Oh. Fenna almost smiled when she remembered the *freezer* – a refrigerated container converted into a torture chamber, hidden in plain sight on a building site in Nuuk.

"So, he owes both of us," she said.

"Yeah. Maybe."

"Well, he can't repay us if he's dead." Fenna wiped the dirt and wet needles from the butt of her assault rifle. "You take the ditch over there." Bahadur looked in the direction she pointed.

"It not very big."

"Neither are you."

"Okay, fuck it. I take little ditch. We wait. Mike sort all this out later." Bahadur took a step backward, turned, and melted into the darkness.

Fenna thought she heard him wriggle into position, but it could have been the wind as it teased the upper branches and the very tops of the pines. She followed the route Alice had taken to the rocks and knelt down beside her. Fenna leaned the rifle against the rock, took out the spare magazines and placed them on the ground, side by side. She unzipped her pocket and pulled out the Glock.

"Did they teach you to shoot at Yuma?"

"No," Alice said, "and neither did my dad."

"But you're American?"

"Right, and every true American girl knows guns?"

Fenna laughed. "Just like every Dane is a Viking."

Alice didn't laugh. She lowered her voice and said, "You are."

The wind caught the trees in another gust, fresh air spiralling down the trunks to flick and tease at their hair. Fenna pressed the Glock into Alice's hand and nodded. "Maybe I am a Viking, and now it's your turn to learn about guns."

"I don't know." Alice let the weight of the pistol press her hand against her thigh.

"I just need you to look in that direction." Fenna waved her hand in an arc toward the trees behind them. "The Glock has a safety in the trigger, here," she said and guided Alice's finger to the trigger. "Can you feel it?"

"Yes."

"It's like a plastic switch in the middle. Be sure you've got it under your finger before you fire."

"You want me to shoot?"

"If someone comes. Yes."

"What if it's your friend?"

"It won't be. He'll come the way we came, or not at all. We'll wait until dawn."

"And if he doesn't come?"

If he doesn't come, Fenna thought, *he's dead*. She said nothing, as she picked up the assault rifle, smoothed one hand across the surface of the boulder, searching for the best firing position with a clear view of the path they had taken and the ditch where Bahadur lay in wait.

"Fenna? What if he doesn't come?"

"He will," she said, and, as she took a breath, the first crack of gunfire ripped through the trees, just a few hundred metres from their position.

Chapter 13

Aim, breathe, squeeze. It was a reflex now, muscle memory, trigger memory, Fenna had discovered a feel for it, a taste even. The rifle jerked in her grasp. She absorbed the kick, compensated with a change in posture, leaned into the butt, and fired. Short bursts of three, designed to keep Vestergaard's men in check, make them think twice.

When Burwardsley crashed into view and fell, Fenna prepared to move. She pointed at her last firing position, ordered Alice to stay put, to shoot at anything that moves within five metres of her, and to keep her head down. Then she was gone, twisting around the trees, a shadow pounding forward into battle. She caught a glimpse of a smaller shadow, Bahadur, as he pressed forward. She copied his stance – bent forward, the rifle an extension of his reach, head down, cheek tucked into the rifle, eyes forward. He was first, curling between the trees, his head never higher than the iron sights fixed before the muzzle of the carbine.

Fenna followed a parallel route, flicking her gaze to Bahadur, slowing when she was ahead of him, stopping when he stopped, stopping to fire. A stray round snapped through the air above her head before it thwacked into a tree, stripping the bark from the truck with a wet rip of woody fibres. She tucked behind the tree in front of her, scanned for movement, and loosed a burst of three rounds to the right of where Burwardsley had fallen. Then she moved, curling her body into shape of the Gurkha. Fenna ignored the scratch of the branches, didn't even feel them. She ripped her hair free of obstruction, tugging away the thin twigs of dead branches, ignoring the earthy resistance, and the silent plea to stop, take cover, hide. If that thought existed, she buried it. She moved on, watched as Bahadur reached Burwardsley. The Gurkha confirmed that his boss was alive, and then pushed forward, firing, blistering the trees with a mix of short bursts and full automatic when he located a target too close for finesse. Fenna heard the thud as one of Vestergaard's men collapsed beneath Bahadur's assault, and then a scream, "Ayo Gurkhali!" as Bahadur tossed his carbine at the dead man's feet and drew the kukri blade from his belt. It flashed once, and then he was gone, the wild sporadic bursts of enemy fire the only indication of the direction of his movement. Fenna pushed on and slid to a stop beside Burwardsley.

"How bad are you hit?" she asked as she ran her hand over Burwardsley's chest, pausing at each pulse of blood over her fingers. She tucked the assault rifle into her shoulder, her left hand trembling with the weight.

"I told you to go."

"Sure you did. Now shut the fuck up and tell me how bad you're hit."

"Konstabel," Burwardsley said, as he reached for her hand.

"What?"

"Go. I'm fucked. Just go."

"No," she said. Fenna grasped his hand, slippery with blood. "Not this time."

A scream from the woods and a sickening wet thud made both of them pause. Then the woods erupted with a fresh onslaught of bullets – new arrivals, more men from the meadow.

Fenna let go of Burwardsley, unclipped the sling from his carbine, and tied it around his chest. She tossed his empty weapon to one side, reached beneath his back and grabbed the sling. Fenna started to pull. Burwardsley groaned.

"Stop fucking moaning and help me," she said. The bursts of weapons fire intensified. Fenna could see the muzzle flashes, could see the arc of fire narrowing as the tracer rounds burned between the trees like green comets. The field of fire was narrow. They had found the Gurkha. Burwardsley pushed at the ground with bloody palms as Fenna pulled him behind her.

"How many?" she said.

"I killed three." Burwardsley paused between words. "There are two teams of four."

"Thomas?"

"Dead." Burwardsley stopped pushing as the roar of lead missiles diminished and the forest absorbed the sounds of battle. "Fenna," he whispered.

Fenna knelt down behind Burwardsley. She propped his body against her thigh and stomach, his head rested on her bended knee. The irony of Burwardsley's body being her only cover crossed her mind, before she switched her grip on the assault rifle and scanned the dark woods through the scope.

"It's quiet," she whispered.

"They'll be there."

"Seven?"

"Yep."

Burwardsley shifted to pull the Browning from his belt. Fenna heard him grimace as he raised it, the heavy pistol wobbling in his grasp.

"There," he said, and pointed. Fenna fired, the bullet casings ejecting from the port in the rifle in high speed brass spins. The man dropped to the ground before he could fire. Burwardsley grunted, as Fenna shifted position.

"Keep looking," she said, and was still, as quiet once again descended on the woods.

Six, she thought. *No. That's four left. Bahadur dropped one, killed another with that sword of his*. She remembered the prick of the tip of the kukri when Burwardsley, the man bleeding at her feet, had stretched and stripped her in the house on Greenland's east coast.

"You're thinking," he whispered. "I can feel it."

"Shut up."

A scream, maybe fifty metres to their right, snapped Fenna's head in that direction, the rifle following her head as she synced her body to the fight. The second scream was duller, wetter, and Fenna remembered the kukri, the bent blade – Bahadur's sword.

"Three," Burwardsley said, his voice thick with blood. "Bad's having a good night."

Fenna spun slowly back to scan the shadows and trees in front of them. She could feel the soft bed of pine needles beneath her knee, they slipped as she repositioned the foot she was sitting on. The wet scent of damp humus tickled her nose, but did little to disguise the more sinister smell of blood. She wanted to look back to the rocks, to see Alice, but there were still three men in the woods. Three enemy combatants. Vestergaard's men. And Burwardsley was bleeding at her feet. "I have to get you to the rocks," she whispered.

"Forget it, Konstabel." Burwardsley paused for breath. "I've my gun. Just go."

Fenna thought about responding, telling him what she promised herself she would, if they ever saw each other again, that he had, in fact, become a friend, and she wasn't about to leave him. Instead, the snap of brush twigs beneath the trees forced her to act. She flung Burwardsley to the ground and rolled to her left. Fenna's elbows slipped in the carpet of needles as she tucked the assault rifle into her shoulder and fired at the man running toward them. Her first burst forced him into cover, further left. He tripped, stumbled, and lost his grip on his weapon. Fenna's second burst caught him in the chest as he pitched head first into a tree. The air was still thick with gun smoke as Fenna kneeled and fired one more burst into the man's body. He was dead, but he wasn't alone.

A wild burst of fire ripped into the ground between Fenna and Burwardsley. Fenna swung the assault rifle up and aimed, only to pull the trigger on an empty magazine. She swore, dropped the rifle, and reached for her pocket with the Glock.

Empty.

"Fuck." She gripped the rifle and jumped to her feet.

The man sneered as she charged. He lifted his rifle and waited for her to close the distance from five to four, and then three metres. He waited too long. Fenna stumbled as the man's chest erupted in a spume of blood and he dropped his rifle. She turned to see Burwardsley shake his head. He pointed a bloody finger at Bahadur, as the Gurkha slammed a boot onto the man's back and shot him twice in the head with his pistol.

Fenna realised that the night was drawing to a close when she saw the blood dripping from Bahadur's wrist and onto the blade of the kukri in his hand. There was enough light to see his face too, and the Gurkha was smiling.

"I save you again, Konstabel Fenna," he said.

"Yes," she said.

"How many times shall I…"

The question died on the Gurkha's lips as a burst of bullets punctured his chest and dropped the short Nepalese man to his knees. His breath caught in his throat as he choked. He dropped the Glock, pressed the tip of the kukri into the earth and leaned on it. The last of Vestergaard's men stepped out of cover, ejected the empty magazine, and reached for a new one from his belt.

Fenna moved fast, as Bahadur drew his last breath, wrenching the kukri from his grip and flinging herself at the man as he jammed the fresh magazine into his weapon. He swung the rifle up to his shoulder, but Fenna slapped it to one side with the flat of the kukri blade. He reeled, took a step backward, as Fenna kicked him in the knee, raised the kukri, and swung the bent blade into the man's shoulder. It dug deep, stuck in the bone, and she let go to punch him in the face. The man slumped against a tree, fumbling for the pistol holstered below his belt around his thigh. Fenna grabbed his wrist, twisted it, and slammed her knee into his groin. As he slipped down the tree she pulled the kukri from his shoulder. He looked up, as she curved the blade in an arc into his neck. Fenna left the blade there, left the man to bleed as she crawled back to Bahadur, turned him onto his side, and cradled his head against her thighs. Bahadur blinked once, curled his lips into a half smile and died with the last rattle of air that spluttered from the ragged holes in his punctured lungs. Fenna closed his eyes with her palm and laid his body on the forest floor. She wiped her bloody hands on her trousers and stood up. The first face she saw was Alice's. The Glock, she noticed, twitched in the young woman's hand.

"It's okay, Alice. We got them all." Fenna followed Alice's gaze and nodded. "Yes," she said, "he's dead." She stepped around Bahadur's body and took the Glock from Alice. Fenna stuffed it into her pocket. She held Alice's hands, and said, "Are you hurt?"

"No."

"Are you okay?"

"No," Alice said, and shook her head. "The smell…"

"It's blood. Don't think about it."

"How can you say that? How can you…"

Fenna pulled Alice into her body, pressed her hand onto the back of her head, and held her tight.

"It's okay," she whispered. "I'm going to get you out of here. Keep you safe. Do you believe me?"

"Yes," Alice said, her voice muffled, her body trembling.

Fenna kissed the side of her head and said, "I need to go see Mike. Will you help me?" Alice nodded. "Okay then." Fenna took Alice's hand and guided her to where Burwardsley lay on the floor. He lifted his head as Fenna knelt beside him. "Bahadur's dead."

"I figured," Burwardsley said. He let his head fall onto his arm. His fingers were still gripped around the Browning pistol, and Fenna tugged it gently from his grasp. He watched her.

"I have to see where you are hit," she said and turned him onto his back.

"Any excuse," he said and smiled. A trickle of blood ran from the corner of his mouth.

Fenna worked quickly, opening the Marine Lieutenant's jacket and shirt, lifting his arms, and rolling him, gently, from side to side with Alice's help. She found one of the bullet wounds beneath his left armpit. She sent Alice to grab the first aid kit from her pack. Fenna undid Burwardsley's belt, unzipped his trousers.

"I didn't see him die," Burwardsley said.

"He took a burst to his chest." Fenna struggled to lift Burwardsley's hips. "Help me," she said to Alice when she returned. She pressed a bandage into the entry wound, and bound it around his chest. Between them they lifted his hips, tugging his trousers and underpants to his knees. Fenna slipped her hands inside the cuffs of his trousers to the collars of his boots, found no more wounds, and decided to leave them on. There was another wound in his thigh, and the bullet was visible. "I have to get that out," she said.

Alice reached around her belt and pulled a multi-tool from a webbing pouch. "My dad's," she said and handed it to Fenna. "He had a climbing pack in a friend's garage. They climbed together. I snuck in and took it. I needed something of his."

"It was a risk," Fenna said and opened the tool. "You could have been caught." She fastened the pliers around the bullet and waited for Burwardsley to nod. She pulled, lost her grip, and pulled again, tugging the bullet out of Burwardsley's flesh as he groaned. "There's dental floss and a needle in the first aid kit," she said. "Alice?"

"I shouldn't have looked. I feel sick."

"Take a breath," Fenna said and smiled. "You're doing fine."

"Where did you learn that?" Alice asked, as she handed Fenna the first aid kit.

"Sirius," she said, and threaded a length of dental floss through the eye of a curved needle. "They didn't actually teach us to remove bullets, but we had to sew up the dogs after fights, clean our own wounds…" she paused to pinch Burwardsley's skin between her bloody fingers. "Pull teeth." The skin was slippery and she set the needle to one side to grip the skin in both hands. "Alice."

"Yes?"

"Your hands are dry. I need you to sew."

"No. No freaking way," Alice said, her face pale.

"It's alright, kid," Burwardsley said. He stared up at the grey light as it filtered through the branches above. "Just get it done." Fenna nodded, and Alice picked up the needle. Burwardsley gritted his teeth at the first prick of the needle in his skin, muttering a stream of soft curses.

Alice sewed under Fenna's direction. The tip of her tongue was visible between her lips, and Fenna stifled the urge to chuckle at the young woman's concentration. She explained how Alice should tie the knot at the end of the stitching.

"He'll never get it out," Alice said, as she looked at her needlework.

"Right now, it doesn't matter. But we do have to clean it."

"With what?"

Fenna pulled a small bottle of alcohol gel from the first aid kit. She squirted it onto Burwardsley's wound and he grunted. Fenna had expected a scream, and told him so.

"Konstabel," he said through gritted teeth.

"Not anymore," she said, as he scowled at her. "I decided something, with a little help from Alice."

"What's that?"

"You call me Fenna from now on, because that's what friends do."

"We're friends? That's cute, *Konstabel*."

"Don't fucking spoil it, you ape," Fenna said and splashed more sterilising gel on Burwardsley's thigh. He cursed, and she waited until he was finished. "Besides, if we weren't friends, I would have left you to die." She looked at Alice. "You'd think he would be grateful."

"He should be," Alice said, as she rocked back on her heels.

"Listen, ladies, I *am* grateful, but I am also naked. And unless you fix the hole in my chest, I will probably die naked."

"Probably," said Alice.

"Well?" he said. "Fenna?"

But Fenna was silent, because the grey light of dawn was brightening, and she could see the outline of a fire road in the distance, between the trees. *We're close*, she thought. *One more country, and then Greenland.* Fenna sighed as she capped the bottle of gel and moved closer to the wound in Burwardsley's chest. *We're going to need a miracle to get out of Canada. A miracle, or magic.* "Fuck," she said as she knelt beside Burwardsley.

"What?" said Alice.

"I know what we have to do," she said and looked at Burwardsley. "You're not going to like it."

Chapter 14

"No," Burwardsley said. He tried to turn away from Fenna, but she pushed on his shoulder, forced him to lie still.

"I have to clean this, and sew it up."

"That's not what I mean."

"I know. It's the thing with Vestergaard."

"Too fucking right it is."

"But how the hell else are we going to get across the border? How are we going to get out of Canada?" Fenna said, and rocked back on her heels.

"I'm working on it."

"No. You're not. You're bleeding to death. Pretty soon this will be my problem, and mine alone."

"Well, love, it's a lousy fucking solution."

Alice helped Fenna lift Burwardsley. "I don't understand. What are you talking about?"

Fenna removed the dressing and cleaned the wound with water from a second bottle in her pack. They lay Burwardsley on the ground, turned him onto his side, and Fenna cleaned the exit wound. It was smaller than she'd anticipated, and better for it. She sterilised it, sewed it shut, and sterilised it again. Burwardsley said nothing beyond a few suppressed groans. Alice handed Fenna the items she asked for, but was otherwise quiet, waiting for Fenna to finish working on Burwardsley, waiting for an answer. The dawn sky lightened and lit the scene of battle on the forest floor. Alice kept her back to the dead bodies.

"Tell her," Burwardsley said.

Fenna removed her jacket and draped it over Burwardsley's shoulders. She picked up the Browning and pressed it into his hand. She held on as he took it.

"You know I'm right," she said, and let go of the pistol.

"Right about what?" Alice stood up, as Fenna dug in her backpack for a change of shirt. The one she was wearing was soaked in blood. Once she had changed she beckoned for Alice to step away from Burwardsley.

"He wasn't always my friend," she said. Alice frowned but said nothing. "We met in Greenland, on the ice, and he did his very best to get information out of me, and to clean up once he was done."

"To clean up?"

"Yes," Fenna said. She bent down to pick up their belongings littered on the forest floor. "He was ordered to kill me by a splinter faction of the Canadian intelligence service. I don't know what they are called, and it doesn't really matter. All you need to know is a young Greenlander killed herself because of what happened, and both he and I," she said and nodded at Burwardsley, "feel responsible. That's what brought us together. That and you."

"Me?"

"Yes." Fenna pointed at a few more things lying on the ground behind the rocks, items of gear that had fallen from the pack as Alice had dragged it over to where they were working on Burwardsley. "I couldn't save Dina, the Greenlander, and when I met you, when I saw how you were being treated, it struck a chord. I made a promise, to myself more than anyone, that I wouldn't let another girl die, not if I could help it."

"But why me?"

"Because, there's a man who is responsible for all this." Fenna gestured at the bodies sprawled between the trees. She paused at the sight of Bahadur, then moved on, grateful to look at Alice. "I know because he interrogated me, and, ultimately recruited me. He sent me to the desert. He put me in the same place, at the same time, as you. There was even a time when they considered me for the role you played." Alice looked away and Fenna grasped her arm. "But here's where it gets difficult, and this is what Burwardsley, *Mike*, wanted me to say."

"Which is what?"

"That I used you, the knowledge of where you might be hiding, to bargain for my life."

"I don't understand."

"I told them I knew where you were, and that I would come and get you, – *we* would come and get you," she said and pointed at Burwardsley.

"You're going to give me to these people?" Alice said, recoiling from Fenna's touch.

"No. Never."

"How can I believe you?"

"You can't, but I won't. I won't ever give you up. I will make sure you are safe."

"But what Mike said…"

"Shit." Fenna twisted the gear in her hands as she spoke. "We can't keep running. Vestergaard – these are his men – will keep sending teams after us. He knew where you were. He put Nicklas in that cabin with you. He is always, and will always be, one step ahead of us. And I can't…" Fenna cleared her throat. "I can't protect you like this. I need to get us to a place where I am in control, a place I know and can use to protect you."

"Like Greenland?"

"Exactly. I know Greenland. I know the environment, the people, I even have friends there, people who can help." She thought of David Maratse lying in a hospital bed, and wondered just how much help he could possibly be. And then another thought, the image of a hunter and his dogs, shivered into focus and she smiled. "And it's so far away from everything, so remote… I can protect you. I know I can. But I need to pretend to give you up, to get us there. All of us."

"You're going to give me up?"

"No. I'm going to pretend to. That's all." Fenna tried to smile, but Alice turned away.

The wind caught in the treetops, whistling down the trunks, showering them with soft needles, green and brown, new and dead. Alice spoke softly, her words barely louder than the whisper of needles, "It's not like I have much choice."

"No."

"How will it work?" She turned around. "What will you do?"

"As soon as we get to that gas station, I'll contact Vestergaard. We'll be in Canada. But you'll still be on the most-wanted list. We'll have to play it smart."

"But he'll just pick us up, and it will all be over."

Fenna shook her head. "Nicklas told me what is going on, that the countries using Vestergaard – his clients – are getting worried. They are starting to distance themselves from him. He needs leverage, and you're it."

Alice frowned. "I still don't get it. He'll want to pick us up. To bring me in."

"But he will want to wait until he gets you out of the country. He needs you somewhere safe and quiet just like I do. He even suggested a place."

"In Greenland?"

"Yes," Fenna said. She noticed movement to one side and watched as Burwardsley struggled into a sitting position and pulled on his shirt. He fiddled with the buttons and then, slowly, stood up.

"But I don't understand. Really, I don't. If he suggested this place, then he controls it. We're as good as trapped. And then, what's the difference? Dead here or dead there? He has control."

"We have to make him think that, yes," Fenna said. "We will agree to all his terms, so long as he gets us there."

"And what's to stop him killing or using us once we're there?"

"The Greenlanders," Burwardsley said. He leaned against a tree, the Browning still in his hand. "They are resourceful. They will help her," he said and nodded at Fenna. "Don't ask me why, but she has a way with them. She's earned their trust somehow."

"Fighting with you, mostly," Fenna said. "How are you feeling?"

"Stiff, sore. I need to pee."

"You need me to hold your hand?"

"Fuck off, Konstabel," Burwardsley said. He turned his grimace into a grin, and said, "Fuck off, *Fenna.* Is what I meant to say."

"So, we're friends now?"

"One step at a time, love."

Burwardsley pushed off the tree and took a few steps away from them. Fenna noticed the stiffness in his movement, wondered how far he would be able to walk, and then she heard him unzip his trousers. She took Alice's arm and walked her back to her pack, and the assault rifle. The ground was littered with bandages, shell casings, and patched with swathes of blood. Burwardsley grunted as he walked past them.

"Where are you going?"

"To see to Bad. You get our gear, and we'll put this crazy plan of yours into action." He staggered off. Fenna watched him as he paused to kneel beside Bahadur's body. She turned away to give him some privacy.

"I still don't understand," Alice whispered. "How are we going to get to Greenland, and how are we going to stop this man…"

"Vestergaard."

"Yeah, him. How do we stop him from using me, and killing both of you?"

"There's a charter flight from Iqaluit in Nunavut," she said, as she cleaned up the area and collected her gear into a pile. "It's an evangelist flight. They fly direct to Qaanaaq at the top of Greenland. I read about it in a magazine a while ago. Converting heathens, I guess, although the Lutheran church is dominant in Greenland, like it is in Denmark. There are close connections between the Inuit of Canada and the Greenlanders – in some cases, the Greenlanders in the north consider themselves more Inuit than Greenlander. Vestergaard can get us on that flight. It's private. It avoids the main hub, and it means we don't have to fly out of the States and into Europe. All other flights to Greenland are routed through Copenhagen, and we can't risk that. Neither can Vestergaard. He needs you in a country where extradition is difficult or time consuming. The more remote and challenging it is to get to you, the better. He'll want you there, and I will promise to deliver you."

"And once we're there, at this safe house of his, are you just going to leave me there? Job done."

"No. I won't do that. And neither will he," she said and gestured at Burwardsley. "Come on." Fenna shouldered her pack. "I'll tell you what I'm thinking later. Right now we need to bury a Gurkha warrior and cross the border."

Fenna led Alice to where Burwardsley knelt beside the body of his friend and fighting comrade. He nodded when Fenna suggested they bury him, pointing at the shallow ditch behind them, the same one that Fenna had ordered Bahadur to take as his fighting position. She dumped her pack, and encouraged Alice to help her carry Bahadur to the ditch. The young woman was willing, but Fenna could see she was struggling. The forest floor was littered with bodies, and Alice was finding it difficult to breathe.

"I'll need his kukri," Burwardsley said, as Fenna and Alice laid the body in the ditch.

"I'll get it," Fenna said. "I know where I left it."

She heard the scrape of soil, as Alice started to cover Bahadur's body. *He's dead*, Fenna thought, and realised that the sense of justice she might have felt that her partner's killer had been killed, was not there. She felt empty, not satisfied. *He was just following orders. He was good at that, and it killed him in the end – following my orders*. She stopped at the tree where the man was slumped, Bahadur's kukri buried in his neck, just where Fenna had left it. She gripped the handle and the man's eyes twitched open. Fenna caught the gasp in her throat, gritted her teeth and removed the blade. The man's head lolled forward onto his chest, and the last of his blood splashed from his neck. Fenna wiped the blade on his trousers.

"What have I become?" she whispered.

She didn't wait to think of a response, choosing instead to remind herself that she did what she needed to do, and if she hadn't, she would most likely be dead. Fenna picked up her pack and carried the knife to Bahadur's shallow grave. Alice had already covered his body with what little ground cover and top soil was available. Burwardsley asked Fenna to chop some of the lower branches with the kukri, and they arranged a blanket of pines over the grave. Fenna gave Burwardsley the kukri, and he buried the blade halfway into the ground just above Bahadur's head.

"I never thought the little runt would die. He didn't have it in him," Burwardsley said and laughed. His voice faltered, and he said, "Goodbye friend. Ayo Gurkhali." And then. "Give 'em hell." He tossed the Browning into a patch of young pine trees, and waited for Fenna to ditch her weapons. "We won't need them," he explained to Alice.

Fenna adjusted the straps on her backpack and nodded that she was ready. Alice led the way, picking a route between the trees to the fire road. Fenna wondered if she was going to run at the first chance, wondered if she had lost the young woman's trust. *And why not? Hell, I wouldn't trust me.* But each time Alice turned to check on their progress, to see if Burwardsley needed a break, she would smile, and Fenna allowed herself to be reassured, that there was still something that bonded them, that would allow them to trust one another.

They reached the fire road, and paused to remove or disguise the signs of battle. Burwardsley protested at the idea that he should remove his clothes, choosing instead to tie Fenna's jacket around his waist, and to hide the blood on his shirt with mud from the edge of the road. They walked on and heard the first car on the asphalt road just half an hour since walking out of the forest.

"There it is," Alice said and pointed at a small gas station less than a kilometre away. Fenna noted the single pump, and the wooden shop tacked onto a brick garage.

"And it's inside Canada?" she asked.

"Yes, and so are we." Alice took a breath and said, "I'm not a fugitive here. It feels good to be free."

"You're not free, kid," Burwardsley said.

"Not yet, she's not." Fenna took Alice's hand. "But I'm working on it." She lifted Alice's hand and pointed at the gas station. "You think your dad left any Smarties?"

"Yeah, I'm pretty sure," she said. Alice and Fenna walked a little faster, and Burwardsley let them go. Alice stopped to wait, but he waved her on.

"I know where you're going," he said.

A second car passed as they walked along the side of the asphalt road. Fenna tried not to laugh, but the absurdness of the situation, the gunfight in the woods, it took hold and she had to stop and let it out.

"What?" Alice said. "You going to tell me?"

"Give me a second."

"Fenna? Come on." Alice smiled, and then the smile broadened, dimpling her cheeks. She laughed beside Fenna, laughed until Burwardsley caught up with them.

"What did I miss?" he said.

"Well," Fenna said, as she curbed the last bout of laughing. "It's just, when I saw the last car that passed us…"

"The Jeep?"

"Yes, whatever, it doesn't matter. I just imagined the driver picking us up and driving us into town. Chatting, you know, asking where we'd been, what we'd been doing."

"And that's funny?"

"In a way, yes. I mean, what would I say? What would I tell him? That we climbed a mountain to pick up the President's assassin, fought our way into the forest and buried a friend, and now, we're going to call the most evil guy we know to see if he can hook us up with a flight to Greenland. I mean, is that what I would tell him?" She laughed, and added, "Oh, and by the way, how was *your* weekend?"

Alice giggled as Fenna continued laughing. They looked at Burwardsley's face and spluttered at his dead-pan expression. He scowled at both of them, bit back a wave of pain, and said, "Alright, Konstabel. But remember, before you lose it completely, remember, it was your fucking plan." He brushed between them and continued on to the gas station. Alice followed, once she had contained her laughter. Fenna waited a few minutes more.

She looked back at the mountain, thought about the location of Bahadur's grave, tried to place it in the trees. The thought sobered her. She tugged the straps of the pack higher onto her shoulders, took a last look at the mountain, and said, "Okay, let's finish this."

Chapter 15

FRASER VALLEY, BRITISH COLUMBIA, CANADA

The helicopter must have arrived in the night. The dark blue Bell 206A JetRanger was tucked in behind the gas station. Burwardsley had seen it, and he waved at Fenna to slow down. Alice was visibly trembling, and Fenna could do little to reassure her when she caught up with them, one hundred metres before the gas pump. *This is it then*, she thought and reached for Alice's hand. Alice pulled back, her eyes darting from one side of the road to the other. Burwardsley caught Fenna's eye and looked at Alice. Fenna nodded. *I won't let her run.* The gas station door creaked open and a woman wearing a thin down jacket, plum-coloured, stepped out, followed by two men, the last of which gave Fenna pause; he looked Greenlandic. *Canadian Inuit*, Fenna thought, but she couldn't help thinking of Maratse.

The woman walked past the pump and stopped. The men flanked her, taking positions to either side, and opening their black waist-length jackets to reveal pistols in shoulder holsters. Fenna turned her attention to the woman, twice her own age with flame-red hair coiled in a tight bun at the back of her head. The woman's stance concerned Fenna more than the two men, she was indifferent somehow, casual, and yet there was no mistaking the woman's agenda as she stared at them.

"It's going to be a lovely day," the woman called out. Fenna relaxed for a second as she identified her as Canadian, not American. But only for a second. "We've been waiting for you. Why don't you come over?" The woman stuffed her hands inside the pockets of her jacket and waited.

"Fuck," Fenna whispered. She reached for Alice, but the young woman shied away again. "Alice, you have to stay with us." Alice tensed and flicked her head toward the trees on the side of the road.

"Fenna," Burwardsley said.

Fenna opened the buckle on the waist belt of her backpack, so that the moment Alice bolted, she was able to dump the pack and race after her. Alice was fast, but Fenna couldn't let her run, wouldn't give anyone the excuse to shoot her. Her heart pounded in her chest as her body began to compensate for Alice's flight, and the fight that Fenna knew was coming. Alice was just a few metres from the trees when Fenna tackled her. They slammed into the ground and the air whumphed out of Alice's body as Fenna landed on her. The girl might have been lighter on her feet than Fenna, mountain fit, but Fenna was all muscle, and she pinned Alice to the ground.

"Let me go," Alice cried. "Just let me go."

"I can't."

"You can. I don't want this. I never wanted this. Let me go."

Alice's body heaved between sobs. Fenna couldn't see her tears, but she could feel her own streaming down her cheeks, cleaning a path through the dirt, the blood, and the pine sap of the violent hours they had spent in the forest. *It wasn't meant to be like this*, she thought. *It was never meant to be like this.*

Fenna heard the swish of boots through the grass and felt rough hands on her arms. She let herself be pulled off Alice's body and onto her feet. The Inuit man whispered in her ear, something about stopping Alice being the first smart move she had made since arriving in North America, but she ignored him, her focus was on Alice, as another man, a white Canadian, pulled her to her feet, and cuffed Alice's hands with thick plastic ties. Fenna recalled the feel of them, the bite of the edges, and then the memory was all too real, as the Inuit snicked ties around her own wrists, and marched her back to the road. He pushed her all the way to the gas station, shoving her back with a flat palm each time she tried to turn to see Alice. He grabbed the ties securing her wrists and pulled her to a stop in front of the woman with the flame-red hair. Fenna noticed that Burwardsley was sitting on the bench beside the door, flanked by two more men; one of them was working on his wounds. She heard Alice sniff as she was marched past her, all the way to the helicopter, and then the woman stepped in front of Fenna and blocked her view.

"Konstabel Fenna Brongaard," she said, "I have waited a long time to meet you."

It was the *you* that confirmed it, the *Canadian raising*, she wasn't American. Of course, that didn't mean she wasn't working for them, but Fenna had anticipated more drama, more flashing lights, more guns. This all seemed very low-key, making it even more menacing.

Fenna lifted her chin and said, "You're with Vestergaard?"

"Klaus Vestergaard?" The woman laughed. "Now what would make you say that?"

The Inuit shifted his stance, and Fenna heard the gravel crunch beneath his boots. She looked at the woman, caught the flicker of emotion in her eyes, and the tightening of the skin around her mouth. She was good, professional, but clearly very excited, and Fenna hoped that was in their favour.

"I would think he was a person of interest."

"Really?" The woman pointed in the direction of the helicopter. "You don't think she is more interesting?"

"Alice? No," Fenna said with a shake of her head. "She's just bait, or a bargaining chip, depending on how you want to play this."

"My, my, you have come a long way since running around with dogs, eh? Oh, yes," she said, as Fenna tensed, "I know all about you. Your history. Of course, the past several months is perhaps the most interesting."

"Then you'll know why I am here?"

"I certainly intend to find out." A weak gust of wind played with the gas station sign by the roadside. It creaked and the woman glanced at it. She looked beyond Fenna toward the mountains. "Do you know how much time it takes, how many resources, to clean up after you, Konstabel?"

"I can imagine."

"Then you'll appreciate that tolerance for your actions – in general, I might add – is growing thin among the community."

"What community is that?"

"Intelligence, of which you do seem to possess a fair share. That's why we're talking, just now. But I am not against using the full palette of options at my disposal."

"And I thought Canadians were supposed to be nice," Fenna said.

"We have a reputation for being polite. There's a difference. But let's not go there, Konstabel. I'm sure we can work things out."

"What is it you want?"

The woman smiled, and Fenna noticed a crooked tooth, one that she tried to conceal with a conscious dip of her top lip. Her lipstick caught on the edge of the tooth, and the woman licked it away with the tip of her tongue. It was a refined move, practised, and Fenna realised that a woman who was attuned to such small details, was likely to be equally tuned-in to the bigger picture. *She already knows my history*, she thought, *and quickly changed the subject from Vestergaard to Alice. Careful, Fenna.*

"What I want? What do I want, Yuka?"

The Inuit man let go of Fenna. He prodded her shoulder as he walked around her. Yuka, Fenna realised, was nothing like the Greenlanders she knew. While his skin was a similar tone, he was thinner in the face, his beard wispier, eyes narrower. He seemed sterner, and she had yet to see him laugh. She thought about Maratse and the hunter, remembered the way they laughed, remembered Maratse's boyish enthusiasm as they raced across the ice in the police Toyota. *And now he is recovering in hospital*, she thought. *Because of me.*

Yuka stared at Fenna, and said, "You want to finish this, Ma'am?"

"I do," the woman said, "that's right." She took a step closer to Fenna. Her perfume was subtle, but confirmed that if she had ever been in the field, it was a long time ago. Fenna thought of her own subtle fragrance, and almost smiled as the woman stepped back.

"Sorry," Fenna said, and smiled. "It's been a long time since I smelled sweet."

"Do you like this life, Konstabel?"

"I don't have much choice. And the longer we spend talking around the subject, the less choice I have."

"Choice?" The woman laughed. "It amuses me to think that you believe you have a choice."

"I believe I have a future, or, at least a purpose."

"And so do I, Konstabel."

"Then let's stop dicking around, and get right to it, shall we?" Fenna looked from the woman to Yuka and shrugged. "Whenever you're ready. Or do we have to wait for someone with more authority?" *Easy, Fenna. Don't piss them off.* From the look on Yuka's face, she knew it was too late.

"Dicking around, eh? Nice choice of words. Amusing, almost." The woman nodded, and said, "Leave us for a moment, Yuka."

"Ma'am," he said, and walked over to join the men guarding Burwardsley. Fenna watched him, studied his gait, looking for a weakness. She found none.

"You're smart, Fenna. I'll give you that. But you've made a series of mistakes, one after the other."

"I had no choice."

"Choice. That word again. Women always have a choice."

"Not in our line of work."

"You're wrong. But you're also young. And I have to remember that. I was, believe it or not, an agent in my younger days."

"RCMP?"

"Ah, no. I was not like your friend, Nicklas." She paused to study Fenna's face. "He was your friend, wasn't he?"

"Yes."

"And now?"

Fenna said nothing. She ignored the image of the lookout cabin, their last rendezvous.

The woman continued, "I'm not RCMP. I'm something else. You can call me Meredith. It's not my real name, of course, but it will do for now, until we get to know one another." She paused to pull her Smartphone from the pocket of her jeans. "Just give me a moment."

Meredith walked toward the pump and leaned on it as she made her call. Fenna smiled as she remembered the signs warning people not to use mobiles when filling their cars with petrol. She wondered if that wouldn't be the easiest solution, for them all to just blow up in an explosion. *But nothing about this is easy*, she remembered. And then she looked at Alice in the helicopter. Her head was against the glass, her beanie pulled low over her eyes.

"Let's get something to eat," Meredith said, as she walked back to Fenna. A large SUV appeared around the corner in the road, and Fenna realised there were probably more arranged in a road block, just out of sight.

"Okay," she said.

"This is going to take a while to clean up, and I could do with some pie."

"And my friends?"

"I'll make sure they get something to eat."

"That's not what I mean."

"I know. But then you don't have much choice."

She was right, of course, *but I don't have to like it.* Fenna tensed as Meredith opened a folding knife and cut the plastic ties from her wrists. There was a second when Fenna considered her options, but one look at Yuka suggested that she really didn't have any, and then the SUV pulled into the gas station, and Fenna was ushered inside by two female agents.

"Yuka is loyal," Meredith said, as she got into the back of the car beside Fenna, "but I like to have as many women on my team as possible." The agents climbed into the front of the SUV, and they pulled away from the gas station and onto the road, heading north. Fenna caught a glimpse of Burwardsley as he stared at the SUV. Her stomach cramped for a second, as she wondered if she would see him again.

"It wasn't supposed to end like this," she whispered.

"No?" said Meredith. "How did you imagine it would end?"

"I don't know. I don't tend to plan that far ahead."

Fenna was quiet until they pulled into a small diner. She smelled waffles as they entered, and coffee. Meredith showed her to a small table by the window. The mountains were visible in the near distance, but clouds threatened to obscure the view of the peaks. Meredith ordered coffee and pie, bantering with the waitress that it was never too early for pie. Fenna slumped into the seat, it had been a long time since she rested. The coffee, when it arrived, lifted her for a moment. It was black, and strong, it almost reminded her of home.

"What are you thinking about?"

"Denmark," said Fenna, as she turned the mug on the table.

"I went to Sweden once. Malmö."

"Sweden is nice. Denmark is…"

"*Hyggelig*? Did I say that right?"

"Yes," Fenna said. The waitress brought the pie and she started to eat.

"I read a book all about it," Meredith said. She picked up her spoon, and said, "But isn't it just a Danish way of being cosy? I mean it's not rocket science. Just light a few candles and eat cake." She waved her spoon at Fenna's pie. "How is it?"

"It's good."

"When I knew we were on our way down here, I wanted to find somewhere…"

"Listen, Meredith, can we just get on with it?" Fenna set her spoon down on the plate. "We don't really have time for small talk. We're not going to build a relationship. Honestly," Fenna picked at a crust of blood on her cheek, "I'll tell you whatever you want to know."

"Why would you do that?"

"Because you obviously need me."

"Based on what assumption?"

"I'm not dead."

Fenna sipped her coffee and cast a glance at the female agents smoking by the side of the SUV. They were about the same age as Fenna. She was sure they could shoot, *but can they kill?* Fenna thought about the man she had killed with Bahadur's kukri. She took another sip of coffee.

"Alright, Konstabel. I'll get to it." Meredith put down her spoon. Fenna noticed she had not touched her pie. "We have a mutual acquaintance."

"Living or dead?"

Meredith laughed. "Living. God, I didn't imagine you to be such a cynic. You've really been through some shit, haven't you?" Fenna shrugged, and Meredith continued, "Vienna Marquez. Do you remember her?"

Alpaca wool, a beautiful apartment, and a shitty little dog, *yes*, Fenna thought, *I remember Vienna*. "We met on *The Ice Star*. How do you…" Fenna put down the mug of coffee. It occurred to her then that another name would connect Meredith and her, and it would be a stronger connection.

"Ah, I see that mind of yours is connecting the dots."

"You don't care about Vienna."

"No," said Meredith. She picked up her spoon and took a tiny piece of pie. She ate while Fenna talked.

"I know who you work with," she said.

"Worked. The past tense is more appropriate."

And then it all made sense, so much sense. It wasn't Vestergaard cleaning up on the mountain. They weren't his men blocking Nicklas, preventing him from leaving with Alice.

"They were your men," Fenna said. Meredith raised her eyebrows – refined, plucked, and with just the right amount of make-up – and spooned another small piece of pie into her mouth. "You wanted Nicklas dead."

"And yet, it was your little Gurkha who killed him."

"To protect me, and Alice. But you wanted vengeance."

"And I got it," Meredith said. Her spoon clattered on her plate as she curled her fingers around the coffee mug, the tips of her nails tapped on the glazed surface. "I don't condone what you did in Toronto, when you castrated my colleague with a bullet."

"You worked with Richard Humble," Fenna said. Her voice quavered.

"I did, and, despite his evil nature," she said, and shrugged, "he was effective, and devious. It was his deviant ways that got him into trouble, of course."

"So, this is personal?"

"Isn't everything?"

"And you wanted Nicklas dead, because he finished off Humble."

"That's right."

"But he was acting on orders. To protect me."

Meredith sipped her coffee. She wiped her lipstick from the rim of the mug with a napkin. She let Fenna think for a moment more, and then said, "Have you ever wondered, Konstabel, just how many times people have died to protect you and your identity?" She didn't wait for Fenna to respond. "Perhaps I should be thankful, because now I have you, and I can use you. You are *useful* to me."

"And that's why I am alive."

"Yes."

"And you want me to kill someone."

"Yes."

"You want me to kill Vestergaard," Fenna said, and smiled.

"Do you think you can do that for me? Konstabel?"

Fenna took another spoonful of pie. She almost choked on the cream, as it slipped the wrong way down her throat. Whether it was fatigue or euphoria, she couldn't tell, but suddenly, here in the Fraser Valley, she could see a way out. There was hope. "You'll get us to Greenland?" she said.

"You," said Meredith. "I'll get *you* to Greenland."

The Arctic

INUIT GOVERNED AREAS, CANADA & GREENLAND

Chapter 16

IQALUIT AIRPORT, NUNAVUT, CANADA

The de Havilland Dash 7 was cramped. Fenna bumped against Alice's shoulder as Burwardsley sat down, squashing his huge frame into the seat. He grumbled something about his knees, huffed for a moment, and then settled. Fenna grinned at him as the evangelists chatted and sang around them, cramming the overhead lockers with sports bags and backpacks, shopping bags of groceries, fruit they could entice the Greenlanders with, and cheap plastic toys for the children. *They'd rather have a Smartphone*, Fenna thought, as a large woman bent over to pick up a collection of plastic cars that had fallen out of her shopping bag. Fenna nudged Alice with her elbow, but she ignored her. Burwardsley was, however, open to distraction, and Fenna decided she could work on Alice later, during the flight.

"Don't," Burwardsley said, as Fenna opened her mouth to speak.

"What?"

"It looks like you're going to take some kind of credit for getting us on this flight."

"And why shouldn't I?"

Burwardsley pointed at Yuka sitting two rows in front of them. "That's why."

"They weren't going to let you leave. I don't know about Alice, but you would be dead already. I had to make a deal. He is part of it. I had to agree that Yuka would come with us. My chaperone," she said and laughed.

"Listen, love, you made a deal with the devil."

"Hey," Fenna said, and shushed him. "Don't mention him here."

"You are fucking kidding me," Burwardsley said. He turned in his seat, but Fenna clamped a hand on his mouth, giggling as she wagged her finger in front of him.

"And no swearing." She let go of him. Alice stirred beside her, and Fenna hoped she was smiling, at least for a moment. *That would be enough, for now.*

The steward announced that they would be taking off soon, and Fenna took a last look at the new terminal, a 300 million dollar project expected to put Iqaluit firmly on the map. She thought about similar projects in Greenland, and how the Greenlanders had been able to preserve their language to a far greater degree than the

Canadian Inuit. The difference between using Latin letters and symbols, was, Fenna imagined, crucial in making the language accessible for later generations, especially in the digital age. And yet Greenland was split between those who could and those who couldn't speak Greenlandic. *Like the Inuit in Qaanaaq*, she remembered, *they speak a dialect that has more in common with the Canadian Inuit than the Greenlanders on the west coast.* It was a point of contention that ostracised the Inuit in the far north of Greenland. *As if life wasn't difficult enough.*

The roar of the Dash 7's four turboprop rotors forced the evangelists into their seats, and Fenna smiled at Yuka's obvious discomfort as the passenger next to him tried to engage him in conversation. It was going to be a long trip for the Inuit intelligence agent, and Fenna realised she didn't care. There were other things to worry about. She wished, for a moment, that Burwardsley could speak Danish, but whatever plans they needed to discuss would have to be talked about in the open. Discreetly. And, as he had often reminded her, *I don't do discreet.* Fenna leaned back in her seat as the Dash 7 taxied off the apron and roared down the runway, lifting off in under twenty seconds.

The journey to Iqaluit had been uneventful, almost anticlimactic. If Alice had opened up, and given Fenna the chance to explain, then it might even have been pleasant. Meredith, whoever she was, clearly had enough information on all of them, that no interrogation was necessary. She seemed to be on the clock, and they had been swept along in the urgency of her operation. Stopping Vestergaard seemed to be her sole motivation, and Fenna began to wonder why. *What was he planning?* Meredith's motive of revenge was a thinly-veiled cover for something greater, more sinister. And, while she had been reluctant to give up Alice, that same urgency seemed to drive her decision-making process. Fenna hadn't seen her make any calls, it appeared that Meredith's decision was final, there was no superior to check in with. *And that should worry me*, she thought.

"There's just one problem," Meredith said in the motel room, the night before the flight from mainland Canada to Iqaluit, Baffin Island.

"Thule Base," Fenna said.

"You have to fly over it get to the Uummannaq fjord area, and your final destination – the so-called safe house."

"Yes."

"The base is American."

"I know."

"And if there is bad weather…"

"We can be forced to land. I know."

Meredith shook her head. "That can't happen. These," she said and tapped her fingernail on the stack of three passports in front of her, "will only get you so far. If they question you… if they recognise Alice..."

"We"ll colour our hair."

"You and Alice?"

"We've been mistaken for one another before. I can mislead them long enough to stall them."

"Long enough for me to help you, you mean?"

"Maybe." Fenna shrugged. "At least this," she said, picking up a bottle of chestnut-coloured hair dye, "is my natural colour." *I get to be me again.* "Besides, they won't be looking for Alice in Greenland, and certainly not in Thule."

"You've considered everything. Haven't you?"

"Not everything." *I haven't even begun.*

As the pilot throttled back, and the engines settled into a rhythmical drone, Fenna looked at Alice, saw the wisps of chestnut hair sticking out from the hem of her beanie. She tried to catch her eye, but Alice ignored her.

"We need to talk at some point," she said.

"I know. But not now." Alice turned to look out of the window, tracing the outlines of icebergs, in the sea below, on the window with her finger.

The steward served coffee. A passenger at the front of the cabin plucked at his guitar, and Burwardsley swore.

They didn't speak for the rest of the flight. Each lost in their own thoughts. Burwardsley kept an eye on Yuka, and, when he wasn't sleeping, Yuka stared at Fenna.

"You'll want to watch him," Burwardsley said, as the pilot announced they would be landing soon in Qaanaaq.

"I know. But he's here for her," Fenna said.

"I'm not so sure."

The wheels of the Dash clunked into position as the pilot

lowered the undercarriage, and then they were approaching, hurtling onto the gravel airstrip just four kilometres outside the village of Qaanaaq. Fenna caught a glimpse of Herbert Island in the fjord to the right as the pilot applied the airbrakes and wrestled the aircraft to a stop beside the airport building. Fenna enjoyed the sight of the familiar blue sidings, the red-striped yellow *Mittarfeqarfiit* pickups favoured by the airport authority. She spotted the standard dark blue police Toyota in the car park, and then she forgot all of it, and focused on the ice.

Qaanaaq is served by two supply ships each year, the first in July, and the last in August. The last ship even included Christmas trees, real ones, stored until December. To buy them, the locals had to order them in advance. The needles fell off the moment they brought them inside the house, but that hardly mattered. It was the thought that counted, and now Fenna's thoughts were focused on the ice, and the extent to which it covered the sea, greater than expected in these times of extreme climate change. The passengers had noticed too, even Yuka showed a passing interest before staring at Fenna once more.

The ice was a popular topic of conversation, and it continued as they disembarked and walked the short distance, beneath the wingtips, and into the airport building. The luggage carousel was a single track of rubber encased in metal. It was just a few metres long, and, from the looks of it, rarely switched on. The ground crew emptied the Dash's hold into shallow skips carried by a forklift truck. Fenna smiled as the passengers commented on how quaint it all seemed, before they entered the airport waiting lounge, and were given further instructions by the policeman and his assistant.

"Here we go," Burwardsley whispered as Yuka joined them. He stuffed his hands in his pockets and stood to one side.

Alice found a chair and sat down as they waited for their gear. Fenna joined her, only to pause as she pulled out a chair. There were two men sitting at the table in the corner, furthest from the carousel strip, but still no more than fifteen metres from the exit. They stared at Fenna and then started speaking quietly, the words barely escaping their beards. Fenna recognised their type immediately. Her stomach cramped again as she took in their tanned faces, the white stripes of skin where the sunglasses sat above their ears. They wore wool sweaters, worn and patched, and their trousers were military grade cotton with large cargo pockets – she looked down – much like her own. Burwardsley spotted them too, and he took Fenna's elbow.

"What the fuck are they doing here?" he said.

"You think I know?"

"It's not even September. Shouldn't they be fucking around with dogs in Daneborg?"

"Yes."

"But clearly, Konstabel, they are not."

"Don't call me that," she said. "Not now."

"What? You think they might recognise you?" Burwardsley let go of her elbow. "Bit late for that. They're coming over." He stepped back and stood beside Yuka, flicking his gaze from Fenna to the two tall Danes of the Sirius Sledge Patrol.

The men smelled of dog, and Fenna took a step toward them, standing between them and Alice. But it was Burwardsley they were more interested in, him and Fenna. They spoke Danish as they approached, but they dispensed with any form of greeting, starting instead with a variety of accusations.

"Heard you were dead," said the taller of the two Danes. Fenna considered him to be the more experienced of the two. He was familiar, but she couldn't quite place him. The shorter man, by just a few centimetres, was the *fup*, the new guy, just starting his first year.

"That depends on who you think I am," Fenna said. She felt Alice stir behind her, heard the squeak of her chair on the floor.

"Who do we think you are? Hah," the man laughed. "You're a legend, Konstabel Brongaard." He turned to the first year man. "This is the one who killed her partner, Mikael Gregersen."

"Is that what they told you?" Fenna worked hard to keep her tone level, measured, as neutral as possible, but she could feel the adrenaline charging through her veins. *This isn't the place, it's not about Mikael anymore.* And yet, she knew it was, and that it always would be for the Sirius Patrol.

"They told us nothing. The first we heard of it was when Kjersing blew his own brains out. Then we heard that Mikael was dead, and you were lost at sea. Apparently, you and your team fell through the ice. That's what we heard. Then," he paused to point at Fenna, "we heard about some PET scuffle in the mountains around Nuuk. A mine was set on fire, and some Chinese men were killed. Along with a couple of Danes. Oh, and there was a car chase, which…" he paused to laugh, "is pretty fucking funny considering how little road there is in Nuuk." He stopped talking and jabbed another finger at Fenna. "But I don't see you laughing, *Konstabel*."

"Okay," she said. "It's me. I didn't fall through the ice. But before I tell you what happened, tell me, Noa Andersen – that's you, isn't it?"

"*Ja*," he said.

"Your beard was thinner when I met you."

"And I was fatter. Go on."

"What are you doing here?" Fenna glanced over her shoulder, as Burwardsley moved closer.

"We're looking for dogs. Daneborg needs new breeding stock."

"You usually don't go this far north."

"No, but hunters are shooting their dogs along the coast. Too many winters with poor or no ice," he said, pausing to nod in the direction of the fjord. "Ironic, really, as this winter looks like it's going to be a good one." He looked from Burwardsley to Fenna. "Your turn, Konstabel. What are you doing here? And, more to the point, why'd you come back?" Andersen waited, his eyes fixed on Fenna, but flicking occasionally in Burwardsley's direction as the Royal Marine moved closer.

"I can't tell you."

"*Ja*, of course," Andersen laughed. "How convenient."

"She means it," said Burwardsley. "Whatever it was she just said."

"Hey, man," Andersen said in English, as he took a step towards Burwardsley. "Just who the fuck are you?"

"Me?"

"Don't," Fenna said. She glanced around at the evangelists as they collected their baggage. She could see their own gear on the luggage belt and tapped Alice on the shoulder. "Can you get our gear?"

"Sure," Alice said, happy to move away from the men crowding around the table.

"You didn't answer my question," Andersen said.

"You didn't ask nicely."

"Oh, for God's sake," Fenna said. She turned on the first year man. "Who are you?"

"Hansen," he said. "Konstabel."

"Great. Hansen meet Burwardsley," she said and grabbed the *fup* by the arm, dragging him between the two men. "I don't have time for this testosterone Navy bullshit."

"Navy?" said Andersen, as he shoved his partner to one side. "British?"

"Royal Marines," Burwardsley said. "Heard of them?"

It was Fenna who threw the first punch. A brawl seemed inevitable, and, with Alice safe collecting their gear, she decided it was best to get it over with. *Besides*, she mused, as she curled her fingers into a fist, *there's no better way to break the ice. And*, she added as an afterthought, *we might need them*. Fenna extended her middle knuckle and slammed her fist into Burwardsley's ribs, just below his bullet wound, just enough to slow him down. She whispered in his ear as he grunted, "Let me handle this. Stand down."

Burwardsley staggered backward into Yuka, creating a gap large enough for Fenna to stand between them. As Yuka shoved Burwardsley onto a chair, she whirled toward Andersen, knees bent, adopting her preferred fighting stance, projecting just enough attitude for a large opponent to take her small frame seriously. She glared at him as he opened his mouth.

"Not one fucking word," she said in Danish, "or I will drop you like a sack of shit."

He lifted his hands and took a step backward. Hansen leaned against a table near the window. The ground crew had stopped working on the Dash, and were gathered at the glass, on the outside of the building.

"Mike?" Fenna said, switching to English. She kept her gaze fixed and focused on the two Sirius men. "Are you alright?"

"I am bleeding. Again. Thanks to you."

"Sorry about that..."

"He's bleeding?" said Andersen. He switched to English. "Why is he bleeding?"

"Because we pulled at least two bullets out of him," said Alice, and she dumped their gear onto the table. "And before you ask *how* or *why*, or some other dumbshit question, then let me tell you…" She paused to look at the two men. "It was to protect me. Now," she said, "if you've got nothing better to do, you can help us with our gear. It's been a long flight. I'm tired, and I can't remember when I last had something to eat." Alice sighed. She looked at Fenna.

"What?"

"Just you," Fenna said, and smiled. She lowered her fists, relaxed her stance, and laughed.

"You're laughing?" Alice said.

"And you will too, if, you know…"

"What?"

"If you want to."

"Yeah, I want to," she said, and smiled.

Fenna bit her lip to stop laughing as the policeman walked over to their table. He tucked his hands into the broad belt around his waist and looked at each of them. He paused to nod at Yuka, and then stopped to focus on Fenna. She decided she liked him.

"*Allu*," he said. "*Ajunngilaq?*"

"*Aap*," said Fenna. "*Ajunngi*."

"You speak Greenlandic?"

"A little," she said.

"And everything is alright here?" he said, and again in English.

"We're fine," Fenna said.

"*Torrak*. Good then." The policeman nodded in the direction of the exit. "My name is Akisooq Jessen. Welcome to Qaanaaq."

Chapter 17

QAANAAQ, GREENLAND

The ground crew drifted away from the window and Akisooq stood to one side, making room for the airport leader. The Danish man glanced at Fenna as he talked to Andersen.

"Air Greenland called. Your flight's been cancelled," he said.

"Shit."

"Technical problems."

"Should've gone with *Flugfélag*."

"They call them Air Iceland today, boss," said Hansen, his smile barely hidden beneath his beard.

"Thanks, whelp," Andersen said and slapped him in the stomach. "But they've still got *Flugfélag* written on the side of the plane. Until they change that… Well," he shrugged. Andersen scratched at his beard as the airport leader returned to the office. "I guess we're stuck in Qaanaaq one more night." He looked at Fenna.

The policeman checked their passports, passing quickly over Fenna's to concentrate on her companions. He spent a long time with Yuka's, flipping the pages back and forth, before handing it back. He looked at Burwardsley, and nodded at the blood seeping through his fleece. "Do you need assistance?"

Burwardsley lifted his arm and prodded at the area. He winced, and said, "Might be a good idea."

"Then I'll give you a ride to the hospital. Where are you staying?" he asked, and looked at Fenna.

"We don't know yet," Fenna said. "We also need a ride south. Noa?"

"*Ja*?"

"How many dogs have you got on your flight?"

Andersen shook his head. "Not gonna happen," he said, and switched to Danish, "You can't just come back from the dead, Konstabel, and expect to roll back into your previous life."

"No?" Fenna lifted her chin. "But you're curious, aren't you?"

"About what?"

"The truth," she said. "Give us a ride south, and I'll give you all the details."

"Like I said, Konstabel. The last I heard, you were dead, and then you were working for PET, maybe. Now you turn up on a flight from Baffin Island with a Royal Marine, a pretty girl, and a Greenlander lookalike." He paused to lean close to Fenna. "Do the words *untrustworthy bitch* mean anything to you? Or are you so far gone, so damaged, that this all seems perfectly normal?"

Fenna almost smiled. "Normal doesn't quite cut it anymore, Oversergent."

"Apparently."

Andersen pulled Hansen to one side. He stared at Fenna as they talked, soft words through long matted whiskers. She pictured them both with ice clinging to their beards, sparkling in the sun, their breath misting into clouds before freezing into another layer of ice. She smoothed a hand over her chin, remembering how the wind, the snow, the freezing temperatures had hardened her skin, rubbed it raw. She had envied her partner's beard during each day on patrol, and teased him about it each night as he plucked food from his whiskers. *I miss it*, she realised, as she watched the two Sirius men talk. The thought of flying south, stuffed in the cabin – seats removed to make space for dogs and gear, thrilled her. *It was what I was meant to do.* She looked at Burwardsley. *Before him.* And then at Yuka. *Before them.*

"I can give you a lift into Qaanaaq," Akisooq said. "They…" he pointed at the bearded Danes, "have their own vehicle. From the hotel."

"There's a hotel?" Alice asked.

"Yes," Akisooq said. "Very small. And full," he said, "of evangelists. We will have to find somewhere else for you to stay."

The small airport emptied. Akisooq showed them to the Toyota, and they loaded their gear into the back. Burwardsley pulled Fenna to one side, nodding at the Inuit intelligence officer as he walked beside Alice.

"We're going to have to deal with him, and soon," he said, his voice low, hidden beneath the crunch and scuffle of gravel at their feet.

"I know."

"And you know it has to be you, right?"

"Me?"

"Fenna," Burwardsley said, "look at me." He lifted his arm to show her the blood seeping through his clothes. The stain was bigger than when he was sat in the chair. "I need to get fixed up before I can do any of the fun stuff. You're on your own, love."

Again, she thought. Fenna stopped at the car and helped Burwardsley with his gear. Yuka was the last to shove his pack into the car, and, when the policeman tried to make conversation, he ignored him and climbed into the back seat. Fenna opened the passenger door and got in. With a quick glance at the two Sirius men as they got into the hotel pickup, she shut the door. Akisooq backed up and drove away from the airport, the grit of the gravel road peppered the Toyota as he accelerated. They passed small groups of Greenlanders, families, children, young couples out for a walk. Akisooq slowed as they passed each group.

"I usually have a car full," he said.

"You still do," Fenna said.

"Right."

The ice sheet was just visible on the plateau of the mountains running parallel to the road. The hard granite sides seemed closer with the dusting of snow, it reached all the way to the lower slopes, close to the road and the village. Fenna pointed, and said, "Winter is coming early this year."

"Maybe."

Fenna looked out at the sea, at the ice just beyond the shore. She thought about global warming, and the anomalies that can't be explained, the ones that buck the trend. *Perhaps this year will be one of those years?* She forgot all about the ice when she saw Yuka staring at her in the wing mirror. She stared back.

"Your passports are all in order," Akisooq said, breaking the contact between Yuka and Fenna. "But I still don't know what you were doing on the charter flight. You're not evangelists."

"No, we're not," Fenna said.

"We're students," Alice said and leaned forward in the gap between the seats.

"You don't look like students."

"Yeah," she said, with a flash of a smile at Fenna. "We're not *all* students. I guess it is just me, really, and my sister is along for the ride. Together with her guy." Alice said and punched Burwardsley on his thigh.

"And you?" Akisooq said, as he turned the rear view mirror to look at Yuka. "You look familiar. Have you been to Greenland before?"

Yuka leaned back in his seat and raised his eyebrows.

"When?"

"2016," Yuka said, and turned away.

Akisooq looked at Yuka for a moment longer, and then repositioned the mirror.

They entered the village, driving past wooden houses – brightly painted, sorely loved. The climate blistered the walls, and a lack of money shifted priorities from furnishings and fittings to food. *Nothing was cheap in Greenland*, Fenna remembered. Akisooq stopped outside a yellow house on a curve in the gravel road. The neighbour had dogs chained to the rocks between the two houses. The policeman's house was exposed on the eastern side to the gradual granite slope leading to the mountains, with a line of three newly-built wooden houses above it. The first house, painted dark blue, sank each summer to the permafrost, only to rise again each winter. Akisooq said as much when he turned off the engine.

"Those houses are fit for Danish summers."

"Then why did they build them here?" said Fenna.

He shrugged, and said, "Somebody did somebody else a favour. They should never have been built." He turned in his seat. "You can stay here. It's the police house, but I am just the summer replacement. My family is in Maniitsoq. There's plenty of room. If you get out, I will take your friend to the hospital." He got out of the car and walked over to the house, opening the door as Alice and Yuka emptied the boot and carried their gear inside. Fenna pretended to have lost something inside the car.

"He's not stupid," Burwardsley said. "He knows you want to talk."

"You're right," she said and looked at Yuka waiting by the door. She started to speak but stopped when Andersen pulled up alongside them in the hotel pickup. He wound the window down and Fenna did the same.

"Hansen and I have had a chat, and, seeing as we're all trapped in this wonderful town for the night, how about we start again? We're staying in a house just up from the hotel. We'll cook. We even have beer. What do you say, Konstabel?"

"You have beer?"

"Brought it with us. No one can afford what they have in the store."

"Right," Fenna said. She looked at Burwardsley. He nodded, and she said, "What time?"

"About sundown?" Andersen said, and laughed.

"Fucking hell, he's a comedian," Burwardsley said. "I liked him better when he was an arrogant Dane."

"Shut up, Mike," Fenna said. "Alright, we'll be there for dinner."

"Good. We can talk about your flight, tomorrow," he said. Gravel and grit spewed out from beneath the wheels as he accelerated up the slight rise in the road.

Fenna watched him drive away. Two of the neighbour's sledge dogs lifted their heads for a moment, only to rest on their paws as the pickup disappeared between the row of houses leading to the hotel. Fenna heard the pickup stop, and wound up her window.

"Tonight then," Burwardsley said.

"Yuka?"

"Yep."

Fenna nodded. She opened the door and got out. Akisooq was waiting by the door to the house. He stopped Fenna as she approached.

"You're not students," he said.

"No." Fenna waited for him to say more. She noted the way he wore the USP Compact on his belt. There was fluff between the snap of the holster and the grip. *He doesn't clean it very often. Doesn't need to.*

"I can't place your strange Canadian friend," he said. "But I have seen him before. As for the rest of your friends – you are a strange mix."

"Yes, we are." She wondered where their conversation was taking them, wondered if their strangeness was what encouraged him to offer them a bed in the police house. *Why not the police station?* She mused, and remembered the single cell in Ittoqqortoormiit. *Not enough room.*

"Greenland is a small country," he said.

"Yes."

"And did you think you could come back, without people recognising you?" he said with a nod in the direction of the hotel.

"I came back to finish things."

"What things?"

"I can't say."

Akisooq sighed, and said, "I could lock you up."

"For what?"

"I could think of something."

"But you're alone."

"Was that a threat?"

"An observation."

A group of children clambered across the rough ground beside the house. They were full of energy, buoyed by the thought of the evening's evangelical entertainment. Fenna heard them chattering, and imagined the stories they might tell their younger brothers and sisters. They stopped talking when they saw Fenna, clustering around her and the policeman.

"I'm not alone, Konstabel," he said.

"Hey," Fenna said, as one of the girls tickled her leg. The girl giggled, as Fenna tickled her back. Soon, she was surrounded, and it was all she could do to keep them at arm's length. Akisooq retreated to the car, waving as he sat behind the wheel. "You're just going to leave me?" she said, as she picked up the smallest of the boys, and tucked him under her arm. The children giggled, regrouped, and attacked, as Fenna whirled the boy around her body. He whooped and she set him down on the ground. A girl immediately filled the vacant spot, lifting her arms for Fenna to swing her too.

"They should keep you occupied until I return," Akisooq said. He drove away, as Alice stepped out of the house.

"What's going on?" she said, only to back away as the children split up to engage both targets at once. "Fenna?"

"We're outnumbered, Alice," she said and made the mistake of sitting on a large boulder by the side of the road. Three children crawled onto her lap and they toppled into a heap on the ground.

Alice staggered over to Fenna, with one boy wrapped around each leg and a girl pushing her from behind, her tiny hands hooked into the belt loops on Alice's trouser. Yuka watched from the door, before retreating inside the house. Fenna saw him go, before the two boys on Alice's legs let go of her and leaped onto Fenna. Alice giggled as Fenna groaned beneath a pile of children.

The girl pushing Alice from behind slipped her hand inside Alice's and beamed at her. She pointed at the boys, and said, "Ungaaq, Kaaleeraq, Luka."

"Okay," said Alice.

"Birgithe, Frederikke," she said, and pointed at the girls.

"And you?" Alice tugged at the girl's hand.

"Pipaluk."

"Hi, Pipaluk. I'm Alice."

Pipaluk smiled and tugged on Alice's hand, pulling her forward until they were close to the squirm of children crawling over Fenna. She pulled her down until Alice sat on the boulder. Fenna said something in Danish, something else in Greenlandic, and then, finally, she said stop, in English. The children crawled off and giggled as Fenna stood up.

"I guess," Alice said, as Fenna dusted herself off, "stop is the same in any language."

"Right," Fenna said, licking at the dirt on her lips. The children started talking. They scrabbled about on the rocks and Pipaluk let go of Alice's hand. She chased one of the boys until they were all involved in a seemingly random and altogether confusing game of tag.

"Do you ever think about children?" Alice said, as they watched the game develop.

"Like having kids, you mean?"

"Sure," she said and moved to make space for Fenna on the boulder.

"Maybe. I don't know. It's seems trivial somehow."

"But nice." Alice brushed a patch of dirt from her knee. "Dad said I should have kids. He said it the day before he died. Something about seeing life in a different light once you have a child. I don't know about that. It's difficult to imagine life – a different life to this one. And there's no light. I mean," she paused to shrug. "Sure, here, there's lots of light."

"It won't start to get dark before sometime in September."

"Really?"

"That's right. And then the sun disappears late October, and the light gradually diminishes until it is pitch black."

"I can't imagine it."

"It takes some getting used to," Fenna said. She looked at the house, saw Yuka at the window, frowned as he lowered the blinds. "But," she said, "so long as you keep busy, try to maintain a routine, try to adapt…" Fenna stood up.

"Fenna?"

"Stay outside, with the children."

"What are you going to do?"

"Don't let them come into the house."

"Fenna?" Alice moved to stand up, but Fenna pressed her hand, gently, on her shoulder.

"Stay here. I am going inside. Don't come in, no matter what you hear."

"You're scaring me," Alice said, as Fenna walked toward the house. "Fenna?"

The interior of the house was not dark, the light streamed in from around the blinds, through the gap beneath the door. Fenna saw the strip of light on the toes of her boots as she stepped inside the house, shut and locked the door. She heard the children playing, calling Alice's name. She pictured them crawling over the rocks, scuffing the palms of their small hands on the rough clusters of black lichen. She knew the touch, could almost hear the dry crunch of the thicker patches of lichen as one stepped on them. *Black*, she thought. *And stubborn*, surviving each winter despite the desiccating cold, the evaporating wind, and the long dark night. *A survivor then*. Fenna turned at the sound of soft footsteps on the linoleum floor. Yuka stepped into view, blocking the door to the kitchen. Fenna recognised the fighting posture, looked for an edge, saw the kitchen knife.

Chapter 18

Yuka was the first to move. The kitchen knife blurred in his hand as he attacked. Fenna dodged to the right and tripped over the shoes and boots littering the floor. Yuka spun on his heel and stabbed at Fenna's thigh. The tip of the blade caught in her trousers, peeling a triangle of material from the pocket and nicking her skin. Fenna rolled onto her back, hooked her foot around Yuka's ankle, and slammed her boot onto his shin. He swore as he kicked free of her grip, giving Fenna time to find her feet. She lunged after Yuka's knife hand, gripped his wrist, and bent his hand backward until he dropped the knife. It clunked onto the floor and Fenna kicked it to one side. She moved, searching for a better position and grip, but Yuka grabbed her hair with his free hand and yanked her head backward. She released his wrist and he jerked his knee into her stomach.

There was nothing pretty to the fight, but it was bloodless, until Fenna slammed an elbow into Yuka's nose. He let go of her hair, and she twisted to grab his bloody nose between her fingers. His head followed his nose, his body followed his head, and Fenna pulled him across the short floor of the hall into the living room.

She hadn't thought about the door frame, or how he might grip both sides with his hands and yank his nose free of her bloody fingers. Fenna toppled into the living room, and Yuka followed, lunging at her body, slamming into her back. They crashed through the glass surface of the coffee table, the shards cutting their faces and hands, and slicing through their clothes. Fenna scrabbled across the floor, grabbed a shard of glass, and thrust it into Yuka's face as he found his feet. The shard tore a flap of skin from his cheek. He ignored it, powering inside Fenna's defence. He wrapped his arm around Fenna's and punched her in the face. She spluttered blood, gasping for breath as he punched her again.

Yuka held her arm above her head, pausing for a second at the sound of a knock at the door. Fenna reached for another shard, but Yuka slammed his boot on her hand, pressing jagged pieces of glass into her palm. She wanted to scream. The thought of a handful of glass, embedded in her hands like nails, made her sick. She bit back on the first convulsion, tensed the muscles in her legs.

The knocking changed to a steady pounding, vibrating through the house. Yuka glanced again at the door, then focused on Fenna.

"You really thought we were going to let you go?" he said through gritted teeth.

Fenna said nothing. Her blood was raging in her temples. She rasped each breath into her lungs through bloody teeth, yanked her hand out from beneath Yuka's boot, heaved down on his grip and lurched to her feet. She slashed at his face with the palm of her hand. He let go of her arm, swatting at her hands, as she gripped the back of his head and pushed his face into her palm of glass. Yuka cursed her as the glass ripped through his flesh. He staggered back and Fenna kicked his legs out from under him, following him down onto the floor, never letting go. She could feel the blood streaming from his face, down her wrist. She could taste it in her mouth, or perhaps it was her own, she didn't know, didn't care, until she felt strong hands grip her arms and pull her up and off Yuka.

"Easy, Fenna, easy," Burwardsley said. She squirmed in his grasp until he let her go, shoving her into the corner of the room as Akisooq wrestled Yuka onto his back, and slipped a pair of handcuffs around his wrists. He sat on the floor beside the Canadian, as Yuka spat blood and shifted his head from side to side until he found Fenna. He snorted blood as it bubbled beneath his nostrils as he glared at her.

"It looks like this man attacked you, Fenna, is that right?" Burwardsley said.

"I…" Fenna started to speak, but Burwardsley cut her off with a look.

"This man joined our group in Iqaluit. We don't know who he is beyond his name. I think it best if you arrest him," he said, and looked at Akisooq.

Yuka spat and laughed, as he rolled onto his side. He sneered at Burwardsley, and said, "You should be an actor. What a perf…"

Burwardsley slammed the toe of his boot into Yuka's chin, snapping his head back and silencing him. He bent over him to check Yuka was still breathing and then apologised to Akisooq. "I am sorry. I thought he was going to attack again."

Akisooq raised his eyebrow and glanced from Burwardsley to Fenna. He stood up, brushed shards of bloody glass from his knees and cast a glance at the door. "First time I've ever had to break into my own house," he said.

"Clearly, he had it all planned," Burwardsley said.

"Mike," Fenna whispered. "Cut it out."

Akisooq gripped his belt and looked around the room. Fenna followed his gaze from the bloody remains of the coffee table, to the spots of blood leading past the kitchen knife to the front door. A picture frame had smashed on the floor, she didn't remember that. The door frame was splintered, and, framed in the light that streamed in from outside, was Alice, and a clutch of children staring around her legs.

"Go home," Akisooq said. "Now." The children let go of Alice. Fenna heard them chatter down the road as they ran away from the policeman's house. He nodded at Burwardsley. "Help me get him into the car."

"I can help," Fenna said, as the men started to lift Yuka's body.

"It would be best," Akisooq said, "if you worked on your part as the defenceless victim. Don't you think?"

"Okay," she said, watching them as they carried Yuka toward the door. She sat down as Alice stepped out of the way and joined her.

"It was you who locked the door," Alice said, "wasn't it?"

"Yeah, that was me."

"Why?"

"I thought I could take him. I was wrong."

"Sure, maybe, but he's the one they are carrying into the police car."

They sat quietly as Akisooq started the engine and drove away. Fenna waited for the sound of Burwardsley's boots, but heard nothing more than the muted rattle of a chain as the dogs settled again after all the excitement.

"Let me see your hand," Alice said. She rested Fenna's hand on her lap and peered at the glass sticking out of it. "I need more light," she said and stirred.

"No," Fenna said, "don't open the blinds. Not yet."

"Okay, but I can only see the big stuff."

"Then start with that."

Fenna sucked a sharp breath through her teeth as Alice teased the largest shard out of Fenna's palm. When it was free she looked around for somewhere to put it, and then tossed it onto the floor of the living room.

"He'll be missed, won't he?" she said.

"Yes."

Alice pulled another shard from Fenna's palm, and said, "Why did you do it?"

"What? Attack Yuka?"

"No. Not that. Why did you talk them into letting me come to Greenland?"

"I wasn't going to leave you behind."

"But why here?"

Fenna winced as Alice worked at a stubborn shard, the jagged edge ripped at her skin until Alice tore it loose.

"Well, we're not there yet. We have to fly south."

"With the Danes?"

"Hopefully, yes."

"Where to?"

"There's a house in a small settlement – maybe seventy people live on the island."

"Whose house?"

"It belongs to a shaman."

"A shaman?" Alice laughed. "As in Native American? A medicine man?"

"Sort of," Fenna said, and smiled. "I don't know for sure, but that's what I was told."

"By who?"

"Vestergaard. He chose the house."

Alice pulled Fenna's hand onto her own lap. "I really need more light," she said, and stood up. Fenna squinted as Alice opened the blind and disappeared into the kitchen. She returned with a wet cloth and a towel. "Neither of them are clean," she said, and sat down. She took Fenna's hand and inspected it. She talked as she turned Fenna's palm in the light. "This man, Vestergaard, he's the same one you talked about before, right?"

"Yes."

"The one who wants to use me and kill you?"

"That's right."

Alice wiped the blood from Fenna's palm. The tip of her tongue was visible as she worked and Fenna tried not to smile. "What I don't get," Alice said, "is why we are going to a house that Vestergaard suggested. Why not go somewhere else?"

"There is nowhere else, Alice."

"Nowhere?" she said, and wrapped the towel tightly around

Fenna's hand.

"No," Fenna said. She sighed and said, "I'm sorry."

"It's okay, I guess." She bent Fenna's hand at the elbow and pressed it to her chest. "Keep it elevated." Alice stood up and paced the length of the living room, stopping at the far window to stare at Herbert Island in the distance. The snow dusted the spine of the island, making it look like the back of some great sea beast, breaching the surface and breaking through the ice. Fenna joined Alice at the window, taking her hand and squeezing it.

"I'm sorry," she said.

"I know."

"But, if we can just get to the house, we can make things right."

"How?" she whispered. "Yuka almost killed you."

"I wasn't ready. He had the advantage."

"And Vestergaard doesn't? He knows we are coming, and where we are going?"

"Yes, but I'll be ready. More prepared."

"I don't know, Fenna."

They turned at the sound of the police car pulling to a stop outside the house. They listened as Burwardsley kicked the grit from his boots and stepped inside. He joined them in the living room, the keys to the car hooked around his little finger.

"How's your hand?" he said.

"Alice fixed it. Where's Akisooq?"

"Processing our friend at the police station." Burwardsley laughed, "more of a house, really. We took him to the hospital, then Akisooq called his assistant, and they took him to the station. I've got the spare car."

"One policeman, and two police cars?"

"This is an old one. Apparently, it would cost more to ship it out than to keep it running."

Fenna nodded. *Typical Greenland*, she thought. "Did Akisooq say anything?"

"We agreed you were lucky, but it's Yuka who is going to be scarred for life. He's not going to forget you, love."

"But what about us? Akisooq could probably arrest us for disturbing the peace."

"I've been wondering about that." Burwardsley sat down on the sofa. "Greenland is a small place, small community. Everyone knows everyone else, despite the distance. What are the odds that he knows your friend from Ittoqqortoormiit?"

"Maratse?" Fenna said, and shrugged. "He probably does."

"That's it then."

"And you think he'll let us get on that plane tomorrow?"

"With the Sirius boys? Fenna, I think he'll drive us to the airport just to make sure we do get on it. He's got enough paperwork to sort out with Yuka. He can't keep an eye on the village and deal with us." He drummed his fingers on his knee. "Which reminds me, I bumped into the boys on the way back from the hospital."

Fenna cringed, and said, "Just bumped into them?"

"Christ Fenna, what do you take me for? I'm hardly going to mix it up with them in the street. Can you imagine it? Oh, by the way, I'm the guy who offed your pal on the ice..." Burwardsley paused. "Sorry, love."

"It's okay." She frowned and said, "But you are pretty upbeat for someone with a couple of bullet holes in them." Then she laughed. "Ah, they gave you something at the hospital, didn't they?"

Burwardsley reached into his pocket. "They gave me a whole bottle," he said, and shook it between his fingers. "I have to say, Konstabel, I probably feel better than you do right now." He looked at Alice. "What about you? Ready to party?"

"Party?"

"It's Friday night. Did you know that? Eh?" He stood up. "I saw the beer they bought, and I don't mind admitting that Carlsberg is equal to the best of British lager, so long as it's cold. Oh, and we're eating whale steaks tonight."

"Mike?"

"Yes, Konstabel?"

"How many pills did you take?"

"Shit, I don't know," he said and stood up. "They said I should take some for the pain. They didn't say how many." He stuffed the bottle in his pocket. "You going like that?" he said and nodded at Fenna's hand. Blood was seeping through the towel.

"It's either that or the hospital."

"Fine. Grab another towel, there's beer to be drunk." Burwardsley walked out of the living room and waited for them at the front door.

"He's going to be impossible, isn't he?" said Alice.

"I think he is." She tugged Alice across the floor, doing her best to ignore the crunch of glass beneath her feet as they walked out of the house. "Are you going to be alright with this?"

"A party?"

"Parties in Greenland can get a little rough," Fenna said. Burwardsley got in behind the wheel and waved at them to hurry up.

"Rough? Did you just say that?"

"I guess I did."

"Amazing," Alice said, "with all we've been through." She let go of Fenna's hand and jogged to the car.

"Hey," Fenna called out. "Remind me? What's the drinking age in America?"

"Who are you? My mother?" Alice said as she opened the passenger door. She called out, "Shotgun," and climbed in beside Burwardsley.

Once Fenna was in the car, they drove less than half a kilometre, before Burwardsley stopped and announced they had arrived. Fenna smiled as she stepped out of the car and saw nine sledge dogs secured to a travelling chain stretched along the road, secured at both ends to rusted fuel drums full of rocks. Each dog had a short length of chain clipped to a collar and attached to the long chain between the drums. One chain was missing a dog.

"If they work together they can pull those barrels down the street and escape," Andersen said, as he stepped onto the porch outside the wooden house. He had an open beer in one hand, and three cans stacked in the other. He gave Alice and Burwardsley a beer each as they stepped around the dogs and walked inside the house. Fenna dawdled by the dogs, fussing each of them with her good hand, appraising them for size and weight, the condition of their fur, how hydrated they were. "If you keep pinching their skin like that, they'll bite, Konstabel."

"Maybe," she said and fussed another dog as she worked her way along the line.

"Do you miss it?"

"You can tell?"

"*Ja*, I can tell," Andersen said and gave Fenna the last can of Carlsberg. "*Skål*," he said and took a slug of beer.

"*Skål*." Fenna popped the can and drank.

Andersen smiled as a neighbour cranked up a radio, and the

revellers inside raised their voices over the distorted sounds of Johnny Cash. The dogs twitched at the ends of their chains, and Andersen knelt to make a fuss of the one between him and Fenna.

"Friday night in Qaanaaq," he said and crushed the empty can in his hand.

Fenna nodded and looked at the house. She heard Alice giggle, and smiled at the thought of winding down, for one night at least. She gestured at the chain.

"Just nine dogs?" she said.

"Nah," Andersen said and grinned. "There's one more inside."

"A bitch?"

"*Ja.*"

"And she's in heat?"

"She is."

"Well," Fenna said, and laughed, "us girls can be a handful."

"I've heard that," Andersen said. He nodded at the towel around Fenna's hand. "You weren't wearing that before."

"No," she said. "No, I wasn't."

"Want to talk about it?"

"Inside, maybe."

"Come on, then." Andersen tossed the empty beer can in the direction of the bin, muttering something about cleaning up in the morning.

He led Fenna up the stairs to the house, and she heard Alice giggle again, before a twenty-kilo bundle of energy, fur and claws, skittered across the floor and leaped into Fenna's arms.

Andersen laughed, and said, "What were you saying? Something about girls being a handful."

Fenna pulled the bitch into her chest and held it tight, as it licked at her face. *It feels good*, she thought, *to be with friends, for as long as it lasts.* She slipped the bitch onto the floor and gave it a soft kick on the rump to send it back inside, and away from the dogs straining at the chain behind her. Fenna waved at the dogs and closed the door. She took a breath, let go of the handle, and joined the party.

Chapter 19

The bitch finally settled at Fenna's feet as the neighbour's music beat through the thin wooden walls, and the Sirius men found another crate of beer to wash down the rich, dark whale meat. Fenna rubbed the fur between the bitch's ears, teasing one ear between her fingers. She listened to Hansen tell Alice about his first year in Sirius. Fenna guessed that he was only a year or two older than the American, about the same age as Fenna had been when she tried out for the sledge patrol. Andersen, she noticed, was far more interested in Burwardsley, although he cast a furtive look in her direction more than once during his conversation with the Marine Lieutenant. He was pumping Burwardsley for information, she knew, but trusted that the Englishman would be guarded. Despite the pills he had taken, Burwardsley had hardly drunk any beer, unlike Andersen. *But then what's a Dane to do on a Friday night in Qaanaaq?* she thought, as the corners of her mouth curled into a smile.

Fenna leaned back against the wall, her legs stretched flat on the floor. She curled her hand around the base of the bottle of beer, pushing it back and forth along the floor as the bitch turned on her side and slumped against her legs. Fenna laid her arm along the bitch's flank and smoothed her fingers between the dog's matted fur. She couldn't remember the last time she had felt so safe, so relaxed. *It feels good. How long will it last?*

The scrape of a chair leg vibrated through the floor and Fenna looked up as Alice walked to the bathroom. She smiled at Fenna as she passed, blushing as Andersen said something about not leaving, because Hansen was going to be inconsolable if she left without a kiss. It was all so very far removed from the bullets, the blood, and the bursts of adrenaline that typically defined Fenna's more recent experiences. She heard the bathroom door click as Alice turned the key in the lock. Hansen went outside to smoke, and Burwardsley joined him.

"He's a close one," said Andersen, as he opened another can of beer and joined Fenna on the floor. "He knows Greenland, and he's been around, but he won't say where, or when… I can't get anything interesting out of him."

"And what do you want to know?" Fenna said and took a sip of beer. It was warm. She didn't care.

"About you. How he knows you."

"Why?"

"Because nothing adds up, Konstabel. Gregersen, a car chase in Nuuk – nothing makes any sense."

"That's PET for you."

"No." Andersen shook his head. "I don't buy that."

"But you'll have to. I can't tell you anything."

"That's your problem then," he said.

"What do you mean?"

"Well, unless you open up, I've got no incentive to put you on my flight, tomorrow." He took a slug of beer, wiped the froth from his beard, and said, "None."

The bitch twitched, and Fenna stroked it as she thought about what to tell Andersen. *How do I tell him that the man responsible for Mikael's death is sharing a smoke with his* fup*?* She bit at her lip, wondering what had changed. *Because I need him*, she realised, and almost laughed at the irony.

"What's so funny?" Andersen asked. He stretched his legs and rested his arms on his knees. Fenna saw the holes he had patched in his trousers, recognised the ragged hems for what they were – wear and tear on patrol, and wondered at the route he had chosen, and which cabins he had visited.

"Are they going to rebuild *Loch Fyne*?"

"They've talked about it. There's not much left. It'll have to be rebuilt from scratch."

"It's a good location."

"Which is why they're talking about it."

If she closed her eyes, Fenna knew she would see Bahadur pressing her Glock to the back of Mikael's head, hear Burwardsley give the order, and then turn away as her partner's body slumped to the floor. If she closed her eyes. She chose to look at Andersen instead, and, as the bass from the neighbour's stereo diminished in favour of a raucous chorus of English songs from the seventies, Fenna decided to tell the Sirius man what had happened that day on the ice, with just one omission, Burwardsley.

Alice returned as Fenna finished her account of the shootout at Loch Fyne, her capture, how the helicopter crew had doused the cabin with aviation fuel, right before they drugged her.

"And that's when my interrogation began," she said. "When they woke me up."

"Jesus," Andersen said. He glanced at Alice, and then said, "No wonder Kjersing killed himself. If he was privy to what was going on…"

"It was a test. He was being used."

"That's no fucking excuse. He was a traitor."

Fenna took another sip of beer, studying Andersen's reaction as she lowered the bottle from her lips.

"What happened next?" he said, and, with another glance at Alice, he switched to English. "You were interrogated?"

"By a Dane, or so I thought."

"Vestergaard? You mentioned him before."

"That's what he called himself. He's also called *the Magician.*"

Andersen bit at the longer whiskers of his beard, the ones curling into his mouth. "And you got away?"

"I had help."

"Who?" he asked and nodded at Burwardsley. "Him?"

"No. Mike helped me later," Fenna said. "It was a Greenlander, two in fact. A policeman called Maratse, and Kula, a hunter."

"We heard about an anti-terror exercise…"

"That was the cover story, yes."

"And a car chase across the ice," he said and raised an eyebrow. "Really?"

"The truth is stranger than fiction."

"No shit."

Alice excused herself, and joined the men talking outside. It was past midnight, but, with no visible difference in the light, the night seemed like it would never end. *If only that could be true*, Fenna thought. *But the winter dark will come, and I need to be prepared for what it might bring. If we live that long*, she added. She watched Alice as she walked across the floor and stepped out onto the deck. Fenna turned back to Andersen.

"You want to know why I'm here?" she said.

"*Ja.* I do."

"The girl."

"Girl? She's not much younger than Hansen." He snorted and lifted the can to his lips. Andersen licked beer from his lips and said, "What about her?"

"I need to her to get to Vestergaard."

"Her?"

"Yes," Fenna said. She took a moment to explain what Vestergaard wanted with Alice, finishing with a plea for help. "We need to go south, as far as Uummannaq, and then into the fjord."

"I can get you as far as Qaarsut. We can land there before going on to Ilulissat."

"That works. We can get a boat to the settlement."

"Which one?"

"Nuugaatsiaq, I think. I'll know when we get there, when I call the Magician."

"You're actually going to call him?"

"He has a safe house arranged for us. The girl is important to him."

"Why?"

"It's complicated."

"See," Andersen said and crossed his legs. He lifted the can of beer, one finger extended, pointing at Fenna as he spoke. "This is what I don't understand. After all you've told me, you are going to call the man that ultimately got Mikael killed, and tell him… tell him what, exactly?"

"That he can come and pick up Alice."

"You're going to give him the girl?"

"No. I'm going to kill him." Fenna leaned forward, a frown on her brow, as she looked at Andersen. "You don't think I can?"

"Fenna…" he started. "Have you heard yourself, lately? I mean, this is not normal talk, even for the first female Sirius *fup*. It's like you're deluded, or something. Have you considered getting help?"

Fenna waited for Andersen to laugh. Only to realise, when he didn't, that her own reality had shifted tectonically from what even the elite Sirius Sledge Patrol considered normal. *It's a whole other world*, she thought, and looked at Burwardsley as he bummed another cigarette from Hansen. Alice was by his side, swapping glances with the young Sirius man. Burwardsley turned and caught Fenna's eye, and that connection, however brief, grounded her in that other world, the one so far removed from Andersen's.

"I don't expect you to understand," she said, her focus still on Burwardsley. "But I do need your help."

"To kill a man?"

"Oh, I don't think he will send just one."

"Jesus," Andersen said. He ran a hand through his long, greasy hair, so matted and twisted from the trail that the division between his hair and his beard was indistinguishable. Fenna looked at him as he tried to process what she had told him. He laughed, suddenly, just as the neighbours stopped singing and found another CD for the stereo. Andersen coughed, nodded once, and said, "Of course, it's all a joke, right? A story?"

"Sure," Fenna said, and smiled as she recognised one of Alice's words slipping into her vocabulary. "It's all a joke."

"And the stuff about Mikael? What really happened on the ice? That's a joke too?"

"No, that's real enough, but you'll never see it written, or hear it said in public." She held the bottle of beer at the mouth and tapped the base on the floor. "Only a few people know. And most of them are dead," she added, in a whisper.

"Well," Andersen said, as he stood up, "true or not, the story is worth a lift to Qaarsut. I'll have to put your names on the manifest, but the pilot owes me a favour. We just have to have things in order, especially as we're flying over Thule Base."

"But not stopping? Right?" Fenna said and looked up. Andersen towered above her. He and Burwardsley were the same height, she realised.

"We'll fly to Upernavik. Touch down, and then on to Qaarsut. We'll only stop in Thule if there's…"

"Bad weather. I know." Fenna looked out of the window, scanned the clouds and then looked at Alice. *She looks happy*, she thought, laughing at something Hansen said. Burwardsley came in and closed the door behind him.

"Three's a crowd, and all that," he said and smiled at Fenna.

"*Ja*," said Andersen. "They'll be talking all night, but I need my bed," he said and yawned. "You'll see yourselves out?"

"Yes," Fenna said, as the bitch stirred beside her. "Thanks, Noa."

"My pleasure. Of course," he said and looked at Burwardsley, "we'll be sharing the plane with the dogs."

"I figured that," he said. "Just glad for the lift."

"*Ja*," Andersen said. He walked to the bedroom door, paused, and turned around. "What about the Inuit guy? Where is he? Has he got family in Qaanaaq?"

"Something like that," Fenna said. "He'll be staying here."

"Fair enough. Goodnight."

Andersen walked into the bedroom and closed the door. Burwardsley pulled out a chair and sat at the table. Fenna got up off the floor and joined him.

"Everything alright, love?" he said.

"Everything is fine."

"You got us on the plane."

"Yes."

Burwardsley lowered his voice. "Tell him anything interesting?"

"A little," Fenna said, and then shook her head. "Not about you though," she breathed.

He nodded and rooted through the open cans and bottles of beer for one last mouthful. He gave up and plucked Fenna's bottle from her hand. "Thanks, Konstabel," he said, and finished her beer.

"You're quieter than earlier," she said. "Pills worn off?"

"Yep, that and jetlag. I'm tired," he said.

"We haven't stopped since, Nuuk."

"Nope."

Fenna's chair creaked as she leaned back. She looked around the walls. They were bare, stained with cigarette smoke, faded by the long low sun of summer. Alice giggled, and Fenna turned to look, just as the young Sirius man made his move. She watched as they kissed, as Alice curled her hand around Hansen's neck and pulled him close. *What would he think*, she wondered, *if he knew he was kissing the woman who killed the President of the United States of America?* Fenna smiled. She looked at Burwardsley and laughed.

"What?"

"It's all so surreal."

"Yep," he said.

Fenna rapped her knuckle on the table. "Let's go for a walk," she said. "See the sights."

"Sights? This town is an armpit, Konstabel."

"Surrounded by glaciers, with the ice sheet just up there." Fenna pointed toward the front door.

"I'm not walking up the bloody mountain, just to see the ice sheet. I've seen enough ice for a lifetime."

"Fine. We'll walk down to the beach," she said, and stood up.

Burwardsley put the bottle down on the table and nodded at

Alice. "We're just going to leave her here?"

"Let her have some fun," Fenna said.

Burwardsley grunted and followed Fenna to the front door. The dogs tugged at the chain as they shut the door behind them, fidgeting and wagging their tails as Fenna made a point of fussing over each of them. Burwardsley shook his head, "I haven't got all night, Konstabel."

"Yes, you have," she said, and nodded at the sun low in the sky.

"Smart arse," he said and started walking along the length of chain link fence that separated the front yard of each house in the row. Children tramped along the bitumen roofs of the wooden siding insulating the water pipes above the ground. They chattered and waved at Fenna, before chasing each other down the street.

"It's almost two o'clock in the morning," Burwardsley said. "What are they doing up?"

"They're playing."

"They should be in bed."

"Why?"

"Because…" He stopped and shrugged. "What do I know, eh? Not my culture. Not my kids."

"Exactly," Fenna said.

They walked down the main street, past the store, painted red, and the bar, spilling drunks onto the dirt. The tide was out and the fishing dinghies and small skiffs were stranded on the sand between sharp boulders of ice. Fenna explored the *qajaq*s on the wooden rack, as Burwardsley picked his way between the boats, leaning against one closest to the sea. Fenna watched as he pressed a hand to his side and checked for blood.

"Does it hurt?"

"It's sore."

"What about your thigh?"

"That's just stiff. You did a good job sewing it up."

"It was Alice."

"That's right, now I remember."

A raven cawed above them, settling on the beach to pick at a rotten seal carcass. Fenna watched as the raven tore at the flesh, tugging at it with its beak. Now she had seen the carcass, the smell reached her nose, the smell of death.

"We're still going through with this?" Burwardsley asked.

"Yes."

"Good," he said.

Fenna thought about the evangelists, wondered where they were, what they were doing, or planning. *Bringing God to the godless*, she mused, *in this godforsaken land*. But in truth, despite the harshness of it, the extremes of winter and summer, Greenland was as close to God as she imagined any country to be. There was little to distract the people from their belief, their faith, no interference, just a very thin and fragile boundary between life and death. *Death*.

"You're thinking, Konstabel. I can hear you."

"Yes."

"Well? What about?"

"Death," she said.

"We all have to die sometime," Burwardsley said. "Hell, I feel pretty lucky to have gotten this far, all things considered. This past week…"

"Yes," Fenna said. "This past week…"

Burwardsley pushed off the boat and stood up. The raven cawed and flapped a couple of metres along the beach, before stalking back to the carcass.

"Are you ready to die, Konstabel?"

"Yes."

"Then let's get on with it."

Burwardsley rapped the hull of the boat with his knuckle, and starting walking back up the hill. Fenna waited a moment longer, staring at *Politiken's Glacier* on the other side of the fjord. She stifled a yawn, turned her back on the sea, and followed Burwardsley up the hill.

"It's time," she said.

Chapter 20

All but six seats had been removed from the interior of Nordlandair's de Havilland Canada DHC-6 Twin Otter. Fenna recognised the cramped interior as an older airframe with a new livery. *Lucifer bit me in this old bird*, she remembered as she grabbed the collars of each dog in turn and lifted them into the aircraft. Andersen and Hansen secured the dogs, relying on a passive temperament and a warm cabin temperature to pacify the sledge dogs from Qaanaaq. Burwardsley made a point of teasing Alice as they watched Hansen bumble around the Twin Otter's interior, only to spur into action each time Andersen barked an order in his direction. Alice blushed, tugging the collar of the young *fup*'s jacket up to her cheeks and peering over the greasy stitching.

They loaded the aircraft within an hour of it landing. As Andersen closed the door on the dogs and Hansen, the pilot did a visual check of the aircraft while Fenna waved at the policeman. He nodded for her to step to one side so they could talk.

"Your Inuit friend has been asking about you," he said. "I can't hold him much longer, unless you press charges."

"Okay."

"Do you want to press charges?"

"That depends. Can you give us time to get airborne?"

"*Aap*."

"And when's the next regular flight out of Qaanaaq?"

"Wednesday."

"Then I don't need to press charges."

"Good," Akisooq said. The first of the Twin Otter's engines fired, and he looked around Fenna's shoulder, as Andersen helped Alice climb onboard. "Your passports are in order," he said, "but I could keep you here for all kinds of reasons." Fenna waited for him to continue. "Do you understand?"

"Yes."

"The thing is," he said, as he rested his hands on his belt, "we have a mutual friend."

"Maratse," Fenna said.

"*Aap*. We studied together at the police academy in Nuuk, several years ago."

Fenna saw a spark light up the policeman's eyes, and she

wondered just how much hell they had raised in class, and on the weekends. Akisooq disclosed nothing, and Fenna was left with the hope that one day she might be able to ask Maratse, to tease him about his days as a cadet.

"He told me about what happened in Uummannaq, about Dina," Akisooq said. "Are you sure you want to go back there?"

"I don't have much choice. We need to finish this," she said, "for Dina, for Alice…" Fenna glanced at the Twin Otter as the pilot started the second engine. Andersen waved for her to hurry.

"But what about you? Will *finishing this* bring you peace?"

Fenna shrugged, "One way or the other."

"Then go," Akisooq said. He looked up at the sky. It was a brilliant blue, with just a few cirrus clouds and mare's tails, above the Twin Otter's preferred flying altitude. "If you leave now, you should pass Thule without any problems."

"Thank you," Fenna said, and shook the policeman's hand. She whispered in his ear before letting go, "Sorry about your living room."

"I didn't like the table anyway," he said. "Good luck, Konstabel."

"Thank you." Fenna turned toward the aircraft, but Akisooq caught her arm.

"I can probably have your Inuit friend deported."

"Thank you."

"You're welcome, but remember, whatever part he has to play in this – and, really, I don't want to know – it is personal now. You made it so when you cut up his face."

Fenna bit her lip. Andersen shouted from the aircraft. She looked at Akisooq one last time, turned, and jogged to the Twin Otter, grabbing Andersen's outstretched arm as she reached the cabin door. He pulled her inside, secured the door, and pointed at an empty seat next to the window. Fenna sat down and closed her eyes, picturing the ragged mess of skin Yuka now wore as a permanent reminder of her. *Great. Just one more man determined to get even*. The word *driven*, came to mind, and she regretted the fact everything always became personal. She almost laughed, for what was more personal than her own need for vengeance?

The pilot turned the Twin Otter in a tight circle, taxied on huge tundra wheels a short distance from the airport building, before accelerating down the gravel runway, pulling back on the stick, and guiding the small aircraft into the blue sky above Greenland's most northerly village. There was a smaller settlement fifty kilometres or so to the north and west, but Fenna had never been there. She took a last look at Herbert Island before closing her eyes once more, making herself comfortable, and succumbing to the stuffy, doggy interior of the cabin. Andersen said it would take a couple of hours to reach Upernavik, she would sleep until then.

Fenna didn't wake up until the pilot bumped the Twin Otter onto the asphalt runway on the island of Upernavik. She opened her eyes just as Andersen stirred in the seat opposite her. Fenna looked over her seat to see Alice curled onto Hansen's shoulder, and Burwardsley, doing his best to ignore them. He looked like he was the only one who hadn't slept. The pilot shut down the engines and clambered out of the cockpit. He shoved a dog to one side with his boot and stepped inside the cabin.

"We have an hour," he said, his Danish laced with Icelandic roots. He pointed at the aircraft building. It was quiet, with only a few ground personnel waiting to receive them. "There's coffee inside." He stepped over the dogs and opened the cabin door. "Make sure they piss," he said, and hopped out onto the apron.

"Pee break," Andersen said. "Everyone grab a dog."

The dog at Fenna's feet growled and she cuffed it on the nose. There was not enough space for a dogfight. *Finish it before it gets started*, she thought, smiling at the idea that it was a pretty good mantra, one she might consider adopting. Burwardsley grunted something about hating dogs, as he stumbled over a large male fidgeting in the tiny aisle between the seats. The cool air from outside had woken them up, and the cabin began to fill with whines and growls. Alice stirred as Andersen leaned over her to thump his partner awake.

"Wake up, Romeo," he said. Hansen stirred and Andersen squashed Alice as he tugged at the *fup*'s beard. "There's work to be done." He grinned at Alice as he backed into the aisle and arranged with Fenna which dogs should pee first.

Fenna walked two dogs on short leads to the flat area overlooking the sea. The top of the mountain on Upernavik island had been blasted flat to build the runway. The Danes living on Upernavik had dubbed the island the aircraft carrier. Seen from the air, it was easy to understand why. Fenna was less interested in the island, and far more occupied by the sight of pancake ice clustering around the island's rocky coastline. It did feel colder, and she had once seen snow in September. But she was still surprised. *Already?* Even if the ice began to form, the wind would determine its reach, and how quickly it would settle. Experienced hunters were known to sledge across newly formed ice barely a few centimetres thick, only to have to wait another week or month after a period of autumn winds broke up the ice, and grounded the dogs. The autumn and winter storms also tended to wreak havoc on the sea ice, but deeper in the fjords, even in this period of global warming, it was not unheard of for ice to form in more sheltered areas earlier than expected. *I wonder*, she thought.

"You're thinking of ice," Andersen said, as he approached. "I can tell."

"It's colder, isn't it? You can feel it."

"*Ja*, but it's probably just a freak cold spell. I wouldn't get your hopes up."

"Wasn't the winter of 2008 a good one? I thought they told us that in training."

"I remember it pissed a lot of journalists off," he said. "Something about wanting to record climate change in progress, but all the locals wanted to do was get out and hunt."

"Maybe this winter will be a good one."

"Planning to get out on the ice, Konstabel?"

Fenna didn't answer. She took a last look at ice crusting the rocks below her, and walked back to the aircraft. The pilot was already there, sipping coffee as he watched Alice help Hansen with the dogs. Fenna waited for Andersen to catch up, and they loaded the last dogs before climbing into the cabin. Burwardsley was already seated, slumped as he was with his chin on his chest. *His turn to sleep*, Fenna thought, as she buckled into her seat. Andersen closed the door as the pilot talked to the tower. They took off just five minutes later.

Fenna swapped places with Andersen so she could look at the snow-clad cirque glaciers of the Svartenhuk Peninsula to the north of Uummannaq fjord. The dark bands of exposed granite in stark contrast to the snow and ice leaped out at her, and Fenna pressed her nose to the glass. She heard Andersen laugh over the drone of the propellers. She turned and said, "What?"

"You," he said, "you're like a kid in a toy shop."

Fenna flicked him the finger and turned back to the window. There were muskoxen down there, one of the nine areas in Greenland where they could be hunted and harvested. She lifted her nose from the glass and warmed it with her hand. Then the Twin Otter began to descend and Fenna's stomach began to churn. Her fascination with the glaciers and the wildlife surviving in the harsh arctic environment below would have to wait; it was her own survival that was at stake now. She thought about the phone call she was about to make, and the actors and elements that call would set in motion, all the way into their approach to Qaarsut airport. Fenna barely felt the wheels bump down on the gravel runway. She almost didn't react when the pilot parked the aircraft and shut down the engines. It was Burwardsley's hand on her shoulder that startled her into action. She looked up and realised they were alone in the aircraft, the Sirius men and Alice were walking the dogs.

"You alright, love?" Burwardsley said.

"I think so."

"Okay," he said, but the frown on his brow suggested he wasn't sure. This was the fjord they had sailed into on *The Ice Star*, and just thirty kilometres from here was the cabin where Dina had killed herself. Burwardsley sat on the edge of the seat opposite Fenna and waited for her to speak.

Fenna began to nod, slowly, rhythmically, as she processed the next steps. "We'll need a boat to get into the fjord. I'm not waiting for a helicopter."

"I'll find us a boat."

"Maybe call in at Uummannaq first, get some supplies."

"I'll make a list."

"Right," Fenna said. She unbuckled her belt and clenched her fists on top of her knees. She looked at Burwardsley and said, "I'll find a phone. I'll make the call."

Fenna stood up and climbed out of the cabin. She ignored Andersen's shouts, and the concerned look on Alice's face. Fenna walked to the airport building, past the patches of early snow on the ground, opened the door, and looked for a phone. There was an old payphone on the wall, and she searched in her pockets for change. She looked at the five, ten, and twenty kroner coins in her palm, and figured she had enough for a few minutes. *Plenty of time to arrange my death.* Fenna picked up the phone, pressed the coins into the slot, and dialled the number she had written on a slip of paper tucked into her passport.

The line buzzed with static and the long rumble of cycling digits before a ringtone sounded in her ear. The voice that answered was distant, but no less destructive. Fenna's stomach cramped when he said, "Hello."

"It's me," she said, and waited.

"I see." Fenna heard movement in the background, as if the man she was talking to was moving to a more private location, or just making himself comfortable. "I've been expecting your call."

"Yes."

"Any problems?"

"No."

"And everyone is with you?"

"Yes," she said, and pressed more coins into the slot. The grip the man's voice had on her stomach tightened as each coin fell.

"You are in Greenland? I assume that is why you are calling."

"Yes."

"And you want to know who to contact?" he said and paused. "Do you have a pen, Konstabel?"

"No. Just tell me."

"Very well." More muffled noises, and a beep on the line, as if he muted her for a moment. When he spoke again, the man's voice was clearer, but there was another sound on the line. Fenna didn't think they were alone. "You need to get to the settlement of Nuugaatsiaq. It's the most northerly settlement in the fjord."

"I know that."

"Ask for the shaman. I honestly can't pronounce his name, so I won't try."

Fenna said nothing, aware only that someone was standing next to her, but too intent on the man at the other end of the line to look. *It's Burwardsley*, she told herself. *And he's probably found a boat already.* But there was one more pressing detail to have in place, and she wasn't going to hang up before she heard the man say it.

"Vestergaard?" she said, at last.

"Yes, Konstabel?"

"You'll be there, won't you?"

She waited for his answer. The cramps in her stomach were gone, just as Burwardsley, standing right behind her, was as good as gone. It was as if nobody else could exist in that moment, everything hinged on the answer, whether he was telling the truth, or just stringing her along, Vestergaard's answer would define her next move, perhaps even her last. She could taste it, the end, the moment when one or the other of them – perhaps even both at the same time – pulled the trigger, plunged the knife, wrapped bloody fingers around one another's throats. It didn't matter how, it just had to end, and she had to know that the end was coming. She had to hear it, taste it, believe it, and so, she waited.

The phone began to beep as the credit for the call expired. Fenna pressed the receiver closer to her ear, clapped her hand on her other ear, took a step closer to the payphone, and stared – she stared through the wall, picturing Vestergaard – standing, sitting, it didn't matter – she saw him take a breath, open his mouth, move his lips, and then she heard the words.

"Yes, Konstabel. I'll be there. You can count on it."

The line went dead, and Fenna started to tremble. Burwardsley put his hand on her shoulder. He tugged the phone gently from her hand, turned her body toward him, and gripped her shoulders in his hands.

"Fenna?"

She looked up. "He's coming," she said.

The Icefjord

UUMMANNAQ FJORD, GREENLAND

Chapter 21

NUUGAATSIAQ, UUMMANNAQ FJORD, GREENLAND

The fisherman driving the boat smoked a cigarette as they sailed toward the settlement of Nuugaatsiaq. They hugged the coastline, close enough to reach it in an emergency, but not so close they might be swamped with waves reflecting off the rocks from a calving iceberg. Burwardsley chatted with Alice, the driver stared straight ahead, and Fenna zipped her jacket all the way to the top of the stiff collar. She always seemed to be caught out by the cold at sea, as if her knowledge of cold weather clothing was limited to the land. *And yet the sea is an extension of the land when it freezes*, she thought. Further thoughts of sledging, the dogs that Noa and his partner had bought for Sirius, and the training runs along the east coast beaches, occupied her for another few minutes until the hull of the boat clunked against ice debris. Fenna peered over the side as the fisherman eased back on the throttle. It wasn't debris from an iceberg, she realised, but softer pancakes of ice clumping in sheets across the flat surface of the sea. Each pancake was clear in the centre, and white at the edges, as if the sugar frosting had been spread to the sides. Fenna caught the fisherman's eye and nodded at the ice.

"What do you think?" she asked in Danish. "Is winter coming early this year?"

"*Imaqa*," he said. "Maybe." He flicked the butt of his cigarette into the water and increased the throttle with a turn of his wrist. The bow of the boat lifted gently like a mini-icebreaker, pressing the hull down on the ice and ploughing a path to the settlement.

"What's up?" Burwardsley said.

"Nothing," Fenna said. "Just the ice. It's forming early."

"It's also colder than I remember this time of year."

"An anomaly."

"No, just cold." Burwardsley shifted on the bench seat stretched across the centre of the small vessel. He made room for Fenna to one side, Alice sat on the other. "Best I sit in the middle I think, love."

A glance at Alice revealed the young woman's delight at sailing between icebergs. She remembered the time she saw icebergs for the first time, and felt a pang of longing, wishing that this was her first time too, and that the circumstances were different.

"You said he was coming?" Burwardsley said.

"What? Oh, yes I did."

"And what do you intend to do when he arrives?"

"That all depends on when," Fenna said and studied the coastline. She could see the brightly-painted houses and buildings of Nuugaatsiaq in the distance, and the deep tongue of the fjord stretching toward the glaciers calving into the sea to the right of the settlement.

"When?"

"If the ice does form early, even just a thin layer, I'll lead him away from the settlement."

"Just like that?"

"Yes."

Burwardsley scoffed and shook his head. "And what happens if that doesn't work?"

"That's where you come in."

"Me?"

"I need you to plan our last stand."

"There?" Burwardsley said and pointed at the settlement as they approached it. "Christ, Fenna, we've got no weapons to speak of, and we can't exactly make a stand inside any of the buildings – they're all made of wood."

"We'll find weapons."

"Really? Where?"

Fenna looked around the boat, slapping Burwardsley's knee when she spotted a hunting rifle nestled between ropes and fishing lines in the bow of the boat. "That's a .30-06," she said. "I bet there's at least one rifle in every boat and another in every house on the island. There'll be ammunition in the store, maybe even a shotgun or two to buy."

"Vestergaard and his men will have automatic weapons. You want us to make a stand with a bunch of rusted saloon rifles and the odd high calibre rifle?"

"Yes," Fenna said and pointed toward the mountains on the island as the fisherman throttled down in anticipation of beaching the boat on the narrow strip of sand in front of the schoolhouse. The ice was thicker near the shore, slowing the boat, and forcing the fisherman to pick his route carefully, following the channel ploughed by the locals. Fenna pointed again and said, "There's plenty of high ground, and good cover if it comes to that. We can draw Vestergaard away from the village and pick him and his men off as they climb after us."

"And if they have a helicopter, Fenna? What then?"

She shrugged. "We'll think of something." Any further discussion was cut short as the boat bumped onto the beach and two Greenlanders walked down to the water to steady the boat as they climbed over the side and unloaded their gear. Fenna spotted an older Greenlander wearing a cornflower-blue smock and thick cotton trousers. He watched them from where he waited beside the schoolhouse. She risked a wave and was rewarded with a smile.

"Do you know him?" asked Alice as she took her holdall from the fisherman. She thanked the Greenlanders as they took it from her and carried it up the beach.

"No, but I have an idea that he has been waiting for us."

"He has been waiting a long time," said the taller of the two Greenlanders. He smiled at Alice as he introduced himself to her and Burwardsley. "My name is Inuuteq, and that man is my father, Tulugaq."

"Tulu…?" said Alice. The name caught upon her tongue and Inuuteq laughed.

"It means raven," he said. "My father is a shaman, if you believe in such things."

Fenna looked at Tulugaq, as his son continued chatting with Alice. She might have been impressed by his English language skills, had it not been for the fact that Inuuteq's father was the shaman, and suddenly everything was coming full-circle. "Right before the end," she whispered.

"…and this is Fenna," Burwardsley said, punching her on the arm, as he introduced her to Inuuteq. "Come on, love, be polite."

"What?" Fenna frowned as Inuuteq clasped her hand. He let go just as quickly, waving at his father and beckoning him onto the beach. Burwardsley paid the fisherman and helped him push the boat back into the water. Fenna did nothing, said nothing, just watched the shaman approach and waited for him to speak. When he did, it was in Greenlandic. She shook her head, and he switched to English.

"I am not so good as my son. Only enough to sell things to tourists," he said.

"What about Danish?"

"Better."

"Good," Fenna said, "because my Greenlandic is terrible."

Tulugaq smiled, and Fenna caught the twinkle in his eye as the late summer sun reflected on the ice crowding the bay. For a brief moment Fenna thought she saw something else reflected in the old man's eyes, *a sadness*, she thought, only for it to disappear as he led them up the beach, past the schoolhouse, and onto the path leading to the store. The shaman's house was opposite the store, looking out onto another beach on the north-western side of the island. A bony finger of rock stretching from the island into the sea provided a natural but low wall protecting the beach in front of the schoolhouse.

The shaman led them between fishing boats and broad sledges, and it wasn't long before they were surrounded by sledge dog puppies of all sizes. The smaller ones tumbled between the legs of those just a few weeks from being put on a chain. Alice bent down to tickle the pups and was bumped to the ground by three of the larger dogs. She laughed as she fell, protesting that she was okay as Inuuteq scared the pups away and helped her to her feet.

"We can't take her anywhere," Burwardsley whispered to Fenna.

"No," she said, as she caught the look in Inuuteq's eyes as he brushed the worst of the dirt from Alice's jacket. *We really can't*, she thought as the young man suddenly realised he was touching parts of the young American that he probably shouldn't. He pulled his hand away, hiding the colour in his cheeks with a few quick commands in Greenlandic aimed at the dogs. Alice forced more colour into the Greenlander's face with a smile, and he was lost. Fenna saved him with a few questions about the dogs. "They look well fed," she said.

"Yes," he said. "You won't find any skinny dogs on the island." He nodded at the ice lapping the beach in crusts of varying thickness. "We might get the first ice a few weeks from now, if the temperature continues to fall."

"What about the wind?"

"We're a bit more sheltered here," Inuuteq said, as he picked up Alice's holdall. "The ice forms deeper in the fjord, and it can stretch all the way here if the conditions are right."

"This early in the year?"

"It is September," he said. "If we are lucky, we might have ice in the fjord by October, and a thin layer surrounding the island."

"October," Fenna said. She looked at Burwardsley, and hoped

that Vestergaard would take his time to get here. *Maybe the shaman knows?* she thought, as they walked to the house.

Fenna was the last to enter. Tulugaq ushered them past the tupilaq on the shelves in the kitchen. Alice lingered beside one carved figure in particular, hiding an embarrassed laugh behind her hand as Inuuteq commented that the figure was a self-portrait. Fenna waited in the kitchen as the others sat down in the living room. She was alone with the shaman in the kitchen, as he poured water from the plastic container into a pan and put it on the stove to boil.

"We collect our water from the tank," he said, "but the house has electricity from the generator."

"One generator powers all the houses?"

"Easily, but," he said and shrugged, "sometimes it breaks down."

Fenna watched as he wiped the lips of dirty mugs with a tea towel. She heard Inuuteq and Burwardsley swapping stories about travelling in Greenland, together with a laugh or two from Alice, as the Greenlander said something funny or mispronounced a word. She corrected him, gently, and they laughed again.

"He studied in America," Tulugaq said. "An exchange."

"That must have been expensive," Fenna said.

The shaman wiped the last mug and nodded at the tupilaq on the shelves. "How many do you see?"

"Nine," Fenna said, after a quick count.

"There were forty more before the last cruise ship came."

"You nearly sold out?"

"*Aap*," he said. "And this year was the worst of the last three years."

"So, you paid for Inuuteq's exchange by selling carved figures?"

"With help from a government grant. What I have left, I send to my wife in Nuuk."

Tulugaq stopped talking as the water boiled. He made tea in one big pot, and pointed at the bowl of sugar cubes on the counter beside the mugs. Fenna carried them into the living room, and smiled as Inuuteq taught Alice how to take her sugar in tea in Greenland, pinching the cubes between finger and thumb, before dipping them in the tea and popping them in the mouth.

Fenna waited until they were all quiet before speaking in English. "You were expecting us, weren't you?"

"*Aap*," Tulugaq said. He looked at Inuuteq and the young man nodded.

"My father asked me to explain," he said. Inuuteq put down his tea and folded his hands in his lap. "First, he wants you to know that you are welcome in this house. All of you," he said, looking at each of them in turn. "But especially you, Konstabel Fenna Brongaard. My father was told you would be coming, and he has been looking forward to your arrival."

"The sea told me when you would arrive," Tulugaq said. "It tells me many things, so long as I keep her happy."

"*Sassuma Arnaanut*," said Inuuteq. "The mother of the sea."

"Sedna," said Alice, as she sipped her tea.

Inuuteq nodded, and continued. "My father also wants you to know that you are in grave danger, and that you are not safe here." He paused as Tulugaq stood up and walked to his desk by the window. Fenna watched as he pulled a figure from the drawer. He sat down, the figure half hidden between his fingers. Fenna stared at it, almost drawn to it, as Inuuteq spoke again. "There is a Danish man who wishes for you to be killed – all of you – and he has arranged for that to happen."

"It's alright," said Burwardsley. "We know. In fact, that's why we're here."

"Yes," Inuuteq said, "we know you know, but you cannot possibly beat this man. You cannot possibly survive. He has many resources, and once he knows you are here, he will come."

"We're counting on it," said Fenna.

"Yes, I know," Inuuteq said. Fenna caught the urgency in his voice and pulled away from the figure to look at him. "But you cannot win."

"The plan is not to win," she said, "but not everyone has to die." She shrugged. "Just him. Just Vestergaard."

"But how will you do this?" Inuuteq frowned. "I have seen this man. He has bodyguards with automatic weapons, and probably a whole army."

"Probably," said Burwardsley. "Is there more tea?"

"More tea?"

Fenna laughed, and said, "Don't mind him, he's British." She felt the pull of the figure in the shaman's hands and focused on it, as Inuuteq sighed and said something in Greenlandic.

"My son does not understand," said Tulugaq. He spoke in

English, the words slow, cumbersome, but clear. "He thinks you have come here looking for somewhere to hide."

"You know different," said Fenna.

"*Aap*," he said. "You came here to wait."

"Yes."

"You are waiting for him."

"And whoever he brings with him," said Burwardsley.

The shaman smiled. He looked at Alice and said, "My son knows where it is safe on the island. When the time comes he will take you there."

"Thank you," she said and looked at Fenna, "but I will stay with my friends."

"*Imaqa*," said Tulugaq. "Maybe. But I think it would be best to hide." He looked at Fenna, uncurling the fingers of his hands as he spoke. "And what about you? Will you hide?"

"No, I will fight."

"Then you will need this."

Tulugaq revealed the crude bone figure in his hands. Roughly ten centimetres tall, it was bound in the shape of a woman. The legs and arms were made of bone, held in place by lengths of grass stems and a single strand of orange plastic fishing line. The figure had small shells for breasts, a crude bone-carved face, and a brush of black hair tacked into its skull with two slim slivers of metal bent at right angles. Fenna didn't need the shaman to tell her – she knew the figure was carved in her likeness. There was only one thing that she couldn't explain.

"You are wondering if it is your hair," Tulugaq said.

"Yes."

"It is yours. The man you call Vestergaard gave it to me."

"What do you call him?"

"*The Magician*," Tulugaq said, and laughed. "But his magic is not as powerful as mine. It has no soul." He reached out to give Fenna the tupilaq.

"But yours does?"

"Yes," he said, pulling the figure back as Fenna reached for it, "if you believe in such things."

"I might," she said. Fenna wrinkled her nose at the smell of the figure. It was rank like rotten seaweed, with something deeper, an odour that was dark like the earth, like powdered brimstone mixed with old leaves. It smelled of ancient magic, unrefined, wild like the sea. *Wild like me*, she thought.

"This is a tupilaq. A real one. The Magician asked me to make one to use against you. I was to throw it in the sea, to turn *Sassuma Arnaanut* against you, but I could not. This man is evil, and I could not turn such a thing loose without meeting you. Without knowing you. This then is my gift to you. Part of you is bound to it, as is my magic, and if you take it, it will make you strong. Do you believe me?"

"Yes," Fenna said, amazed that she did.

"Then take it. You will need it."

Fenna took the figure from the shaman's hand, cursing under her breath as she tried to explain the tingling in her fingers. *Adrenaline*, she thought, *that's all it is*. But there was something deeper, something buried beneath the smell, and the touch of the tupilaq. It was as if some earthly magic from the roots of Greenland was twisted within the fibres and bones of the figure and was now seeping into her fingers. She looked up as Burwardsley clamped his hand on her shoulder.

"That's enough magic for one day, love." Burwardsley let go as Fenna stood up. She slipped the tupilaq into her pocket, and whispered thank you to the shaman.

"Okay," she said. "I'm ready."

"Good," said Burwardsley, "because now we've got to turn this village into a death trap."

Chapter 22

Fenna closed her hand around the tupilaq in her pocket. The grass, hair, and fishing line tickled her palm, as she stood on the beach and breathed in the scent of the ice-choked sea. Chunks of ice from calving icebergs bobbed in a broad swathe of white, arced like the path of a scimitar's swing, and grinding against the curve of rock breaching the water's surface. Fenna wondered what would happen if she was to toss the tupilaq into the sea. Would Sedna rise against her? Would the ice weaken beneath the runners of her sledge? She let go of the tupilaq and pushed the thought from her mind. *Sedna can wait*, she decided. *There are other things to take care of.* She took her hands out of her pockets, felt the tiny hairs on her skin begin to prickle in the cool wind, and nodded to Burwardsley that she was ready. He was waiting further along the beach, chatting with a hunter, admiring the rifle in the man's hands.

"Fenna," he said, as she approached, "this is Svend. I am going to buy his rifle."

"Hi," Fenna said, and smiled. The hunter raised his eyebrows. "How much?"

"We were just getting to that, but I don't speak Danish." Burwardsley leaned in close and whispered, "We can't buy all the rifles in the settlement, and I've already spent what cash we had left on the 12 gauges from the store. See if we can do a deal – we borrow the rifle, and he keeps the shotguns once we're done."

"Once we're done?"

Burwardsley shrugged and said, "Yeah, done. I didn't want to say dead."

"But you were thinking it…"

"Come on, love, just make the deal." Burwardsley took a step back and let Fenna finish negotiating. He leaned against an upturned boat and surveyed the row of houses along the shoreline. The wooden houses were barely two deep, with the majority clustered around the store near the shaman's house built on the thick finger of land pushing out into the fjord. Fenna completed the deal with the hunter, thanking him as he pressed the rifle into her hands together with a box of 7.62 ammunition.

"We're borrowing it," she said, and laid the rifle on the boat's hull. She gave Burwardsley the box of ammunition and pointed at the dogs chained just above the beach. "He has a team I can borrow too."

"And how much did that cost us?"

"The other shotgun."

"Fair enough," Burwardsley said and looked out at the fjord. "You really think the ice will come early?"

"I don't know, but the signs are here. There's a nip in the air, little wind. We might be lucky."

"Maybe."

Fenna waited for a moment before pulling Burwardsley away from the boat. "Come on. Let's go have a look at the dogs."

Burwardsley picked up the rifle and followed Fenna along the beach. They climbed up the embankment, picked their way around the lumps of shit between stumps of grass and approached the team of sledge dogs.

"I'll wait here," Burwardsley said, and sat on a weathered crate. The side of the crate had been removed and two fat puppies were snoring inside. They fidgeted as the crate creaked under Burwardsley's weight, rolled over, and ignored him. Fenna stepped inside the circle of the first pair of dogs, their chains running long and free from a metal swivel wedged into a hole bored in the rock.

"Down," Fenna said, cuffing them on the nose and pushing them down onto the ground as they jumped up to greet her. She grabbed one by the collar, lifted her leg over its back and clamped the dog's body between her knees. She inspected the dog's paws, teeth, pinched the skin on its flank to see how well hydrated it was, nodding as the skin flashed back into position. *This hunter looks after his dogs*, she thought. Fenna looked up and saw the hunter drinking coffee on the deck outside his house. He waved and she waved back before releasing the dog and checking its partner.

"Well?" Burwardsley said, after Fenna had checked the ten dogs chained outside the hunter's house. She ignored the puppies, brushing them away with soft sweeps of her foot.

"They're in good condition. A little thin, but that's to be expected after the summer."

"And the sledge?" Burwardsley said and nodded at three sledges stacked one on top of the other, the largest at the bottom.

"The one in the middle looks lightest," Fenna said, as she walked over to them. "Metal runners, tight bindings," she said and plucked at the cord securing the thwarts. "It'll be fine." She straightened her back at the sound of footsteps on the packed earth that served as a footpath. The shaman smiled as he walked toward her, a clutch of children bobbing around his legs. The children descended on Fenna like a wave crashing onto a beach, and she was reminded of the kids in Qaanaaq, when she and Alice had tumbled with them outside the policeman's house, just before she had fought with Yuka. She paused as the image of his face, the stitches holding the flaps of skin together on his cheeks, flashed before her, only to be erased as the children tugged at her clothes and tried to drag her away from the sledges.

The shaman said a few quiet words in Greenlandic and the children let go of Fenna. They drifted away to play with the puppies, pointing and laughing at Burwardsley, as they stood on tiptoes and spread their arms to mimic his height and reach. Fenna laughed with them and the shaman took a step closer.

"You don't have children?" he said.

"No. Not yet."

"But maybe one day?"

Fenna bit her bottom lip as Burwardsley rose up from his seat on top of the crate, spread his arms and growled, chasing the children around the dog yard. They shrieked and giggled as he stumbled around the rocks, stepping over the chains, as the dogs joined in. She realised she had never seen him around children.

"I don't know," Fenna said. "I haven't had time to think about a family."

"One day, then," the shaman said. He gestured for Fenna to join him, and they walked along the path away from the chaos of kids, puppies, and one Royal Marine Lieutenant clearly out of his depth. "He will be alright," he said. "I have something to show you."

The children's cries and giggles carried on the cool wind from the fjord, pressing at Fenna's back as she followed the shaman out of the settlement. They moved on beyond the makeshift landing pad and the digger used to carry luggage and mail from the helicopter to the store. Then they climbed up a narrow path on the side of the mountain. The path wound its way up and onto a plateau beneath the steep sides of the mountain. The shaman stopped beside a cairn overlooking the settlement behind them, and the icebergs crowding the glacier just beyond the very tip of the island. Fenna held her breath at the sight of so much debris and the blue-white walls of the glacier, but it wasn't the ice the shaman wanted her to see. He took her arm and led her around the cairn to a slab of rock, Fenna could see there was a cavity beneath it.

"Take a look," the shaman said, gesturing for Fenna to crouch on the rock and peer through the crack in the surface.

Fenna kneeled on the slab and pressed her face to the crack. She saw bones resting on the earth inside, and at least one skull, maybe two. She shifted to one side to confirm that this was the resting place for more than one person.

"Our ancestors chose this place for the hunting."

"Not the view?" Fenna said and stood up.

"*Imaqa*," the shaman said and shrugged. "I don't know, but can you think of a better place to be buried?"

"No." Fenna looked at the glacier, breathed the chill of the ice deep into her lungs.

"I will die here," he said. "That is my choice. But, Konstabel, I think you should choose a different place to die."

Fenna looked at the shaman and said, "I will draw Vestergaard away from here. I won't let anything happen to the people of Nuugaatsiaq."

"That is not what I mean. The people are my responsibility," he said and pointed back to the settlement. "Do you see the red house, standing by itself, away from the village?"

"Yes."

"That is also my house. It is old, but strong. When the time comes, we will gather there."

"Okay."

"And your friend, the young woman…"

"Alice."

"*Aap*. She will come with us." The shaman laughed. "I think my son is falling in love with your friend."

Fenna smiled as she remembered the way Inuuteq had looked at Alice when they first arrived, when he had carried her bag. "Yes," she said.

"Then she will be safe. He will make sure of that."

"Thank you."

"But your other friend, the big soldier.

"Yes?"

"I think he should come here, to this place. It has a good view of the village, and it is protected from behind by the mountain. It is a good place from which to fight."

"Yes, it is," said Fenna, and she turned a slow circle to fully appreciate the shaman's eye for a good, defendable position.

"It is also a good place to die," he said. The shaman turned and walked along the path in the direction of the glacier.

"What?" Fenna said and followed him. "Do you think he will die?"

"It is not his death you should worry about, but your own." He stopped at another rise in the path, and drew an arc with his arm from one side of the glacier to the other. "You can see that the ice is forming here. The glacier has slowed for the winter, and soon it will stop. Winter has come early this year, and it will be to your advantage."

Fenna followed the shaman's direction and noticed the thicker ice trapping the smaller icebergs in front of the glacier. The larger bergs were still in motion, moving in and out of the bay on the tide. But even they were slowing as the sea thickened around them. *The early winter might be an anomaly*, she thought, *but I'll take every advantage I can get.* Fenna traced an imaginary route to the glacier wall, picturing the journey she would make with Svend's dog team. The shaman nodded, as if reading her thoughts.

"Svend's dogs are good," he said. "They are used to pulling on thin ice. Svend is the first on the ice every winter, and the last to leave."

"But the fjord is not frozen yet," Fenna said.

"You have time. I have consulted with the mother of the sea. I have read the signs. You have time."

"How much?"

"Enough," he said. The shaman began walking back to the village. Fenna took one last look at the glacier and turned to follow him.

Burwardsley was sitting beside the cairn when they reached it. The rifle was in his lap. He wiped the scope with the corner of his shirt and nodded as they approached.

"It's a good spot," he said. "Good visibility."

"*Aap*," the shaman said. He waved at Fenna as he passed the cairn, and she let him go on to the settlement alone, choosing instead to sit beside Burwardsley.

"It's a nice view too," she said. "You've seen the glacier?"

"Hard to miss it."

"There's bones beneath the cairn," Fenna said.

"Human?"

"Yes."

Burwardsley nodded. "Yep," he said, and looked around. "There are worse places to make a last stand."

"You really think this is it?"

"Don't you? I thought that was the plan?"

"Sure, I mean..." Fenna paused. "Yes, it is the plan. Draw him here. Finish this."

"But now?"

"Now..."

Burwardsley lifted the rifle from his lap and rested it against the cairn. He took a breath. "We've been through a lot in a short space of time, Konstabel. If this is the end, then let's accept it and just get on with it. God knows, the journey here wasn't pretty. But this..." he said and looked out at the fjord, "...this is as beautiful as it gets. It's peaceful, and maybe we'll find peace here."

"You think so?"

"Why not?" he said and smirked, "Alice certainly has."

"What do you mean?"

"She's out in the bay with the shaman's son. He's showing her the sights."

"She is?"

"Yep," he said. "Although, I'm confused. I thought she had the hots for that young Sirius fella, but what do I know..."

What do *we know?"* Fenna wondered. She remembered the shaman's words, *she will be safe*, and she sank onto the rock, letting her body sag against Burwardsley's. *We've done it*, she thought. *She's safe.*

"Mike," she said. "Does this even things out?"

"What do you mean?"

"Alice. If we save her, does that make up for Dina? Is it enough?"

Fenna trembled as Burwardsley took a deep breath and sighed. He was quiet for a long time, and Fenna didn't prompt him, focusing instead on the wind that tugged at the strands of her hair. Finally, he spoke, and Fenna closed her eyes, listening to his words as the deep bass of the syllables flooded through his body and into hers.

"It will never be enough, love, but it's a step in the right direction."

"But we tried, didn't we?"

"To save Dina?"

"Yes."

"You did," Burwardsley said. His voice drifted on the wind and he was silent for another moment. Then he said, "Bad would have liked it here. The little runt would have been up and down the mountain already."

Fenna felt her muscles tighten at the sound of the Gurkha's name, but she resisted, and willed herself to relax, enjoying instead the sight of the glacier, and the cool wind that filtered her thoughts.

"I am sorry he died," she said.

"You don't have to be," Burwardsley said. "He killed your partner after all."

"I know."

"Just as long as you don't blame him," I think he will be alright with that."

"And what about you?" Fenna said. She moved her body, turning to look at Burwardsley. She reached out for his hand, slipped her fingers within his, felt his rough skin brush against her own. "What about us?"

"I don't know, love. If I had done my job right, you'd be dead."

"Yes. I know that. But what about now?"

Burwardsley took a breath and smirked. "Let's take it one step at a time, eh? If we get off this rock – alive – then I'll be happy to say I've done my bit, and if you want to say that we're quits, I won't argue. But that's another day, Konstabel," he said and stood up, tugging his hand free of Fenna's fingers. "I want to walk to the end of the island. If you really intend to sledge to the glacier to finish this, well, maybe I can cover you, at least before you get too far from the shore."

"That all depends on the ice, but yes, let's do that."

"Of course," Burwardsley said, as he picked up the rifle. "Vestergaard might never come, and we'll be stuck on this island, just waiting."

"There are worse places to wait," Fenna said. "You said as much."

"I did. But that was before I realised the Internet was lousy, there's only one channel on the TV, and all the women are taken."

"The women?"

"No offence, Konstabel, but no matter how good you clean up…" Burwardsley grinned as Fenna clenched a fist to throw a punch, "and even if you were the last woman on the island…"

"Yes?" Fenna said, a smile playing across her lips as she positioned her feet and bent her knees, slightly – a fighting stance.

"You still smell of dog."

Fenna relaxed, smoothed her hands along the sides of her trousers and laughed. She followed Burwardsley, as they walked along the path parallel to the shoreline, identifying good defensible positions and rally points. They joked, but it was all business, *the killing business*, Fenna thought, as they passed one more boulder on a rise in the path. She glanced down at the ice brushing against the rocks below them, stopping to study a figure in a small boat. Burwardsley walked on, increasing the distance between them as Fenna studied the man in the boat, recognised the familiar cornflower-blue smock, and wondered at the shaman's actions as he beat a slow rhythm on a sealskin drum. She was surprised that she could hear the beat, and then realised that she couldn't just hear it – she could feel it. Fenna slipped her hand inside her pocket and curled her fingers around the tupilaq. She felt a surge of energy through her body and shook her head to clear her mind.

"Get it together, Fenna," she whispered.

The drum continued to beat through the hull of the boat, through the water, into the earth and up the sides of the mountain. She could feel it in her toes, thudding through her soul. She glanced at Burwardsley as he called out her name, hurrying her along the path. Fenna waved that she was coming, let go of the tupilaq, and jogged along the path to join him. The beat continued until it was lost beneath the pounding of her boots on the packed earth. Lost, but not forgotten.

Chapter 23

It was the children who saw the ship first, five weeks and one centimetre of sea ice later. The autumn storms had been mild, and the warm winds skirted the island with what Fenna imagined to be a supernatural reverence, almost as if the island was marked and somewhere to be avoided.

Life on the small Arctic island, so Fenna had come to appreciate, was a healthy mix of claustrophobia and cosiness. There were birthdays to attend, celebrated in the traditional Greenlandic *kaffemik,* where a steady stream of guests visits the house of the birthday girl or boy, man or woman, giving small presents and sitting at the savoury table of traditional Greenlandic food. Then it is time for the cake table, drinking strong black coffee before slumping on the couch with chocolates and spirits. Reluctant to let them leave, the children were quick to drag Alice and Fenna from the sofa and back to the cakes. Burwardsley was too heavy and too big to pull off the sofa, but they tried anyway, and it was during one last concerted and combined effort that the ship was spotted by one small girl, Nuka, as she skipped along the path to the *kaffemik*. Fenna caught the change of mood among the guests as she announced the arrival of the ship in Greenlandic, and one of the men left to fetch Tulugaq. Fenna pulled Alice to one side, away from the cake table.

"This is it then," she said, "you remember what we talked about."

"Yeah, but I don't agree. This is as much my fight as yours."

"Alice, stop," Fenna said. "You'll go with Tulugaq and Inuuteq. You will stay in the house with the children, keep them safe, just as we agreed."

"But it's me he wants. I'm the reason he's coming here." Alice began to tremble. She looked at Burwardsley as he joined them.

"Listen to Fenna," he said. "We'll take care of the rest."

"No…" Alice started, but Burwardsley silenced her with a look.

"Christ, she thinks this is a democracy," he said and looked at Fenna. "Deal with this. I'm going to have a look outside." He brushed past the children, stepping to one side as Inuuteq clomped up the weather-beaten stairs and onto the deck before entering the house. The young Greenlander kicked the snow from his shoes and walked inside, nodding at Burwardsley as he searched for Alice.

"We have to go," he said, as he skirted around the table to take Alice's hand. She pulled back, resisting, squirming her stockinged feet onto the floor into a firmer stance, only to succumb to Fenna's hug as she wrapped her arms around her and whispered in her ear.

"Go," she said. "Do this for me. Live a long, beautiful life, raise six kids, love them so hard they melt. Do that for me. Go."

"I can't."

"Yes," Fenna said, as she smoothed her hands down Alice's arms and stepped back, "you can." She nodded at Inuuteq. "She's ready. Look after her."

"Yes," he said, and took Alice's hand.

Fenna waited until the room was empty, and the *kaffemik* was officially over. She picked her way around the chairs, grabbed her jacket, stuffed her feet inside her boots, and left the house. She found Burwardsley on the rocks above the surface of the sea ice at the far end of the settlement, past the store, beside the oil tanks. The snow crunched beneath her feet as she stepped off the worn path that led to the store entrance, and followed Burwardsley's tracks to the ice. The hunter's rifle was slung across his chest, and he was looking through a cheap pair of binoculars he had bought in the store.

Fenna took a breath of crisp air, used it to slow the adrenaline racing through her body, and looked toward the horizon. There was the ship. Red-hulled, a prominent bow, curved for the ice. The stack was white, and it could have been just another ship of the Royal Arctic Line servicing the towns, villages and settlements of Greenland. It could even have been a Canadian or American Coast Guard vessel, but Fenna knew it wasn't. She knew it was him.

She watched as the ship sailed closer. She could almost hear the soft crumpling of thin ice as it nosed its way forward, effortlessly. The ship could easily sail all the way to the island, she realised, even as far as the glacier if it wanted to. *But it won't, it's too dangerous.* Fenna looked over her shoulder at the glacier in the distance, beyond the island. She turned back to the ship at a grunt from Burwardsley.

"What is it?" she asked.

"They are stopping."

"Let me see," she said. Burwardsley handed her the binoculars and she looked through them, adjusting the focus with her fingers, aware of the cold pinching her skin.

The binoculars revealed the detail of the ship, the helicopter landing pad at the stern, but no hangar, and no sign or sound of the aircraft itself. There was activity at the rails, and, as the ship turned to starboard, the port side was exposed, and Fenna saw the crew lower a staircase and organise a small floating dock that they pushed onto the surface of the ice.

"Talk to me," said Burwardsley. Fenna heard the scratch of cotton as he stuffed his hands inside the white smock he wore on top of his thermal and fleece layers.

"The ship has stopped. The crew are getting ready to put something on the ice," she said. "Either they are concerned about getting too close to the glacier or…"

"It's a blocking action. They are sealing off the fjord."

"But then how are they going to get…" Fenna paused. She adjusted the binoculars, tried to hold her breath to stop the mist obscuring her view. "Dogs," she said. "They are putting teams onto the ice."

"Teams? How many?"

"Three sledges so far. Sleds, actually, the toboggan kind." She handed the binoculars to Burwardsley. "They are running Nome traces behind narrow sleds."

"That's great, love. Now what does it mean?" Burwardsley looked through the binoculars.

"Nome traces means they are running the dogs side by side, Alaskan style. They also have Alaskan Huskies, by the looks of it."

"Which means?"

"Mixed breed, bred for speed."

"So, fast dogs?"

"Yes, and banned in Greenland. The Greenlandic Sledge Dog is pure bred, the closest thing to a wolf. No other dogs are allowed above the Arctic Circle or on the East Coast. This is against the law…"

"Fenna."

"Yes?"

"Focus," said Burwardsley. "Tell me what it means."

"It means they will run fast and smooth all the way to the island."

"And the good news?"

"If the ice breaks they are screwed." Fenna remembered the time Mikael had plucked her from the sea when their team, running Nome traces, had broken through a patch of thin ice. "Sirius runs with Nome traces on land, switching to fan traces on the sea ice, mostly, unless the ice is really good."

"But this ice is new and thin."

"Which means they are sacrificing safety for speed."

"I like that," Burwardsley said and lowered the binoculars. "Get your dogs ready, Konstabel. I am going to grab my gear and find a position to start picking off the leaders. Give them something to think about." He offered Fenna the binoculars. "One last look?"

"No," she said.

"Take them anyway. I have the rifle scope."

"Alright." Fenna slipped the strap around her neck and stuffed the binoculars inside her jacket. She pulled the zip to the top of the collar and looked at Burwardsley. She could feel her eyelashes crisping in the cold and chose to focus on that rather than her emotions. *Is this the last time we will see each other*, she wondered.

"Stop thinking so hard, love," Burwardsley said. He smirked and reached out to touch her hair, pinching the rime ice frosting the very ends of the strands framing her cheeks. "There was a time," he said as he let his hand fall, "when all I could think of was putting a bullet in your brain, Konstabel."

"Thanks," she said, choking on a laugh.

"It was completely professional, you understand? I was given one job, by that man." Burwardsley hiked his thumb over his shoulder in the direction of the ship. "Perhaps the instruction was from someone else, but he was the one who spelled it out. We know that. But you were so fucking stubborn. You just wouldn't die."

"You say that like it was a bad thing." Fenna smiled, but her lips flattened as she saw the look on Burwardsley's face.

"Be stubborn, Konstabel," he said. Burwardsley nodded once, tugged at the rifle sling across his chest and walked past Fenna toward the shaman's house.

"Mike," she called out, but he didn't stop. She watched him all the way to the steps of the house opposite the store, and then she turned to look at the ship. There were three black stripes on the ice, three teams, all of them moving, and moving fast.

Fenna turned and ran to the hunter's house, his dogs were howling, fidgeting, biting, raring to go, as he gripped each one between his knees and slipped a harness over its head. He bent the dogs' front legs at the elbow and slipped them through the harness. Once they were in harness he attached them to their traces, and made them ready for Fenna to attach the fan of dogs to the sledge. Fenna thanked him as she raced past the dogs and stopped at the sledge bag hanging between the uprights at the rear. She opened the envelope flap and pulled out her sledging gear, stripping on the snow behind the sledge as the hunter continued preparing the team. The dogs whined with enthusiasm, yipped and half-barked. Fenna could have been alone for all the attention anyone gave her as she peeled off her layers down to her bra, building the layers up again with a thermal top, leggings, fleece, and military trousers. She checked the contents of the cargo pockets, tightened the belt around her waist, tested the snap securing the knife in its sheath, pulled on her socks, and tightened the laces of her boots. Fenna left her jacket on the ground, favouring instead the waist-length padded canvas jacket she had seen a young mother wearing in town. She had bartered for it, and now enjoyed the snug fit around her waist and the thick ruff of dog fur the woman had sewn onto the hood. She hung the sealskins mitts – a gift from the same woman – on a length of cord around her neck, checking the rifle in its canvas holster with bare fingers. She pulled the rifle out, worked the bolt, checked the magazine, and slid it home again. The holster was secured to the right-hand upright, reminding Fenna, as it always did, of a cowboy's rifle wedged beneath the straps of his saddle. *Or hers*, she thought. *Women can fight too, and this one has too.* She fished a fleece neckie from her cargo pocket, pulled it over her head, and tugged a thin beanie over her hair. Fenna took a long breath and then brushed her fringe beneath the rim of the beanie. *I'm ready.*

Inuuteq appeared on the path, sliding along the packed snow in sealskin *kammiks*. He said something fast in Greenlandic to the hunter, and then turned to Fenna. "Burwardsley said to hurry. They are almost within range of the rifle."

"Right," Fenna said and nodded to the hunter. She was just about to release the rope anchoring the sledge to a thick hawser wrapped around a boulder, when she remembered the tupilaq. She reached down and pulled it out of the jacket laying on top of her discarded clothes. Fenna studied the tupilaq for a moment before zipping it inside one of the cavernous pockets on the front of her jacket.

"Fenna, you must go," Inuuteq said, as he helped the hunter attach the dogs to the sledge.

They all paused at the sound of the first gunshot, rallying on the second, and tugging the dogs and sledge down to the ice on the third. Fenna hoped Burwardsley was thinning the field, as the hunter dragged the lead sledge dog up and over the ice foot where the land met the sea. Inuuteq helped Fenna bump the sledge over the same icy obstacle as the dogs gathered on the ice.

"Go back to the house," Fenna said to Inuuteq. "Svend will help me with the dogs. You must look after Alice."

"What about you?"

"It's me he wants. Burwardsley and me. When the men come, they will ignore everyone else. But just make sure you keep Alice hidden. If she can't be seen, she will be safe."

"There is a space beneath the floorboards."

"Good. Use it. I will draw them away from the settlement."

Another gunshot rattled the dogs into a frenzy of excitement. Fenna pushed Inuuteq in the direction of the house, insisting that she would be fine. Then she turned her attention to the hunter as he explained for what seemed to Fenna like the hundredth time, that the ice was still too thin to stand still just beyond the island, thickening only once they got close to the glacier. Fenna knew he had tested it each day since the ice had begun to settle. She had watched him go out to set his longline from a hole dug in the ice, checking each day to brush the newly formed ice up and over the wood he had placed on each of the four sides.

"Follow my tracks," he said. "Once you are past the longline, the ice will be thicker. But beware of the icebergs, they are not settled yet."

Not settled. Fenna thought about it, remembering the bergs that were locked in the ice on the east coast, new bergs and new positions each winter. Until the temperature really dropped, there was still plenty of movement to cause an iceberg to roll, presenting Fenna with a hazardous opportunity. *If all else fails, I'll draw them close to the bergs and…*

The thought vanished at the sight of the first of the three dog teams as it slid around the corner of the island. The team had been thinned, and Fenna could see where dead dogs had been cut from their traces. Burwardsley had been busy, but he had not stopped them. She risked a glance toward the mountain, and saw the big Marine Lieutenant pounding up the path, a rifle in each hand. He would be running for the cairn, where they had cached supplies and ammunition in anticipation of Vestergaard's arrival. *And now he is here*, she thought, as she took one last look at Burwardsley.

"*Tuavi*," Svend shouted. "Hurry." He tugged at the dogs, leading them out onto the thin ice. Fenna followed, slipping the soles of her boots along the icy surface, avoiding pressing her toes downwards, keeping her feet flat, balanced, spreading her weight.

The first crack of automatic weapons fire spurred her and the team into action. She heard a cry, felt the slap of the hunter's hand on her back as she shushed past him, and then she was on the ice, leaping onto the sledge and reaching for the whip, as the dogs dug their claws into the pitted surface and followed the familiar lines left by the runners of the hunter's sledge.

The shushing sound changed to a harder, more brittle grating, as the metal runners slid along ice, clean of snow, black, almost transparent. Fenna kept her head down at the crack of gunfire. She checked that Vestergaard's sled teams were following her, and felt the familiar extra thump of her heart at the sight of her quarry. He was there, in the lead sled, riding in the bucket as two of his men skied by the side, one hand on the curved handle attached to the uprights, the other curled around the grip of a Heckler Koch MP5 submachine gun. The echo of each burst of 9mm urged Fenna's dogs to claw at the ice, fantailing the sledge and forcing Fenna to make corrections with the heels of her boots and the wooden butt of the whip. She whooped and encouraged the dogs with clicks and whistles, as the hunter did, ducking every so often at another burst of lead above her head.

"Come on, boys," Fenna yelled. "Let's go."

Fenna's team was fresh, they were following a familiar route, and the sledge was broad and light. She felt the cold pinch her cheeks and allowed herself a smile. The plan was working.

Chapter 24

Burwardsley could see Fenna from his position in front of the cairn. He watched her bump and steer the sledge onto the track leading to the hunter's fishing hole in the ice. There was one team following Fenna, and he was sure he had glimpsed Vestergaard sitting in the basket seat of the sled. That left two teams for him, the first of which he could see through the rifle scope as they left their dogs at the beach and spread out between the houses. Two teams of dogs, six men, all of whom carried MP5 submachine guns. Burwardsley recognised the sound and calibre of the weapon, the same he had trained with so many years earlier.

It's a good weapon for short range, he thought, as he wormed his body into the snow and tracked the first of the men. The trick to taking on six men armed with submachine guns with only a hunting rifle, Burwardsley realised, was to lull them into a group, to bring them closer before taking out the man at the rear. Burwardsley waited, letting the lead man climb the slope, and focusing on the third and fourth man in the group. He lifted his hand from the grip of the rifle to check the position of the shotgun. He would take the first man out with a scatter of pellets, then pick off the last of the group with the rifle. He spared another second to picture the location of the second shotgun further along the track in what he had dubbed his *last stand position.*

"If I make it that far," he whispered.

He heard the lead man slip on the slope just below him, switched the rifle for the shotgun, kneeled and fired as soon as the man's torso was in plain view.

The blast of the 12-gauge shotgun caught the man squarely in the chest, pitching him backwards over the lip of the rise. Burwardsley lunged forward to grab the sling of the man's MP5, only to miss. He was rewarded with a burst of fire over his shoulder, a single bullet of which singed his neck as it sped past him. He swore as he squirmed back into his firing position, tugged the butt of the rifle into his shoulder and searched for a target further down the slope. He saw the last of the group exposed on the open ground between the houses and the start of the incline. He tracked the man through the scope, as he dashed for cover behind the digger that was gathering snow by the side of the landing pad. Burwardsley's first bullet caught the man in the back of the thigh, his blood spraying the side of the digger, then Burwardsley jacked another round into the rifle and shot the man through the spine.

"Two," Burwardsley said, as he chambered another round in the rifle.

He sensed movement to his left, pictured the terrain he had explored to that side of the slope, and remembered how steep it was. Burwardsley crouched in the snow, slung the rifle around his chest and grabbed the shotgun. He pumped a shell into the chamber and moved closer to the slope, firing when he saw the top of the man's head. The man ducked and Burwardsley fired again. He missed, but the man lost his footing and started to slide down the slope. Burwardsley fired a third time and helped the man on his way, the impact of the shotgun blast propelling the man down the side of the mountain. Burwardsley pumped another shell into the chamber and moved backward in a crouch toward the path.

He knew the path well, having studied the terrain over the previous month, in all kinds of weather. He knew where to run, where to slide, where to jump, and made good progress. But the men following him were younger, faster, and likely had fewer wounds than he did. Burwardsley could feel the recent gunshot wounds protesting as he moved, he grunted and tried to ignore them. It was his shoulder that bothered him the most, and each time he pulled the butt of the rifle or the shotgun into his body, the recoil reminded him of when he had last been in combat, when he had last been hit. Even if his memory had failed him, he didn't have to wait long for the familiar burning pain that tore through his upper body as a three-bullet burst bit into the ground and a single bullet ricocheted off a lichen-crusted boulder and into his ribs.

"Fuck." Burwardsley stumbled, and a second burst of lead tore through the snow behind him into his right leg. He stumbled, rolled onto his back and fired the shotgun back up the path, catching the first man to run into his line of fire. The man cartwheeled into the snow in front of Burwardsley, bleeding profusely but alive. His MP5 was within Burwardsley's reach, and the Royal Marine Lieutenant considered grabbing it, only to hear an inner voice chide him that cover was better, and that he should get going. He rolled onto his knees, used the shotgun to lever himself up onto his feet, ignored the pain, and ran.

Burwardsley focused on the trail to quash the pain in his ribs and leg. He picked out his visual markers, and realised he was just a few hundred metres from a more defendable position. He was close to the end of the island, and had even chosen a spot that meant he could cover Fenna from the land if she needed help. But a few hundred metres was a long way for a wounded man. He pushed on, aware of the scrape of the men's boots over the lichen and rocks behind him, and the softer tread of their soles through the deeper patches of snow.

The wind blew spindrift into Burwardsley's face, and he spared a kind thought for the sudden cloud of snow and stars of ice masking his descent toward the tip of the island.

The only thing I don't understand, he thought as he ran, *is why they pushed so hard so fast. Why didn't they take their time? Why didn't they try to flank me?* The question occupied him for another hundred metres, and he even picked up the pace, only to slow as he realised the answer. *They don't have the time. This has to be done fast.*

The opposite side of the island and position of Vestergaard's ship in the fjord was obscured from view by the mountain. Burwardsley didn't have the vantage point he needed to second-guess why his pursuers had abandoned caution in favour of speed. But, he had to admit, speed was something they did have, and they were gaining on him. Two three-round bursts convinced him to stop thinking and start running. He pounded down the path only to stumble over a boulder. For the first time since they had sledded into the settlement, the men slowed, choosing two firing positions from which to torment the Royal Marine with a bullet from each position into his thighs.

"You bastards," he yelled. Burwardsley bit back a cry of pain and looked ahead. The position he had chosen for his last stand was only fifteen metres further on, through the snow, down the slope. "But I won't make it," he said, his words jarring through gritted teeth. The path was still high enough that there was a steep slope to his right, running all the way to the ice below. Burwardsley heard the soft click of metal as the men changed magazines, and that's when he pressed the barrel of the shotgun flat against his chest and pushed off over the edge of the path.

Burwardsley laughed as he heard the men swear, but the first boulder he hit with his ribs forced him to concentrate on rolling, or falling as it appeared to the men above him. They tried a few single shots, anticipating where he might be before he rolled into their line of fire, but the slope was uneven, and two sudden drops saved Burwardsley from more bullets in his body, only to knock the wind from his lungs as he slammed onto the rocks below. Snow plumed and geysered around his body as he fell, until the slope smoothed and he rolled and slid the last twenty metres to the ice foot that braked his fall.

The snow settled around him. Burwardsley took a moment, and then spat snow from his mouth. He rolled onto his back, ignoring the pain from the bullets and the fall. He watched as the two men picked their way down the slope, slipping around the larger boulders and stumbling over the smaller ones. When one of the men slipped and pitched forward, Burwardsley pushed himself up, levelled the shotgun and fired.

The hammer clicked but the weapon did not fire. He tossed it away and groaned onto his feet as the man regained his footing and ran down the last few metres of the slope. He crashed into Burwardsley and they fell backward over the ice foot and onto the slippery surface of the sea ice. Burwardsley's opponent was first onto his feet. He moved backward a step, reaching for his weapon, only to tug at an empty sling.

"That's just too bad," Burwardsley said as he pressed one foot down onto the ice, and kneeled. The man kicked at him, and Burwardsley caught his foot and pulled him off balance. The combined weight of the two men and the sudden impact splintered the ice. The current streaming through the water was strongest at low tide, it degraded the ice from beneath, thinning it. The man was masked, like his teammates, but his eyes were visible. They no longer focused on Burwardsley, but on the black water beneath them. Burwardsley looked at the man, lifted his elbow, and slammed it into the ice.

"No," the man shouted, as he struggled to pull free of Burwardsley's grasp. Burwardsley slammed his elbow again, and again, until it splashed through the ice and the frigid water of the fjord swelled onto the thin frozen surface. "What are you doing?" the man cried.

"Killing you," Burwardsley said, and rolled the man onto his back, pushing down on his chest until the water was rising around the man's neck. Burwardsley ignored the man's kicks and cries. He ignored the cold water turning his fingers and hands to wooden implements, unable to bend or feel, only push. "What's the rush? Who's coming?"

The man said nothing. He tried to kick, but Burwardsley's weight was too great. The water rose to the man's cheeks and he yelled at Burwardsley to let him go, but he kept pushing, until the man's forehead was below the surface. Burwardsley could feel his knees beginning to cool as the ice bowed beneath the weight of the two men. He pushed once more and the man's head disappeared beneath the water. Burwardsley held him there as the last of his breath bubbled through the fibres of his ski mask.

"I asked you a question. Answer me." Burwardsley started to pull the man out of the water, to lift his head, but he had forgotten the man's partner, at least until he felt the butt of the MP5 crack on his head. He slumped down onto the man beneath him, trying to focus on the icebergs in the distance, where he imagined he might see Fenna, just one more time, as she sledged toward the glacier wall. He forgot all about the man beneath him, thinking only of how much his head hurt, and how much more it hurt as he received another blow. Burwardsley's head slumped into the sea, he tasted the salt on his lips, felt its cool kiss on his cheeks, and in the blackness beneath him, he saw a young Greenlandic woman, her hair so black, so long, it twisted around her naked body, beckoning him to join her.

"Dina," Burwardsley said, the seawater bubbling from his mouth and onto the man's chest. "It's you."

"*Iiji*," she said, in her native Greenlandic tongue.

"You can speak."

"Yes." Dina smiled, beckoning once more. "Come."

"I will," he said. "I'll be right there, only, just give me a minute." Burwardsley spluttered as the last of the team sent to kill him pressed his foot onto his back. "I just need a minute." He coughed. "I just need to see Fenna. Just one more time. To say I'm sorry."

"She knows," Dina said. "Come."

"Yes. I'll be right there, love. I will. I promise. Just one minute." He coughed another mouthful of sea water, and the man pressed him down, harder, kicking him again and again. But Burwardsley resisted, spreading his hands flat against the surface of the ice, a cold crucifixion as he tried again, one last time, to scour the ice for a sign, a trace, a glimpse of the young Sirius woman, Fenna, as she sledged to the glacier.

"Come," Dina called again, beckoning him to the depths. "It will be alright," she said, as she curled her slim hand around his neck and pulled him down beneath the ice, until his body was immersed to his boots. The man on the ice kicked at Burwardsley's hands, propelling him down into the water where Dina took care of him, rolling him onto his back so that he might have one last look at the sky.

Vestergaard's man, the last of the team of six, stepped back from the hole in the ice, slid the soles of his boots on the surface until he felt confident he could turn his back on the ice and walk to the safety of the land. He frowned at the sound of tapping on the air, checked the swivel mount securing his weapon to the sling, pressed his hands over both attachment points and paused on the ice to search for the source of the noise. He found it when he looked up and saw a man in a cornflower-blue smock tapping a thin bone instrument against a sealskin drum. The man cocked his head to look, exposing the side of his neck, and giving the shaman a perfect point at which to strike. The tapping noise stopped when the shaman plunged the length of bone into the man's neck and kicked his body back toward the hole in the ice. It was just one more thing that Fenna did not see, but then, as the shaman knew, she was fighting for her life.

Chapter 25

Fenna's dogs slowed as they passed the fishing hole and entered the ice fjord. The light was failing and the shadows from the icebergs created pockets of darkness, as long as the icebergs were tall. The team pursuing Fenna loitered at the fishing hole, as the men checked their gear before entering the maze of icebergs. Fenna let her team rest as she watched her pursuers through the binoculars. She saw their breath steam through their ski masks and imagined it freezing on the swathe of ice clinging to the fibres of the masks. Only Vestergaard's face was unmasked, and she studied him, the raw colour of his cheeks struggling to cope with the cold. He looked like a Russian, with the arms of his glasses tucked behind his ears, beneath a large fur hat. She wondered for a moment if there was a connection, another group in the shadows, pulling on strings, before deciding it really didn't matter anymore.

From her position, she could just see Vestergaard's ship beyond the island. It had turned, the gantry and floating deck had been retrieved and stowed, and it seemed to be moving slowly toward Nuugaatsiaq. Fenna thought she could hear the sound of a helicopter approaching, and a quick glance at Vestergaard through the binoculars suggested he had too. She watched as he hurried the two men with sharp gestures and trails of mist from his nose and mouth. *He looks like a dragon*, Fenna thought. *Let's see if we can put that fire out.*

She stuffed the binoculars inside the sledge bag and got off the sledge. The dogs were uncertain among the icebergs, and the air was colder, as the dense behemoths of ice pushed the temperature several more degrees below zero. Fenna imagined it to be close to minus twenty degrees Celsius. She walked to the front of the team, tracing slow circles with the tip of the whip on the ice. The dogs fidgeted as she bent down to fuss over the lead dog.

"Hey boy," she said, and smiled at the lead dog. Its face was scarred with the challenge of being an alpha dog and keeping the job. Ice beaded the fur around its eyes, and hung from its muzzle in the same way it hung from a man's beard. Fenna could feel the same tiny beads of ice clinging to the fine hairs on her face, could feel the crust of ice on her neckie each time she moved her chin, and she knew the tips of her hair were frosted white like icing. She pressed her forehead to the dog's and whispered, "I need you to follow me, keep the team in check, and we'll be alright." She lifted her head and looked at the dog. "Deal?" The dog licked at the ice on its muzzle and Fenna took that as a *yes*.

She stood up, and in the lull between the supernatural creaks and groans of the icebergs settling, she could hear the shush of the approaching dog team.

"Trust me," she said to the lead dog.

Fenna scanned the ice between two large icebergs. It was convoluted, a mess of jagged shards like toffee broken from a pan. Between the shards she saw patches of free plates of ice, bobbing in a white mass. The route she was considering was not frozen solid, far from it. There were larger plates of ice that were frozen in place, but the gaps between them were not be trusted. It was unlikely they could bear the weight of a sledge.

"Perfect," she said, even though the tumult in her stomach and the jag of adrenaline that peaked at the thought of venturing between the icebergs suggested otherwise. Fenna lifted her chin, ignored the sound of the runners grating across the ice behind her, and led her team between the bergs.

She took a step and heard her team follow, the creak of the hunter's wooden sledge magnified by the amphitheatre of ice. She took another step, picking her route toward a large floe that was flat, big enough for her team. She hoped the jagged shards and smaller bergs littering the route would provide ample cover from Vestergaard's men and their submachine guns, and counted on the fact they would be forced to follow. She pushed on, avoiding a smooth chunk of ice the size of a washing machine as it rolled within a chilly soup of small clumps and grains of brash ice. One of the dogs was not so observant. Fenna heard the splash as it slipped. She turned, lunged for the gangline and pulled it out of the water. There was more ice than water, and the dog had been lucky. *I'll check his paws later*, Fenna thought, and continued."If there is a later."

Fenna reached the large floe and stopped to choose the next leg of her route. That was when she heard Vestergaard's voice, and felt a chill greater than the air freezing and pressing at her body.

"Where are you going, Konstabel?" he shouted, his voice reverberating between the icebergs. "There's nowhere to go. You might as well stop, and we can put an end to this." He paused and Fenna assumed he was giving instructions to his men. "You're only making this more difficult on yourself, Konstabel."

Vestergaard's voice echoed once more until it was replaced by the sound of dogs following Fenna's route. She scanned ahead, quickly, picked her route and jumped on the sledge.

"Let's go," she shouted, and cracked the whip to the right of the team, pushing them left. The lead dog took up the slack as Fenna knew he would, and the team followed. *Tough dog*, Fenna thought. *There's a reason he has those scars. Thank God.* She knelt on the wooden thwarts of the sledge, wishing she had brought a reindeer skin to protect her knees and provide some warmth, but there had been no time. She held her breath to stop it misting in front of her face, just for a moment, to better see her route.

"Shit."

The lead dog pulled them onto a floe that began to wobble. Fenna cracked the whip to the left, urging the team to the right, whistling and clicking to get them to go faster. The route was uneven, the path obscured with ice that trapped the sledge runners. Fenna coiled the whip around an upright, leaped off the sledge and grabbed both uprights in her hands. She pushed, guiding the sledge from the rear, as the dogs pulled from the front.

"Come on," she said, risking a glance behind her and seeing the black muzzles of the dogs leading Vestergaard's team. The bucket seat of the sled was empty, she noted, and there was only one man standing at the rear of the sled. *And it's not him.*

The team behind rallied at the sight of Fenna's dogs. They had been chasing the scent, and now they had them in sight. The man at the rear of the sled tried to slow their speed by stamping down on a metal brake designed for snow on forest trails, not for sea ice. If Fenna had heard it, she would have enjoyed the sound of the metal brake being torn from the sled. She heard only the man's cry of alarm, and mistook it for a challenge, a command for her to stop. She pushed on, driving the team onto another patch of uneven ice where the larger slabs were angled at forty-five degrees. The dogs skittered onto the ice, the sledge slid sideways and Fenna slipped. She fell as the dogs and the sledge slid down the ice floe, the sledge crunching into Fenna's knee and trapping her for a moment against a large boulder of ice.

"Shit." Fenna tried to push at the sledge, but didn't have the angle. She reached instead for the flap of the rifle holster, fumbling at the quick-release knot she had tied that was now frozen. She opened it as the first of the foreign dogs clawed their way over the ice, grasping the butt of the rifle and pulling it free of the holster. Fenna leaned back against the ice, her body twisted and protesting with a sharp pain in her back. She ignored it, chambered a round into the rifle, tugged it into her shoulder and aimed at the spot she imagined the driver of the team would appear. But the foreign dogs, eight or nine of them, were too excited to stop, and the man lost control as the two teams of dogs fought, friend and foe alike, as canine teeth ripped through the fur and flanks closest to them.

The dogs of both teams fought almost silently, the teeth too engaged to allow unnecessary sounds through the mouth. The sled slipped down the ice and crunched into Fenna's sledge, putting more pressure on her knee. Then she saw the driver of the team, as he slipped on the ice, scrambling for a solid grip with his boots, as he aimed the MP5 at Fenna. She shot him through the chest, crying out as the recoil and the combined weight of the sledges and teams jarred her knee. She couldn't move.

The dogs ignored the gunshot and continued to lunge at the throat of the nearest opponent, any opponent. The ganglines stretching from the sledge and sled to the dogs were twisted and knotted and rethreaded as they fought. But as the fight progressed and Vestergaard's team dragged their sled off Fenna's sledge, she felt the weight shift from her knee, and slammed the rifle butt against the ice to push herself free and onto her feet. Fenna slung the rifle across her chest, pulled the knife from the sheath on her belt and hobbled into the mess of lines, teeth, and dogs. She sawed at the ganglines attaching Vestergaard's team to one another, and then severed the gangline from the sled. Once his dogs were free she knew they would have the advantage over her own, but then they could also escape, and she counted on the wild, raw nature of the Greenlandic dogs being more than a match for the Alaskan breed, bred for speed not survival. The dogs took a moment to realise they were free, and then leaped back from the frenzy of the fight. Half of the dogs lingered, looking for another angle of attack, Fenna shooed them away with sharp words and kicks that jarred her knee and brought a tear to her eye. Her tears froze as the dogs ran and she gritted her teeth while pulling the sled off the sledge.

Fenna sorted out her own dogs next, cuffing them with thumps of her fist, and then the butt of the whip when she remembered to use it. The dogs relented, content with a snarl or two before Fenna reminded them again who was boss. She swore as she moved, favouring her good knee and limping around the dogs as she worked her way back to the sledge. She sheathed the knife and scrambled up the floe to scavenge what she could from the dead man's body. The sling of his weapon was trapped beneath him, so she cut it away, and took the submachine gun. She checked the magazine. It was light, only half full. She took it anyway and slid back down the floe, cursing as she crashed into the sledge. Fenna picked herself up and stuffed the MP5 into the sledge bag.

"Okay, boys," she said. "You've had your fun. Let's go."

Fenna pushed at the sledge and the lead dog, blood frozen around its chops, took up the slack and led the team off the floe and onto a stretch of smooth ice, much to Fenna's relief. She squirmed the toe of her boot beneath the sledge bag and leaned over the uprights to let the dogs carry her weight across the ice. She could see at least thirty metres of good ice ahead, and chose to let the dogs run the length of it, before slowing and stopping to pick her route. There was blood on her lip, and she didn't know if it was human or dog. She realised she didn't care. Fenna winced at the pain in her knee, but considered herself lucky.

"Still alive," she said. "Still stubborn." *Burwardsley will be pleased.*

Two black shapes in the distance caught her eye, and she slowed the team with soft commands, using her feet to add more friction until the sledge slowed to a stop. One of the men was Vestergaard. She recognised the shape of the fur hat. *He must have found a better route*, she mused, *for him and his man.* They started to walk toward her, and Fenna decided to wait until they were closer.

She slid the rifle off her chest, worked the bolt and chambered a round. She rested the barrel on top of the sledge bag, changed her stance to ease her knee, and waited. Vestergaard's man chose a position behind a low boulder of ice frozen into place. Fenna watched as he changed magazines, and took aim. His boss continued walking toward Fenna, and she noticed the pistol in his hand. He stopped within ten metres of her, close enough for them to kill one another. Vestergaard was the first to speak.

"You never could stick to a plan, Konstabel," he said. "You always have to make things difficult."

"That's the kind of girl I am," she said. "You should know. You had me trained this way."

"No, that's where you are wrong." Vestergaard's breath steamed around his face as he sighed. "I never wanted you to be like this. It was Jarnvig who said you had potential. He had you trained and this is what I got. I should never have listened to him."

Fenna tapped her fingers on the rifle, aware of the cold cramping her grip, she stuffed her hands in her pockets, choosing warmth over the chance for an impetuous shot. She felt the tupilaq in her pocket and curled her fingers around it, as Vestergaard continued.

"I understand you met my colleague in Canada?"

"Colleague?"

"Meredith. We worked together once. But now, I suppose she is less inclined to cooperate." Vestergaard paused to nod. "Now there's an opportunity, Konstabel. How would you like to make some money?"

"This has never been about money," she said.

"That was your mistake, not mine. But, seriously, we could come to an arrangement." He turned his head at the sound of a helicopter approaching. When he spoke again, Fenna thought she detected a sudden urgency in his voice. "If you were to report a successful mission to my Canadian friend, then you would be in a position to tidy up one more loose end. That's what I have used you for in the past, and, despite the mess, that's one job you have been adequate at performing."

Fenna smoothed her thumb over the bone limbs of the tupilaq. She squeezed it, wondering at the power the shaman had locked within it, wondering if that power was hers, if she could use it, if it would make a difference.

"Well, Konstabel?" Vestergaard tapped the pistol against his leg. "You don't really want to die here, do you? Because that's the alternative, the only alternative." He glanced again in the direction of the settlement as the helicopter approached Nuugaatsiaq.

Fenna lifted her chin and said, "Friends of yours?"

"A nuisance. Nothing more," he said. "Not unlike yourself." Vestergaard raised the pistol and pointed it at Fenna.

She laughed and said, "I think you'll find I can be far more than that." Fenna pulled her hands out of her pockets and grabbed the whip from the sledge.

Chapter 26

The dogs lurched into a run as Fenna cracked the whip on the ice behind them, just before she dived to one side, sliding across the ice to stop behind a boulder. She heard Vestergaard curse and yell a command to his man. *The one with the submachine gun*, Fenna thought, sighing at the fact that all her weapons were on the sledge. *Not all of them*, she remembered and drew the knife from its sheath. She sat up and coiled the dog whip around her chest, it would be useless in a fight. She buried any insecurities she might have about her knife-fighting skills, and chose to remember instead the first man she had killed, with his own knife, in the desert.

"The Arctic is a desert too," she whispered and shifted position to peek around the boulder of ice. The dogs had stopped just beyond Vestergaard. They shifted and fidgeted for lack of purpose and direction in an unfamiliar and intimidating environment. Fenna looked at the leader and whispered, "Just stay there. Just a little longer." The sound of rubber soles slipping on the ice to her left caught her attention, and she turned away from the dogs.

Vestergaard's last man was cautious. He held his MP5 in a tight grip, a textbook position for close-quarter combat. The iron sights of the submachine gun moved in sync with his head. Where he looked, he aimed. *Which is just fine*, Fenna thought, *when you're standing on solid ground. But here…*

Fenna waited until she was sure the man was as close as he dared, before jumping up and throwing the knife at him. She didn't care if it hit him, she just needed a few seconds to vault over the ice boulder and slam her knee into his crotch and her fist into his chest. She was lighter than him, lighter than any of her opponents, but the glassy nature of the ground beneath the man's feet played to her advantage and he slipped onto his back, grunting as a spear of ice punctured his shoulder. He was pinned for a second, and Fenna didn't need much longer than that. She gripped his chin and pushed his head back as she squirmed on top of him, ignoring the pain in her knee, and the burst of bullets he fired from the gun as he tried to blast her off his body. The bullets boomed past her head, leaving a ringing sound in her right ear and the taste of cordite on her tongue. She slapped at the weapon, as she tried to get her knees onto his chest and press his shoulder down on the spear of ice protruding from the jagged shard beneath him. She stopped when she saw the ice pierce his skin and push through his jacket. Fenna shifted her focus to the man's head, slamming the base of her fist into his forehead until she felt and heard his neck snap. The man's head lolled back on the ice and he dropped the MP5. Fenna reached for it, only to be spun onto the ice with two bullets into her right arm. She landed, gasping for air as it was knocked out of her lungs. Vestergaard stepped into view, and aimed the pistol at her head.

"Always so brutal, Konstabel. Why?"

Fenna filled her lungs with icy air as the shock of the bullets piercing her arm, and the impact of landing on the ice subsided. She was about to say something, anything, when she felt the ice move beneath her.

"Never mind," Vestergaard said. "Let's just finish this, shall we?" The sound of the helicopter increased, the *whop whop* of its thick blades beating the Arctic air between the island and the icebergs leading to the glacier. "And quickly, I think."

Fenna caught a glimpse of the helicopter's searchlight as it beamed through the gloom and lit the route she had taken into the ice fjord. She looked at Vestergaard as he twitched at the proximity of the helicopter. The ice shifted again beneath her and she cleared her throat.

"What's that?" Vestergaard said. He bent down over Fenna grabbed the whip looped around her chest and pulled her upward as he pressed the muzzle of the pistol to her head. The tip of the whip wedged between a crack in the ice. "Got something to say?" he said and sneered.

"Yes," she said, and grabbed his wrist and the belt around his waist. Fenna kicked at a solid clump of ice, and took a breath as she felt the small floe upon which she lay shift and topple. She splashed into the water and dragged Vestergaard with her.

Vestergaard cried out and dropped the pistol, as he braced his hands on the solid ice either side of Fenna. His knees slipped into the water, and Fenna tugged at his belt, clawed at his face, and pulled his glasses off. Her teeth chattered as she grabbed at his neck and pulled him down toward her face. The only thing stopping her from slipping under the water and beneath the ice was Vestergaard. She tried to hook her leg through his and pull him down, but again, her weight was against her.

"Too light," she spluttered, as the black icy water lapped at her mouth.

"This is a stalemate, Konstabel," Vestergaard shouted. "Just let go and die."

"Okay," Fenna said. She slipped her hand from his belt and, muscles cramping, she shoved it into her pocket. She pulled the tupilaq out of jacket and pressed it into Vestergaard's face. "Do you recognise this?"

"Hah," he said, as he shifted his grip on the ice, and tried to shake off Fenna's grip. "You believe in magic now? Really, Konstabel, after all we've been through, I thought you would know better."

"But they call you *the Magician*. Don't they?" Fenna's words trembled over her frozen lips. But as the helicopter approached, and before she lost control of her lips, Fenna whistled, long and low, faltering toward the end as Vestergaard laughed.

"*The Magician* is just one of many names, Konstabel. But the last one you will hear," he said, as he pulled his leg free of Fenna's. He turned at the sound of runners grating across the ice and Fenna saw the frown on his brow as the hunter's lead dog clawed across the ice and into view. It sniffed after Fenna, pressing its paws and its weight onto Vestergaard's back. Fenna felt her head dip below the surface of the water, felt the pinch of cold around her forehead, but she smiled at the sight of the dog, all forty kilos of it. She made one last grab at Vestergaard and pulled him under the ice as the dog sprang back from the hole.

Vestergaard's body sank faster than Fenna's as her descent was arrested by the tip of the whip clamped in a crevice of ice on the surface. Fenna still had the tupilaq between her fingers, and she kicked at Vestergaard's body, barely aware of how fast he was sinking as she dragged herself up the whip with frozen fingers. She kicked with what little strength she had left as she broke through the surface, and clawed her way out of the water.

She saw the dogs, saw the sledge, and pulled her way toward it, ignoring the bullet wounds in her arm, ignoring her knee, ignoring the cold. There were spare clothes in the sledge bag, she knew it. There was even food, she could almost taste it, a whole bar of chocolate, already unwrapped, bagged only, waiting to be eaten. The dogs fidgeted as she crawled onto the sledge, her body shivering so hard the sledge shook and creaked. The lead dog mistook the movement for a command and pulled the team and Fenna away from the hole in the ice and back toward the settlement. With no counter-commands, the lead dog trusted to what it knew about ice, and chose only the safe, flat, thick floes locked together between the icebergs.

The helicopter passed to their right, and Fenna watched as it circled around and played the searchlight across the ice until it found the bodies of Vestergaard's men. It couldn't land, she knew, but it hovered long enough to confirm that the men were dead and to document the scene. *They will probably return in the morning*, she thought, *whoever they are.*

A new sound cut through the beat of the helicopter's rotor blades as the pilot switched on the loudspeaker mounted beneath the cockpit. Fenna fumbled the chocolate from the sledge bag into her mouth, chewing through teeth that chattered as she listened to a familiar voice distorted just a little by the noise of the helicopter.

"Konstabel Fenna Brongaard, this is Oversergent Noa Andersen of the Sirius Sledge Patrol. Let us help you. Show us where you are."

She considered it, for a moment, as the dogs increased speed away from the metallic beast buffeting the air between the icebergs. She imagined being rescued by the Sirius men, the warm blankets, the hot coffee and the interrogation, and a very uncertain life. But it was Andersen's next words that confirmed her decision, as darkness descended on the thin sea ice leading into the fjord.

"Burwardsley is dead. You don't need to die out here. Let us help you."

"Somehow, I knew," she said, as she removed the whip and stripped off her jacket and the sodden icy layers clinging to her upper body. "But I don't have to die out here. He wouldn't want that."

She talked to herself as she dressed, as if the words would make her actions easier. She checked the bullet holes in her arm, grazes really, they stung more than they bled. A bandage could wait, a hat was more important, and she pulled a dry woollen hat over her head. The helicopter began circling the hole in the ice, increasing the diameter of the search with each pass. Fenna willed the dogs onward as she pulled a sleeping bag from the sledge bag and crawled inside it. She stuffed her hands inside the sealskin mittens and shivered as she thought.

The lights of Nuugaatsiaq beckoned and the dogs nosed for

home, until Fenna cracked the whip and turned them away from the settlement, and deeper into the fjord. She would avoid the village and sledge straight for the airport at Qaarsuut. *Perhaps everyone would think she was dead?* She smiled at the thought, her feelings buoyed and her body warmed at the idea of being free. The dogs pulled the sledge past the settlement and Fenna closed her eyes, until she was sure they were past the island, swinging wide of the ship, and sledging away from her past and into the future.

Alice is safe, she thought, *and Dina…*

She remembered Burwardsley's words, about saving the living, so that the dead might find peace. He had said something like that, and it sounded good, it sounded right. Fenna smiled as the wind burned at her cheeks and she opened her eyes, staring at the vast expanse of thin ice ahead of her, and a world of opportunities.

LONDON, ENGLAND

It was a terrible connection, and the clatter of mugs, the chatter of customers, and the hiss of the coffee machines, didn't help matters. Fenna pressed the receiver of the payphone closer to her ear and smiled at the familiar voice who answered in Greenlandic. It was late evening in London, but Tulugaq and his family were just sitting down to dinner.

"Hi," Fenna said in Danish. "It's me."

"I know who you are," Tulugaq said, and Fenna could almost see the knowing smile crease his face. "Shall I keep it between us?"

"Yes."

"Good," he said. "It is better this way."

Fenna nodded as she pressed several more coins into the payphone. "Is she alright?"

"Alice? *Aap*, she is fine, although my son is frustrated."

"She is playing hard to get?"

"Very, but the children are happy with their new English teacher."

"That's good," Fenna said. She paused for a moment before saying, "What about my friend? Did you find him?"

There was a pause and a rattle at the other end of the line, and Fenna imagined the shaman moving to a quieter part of the house. "He is at peace," he said.

"But you never found his body?"

"*Naamik*."

Fenna let the receiver slide down her cheek as she thought about what to say next. There were no words, only the brief tears she allowed herself before Tulugaq's voice urged her to listen.

"He is at peace, he is with *Sassuma Arnaanut*, the one you call Sedna."

"Beneath the ice?"

"*Aap*."

Safe, Fenna thought. And then she smiled. He has an eternity to torment Vestergaard. She almost laughed at the thought, and then remembered to thank Tulugaq for everything he had done.

"Be safe," he said, before ending the call.

The connection was severed, and it took a moment for Fenna to realise she was alone, cut off, and removed from the world she once knew, and ready to explore another. *But where?*

Fenna placed the receiver on the hook and ordered a coffee. She found a seat by the window, and enjoyed the warm glow from the Christmas lights that lit the raindrops on the glass. *Too warm for snow*, she mused as she sipped at her coffee. *But perhaps I have seen enough snow for a lifetime.*

She put the mug on the table and studied her hands, ignoring the small scars on her skin, and focusing instead on the length of her nails. No longer were they broken and pitted, scratched or covered in mud, *or worse*. Fenna held them up to the light and imagined, for once in her life, that these were the hands of a lady. She looked at her jeans, the small feminine boots she had picked out in the second-hand store. She smoothed the fabric of her shirt between her fingertips, felt the soft fibres of the cardigan that she wore instead of a fleece. Only the creak of her leather jacket reminded her of her former life, as she imagined the sledge shifting within its bindings.

I probably still smell of dog, she thought, and smiled. She looked up at the sound of someone sitting down at a table near hers. Three people, a couple and a single man. The man smiled at her, and Fenna dared to imagine another future, a possible future, that might one day even include a man. She smiled back and returned to her coffee, more than a little self-conscious all of a sudden, and enjoying the feel of it.

The Christmas lights flickered as a fresh gust of wind played at the cables hung between the shops on the cosy backstreet she had found. The man selling roasted chestnuts grabbed at his hat, and Fenna watched him for a moment, only to be distracted by the sight of another man, a reflection in the window, from inside the coffee shop.

She recognised the face, almost Greenlandic, with a patchwork of ugly scars criss-crossing the man's cheeks. Fenna stared at the man's reflection, putting a name to the face of Yuka, realising at the same time that the life she might have imagined, the life of freedom, was short-lived, and the life she knew only too well, had caught up with her once again.

THE END

ACKNOWLEDGEMENTS

I would like to thank Isabel Dennis-Muir for her invaluable editing skills and feedback on the manuscript.

Once again, while several people have contributed to *The Shaman's House*, the mistakes and inaccuracies are all my own.

Chris
December 2017
Denmark

ABOUT THE AUTHOR

Christoffer Petersen is the author's pen name. He lives in Denmark. Chris started writing stories about Greenland while teaching in Qaanaaq, the largest village in the very north of Greenland – the population peaked at 600 during the two years he lived there. Chris spent a total of seven years in Greenland, teaching in remote communities and at the Police Academy in the capital of Nuuk.

Chris continues to be inspired by the vast icy wilderness of the Arctic and his books have a common setting in the region, with a Scandinavian influence. He has also watched enough Bourne movies to no longer be surprised by the plot, but not enough to get bored.

You can find Chris in Denmark or online here:

www.christoffer-petersen.com

BY THE SAME AUTHOR

THE GREENLAND TRILOGY
featuring Konstabel Fenna Brongaard

Book 1
THE ICE STAR

Book 2
IN THE SHADOW OF THE MOUNTAIN

Book 3
THE SHAMAN'S HOUSE

and

THE GREENLAND CRIME SERIES
featuring Constable David Maratse
set in Greenland

Book 1
SEVEN GRAVES, ONE WINTER

Book 2
BLOOD FLOE

Book 3
WE SHALL BE MONSTERS

Short stories from the same series
KATABATIC
CONTAINER
TUPILAQ
THE LAST FLIGHT
THE HEART THAT WAS A WILD GARDEN

and

THE DARK ADVENT SERIES
featuring Police Commissioner Petra Jensen
set in Greenland

Book 1
THE CALENDAR MAN

Book 2
THE TWELFTH NIGHT

and

THE SIRIUS SLEDGE PATROL SERIES
featuring Sirius Patrolman Mikael Gregersen
set in Greenland

Story 1
PITERAQ

and

THE JON ØSTERGÅRD SERIES
featuring Wildlife Biologist Jon Østergård
set in Denmark

Book 1
PAINT THE DEVIL

and

THE MADE IN DENMARK SERIES
featuring Milla Moth
set in Denmark

Story 1
DANISH DESIGN